The Researcher's Guide
to American Genealogy

The

Researcher's Guide

to

American Genealogy

Val D. Greenwood

4th Edition

Genealogical Publishing Co., Inc.

Library of Congress Catalog Card Number 2017954692

ISBN 978-0-8063-2066-3

Made in the United States of America

Dedication

*To the faithful and devoted students who are better
family history researchers because of this book*

Contents

Illustrations and Charts xi

Preface.. xiii

Part 1
Background to Research

1. **Understanding Genealogical Research** 3

    The true nature of research—Genealogy and science—Completing
    the family picture—Genealogy and historical background—
    The importance of places—Nothing but the facts—What is expect-
    ed?—Educational opportunities—A realistic perspective—Family
    history professions—Conclusion

2. **Language, Terminology and Important Issues** 29

    Language changes and handwriting—Changes in the language—
    Naming practices—The calendar

3. **Surveying, Analyzing, and Planning** 57

    Secondary research: your preliminary survey—Preserve prelimi-
    nary survey results—Pedigree analysis—Get everybody—Jurisdic-
    tions—Locality analysis—Tradition, common sense, and helpful
    clues—Additional help

4. **Evidence**.. 79

    Basic definitions—Standard of proof—Types of evidence—Sources
    vs. evidence—Original and derivative sources—When evidence
    does not make sense—Conflicting evidence—More information
    on evidence

5. **Libraries and the National Archives (NARA)** 99

    The purposes of library research—Some important libraries—
    FamilySearch libraries—A library's online catalog—Library
    classification systems—The National Archives and Records
    Administration (NARA)—Final observation about library use

6. **Reference Works** 115

    Guides to locality data—Guides to non-original sources—Guides
    to original sources—Conclusion

7. **Organizing and Evaluating Your Research Findings** 143

The reasons and the requirements—Note-keeping methods—
Research logs and notes—Organizing your research notes—Special searches—Evaluating the information in your notes—One
more step: the research report—Reminder notes—Abstracts and
forms—Card files and computer indexes—Records relating to correspondence—Concluding thoughts

8. **Successful Correspondence** 165

Filing documents acquired by correspondence—Analyzing your
correspondence results—Review of research note requirements—
Writing your letter—Appearance matters—To whom do I write?—
Conclusion and checklist

9. **Computer Technology and Family History** 175

Concepts and definitions of modern technology—Technological
resources important to family history—Conclusion

10. **Family History on the Internet** 201

Significant steps and a current perspective—Keeping on track—
Major family history websites—Enhancing your search results on
these major sites—Other important websites—Conclusion

11. **Family History: Going Beyond Genealogy** 237

The what and why of family history—Sources—Historical considerations—African American family history and the Freedmen's
Bureau records—Writing family history—Objectivity

Part 2
Records and Their Use

12. **Compiled Sources and Newspapers** 255

Family history and compiled sources—Newspapers—Limitations
of compiled sources—Final observation

13. **Vital Records** 279

Beginning and background—Using vital records for family history—Securing copies of the records—Town meeting records—
Record problems—Final observations

14. **Census Returns** 315

What is the census?—Where are the census population schedules?—Special census indexes—Military service information in
the census—Colonial censuses, special enumerations, and state
censuses—Important non-population census schedules—Glossary
of census terms

15. **Using Census Records in Your Research** 379
Benefits and uses—Limitations of the census as a family history
source—When should the census be searched?—Examples of
census use—Conclusion

16. **Understanding Probate Records and Legal Terminology** 399
Definition and background of probate records—Content and
genealogical value—The limitations of probate records—Legal
terminology—Important details

17. **What About Wills?** 423
Kinds of wills—Proving (probating) the will—The contested
will—The value of wills—Record problems—Finding and using
wills—Help with a difficult problem

18. **The Intestate, Miscellaneous Probate Records,
and Guardianships** 447
The intestate and the probate process—Miscellaneous probate
records—Guardianships—Conclusion

19. **Government Land: Colonial and American** 469
Background—Land from the colonial government—After the Rev-
olution—History of land entries in the public domain—Records
created by land entry in the public domain—Land patents from the
BLM—Texas—Other state-land states

20. **Local Land Records** 495
Land titles—Records that relate to land—Using land records—Tax
records—County land ownership maps—Availability of local land
records—Conclusion

21. **Abstracting Probate and Land Records** 529
Abstract vs. extract—The nature of the abstract—Abstracts of
deeds—Abstracts of wills

22. **Court Records and Family History** 547
Background and definition—A misconception—The American
court system—Records and our access to them—Legislative
records—Adoption records—Note on Virginia's independent
cities—Case reports, reporters, and digests—Conclusion

23. **Property Rights of Women as a Consideration** 575
Background—Real estate conveyances—Laws and customs relat-
ing to inheritance—Conclusion

24. **Church Records and Family History** 585
Types of records—The nature of the records—Locating church records

25. **Immigrant Ancestor Origins: American Finding Aids** 625
Immigration records: their nature and value—Locating and using immigration records—Passport applications—Conclusion

26. **Military Records: Colonial Wars and the American Revolution** 653
Background and history—The records—Colonial wars—The Revolutionary War—Using Revolutionary War records—Loyalists and the Revolutionary War

27. **Military Records: After the Revolution** 689
Between the Revolution and Fort Sumter—The Civil War, 1861–65—Military actions following the Civil War—The Regular Army or Regular Establishment—World War I and beyond—State military records and records relating to civilians—Printed military sources—When to use military records—Conclusion

28. **Cemetery and Burial Records** 727
Background—Gravestone and monument inscriptions—Access to cemetery records—Sextons' records—Help in finding the records—Records of funeral directors—Conclusion

Index 739

Illustrations and Charts

The research process 8
Some early modern English writing with its many unfamiliar characters.... 32
Some scribes developed their own brands of shorthand 34
A document with extensive abbreviations 37
The will of Jeremiah Willcox 43
A typical family group form... 63
Pedigree of John Samuel Kelly 64
Part of southeastern Kentucky showing Owsley County 75
A research log 151
Important dates in the history of birth and death registration:
    United States 285
Standard certificate of birth 288–289
Standard certificate of death 290
Standard certificate of marriage 291
Census content chart (1790–1840) 318
Census content chart (1850–1870) 319
Important census data 320–331
The 1790 federal census 332
The 1800 [and 1810] federal census 333
The 1820 federal census 334
The 1830 federal census 335
The 1840 federal census 336
The 1850 federal census 337
The 1860 federal census 338–339
The 1870 federal census 340
The 1880 federal census 341
The 1900 federal census 342
The 1910 federal census 343
The 1920 federal census 344
The 1930 federal census 345
The 1940 federal census 346–347
The 1890 federal census 352–353
Application for search of census records 355–358
A card from the 1880 Soundex 362
A page from a mortality schedule, 1850 census 372
Relationships and degrees of relationship according to *civil law*
    and canon law 407
A petition for probate 448
Decree of distribution (assignment of real estate) 449
Settlement (final account) 463

Numbering townships and ranges from the base line and principal
meridian 475
Numbering and dividing the sections of a township.................................. 476
BLM land patent record 492
Kentucky tax lists.. 513–518
Land ownership map for part of Dutchess County, NY
(1:42, 240—1850—J.C. Sidney).. 520
A page from a grantor index 526
Standard certificate of divorce or annulment 559
Presbyterian baptism records 610
Customs passenger lists manifest for the port of New York 630
Veteran's declaration as part of a Revolutionary War pension
application 661
A page from *Index of Revolutionary War Pension Applications*,
prepared by the National Genealogical Society 666
NATF form 85 669
Muster roll notation from the compiled service records of the
Mexican War 697

Preface

I t was in 1969 at the first World Conference on Records in Salt Lake City that I delivered the manuscript of the first edition of this book to Keith Kern of Genealogical Publishing Company in return for his promise to give it serious consideration. That was a significant promise because Genealogical Publishing Company had never published anything like it before. Never had they published an original work—only reprints.

It was four years later when 1,000 copies of *The Researcher's Guide to American Genealogy* finally came off the press. The publisher was hopeful and so was I. GPC editor, Dr. Michael Tepper, informed me that the company had printed that many copies as an experiment they hoped would be successful. "We believe," he explained, "that if we can sell all of these within five years, it will be a profitable venture and worth the cost."

The long wait after my 1969 meeting with Keith Kern was difficult for me. I wondered what was going on, but I have learned that there were serious deliberations about the wisdom of this venture by a company that was built on a foundation of reprinting important genealogical publications and not on publishing original works—especially original works by unknown authors.

GPC sent out copies of my manuscript for review by prominent genealogists to see if they felt there was merit in a book of this kind. I understand that the response was mixed, but the majority felt there was need. One eminent genealogist, Milton Rubincam, expressed his opinion that the book was good and that it was needed; he also offered to write the foreword for the book.

Even after the decision to proceed was finally made, there was still concern about economic feasibility. Because of that concern, I received a phone call from Dr. Tepper in the spring of 1972 asking if I would be willing to type the manuscript so that it was camera ready for the printer. GPC would rent an IBM Executive typewriter for me and provide the paper. This typewriter had the unique capability—certainly unique in 1972—of being able to justify the lines on the page. In order to do this, however, every page had to be typed twice. Being anxious, as I was, to see the book in print, I agreed to the task.

Thus, in the summer of 1972, between my first and second years of law school, I used that magnificent machine to type the entire 535 pages of the first edition (including all charts, tables, and non-photographic illustrations).

The exacting process was interesting. Before I describe the procedure, however, I need to explain that the exact position of the desired right margin was already marked on every page. That was helpful. Thus, after typing each line, I used either the space key or the backspace key to count the number of keystrokes—plus or minus—that the line I had just typed either fell short of or extended beyond the marked ending place. I then penciled in, in the margin, the plus or minus difference of the line I had just typed from the marked place where that line should have ended. After each full page was typed using this method, I retyped it, adding or deleting the designated number of spaces at various places within that line to make it the desired length. All of this was possible because the typewriter had two space keys, the two-space key (which was the standard) and a one-space key.

If the original line was too long, the deleting was accomplished by using the one-space key between two words *instead* of the two-space standard key. If the line was short, I added the appropriate number of one-space tab keys *in addition to* the standard two-space keys. Whenever possible, I made my deletions and my additions at the ends of sentences or in connection with other punctuation. When the typing was completed, the typewritten master pages were then photographed by the printer at 85 percent of their original size to create the printing plates for the offset press.

It was a long summer with time for little else, and, because I am not an expert typist, I became an expert at using stick-on correction tape; I went through *many* rolls of it.

I have described this tedious process in some detail here, not to impress anyone with what I accomplished that summer (and into the fall), but to illustrate how far technology has come since 1972. Modern computer word-processing programs do everything I did—except the actual typing—with a few simple settings put in place by a keystroke or the click of a computer mouse. And, in addition, they can automatically check the spelling and superficial aspects of grammar. Perhaps my experience with what was then considered a remarkable typewriter gives me a greater appreciation for the marvelous technology we take for granted today.

It is not an exaggeration to say that computer technology is a wonderful tool, and, because of my experience in that long ago summer of 1972, I probably have a greater appreciation for the technology described in this fourth edition of *The Researcher's Guide to American Genealogy* than do most other people who now benefit from it. Many of those who are reading this do not even remember the world before personal computers.

Since those first 1,000 copies of that first edition came off the press in 1973, *The Researcher's Guide*, through three editions, has sold more than 110,000 copies and is considered by many to be a classic. I am humbled and honored by its success.

This fourth edition has been a long time in coming. There have been so many extraordinary technological innovations since 2000, when the third edition was published, that the job of updating seemed overwhelming. There was even some thought by some at Genealogical Publishing Company that the task was too great for me and that I would not be able to do it. And I had some of those same thoughts as I considered the task.

On top of that, technology is still advancing at such a rapid pace that much of the information in this fourth edition will likely be outdated very quickly. In fact, I have experienced some of the frustrations of that phenomenon during the two years I have been working on this edition. Many things have had to be updated from the way they were expressed in my first go-through—and even my second go-through. There have also been multiple other situations where I had to go back to specific places in the text and add information about newly available resources. And, even with all I have done, there are surely some things I have missed. And, as surely as I am writing this, I am sure that much more will be outdated before the book is finally in print—and much more by the time you read it.

In spite of all of this, I felt driven to go forward with this edition—an exercise that has consumed my life almost full time for more than two years. However, I believe the final result—the book you now hold in your hands—was worth the effort. I hope you feel the same.

Before concluding this preface, I also need to mention/explain the Internet page references (website addresses or URLs) I have included throughout the book. There are many of them, and I believe they are important and will be useful. To make them stand out within the text, I have put them in italics. I first thought I would also underline them so that they would stand out, but I decided against that for a number of reasons that I will not take time and space to explain here.

I wish you could click on them as you would links on the Internet and go to the referenced pages, but that is not possible. I am sorry to say that some of them are long, and it will require extra effort for you to look at them. Some others I did not include because they were so unreasonably long that they were totally impractical.

As time passes, I am sure there will be some of these website URLs that will no longer work. In such cases, please use your Internet search engine to find the sites you seek—if they still exist. The process for using search engines is explained in Chapter 9, in case you need an explanation. As time passes, there are sure to be other resources you will find that are better than those I have listed.

The Internet is a marvelous resource for genealogical research, as it is for many other areas of study. Using the resources now available, you can—in many cases—accomplish more research in a few minutes than you could previously do in several hours. But though it is a great boon to this work, it is still an imperfect tool. Many important records relating to your ancestral families and their genealogy are not on the Internet, and some of those records will never be there. In addition, the indexes to those records that are on the Internet are also imperfect—some of them very imperfect—because they were created by imperfect people who were reading and interpreting records that are also imperfect, as well as being difficult—and sometimes impossible—to read.

In spite of what you may have been told and what is endlessly preached by the uninformed, I regret to say that if you do thorough, quality research, much of what you do will involve records that are not available on the Internet. However, even though many important sources of critical evidence are not online, we can (and must) still use the Internet for the considerable merit it has and the resources it puts literally at our fingertips. Nevertheless, when all is said and done, the principles of thorough and sound research are still important because accuracy is still paramount, facts are still facts, and our prime objective in research must be to get it right even if it takes longer.

We must be faithful to the principles of complete research and to the facts that complete research will produce. After all, these are our ancestors we are dealing with, and we owe it to them to get it right.

My final comment, as I conclude this preface, relates to the many quotations used throughout the book. In every case, I have used the spelling, grammar, punctuation (and lack thereof), and exact wording of the original sources, regardless of style or any grammatical imperfection that may be contained therein. In a few cases, I have added a word or two in brackets [ ] for clarification. I trust you will accept this approach in the spirit in which I have done it and acknowledge it as an indication of the authenticity of the sources cited. What you see in these patterns of usage and the grammar in these quotations is also a foreshadowing of what you will experience in your research.

Part 1

Background to Research

1

Understanding Genealogical Research

The word "genealogy" (jēnēˈaləjē) is a noun. When I checked a multitude of web-based dictionaries recently, I discovered that the consensus of most definitions concentrated on two ideas. One of these said, essentially, that a genealogy is a table or chart showing ancestral descent. The second defined genealogy as a study of families and their relationships. Genealogy, based on the second of those definitions, is the object of this book. However, as we follow that line of study, it should lead us, ideally, to produce a well-researched and carefully documented product that fits the first definition.

In recent years, another term has emerged in place of "genealogy." That term, "family history," has been widely accepted and extensively used. Certainly, genealogy is a branch of history that relates to families, so the term "family history" also fits our subject. It is a "softer" and more comfortable term, and it has a more familiar feel that invites people to get involved or, at least, does not scare them away. It intimates that we are dealing with personal connections and not just cold, hard data.

The term certainly has merit and, in fact, few people object to it—except the purists. And, after all, the more I know about my family's history, the more I know about myself. Keep in mind, however, that merely changing the name from *genealogy* to *family history* does not magically change the nature of what is required; it does not simplify or change the nature of the work. There are recent technological developments that have made many things easier, but we need to be careful that we do not succumb to the false notion that they are foolproof or that everything we find on the amazing family history Internet websites is of unquestioned accuracy.

The primary purpose of this book is to help you become a family history researcher—even a good family history researcher. I use the term "family history researcher" here rather than "family historian" because my intent is to make you more of a researcher than a historian. Chapter 11, later in this book, is designed to help you think more in terms of the family history angle and not strictly about the names, dates, and places of genealogy. Both, however, are important.

In this connection, I cannot go on without sharing the definition of genealogy on the website of the Board for Certification of Genealogists. It speaks to the essence of the work we are doing.

> Genealogy is the study of families in genetic and historical context. Within that framework, it is the study of the people who compose a family and the relationships among them. At the individual level, it is biography, because we must reconstruct each individual life in order to separate each person's identity from that of others bearing the same name. Beyond this, many researchers also find that genealogy is a study of communities because kinship networks have long been the threads that create the fabric of each community's social life, politics, and economy.[1]

That is a very insightful definition, and I like it a lot. That having been said, I hope you will not think it presumptuous for me now to offer my own definitions:

Genealogy/Family history: A branch of history that encompasses the determination of family relationships and enlarges, insofar as possible, the researcher's understanding of the lives of his ancestors.[2]

Research: An investigation aimed at the discovery of facts, as well as the analysis and interpretation of those facts. It also often includes the revision of accepted theories (the "facts" of the past) in light of newly discovered evidence.

The family history researcher must not deal with a genealogy/family history challenge in the same way you and I might have dealt with an assignment years ago in our high-school history classes. As history students, if we had an assignment to study the American Civil War, for example, we probably read an assigned chapter and perhaps checked an encyclopedia. If we were diligent, we also read about the subject in another history book or two. If you are younger than I am, you likely spent most of your time checking sources on the

---

[1] "Definition of Genealogy," Board for Certification of Genealogists, http://www.bcgcertification. org/certification/faq.html#5 (accessed January 4, 2017).

[2] Please note that my use of "his," in this instance and similar uses of masculine pronouns throughout this book, is not intended to demean or offend women. This usage is merely for the sake of simplicity, and I intend for it to relate to both males and females. In other words, I am choosing not to be fettered by the complicated and nonsensical demands of political correctness that have so mercilessly complicated our communications.

Internet. But, either way, most of us took someone else's word for everything we read on the subject.

With a genealogical/family history problem, we may *begin* in the same place we did as high-school history students. We may read printed or published genealogies and family histories, and we may find pedigrees on the Internet—as well we should. However, the notion that when we are copying the results of someone else's work we are doing family history research/genealogy is a misconception. Published and compiled works—whether in books or on the Internet—are, after all, *only* the report of someone else's research. Without further investigation, we do not know whether that research was good or bad. Yes, it is important that we find what information is out there about our families—to know what others have already done—but we cannot take the results of their research at face value. If we are fortunate, they will have documented their work so we can more easily verify its correctness.

As family history researchers, we need to pursue our work in the same way that we hope the author of the textbook we used as history students pursued his work. We must immerse ourselves in the process of searching out and studying original documents and accounts. We might search original records on microfilm or digitized documents on the Internet—or perhaps delve into records in some courthouse or another repository of original records.

Next, when we have completed our investigation, we will take the information found in those sources and analyze whatever evidence we found that relates to our objectives. After this, we will compile our results into an understandable and usable format. Finally—and this is critical—we will take pains to see that all of those facts, and our conclusions based on those facts, are well documented for the benefit of those who will follow after us.

In contrast to the research of the historian, we cannot make a brief general summary of a historical period. Instead, we must consider the critical details of each ancestral problem—each family connection—thoroughly and individually, both while we are searching the records and while we are preserving the results of our research.

I. THE TRUE NATURE OF RESEARCH

In this section, I will take the liberty of comparing the genealogist/family history researcher to a research chemist, but the comparison could just as easily be made with any person involved in nearly any kind of research. As I anticipated this fourth edition of *The Researcher's Guide*, I thought about changing this section relating to the true nature of research. My thinking was that, with all the technological innovations that have taken place since the third edition, the nature of research is somehow different. However, the more I have looked at the issue, the more I am convinced that the true nature of research is unchanged—we just have some incredible tools now available to us that often expedite the process. And I add the caution that speed can entice us to short-circuit the process. We must not cut corners or do less than good research requires.

No matter the state of available technology, once a decision is made on the focus of our research, the steps we follow will not change. We may be able to complete some of those steps faster and more easily, but each step is still important and must be taken. What the chemist does in this example, we must do also:

1. Before the chemist begins work on an actual problem, he must find out what others have done with the same problem. This process is called secondary research. (In family history, it has been called the "preliminary survey.") The chemist will seek, carefully and systematically, to learn everything he can about what others have already done. How foolish it would be for him to spend ten years (or even one year or one month) on a particular project only to discover, upon presenting his findings to his colleagues, that someone else had already accomplished the same work. It is no less foolish for us to do the same thing in our family history research.

2. As the scientist completes this secondary research, he will analyze what he has found and make a judgment about its validity. He must very carefully study the information that relates to what has already been done. If he agrees that the results and the conclusions drawn from the previous research are sound, he is ready to begin his own research where his predecessors left off. However, if he questions part of it or rejects it totally, his starting point will be quite different. In any case, his approach will be influenced significantly by what has already been done. The same applies to the family history researcher.

   As a side note here, I must also say that I do not believe we should *never* repeat a search that has been previously made. Nevertheless, if and when we repeat a search, we need to be aware we are doing so and know why. In fact, there will be times when we repeat searches we have made ourselves because newly discovered evidence tells us it needs to be done.

3. The chemist's next step, based on his analysis, will be to determine his research objectives and prepare a plan for primary research. He knows by now what his problems are and can decide what steps to take as he seeks to solve them. The family history researcher must do the same.

4. He begins his research, gathering information from primary investigation, and he records that information, systematically creating complete documentation of everything he does. His approach will be logical and in complete agreement with his predetermined plan. The only difference between what the chemist does and what the family history researcher does is in the basic nature of the research performed. The chemist's sources are his hands-on research and experimentation while the family history researcher's sources are records and documents.

   In connection with this step, I emphasize the great forward leaps taken in recent years to facilitate access to many of the records that family history research requires. Computer technology and the work of many dedicated people have made some important original source materials *much* more accessible than ever before. Many important records have been digitized, and many of these digitized records have been indexed so we can examine digitized original images of those records on our computer screens with a few mouse clicks.

The fact that the indexing and digitizing of records are mammoth-sized tasks has not caused hesitation. These processes have high priority, and they are getting done faster than anyone thought possible. That which has been completed is already a boon to this work, and there are careful explanations later in this book—as we discuss computer technology—on how to access these important resources.

5. Once the relevant evidence has been gathered according to our chemist's objectives and plan, he will carefully evaluate that evidence. He will analyze his research results to ascertain whether his objectives have been attained. He will then synthesize all findings into a meaningful form.

   If the desired objectives have been achieved, the cycle will start again, working on a new problem with new objectives. If not, the cycle will also start again, but skipping the secondary research step unless sufficient additional evidence has been found to make that step profitable. If that is the case, the quest will continue with a fresh analysis of the problem in light of the recent failure—but with added insight. This is what we too must do as family history researchers.

6. A sixth step—not a part of the actual research process, yet essential to it—is to make the results of our research findings available to others (perhaps by publication). In today's world, there are some simple ways to do this. One way is to post our findings, along with our documentation, in an appropriate place on the Internet. In Chapters 9 and 10, you'll find much more information about the Internet and the technological resources that are now of such great value to the family history researcher.

These six steps comprise the research cycle; they are the essential steps in the process. Understand, however, that the process as I have explained it here is oversimplified; the steps are not always clearly separated. I have divided them for the purposes of clarification and discussion only. It is my hope that this analysis will illustrate that the basic processes are the same whether the researcher is a chemist, a geneticist, a research psychologist, or a family history researcher.

Also, note that dividing the research process into its component parts enables our observation of some other interesting phenomena. Note that of the six steps listed, three of them (the second, third, and fifth steps) involve some type of analysis. Thus, it becomes apparent that a significant requirement in most research is the ability to evaluate information and analyze it correctly. Almost anyone can search records if told what to search, but to make a correct

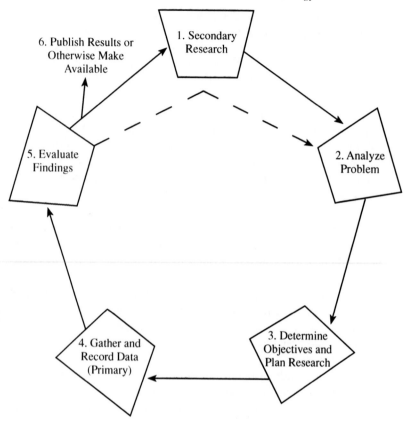

FIGURE I—THE SIX STEPS OF THE RESEARCH PROCESS

analysis of what has been found is a more difficult task. Likewise, the tasks of setting realistic objectives and making plans to achieve those objectives are also more difficult than searching records. These skills require both aptitude and training, and improve with experience.

Many would-be family history researchers do not complete all the steps that good research requires. Too many spend their entire efforts on secondary research, thinking they are doing everything that needs to be done when they search old family history books and/or copy other people's pedigrees off the Internet.

A woman once (actually, I am sure this has happened more than once) approached the reference desk at a large genealogical library with a printed family history open in each arm. She carefully laid the two books on the counter and then, apparently quite upset, queried the reference librarian about two conflicting entries. One book said the father of a certain individual was one man while the second claimed it was someone else. The librarian examined the two books and then told her she would need to check original sources for her answer. Her reply: "I don't have time to do that!" And it is not likely she pursued that course; such a task was beyond the parameters of her agenda. Perhaps she solved her inconvenient dilemma by flipping a coin or by following some other equally unsound course of action.

There are others (though not nearly so many) who believe non-original sources are too unreliable to be consulted at all and thus spend all their research efforts in original records without concern for what others may have done before. That, too, is a serious mistake.

II. GENEALOGY AND SCIENCE

Thus far, I have made no explicit claim that family history research is a science, though I have suggested that such is the case; I hope you caught that message. However, let me pursue the idea a little further.

First, it is important to define *science* and look at its etymology. The word comes from the Latin term *scientia*, which means "having knowledge." My dictionary gives six definitions for science, two of which seem particularly relevant to our subject:

- Systematized knowledge derived from observation, study, and experimentation carried on to determine the nature of what is being studied or those principles relating to it.
- Any specific branch of scientific knowledge, esp. one concerned with establishing and systematizing facts, principles, and methods, as by experiments and hypotheses.[3]

Both of these definitions apply to family history research when it is practiced correctly. Sadly, however, as practiced by many, there are significant gaps. I believe that family history research *should* be a science—it deserves to be a science. Unfortunately, the methods of some devotees tend to lower it to the level of a mere pastime—even a pastime built on unstable ground. Thus, with that thought in mind, I want to modify my earlier definition to state as follows:

Genealogy/Family history: A branch of history that encompasses the *scientific* determination of family relationships and enlarges, insofar as possible, the researcher's understanding of the lives of his ancestors.

Family history will achieve respectability among the sciences only as those of us who do the research adopt scientific principles. First, we must employ every step that scientific research requires. Then we must carefully consider all relevant evidence in our efforts to reach correct, well-documented conclusions. No scientist would do less. And if you and I are ever tempted to do less than our best, we should remember two things:

1. Those who come after us will eternally judge us by what we actually produce rather than by our ability.

---

[3] *Webster's New World College Dictionary*, 5th ed. (New York: Macmillan USA, 2014).

2. An error on an ancestral line that is extended many generations is far-reaching in its effect. An incorrect ancestor on one of our lines, if extended five short generations, will have those who follow working on thirty-two wrong lines, and that number doubles with each additional generation.

These are our ancestors we are talking about here; we owe it to them to get it right.

III. COMPLETING THE FAMILY PICTURE

I am often asked to name one procedure that, if followed, would have the greatest effect in improving the quality of family history research. My answer to that question is simple: it is concern for complete families on our direct lines rather than just individuals. The histories of our families involve much more than just pedigrees with names, dates, and places. Though such pedigrees are essential, they can—if that is all we have—limit our ultimate success.

For example, if a man was born in 1845 and his father in 1780, that sixty-five-year gap makes the connection suspect. However, it does not seem so far-fetched once we discover (by gathering evidence on the complete family) that the man's mother was his father's second wife, his father was twenty years older than his mother (born 1800), and he was the youngest child in a large family, the eldest child being born in 1825. These facts help put the problem into proper perspective, and the connection does not seem particularly unusual. However, this is true only because we can see the complete picture.

Other situations can also give us a false sense of accuracy. When we look at only one child in the family—our direct ancestor—a pedigree connection might appear entirely logical but quickly becomes suspect when we compile the complete family. Once all the brothers and sisters are identified, we might easily notice that some of the children were born after the alleged mother's childbearing years. Or, in a different case, we might find some of the children born when the alleged mother was still herself a child. Unless we compile complete families, erroneous connections might be readily accepted—an error we cannot afford to make and that can be so easily prevented.

Reputable family history researchers agree on the importance of compiling complete families with complete data on all family members. The late Donald Lines Jacobus,[4] writing on this matter, said:

> For many reasons, it is advantageous in doing genealogical research to consider the family group, not to look upon each ancestor as an isolated individual or as a mere link in a chain of descent. One of the most important reasons is that it enables us to check the chronology. Very often, the relations

---

[4] Mr. Jacobus (1887–1970), whose name is legendary among genealogists, was considered the dean of American genealogy during his lifetime. *The New Haven Genealogical Magazine*, which he established in 1922, became *The American Genealogist* in 1932. He served as its editor and publisher until 1966.

of dates determine or negate the possibility of an alleged line of descent, or provide clues that might otherwise elude detection. It is a good idea to write out the full family history, or chart of relationships, while working, inclusive of "guessed" dates where specific dates are not known. It is an aid to the memory as well as to the imagination if the eye can see the members of the family grouped together.[5]

There is an unfortunate tendency among some ancestor hunters to put greater value on the length of their pedigrees than on the accuracy. There seems to be a sense of magic in the pedigree that goes back a long way—even to Father Adam. And people are enthralled by pedigrees that connect to royalty.

Perhaps this is the sort of thing the Apostle Paul was writing about in his Epistles to Titus and Timothy when he instructed them to not "give heed to . . . endless genealogies" (see Tim. 1:4 and Titus 3:9). In more recent times, people have gotten excited about computer programs that show how they are related to famous people. Besides being a curiosity, they have no value unless the connections made are accurate—which many are not.

Another tactic that will add to the quality and success of our research—and also assist in our quest to compile complete families—is concern for every person of the surname(s) of our interest who lived in the same localities where our ancestors lived during the same time period our ancestors lived there. This practice, as you can understand, is closely allied to the compiling of complete families because it is impossible to compile families without first identifying all potential family members.

As we search the records of those places where our ancestors lived, we must consider every relevant document relating to every person with our ancestral surname(s)—including all spelling variations. We should also carefully extract all pertinent information from those records into our research notes, by whatever method of record keeping we use. The connection of all these people to our ancestors may not be immediately apparent, but most of them will likely fit into the picture as we analyze our findings and put families together.

If the surname we are researching is common, we may find many people who do not seem to fit into our family picture. We will likely also find people who are definitely *not* related to our ancestors, and this is also useful.

As an example of this principle, let us consider a hypothetical (though common) situation: We are searching records relating to our ancestor Charles Pebble in Mugwump County, in an effort to identify his father. We find nothing. However, if we had searched the Mugwump County records for everyone named Pebble (all possible spellings), we would have found the will of one John Peppell in 1805. In his will, John named "my brother Charles" as executor and also bequeathed to his son James "the old saddle I bought from my father, Thomas Peppell."

---

[5] Donald Lines Jacobus, "Genealogy and Chronology," *Genealogical Research: Methods and Sources,* Vol. I. Rev. ed., edited by Milton Rubincam (Washington, DC: American Society of Genealogists, 1980), 28. Used by permission.

This may or may not be our Charles Pebble who was referred to by John Peppell as his brother. This information would need to be carefully analyzed as it relates to other evidence, but the possibility is obvious.

If two people are related, the records of the places they lived will often tie them together, but we *must* exhaust the records for everyone of that surname. Likewise, we must not be too concerned if we find the name spelled a variety of ways (Pebble, Peppell, Pebbel, Pepple, Pebell, Peble, Peple, Pebel, etc.). It is helpful if we can think about what variant spellings there might be and then look for those spelling variations in the records. If our ancestor could not write (as was common in early periods), his name will be spelled the way it sounded to the person who happened to be making the record. Spelling was not an exact science. (Challenges associated with spelling are discussed in greater depth in Chapter 2.)

We have use of the wonderful digitized records and the indexes relating to them that are on the Internet today, but it is unfortunate that the very nature of the way the records are set up tends to take us away from our objective of gathering evidence relating to everyone of our surname(s) of interest. That principle is so fundamental to good research that it is essential for us to take the extra time and make the extra effort necessary to accomplish this task. Otherwise, our research is incomplete.

IV. GENEALOGY AND HISTORICAL BACKGROUND

Genealogy and history (religious, economic, social, military, political, etc.) cannot be separated. Our ancestors cannot be detached from the times in which they lived or the places where they lived and still be understood. It is impossible to recognize the full extent of research possibilities unless we are aware of the historical background from which our people came.

History and circumstances dictated the types of records kept, as well as the format and content of those records. They also influenced the records not kept, as well as those lost or destroyed. History dictated social stratification, patterns of migration and settlement, and even occupations. Hostile Indians, wars, land policies, political figures, legislation, persecutions, disease, epidemics, droughts, fires, and religion: all these factors and many more had a profound effect on our ancestral families and those records in which we find information about them.

If we can understand the forces that shaped people's lives, we can better understand those people. If an ancestor was of age to fight in the Civil War, it would be a mistake not to investigate records of that war. Then, if we find he did not serve, perhaps his religious affiliation should be examined to see if he may have been a conscientious objector on religious grounds (as were the Quakers). This, too, would be significant and might lead to other relevant records. Alternatively, it would be interesting to know if he suffered from serious disability that prevented him from serving.

Family history research is event oriented. Much of our success depends on our understanding of the events that were part of, and that otherwise affected, our ancestors lives. We must identify the events in which they may have been involved. We must also learn whether their participation in those events was recorded, and, if so, we need to find those records. Finding records that relate to an ancestral family, extracting from those records all pertinent genealogical/historical information, and then accurately determining the correct meaning and the significance of that information as it relates to our ancestor(s) are the very essence of family history research success.

V. THE IMPORTANCE OF PLACES

Considering the relevance of events to family history research, we must understand that it is usually necessary to know where an event occurred before we can find any record of it. Events do not occur in a vacuum but, rather, in specific places. Moreover, it is in those places—within established record jurisdictions—that those events were recorded. The more precisely we can identify the location of a critical event, the better are our chances for research success. There is a detailed discussion of places in Chapter 3.

VI. NOTHING BUT THE FACTS

Do we fear the facts? Are we afraid of finding skeletons in our ancestral closets? If we are ashamed to have ancestors who may not meet our personal social standards, we should probably stay away from our family history. There are out-of-wedlock children in the best of families—none of us is free from this. An outlaw or a horse thief might also turn up on any family tree, but we will also find the opposite—nobility and social status. Whatever we find, it is not our place to judge. Consider the observation of Sir Thomas Overbury, the seventeenth-century English poet, in his *Characters*: "The man who has not anything to boast of but his illustrious ancestors is like a potato—the only good belonging to him is underground."

It is also true that some of the most shameful carryings-on took place in the most illustrious families. Geoffrey Chaucer, whom many consider to be the father of English literature, put it nicely in his "Wife of Bath's Tale":

> It is clear enough that true nobility
> Is not bequeathed along with property,
> For many a lord's son does a deed of shame
> And yet, God knows, enjoys his noble name.
> But though descended from a noble house
> And elders who were wise and virtuous,
> If he will not follow his elders, who are dead,
> But leads, himself, a shameful life instead,
> He is not noble be he duke or earl.
> It is the churlish deed that makes the churl.[6]

---

[6] Geoffrey Chaucer, "The Wife of Bath's Tale," *The Portable Chaucer*. Translated and edited by Theodore Morrison (New York: The Viking Press, 1940), 250–251. Used by permission.

Regardless of what our research reveals, our first responsibility is to the truth. An accurate report, unaffected by the nature of the facts, is the responsibility of the family history researcher, as it is the responsibility of any historian or scientist. Those who attempt to alter or color the truth are a liability to the science of family history. They do not deserve the title of either genealogist or family history researcher. However, I also add this warning: in our dedication to truth, we also have a responsibility to present that truth objectively, tastefully, and in proper perspective. I advise careful consideration of those standards recommended by the National Genealogical Society that you will read near the end of this chapter.

We must never be ashamed of either the truth or our ancestors. After all, who knows how they might feel about us!

VII. WHAT IS EXPECTED?

Two questions become apparent:

- Is it necessary to be professional genealogists to be successful in locating our ancestors?
- Might it be best to leave all of this work to the professionals?

The answers to both these questions are the same—a resounding *NO!*

With proper instruction and discipline, many people become proficient family history researchers and, as such, have the deeply satisfying experience of seeking and finding ancestors, both their own and those of other people. However, whatever reasons we have for learning to be good family history researchers, the requirement is the same: to be successful, we *must* know what we are doing.

Remember, also, that no matter how good our tools may be and how complete our tool collection, these are of little worth if we are not skilled in their use. If I were to suffer a severe attack of appendicitis in some remote place with no hospital available, I would be grateful for the surgeon who chanced to come by with a tin can, a pocketknife, and a needle with thread (all of which he would boil to sterilize) to take care of my problem. In fact, I would prefer this to being in a modern hospital with state-of-the-art tools where the hospital custodian was called on to perform my surgery.

When we get down to bare facts, tools—though important—are not the most important thing. Knowledge is. However, after we have the essential knowledge, there is much to recommend being properly tooled. There is no arguing the point that, when a critical need arises, the preferred situation is to have both the skilled professional *and* the best tools. The same principle applies to our family history research.

We would not turn a person loose to do research (of even the most fundamental type) in a chemistry lab filled with equipment and chemicals without some instruction. We would instruct him carefully about both the equipment and the chemicals; the more he knows about these things, the better are his chances of achieving success. Lack of knowledge may not only result in failure, but it has the potential of producing disastrous results. Yet how often does a person with a similar lack of genealogical experience and expertise undertake "research" in the historical and documentary laboratory? Though there are many tools available to facilitate research—more of them than ever before—knowledge of fundamentals is still critical to the best results.

Is it any wonder that some people get discouraged or that their "research" results are unsatisfactory—even disastrous? Should we be surprised that so many compiled family history records lack credibility and so many published family histories and genealogies are less than reliable?

If you have an aptitude for history and the social sciences, are good with details, and enjoy intellectual problem-solving, you have the necessary talents to become a family history researcher. You should be able to learn readily what you need to know about using the available tools; you merely need a guide. Proper instruction, together with the empirical knowledge that comes with experience, can prepare you to be a competent researcher, even though you do not pursue family history research as a profession.

Take comfort in the fact that we need not be experts in all phases of family history research to do good work. We need only be experts on research in the geographical locality (the place) where our current research problem is centered. As we go from one problem to the next, we can become experts one step at a time.

VIII. EDUCATIONAL OPPORTUNITIES

In addition to personal, on-the-job experience (which, of course, is essential), there are some significant resources available to help us learn what is necessary and to hone our skills.

A. Genealogical societies

Genealogical societies everywhere hold regular meetings to explore significant advances and for members to help one another. Most of these societies also hold conferences where they invite knowledgeable guest speakers. It is good to belong to these organizations, both for their educational benefits and to lend support to their programs and projects.

Some societies are large and have a far-reaching influence. We should become aware of these and, if we can, be involved with one (or some) of them. Many societies also have specific areas of focus that might be relevant to our research. Of note are those associated with specific ethnic groups.

I will mention a few of the most important larger societies.

1. **The National Genealogical Society (NGS),** founded in 1903, is one we should note, and we should also acquaint ourselves with the soci-

ety's website (*http://www.ngsgenealogy.org/*). There is more information about classes offered by NGS later in this section under "Courses and Classes."

2. **The New England Historic Genealogical Society (NEHGS)**, located in Boston, Massachusetts, is also important. It is the oldest genealogical society in America, founded in 1845. Website: *https://www.american ancestors.org/*.

3. **The Federation of Genealogical Societies (FGS)** is an organization you should also know about. Though devoted primarily to the needs and success of genealogical societies, FGS has much to offer the individual researcher. The Society website (*https://fgs.org/*) has some significant helpful resources, including *Forum* (which is a quarterly interactive electronic magazine), an exhaustive list of genealogical and family history societies, information on various conferences and publications, webinars, and a useful blog.

B. Conferences, seminars, and workshops

NGS sponsors a major annual conference for researchers. The National Genealogical Society Family History Conference, a four-day event, is held in a different U.S. city each year. Genealogical societies in the states where these events are held host the conferences. You can learn more at *http://conference. ngsgenealogy.org/*.

NEHGS also offers significant educational opportunities, including an annual one-day research seminar and a three-day Research Getaway. More information about these programs and other available services is available at *https://www.americanancestors.org/Education*.

There are also other significant conferences, including the following:

- The Institute of Genealogy and Historical Research (IGHR), a significant six-day institute, which was hosted by Samford University in Birmingham, Alabama, from 1965 to 2016. It is now hosted (beginning in July 2017) by the Georgia Genealogical Society at the Georgia Center for Continuing Education in Athens, Georgia. Go to *https://www.facebook. com/IGHR.Georgia/* for more information.

- The Genealogical Institute on Federal Records (Gen-Fed) in Washington, DC. (It was formerly named—until November 2015—the National Institute on Genealogical Research [NIGR].) It has offered a five-day annual conference since 1950 (except in 2015). This conference, which convenes at the National Archives, is an intensive program featuring on-site examination of federal records for experienced researchers. It is not an introductory course. More information is available on both the history and the future at *http://www.gen-fed.org/home/about-gen-fed/history-of-gen-fed/*. Some scholarships are available.

- Salt Lake Institute of Genealogy (SLIG), sponsored by the Utah Genealogical Association (UGA), is a five-day conference held annually each January. SLIG primarily offers courses on high intermediate and advanced levels, with a handful of classes for intermediate and transitional researchers. Information is available on the UGA website, *https://infouga.org.*

- The Federation of Genealogical Societies (FGS) offers conferences as well—sometimes even cruises. The FGS website says that the society's conferences are open to anyone with an inkling of finding their past and provide a unique setting to interact, connect, and learn from many of the world's expert genealogists. Drawing people from all over the U.S. and around the world, FGS conferences promise to deliver an unparalleled educational and enlightening experience for everyone year after year.[7]

  For more information on FGS conferences, go to the society's website at *https://fgs.org/.*

- Roots Tech is a three-day conference held in Salt Lake City each February, featuring all levels of instruction. FamilySearch is the conference host. Website: *https://www.rootstech.org.* This is by far the largest family history conference in the United States and offers a broad spectrum of classes, with its main focus on the novice.

- Brigham Young University (BYU) Conference on Family History and Genealogy, sponsored by FamilySearch and the International Commission for the Accreditation of Professional Genealogists (ICAPGen), is a four-day annual conference held in July. It focuses on the needs of Latter-day Saint family history researchers but also has much of interest for others. The website is *https://familyhistoryconferences.byu.edu/.*

- The International Association of Jewish Genealogical Societies (IAJGS) sponsors an annual conference for researchers of all skill levels. The conference includes lectures, workshops, and presentations of various kinds, including hands-on help with the latest technology, databases, and search tools. The aim of these conferences is to assist those with Jewish ancestry. IAJGS is an umbrella organization of more than 70 national and local Jewish Genealogical Societies (JGS) around the world. The association's website is at *http://www.iajgs.org.*

- The Genealogical Research Institute of Pittsburgh [GRIP] holds two separate weeklong courses at La Roche College in Pittsburgh, Pennsylvania, each summer. Each course is different from the other. More information is on the GRIP website, *http://www.gripitt.org.*

- The Midwest African American Genealogy Institute (MAAGI) has been holding an institute offering family history instruction annually since

---

[7] "Who attends a FGS Conference?" *Federation of Genealogical Societies: Linking the Genealogical Community*, Federation of Genealogical Societies, https://fgs.org/cpage.php?pt=43 (accessed January 4, 2017).

2013, initially at the Harris Stowe University in St. Louis and more recently at the Allen County Public Library in Fort Wayne, Indiana. Information is available on the MAAGI Institute website at *http://www.maagiinstitute.org/*.

- The National Archives sponsors many workshops throughout each year at the regional National Archives. A list of workshops is at *https://www.archives.gov/research/genealogy/events*. A list of the regional National Archives, with their addresses and contact information, is in Chapter 5.

The above events are some of the most noteworthy, but there are many more.

C. Courses and classes

Brigham Young University (BYU) in Provo, Utah, offers both certificates and bachelor's degrees in family and local history. Both BYU and BYU-Idaho in Rexburg have broad and diversified genealogical curricula. Other institutions offering courses in genealogy include American University in Washington, DC; Boston University in Boston, Massachusetts; Western Illinois University in Macomb, Illinois; and BYU–Hawaii in Laie, Hawaii. Some others also offer home-study courses. The University of Washington has a certificate program in genealogy and family history. It is a nine-month course offered in the evenings by the university graduate school.

The National Genealogical Society (NGS) is a major player in the education area, as it relates to American research, with its independent study and cloud-based[8] home-study classes. What it previously offered as an excellent home-study course in American genealogical research has now been replaced by the American Genealogical Studies series. The courses in the series include:

- American Genealogical Studies: The Basics
- American Genealogical Studies: Guide to Documentation and Source Citation
- American Genealogical Studies: Beyond the Basics
- American Genealogical Studies: Branching Out

Before you can enroll in either the "Beyond the Basics" or the "Branching Out" courses, you must successfully complete both "The Basics" and the "Guide to Documentation and Source Citation" courses.

Beyond these courses, NGS offers what it calls "Continuing Genealogical Studies for those who are interested." The specific home-study classes include:

- Continuing Genealogical Studies: Genetic Genealogy, the Basics
- Continuing Genealogical Studies: Introduction to Civil War Research
- Continuing Genealogical Studies: Researching Your Revolutionary War Ancestors

---

[8] There is a discussion and an explanation about "the cloud" in Chapter 9.

- Continuing Genealogical Studies: Researching Your World War I Ancestors
- Continuing Genealogical Studies: Genetic Genealogy, Autosomal DNA
- Continuing Genealogical Studies: Special Federal Census Schedules
- Continuing Genealogical Studies: Effective Use of Deeds

More details on the above courses and the fees associated with them are on the NGS website (*http://www.ngsgenealogy.org/*). For those who are willing and able, these courses can help them become better researchers.

There are also both independent study and online courses—they call these webinars—in various aspects of family history offered on a regular basis by Family Tree University (*https://www.familytreeuniversity.com/catalog*) and various other organizations. The webinars are of varying lengths, depending on the class—usually either two or four weeks. They are aimed at those with different levels of expertise.

Adult education classes are available in many communities. Also, useful education and training in various aspects of research are available on an almost-daily basis at the Family History Library in Salt Lake City. Similar instruction is also available at the Family History Centers but with less frequency. To get a sense of what is happening with home-study classes, try entering "home study genealogy courses" or "home study family history courses" in your Internet browser. I think you will be amazed.

D. The Family History Guide

A website called The Family History Guide (*http://www.thefhguide.com/*) is a new and unique resource for those involved in family history research on any level. Its scope and its functions are amazing. Details about this website are at the end of Chapter 10 as part of our discussion on family history websites, so I will provide no detail here.

E. Genealogical and historical periodicals

Genealogical periodicals are important to know about and use as we hone our skills as researchers. I will say no more about them here because Chapter 12 lists many of them and discusses them in some detail. However, this is a good place to mention *Family Tree Magazine* (*http://www.familytreemagazine.com/*). This publication is in tune with modern technology and is a helpful guide to other valuable resources. It is available in hard copy and online.

IX. A REALISTIC PERSPECTIVE

With the recent advances generated by computer technology and the surge of record indexing and the digitizing of important records, some people claim that the very nature of "research" has changed. They are convinced—based on the cyber-electronic revolution with all of its apps, wikis, databases, etc., and with the availability of so many indexes and digitized records—that we need a new definition. Modern family history research, they say, is much less complicated—much simpler—than the genealogical research of the past. They believe they can sit down at their computers, with high-speed Internet connections, and do everything that family history research requires.

I am thrilled to say that there truly has been a miraculous transformation, and we are privileged to see it all happen as we look on in amazement. It is true that billions of important digitized records are now available on the Internet, and this is wonderful. It is also true that important computerized indexes are available to facilitate our research. Much has indeed changed and many things are much simpler and less time-consuming than they have ever been. Also, though nothing happens instantaneously, everything is faster and many things do take only a fraction of the time they once took.

Another benefit is that access to other people (our distant relatives) and to the fruits of their research is greatly simplified.

Everything that has happened thus far and all that is yet to happen—for there will surely be much more—is awe-inspiring and miraculous; we are all thrilled to see it unfolding before us as it is. And it is impossible even to imagine what the future holds.

However, as enthusiastic as we are about the current state of this work, it is still important to face this one important fact: In spite of the great blessing and the godsend this modern technology is, family history research still requires everything that we discussed earlier as part of the research cycle. The steps involving actual research—both primary and secondary—are greatly facilitated and enhanced, but the technological enhancements do not get us all the way to our desired destination. It is still essential to search all available records for all persons of our surname(s) of interest and to analyze/evaluate carefully all the information we find to determine if and how it provides evidence that relates to our objectives.

We must still be careful that we do not draw incorrect conclusions and make erroneous connections. And, as we complete all the steps of our research cycle, the steps may be simple in many cases, but in other situations they may be even more difficult and the chances for drawing erroneous conclusions must be recognized and carefully dealt with. We must follow every step carefully.

In light of all of this, I encourage you to read carefully, take to heart, and abide by the National Genealogical Society's "Guidelines for Use of Computer Technology in Genealogical Research" referenced in the "Conclusion" (section XI) to this chapter and quoted verbatim at the end of Chapter 10. These standards are excellent; they are insightful, and they are relevant for our present time. If we follow them carefully, they will help us avoid pitfalls and gain the greatest possible benefit from everything genealogical we find on the Internet. You would do well to read them now, again at the end of Chapter 10, and periodically throughout your research experience.

X. FAMILY HISTORY PROFESSIONS

I have said much about professionalism, but I want to stress that one does not have to be a professional to do professional-quality research. However, for those who actually wish to become professionals, I offer the following information about some major areas of professional employment.

A. Professional family history researcher

If one wants to become a professional family history researcher, the requirements are the same as for the hobbyist, only they are more intense. He must have the proper instruction and plenty of practical experience while he is learning. Beyond this, he must be able to devote himself wholeheartedly to the pursuit of information.

He must be more than a scientist; he must also be a detective. He must be able to remember and to categorize details. He must be extraordinarily painstaking as he records information and sources. He must be able to report his research findings clearly and accurately to his clients. In addition, he must be able to do all of these things expeditiously. These qualities, of course, are improved with practice, but he must be fully aware of their necessity before he embarks. As the satisfactions are great, so are the demands.

What can the professional genealogist do? Can he find work? If so, where? These questions are legitimate and are often asked. There are, in fact, a few possibilities:

Anyone who lives almost anywhere can do research on a freelance basis for those wishing to engage his services. Though the Internet now allows him to do much work from his home, it is usually to the freelancer's advantage to live near and have access to important record repositories, libraries, or other genealogical research facilities. However, if travel is not an obstacle, this is not necessary. Some cities, especially Washington, DC, and Salt Lake City, have significant advantages, but living there does not fit everyone's circumstances. I observe, however, that airfare is becoming very expensive and airport security procedures are a nightmare.

Most freelance researchers build up clientele by their reputations for good work. If their work is of high quality, their satisfied clients tell others. Thus, once established, they will have no problems as long as they continue to do good work. Many researchers have several months' work ahead of them.

There are also companies that specialize in research for paying clients; many of these have jobs to offer. Those who are employed by them do not have to worry about routine business details, but there are some limitations. All work is by assignment, and the potential financial rewards are less. In fact, many researchers who work for these companies have other employment and do their research on a part-time basis. However, working for others instead of owning the company has its pluses. It eliminates the need for jumping through government hoops and such issues as payroll taxes and withholding requirements.

Some readers are aware that, for many years, the Family History Library in Salt Lake City had a program for accrediting qualified genealogical professionals. With an Accredited Genealogist (AG®) credential, the genealogist could offer this qualification to the public as proof of competence.

Several years ago, when the Family History Library discontinued its accreditation program, the process was taken over by a private group called the International Commission for the Accreditation of Professional Genealogists (ICAPGen). Under the sponsorship of ICAPGen, the accreditation program has continued without interruption. Those who qualify in various geographical areas are accredited to do research in those areas; their names are available on a list of "recommended" researchers.

Those who feel qualified to seek an AG® credential for a given geographical area, and who have had a minimum of 1,000 hours of combined genealogical research and education experience associated with that area, may apply to take the appropriate examination. Also, there are three different levels of accreditation, based on experience and expertise. Qualifications for each level are certified by testing.

A researcher may seek accreditation in more than one geographical area, and renewal is required every five years. All details relating to accreditation are available on the ICAPGen website (*http://www.icapgen.org/*).

Also, the Board for Certification of Genealogists (BCG), a private organization formed in Washington, DC, in 1964, has an excellent program for verifying research expertise. A Certified Genealogist (CG®) credential from the BCG adds considerable prestige to the researcher's professional status. The board grants certification for renewable five-year periods, and applicants may qualify as:

- Certified Genealogists (CG®)
- Certified Genealogical Lecturers (CGL®)

Those who certify as lecturers must first have CG® certification. Other areas of certification used in the past are no longer applicable.

The BCG has also adopted a "Code of Ethics and Conduct" that is widely accepted. Every CG® signs his name in acceptance of this document. I recommend that every family history researcher become familiar with it and embrace its principles:

CODE OF ETHICS AND CONDUCT

As a practicing genealogist, mindful of responsibilities to the public, to the genealogical consumer, and to scholarship, I hereby pledge

- To strive for the highest level of truth and accuracy in all phases of my work;
- To act honorably toward other genealogists and toward the field as a whole;

- To adhere to the Board for Certification of Genealogists' Standards of Conduct; (and, if engaged in research for others)
- To act in my client's best interests; and
- To protect my client's privacy.

To protect the public

- I will not publish or publicize as fact anything I know to be false, doubtful, or unproven; nor will I be a party, directly or indirectly, to such action by others.
- I will identify my sources for all information and cite only those I have personally used.
- I will quote sources precisely, avoiding any alterations that I do not clearly identify as editorial interpretations.
- I will present the purpose, practice, scope, and possibilities of genealogical research within a realistic framework.
- I will delineate my abilities, publications, and/or fees in a true and realistic fashion.
- I will keep confidential any personal or genealogical information disclosed to me, unless I receive written consent to the contrary.

To protect the client (paying or pro bono)

- I will reveal to the client any personal or financial interests that might compromise my professional obligations.
- I will undertake paid research commissions only after a clear agreement as to scope and fee.
- I will, to the best of my abilities, address my research to the issue raised by the client and report to that question.
- I will seek from the client all prior information and documentation related to the research and will not knowingly repeat the work as billable hours without explanation as to good cause.
- I will furnish only facts I can substantiate with adequate documentation; and I will not withhold any data necessary for the client's purpose.
- If the research question involves analysis of data in order to establish a genealogical relationship or identity, I will report that the conclusions are based on the weight of the available evidence and that absolute proof of genealogical relationships is usually not possible.
- If I cannot resolve a research problem within the limitations of time or budget established by contract, I will explain the reasons why.
- If other feasible avenues are available, I will suggest them; but I will not misrepresent the possibilities of additional research.
- I will return any advance payment that exceeds the hours and expenses incurred.

- I will not publish or circulate research or reports to which a client has a proprietary right, without that person's written consent; I will observe these rights, whether my report was made directly to the client or to an employer or agent.

To protect the profession

- I will act, speak, and write in a manner I believe to be in the best interests of the profession and scholarship of genealogy.
- I will participate in exposing genealogical fraud; but I will not otherwise knowingly injure or attempt to injure the reputation, prospects, or practice of another genealogist.
- I will not attempt to supplant another genealogist already employed by a client or agency. I will substitute for another researcher only with specific, written consent of and instructions provided by the client or agency.
- I will not represent as my own the work of another. This includes works that are copyrighted, in the public domain, or unpublished. This pledge includes reports, lecture materials, audio/visual tapes, compiled records, and authored essays.
- I will not reproduce for public dissemination, in an oral or written fashion, the work of another genealogist, writer, or lecturer without that person's written consent. In citing another's work, I will give proper credit. (© Copyright 2007–2015 Board for Certification of Genealogists®. All Rights Reserved.)[9]

Information about certification is available on the BCG website (*http://www.bcgcertification.org*).

B. Freelance record searcher

Record searchers do nothing more than the mechanics of the research—locate records/documents, search them, make copies of relevant documents and/or take notes on what they find, and report their findings back to those who hired them. Their function is critical because many people without personal access to needed records want to have records searched. Above all, record searchers must be able to follow instructions and do precisely what they are asked. Though they might make suggestions, they must never make unauthorized searches and expect to be paid for making them. Record searchers do not usually make as much money as genealogists. However, good record searchers, especially those who are free to travel, are in high demand. If they are good, they can command a good price. Note, however, that the role of the record searcher will likely diminish—or change significantly—as more and more records are digitized and become more accessible on various Internet

---

[9] "Code of Ethics and Conduct," Board for Certification of Genealogists, http://www.bcg certification.org/aboutbcg/code.html (accessed September 15, 2016).

websites. Some tell us that the role of the record searcher is already diminishing significantly.

Like researchers, many record searchers are usually located near large family history collections or libraries. At present, there is a need for record searchers who will read microfilm and who will go into courthouses, churches, cemeteries, and other places where working conditions may be cramped, uncomfortable, and dusty. Certification of Genealogical Record Searchers (CGRS®) is no longer available from the Board for Certification of Genealogists (BCG).

C. Library and archives work

Many libraries, genealogical societies, historical societies, patriotic and hereditary organizations, and archives hire employees knowledgeable in family history research. They seek people who can take care of their collections, assist patrons, and answer correspondence and telephone inquiries relating to family history matters. If you are interested in this phase of family history work, you should consider the study of what is now known as library and information science in addition to your study of family history research procedures.

D. Editorial work and/or writing

Large numbers of genealogical and historical periodicals are currently being published in the United States. These not only demand qualified editors but are also an endless market for good, well-written material. Many people involved in other areas of family history work do free-lance writing for these publications. However, to do any kind of writing you need above-average command of English and a reasonable level of writing skill. Also, note that those who write genealogical articles do so because they like to write them and not for monetary reward. One word of caution for those most enthusiastic: Never submit the same article to two publications at the same time.

E. Computer technology

With the breathtaking incursion of electronics and computer technology into the field of family history, there is a growing need for those who have training in computer science and mathematics as well as family history research. If you are interested in this area, you should plan your schooling accordingly. Future possibilities in this field seem excellent. Consider, for example, the technical needs of the many online family history websites.

F. Teaching

The market for full-time family history teachers is scant but growing. If you desire full-time teaching, I recommend that you pursue an advanced degree in some related social science field—perhaps history, library and information science, or law—in addition to your family history training and experience. But, above all, qualify yourself as both a family history researcher and a teacher.

With regard to teaching, I also refer you back to subheading "C. Courses and classes" in Section VIII of this chapter. Because people want to know how to find their ancestors, community education classes are always in demand and qualified teachers are needed for them. In addition, all of those seminars, conferences, and workshops being offered require instructors. There are many opportunities for those who are qualified and enjoy teaching. However, most of these opportunities are not full-time teaching positions and are filled by knowledgeable people, both amateur and professional, whose lives are also involved with other things.

XI. CONCLUSION

Whatever may inspire you to pursue the study of family history, one point is clear: Success and competence are dependent on *both* good instructional guidance and practical experience. Remember that a book, no matter how good, can go only so far. A good cookbook does not make a good cook, though it helps. Edwin Slosson, a noted magazine editor and scientist of a century ago, summarized this issue appropriately:

> Of course, one cannot become a scientist by merely reading science, however diligently and long. For a scientist is one who makes science, not one who learns science. A novelist is one who writes novels, not one who reads them. A contortionist is one who makes contortions, not one who watches them. Every real scientist is expected to take part in the advancement of science, to go over the top. . . . But, of course, the number of those who are in reserve or in training must always outnumber those at the front.[10]

The way is clear, and the goal is attainable. It is possible for you to become a good family history researcher, amateur or professional, if you are willing to pay the price and adequately prepare—not just here and now, but all along the way. If you are good, the personal satisfaction can be great. Your work can also bring pleasure and satisfaction to many others. However, much is required of you because expectations are high.

Before concluding this discussion, let me mention that the National Genealogical Society (NGS) has promulgated five lists of guidelines for family history researchers that I believe will be of significant value to you. They are:

1. Guidelines for Sound Genealogical Research (quoted below)
2. Guidelines for Using Records Repositories and Libraries
3. Guidelines for Use of Computer Technology in Genealogical Research (quoted at the end of Chapter 10)

---

[10] Slosson, Edwin E. "Science from the Side-Lines," *Chats on Science* (New York: Appleton-Century-Crofts, 1924), p. 140. By permission.

4. Guidelines for Sharing Information with Others

5. Guidelines for Genealogical Self-Improvement and Growth

The NGS website (*http://www.ngsgenealogy.org/cs/ngs_guidelines*) provides ready access to all of these guidelines. All are excellent, and I recommend them for your serious consideration.

In the spirit of all my preaching, I close the chapter by quoting the following:

Guidelines for Sound Genealogical Research
Recommended by the National Genealogical Society

Remembering always that they are engaged in a quest for truth, genealogists and family history researchers consistently

- recognize that information relevant to answering genealogical questions can come from various types of sources, including but not limited to documents, artifacts, and genetic test-reports.

- record the source for each item of information they collect;

- test every hypothesis against credible evidence, and reject those that the evidence shows are incorrect;

- seek original records as the basis for their research conclusions or reproduced images of original records when there is reasonable assurance the records have not been altered in their reproduction;

- use compilations and published works primarily for their value as guides to locating original records and for analysis of the evidence discussed in them;

- state something as a fact or as a proven conclusion only when it is supported by convincing evidence, and identify the evidence when communicating the fact or conclusion to others;

- limit with words such as "probably" or "possibly" any conclusion not based on convincing evidence, and explain their reasoning;

- avoid distributing or publishing inaccurate information and unsupported conclusions in a way that may mislead other researchers;

- state carefully and honestly the results of their own research, and acknowledge all use of other researchers' work;

- recognize the collegial nature of genealogical research by making their work available to others through publication, or by placing copies in appropriate libraries or repositories, and by welcoming critical comment;

- consider with open minds new evidence and others' comments on their work; and

- become familiar with research and ethical standards set by other genealogical organizations, such as the Board for Certification of Genealogists, the Association of Professional Genealogists, the International

Commission for the Accreditation of Professional Genealogists, the International Association of Jewish Genealogical Societies, and the Genetic Genealogy Standards Committee.[11]

Enjoy the journey!

---

[11] "Guidelines for Sound Genealogical Research Recommended by the National Genealogical Society," National Genealogical Society, 2016, http://www.ngsgenealogy.org/cs/ngs_guidelines (accessed January 4, 2017). © 1997, 2002, 2016 by National Genealogical Society. Permission is granted to copy or publish this material provided it is reproduced in its entirety, including this notice.

2

Language, Terminology, and Important Issues

Every branch of learning—be it physics, chemistry, geology, sociology, medicine, law, photography, communications, or whatever subject we name, including family history—has its own principles and related vocabulary. In order to be a good family history researcher, a person must be familiar with the principles and vocabulary of family history.

Many years ago, I had an acquaintance who came from Sweden. Before he passed away, I would take to him all my questions about the puzzling terms I encountered in my Swedish research. I found that some of those terms were also unfamiliar to him, even though he was born and raised in Sweden. This is not an issue of his not understanding Swedish but rather of not being familiar with the vocabulary associated with Swedish family history. There are also English language terms associated with family history research that are unfamiliar to the average American. One of my reasons for writing this chapter is that gap in understanding.

With the technological revolution going on today, there are many words and expressions common today that were unknown just a few years ago—and vice versa. As we get involved in family history, many of these new terms—and the old ones—are important, and it is essential for us to become familiar with their usage and application.

My second reason for writing this chapter is to explore some of the common issues and problems inherent in family history research. Understand, however, that I will not cover every potential topic here. Various terms and concerns are discussed in every chapter of this book.

I. LANGUAGE CHANGES AND HANDWRITING

Some people wonder why handwriting is discussed in an American research textbook. They suppose that American records—going back only a few hundred years—are recent enough that handwriting and its related issues are not a concern. I wish that were the case, but it is not. There are enough differences in handwriting, both in the records of the colonial period as well as in later records, that a brief discussion is appropriate. Even in our own time, handwriting can be a problem because some of us write in such a way that others have difficulty reading what we write. (In fact, I sometimes have difficulty reading my own handwriting after it gets cold.)

If our ancestors were in America in the 1600s, and even in the early 1700s, there is enough carry-over from what is called Early Modern English that a study of its unique features—including the development of conventional spellings—can be very helpful. What is now known as Early Modern English was the language used during the Tudor period, between 1485 and 1603, but the transition to the Modern English we know today did not take place quickly. The following quotation from Wikipedia (one of the simplest and most succinct explanations I have found) helps put the situation into perspective. Note that, in this quotation, I have enlarged the size of the letter examples and added two brief explanations that you will see in brackets. I have also deleted (as shown by ellipses [...]) some unnecessary detail.

Early Modern English orthography [i.e., the way words are spelled] had a number of features of spelling that have not been retained:

- The letter <S> had two distinct lowercase forms: <s> (short *s*) as used today, and <ʃ> (<u>long *s*</u>). The short *s* was always used at the end of a word, and many times in other parts of the word, and the long *s*, if used, could appear anywhere except at the end. The double lowercase *S* was variously written < **ff** >, <fs>, or <ß> (cf. the German <u>ß</u> ligature) ...

- <u> and <v> were not yet considered two distinct letters, but different forms of the same letter. Typographically, <v> was frequently used at the start of a word and <u> elsewhere; hence *vnmoued* (for modern *unmoved*) and *loue* (for *love*). The modern convention of using <u> for the vowel sound(s) and <v> for the consonant appears to have been introduced in the 1630s. Also, <w> was frequently represented by <vv>.

- Similarly, <i> and <j> were not yet considered two distinct letters, but different forms of the same letter, hence *ioy* for *joy* and *iust* for *just*. Again, the custom of using <i> as a vowel and <j> as a consonant is first found in the 1630s.

- The letter <Þ> (thorn) was still in use during the Early Modern English period, though increasingly limited to hand-written texts. In Early Modern English printing <Þ> was represented by the Latin <Y> ... , which appeared similar to thorn in blackletter typeface <ꝧ>. Thorn fell into near-total disuse by the late Early Modern English period; the last vestiges of the letter were its ligatures, **y**ᵉ (thee), **y**ᵗ (that), **y**ᵘ (thou), which were still seen occasionally in the King James Bible of 1611 and in Shakespeare's Folios.

- A silent <e> was often appended to words. The last <u>consonant</u> was sometimes doubled when this <e> was appended; hence *ʃpeake*, *cowarde*, *manne* (for *man*), *runne* (for *run*).

- The sound <ʊ> was often written <o> (as in *son*); hence *ʃommer, plombe* (for modern *summer, plumb*).
- The final syllable of words like *public* was variously spelt, but came to be standardised [*sic*] as *-ick*. The modern spellings with *-ic* did not come into use until the mid 18th century.

Much was not standard, however. For example, the word "he" could be spelled "he" or "hee" in the same sentence, as it is found in Shakespeare's plays.[1]

Various other explanations are more detailed than our discussion here requires. However, you may find them both interesting and helpful. If you want more information, there is a detailed description of Early Modern English in the public online *Oxford English Dictionary* (*http://public.oed.com/page-tags/early-modern-english/*).

Some early American records were not written in English at all but in various European languages—the languages of the emigrants from those countries. However, this is a separate issue and is not addressed here. The best solution, if you encounter this problem, is to seek the help of someone who knows the language involved.

Sometimes, when working with records of past generations, we get the impression that the most important qualification for a public records keeper was to be able to write so no one could read it. However, much early handwriting is carefully written and very legible. In fact, most of the earlier scripts can be read (often quite readily) once we are aware of a few routine practices.

A. Abbreviations/contractions

One common, and often confusing, practice in earlier American documents was that of abbreviating—a carryover from the practice of abbreviating in Latin (the official formal record language of early England). Although England passed a law in 1733 forbidding the use of Latin in parish registers, some Latin persisted, as did the extensive use of abbreviations. Many writers used abbreviations, usually with contractions, just to decrease the amount of writing they had to do; the quill pen was not an instrument of great writing pleasure.

Most abbreviations are recognizable if we are aware that the writer was using them and we watch for them. What we would call "standard" abbreviations were very few, and many words were abbreviated several different ways, depending on the writer. However, the following abbreviations were typical:

accomptant (an old word for accountant) accompt[t]
according   accord[g]
account or accompt   acco[t], acc[t]
administration   admin[ion], admon., admon:

---

[1] "Early Modern English, Orthography," *Wikipedia*, July 31, 2016, https.://en.wikipedia.org/wiki/Early Modern_English (accessed September 19, 2016).

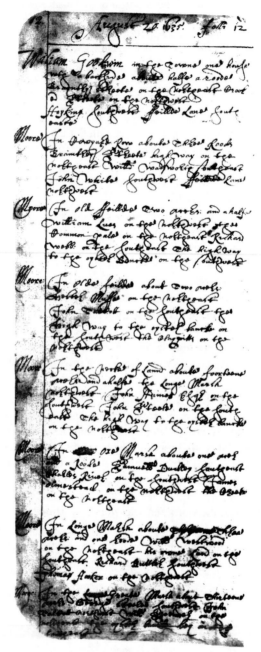

FIGURE I—SOME EARLY MODERN ENGLISH WRITING WITH ITS MANY
UNFAMILIAR CHARACTERS

administrator	admin^r
administratrix	admin^x
aforesaid	afors^d, fors^d, afors:, afsd.
and	&
and so forth [*et cetera*]	&c, etc.
captain	captn, capt:, capt^n
church	chh, ch^h
daughter	dau, dau^r
deceased	decd, dec^d
ditto	do, d^o
Esquire	Esq:, Esqr, Esq.
executor	exec^r, ex^r, ex^{or}, exor:
executrix	exec^x, ex^x, ex^{ix}
Gentleman	Gentl^n, Gent:, Gent.
honorable	honble, hon:
improvement	improvem^t, improv^t
inventory	inventy, inv:, inv^y
Junior	Junr, J^r, Jun:
Messieurs	Messrs, Messrs
namely [*videlicet*]	viz, viz:, vizt
paid	p^d
pair	p^r
per	p^r
personal	personl, p'son^l
probate	probt
probate register	p. regist^r
received	rec^d, recv^d
receipt	rec^t
record	rec^d, rec:
register	reg^r, regist^r
said	sd
Senior	Senr, S^r, Sen:
testament	testam^t, testa:
the	ye, y^e (This usage was a remnant of the ancient Anglo-Saxon letter *thorn* [Þ] common in Early Modern English. Apparently, there was no *thorn* [þ] in the printer's typeset drawer and the y became its substitute. The thorn was pronounced as we pronounce *TH*. Other words beginning with this sound were frequently written thus: y^{at}, y^{em}, y^{en}, y^{ere}, y^{is}, y^{us}, etc.)

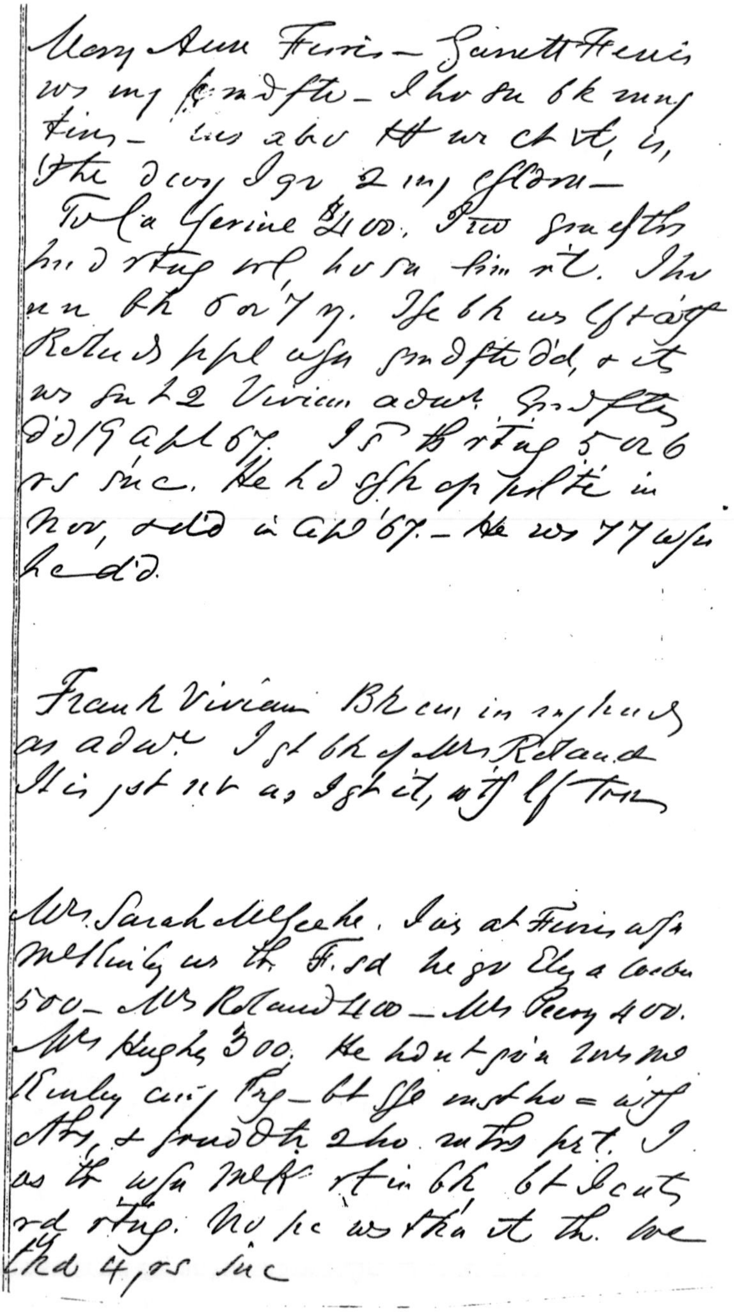

FIGURE 2—SOME SCRIBES DEVELOPED THEIR OWN BRANDS OF SHORTHAND

A good illustration of the use of abbreviations is found in the account of Elizabeth Hodsdon's administration of her late husband's estate in 1763 in York County, Massachusetts (now Maine):

> The acco^t of Eliz^a Hodsdon of her admin^{ion} of the Estate of her late Husband John Hooper the third late of Berwick in ye County of York dec^d Intestate. The S^d accompt^t chargeth her self with the person^l Estate of S^d Dec^d as p^r Invent^y £21·13·-.

Let me point out a few important things about this example. Note that most of the abbreviations were formed by merely shortening the words, sometimes even as we might abbreviate them today, but then putting the last letter of the word (sometimes even two or three letters) in an elevated position at the word's end. This is *superior letter* abbreviation. It was also used with names, as with the name Elizabeth (Eliz^a) in the above example. (See "Name Abbreviations," below.)

Another type of abbreviation (one not found in this document) is *termination*—that is, merely cutting the word short and putting a period (.) or a colon (:) after it, or by drawing a line through it like this: ~~Tho~~ (for Thomas). There are instances in some early writing where only the single first letter of the word was used to form the abbreviation.

Another common abbreviation form was *contraction*. A word like *parish* might be contracted to *p'ish,* or the word *present* to *p'sent.* In these examples, an apostrophe (') is used, but at other times contractions were made by putting a curved line like a tilde (~) above the contracted word, like this: *psẽnt.* Sometimes a word with a double consonant was written with a single consonant and a line drawn over that consonant to show it should have been doubled. For example, *common* might have been written as *com̄on.* This practice was especially common with the letters *m* and *n,* and the line was sometimes like a tilde, as *com̃on.*

Many words were abbreviated in many different ways—all depending on the person doing the abbreviating. In some instances, the abbreviations used for two different words were the same, but the intended word can usually be identified by its context.

B. Name abbreviations

Given names were often abbreviated, as was Elizabeth (Eliz^a) in our Hodsdon example. Names were usually abbreviated in the same ways as other words, but there were also exceptions to this. Following are a few common name abbreviations:

Aaron	Aar ^{n}
Abraham	Abra^m
Andrew	Andr^w, And^w
Arthur	Art^r, Arth^r
Barbara	Barb^a

Benjamin	Benjn, Benj^a, Benj:
Charles	Chas, Char^s, Chas:
Christopher	X^r, Xopher, Xofer
Daniel	Danl
David	Dav^d
Ebenezer	Eben^r
Elizabeth	Eliz^a, Eliz:
Franklin	Frankl^n, Frank^n, Frank:
Frederick	Fred^{ck}, Fredr^k
George	Geo:, G^o
Gilbert	Gilb^t, Gil^{rt}
Hannah	Hañah
James	Ja^s, Jas:
Jeremiah	Jer^a, Jerem^a, Jer^{ah}, Jer:
Jonathan	Jonath^n, Jon^n, Jon:
John	Jno, Jno:
Joseph	Jos, Jo^{ph}, Jos:
Leonard	Leon^d
Margaret	Marg^t, Marg:
Nathan	Nath^n
Nathaniel	Nathl, Nathan^l
Patrick	Patr^k, Pat:
Richard	Rich^d, Rich:
Robert	Robt, Rob:
Samuel	Saml, Sam:
Stephen	Steph^n, Steph
Thomas	Thos, Tho:, ~~Tho~~
Vincent	Vinc^t, Vin^{nt}
Virginia	Virg^a, Virg:
Wilford	Wilf^d, Wilf:
William	Willm, W^m, Will:
Zachariah	Zach^a, Zachar^a, Zach:

Many other names were also frequently abbreviated (and many of those shown were often abbreviated in different ways), but most of these abbreviations can be easily recognized. Nearly every given name of any length—and even surnames—were abbreviated at one time or another. When we have trouble identifying a name, we try to find it written out some other place in the same document.

C. Capital letters

There was a tendency among early writers to capitalize words—almost any word—for no apparent reason, and capitalized words might be found anywhere within a sentence. There was a tendency to capitalize nouns, but the

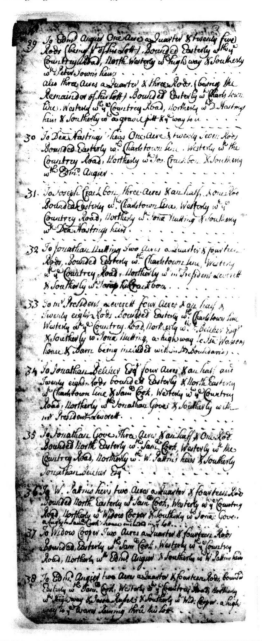

FIGURE 3—A DOCUMENT WITH EXTENSIVE ABBREVIATIONS

pattern was not consistent. Some writers capitalized certain letters whenever those letters were the beginning letters of words. There was no apparent consistency from one writer to another.

D. Punctuation

Perhaps you noticed that the only punctuation marks in the earlier Hodsdon example were the periods at the ends of sentences. This is not unusual. However, there are three main exceptions to this kind of punctuation in early records:

- Occasional commas
- No punctuation
- Dot (•) punctuation

Item number 3 (dot punctuation) was a practice common to many writers. The dots identified pauses. Typically, if placed low (‚), it marked a brief pause. If placed directly between the words (•), it indicated a phrase separation. If placed above the level of the writing (˙), it marked a full stop. Such dots, when used, replaced all other punctuation.

E. Look-alike letters

Another challenge faced by the researcher, only partially observable in the sample documents shown in this chapter, is that some letters appear to be identical to other letters. As mentioned in our discussion of Early Modern English, the letter *I* is interchangeable with *J*, and *U* is interchangeable with *V*. They are indistinguishable. The capital letters *L* and *S*, as well as *T* and *F*, are also easily confused. However, much depends on the person who did the writing. There are also other frequently confused capital letters, but again, much depends on the writer.

When confronted by unreadable handwritten words, the best approach is to carefully study the writing in the rest of the document to see if you can make a distinction. Look for matching letters in other words—words you can identify within their context. This approach should enable you to decipher almost any word. However, initials in names are especially difficult when you are dealing with census returns (even in the nineteenth century) and other records with lists of names.

An additional challenge is the fact that many writers used more than one form of some of their letters, especially capital letters. *A*s, *F*s, *I*s, *J*s, *L*s, *S*s, and *T*s especially lent themselves to this tendency. Because of this, some writing—especially names—requires even more than usual caution. This is also one reason there are no perfect indexes.

Some lowercase letters also cause misunderstandings. Decorative flourishes above the line on the letter *d* and below the line on the *y* and the *g* can be troublesome because they so often invade the space of words on other lines. However, these will not usually cause trouble if we recognize them for what they are.

Another troublesome character, because it is unfamiliar to us, is the long *s* (ſ), as observed in our discussion of Early Modern English. To the inexperienced, this can be confusing and may appear to be an *f* or a *p*. When there is a double *s* (ſſ), it may appear to be a double *f* (*ff*) or a double *p* (*pp*). Challenges relating to the letter *s* persist in writing into the middle 1800s.

One more challenge related to Early Modern English is that the small *e* was made to resemble the modern-day *o* and can cause us to err if undetected. Another potential problem is the similarity of the *n* and the *u*—and all other letters (including *r* and *i*) with up-and-down strokes (minims) in a series. We still struggle with these in our modern handwriting. The name *Drury* ( ) provides a good example. Some writers in the 1600s would put a crooked line (ſ) above one letter (especially *n*s) if there was more than one letter in sequence with these up-and-down strokes. For example, *punish* might appear as *puñish*.

F. Word divisions

If a word was divided at the end of a line, it was not usually divided with a hyphen (-) as in modern usage, but rather with an equals sign (=) or a colon (:). And this mark was often placed in front of the last part of the divided word. Some writers, however, placed the mark both at the end of the first line and at the beginning of second. Also, do not forget, as mentioned earlier, that colons were also frequently used in suspension abbreviations. Do not confuse these two usages.

G. Number problems

Numbers also cause difficulties. Many Arabic numerals, as written two or three hundred years ago, looked quite different from those same numerals as written today.

Dates and other numbers written in the Arabic form should be examined carefully to ensure your reading is correct. Sometimes numbers do not look like numbers at all, and people erroneously try to read them as words. The number *8,* for example, often lies almost flat on its side, and most scribes wrote numbers in a series (such as a year) without lifting pen from paper. Also, because Roman numerals were frequently used in many older records, you need to be able to read them. If you have trouble, conversion tools are available on the Internet. One such tool is "The Calculator Site" at *http://www. thecalculatorsite.com/*.

H. Latin terms

You may also encounter unfamiliar Latin terms and/or abbreviations of these terms. Latin was not used extensively in American records but, as a carryover from British and European practice, it appears with sufficient frequency that you should be aware of the more common terms. Latin terms are frequently used in legal and court records, but you may also see them in other places. Following is a list of some oft-used Latin terms, with some customary abbreviations in parentheses:

Anno Domini (A.D.)	in the year of our Lord
Circa (c., ca., circ.*)*	about
died *sine prole (d.s.p.)*	died without issue
et alii (et.al.)	and others
et cetera (etc., &c)	and so forth
item	also, likewise
liber or *libro*	book or volume
neptis	granddaughter
nepos	grandson
obit (ob)	he/she died
obit sine prole (o.s.p.)	he/she died without issue
requiescat in pace (R.I.P.)	may he/she rest in peace
sic	thus (used to indicate that something incorrectly written is intentionally unchanged from the original)
testis / testes (test.)	witness / witnesses
ultimo (ult.)	last
uxor (ux, vx)	wife
Verbi Dei Minister (V.D.M.)	minister of the word of God
Videlicet (viz., vizt*)*	namely

Latin terms can be interpreted easily using the Internet. For a quick answer, type the unfamiliar Latin word into your Internet search engine, and the definition will be quickly provided. Or, you can go directly to a website called "Google Translate" at *https://translate.google.com.*[2]

The likelihood of encountering American records/documents written entirely in Latin is remote, but the possibility is not excluded. Should you find such records, do not attempt to translate them yourself, even when some words seem familiar, unless you have a background in Latin. In Latin, word endings significantly affect their meanings, and the way one word ends can change the meaning of an entire sentence. The sequence of words means little, but word endings are all-important. My advice is to seek counsel from someone familiar with the language.

I. Non-originals and indexes

When using sources that are not originals, whether published or not, remember that those sources are subject to errors—both those errors we have been discussing and those that occur because the people who extract and/or abstract original documents are not always wholly qualified to do so. Also, remember that even those who are qualified are not error-exempt; they can

---

[2] There is a detailed discussion in Chapter 9 about the use of Internet search engines in family history research.

and do make honest mistakes. In either case, the effect is the same. Human error is always an issue.

Whenever you use an index or a published, handwritten, or typewritten copy of a document, you must face the possibility of mistakes. Names in documents being indexed or copied are easily misread. This is true of indexes even when two separate individuals—independent of each other—index the document and a third person acts to mediate discrepancies. As I have observed this process, I have noticed that, under the pressure of time, most mediators are not meticulous in that role. As good as this process is, it is not perfect. In fact, I have two good examples of such incorrectly indexed names relating to my own family. The index to the 1940 U.S. census has an incorrect name for one of my brothers (Noah instead of Noal) as well as for my father-in-law (Roy instead of Ray). There is also the possibility of a name in a document or even an entire document being inadvertently missed by the indexer.

I do not raise these issues to minimize the value of indexes. However, as wonderful and useful as they are, and as helpful and important as they are to our family history research, indexes are imperfect and must be used with due caution and a significant amount of imagination.

I would be remiss here if I ended this discussion of indexes without noting that our amazing modern technology has linked computer-readable copies of some extremely valuable records directly to their indexes. For example, with the computerized 1940 U.S. census index, I can, with one click of my mouse, go directly from the index to a digitized image of the actual census record relating to my indexed ancestor. That is an incredible boon to my research. But, at the same time, it is of no help to me if my ancestor's name was incorrectly indexed and I missed finding the entry.

J. A useful general rule

The best approach, when a document/record is hard to read, is to carefully study the handwriting in that record and learn how to read it. This procedure is worth whatever time it takes if the document contains needed information. Study the handwriting carefully, read and "translate" it word-by-word, and note how the various letters are formed. Consider difficult words letter-by-letter, comparing individual letters to similar letters in other words until you recognize the word in question. This is especially important when reading names, as in a census, because some names, at first glance, are easily mistaken for other names. Also, when searching legal records, it is helpful to know that legal documents of the same kind contain much standard phrasing that varies little from one document to the next. It is helpful to become familiar with these words and phrases before attempting to read legal documents in any early script.

When working with vital records (certificates of births, marriages, deaths), it is hard to apply these rules in their entirety because the document of interest will be the only example you have of the handwriting in question. We do our best with what we have, but we must be very, very careful. It may also help to seek other opinions.

For help with handwriting issues, I recommend a book by Kip Sperry: *Reading Early American Handwriting* (1998; reprint, Baltimore: Genealogical Publishing Company, 2008). This book is invaluable for those dealing with handwriting issues.

K. Spelling

The use of phonetic spellings and the lack of conventional or standard spellings can also be thorny problems. If we go back just 150 years (or even less), a significant percentage of the U.S. population could not read, more still could not write (many could write only their own names), and even more could not spell. Most of those who did write were not concerned with so-called standard spellings; they spelled words as they sounded—phonetically—and as skewed by their local accents. Also, insofar as accents are concerned, remember that the early settlers of America came from many foreign lands. When a record was made, the writer wrote what he heard, accent and all. Also, remember that standardized spellings are a recent phenomenon. (Note that all examples of various documents in this book have retained original spellings.)

What is the significance of these facts? It just means that, as researchers, we need the ability to decipher writings with unique spellings in the unfamiliar handwriting of many different scribes.

Another problem quite surprising to the uninitiated is the multitude of spelling variations in names (especially surnames) and places. In his will, made in 1754 in Pasquotank County, North Carolina, Jeremiah Willcox's family name is spelled two different ways—Willcox and Willcocks (see Figure 4). In other documents, it is spelled in still other ways—Wilcox, Wilcocks, Wellcox, Wellcocks, Welcocks, etc. Because Jeremiah could not write (he made a mark for his signature), he had no idea about the correct spelling of his name, if it was ever spelled correctly, or if there even was a correct spelling. The spelling of his name was entirely at the mercy and discretion of the person who chanced to write it.

Jeremiah Willcox's situation illustrates the fallacy of believing, as so many people do today, that if a name is not spelled in a certain way, those persons with different spellings have no connection to "our family." By embracing that false notion, they overlook much valuable family history information. We must not worry if a name is spelled with an *a* instead of an *e*, with an *ie* rather than a *y*, or with only one *n*. Of course, the connection to our family is not guaranteed, but neither is it guaranteed when the spellings are the same. In both cases, we have to do the research and carefully weigh the evidence.

While we are still discussing the spelling issue, I want to return to the subject of indexes and how we search them. When searching an index, we must consider every possible spelling of the name we seek. It is so very easy to overlook some of the less logical (to us) possibilities and thus neglect valuable

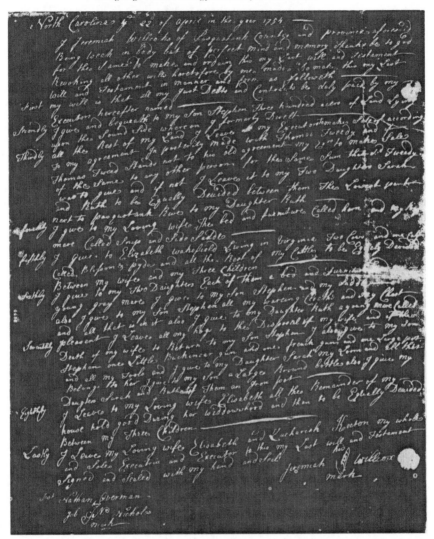

FIGURE 4—THE WILL OF JEREMIAH WILLCOX

records. Because local dialects and foreign accents often make a significant difference, the pronunciation of a name might have been quite different in Massachusetts than in Georgia, and so might the way it was spelled in the records.

In legal practice, there is a rule called the Rule of *"Idem Sonans."*[3] This rule says (and this gets complicated) that in order to establish legal proof of relationship from documentary evidence it is not necessary for the name to be spelled absolutely accurately if, as spelled, it conveys to the ear, when pro-

---

[3] The Latin term *Idem Sonans* means "having the same sound."

nounced in the accepted ways, a sound practically identical to the correctly spelled name as properly pronounced.

Several years ago, I worked on a problem where the family's surname was spelled twenty-four different ways in the same locality. Some of those variant spellings even began with different letters of the alphabet. The correct spelling of the name (supposedly) was *Ingold,* but the following variations were found: Ingle, Ingell, Ingles, Ingells, Ingel, Ingels, Ingeld, Inkle, Inkles, Inkell, Ingolde, Engold, Engolde, Engle, Engell, Engles, Engells, Engel, Engels, Engeld, Angold, Angle, and Ankold. Would you have considered all of these? Or would you have stopped with those beginning with the letter *I*—or even all of those listed?

Other spelling possibilities are *Jugold* and *Jugle.* Such variations could easily occur in an index because of the similarities between the capital *I*s and *J*s and the small *n*s and *u*s. There may also be other logical possibilities.

Another family changed the spelling of its name from Beatty to Baitey when moving from one locality to another. In another instance, the name Kerr was found interchanged with Carr. Whether these spelling changes were intentional is unknown, but intention makes little difference. In one family, three brothers deliberately spelled their family surname differently—Matlock, Matlack, and Matlick—which is actually quite common, even in our day. In his history of the Zabriskie family,[4] George O. Zabriskie reported having found 123 variations of Zabriskie, though not all in the same locality or same time period—and I should mention that many of these were not in the U.S.

L. Marks and signatures

Very often, the records we use (even "official" records and digitized copies of official documents) are not original documents but are, instead, records copied by hand *from* the original documents into official record books by recorders and/or clerks. Thus, the signatures on these official documents are only copied signatures with no value in identifying the signer. But, even then, we can get an important clue if the person concerned (the ancestor) could not write. That value lies in the nature of the mark he used to "sign" his name. This is true because the clerk usually tried to copy the unique mark into the register. If the mark was an *X,* the value is minimal because so many people used *X*s. However, if a different type of mark was used, it might prove useful for identification purposes, especially if the ancestor had a common name. Those with the most common names often used the most distinctive signature marks in their striving for identity and individuality.

If we can positively identify our ancestor in a deed (or another record) where he signed with his distinctive mark, we have valuable circumstantial evidence if we find that same mark associated with a person of the same name in another contemporaneous document. Almost anything except an *X* can be

---

[4] George Olin Zabriskie, comp., *The Zabriskie Family* (Salt Lake City: Publishers Press, 1963).

helpful. And we cannot even rule out the possibility of an *X* being useful in the right circumstances. Consider this possibility when there is other evidence of identity, and our ancestor was the only John Brown who signed with an *X*.

When original documents are available, signatures can be used in the same way, but only if the party concerned signed his own name or used a distinctive mark. However, this can also be tricky, and you must be careful about not reading too much into a signature. Also, keep in mind that it is not unusual for a person's signature to change over time.

M. Poorly preserved records

Unfortunately, we often discover that the records we need have not survived the assaults of nature, the ravages of time, or inadequate care. It is sad to say that, in addition to acts of nature, some records custodians and/or records users have been careless. There is not much we can do if the records we need have been destroyed or badly damaged, but we can be more careful about our own use of the records so that same fate does not befall them. Carelessness on the part of record users is one of the chief reasons many records are either severely damaged or non-existent. It is also the reason many records custodians are disinclined to allow public access to their records.

If you are privileged to handle old original documents, please treat them gently. *Do not touch them!* No matter how clean your hands are, your skin oil will—in time—darken the paper in every place you touch. Turn pages with the eraser end of your pencil or with a rubber finger. Keep pens and pencils off the records; do not even take a pen with you. There is no good reason to leave any mark on any document. Proper care of documents is your responsibility.

To clarify the responsibility we have for the proper care of valuable records, the National Genealogical Society has developed "Guidelines for Using Records Repositories and Libraries." I include those guidelines here and hope we can all follow them. They deserve our careful attention.

Guidelines for Using Records Repositories and Libraries Recommended by the National Genealogical Society

Recognizing that how they use unique original records and fragile publications will affect other users, both current and future, genealogists and family history researchers routinely

- determine before visiting a records repository or library what is available and what they will need from the facility;
- are courteous to records repository and library personnel and to other researchers, and respect the personnel's other daily tasks;
- follow the rules of the library or records repository without protest, even if the rules have changed since a previous visit or differ from those of another facility;

- dress appropriately, converse with others in a low voice, and supervise children;
- use only work space and equipment, such as readers and computers, intended for patron use, respect off-limits areas, and ask for assistance if needed;
- treat original records at all times with great respect;
- treat books with care, never forcing their spines, and handle photographs in accordance with the facility's rules;
- never mark, mutilate, rearrange, or relocate any record or artifact;
- never remove any item from the facility except as allowed by the facility's rules;
- learn and observe the repository or library policy on photographing, scanning, or photocopying;
- use the repository or library's acceptable methods for identifying records for photocopying, avoiding use of paper clips, adhesive notes, and other means not approved by the facility;
- use only procedures prescribed by the repository for noting corrections to errors or omissions found in published works or records, never marking the work or the record itself;
- return volumes, records, and files only to locations designated for that purpose; and
- before departure, thank records repository and library personnel for making the materials available and for assistance received.[5]

II. CHANGES IN THE LANGUAGE

Whenever we deal with writings or language from an earlier time, there are potential problems associated with changes in the meanings of words. The history of linguistic development is the story of constant change; meanings and usages are not static. They have changed in the past, they are changing today, and they will continue to change. You and I have seen the meanings of some words change completely during our lifetimes.

Because early American colonization was somewhat concurrent with the publishing of the King James Bible in 1611, I will use two simple examples from the Bible to illustrate this point. In the King James translation, part of Mark 10:14 reads: "Suffer the little children to come unto me." This same verse in a more recent translation says, "Let the little children come to me."[6]

---

[5] "Guidelines for Using Records Repositories and Libraries Recommended by the National Genealogical Society," National Genealogical Society, 2016 (accessed January 4, 2017). © 1997, 2001, 2016 by National Genealogical Society; includes material ©1995 by Joy Reisinger, CG. Both copyright owners grant permission to copy or publish these standards, provided they are reproduced in their entirety, including this notice.

[6] *Holy Bible, New International Version (NIV®)*. ©1973, 1978, 1984, 2011 by Biblica, Inc.® All rights reserved worldwide.

The second example comes from the 23rd chapter of Acts, where Paul had spoken out against Ananias, the high priest, and was taken to task for so doing. In verse 5 of the King James version, Paul replied, "I wist not, brethren, that he was the high priest: for it is written, Thou shalt not speak evil of the ruler of thy people." The issue here is the meaning of the word "wist." In another, more recent translation of verse 5, this passage says, "Brothers, I did not realize that he was the high priest. . . ."[7]

This is the issue we deal with, and only when we realize that a word might have a different meaning than the one we ascribe to it (if we recognize the word at all) can we fully grasp the possibility that we might be misled.

Let us look at some of the more common usage variations as they affect American family history research.

A. Relationships

Relationships and the terms connected with them can cause trouble. The words *senior* and *junior* are generally understood today as indicating a father-son relationship, but in early records, this was not necessarily true. These terms were often used merely to distinguish between two persons of different generations who had the same name and who lived in the same locality. They were often uncle and nephew rather than father and son. In some parts of the United States, particularly the South, it was as common for a man to name his sons for his brothers as for himself.

We should also watch for changes in the actual meanings of such words as *junior* and *senior*. A man once known as a *junior* often became *senior* after the earlier senior was gone and the next generation was growing up. Then, someone with that name in the next generation might have become the new *junior*.

Be careful here, and always consider the possibility of this usage. I once checked a Daughters of the American Revolution (DAR) lineage based on a senior-junior/father-son assumption, where the junior was allegedly the son of the senior who served from Virginia in the Continental Line. Careful research proved this to be an uncle-nephew connection.

In-law relationships and *step relationships* can also cause confusion. In earlier times, some records stated that there was an in-law relationship when there was actually a step relationship. The following excerpt from a release executed by the heirs of William Bryer, 1738/9, in York County, Massachusetts (now Maine), provides an example:

> Know all men by these Presents that we William Bryer Shipwright Richard Bryer Weaver Andrew Haley husbandman and Mary his Wife Caleb Hutchins Caulker and Sarah his Wife Joseph Hutchins Weaver and Elizabeth his Wife William Willson Weaver and Eadah his Wife John Haley Husbandman & Hephzib[a] his Wife all of Kittery in the County of York in the Province of the Massachusetts Bay in New England and William Tapley Taylor of New Hampshire

---

[7] Ibid.

& R [*sic*] his Wife Do forever acquit exonerate and discharge *our Father in Law Benjamin Hammond* of Kittery & Province afors[d] and our Mother Sarah Hammond lately call'd Sarah Bryer from the Demands of us or our or either of our Heirs in and unto any part of the Cattle or Household Goods or moveable Estate of our hon[d] Father William Bryer late of Kittery afores[d] dee[d] . . . this 31st Day of January Anno Domini 1738/9. [Emphasis added.]

Another example of this practice is found in the will of Francis Champernoun, dated 16 November 1686 in the same county. I quote in part:

I give and bequeath & confirm unto *my Son in Law* Humphrey Elliot & Elizabeth his now wife and their heirs forever the other part of my s[d] Island, which I have allredy given by Deed under my hand and Seal to the s[d] Humphery & Elizabeth his wife—Item I give and bequeath unto *my Son in Law* Robert Cutt *my daughter in Law* Bridget Leriven *my daughter in Law* Mary Cutt and *my daughter in Law* Sarah Cutt and their heires forever all that part of three hundred acres of land belonging unto me lying between broken Neck and the land formerly belonging unto Hugh Punnison. . . . [Emphasis added.]

It is easy to see the confusion this usage might cause for those unaware of the possibility. However, this type of problem cannot be predicted. The records usually mean what they say in this regard—they say "in-law" and mean just that. We just need to be alert to possible exceptions.

The family relationships of *cousin, brother,* and *sister* are also significant because of their varied usage. Donald Lines Jacobus gave the following explanation concerning these three words:

The term "cousin" is perhaps the one most puzzling to the untrained researcher. It was applied loosely to almost any type of relationship outside the immediate family circle. It was most frequently used to denote a nephew or niece, but it could be applied to a first cousin or more distant cousin, or to the marital spouse of any of these relatives, and sometimes to other indirect connections who were not even related by blood. The first guess should be that a nephew or niece was meant; if this does not work out, then try to prove that cousin in our sense of the word was meant; if this also proves impossible, it may require long and profound study to determine just what the connection was. This applies, generally speaking, to the use of the term in the colonies prior to 1750. No definite and exact date can be fixed, for the terms nephew and niece gradually supplanted cousin to denote that form of relationship. . . .

. . . Husband and wife were identified as one person. Hence, when a man writes in his will of "my brother Jones" and "my sister Jones," he may be referring to his own sister and her husband, to his wife's sister and her husband, or to his wife's brother and that brother's spouse.

It is not always possible to decide, in the will of a puritan around 1650, whether the "Brother Peck" and "Brother Perkins" whom he appointed overseers of his estate were relatives by marriage or merely brothers in the church. The expression *"my* Brother Peck" makes it sound a little more like a relationship, but is not conclusive. The same uncertainty attaches to the use of the term "Sister" in these early wills.[8]

We occasionally see the word *german* (sometimes spelled *germane)* used in connection with various relationships, especially brothers, sisters, and cousins. Brothers or sisters german are children of the same parents (as opposed to half-brothers or half-sisters), and cousins german are the children of brothers and sisters, i.e., first cousins.

The terms *niece* and *nephew* can also cause confusion as used in some of the earliest American records. They did not always have the meanings we attach to them. Niece derives from the Latin word *neptis* and nephew from the Latin word *nepos,* which actually mean granddaughter and grandson, respectively. The usage of niece for granddaughter or of nephew for grandson is rarely found but is not unknown. In most cases these relationships, when stated, mean the same as they do today—but be careful.

During the evolution of meaning, you might find the words niece and nephew used in either sense but, after 1690, I have found no cases where they relate to grandchildren while finding frequent use of the terms grandson and granddaughter. Note, however, that if you encounter the Latin words *nepos* or *neptis,* you can almost count on them meaning grandson and granddaughter. Look carefully at all of your evidence in these cases and be sure to make the right connection.

The term *now wife* is very often misunderstood as it appears in various records. It is frequently misinterpreted to mean that the person to whom it applies was previously married (as in the will of Francis Champernoun where he mentioned "my Son in Law Humphrey Elliot & Elizabeth *his now wife*"). Whether the person in this example (Humphrey Elliot) had been previously married was of no concern to Francis. When he used that wording, his intention was to place a limitation on inheritance that the court would recognize when he was not around to explain. This phrase was used to block any claimed inheritance rights of a *future* wife in case the "now wife" should die and her husband remarry.

B. Titles

There were other terms in frequent usage in earlier periods that should be noted. Because British America, during colonial times, was naturally caught up in many British traditions, customs, and usages, the terms of British social rank were also used here, but usually without the strict social implications of gentility attached to them in the mother country. In many records (some of them quite recent), we find men referred to as *Esquire (Esq*r) or *Gentleman (Gentl*n).

---

[8] Donald Lines Jacobus, "Interpreting Genealogical Records," in *Genealogical Research: Methods and Sources,* edited by Milton Rubincam (Washington, DC: American Society of Genealogists, 1960), 22–23. Used by permission.

In Britain, a man with the title "Esquire" after his name was able to bear arms and was next in social precedence to a knight. If the title "Gentleman" followed his name, he was also of gentle birth but one more step down the social ladder.

The use of these terms became quite loose in England, but especially so in America. However, even here, the earlier the period, the more strict the usage. The terms were primarily used as titles of courtesy to designate the most influential and/or prosperous persons of the community. They were most often used by the social elite—lawyers, physicians, notable political figures, clergy, large landowners, magistrates, and justices of the peace—but with no precise meaning. You will occasionally find these terms used by some public officials such as justices of the peace, magistrates, and church leaders even as late as the middle 1800s. The most significant thing about the use of these titles in America is that they often provide an additional means of identifying the person so designated by separating his identity from contemporaries of the same name.

Many of the southern planters also frequently used the title *Colonel*, and, though it had nothing to do with military rank, it is useful for identification purposes.

Among the early colonists, the terms *Mr.* and *Mrs.* followed the English precedent and were used only by the upper classes of society—usually those with "Esquire" and "Gentleman" after their names. In this connection, Mrs. was not a term used to identify a married woman but rather a title of courtesy for a woman of "gentle" birth, married or single. In this sense, it was ordinarily used before both the given name and surname of the unmarried woman, as *Mrs. Sarah Parsons.* However, it was not long before our current usage became the standard usage.

We may also find the terms *Goodwife* (often shortened to *Goody*) and *Goodman* used in older records. These titles mean mistress of a household and head of a household, respectively.

III. NAMING PRACTICES

A. Given names

Because we have already discussed problems relating to the spellings of surnames, we need also to consider familiar practices relating to given names. In both New England and the South, Bible names were popular. However, New Englanders used both common and uncommon Bible names while their southern cousins stuck with the more conventional. New Englanders were also known for giving their children names representing various qualities of the soul or spiritual gifts. This was perhaps partially due to their dislike for old, traditional English names. Faith, hope, and charity were more than just words to live by—they were common female given names. Other popular names for girls included Prudence, Patience, Sympathy, Mirth, Kindness,

Mercy, Constance, Submit, Silence, Benevolence, and Deliverance. Favorite male names included Remember, Resolved, Comfort (sometimes also feminine), Ransom, and Consider.

Given names of the past also tended to be carried on in a family from generation to generation more so than today, though we still have some tendencies in this direction. Even very unusual names were passed on—a practice that often provides circumstantial evidence for family connections. We must be careful, however, never to accept a connection on this basis alone. There must be sufficient evidence that such a connection was a fact.

A child was frequently given the name of a grandparent. (This custom was more common in some other countries than in America, but it was also common here among certain ethnic groups.) A boy may have been given his mother's maiden surname as his given name or, perhaps, the name of one of his parents' brothers. A girl might have been given the name of one of her parents' sisters. Thus, if a man and his brothers all had large families and came from a large family themselves, there will be many contemporaneous cousins with the same given names—often making it very hard to separate one from the other or to determine to which parents they belonged as we encounter them in our research.

Names can be tricky and simple answers are enticing. However, we must not succumb to the temptation of accepting a family connection because the names are the same. It is essential for us to gather all the evidence we can in such cases and then evaluate it carefully, never accepting a connection just because the names are right. Too many connections look good on the surface but fail when all the facts are known.

Changing the subject slightly, it was not unknown for parents to give the same name to more than one child. It was, in fact, common in cases where the first child of that name died. Occasionally, however, there was more than one living child with the same given name. This occurred mostly in German or Dutch families or when there was a significant age difference between the two children—perhaps children of different marriages of their father. My mother had an older brother and a younger stepbrother with the same given name.

Several children in the same family were often given the same middle name (after middle names became common). It was not unusual for their mother's—or even a grandmother's—maiden surname to be used. This practice, however, does not date back quite so far as some of the others.[9]

Unlike today, names of the past were usually (but not always) indicative of gender, and most names can be identified as being either masculine or feminine. However, a few names were given to persons of either sex. Consider names like Christian, Evelyn, Sharon, June, and Shirley. The names Francis

---

[9] For further discussion on names (especially in New England), see chapter 5 of Donald Lines Jacobus, *Genealogy as Pastime and Profession*, 2nd ed., rev. 1968 (reprint, Baltimore: Genealogical Publishing Co., 1999).

and Marion are usually considered masculine, while Frances and Marian are considered feminine. However, there are many exceptions to both of these, and it is not safe to make assumptions about a person's sex based on that distinction.

Because names we think clearly belong to one gender or the other are sometimes found borne by members of the opposite sex, be careful about conclusions of a child's sex based solely on the person's name. If there is any doubt, look for more evidence. Can you believe that many people who do not know me believe that I am a woman?

B. Nicknames and pet names

Some nicknames were given because of a specific characteristic of an individual, like Shorty, Slim, and Red. There are also nicknames that are familiar (and often diminutive) forms of proper names, such as Jim for James, Beth for Elizabeth, Sally for Sarah, Bob for Robert, Phil for Philip, Sam for Samuel, and Bill for William. Other nicknames are pet names given as an expression of endearment, such as Muffy, Pinky, Winky, and Buddy.

Nicknames are often found in records in place of actual given names, and some people can be identified more easily if you are aware of the possibility. Sometimes a person's nickname was so widely used that his real name was unknown outside the family circle. If you are unaware of traditional nickname patterns, confusion results and gives the illusion of two people when there is only one. Note that the following female names and their traditional nicknames were often used interchangeably:

Abigail	Abby
Agnes	Nancy
Charlotte	Lollie and Lottie
Elizabeth	Betty, Beth, Liz, and Lizzy
Margaret	Peggy, Maggie, Mitzi, and Meg
Martha	Patsy and Patty
Mary	Molly and Polly
Melissa	Missy
Nancy	Ann
Obedience	Biddy

Traditional male nicknames were also frequently interchanged with given names, including the following:

Alonzo	Lonnie
Alexander	Alex and Sandy
Edward	Ted and Ned
Francis	Frank and Fran
Henry	Hank and Hal
Harold	Hal and Harry

John	Jack
Isaac	Ike
Richard	Dick, Rick, and Ricky
Robert	Bob, Bud, and Dob
Thadeus	Tad and Thad
Theodore	Ted
Wallace	Wally
William	Bill, Billy, and Willy

The above are some common nicknames but, of course, there were many others. Just be aware of the possibility and do not be confused when you encounter name challenges. Remember that there were patterns relating to nicknames, but no hard-and-fast rules. Some people had nicknames totally unrelated to their given names—just as today.

IV. SYMBOLS

It seems wise to list here some symbols that are widely used by those who compile and publish genealogies. We encounter these symbols in various published sources, but not in the original records. Some of the main symbols are:

* * – born
* (*) – born illegitimate
* X – baptized or christened
* ⊂⊃ – baptized or christened
* ∿ – baptized or christened
* O – betrothed
* OO – married
* O/O – divorced
* O-O – common-law marriage
* † – died
* ⊬ – died
* ☐ – buried
* ☐ – buried
* †† – no further issue
* (†) – no further issue

IV. THE CALENDAR

The fact that there are calendar issues surprises many beginning researchers. Most people are unaware of these matters unless they have either studied astronomy or are aware of some interesting, seldom explored, history. However, the transition from the Julian calendar to the Gregorian calendar (and other modifications involved with that change) has an effect on many early American family history problems.

Britain and her colonies (including most colonies in what is now the U.S.) changed from the Julian to the Gregorian calendar in 1752.[10] Remember that year; it is important.

During the long period during which the Julian calendar was used, the Christian church, and the countries within which Christianity was predominant, followed the dates on that calendar. When the Julian Calendar was used, the new year began on March 25 rather than January 1. That day (March 25) was the day of the Christian Feast of the Annunciation (or Lady Day), commemorating the visit of the Angel Gabriel to the Virgin Mary.[11]

An example will show why it is important for the family history researcher to understand this situation. Suppose we have several documents (such as wills) relating to an ancestral family and the dates on these documents are:

November 14, 1718
December 26, 1718
January 3, 1718
January 22, 1718
February 16, 1718
March 5, 1718
March 23, 1718
March 28, 1719
April 12, 1719

The difficulty most people have with these dates is that we are accustomed to beginning the year on January 1. So, when we see a date like one of these (say any date in January or February), we want to put it in the wrong year and, by doing so, we are one year off.

One year is not bad, you say? And you are right, of course, *unless* the one-year error leads you to draw incorrect conclusions. If the record in question happens to be a church register and the christenings of our ancestor's children are recorded in that register, we may have a problem. Suppose, for example, that we find two christenings on the following dates for persons we think might be our ancestor's children:

April 2, 1720
March 22, 1720

If we were unaware that the year 1721 did not begin until March 25, just three days *after* the second of these two dates, what would we think? Would

---

[10] The Dutch in New Netherlands never used the Julian calendar; they had changed to the Gregorian calendar prior to their American colonization. However, they continued using what were called New Style dates in their private records after England took control of the colony. (Note, however, that the examples of Dutch church records in Chapter 24 include an exception to this general rule.) The Quakers began their year on January 1 instead of March 25, but they otherwise accepted the dates of the Julian calendar.

[11] See Luke 1:26–28.

we be confused? Surely, we would question whether it was possible for both of these children to belong to the same parents.

Consider, also, the case of the man who executed his will in October 1692, and records show that the will was admitted to probate in February 1692. What would we think? Would we be a little confused?

To deal with this issue, a tactic called *double dating* was/is used. This means that in records created *before 1752*, whenever a date fell between January 1 and March 24, inclusive, we write that date to reflect both the Julian and the Gregorian calendars. We do this by writing the dates on the previous list like this:

November 14, 1718
December 26, 1718
January 3, 1718/9

January 22, 1718/9
February 16, 1718/9
March 5, 1718/9
March 23, 1718/9
March 28, 1719
April 12, 1719

Also, we write the two christening dates given earlier like this:

April 2, 1720
March 22, 1720/1

The months and years in which the will mentioned above was executed and probated, respectively, are written as October 1692 and February 1692/3.

This double dating helps provide clarity. It shows that the year of the second christening was actually 1720 and then shows that *if* the year had begun on January 1, as on our Gregorian calendar, it would have been 1721.

The Gregorian calendar was first introduced in 1582 and, thus, from that time forward there was significant pressure to adopt it and change the beginning of its year to January 1. Because of that pressure, and because the Gregorian calendar had already been adopted by various other countries, it is not unusual to see double dating in many early American records, especially after 1700.[12] This phenomenon was evident earlier in this chapter in the release executed by the heirs of William Bryer in York County, Massachusetts, on January 31, 1738/9.

There are also cases where double dating was used incorrectly, but do not let this alarm you. You can usually identify the problem and make the adjustment. For example, you may find a date incorrectly written as "April 12,

---

[12] Some Christian countries (France, Austria, Germany's Catholic states, and Hungary) were using the Gregorian calendar in the 1580s. Some other countries (China, Bulgaria, Russia, Estonia, Greece, and Turkey) did not adopt it until the early 1900s.

1718/9." This is much the same problem as you and I have today when we continue writing the old year after the new year has started. The year in this example can be corrected easily to 1719.

You might also encounter some double dating after 1752. This is a case of the writer either having a habit of writing dates that way or just being opposed to change. I have a friend who told me that his father once said, "I have seen hundreds of changes in my life, and I have been against every one of them." That is just the way it is sometimes.

One final note concerning the calendar: Because the Julian calendar year began in March, even though late in the month, March was called the first month. April was the second month, and so on. Hence, when (before 1752) we see a month written as "7ber" or as "8ber," these months are September and October—not July and August. In Latin, September and October actually mean "seventh month" and "eighth month," respectively. The same applies to November and December—they mean "ninth month" and "tenth month," respectively. And, regardless of their names, all the months were numbered differently than they are today, from March (first month) through February (twelfth month). We need to remember this; it can make a difference.

There are other differences between the Julian and Gregorian calendars, but they are not relevant to this discussion. Those who are interested can learn more elsewhere.

3

Surveying, Analyzing, and Planning

I. SECONDARY RESEARCH: YOUR PRELIMINARY SURVEY

Most people understand that it is impossible to arrive at their destinations if they do not know where they are going. The person who does not know where he is going is like the ship that leaves port with no particular destination in mind and drifts aimlessly on the open seas. Without goals, very little of value can be accomplished. In family history research, the process of objectively analyzing your pedigree is what enables you to set meaningful goals (i.e., destinations) and channel your efforts to attain those goals. This analytical process does not actually make your research easier—the work is still there—but it can make the research processes more efficient and more fruitful. It can help you reach your desired destination.

Before you can make an objective analysis of your pedigree and determine what needs to be done, however, some secondary research is required. Secondary research is an examination of what has already been done. Its purpose is to find the answers to three significant questions:

- What is already known about our ancestral families?
- What research have others already done on those families?
- What level of trust can I place in this information?

With the answers to those questions, the researcher is prepared to establish a reasonable destination for his journey.

Your secondary research—what we call the preliminary survey—need not take forever; it is a simple process if properly pursued. However, it is also important to understand that some elements of this preliminary survey will be ongoing and perpetual. This is true because you will always be seeking other relatives—to find out what they know and benefit from any research they have done. You will also be planning to reach other destinations as your research takes you in pursuit of other family lines.

As noted in earlier chapters, the recent advances in technology and the innovations achieved by some very bright people have actually made this preliminary survey process easier to accomplish than ever before. As you proceed, you will be looking for and using the following source types:

A. Home and family sources—both those in your own possession and those belonging to other family members and relatives

B. Secondary sources on the Internet

C. Compiled and published sources—as they are discussed in detail in Chapter 12

Let us now examine what is involved with each of these source types and the reasons why each is critical to the process.

A. Home and family sources

Beginning is easy. We start with what we have in our own home. I will not go into great detail here, but most people have significant records as well as treasured objects (artifacts) relating to their close ancestors (parents and grandparents)—and often to more remote ancestors—right in their homes. In addition, most will likely remember some important things—people and their relationships, family traditions, and family stories. Some stories may already be written down—others may not. And any that have not been recorded should be.

You may find various kinds of certificates and memorabilia relating to events in your family members' lives. There may be birth, marriage, and death certificates. Church certificates of various kinds are also commonplace, as are different types of achievement certificates—perhaps relating to things they and their family members and ancestors did in school. Graduation diplomas might be found as well, and many families have preserved their immigrant ancestors' certificates of naturalization and citizenship as well as land deeds, wills, and various court documents.

There may be old newspapers and news clippings relating to significant events in family members' lives, as well as funeral programs, wedding invitations/announcements, graduation programs, and other keepsakes. There may also be postcards and letters sent by traveling friends and relatives or by family members left behind in countries of origin. There will probably also be some old pictures and photo albums.

There may also be diaries, personal journals, and life accounts of varying size and detail written by family members. And, who knows, you may be fortunate enough to have an old family Bible with specific dates and places of births, marriages, and deaths in one of your ancestral families. You may even discover the fruits of someone else's efforts at family history research.

Finding these things is important, but you will also need to organize what you find so everything can be properly preserved—not just for your own benefit, but also for other interested family members and certainly for your descendants.

Remember, also, that the same kinds of things you find in your home will be in the homes of your relatives. There should be a special interest in probing the possibilities of such treasures in the homes of older family members. In addition to examining their records, you will want to interview these older relatives and preserve their recollections on electronic media. Memories of older relatives might bridge significant gaps besides being an important part of your family's history. Relatives who cannot be interviewed in person can be interviewed on the telephone or on an Internet video chat connection (such as Skype, FaceTime, ooVoo, Google Video, and Tango).

B. Secondary sources on the Internet

Chapters 9 and 10 discuss using the Internet in the process of locating relatives who may have even more informational treasures, including the results of any research they have done. Some—but not all—of these people may be excited to join you in cooperative research efforts.

Computer technology and some resourceful visionaries have provided marvelous resources with virtually unlimited potential. Chapters 9 and 10 discuss and explore those resources and the possibilities associated with them, as they relate to family history.

I will not make any lists of resources here, but suffice it to say:

- These resources exist.
- With the passage of time, those that are most beneficial will be enhanced and become even better.
- Also, with the passage of time, many technological resources now in their infancy will develop to become extraordinary.

Because of the specific purposes of our current discussion on the preliminary survey, I have only scratched the surface of this subject here; however, the current benefits are great and future possibilities are even greater. To give an idea of the magnitude of what we are dealing with, note that *Family Tree Magazine* (*http:// www.familytreemagazine.com/*), a significant online periodical, has, for the last several years, published an annual listing of what its staff considers the "101 Best Genealogy Websites." The 2016 listing featured fifteen separate categories of family history websites, among which was a category entitled "Best US Genealogy Websites in 2016." That list includes twelve sites (the names of which are really not important here[1]), each with unique characteristics that make it valuable. In addition to the 101 sites on the main list, there are many more—and most of them are getting better all the time. You can also be assured that the survivors will absorb many of those that disappear.

---

[1] These twelve websites are named in Chapter 10, "Family History Websites."

In addition to this, *Family Tree Magazine*'s December 2016 issue had an article entitled "America the Digitized" that listed seventy-five free, state-focused websites with digitized records.[2] Sites are listed for all fifty states but none for the District of Columbia.

Another resource is a Google website called Family History Internet Sites. It was prepared and is kept updated by Kip Sperry. This list is divided into thirteen categories, and each listed site is accessible with a clickable link. It is online at *https://sites.google.com/site/familyhistoryinternetsites/*. There is more detail in Chapter 10.

Also, be aware of Cyndi's List of Genealogy Sites on the Internet (*http://www.cyndislist.com*). Perhaps the best way to describe Cyndi's List is to quote the website itself, where the following description of site resources is given:

- A categorized & cross-referenced index to genealogical resources on the Internet
- A list of links that point you to genealogical research sites online
- A **free** jumping-off point for you to use in your online research
- A "card catalog" to the genealogical collection in the immense library that is the Internet
- Your genealogical research portal onto the Internet[3]

As part of our preliminary survey, there are also some resources from the past that have been preserved and made more accessible on the FamilySearch website. FamilySearch lists these files and describes them as follows:

Guild of One-Name Studies: A collection of lineage-linked sourced genealogies from this international Guild launched in Great Britain in the 1970s.

Oral Genealogies: A growing collection of genealogies obtained by interviewing people in various parts of the world. Entries include names, family relationships, and dates and places of events. No corrections or merges have been made.

Pedigree Resource File: A growing collection of genealogies submitted by users including hundreds of millions of ancestors. Entries include names, family relationships, and dates and places of events. No corrections or merges have been made.

Ancestral File: A static collection of genealogies submitted by users, prior to 2003, including 40 million ancestors. Entries include names, family relationships, and dates and places of events. Submissions were merged to eliminate duplication.

---

[2] Rick Crume, "America the Digitized," *Family Tree Magazine*, 17, No. 7, December 2016, http://www.familytreemagazine.com/ (accessed December 3, 2016).

[3] "Welcome to Cyndi's List," Cyndi's List: A Comprehensive, Categorized & Cross-referenced List of Links That Point You to Genealogical Research Sites Online, http://www.cyndislist.com (accessed September 20, 2016).

International Genealogical Index (IGI): Information for over 430 million ancestors contributed by members of The Church of Jesus Christ of Latter-day Saints. Each record contains one event, including birth, baptism (christening), marriage, or death.

Community Trees: A collection of sourced genealogies from specific times.[4]

The final category on this list, "Community Trees," is a collection of genealogies submitted by various researchers, on a current basis, in response to an invitation on the website. It relates to various communities in different parts of the world, including the United States. It is no longer an active file.

An automated search of all six of these files in one search operation can be initiated at *https://familysearch.org/family-trees*. The information in these records is easily accessed and represents a significant amount of information that was available previously only on CD at LDS Family History Centers and a few other libraries. However, none of this information has been verified for accuracy, and it should not be taken at face value.

C. Compiled and published sources

Printed/published genealogies relating to our ancestors are important. If they exist, they should be identified, located, and explored for the relevant family information they contain. Those books in the extensive collections of the LDS Family History Library can be identified and found by using the FamilySearch Catalog (formerly called the Family History Library Catalog), which is part of the FamilySearch program and available online at *https://familysearch.org* (choose "Catalog" on the "Search" menu).

All library materials are listed in the FamilySearch Catalog—both those compiled sources we will explore as part of our preliminary survey and the vast collections of microfilmed and digitized original records available for our primary research.

Also, of great significance to family history researchers is a partnership agreement struck in 2016 between the Family History Library in Salt Lake City and the Digital Public Library of America (DPLA). This agreement makes digitized copies of some 200,000 online family history library books available in one place online. This collection will join—on FamilySearch, through DPLA's online search portal—books from the Family History Library and from the archives of other important family history libraries throughout the world.

As you use these printed genealogies—and it is important that you do use them as part of your preliminary survey—remember that they are compilations of information and are the results of someone else's research—whether good or bad. The research you do in them is secondary research. The informa-

---

[4] "Search Genealogies," FamilySearch, The Church of Jesus Christ of Latter-day Saints, February 3, 2015, https://familysearch.org/family-trees (accessed December 1, 2016).

tion found in these books is no more reliable than the research that produced it. If you are fortunate, the authors of those sources relating to your ancestors will have carefully documented their work.

Chapter 12 contains a detailed discussion of printed genealogies, family histories, and other compiled sources you will use as part of your preliminary survey.

II. PRESERVE PRELIMINARY SURVEY RESULTS

Before you begin those phases of your preliminary survey beyond home and family sources, you need to pick one family line as your point of focus—one line on which to concentrate your efforts. If more than one line of your ancestors lived in the same geographical area during the same time period, you can focus on two or (on rare occasions) three lines. You can focus on other lines at other times, but the scope of your research must be limited in order to keep it manageable.

It is essential to make a careful record of all information relating to your ancestral family that you find as you progress through your preliminary survey. And you must carefully note where you find every piece of information. This documentation will be critical to your analysis as you move to the next step of the research cycle. At this point, however, you have no idea about the reliability of much of what you have found, but you cannot stop now to evaluate it thoroughly. If you make a faithful record, you will be able to evaluate it properly later. There is a discussion about keeping research notes in Chapter 7.

Except for those original documents uncovered in your home and family sources, every source you use during the preliminary survey will contain only secondary evidence and is no more reliable than the research that produced it. The information may be correct (you hope it is), but at this point you do not know. The object of the preliminary survey is to gather the information; careful analysis will be required later. If the information you find is documented, make sure to also preserve the details of that documentation.

All information found during your preliminary survey needs to be put into a meaningful/usable format. It is helpful to put families together using family group record forms—one form per family—insofar as your findings allow. Organizing survey results into a family format facilitates analysis. It provides a better perspective of what you have found, including inconsistencies, conflicting information, and gaps. The family-based format provides a useful picture of what you actually have and of what you still need. It is also helpful to this analytical process to have your direct line ancestors on a pedigree chart.

Free blank forms (family group records, pedigree charts, and other forms) are available in many places on the Internet. By keying in "family history forms" in your Internet search engine, you will discover many options. It is helpful to choose forms that you can either print out or download directly onto your computer. You will need that flexibility. As you organize your findings into this family format, it is also important to note the source of every piece of information you enter on those family group worksheets.

Once all information found during the preliminary survey and all source information are entered onto family group and pedigree worksheets, you are ready to move to the next step of the research cycle. You are ready to analyze what you have found so you will know exactly what you have learned and its importance.

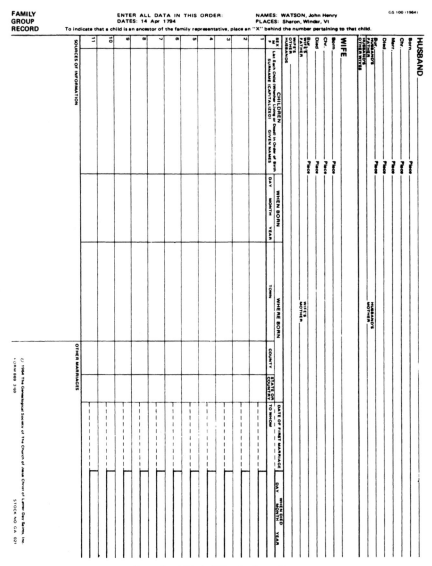

Figure 1—A Typical Family Group Form

Pedigree Chart

No. 1 on this chart is the same as
No. _____ on pedigree chart no. _____

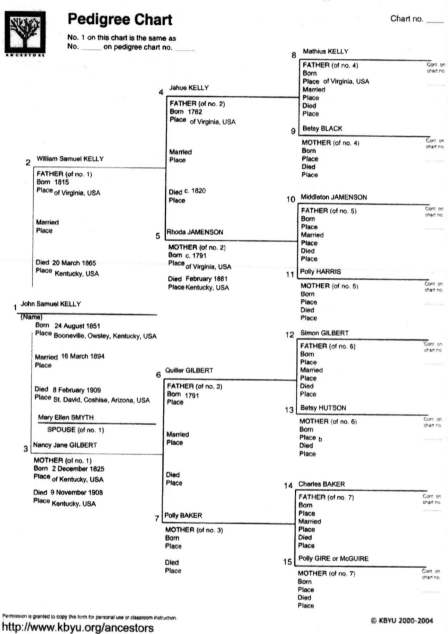

8 Mathius KELLY

FATHER (of no. 4)   Cont. on chart no.
Born
Place of Virginia, USA
Married
Place
Died
Place

9 Betsy BLACK

MOTHER (of no. 4)   Cont. on chart no.
Born
Place
Died
Place

4 Jahue KELLY

FATHER (of no. 2)
Born 1782
Place of Virginia, USA

Married
Place

Died c. 1820
Place

10 Middleton JAMENSON

FATHER (of no. 5)   Cont. on chart no.
Born
Place
Married
Place
Died
Place

11 Polly HARRIS

MOTHER (of no. 5)   Cont. on chart no.
Born
Place
Died
Place

5 Rhoda JAMENSON

MOTHER (of no. 2)
Born c. 1791
Place of Virginia, USA

Died February 1881
Place Kentucky, USA

2 William Samuel KELLY

FATHER (of no. 1)
Born 1815
Place of Virginia, USA

Married
Place

Died 20 March 1865
Place Kentucky, USA

1 John Samuel KELLY

(Name)
Born 24 August 1851
Place Booneville, Owsley, Kentucky, USA

Married 16 March 1894
Place

Died 8 February 1909
Place St. David, Coshise, Arizona, USA

Mary Ellen SMYTH
SPOUSE (of no. 1)

12 Simon GILBERT

FATHER (of no. 6)   Cont. on chart no.
Born
Place
Married
Place
Died
Place

13 Betsy HUTSON

MOTHER (of no. 6)   Cont. on chart no.
Born
Place b
Died
Place

6 Quiller GILBERT

FATHER (of no. 3)
Born 1791
Place

Married
Place

Died
Place

14 Charles BAKER

FATHER (of no. 7)   Cont. on chart no.
Born
Place
Married
Place
Died
Place

15 Polly GIRE or McGUIRE

MOTHER (of no. 7)   Cont. on chart no.
Born
Place
Died
Place

7 Polly BAKER

MOTHER (of no. 3)
Born
Place

Died
Place

3 Nancy Jane GILBERT

MOTHER (of no. 1)
Born 2 December 1825
Place of Kentucky, USA

Died 9 November 1908
Place Kentucky, USA

http://www.kbyu.org/ancestors

Figure 2—Pedigree of John Samuel Kelly

Let us now look carefully at the process of pedigree analysis, which will include the process of choosing an appropriate point of focus.

III. PEDIGREE ANALYSIS

The first rule to remember as we begin our analysis is that we *must work with what information we already know.* (For the sake of this discussion, we will presume that conflicting information and inconsistencies have been properly resolved. We will presume that everything we know in this case is consistent and appears to be correct. We will say, for the sake of discussion, that the information we have appears to be correct.)

Successful research must focus on ancestors about whom you already know three significant details:

- A <u>name</u>
- A reasonable <u>time</u> period
- A reasonably precise <u>place</u>

Your time and efforts will be wasted if these three details are not known. Too many would-be family history researchers begin by finding a "desirable" person—perhaps a noted historical figure—with the right surname and then seek to trace a line of descent from him down to them. The odds of success are not good, perhaps about the same as winning the lottery.

I suggest you prepare for your analysis by making a "T" chart on a blank sheet of paper. It should look something like this:

Above the line and on the left side of your "T" chart, write the question, *What do I already know?*

On top of the line on the right side of your "T" chart, write the question, *What does this suggest?*

Your "T" chart now looks like this:

What do I already know?	*What does this suggest?*

Next, analyze carefully to determine everything already known about the person (or persons) you have chosen as your point of focus—the things you will write on the left side of your chart. Analyze that person's name, the places with which he was associated, the dates of importance, and his relationships to other persons.

You will usually begin your research in the earliest place you find this person, unless you have reason to do research in some later place to get complete information on the family group form you are preparing. The decision you make about where to begin will guide your analysis.

Consider whether the dates associated with your ancestor are historically significant. Might this person have lived at the right time to serve in one of this country's many wars? Might he (or his widow) have applied for a pension because of that service? Did he die when his children were still young? If so, might there be guardianship records for those children? Did he die several years before (or after) his wife died? Might he (or his widow) have remarried? Was he several years older (or younger) than his wife? Might she have been a second wife? Or was he a second husband? Or both? The things you observe about the person(s) who is (are) your point of focus as you study the pedigree and family group records should be carefully noted. Many significant events in an ancestor's life have no doubt been lost to family tradition. But, right now, you are listing the things you know as the basis for careful analysis. This list of things known will suggest other possibilities to help you determine where your primary research will begin. Your research will then explore those possibilities.

As an example, let us consider the family on the pedigree chart on page 64 (Figure 2). First, from what appears on the pedigree chart, we must decide where our research will begin. Should we start with Simon Gilbert? Or with Rhoda Jamenson? Or where?

Careful examination makes it clear that neither Simon nor Rhoda should be our primary point of focus at this point because we do not know enough about them. Though we know a little about Rhoda, we still do not know a locality.

Because there seems to be reasonably complete information on John Samuel Kelly, he would not be our objective unless we need more complete information on his whole family.

It appears that there are actually just two logical possibilities—William Samuel Kelly and his wife, Nancy Jane Gilbert. We can easily combine them into a dual objective because we need further information on both and because the required information on both can likely be found in records of the same locality: Booneville, Owsley County, Kentucky.

To begin our analysis, we need to start by listing a few things we already know about William Samuel Kelly and Nancy Jane Gilbert on the left side of our "T" chart.

As already noted, if we were working on an actual case, we would first deal with any discrepancies and inconsistencies we discovered in the information found during our preliminary survey and would seek to verify all undocumented and inadequately documented information.[5] For this example, however, we will assume that the information we have relating to William Samuel Kelly and Nancy Jane Gilbert is correct and proceed with our analysis, listing the things "I already know" about them.

What do I already know?

1. William is 10 years older than Nancy.
2. William died 43 years before Nancy.
3. William was about 5 years old when his father, Jahue, died.
4. William died 16 years before his mother, Rhoda, died.
5. William's mother, Rhoda, was about 24 years old when William was born, his father, Jahue, about 33.
6. William came from Virginia. (Note: Our use of the word "of" on our pedigree chart indicates that we are not sure of birthplaces; this is the earliest known place of residence.)
7. Nancy came from Kentucky.
8. William and Nancy had a son born in 1851 in Booneville, Owsley County, when he was 36 and she was 26. (Note that this is the earliest known *specific* place of residence we have for them and is thus very significant.)
9. William's mother, Rhoda, also came to Kentucky (she died there in 1881).
10. Both William and Nancy died in Kentucky.
11. We know the names (apparently) of both parents for both William and Nancy.

Now we ask our second question: Do any of the "things I already know" suggest possibilities to be investigated? We can list some suggested *possibilities*, along with the basis of each one, as appropriate. In essence, we ask what answers are suggested by the things we already know:

What does this suggest?

1. Because William was 10 years older than Nancy, he *may* have had a previous marriage.
2. Because Nancy outlived William by 43 years, she *may* have remarried after his death.
3. Because William's mother, Rhoda, outlived his father, Jahue, by so many years, she *may* have also remarried.

---

[5] A "T" chart is also a useful tool to help resolve discrepancies. On the left side of the chart, you can explain each discrepancy, and then, on the right side, you can list those steps taken to resolve the discrepancy and to explain how it was resolved.

4. William and Nancy's marriage *probably* took place in Kentucky since she was from that state and their son, John, was born there. (Under these circumstances, it is much more likely that he came to Kentucky to marry her than that she went to Virginia to marry him.)

5. William and Nancy were *probably* married before 1851 when their son, John, was born.

6. William and Nancy *possibly* had other children besides John, born before or after John was born, or both. (There would have been no children after 1865 when William died—at least not more than nine months after.)

7. *If* William came to Kentucky before his marriage to Nancy, and *if* it was his first marriage, he *probably* came with his mother and her family, *possibly* a stepfather.

8. William and Nancy *possibly* resided in Booneville and Owsley County for more than just the one year (1851) and *our research should begin there.*

9. William's date of death suggests that he *may* have died in the Civil War. Though he was fifty years old, this is still a *possibility*. (Note: Being from Kentucky, a border state, there is no suggestion as to whether this might be a Union or Confederate Army connection. We need to learn more about local history.)

As research begins following this analysis, we know many questions we will seek to resolve, and we will investigate each possibility in the appropriate records.

This is how every pedigree should be analyzed. This method enables the researcher to put the individual, the locality, the records, and history all in their proper perspective. It is important, however, that you keep things as simple as you can. You do not try to find the answers to all questions at once. Make a list of your short-term goals—those questions you want to answer—then choose one of them and work on it. When you have achieved that goal, pick another and work on it. And so on. In your family history research—just as with walking or running—you cannot successfully take more than one step at a time. Any attempt to do otherwise leads to confusion. Or worse!

IV. GET EVERYBODY

I emphasize again that, in most cases, as you do research relating to your ancestors, it is important that you gather *all* information relating to *all persons of the surname(s) of interest* in your locality of interest. If you do not do it, you will someday be sorry and will find yourself coming back to search the same records again. And it will likely be sooner than you think. You may not be able to tell who all of these people are at the outset, but when you begin to synthesize your findings and put them into families, many pieces will fall into place. In fact, the information you find about "unknown" persons often provides some of the evidence needed to extend your pedigree. Some argue that, if the surname is common, this procedure is too time-consuming. But, actually, the more common the name, the more essential this process becomes. Getting all the information on everyone of the surname—with all spelling variations—is the preeminent method of identifying your ancestors and their families.

The Charles Pebble case in Chapter 1 illustrates the value of this procedure. The "easy" way—choosing only those records relating to people on your direct ancestral line(s)—comes up short in actual practice.

Note, also, that before research can begin, you must know what records are available in the locality of your problem during the time period of your problem, and the kind of information you might expect to find in those records that might help you solve your problems. This facet of American research is especially fascinating, and also somewhat complicated, because you can never be sure what information might be found in so many of the available records. Though you can usually get a good idea, there will be times when you are surprised by the actual contents of a record. Because of this, no record should be sold short or overlooked until you have put it to the test. Many facts and family connections are so difficult to prove that you cannot afford to decide on "the facts" until you have considered all the evidence.

V. JURISDICTIONS

It is also necessary to know something about the jurisdictions in which various records were kept, as well as the present locations of those records or searchable copies of them.

By "jurisdiction," I mean the *legal* or *traditional* authority to carry out certain activities. A *legal* jurisdiction is established by law and relates to civil court cases, vital records, land records, wills, censuses, etc.—all those records kept because the law required them to be kept.

Traditional jurisdictions might include churches, private businesses, schools, institutions, fraternal organizations, etc., that carried on activities and kept records of those activities on behalf of their members and/or patrons. For example, a church might have records of christenings (or baptisms), marriages, burials, and other church activities. The family history researcher needs to know who had jurisdiction over certain activities and events so he can locate and use any records those activities and events might have generated.

The most logical approach to almost every American family history research problem is what is called the jurisdictional approach. This approach requires that each locality and each jurisdiction of interest must be examined carefully as to its record-keeping procedures before research begins. Once you know what records were kept, who kept them, and where those records can be accessed, you are ready to proceed. Also, I cannot emphasize too strongly the importance of searching all existing records produced by all jurisdictions within which your ancestors lived—the home, the church, the county, the state, etc.

Probate records (those records relating to the settling of estates after people die) provide a good example of the importance of understanding jurisdictions. In most states, these records are kept in the county, but if you are tracing ancestors in Vermont, you need to know that they are maintained in probate districts that do not always correspond with the counties. In Rhode Island, probate records are kept in the cities and towns. And in Delaware, they are maintained by the state in one central place.

You also need to be careful of jurisdictional changes. Records kept in one place at one time may have been kept somewhere else during another time. In New Hampshire, for example, probate and land records have traditionally been kept by the counties. However, between 1671 and 1771, both types of records were maintained by the colony (this was prior to statehood). You need to be aware of these jurisdictions in order to find the records.

Closely related to jurisdictional knowledge is knowledge about the nature and content of the various sources. On this point, it is helpful to know the reason or reasons a record was kept, as that is the key to understanding its contents. When you search a document, you should have, at least, a general idea of the kinds of information that type of source usually contains. One purpose of this book is to help provide that knowledge. Your research experience will also provide priceless knowledge.

While we use many different kinds of records in our family history research, not one of these records was created for a genealogical or family history purpose. Our task is to take the records that exist, without regard for the purposes for which they were created, and extract from them whatever information they contain that meets our needs. That is not always an easy task.

VI. LOCALITY ANALYSIS

Your understanding of the localities themselves is also important—perhaps even critical—to your success in research. Locality analysis is related to jurisdictional analysis, but it goes beyond the necessity of knowing who kept the various kinds of records in a given place or when they kept them. You must also learn, in some detail, about the history and geography of the places associated with your research.

If you know your great-grandfather lived in Zanesville, Ohio, for example, what do you need to know about that place in order to learn more about him? This is a very simple question with a not-so-simple answer. Let us look at what is involved.

A. Essential tools

Your first step is to determine the county in which Zanesville is located. This is important in the United States because so many records are kept on a county basis. Very little meaningful research can be done unless you know the county.

In the past, we learned the names of counties from gazetteers (geographical dictionaries), postal directories, and encyclopedias. These sources helped us identify the county in which a particular town or city was located and where it was situated within that county. Gazetteers also provided other useful information about these places, and they still have significant value for that purpose. Older gazetteers—perhaps from some time near the time our ancestors lived there—can be especially helpful. However, it is no longer necessary to go to a library to find a gazetteer because they are available on the Internet. Postal directories, however, are mostly outmoded for family history purposes.

Today, the best and easiest-to-use source of locality information is the Internet. When I typed "Zanesville OH" into my search engine, I got 1,480,000 results in 0.74 seconds—much more than I ever wanted to know. And, without opening even one website, I learned that Zanesville is in Muskingum County. Though this was simple, I add the caution that it will probably not be so easy if your ancestor lived in a place that no longer exists. This, however, is not a new problem; we had the same difficulties when we relied on gazetteers and postal directories. But, as difficult as this might turn out to be, it is still something we can do. There is a wealth of information on the Internet relating to just about any place we want to learn about—a marvelous benefit as we seek to learn more about our forebears.

The name of the county is important because records relating to the county are the place where we will begin our research. As our next step in learning more about Muskingum County, I recommend going to an Internet wiki page on the FamilySearch website. By typing "FamilySearch wiki Muskingum County Ohio" into your Internet search engine space, you will go directly to that page.

The page involved here, entitled "Muskingum County, Ohio, Genealogy," tells you practically everything you need to know about the county.[6] Become acquainted with this page and the wealth of information it contains. There are similar wiki pages available on FamilySearch for just about any place your research takes you.

On this Muskingum County wiki page, it tells us that Coshocton, Guernsey, Noble, Morgan, Perry, and Licking are neighboring counties and that Muskingum was created from Fairfield and Washington Counties on 7 January 1804. It also tells us that part of the county was returned to Fairfield County in 1817 and that portions were taken from it in 1810 to create Coshocton and Guernsey Counties and another portion in 1817 when Morgan County was created. All of this is important.

---

[6] There is more information about wikis in Chapter 9. Here I only add the caution that wikis, as important and as useful as they are, should be used with some caution because anyone can add information and anyone can edit information.

Our next step is to find a good map. Maps are critical because they give research problems a perspective available in no other way. Even if you visit the place where your ancestors lived, a map provides a broad perspective you cannot get on the ground. If there is a historical map of the locality, from about the time your ancestors lived there, so much the better. Boundary and jurisdiction changes will be reflected as the old map is compared with a modern one. More is said later about the importance of understanding these changes.

In addition to the information maps provide on boundary and jurisdictional changes, they also help us understand the geographical and physical features that so often affect family history problems. These changes may suggest various patterns of settlement and migration and also eliminate others. A range of mountains is a barrier to movement while a river may aid migratory travel. It is much easier to travel on water than through dense forests and undergrowth; however, in some cases, a river might also be an obstacle to travel because it is hard to cross a large river when not properly equipped.

A map shows us the relationship of a town or county to other towns and counties in the same area. These geographical relationships might also suggest other searches, especially if the place our ancestors lived was near the state or county boundary line. When we cannot see relative locations on a map, we tend to limit our research inappropriately by jurisdictional boundaries. Those who lived there, however, were never thus restricted and went where they pleased and as it was convenient or necessary for them to do so. Some records relating to the family we seek might be found in neighboring jurisdictions.

Detailed local maps, if available, are the most valuable for our purposes. It naturally follows that the smaller the area covered, the more detailed is the map's coverage. As already mentioned, old maps are best *if* they can be found, but modern maps are also helpful.

The Internet once again provides significant assistance. Many maps—both old and new—are available online. You can try keying in the name of your place of interest in your Internet search engine, along with the word "map." Of course, you can add more information to be more specific. Words like "old," "historical," "township," "land owners," etc., often enhance the quality of search results.

One website that specializes in maps is Historic Map Works (*http://www. historicmapworks.com/*), and you can easily find other useful sites in just a few minutes using your search engine. If you want to download a historical map of a locality where an ancestor lived, Historic Map Works will sell you the right to do so. And other websites will do the same.

With the Internet as a resource, there are very few places, even defunct places, that cannot be found. However, if you have difficulty, historical societies and local libraries can often provide information about defunct places and/ or place names. Books on local history can also be helpful.

My experience suggests that the reason people are unable to locate most such places is that the family members who provided the information—and who probably never lived there themselves—misremembered the information passed down by the family. In these cases, the best approach is to begin research at a later, appropriately identified, family location, and then work back until the correct place is identified. Regardless of the reason one is unable to ascertain a viable place of residence, meaningful research cannot go forward until the correct place is identified.

If your ancestor lived in a large city, some research can be very time-consuming because of the large numbers of people. However, if you can locate your ancestor's address in some way—perhaps in an old city directory—your research will be expedited. For example, if you find your ancestor's address in the city directory, and a map of the city shows that address to be in Ward 14, your research task is greatly simplified.

If, for example, you want to find your Philadelphia ancestor and his family in the 1860 census and, for some reason, you are unable to find them in the index to that census, you may want to search the actual census record on the chance that the family name was misindexed. It will be much easier to search the census of just one ward of the city than to search the entire city. You can now do, in perhaps two hours, what otherwise might take several days. The Ancestry website has an extensive online collection of U.S. city directories, covering 1822 to 1995. It is worth your time to use this resource. It is at *http://search.ancestry.com/search/db.aspx?dbid=2469.*

B. The genealogy of places

Because America is a relatively new country, there are unique research problems caused by boundary changes. We have already discussed the need for maps that illustrate these changes, and now we need to consider the importance of understanding a county in its relationship to its parent county (or counties) as well as any offspring. We got a clue about this issue from the FamilySearch wiki page for Muskingum County, Ohio.

Almost every early American family history problem is affected by changes in boundaries. Many families that lived in only one place had county boundaries changed around them—sometimes more than once—making it necessary to search the records of several jurisdictions. For example, if a family lived in Jefferson, North Carolina, for a 100-year period between 1700 and 1800, you might find records relating to them in seven different counties, though the family never moved. You would first find them in Bath County (established 1696), next in Bladen County (established 1734), next in Anson County (established 1750), next in Rowan County (established 1753), next in Surry County (established 1771), next in Wilkes County (established 1777), and finally in Ashe County (established 1799), where Jefferson is still located.

There are many examples of this phenomenon from many states, but let me mention just one more. Western New York—what we know as "Upstate New York," the area now comprising forty-five entire counties and parts of two others—was all within the boundaries of Albany County in 1683.

Understanding this "genealogy of places" is vital; if you do not know it, you will never find the records you need. When a county was divided by the creation of another, the records relating to the divided-off area before the division remain in the original county. It was impossible to separate those records from other records of the parent county because they were all kept in the same record books with no consideration for then-future county divisions.

A useful website for dealing with the issue of county divisions is an Internet website entitled Random Acts of Genealogical Kindness (*https://www.raogk.org*). This site is one you might like to explore, but our primary interest here is in the portion of the site—if you look at the menu at the top of the page—accessed through the link entitled "Genealogy Maps." Clicking on that link takes you to a page on the Random Acts website entitled "Research Guide—US & State Maps." The page's subtitle is "US & State Maps Guide."

When we scroll down the page, we will find a map of the United States. When we click on a state on that map, we go to a page with interactive maps for that state. Here, when we click on any listed year, we bring up a map that illustrates the creation of counties during the year chosen. That map will show any and all new counties created that year, with a brief explanation above the map telling the names of counties created that year and their parent counties.

To explain how this helps, let us consider again Muskingum County, Ohio, which—as discovered earlier—was established in 1804 from Washington and Fairfield Counties, with Zanesville as the county seat. When we click on the Ohio map for the next previous year on the list (in this case, 1803), the map shows how that part of Ohio looked *before* Muskingum's creation. It shows clearly that most of Muskingum came from Washington and only a little from Fairfield. By going back and forth between 1803 and 1804, we can see exactly what happened.

We can also look at the 1808, 1810, and 1817 maps, those years when land was taken from Muskingum County to form other counties. The 1808 map shows what happened when Tuscarawas County was created, and the 1810 map illustrates the result when Coshocton and Guernsey Counties were created. On the 1817 map, we can see the minimal effect on Muskingum County when Morgan County was created. However, there is no indication here of territory going back to Fairfield County, as the FamilySearch wiki says it did. It is also interesting to note that the 1818 map shows a piece of the southwest corner of Muskingum was taken away that year to become part of the newly created Perry County, another fact not mentioned on the FamilySearch wiki. These discrepancies might be significant if our ancestors came from the southwest part of the county instead of from Zanesville.

There is also one more feature of this website that should be mentioned. The interactive maps for each state also show county configuration within each state at the time of each decennial (every ten years) U.S. census. Perhaps you will want to look at these maps later when we focus on census records. Note that some of these maps have overlay maps of the present counties allowing comparison of present counties to the counties as they were at the times of the various census enumerations.

This is a good place to emphasize that, as wonderful as technology is and as useful as all these websites are as we pursue our research, the total accuracy of all their contents is not guaranteed. We *must* exercise due care.

In connection with our earlier Kelly example, it would be significant for the researcher to know that Owsley County, Kentucky, was created from parts of Breathitt, Clay, and Estill Counties in 1843, just eight years before John Samuel Kelly's birth. If either the Kelly or the Gilbert family was in Kentucky before 1843, records relating to them would be in one of those parent counties.

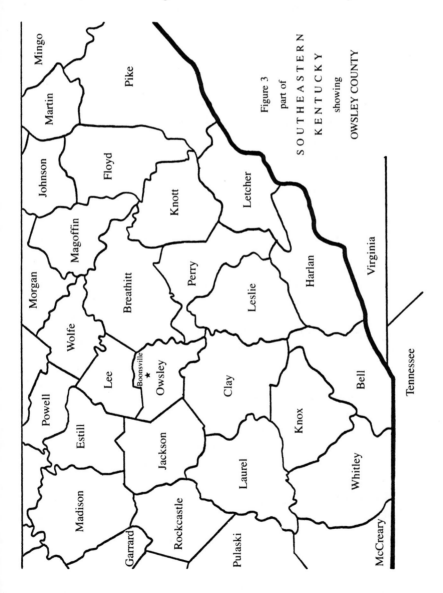

Figure 3
part of
SOUTHEASTERN KENTUCKY showing OWSLEY COUNTY

By going to the Random Acts of Genealogical Kindness website and comparing the interactive maps of Kentucky for 1842 and 1843, it seems most likely that Booneville was in Estill County before Owsley County's creation. However, it is a close call. Also, it may be important to learn more about Lee County, the neighboring county to the north. This is of interest because the FamilySearch wiki for Lee County says it was created on 29 January 1870 from Owsley, Estill, Wolfe, and Breathitt Counties.

When you go to the interactive Kentucky map and look at changes made when Lee County was created in 1870, you see—by comparing the maps—the possibility that the part of Owsley County where Booneville lies *might* actually have been cut off from Clay County. It is hard to tell, because of Booneville's location near to what would have been the line between Estill and Clay Counties. Because we have found no history that provides an answer to this question, and because Booneville is so close to the line, the careful researcher will want to check the pre-1843 records of both Estill and Clay Counties.

As mentioned earlier, another site where you can purchase maps is Historic Map Works (*http://www.historicmapworks.com/*). This site has nearly 1,663,000 maps (2016). It may have one you need.

I should also mention another site—a free site—you might find helpful. This one is different from the others in that it does not have historical maps but rather has maps that can show what the county boundaries were on any given date. This website is called randymajors.com (*http://www.randymajors. com/p/maps.html*). It is worth your time to take a look; it can be helpful in solving many geographical problems.

Before leaving the subject of the "genealogy" of American counties, I need to mention a book that has been a boon for genealogists for generations: George B. Everton's *The Handybook for Genealogists*. It is now in its 11th (and last) edition (2006) because George Everton is now deceased and Everton Publishers is out of business. The book can still be found in both book form and on a word-searchable compact disc (CD). In addition to information on county origins, *The Handybook* has maps showing the counties in every state and giving the county seat for each county. (The county seat is important because that is where the courthouse is and where the county records are kept.) *The Handybook* also contains descriptions and addresses for each state's major record collections and contact information for libraries, repositories, historical societies, and genealogical societies. Much of this kind of information, however, tends to become dated.

Another useful book showing the evolution of American counties at ten-year intervals from 1790 through 1920 is William Dollarhide's *Map Guide to the U.S. Federal Censuses, 1790–1920*. The third edition was published in 1987 and was reprinted in 2012 by Genealogical Publishing Company.

The purposes of our discussion about locality analysis in connection with our pedigree analysis have been twofold:

- To illustrate the need for knowledge of those places where your research problems exist
- To introduce the tools that will help you obtain that knowledge

If the researcher will

1. conduct a proper preliminary survey;
2. accurately document what he finds during that survey;
3. recognize any discrepancies in the information found;
4. analyze the pedigree carefully, taking discrepancies into consideration; and
5. learn everything possible about the locality of interest,

   he will have laid a solid foundation on which to do productive and accurate primary research. His careful work should produce satisfying results.

VII. TRADITION, COMMON SENSE, AND HELPFUL CLUES

Do you know the religious affiliation of your ancestor? His position in the community? Whether he was prominent or obscure? Whether or not he owned land? Whether or not he was considered "well to do"? These are all factors that will affect your approach to your research problem. If the answers to any or all of these questions can be determined, it will be to your advantage. Perhaps your ancestor was a Quaker or belonged to another religious group that declined to bear arms in time of war. This would certainly be significant. Or, perhaps he was loyal to the British king during the Revolutionary War. It would be helpful to know.

Family traditions can also tell us much about family origins; however, such traditions, overall, are notoriously unreliable and should not be accepted at face value. Dr. Ethel Williams said, "They have value but should be evaluated."[7] To that statement, I would add that they should be chewed and tasted but never swallowed. Remember, however, they often contain threads (and sometimes even cables) of truth that, when unraveled, provide useful clues upon which we can base meaningful research.

You must use common sense in your approach. Common sense is practical judgment along with sound reasoning. Much of both of these two commodities is needed by the family history researcher in pursuit of his ancestors. It is best typified by looking at each problem individually, logically, and thoroughly and then proceeding one step at a time to do those things suggested by

---

[7] Ethel W. Williams, *Know Your Ancestors* (Rutland, VT: Charles E. Tuttle Co., 1960), 23. Used by permission.

your analysis. In all of this, however, no connection is ever accepted unless it can be proved by sufficient evidence. Just because a connection is possible—or even probable—does not mean that it is the right connection.

VIII. ADDITIONAL HELP

For those who want more information on research planning and analysis, I recommend the following article. It was written for professional genealogists and takes a different approach than I have taken in this chapter. However, I think you will find it helpful:

Leary, Helen F.M. "Problem Analyses and Research Plans," *Professional Genealogy: A Manual for Researchers, Writers, Editors, Lecturers, and Librarians,* edited by Elizabeth Shown Mills. 2001. Reprint, Baltimore: Genealogical Publishing Co., 2010.

4

Evidence

The events that took place in and around the lives of our ancestors provide the foundation for our family history research. It was those events, after all, that generated the records that enable us to identify our ancestors and learn about their lives. Those records provide information we can use to establish proof of our ancestral connections. If those events—those births, marriages, deaths, sales (or purchases) of land, or military enlistments, etc., etc.—had not been recorded, we would be hard-pressed to trace our forebears and establish our connections to them. But even with all the evidence we can gather, absolute proof is, sadly, frequently beyond our grasp.

Previous chapters of this book have emphasized the relationship between genealogy and history and the significance of that relationship. This chapter goes in a somewhat different direction and essentially explores the relationship between genealogy and the law. This is also a significant relationship when we consider the rules of evidence that the family history researcher must understand as he seeks information about his family roots. The information the researcher finds provides evidence—the evidence that is his stock-in-trade. The better he understands the "rules" relating to that evidence, the more capable he will be of solving his family history problems.

The relationship between genealogy/family history and the law was brought into focus in 1979 by an attorney-genealogist named Noel C. Stephenson in his book *Genealogical Evidence: A Guide to the Standard of Proof Relating to Pedigrees, Ancestry, Heirship, and Family History* (Laguna Hills, CA: Aegean Press). Stephenson's book, a revised edition of which was published in 1989, built on the foundation laid by several of his predecessors, including Donald Lines Jacobus, whom I have previously mentioned and quoted. The book ignited serious discussion and thought that started us on the path to the Genealogical Proof Standard we have today—a standard we discuss in some detail later in this chapter.

This chapter discusses several definitions relating to evidence. These definitions can help us better understand what we are dealing with. Before going to the definitions, however, I want to make it clear that, although definitions are useful in our understanding, they have limitations. Practical experience is far more valuable than any definition or collection of definitions I can provide.

Even though the researcher needs to understand those definitions that relate to the various kinds of evidence, he should not become obsessed with them. After all, the researcher's ultimate objective is to accurately link generations and put families together. It is not to split hairs over the meanings of words. The definitions I give here are provided only to provide a basis for a better understanding of the research processes—not to complicate those processes.

Family history research is difficult and the promise of proof in a given case is uncertain, but I suppose it is that very element of difficulty, after all, that gives family history research much of its appeal. A man once told me that he considered genealogy to be "a fool's errand" because every time one ancestor is found, it gives us two more to look for. But, call it what you may, once you get into it and taste success—once you feel the satisfaction of discovering meaningful information relating to an ancestor—there is no leaving it alone.

Obviously, I am not the first person to write about evidence, nor will I be the last. Many excellent articles, even whole books, have been written on the subject. I am not deluded with the notion that I can cover the subject better than anyone else can. However, I offer my thoughts here with the hope they will be more helpful than confusing. Some other important writings on the subject are listed at the end of this chapter.

I. BASIC DEFINITIONS

Along with the definitions of evidence-related terms given here, I will attempt to provide appropriate explanations. Let me start with the very basics and then go forward:

A. Information

Information is no more than collected data about a specific subject.

B. Evidence

Evidence is what results from of our interpretation of *information* about the point or issue in question. It is the very medium by which *facts* are proved. Helen Leary gave the following explanation and example about the connection between *information* and *evidence*:

> *Evidence* is drawn from information in written records, oral testimony, and artifacts. *Information* is inert and impartial, until we use it to support an assertion about someone's identity, relationship, biographical event, or circumstance. As an example, let us say: according to the 1850 census, John M. owned real estate worth $25,900. That information is neutral—it conveys no

more than exactly what it says. When we interpret the information and assert that "John M. was a wealthy landowner," we have drawn a conclusion. That conclusion is the sum of prior deductions based on our judgment that (a) the census data is reasonably reliable; and (b) $25,900 represents realty of higher-than-normal value. By resting our statement on hitherto neutral information, we convert the data into evidence.[1]

In a court of law, *evidence* might be presented in the form of an object, a weapon, a photograph, a document, a circumstance, an eyewitness account, or whatever else might be relevant. In family history research, evidence may come from the testimony of a living witness who has personal knowledge of the relevant event. However, a particular piece of *evidence* comes more often from a record or document generated in connection with the relevant event. *Evidence* might also come from the existence of a circumstance, such as that of a supposed ancestor *not* being found in the records of a particular area during the time period when his supposed child was thought to have been born there. This situation demonstrates the fact that *what we do not find* may also be significant *evidence*. Someone aptly observed that "Absence of evidence is evidence of absence."

C. Facts

Facts in family history relate to circumstances as they *really* were or to events as they *actually* took place. Facts are absolute realities as distinguished from opinions, presumptions, and suppositions. Although the facts about a particular matter are often difficult to establish, our ultimate objective is, if humanly possible, to prove the *facts* relating to our ancestors and their families. This we seek to do with the *evidence* derived from the information gleaned in research. "Absolute" certainty of some connections can be established only through DNA testing, but that standard of proof—although used more and more today—is not usually required. DNA testing and its use for family history purposes will be discussed in Chapter 9 as part of the discussion on technological innovations.

D. Proof

Proof is the desired effect of *evidence*; facts are proven. Our primary objective is to establish (i.e., prove) *facts* by the use of *evidence*. Once we have gathered all available *information* on the matter in question and have carefully evaluated that information and determined that it is, in fact, *evidence* relating to our problem, it is our hope that proof has been achieved and the *facts* have been established. However, there is more to it than this. *Proof*, as one author put it, "is a process that takes place in the mind and is distinct from the infor-

---

[1] Helen F.M. Leary, "Evidence Revisited—DNA, POE, GPS," *On Board*, Newsletter of the Board for Certification of Genealogists, 4, no. 2 (January 1998): 2.

mation on which it is based."[2] As already noted, few facts can be established with absolute certainty, but we do our best based on our standard of *proof*. Sometimes, I believe, we succeed admirably—other times not so well, because the available *evidence* is not clearly convincing.

II. STANDARD OF PROOF

Our ultimate goal is to prove every family connection with absolute certainty. Total accuracy—absolute proof of the facts—is what we must strive for, insofar as historical information proves to be reliable evidence. I admit, however, that there are many situations where the information found during our research cannot produce sufficient evidence to prove the facts with that degree of certainty. In these cases, we must take whatever time thorough research requires in order to achieve the best possible result with the available evidence—always with the understanding that we can reopen the case as new evidence might be forthcoming.

Because every situation is different, we must approach each case differently. In the absence of that flawless original source that gives us perfect and reliable information about what we want to know, we must never draw our conclusions until we have considered every shred of available evidence. Remember, also, that what we may think is a "flawless original source" might prove to be flawed.

Some have suggested arbitrary rules about "how many" pieces of evidence are needed to establish proof of a fact, but that approach is illogical. It is the quality—not the quantity—of evidence that is at issue, and such numbers mean little or nothing. In each case, we must take whatever evidence we can get, but we must take all of it. We must then carefully weigh and evaluate that evidence before deciding.

In some cases, we may not find sufficient evidence to draw a comfortable and well-reasoned conclusion on the issue. In those cases, our final decisions must wait until more evidence can be found and considered. And, even then, there might not be enough. This leads to the question of how much proof *is* required. How can we know when we have proved our case sufficiently? What, in fact, is an appropriate standard of proof?

In the court of law, two different standards of proof are used depending on the nature of the case. The "beyond reasonable doubt" standard is used in criminal proceedings, and the "preponderance of the evidence" standard is used in civil proceedings. Genealogists have traditionally given lip service to the second of these—the POE standard, as it has been called. However, because it is not always easy to determine what exactly constitutes a preponderance of the evidence, we have sometimes settled for less than we should

---

[2] Donn Devine, "Evidence Analysis," *Professional Genealogy: A Manual for Researchers, Writers, Editors, Lecturers, and Librarians*, edited by Elizabeth Shown Mills (2001; reprint, Baltimore: Genealogical Publishing Co., 2010), 335.

have (and regret it later). Although, in practice, most good genealogists, while giving lip service (as I stated before) to the POE standard, actually embraced a higher standard in their own research.

In 1997, the Board for Certification of Genealogists (BCG) made a decision to renounce allegiance to POE and officially adopt a standard more consistent with good family history research practice. This standard, adopted after extensive discussion and debate about the merits of such a bold move, was named the "Genealogical Proof Standard," or GPS (having nothing to do with global positioning systems). The GPS requires that evidence of a "fact" be "clearly convincing" before we declare that "fact" to be proven.

The BCG, the sponsor and champion of GPS, explains that GPS has five interdependent components. I quote:

- Reasonably exhaustive research—emphasizing original records providing participants' information—for all evidence that might answer a genealogist's question about identity, relationship, event, or situation.
- Complete, accurate citations to the source or sources of each information item contributing—directly, indirectly, or negatively—to answers about that identity, relationship, event, or situation.
- Tests—through processes of analysis and correlation—of all sources, information items, and evidence contributing to an answer to a genealogical question or problem.
- Resolution of conflicts among evidence items pertaining to the proposed answer.
- A soundly reasoned, coherently written conclusion based on the strongest available evidence.[3]

The BCG also explains that a genealogical conclusion is considered to be proved when it meets all five GPS components. Each of those five parts must contribute to the credibility of a proven conclusion:

- *Reasonably exhaustive research* ensures examination of all potentially relevant sources. It minimizes the risk that undiscovered evidence will overturn a too-hasty conclusion.
- *Complete and accurate source citations* demonstrate the research extent and sources' quality. They enable others to replicate the steps taken to reach a conclusion. (Inability to replicate research casts doubt on its conclusion.)
- *Critical tests of relevant evidence through processes of analysis and correlation* facilitate sound interpretation of information and evidence. They also ensure that the conclusion reflects all the evidence, including the best existing evidence.

---

[3] Board for Certification of Genealogists, *Genealogy Standards*, 50th Anniversary ed. (Nashville: Turner Publishing Co., Ancestry, 2014), 1–2.

- *Resolution of conflicting evidence* substantiates the conclusion's credibility. (If conflicting evidence is not resolved, a credible conclusion is not possible.)
- *Soundly reasoned, coherently written conclusion* eliminates the possibility that the conclusion is based on bias, preconception, or inadequate appreciation of the evidence. It also shows or explains how the evidence leads to the conclusion.[4]

The *Genealogical Standards* book, from which the above explanations of GPS were quoted, provides additional guidance. It explains that

> Genealogical results cannot be partly proved. Proof results only when a genealogist's research, conclusion, and presentation of that conclusion reflect all five GPS components.
>
> Genealogical proof rests on evidence from thorough examination of all known sources potentially relevant to solving a research problem. Genealogical proof reflects what that evidence shows after any conflicting evidence is resolved. Such proof, therefore, cannot be overturned by "might-have-beens." Possibilities for which no known evidence exists do not discredit a proved genealogical conclusion.
>
> Meeting the GPS neither requires nor ensures perfect certainty. Genealogical proofs—like accepted conclusions in any research field—never are final. Previously unknown evidence may arise, causing the genealogist to reassess and reassemble the evidence, which may change the outcome.[5]

Helen Leary, in her article in *On Board* (cited earlier), suggested that we might weigh the evidence found in various sources by asking the following three questions. (Note that each question is followed by her comments in brackets and italics.)

- Are these sources generally accepted as reliable? Is the information itself coherent and free of obvious error? [*There are, of course, no "irrefutable" sources. Even a birth certificate may be mistaken in some of its details.*]
- Was the data's significance understood? [*Were its logical, physiological, psychological, social, legal, religious, ethnic, and historical contexts accurately reflected in the evidentiary conclusion?*]
- Is the data being used as *direct* or *indirect* (circumstantial) evidence? [*This judgment depends on how it is used. "John M. was a wealthy landowner" rests on direct evidence taken from the census. The same evidence is indirect when used to support a complex statement about John's identity—e.g., "the land value points to his being the plantation-owning John, not the Baptist minister John."*][6]

---

[4] Ibid., 2–3.

[5] Ibid., 3.

[6] Leary, "Evidence Revisited," 2.

Mrs. Leary has also suggested that judgment about a proof's power to convince depends on the answers to four more questions. Those four questions and her final observation concerning those questions are as follows:

- Was the research for relevant information thorough? Did it include all sources that a reasonably knowledgeable genealogist would expect of a competent search?
- Is the evidence valid?
- Was the evidence assembled correctly? Does all the underlying data concern the same person, event, or relationship? Has it been faithfully portrayed, without distortion or significant omission?
- Does the proof satisfactorily answer questions raised by *(a)* data that conflicts with the genealogical statement; and/or *(b)* information that might have been available in records that were never created or have been subsequently destroyed?

If the answers to these questions warrant our conviction that the statement is substantially true, it is said to be proved. That does not mean that additional data or interpretation that is more precise can never disprove it. It does mean that frivolous challenges, such as "but something else *could* have happened" or "the *History of the M. Family* (undocumented) says otherwise," should not be viewed as sufficiently powerful to destroy the case.[7]

III. TYPES OF EVIDENCE

At this point, I want to discuss some additional definitions. These definitions define and describe various types of evidence as we deal with them in our family history research:

A. Direct evidence

Direct evidence, in family history/genealogical usage, is evidence that, standing alone, gives a direct answer to a specific question; it relates directly to a precise issue. If we find a record or a source that says Samuel McCracken is the father of Seth McCracken, a man we know to be our ancestor, that piece of information is *direct* evidence of the parentage of Seth McCracken. Although the question is answered directly, we really do not know whether the answer is correct. There is always the question of how much evidentiary weight or value we should give to a particular piece of information, but we shall discuss that issue later.

B. Indirect or circumstantial evidence

Circumstantial evidence (the term I prefer) stands in contrast to direct evidence. It relates to evidence or information about facts and/or circumstances

---

[7] Ibid., 2, 5.

from which the existence (or nonexistence) of a fact may be inferred. Our minds must juggle that evidence in order to find its meaning. We must consider and carefully evaluate how it relates to all other evidence on the same issue.

An example of circumstantial evidence is finding two men of the same generation and with the same unusual surname living in the same locality. That circumstance suggests (but does not prove) that these men are brothers. On the other hand, if there were dozens of men of that surname living in that area, this circumstance might suggest, in the absence of other evidence, that the likelihood of these same two men being brothers is more remote.

On my own Greenwood line (if I might be excused for using an example from English research), it has been accepted by some family members that the parents of my third great-grandfather, William Greenwood, are Paul Greenwood and Mary Foster. William's birth date and place have been preserved and handed down through the family as being 1 March 1778 in Heptonstall Parish, Yorkshire, England. However, the case is difficult because Heptonstall Parish records show christenings for five William Greenwoods in the year 1778, all of them later than the date of our William's birth on 1 March. Unfortunately, the parish register provides no identifying birth dates for any of these Williams. The circumstance that family members have relied on in accepting Paul and Mary as William's parents is the singular fact that our William named one of his sons Foster.

This may indeed be a correct connection, but we just do not know. Exhaustive research has produced no other evidence—either direct or circumstantial—to support it. It is also interesting to note that the given name Paul was not perpetuated by William's children or his grandchildren—which in itself gives good reason to question the Paul Greenwood/Mary Foster connection.

In family history research, we rely on circumstantial evidence to help us prove many things, but we must be careful not to rely on it too much or draw conclusions too quickly. And we must never accept something as fact because of one piece of circumstantial evidence—no matter how much we like the answer. Also, when two pieces of circumstantial information are in apparent conflict, that conflict must be resolved before we draw any conclusions. Sometimes, in our desire for answers, we tend to grasp at straws when we find something that even hints at the possibility of a connection. This is an unfortunate tendency among novice researchers, but we must not allow ourselves to do this.

As significant and essential as circumstantial evidence is to the family history researcher, its improper use is one of the most common mistakes made by the neophyte. Too often, a piece of circumstantial evidence is so appealing that it is accepted without giving proper consideration to—or even looking for—other evidence. Indeed, too often other evidence is never even sought and thus never considered. The researcher is so happy to discover this circumstantial evidence that he does not want to find anything that might interfere with his "success." Remember that finding information on a person with the same name as our ancestor is not proof that person is our ancestor.

C. Primary evidence

Primary evidence is original or firsthand evidence. It is (1) from an original source document, and that document was (2) created at the time of the event of which it is a record. A third requirement is that (3) the person who provided the information found in that document was in a position to know the facts of the matter. Primary evidence might come from an original will, an original pension application, an original deed, or an original tax receipt. In addition, I should explain here that, for evidentiary purposes, we also consider photographic reproductions of these records—including microforms, photocopies, and digitized copies of these original documents—as if they were the originals. In actual practice, we encounter very few true original documents in family history research if we are working beyond the second or third generation from ourselves.

I also need to note that today's technology allows photographs and digitized images to be modified and falsified. Thus, we need to be reasonably satisfied that any image we rely on has not been altered.

Non-photographic and non-digitized copies, such as handwritten or typewritten copies and abstracts of records, do not provide primary evidence because of the copying process. They fall into the category of secondary evidence, discussed below.

In legal practice, there is a requirement called the "best evidence rule." The law demands that evidence from original documents be used as evidence because experience has taught that there is less chance of fraud, forgery, or error when evidence comes from an original document. Evidence from any other source document is *hearsay evidence.*

I should also note that, notwithstanding this rule, the term "best evidence" is often used in practice to describe *the best evidence that can be produced* relative to a particular issue, such as the testimony of a credible witness in preference to unverified information from a published genealogical compendium. In this context, the best evidence may not be primary evidence—it is just the best evidence there is in this case.

D. Secondary evidence

Secondary evidence is evidence that is not primary. (That is a strange definition, but it is accurate and is perhaps the best one available.) Secondary evidence is important for us to understand because we deal with a significant amount of it in our family history research. It covers a very broad spectrum of things, from sources that are usually trustworthy to those that are highly questionable, and it includes, as explained above, non-photographic and non-digitized copies, such as handwritten or typewritten copies, as well as abstracts of records. Because of the vast variety of sources from which secondary evidence can come, I have—for the sake of clarity—listed typical examples. Understand, however, that this list is not complete and is given only by way of example.

- *Recorded copies of deeds, wills, etc., before the advent of photocopying technology.* Until quite recent years (well within my lifetime), these records were handwritten by a clerk who was hired to transcribe original documents into the official record books or registers. Because these official records are handwritten copies, the information in them is actually secondary evidence. Although they have potential problems (whether in the courthouse or on microfilm), they are often all that is available and are thus a valuable resource.

- *Published and unpublished compilations of information—including published family histories.* All of these, for obvious reasons, provide secondary evidence.

- *Information on original records that relates to events that occurred long before the record was created.* For example, the date given for your great-grandmother's birth on her death certificate is secondary evidence. There are many other examples.

- *Information on the births, marriages, and deaths, etc., recorded in a family Bible published long after the events themselves.* This is secondary evidence both because of the passage of time and because of the uncertainty about the source of the information.

- *Reports of events by persons who were not participants in those events.* This information is also secondary because such persons were not in a position to know firsthand—even if the source of that person's information was involved in the event. The main difficulty is that we usually have no way to know how or where the person who reported the event got his information or whether he remembers correctly.

- *Information found in copies of copies, abstracts of abstracts, copies of abstracts, abstracts of copies, etc.* These cover a broad spectrum of secondary evidence.

Secondary evidence may be accurate (or not); the difficult thing is that, on its face, it is impossible to determine its accuracy—and risky to try. Some secondary evidence is *more likely* to be accurate than others and might be weighted differently in some cases, but we can *never* take it at face value because we do not know how trustworthy it is. To establish proof, we *always* need additional evidence from other sources.

When considering secondary evidence, we might ask the following questions as we seek to evaluate its potential worth:

1. *How far removed (or how many generations removed, if we can use that term) from the original document is the document in which the secondary evidence was found?* Note: This question is applicable not only when the source of our evidence is a copy but also when a significant amount of time elapsed between the event and the recording of the event.

2. *What was the reason for this record's creation, and did that reason bear any relationship to the information/evidence we are taking from it?* Con-

sider, for example, the date of birth on our ancestor's death certificate. There may be some demographic value in reporting a person's birth date when he dies, but the death certificate's ultimate purpose is to document his death. That information is useful in our research, but we do not accept it unquestioningly until other evidence substantiates it.

3. *Who created the source record in question, and what was that person's interest in making sure it was accurate?* If the evidence of interest is found in a book of will abstracts for an entire county prepared by a volunteer as part of a project, there may have been less incentive for accuracy than if the book contains only abstracts of the wills of the abstractor's own ancestors. The vested interest the abstractor has in the correctness of the information can make a significant difference.

Consider again the birth information on the death certificate. Remember, also, that some informants are better than others; the surviving spouse is probably a more reliable source than is the son-in-law. The clerk who copied deeds into the official deed books in the county courthouse also had the incentive to be careful and accurate because of the nature of the job, but he was still human and such records are not error free.

4. *What were the qualifications of the person who created this source record?* If it is possible to know this, we will find it helpful to know whether that person was a novice or if he was experienced in creating such records. And, if he was experienced, it would be useful (but may not be possible) to know something of that person's reputation for accuracy and care.

5. *If the person who created the record with the secondary evidence was not the person who provided the information contained in that record, what is that informant's connection to and/or interest in the information contained in that record?*

Carefully consider these questions and their answers in each case. They have great potential significance as you evaluate the secondary evidence you have gathered.

E. Collateral evidence

Collateral evidence comes from information that is an integral part of the source record in which it is found but has nothing to do with the reason the record was created. It is valuable evidence and may be used to help establish proof as it might apply. The evidence may be either primary or secondary, depending on its nature and its origin.

A good example of collateral evidence is a deed in which our ancestor, who is selling a tract of land, specifies that the property involved is "the tract on Sinking Creek I purchased from my father-in-law, Frank Sellers." The fact that our ancestor disclosed his father-in-law's identity had nothing to do with the purpose of that deed, but it is still valuable information. If this deed is an original document, the evidence is primary. If it is a handwritten copy in the county deed books, the evidence is secondary. In either case, it carries significant evidentiary weight.

Another example of collateral evidence is our great-grandmother's birth date on her death certificate. It is collateral evidence because it has nothing to do with the purpose of the record. It is secondary evidence, as was already explained, whether the document is an original or a copy, both because the event was recorded so long after the event and because the person who provided that birth information had no personal knowledge of that birth.

The issues of most importance in evaluating collateral evidence are

- the identity and connection of the informant to the event (e.g., the person who provided the birth date on the death certificate), and

- circumstances that might have made the informant privy to reliable information on that issue. Almost every man, for example, knows the identity of his father-in-law, and every husband is likely to know his wife's birth date.

F. Hearsay evidence

Hearsay evidence is any evidence that is outside of the personal knowledge of the source that reports it. The term applies to both written information and spoken information. This means that virtually all documentary evidence used in our family history research is hearsay evidence. This is true because the document itself is not the source of any information we get from it. Because a document is inanimate and knows nothing, it has no personal knowledge of any event (or of anything else). Thus, all documentary or recorded evidence is, by definition, hearsay evidence. The document can tell us only what someone told it. Those who tell us that we must never base our ancestral connections on hearsay evidence do not understand what hearsay evidence is.

In legal practice, there is a rule—called the hearsay evidence rule—that prohibits the trier of fact (the jury or judge) from accepting hearsay evidence if that evidence will be used to prove the facts claimed in a given situation *unless* an appropriate exception to the rule can be found. The hearsay evidence rule *per se* is important to the family history researcher only if he is called upon to establish a family connection in a court of law. In such a case, the rule is critical—especially its exceptions—because hearsay evidence is often all the evidence there is.

More as a matter of interest than for any significant purpose, note that exceptions to the hearsay evidence rule are many and varied. Some that might apply in the case of family history include the "ancient document" exception (which allows use of any document over thirty years old), the "regular course of business" exception, the "dying declaration" exception, the "official record" exception, the "authenticated document" exception, and the "declarations of pedigree and family history" exception. Note, however, that no exception can apply unless the document containing that evidence existed prior to the controversy that requires reference to it.

G. Relevance and weight

For the typical family history researcher, the more important question concerning evidence is not whether a particular piece of evidence is hearsay, but whether it is relevant. If it is relevant to the problem, it must be considered. Then we can decide how much weight it should be given. Its weight depends on many factors, including—but not limited to—whether it is direct or circumstantial and whether it is primary or secondary.

IV. SOURCES VS. EVIDENCE

Not everyone agrees with me on this point, but I believe it is useful for the researcher to think more in terms of evidence than in terms of sources; you can read about the other viewpoint elsewhere. Although some researchers speak in terms of primary sources and secondary sources, I do not take this approach because there are many sources that contain both primary and secondary evidence. They provide primary evidence of some things and secondary evidence of other things. Consider again a death certificate: it usually provides primary evidence relating to the decedent's date, place, and cause of death and other related matters. However, as already noted, the evidence found on that certificate about that person's birth is secondary evidence. Hence, my point is that we are more precise when we refer to primary and secondary *evidence* than we are when we talk about primary and secondary *sources*.

V. ORIGINAL AND DERIVATIVE SOURCES

Although I will not discuss here the topics of primary sources and secondary sources per se, it is still helpful for us to understand something about sources. This discussion focuses on two categories of sources in very simple terms. Records are either *original* or they are *derivative*. An original source is one made at or near the time of the event recorded in it, and the person who was responsible for the information found in that source—the informant—was in a position to know the facts firsthand.

A derivative source is one that does not meet *both* requirements of originalness (if I might coin a word). Donn Devine gives this explanation of derivative sources:

> . . . [T]his class of record or source varies widely in nature. It may be copied or compiled from original materials, or it may be a synthesis of many sources—original and/or derivative—that reflect the conclusions of others. . . . The merit of any source must not only consider whether it is an original or a derivative, but also whether the information is *primary* or *secondary* in nature and whether the evidence contained in that information is *direct* or *indirect*.[8]

---

[8] Devine, 333.

VI. WHEN EVIDENCE DOES NOT MAKE SENSE

There will be times when the evidence, or the lack of evidence, you find in your research does not make sense. It might be a case of people who should be in the records but are not there. Or, it may be a case where internal references within the records do not agree with the facts on the ground. These situations can be frustrating, and sometimes you begin to wonder just what it is you are missing. These cases usually relate to your use of records that have been microfilmed or digitized.

Let us look at a couple of examples. One example is an index (usually a card index) that was microfilmed or digitized rather than the original record. Perhaps the original records were deteriorating and would have been very difficult to reproduce—at least to do so in a time-efficient manner. The custodian of the records justified this approach because the people who created the card index did a good job of extracting "all of the information from the original records." The sad truth is that most such indexes are not only incomplete but also have many indexing errors. Such errors are serious in and of themselves, but they are also compounded when the digitized record is indexed.

To add to your problem, the custodian of the original records will not allow you access to the deteriorating originals because they are available on film or in a database. You will need to be able to make a good case in order to get access to the records you need.

The other case I want to mention is the one where the filmed or digitized record was mislabeled during processing. If you search the records of one location with the mistaken notion that those records actually belong to another place—the place where your ancestors lived—you will never find the evidence you seek. These could be the records of the wrong church, the land records or the wills of the wrong county, or some other case of mislabeled records. This is not a frequent occurrence, but it does happen. Consequently, you always need to examine the headings in the filmed or digitized records you search to make sure there was not an error of this type. If you discover an error of this type, bring it to the attention of the library or archives staff.

With regard to these types of problems, one author wrote the following:

> Do not accept any copies of original records at face value. Analyze every document and its format before accepting the validity of the information.
>
> Take the time to research the place and time. The records must be studied in historical context. This process often uncovers information that helps in understanding the records even if those sources do not include a family's name.
>
> Report errors to record owners and record copyholders. Document the corrections and share your findings.
>
> Lastly, researchers should trust their instincts when something "just doesn't seem right." . . . [R]ecords are not always what they appear. It is worth the time and effort to dig deeper and either confirm or disprove your instincts.[9]

---

[9] Julie Miller, "The Perils of Accepting Copies of Original Records at Face Value," *NGS Magazine*, 42, no. 4 (2016): 23.

VII. CONFLICTING EVIDENCE

One major challenge frequently confronting the researcher is conflicting evidence—when two sources of information disagree on the facts. Some evidence found relating to a particular issue may not agree with other evidence relating to the same issue. In these cases, the researcher faces the task of sorting out the evidence, weighing it carefully, and seeking to determine which, if either, is true. To appreciate fully what I am saying here, consider the differences that so often exist in the testimonies of two eyewitnesses to the same event. Such discrepancies may seem strange to us, even frustrating (why do we not all see things in the same way?), but we must remember that the observations and reports of witnesses are based on the following:

1. Each witness's point of view or his perspective of the event.
2. Each witness's past experiences.
3. Each witness's personal biases relating to the event.
4. The importance of the event to each witness—even any vested interests.
5. The passage of time between the event and the witnesses' reports. Time affects the statements of some witnesses much more than it does others. Also, we all remember some things more accurately than we remember other things. Most of us, for example, tend to remember the place of an event much more precisely than we do the date—unless the date is relevant for some other significant reason.

Example 1:

To illustrate the issue of conflicting evidence, consider the matter of Alvin Smith's death date.[10] This is a minor issue, to be sure, but it illustrates the point. Alvin was the eldest son of Joseph Smith, Sr., and Lucy Mack. He was also the oldest brother of Joseph Smith, Jr., the prophet and founder of The Church of Jesus Christ of Latter-day Saints.

When Lucy Mack Smith wrote the history of her son Joseph, she gave Alvin's death date as 19 November <u>1824</u>. However, the inscription on Alvin's tombstone in the Palmyra (New York) cemetery says Alvin died on 19 November <u>1823</u>.

Which of these dates is more likely correct: the one remembered by the mother or the one on the tombstone?

For many years, the family took the mother's testimony in preference to the date on the tombstone. Errors are often found in tombstone inscriptions, and our sentiment tells us that a mother does not forget this kind of thing. However, additional evidence was found in a notice published in the *Wayne Sentinel,* the local Palmyra newspaper, on 25 September 1824 and in several issues following:

---

[10] This case study comes from Archibald F. Bennett, *A Guide for Genealogical Research* (Salt Lake City: The Genealogical Society of The Church of Jesus Christ of Latter-day Saints, 1951), 108–110.

TO THE PUBLIC: Whereas reports have been industriously put in circulation, that my son Alvin had been removed from the place of his interment and dissected, which reports, every person possessed of human sensibility must know, are peculiarly calculated to harrow up the mind of a parent and deeply wound the feelings of relations—therefore, for the purpose of ascertaining the truth of such reports, I, with some of my neighbors, this morning repaired to the grave, and removing the earth, found the body which had not been disturbed . . . ." Palmyra, Sept. 25th, 1824. Joseph Smith [Senior].

What does all this mean? Well, it is obvious from this last piece of evidence that Alvin could not have survived until November 1824, as his mother reported, and have his body exhumed by his father and neighbors in September of that same year.

Example 2:

This example also comes from the family history of Joseph Smith.[11] It relates to the identity of the man who was Joseph's great-grandfather, the paternal grandfather of Lucy Mack Smith. There are two scenarios. I will present the two as Case A and Case B. If we accept Case A, then we accept Nathan Gates as Lucy's grandfather. Case B suggests that her grandfather was Daniel Gates. Italics have been added in each case to provide emphasis.

Case A:

1. In his later years, Solomon Mack, Joseph's grandfather, wrote the following in what he called a "narrative" of his life:

   In the spring of 1759, the army marched to Crownpoint, where I received my discharge. In the same year, I became acquainted with an accomplished young woman, a school teacher, by the name of *Lydia Gates. She was the daughter of Nathan Gates,* who was a man of wealth, *living in the town of East Haddam, Connecticut.* To this young woman I was married shortly after becoming acquainted with her.

2. *Lucy Mack Smith, the daughter of Solomon Mack and Lydia Gates as well as the mother of Joseph Smith, Jr., initiated baptisms* for the dead in 1841 in Nauvoo, Illinois, on behalf of her deceased parents, Solomon Mack and Lydia Gates (Book A, page 107), and *in behalf of her deceased grandfather, Nathan Gates* (Book A, page 61).

Case B:

1. In the vital records of Lyme, Connecticut (Volume I, page 92), there is a record of the marriage of Solomon Mack, of Lyme, to *Lydia Gates of East Haddam, Connecticut, daughter of Daniel,* of East Haddam, on January 4, 1759.

2. The records of the East Haddam First Congregational Church (Volume 1, pages 21 and 24) show the following baptisms:

---

[11] Ibid., 113–114.

a. "Oct. 29, 1732 Br. *Dan' Gates' child* was bapt. *called Lydia.*"

b. "Mar. 16, 1736 *One of Br. Dan' Gates' children* (bapt.) wch was *called Nathan.*

3. Besides Daniel's son (whose baptism is noted under b above), there is *no other Nathan Gates* on record *in the town of East Haddam, Connecticut*, during this period.

4. In his will, Deacon *Daniel Gates of East Haddam* left inheritances *to his daughter Lydia Mack and his son Nathan Gates* (Colchester County, Connecticut, Wills, Volume 4, pages 155–6):

> The first day Sept. 1769, I give unto my Dearly and well beloved wife Lydia one third part of my movable estate. . . . I give unto *my Loving son, Nathan Gates.* . . . I give unto my *Loving daughters Lydia Mack &* Hannah Gates the remaining part of my Moveable Estate. . . .

This is an interesting case. We have what appears to be credible evidence that tells two different stories. On the one hand, you would think that Solomon Mack should surely have known his father-in-law's name. It seems logical, also, that Lucy Mack Smith should have also known the name of her grandfather. On the other hand, however, it is even harder to argue against the evidence found in the public records—especially when *all* of the evidence in those public records is entirely consistent and in complete agreement on this issue.

It is true that, after careful consideration, we must accept the evidence found in the church and town records. But how can one explain the erroneous information in Case A? Let me suggest some possibilities: First, I think Solomon knew the name of his father-in-law, but that he just made a mistake in writing it down, perhaps doing what many other people do—letting his mind run ahead of what he was writing and thus making an error (thinking ahead about Lydia's brother Nathan while writing about her father, thus inadvertently writing the wrong name). Is that believable? We can only guess.

What about Lucy? Why was she mistaken? Her error is easier to understand when we realize that Lucy never knew her grandfather Gates; he died before she was born. Perhaps she was influenced by her father's narrative.

We have solved this question by analyzing the available evidence, but there is still one unresolved issue in the case. It is unrelated to the identity of Lucy's grandfather but rather to the time of his marriage to Lydia Gates. The vital records of Lyme give the marriage date as January 4, 1759, while Solomon says he was released from the army in the spring of 1759, after which he met and married Lydia Gates. Because Solomon's narrative of his life was written many years later, we might be inclined to place more trust in the vital records. However, for the sake of argument, consider the possibility that, because this marriage was so close to the first of the year, the clerk who created the record mistakenly wrote the wrong year and the marriage actually took place on January 4, 1760.

I am not sure we can resolve this issue, but it might be helpful to know the dates of birth of Solomon and Lydia's first child. Does it help to know that the eldest child, Lovina (or Lovisa), was born *about* 1762? It might, but note that the date of this birth is not documented and really tells us very little. In fact, some reports claim that Lovina and Lovisa are two separate persons. Some other reports say that a brother, Jason Gates, was older than she was (or they were). Are you ready to make a decision about this issue or do you need more evidence?

One other observation about evidence: We frequently see erroneous secondary evidence that agrees with many other pieces of erroneous secondary evidence. Such errors can often be traced to the same origin. The fact that many sources cite each other does not improve the quality of the evidence they contain.

In all of this, I hope you can appreciate the importance of looking at all of the evidence and carefully evaluating what you find before deciding on the "facts." Stopping research too soon, just because the evidence seems convincing, is a serious mistake. "Accuracy is fundamental to genealogical research. Without it, a family's history would be fiction."[12]

VIII. MORE INFORMATION ON EVIDENCE

If you wish to read more on the subject of evidence in family history research, I recommend the following sources. I have listed them alphabetically by author, and I suggest no preferences:

Board for Certification of Genealogists, *Genealogy Standards,* 50th Anniversary ed. Nashville: Turner Publishing Co., Ancestry, 2014. This 79-page manual presents the standards that family history researchers use to guide them in their research and obtain valid results. The book addresses documentation; research planning and execution, including reasoning from evidence; compiling research results; genealogical education; and the ongoing development of genealogical knowledge and skills. The book's six chapters are entitled "The Genealogical Proof Standard," "Standards for Documenting," "Standards for Researching," "Standards for Writing," "Standards for Genealogical Educators," and "Standards for Continuing Education."

Devine, Donn. "Evidence Analysis," *Professional Genealogy: A Manual for Researchers, Writers, Editors, Lecturers, and Librarians.* Edited by Elizabeth Shown Mills. 2001. Reprint, Baltimore: Genealogical Publishing Co., 2010. This brief (14 pages) treatise on evidence provides one of the better explanations of the subject, dealing fairly with all its aspects, including a discussion of the Genealogical Proof Standard (GPS).

Jones, Thomas W. *Mastering Genealogical Proof.* Arlington, VA: National

---

[12] Board for Certification of Genealogists, *Genealogy Standards*, xiii.

Genealogical Society, 2013. This book begins with a discussion of what genealogy is and then goes on to consider the complex principles of the GPS. It concludes with case studies and exercises with worksheets. Included are the subjects of "Genealogy's Standard of Proof ," "Thorough Research," "Source Citations," "Analysis and Correlation," "Resolving Conflicts and Assembling Evidence," "The Written Conclusion," and other topics.

Mills, Elizabeth Shown. *Evidence Explained: Citing History Sources from Artifacts to Cyberspace*, 3rd ed. rev. Baltimore: Genealogical Publishing Co., 2017. This book is a comprehensive guide to analyzing historical sources and properly citing those sources. It begins with the question: *"Why do we invest so much of our energy into the citation of sources?"* It then answers, *"Because all sources are not created equal."* The book explains that there are no historical resources we can trust at face value and that the records we use only offer evidence that may or may not be true. The author suggests that in order to properly analyze evidence and judge what to believe, we also need to consider particular facts about those records where that evidence is found.

Rose, Christine. *Genealogical Proof Standard: Building a Solid Case*, 4th ed. San Jose, CA: CR Publications, 2014. This 72-page revised edition incorporates the 2014 refinements to the GPS. It explains the GPS and how the GPS relates to the analysis and evaluation of evidence. It also seeks to provide a better understanding of the five points of the Genealogical Proof Standard. There are five chapters: "What is the Genealogical Proof Standard?," "Building a Solid Case," "Evaluating the Records," "Case Studies," and "Writing it Up."

5

Libraries and the National Archives (NARA)

Practically every activity in which people participate has special requirements of some kind. Some activities require the use of distinctive tools or equipment. Others are limited to unique places or particular types of facilities. Family history research falls into this last category, and a library is one such facility. In libraries, we can find some of the tools and the materials we need for our research. Even in this age of digitization, when we rely so much on computers and the Internet, libraries are critical to what we do. In fact, the use of computers and digital technology has made it even more critical for us to understand libraries and the role they play in our work. We must understand how to use them effectively and efficiently.

I. THE PURPOSES OF LIBRARY RESEARCH

At the very beginning of this discussion, I want you to know that there is still much we do not understand—and it seems to become more that way every day. Everything we know and everything we do seems to be in transition. We used to be able to say with some certainty that most family history research was not done in libraries—at least not in traditional libraries. However, it seems that nothing can be said with absolute certainty anymore. And what we think we can say with certainty on one day may not be true a few days later. This is not necessarily bad, but it does require us to pay attention so we do not get left behind.

In this time of transition, we must be careful to keep a realistic perspective on what is going on around us. Research is still research. The principles we talked about earlier in this book are still valid and need to be applied. There can, however, be a significant amount of variation in how we apply those principles—all depending on the localities where our problems are centered and the availability of the evidence required to resolve our ancestral issues.

It is still true that those who spend all of their time in libraries searching for and reading published family history books do not comprehend what correct family history research is all about. However, if one is fortunate and if his ancestors happened to live in the right places, many libraries today have resources that accommodate much primary research.

Some libraries mentioned in this chapter—as well as many, many others—have vast collections of original records as well as microform (film or fiche) and/or digitized copies of original records available for research. That fact can change your approach to many of your research problems. The difference is in the availability of critical records, both microform and digitized—as well as the availability of indexes to many of those records. If essential record collections of those places where your ancestors lived are available in a library convenient to you, it would be foolish not to take full advantage of those resources. It would be foolish, even, not to travel some distance if that were necessary to gain access to those valuable records.

Although the collections of most public libraries have significant inadequacies insofar as family history research is concerned, most have a few histories, published genealogies, and other resources that can and should be checked as part of our preliminary survey. Much information and many valuable clues can often be gleaned in a few well-spent hours in a public library. Such has always been the case.

The big difference we deal with, however, relates to the technological advances of the past few years and the innovative people and diligent indexers who are working miracles to make those advances serve the needs of family history researchers. And there are resources available—almost at our fingertips—that have changed the world for us.

Today family history websites, with their vast collections of digitized records, make a significant difference. We can subscribe to these websites and use their resources to whatever extent we desire and can afford. Many of them have significant subscription fees if we use them on the computers in our homes or on our mobile devices, but we can use the library editions of these websites free of charge in many local libraries. These include such vast collections as those of Ancestry, MyHeritage, and FindMyPast.[1] These are available for the free use of library patrons who will come in and use them.

Also, Latter-day Saint Family History Centers have the following online collections available for patron use without charge: NewspaperARCHIVE. com; the "American Civil War Research Database" from Alexander Street Press; Ancestry; FindMyPast; Fold3; HeritageQuest Online; and Historic Map Works (Library Edition).

All you have to do is go to the library or the Family History Center and use them. If you do not have a Family History Center close by, it may be worth

---

[1] The FamilySearch website was not included on this list because it can be accessed and used free of charge—which you can do at home on your own computer or on your laptop or mobile device wherever you happen to be.

your while to check with your local public library to see what they have. If they do not currently subscribe to these websites, perhaps you can convince them of the benefits.

Not only are more family history resources now accessible to us in our libraries than ever before, but most U.S. libraries now have their library catalogs on the Internet so we can check to see what is available before we leave home for our library visit. Section IV of this chapter discusses the use of these online library catalogs.

II. SOME IMPORTANT LIBRARIES

Although most public library collections are inadequate for serious family history research unless they subscribe to the family history websites, you should also know that there are many libraries in the United States with significant collections of printed family history materials as well as archival materials and record collections. Following is a list of a few of these libraries, listed alphabetically by state, along with their addresses and websites.

You can use the website information to their library catalogs. I have placed asterisks (*) before the names of eleven libraries on this list, identifying them as libraries with exceptional family history collections. Libraries from only twenty-five states and the District of Columbia are on this list, so—although it is a very good list—it is incomplete.

CALIFORNIA

CALIFORNIA STATE LIBRARY—SUTRO LIBRARY, 1630 Holloway Ave., San Francisco, CA 94132
(*http://library.ca.gov/about/sutro_main.html*)

LOS ANGELES PUBLIC LIBRARY, 630 W. 5th St., Los Angeles, CA 90071 (*http://www.lapl.org/*)

COLORADO

DENVER PUBLIC LIBRARY, Genealogy Division, 10 W. 14th Ave. Pkwy, Denver, CO 80204 (*https://www.denverlibrary.org/*)

CONNECTICUT

CONNECTICUT HISTORICAL SOCIETY, 1 Elizabeth St., Hartford, CT 06105 (*https://chs.org/*)

CONNECTICUT STATE LIBRARY, 231 Capitol Ave., Hartford, CT 06106 (*https://ctstatelibrary.org/*)

DIST. OF COLUMBIA

*DAUGHTERS OF THE AMERICAN REVOLUTION (DAR) LIBRARY, 1776 D St. NW, Washington, DC 20006
(*http://www.dar.org/library*)

*LIBRARY OF CONGRESS, 101 Independence Ave. SE, Washington, DC 20540 (*https://www.loc.gov/*)

NATIONAL SOCIETY, DAUGHTERS OF THE AMERICAN REVO-
LUTION LIBRARY (See DAUGHTERS OF THE AMERICAN
REVOLUTION LIBRARY)

U.S. LIBRARY OF CONGRESS (See LIBRARY OF CONGRESS)

ILLINOIS

*NEWBERRY LIBRARY, 60 W. Walton St., Chicago, IL 60610
(*https://newberry.org/*)

INDIANA

*ALLEN COUNTY PUBLIC LIBRARY, The Genealogy Center, 900
Library Plaza, Fort Wayne, IN 46802 (*http://acpl.lib.in.us/*)

INDIANA STATE LIBRARY, 315 W. Ohio St., Indianapolis, IN 46202
(*http://www.in.gov/library/*)

KANSAS

KANSAS HISTORICAL SOCIETY, 6425 SW 6th Ave., Topeka, KS
66615-1099 (*http://kshs.org/*)

KENTUCKY

FILSON HISTORICAL SOCIETY LIBRARY, 1310 South 3rd St., Louisville, KY 40208 (*http://filsonhistorical.org/library/*)

LOUISIANA

NEW ORLEANS PUBLIC LIBRARY, Louisiana Division, 219 Loyola
Ave., New Orleans, LA 70112 (*http://www.nolalibrary.org/*)

MARYLAND

MARYLAND HISTORICAL SOCIETY, 201 W. Monument St., Baltimore, MD 21201 (*http://mdhs.org/*)

MASSACHUSETTS

BOSTON PUBLIC LIBRARY, 700 Boylston St., Boston, MA 02116
(*http://www.bpl.org/*)

*NEW ENGLAND HISTORIC GENEALOGICAL SOCIETY, 99-101
Newbury St., Boston, MA 02116 (*http://library.nehgs.org/*)

MICHIGAN

DETROIT PUBLIC LIBRARY, Burton Historical Collection, 5201
Woodward Ave., Detroit, MI 48202
(*http://detroit.lib.mi.us/featuredcollection/burton-historical-collection*)

MISSOURI

KANSAS CITY PUBLIC LIBRARY, 14 W. 10th St., Kansas City, MO
64105 (*http://www.kclibrary.org/*)

*MID-CONTINENT PUBLIC LIBRARY, Midwest Genealogy Center,
3440 S Lee's Summit Rd., Independence, MO 64055
(*http://www.mymcpl.org/genealogy*)

ST. LOUIS COUNTY LIBRARY, 1640 S. Lindbergh Blvd., St. Louis, MO 63131-3598 (*https://www.slcl.org/*) (Note: In 2001 the holdings of the library of the National Genealogical Society [NGS] were added to this collection.)

STATE HISTORICAL SOCIETY OF MISSOURI, 1020 Lowry St., Columbia, MO 65201 (*http://shsmo.org/index.shtml*)

NEBRASKA

NEBRASKA STATE HISTORICAL SOCIETY, PO Box 82554, 1500 R St., Lincoln, NE 68501 (*https://history.nebraska.gov/*)

NEW HAMPSHIRE

NEW HAMPSHIRE STATE LIBRARY, 20 Park St., Concord, NH 03301 (*https://www.nh.gov/nhsl/*)

NEW JERSEY

GENEALOGICAL SOCIETY OF NEW JERSEY, Manuscript Collections at Rutgers University, Alexander Library, 169 College Ave., New Brunswick, NJ 08901-1163 (*http://gsnj.org/*)

NEW JERSEY HISTORICAL SOCIETY, 52 Park Pl., Newark, NJ 07102 (*http://jerseyhistory.org/*)

NEW YORK

BROOKLYN HISTORICAL SOCIETY (formerly LONG ISLAND HISTORICAL SOCIETY), 128 Pierrepont St., Brooklyn, NY 11201 (*http://brooklynhistory.org/*)

BUFFALO AND ERIE COUNTY PUBLIC LIBRARY, Grosvenor Room, 1 Lafayette Sq., Buffalo, NY 14203 (*http://buffalolib.org/content/Grosvenor*)

HOLLAND SOCIETY OF NEW YORK, 20 W. 44th St., 5th Floor, New York, NY 10036 (*http://www.hollandsociety.org/*)

NEW YORK GENEALOGICAL AND BIOGRAPHICAL SOCIETY, 36 W. 44th St., Suite 711, New York, NY 10036-8105. (Note: The genealogical collections of the NYG&BS have been combined with those of the New York Public Library (*q.v.*) to make them more accessible.)

*NEW YORK PUBLIC LIBRARY, Irma and Paul Milstein Division of United States History, Local History and Genealogy, 5th Ave. and 42nd St., 1st Floor, Rm. 121 N, New York, NY 10018 (*https://www.nypl.org/*). (Note: This includes the genealogical collections of the New York Genealogical and Biographical Society.)

NEW YORK STATE LIBRARY, Cultural Education Center, 222 Madison Ave., Albany, NY 12230 (*http://www.nysl.nysed.gov/*)

OHIO

*PUBLIC LIBRARY OF CINCINNATI AND HAMILTON COUNTY, 800 Vine St., Cincinnati, OH, 45202 (*http://cincinnatilibrary.org/*)

WESTERN RESERVE HISTORICAL SOCIETY, 10825 East Blvd., Cleveland, OH 44106 (*https://www.wrhs.org/*)

OREGON

OREGON HISTORICAL SOCIETY, 1200 SW Park Ave., Portland, OR 97205 (*http://ohs.org/*)

PENNSYLVANIA

HISTORICAL SOCIETY OF PENNSYLVANIA, 1300 Locust St., Philadelphia, PA 19107 (*http://hsp.org/*)

SOUTH CAROLINA

SOUTH CAROLINA HISTORICAL SOCIETY, The Fireproof Building, 100 Meeting St.,Charleston, SC 29401 (*http://schistory.org/*)

TEXAS

DALLAS PUBLIC LIBRARY, 1515 Young St., Dallas, TX 75201 (*http://dallaslibrary2.org/*)

*HOUSTON PUBLIC LIBRARY, Clayton Library Center for Genealogical Research, 5300 Caroline St., Houston, TX 77004 (*http://houstonlibrary.org/clayton*)

UTAH

HAROLD B. LEE LIBRARY, Brigham Young University, Provo, UT 84602-6800 (*https://lib.byu.edu/*)

*FAMILY HISTORY LIBRARY (THE CHURCH OF JESUS CHRIST OF LATTER-DAY SAINTS), 35 N. W. Temple St., Salt Lake City, UT 84150 (*https://familysearch.org*). (Note that there are also branch libraries throughout the country and a few FamilySearch Libraries in the Western states. For your information, I have listed those FamilySearch Libraries in the next section of this chapter because of their importance to the family history researcher.) A useful guide to the Family History Library is *The Library: A Guide to the LDS Family History Library*, edited by Johni Cerny and Wendy Elliott (Salt Lake City: Ancestry Publishing, 1988).

VIRGINIA

LIBRARY OF VIRGINIA, 800 East Broad St., Richmond, VA 23219-8000 (*http://www.lva.virginia.gov/*)

NATIONAL GENEALOGICAL SOCIETY LIBRARY, 3108 Columbia Pike, Suite 300, Arlington, VA 22204. (Note: In November 2001, the National Genealogical Society moved its library holdings to Special Collections at St. Louis County Library in St. Louis, MO (*q.v.*), where they are available to the general public by Interlibrary Loan through most local libraries.)

WASHINGTON

SEATTLE PUBLIC LIBRARY, 1000 Fourth Ave., Seattle, WA 98104 (*http://www.spl.org/*)

WISCONSIN

*WISCONSIN HISTORICAL SOCIETY, 816 State St., Madison, WI 53706 (*http://www.wisconsinhistory.org/*)

As already stated, there are many other libraries with genealogical collections—some of which may already be known to you. The libraries of some colleges and universities are of particular note. There are also libraries with limited collections of a very specialized nature—especially those relating to particular ethnic groups or to specific geographic areas—that may have just what you need. Use your Internet search engine to zero in on libraries with specialized holdings. In addition, there is a list of libraries with genealogy collections on a website called GWM: Guide to Genealogy Libraries in the U.S. (*http://gwest.org/gen_libs.htm*).

III. FAMILYSEARCH LIBRARIES

At various locations in the western U.S. (and likely to follow soon in other locations), the Family History Library in Salt Lake City has established facilities during the past few years that they call FamilySearch Libraries. Most of these are in the same physical facilities where branch Family History Centers once functioned. These libraries are publicized as "library class facilities" and are a boon to those living in the areas where they are located. They provide access to the resources of the FHL and are not comparable to the branch libraries that most of them replaced. There are (as of this writing) thirteen FamilySearch Libraries, located in five states. Following is a list of these FamilySearch Libraries with their websites, both the local website URL (where applicable) and the FamilySearch wiki URL:

ARIZONA

MESA FAMILYSEARCH LIBRARY, 41 S. Hobson St., Mesa, AZ 85204
http://mesarfhc.org/
https://familysearch.org/wiki/en/Mesa_FamilySearch_Library

CALIFORNIA

LOS ANGELES FAMILYSEARCH LIBRARY, 10741 Santa Monica Blvd.,
Los Angeles, CA 90025 *http://lafhl.org/index.htm*
https://familysearch.org/wiki/en/Los_Angeles_FamilySearch_Library

OAKLAND FAMILYSEARCH LIBRARY, 4766 Lincoln Ave., Oakland,
CA 94602
https://localwiki.org/oakland/Oakland_California_Family_History_Center Center
https://familysearch.org/wiki/en/Oakland_California_FamilySearch_Library

ORANGE COUNTY FAMILYSEARCH LIBRARY, 674 S. Yorba St., Orange, CA 92869 *http://ocfamilyhistory.org/ https://familysearch.org/wiki/en/Orange_County_California_Family Search_Library*

SACRAMENTO FAMILYSEARCH LIBRARY, 2745 Eastern Ave., Sacramento, CA 95821 *http://www.sacfamilysearchlibrary.org/ https://familysearch.org/wiki/en/Sacramento_California_FamilySearch _Library*

SAN DIEGO FAMILYSEARCH LIBRARY, 4195 Camino Del Rio S., San Diego, CA 92108 *https://familysearch.org/wiki/en/San_Diego_California_ FamilySearch_Library*

IDAHO

IDAHO FALLS FAMILYSEARCH LIBRARY, 750 W. Elva St., Idaho Falls, ID 83402 *https://familysearch.org/wiki/en/Idaho_Falls_Idaho_ FamilySearch_Library*

POCATELLO REGIONAL FAMILYSEARCH LIBRARY, 156½ S. 6th Ave., Pocatello, ID 83201 *https://familysearch.org/wiki/en/Pocatello_Idaho_FamilySearch_Library*

NEVADA

LAS VEGAS FAMILYSEARCH LIBRARY, 509 S. 9th St., Las Vegas, NV 89101 *https://www.lvfamilysearchlibrary.org/ https://familysearch.org/wiki/en/Las_Vegas_Nevada_FamilySearch_Library*

UTAH

LOGAN FAMILYSEARCH LIBRARY, 50 N. Main, Logan, UT 84321 *https://familysearch.org/wiki/en/Logan_Utah_FamilySearch_Library*

OGDEN FAMILYSEARCH LIBRARY, 539 24th St., Ogden, UT 84401 *http://ogdenfsl.org/ https://familysearch.org/wiki/en/Logan_Utah_ FamilySearch_Library*

RIVERTON FAMILYSEARCH LIBRARY, 3740 W. Market Center Dr. (13175 South), Riverton, UT 84065 *https://familysearch.org/learn/ wiki/en/Riverton_FamilySearch_Library*

ST. GEORGE FAMILYSEARCH LIBRARY, 237 E. 600 South, St. George, UT 84770 *https://familysearch.org/wiki/en/St_George_Utah_FamilySearch_ Library*

I should also mention a similar facility in Layton, UT, that is called a FamilySearch Center:

LAYTON FAMILYSEARCH CENTER, 915 W. Gordon Ave., Layton, UT 84041 *https://familysearch.org/wiki/en/Layton_Utah_FamilySearch_Center*

IV. A LIBRARY'S ONLINE CATALOG

When using any library, you must first understand how to use the library catalog; it is the index to the library's holdings. Card catalogs on 3" x 5" index cards that were used in the past are now practically obsolete. Most library catalogs today are interactive computer programs. They are available on the libraries' websites and can be used from your home or on your mobile device. The website will usually have a "search" space to key in an entry of some kind, depending on the search you wish to make. You can usually search for a title, an author, or a subject (frequently designated as a "keyword"). Once an entry has been made in the "search" field and you have clicked on it, the automated catalog displays options from which you can choose. This process provides a "call number" for the book you want, thus enabling you to find that book.

In a library that has a significant family history collection and source materials, the website usually has lists of the library's holdings with clickable links to provide additional information about how to access the materials of interest.

V. LIBRARY CLASSIFICATION SYSTEMS

Most libraries organize their holdings by assigning each book a number based on that book's subject. That number, known as a call number, is written on the book (usually on the spine) and books are shelved with those numbers in consecutive order.

In the United States, two classification systems are in general use—the Library of Congress Classification System (LC) and the Dewey Decimal Classification System (Dewey)—named for Melville Dewey, its originator. Some libraries, such as the LDS Family History Library, use an adaptation of one of these systems. And there are, no doubt, libraries that use other systems. However, it matters little what system is used if the catalog is complete and you know how it works. The purpose of every book cataloging system is to facilitate easy access to books and library resources.

Many libraries have "open stacks" where library patrons are free to go into the areas where the books are shelved and serve themselves. However, in libraries where stacks are closed to public access, the user fills out a book order slip and presents it at a designated station for an attendant to retrieve the book. When the user is finished with the book, it is returned to a designated location for reshelving. In some libraries, most books can be checked out (or circulated, as they call it) for off-site use, but genealogy/family history collections—except perhaps "how-to" books like this one—are sometimes considered to be reference books and are restricted to in-library use only. Some libraries have multiple copies of popular books—some for circulation and some for in-library use only. Most libraries with extensive family history collections reserve the books in those collections for in-library use.

A. Library of Congress (LC) classification

Both LC and Dewey classify by subject, but some consider LC the better of the two systems because it has more latitude for expansion as new areas of learning are developed. It is particularly useful in classifying large collections in some subject areas. Many large libraries consider it a "must," and even many smaller libraries that formerly used the Dewey system are switching. LC is easier for the library because the Library of Congress assigns the cataloging numbers when the books are copyrighted. One disadvantage to this is the amount of time it takes for a copyright to be obtained after the application is submitted.

Knowledge of how the system works is no substitute for using the library catalog. Browsing the library stacks is a hazardous practice because materials significant to your research may be classified throughout the system in places you do not suspect. And, if another user has a book off the shelf, you will never know it exists. I have not provided a list of the LC classification areas because understanding such a list adds nothing to your ability to use the library correctly.

B. Dewey Decimal (Dewey) classification

Dewey is based on ten major subject divisions, each of which is subdivided using Arabic numbers and decimals. Classification in each main subject area is based on a three-digit number; if the subject is a more minute subdivision of the main subject, additional numbers are added after a decimal.

At the Family History Library in Salt Lake City, the Dewey system has been modified so all research source materials are assigned the classification numbers for history—based strictly on locality—instead of using the subject numbers. Though this modification facilitates a limited amount of browsing, that is not where you want to start.

C. The problems with browsing

Knowledge of classification numbers in either the LC or the Dewey system is not an excuse for bypassing the library catalog. The primary purpose of classification numbers is to help us locate the books and other resources in the library. Important works are often overlooked when the researcher checks only those shelves where he thinks the wanted material should be. Also, there may be such a divergence of material classified in one geographic area that the researcher could easily overlook relevant materials unless the specific catalog reference is used in his search. Even though books on one subject are not scattered throughout the library to quite the extent with Dewey as they are with LC, there is still no excuse for not using the catalog. Also, if another library patron happens to be using the book you need, the browser would never even be aware of that book's existence. Finally, the relevant resources that are not in books (microfilms, etc.) cannot be located unless we have their catalog references.

D. Cutter Classification

If there is more than one book on the same subject, they do not have the same exact classification number because library materials are classified according to both authors and subjects. This author classification is accomplished by adding an additional number—a Cutter number (named for Charles Cutter, its originator). The Cutter number is written below the Dewey number.

Many libraries have modified their use of Cutter numbers but, typically, a Cutter number consists of the first one or two letters of the author's surname (depending on the name), followed by a number assigned to that author (determined by formula).[2]

When there are multiple books by one author on the same subject (thus also having the same Dewey classification), an additional letter (or more) is added at the end of the Cutter letter-number combination. This is usually the first letter or two of the first word in the book's title (not including "the" and "a"). For example, if the book title were "The Search for Ancestors" by John Doe, the Cutter number might be something like "D64s." The "D" is for Doe, the "64" is for the number assigned to this author, and the "s" is for "Search," the first letter in the first qualifying word of the book's title. Many libraries follow this procedure as a matter of policy even when the author has only one book. This allows books to be shelved alphabetically by author within each subdivision of the subject and then alphabetically by title. And, who knows when he might write another book?

The LC system also frequently uses Cutter numbers to indicate things other than author, and often a book may have two Cutter numbers (seldom more)—one for the author and one for something else (usually placed before the author number). For example, a Cutter number may indicate a locality, thus facilitating the arrangement of books in a particular class by relevant geographic areas, if pertinent. When double Cutter numbers are used with LC, it is usually to subdivide the subject in some way.

It is not necessary to explain all of the intricacies of the system or all the exceptions to various rules. However, it is necessary to stress once again the necessity of using the catalog.

VI. THE NATIONAL ARCHIVES AND RECORDS ADMINISTRATION (NARA)

A. A significant resource

Although the National Archives and Records Administration (NARA) is not a library in the sense I have described libraries in this chapter, it is one of the most important repositories of records containing family history information. Because of the importance of the collections of that great institution, no

---

[2] The Family History Library in Salt Lake City has modified its use of Cutter numbers so the number refers to record type rather than author. This works well along with the use of the Dewey number also being altered to indicate locality rather than subject.

book on American family history research would be complete without an introduction to NARA facilities. This is especially true because the NARA staff puts forth every effort to accommodate family history researchers and make this vast collection of records accessible for their use.

There are many references throughout this book to documents located in the National Archives. There are also references and quotations from both the 1964 publication *Guide to Genealogical Records in the National Archives,* by Meredith B. Colket and Frank E. Bridgers (Washington, DC: The National Archives, 1964), and the more up-to-date guide that has been published in three editions since that time. Although the Colket and Bridgers work is significantly outdated and no longer in print, the quotations from that book I have chosen to include in this book are still timely and accurate.

As noted, the Colket and Bridgers 1964 *Guide* is essentially outdated. It was replaced in 1983 by a more comprehensive and up-to-date work with a slightly different title: *Guide to Genealogical Research in the National Archives,* by the National Archives Trust Fund Board (Washington, DC, rev. ed., 1983).

Then the 1983 guide was updated by a second edition in 1985 and by a third edition in 2000. This third edition is touted in its Preface as a "complete revision and enlargement"[3] of the previous work. Concerning the need for an update, the 1983 edition explained that it was a

> complete revision and enlargement, [and] . . . includes records not described in the earlier work, particularly records of genealogical value in the regional archives branches [recently called National Archives Field Branches and now known collectively as Regional National Archives]. It also contains illustrations and photographs, citations to microfilm publications, and expanded and clarified descriptions of the records.[4]

The third edition (2000) also boasted of its enhancements, including the following:

- "How to" advice for those beginning their genealogical explorations
- Reference to material available through NARA's website
- Citations to more than 850 microfilm publications, including 300 never before listed
- Information concerning the 1920 Census and earlier Federal census records
- Greatly increased coverage of immigration and naturalization records
- Extensive information on military service and pension records

---

[3] Anne Bruner Eales and Robert M. Kvasnicka, eds., *Guide to Genealogical Research in the National Archives of the United States,* 3rd ed. (Washington, DC: National Archives Trust Fund Board, 2000), vii.

[4] *Guide to Genealogical Research in the National Archives,* rev. ed. (Washington, DC: National Archives Trust Fund Board, 1983), xiii.

- Expanded chapters on African Americans and Native Americans
- Enlarged coverage of genealogical records in NARA's regional facilities[5]

The very nature of these enhancements suggests that, after the passing of more than another decade and a half, another update might be overdue. But, notwithstanding the aging of this third edition, every serious American family history researcher should have access to it.

I would also be remiss, however, if I failed to note that the National Archives Internet website has made the need for an updated version much less critical. You will want to access that website at *https://www.archives.gov/* and explore it both carefully and thoroughly—then go back as needed.

Two additional resources are also available to assist us. The first is the online National Archives Catalog (*https://www.archives.gov/research/ catalog/*), and the second is the online *Guide to Federal Records in the National Archives of the United States* (*https://www.archives.gov/research/guide-fed-records*). The latter, an invaluable work published in a paper version in 1995,[6] has been put online by NARA and updated regularly to reflect new acquisitions of federal records. This is important because the National Archives Catalog is not yet a comprehensive resource. You should become familiar with both the online catalog and this online guide.

Getting back to our discussion about the 2000 edition of the *Guide to Genealogical Research*, I note that it has nineteen chapters in four sections. I shall not take space here to list the chapters, but the four sections are as follows:

1. "Population and Immigration"
2. "Military Records"
3. "Records Relating to Particular Groups" [including, among others, Native Americans and African Americans]
4. "Other Useful Records"

In spite of all the Archives staff does to accommodate family history research, there are certain record inadequacies when we use NARA records for research. The "Introduction" to the 1983 *Guide* lists three significant limitations:

> First, the NARA keeps only federal records. Birth, marriage, and death—the milestones of life and the backbone of genealogy—have never been the first concern of the federal government, and the best evidence of these will be found, if it exists, in family, local, and state records.
>
> Second, the American colonial period is not documented in the National Archives; very few records predate the Revolutionary War. Most of the records

---

[5] Eales and Kvasnicka. back cover.

[6] Robert B. Matchette, Jan Shelton Danis, and Anne Bruner Eales, comps. *Guide to Federal Records in the National Archives of the United States.* 3 vols. (Washington, DC: National Archives and Records Administration, 1995).

. . . pertain to the nineteenth century, a time when the government did not touch the lives of most Americans to the extent it does today. . . .

The third limitation arises from the nature of archives: records are arranged to reflect their original purposes, usually just as they were kept by the agency that created them. They cannot be arranged in ways that might seem most helpful to genealogists, partly because family history is only one of many present-day uses of archives.[7]

With regard to the nature, extent, and arrangement of the records, the 2000 *Guide* tells us that, in that year, there were more than 2 million cubic feet of materials, divided among 545 record groups. These included billions of pages, plus millions of items in every other imaginable form. The record descriptions in the *Guide* are mostly according to series, a subset of the record groups. Most files within the various series are retained by the National Archives in the order that best served the government agency that created them. Although this is not an arrangement that is usually advantageous to the family history researcher, the guides and catalog discussed here help to minimize that problem.

Many of the records of most significance to family history researchers have been microfilmed to make them more accessible. Many have also been digitized, and there is an online list of both those publications that are microfilmed and those that have been digitized by the National Archive's partner websites (*https://www.ancestry.com, https://www.fold3.com,* and *https://familysearch.org*). For each item on the list that is available on microform (film or fiche), the list includes its publication number, its title, the record group number, the record group title, and the number of rolls of film (or fiche or disks) in that publication. That list is at *https://www.archives.gov/digitization/digitized-by-partners.html*. Persons doing research at the National Archives are provided with free access to these partner websites.

Read carefully the "Introduction" to *Genealogical Research in the National Archives* (third edition) to learn all you can about the records, what kinds of information they contain, and how to gain access to those you need.

Each record group is divided into multiple series. Also, smaller bodies of records are "filed together because they relate to the same subject, function, or activity, or because of some other relationship arising from their origin and use."[8]

The National Archives staff has developed many different finding aids to facilitate access to those records relevant to our research. Take particular note of "General Information Leaflet 3," *Select List of Publications of the National Archives and Records Service.* This leaflet is available online at *https://www. archives.gov/files/publications/general-info-leaflets/3-publications.pdf.*

Finding aids of value to the family history researcher are also listed in the

---

[7] *Guide to Genealogical Research in the National Archives,* rev. ed., (Washington, DC: National Archives Trust Fund Board, 1983), 3.

[8] Ibid., p. 4.

2000 edition of *Guide to Genealogical Research in the National Archives* and are cited in appropriate sections of the text.

Because many of those NARA records of significance to the family history researcher have been microfilmed to provide easier access, many of them—as well as many original records—are also available in other repositories, including the Regional National Archives. Many important collections are now also available online.

B. The Regional National Archives

The Regional National Archives are in the following locations:

Anchorage, AK (This Regional Archives was permanently closed in June 2014 and its records transferred to Seattle, Washington, where they are being digitized.)

Atlanta, GA (*Serves Alabama, Florida, Georgia, Kentucky, Mississippi, North Carolina, South Carolina, and Tennessee*): 5780 Jonesboro Rd., Morrow, GA 30260

Boston, MA (*Serves Connecticut, Maine, Massachusetts, New Hampshire, Rhode Island, and Vermont*): 380 Trapelo Rd., Waltham, Massachusetts 02452-6399

Chicago, IL (*Serves Illinois, Indiana, Michigan, Minnesota, Ohio, and Wisconsin*): 7358 S. Pulaski Rd., Chicago, IL 60629-5898

College Park, MD (*Washington, DC, area—known as Archives II*): 8601 Adelphi Rd., College Park, MD 20740-6001

Denver, CO (*Serves Colorado, Montana, New Mexico, North Dakota, South Dakota, Utah, and Wyoming*): 17101 Huron St., Broomfield, CO 80023

Fort Worth, TX (*Serves Arkansas, Louisiana, Oklahoma, and Texas*): 1400 John Burgess Dr., Fort Worth, TX 7614.

Kansas City, MO (*Serves Iowa, Kansas, Missouri, and Nebraska*): 400 W. Pershing Rd., Kansas City, MO 64108-4306

New York City, NY (*Serves New Jersey, New York, Puerto Rico, and the Virgin Islands*): One Bowling Green, 3rd Floor, New York, NY 10004

Philadelphia, PA (*Serves Delaware, Maryland, Pennsylvania, Virginia, and West Virginia*): 14700 Townsend Rd., Philadelphia, PA 19154-1096

Riverside, CA (*Serving Southern California, Arizona, and Clark County, Nevada*): 23123 Cajalco Rd., Perris, CA 92570

San Francisco, CA (*Serves Northern and Central California, Nevada [except Clark County], Hawaii, American Samoa, Guam, and the former Trust Territory of the Pacific Islands [Marshall, Caroline, and Northern Mariana Islands]*): 1000 Commodore Dr., San Bruno, CA 94066-2350

Seattle, WA (*Serves Alaska, Idaho, Oregon, and Washington*): 6125 Sand Point Way, NE., Seattle, WA 98115-7999

St. Louis, MO (*National Personnel Records Center [NPRC]; largest Federal records collection outside NARA's Washington, DC, and College Park, MD, locations. Has more than 100 million military and civilian personnel records beginning in the 19th century*): 1 Archives Dr., St. Louis, MO 63138

For information about these Regional National Archives and other federal records repositories—and for clickable links to their individual websites—go to *https://www.archives.gov/locations.*

The National Archives in Washington, DC (700 Pennsylvania Ave., NW 20408) can provide some research assistance and—for a fee—provide photocopies of records by mail when exact identifying information is provided. Before you visit the National Archives to do research, you should review the information on the Archives website at *https://www.archives.gov/dc-metro/washington/researcher-info.html.*

The regional National Archives sites cannot provide research assistance, but they have many records of importance to the family history researcher, including many important NARA microfilm publications.

VII. FINAL OBSERVATION ABOUT LIBRARY USE

If you need help in locating library materials relating to family history in any library, ask for assistance from a library staff member.

In the next chapter, we will look at some of the materials found in most libraries that can help make your research easier.

6

Reference Works

To begin with, let me define the term *reference works* as used in this chapter. These are the sources we consult as we seek information on specific issues—but not usually the types of sources we read from beginning to end. When they are books, they stay in the library reference section and are not checked out to library patrons. The reference works of value to the family history researcher are those sources he uses to

- help him locate records pertinent to his research and/or
- facilitate his use of those records.

In addition to the traditional type of reference works, this chapter includes a listing of textbooks and various other instructional aids.

There are many problems the beginning family history researcher struggles to solve that can be resolved quite quickly by using some common and readily available reference sources. Thus, one of the main differences between a good researcher and a poor one is his knowledge of, and his ability to correctly use, critical reference works. You will not be surprised when I tell you that many of the reference works discussed in this chapter are not books at all; they are "tools" available on the Internet.

For our purposes as family history researchers, I have divided these reference works (I call them "guides") into four categories, each of which we will explore:

      I. Guides to locality data
     II. Guides to non-original sources
   III. Guides to original sources
   IV. Other useful research guides

At the beginning of this discussion, I suggest—as you look at the works included on these lists—that you go to the WorldCat website to learn which libraries have copies of them. The WorldCat website is at *http://www.worldcat.org/*.

Let us look now at reference works in each of our four categories.

I. GUIDES TO LOCALITY DATA

Previous editions of *The Researcher's Guide* have listed various printed resources to help family history researchers learn what they need to know about the places where their ancestors and ancestral families lived. In the past few years, however (as discussed in Chapters 9 and 10), resources on the Internet have largely superseded some of these once-useful tools. Here we will look at both the books and Internet sources that provide valuable information about American localities. These include (A) atlases and maps, (B) gazetteers, and (C) specialized locality sources.

A. Atlases and maps

The right map is a valuable tool for the family history researcher. Many excellent maps are now readily accessible on the Internet. Here are a few useful Internet websites at the time of this writing:

Historic Map Works (*http://www.historicmapworks.com/*): This website has more than a million and a half maps, all of which can be viewed online (and copies purchased and downloaded if you desire). A clickable link on the website provides access to a Historic Earth™ premium site where 54 percent of the site's maps can be searched by anyone who has a monthly or yearly subscription.

A premium search allows the researcher to search both for specific addresses and for names of people. For an address search on the premium site, you can enter an address, city, or landmark in a space provided and then make a search. Search results will appear on the screen as a list of map results. After choosing a map from that list, a "View Overlay" option is available that allows you to view the selected map overlaid on a modern map.

For a name search, a single surname along with a state, county, and year can be entered in the "Name Search" box under the site's "Tools" tab. Icons showing the locations of all people with that name will appear on the map. You can click on an icon to find maps for that location. An area highlighted in red on a master map identifies a place for which detailed maps are available. You can get a list of those map results by clicking on a red area.

The remaining 46 percent of the maps on Historic Map Works can be searched on a free Historic Earth™ basic site and accessed using the "Browse" and "Search" options at the top of the page. I suggest that you see what success you have with this option before investing in a subscription.

U.S. maps on Random Acts of Genealogical Kindness website (*https:// www.raogk.org/us-map/*): This useful website, already discussed in Chapter 3, has useful interactive maps relating to county creations. It also provides access to much other information. You may want to refer back to Chapter 3 for instructions on accessing the county maps. Though these county creation maps do not have the detailed information found on some other sites, they can be helpful in providing perspective.

Land ownership maps by Arphax Publishing (*https://arphax.com/*): There are two series of map books showing those persons who secured land patents in the covered counties: the *Family Maps* series of Land Patent Books and the *Texas Land Survey Maps* series. Each book is for a single county, with maps—decade by decade—showing the land claimed by the original settlers during each decade. Each map was created using the land acquisitions indexed in the database of the U.S. Bureau of Land Management or in the database of the Texas General Land Office. Because these books represent a significant amount of detailed work, the books are relatively expensive. However, they are valuable resources for families whose ancestors were original patentees. The surnames of patentees in each book are on the website, so you can see if your family surname is included before you buy the book.

U.S. territorial maps (*http://xroads.virginia.edu/~MAP/terr_hp.html*): This site provides an interesting perspective on the development of the state and territorial status of the entire country, beginning in 1775 and going decade by decade until 1920. It provides a "big picture" but is without details.

The US GenWeb Project (*http://usgenweb.org/*): This is a geographically oriented project focused on the individual states and counties and their genealogical/family history resources. It is manned entirely by volunteers. There are many maps for many counties in many states. It is worth your while to visit this site in your search for maps, as well as for other resources to help you with your research. More is said about the US GenWeb Project later in this chapter.

Though the Internet is your easiest option as you look for maps, there are also some important books that deserve mention:

Adams, James Truslow, ed. *Atlas of American History*. New York: Charles Scribner's Sons, 1943. This book, when it can be found, is still a useful tool for the family history researcher.

Andriot, John L., comp. and ed. *Township Atlas of the United States*. McLean, VA: Androit Associates, 1979. This is a useful book but is now out of print and hard to find.

Morgan, Dale. *Rand-McNally's Pioneer Atlas of the American West*. New York: Rand-McNally and Co., 1969.

Thorndale, William, and William Dollarhide. *Map Guide to the U .S. Federal Censuses, 1790–1920*. 1987. Reprint, Baltimore: Genealogical Publishing Co., 2012.

Insofar as the family history researcher is concerned, one of the best collections of American period maps is the collection of county land ownership maps in the Library of Congress in Washington, DC. This collection is located in the Geography & Map Reading Room, Room LM B01, Madison Bldg., Independence Ave. SE, Washington, DC 20540-4650. This is a vast, though incomplete, collection of maps for U.S. counties from the 1800s—with some maps even earlier. Each map shows who owned the various parcels of land in the county at the time the map was prepared.

The Library of Congress produced an inventory of these maps in 1967 that has been available from the Superintendent of Documents, U.S. Government Printing Office:

Stephenson, Richard W., comp. *Land Ownership Maps: A Checklist of Nineteenth Century Land Ownership Maps in the Library of Congress.* Washington: U.S. Government Printing Office, 1967. (LC catalog no.: Z6027.U5 U54; LCCN: 67060091)[1]

Stephenson's book is now difficult to find. There is, however, a list of available maps on a website entitled "Kinquest" (*http://www.kinquest.com/usgenealogy/lom.php*). I have also included additional information about these land ownership maps in Chapter 20, "Local Land Records."

I also recommend that you look for maps on the FamilySearch wiki, for there are many good ones. The easiest way to do this is to use your Internet search engine. Type the name of the state and the words "maps" and "familysearch" in the search engine space. You can also narrow your search by including the name of the county in your search. Not only will you find maps, you will also be referred to relevant books and microfilm collections of maps with call numbers from the Family History Library. For example, the wiki for the state of Georgia lists the following books and microfilms of maps that are available at the Family History Library and its branches:

- Georgia Surveyor General. *Surveyor-General's Maps and Maps of Counties of Georgia, Arranged in Alphabetical Order* (FHL films 465171-2).
- Library of Congress. Geography and Map Division. *Ward Maps of United States Cities* (FHL film 1377700, fiche 6016567).
- James C. Bonner. *Atlas for Georgia History.* Milledgeville, GA: Georgia College Duplicating Department, 1969 (FHL book 975.8 E7b).

---

[1] This book is in several libraries and is for sale at Amazon.com. It is also supposed to be for sale at the Government Printing Office, but I had no success in finding it there.

- Pat Bryant. *Georgia Counties: Their Changing Boundaries.* 2nd ed. Revised by Ingrid Shields. Atlanta, GA: State Printing Office, 1983 (FHL 975.8 E3b).[2]

This source also has lists of Georgia maps and atlases available in other libraries and archives. And what is true for Georgia is also true for many other states.

B. Gazetteers/geographical dictionaries

There are some gazetteers that have potential value for us, and many of them are now on the Internet. In many cases, they are valuable because they are old, as you will note from the following list. Some of the more recent gazetteers are also valuable because of their coverage and completeness. Note, also, that many of those listed are available online. In many cases, you will be able to identify other gazetteers on the Internet that relate to the specific places of your research interest by using your Internet search engine.

UNITED STATES GENERAL

Abate, Frank R., ed. *American Places Dictionary: A Guide to 45,000 Populated Places, Natural Features, and Other Places in the United States.* 4 vols. Detroit: Omnigraphics, 1994.

———. *Omni Gazetteer of the United States of America: Providing Name, Location, and Identification for Nearly 1,500,000 Populated Places, Structures, Facilities, Locales, Historic Places, and Geographic Features in the Fifty States . . .* 11 vols. Detroit: Omnigraphics, 1991.

Cohen, Saul B., ed. *The Columbia Gazetteer of the World.* 2nd ed. New York: Columbia University Press, 2008.

de Colange, Leo. *The National Gazetteer: A Geographical Dictionary of the United States.* London: Hamilton, Adams & Co., 1884. This book is online at *http://archive.org/stream/nationalgazettee00cola#page/n5/mode/2up.*

Hayward, John. *A Gazetteer of the United States of America.* Hartford, CT: Case, Tiffany, and Co., 1853. This book can be either read online or downloaded at a website, the URL of which is too long to include here. To locate it, enter the author and title in your Internet search engine space.

CONNECTICUT and RHODE ISLAND

Pease, John C., and John M. Niles. *A Gazetteer of the States of Connecticut and Rhode-Island, Written with Care and Impartiality, from Original and Authentic Materials.* Hartford, CT: William S. Marsh, 1819. Copies are in

---

[2]"Georgia Maps," *FamilySearch,* March 18, 2014, https://beta.familysearch.org/wiki/en/Georgia_Maps (accessed September 30, 2016).

various libraries, including the Connecticut State Library. It is also online at *https://babel.hathitrust.org/cgi/pt?id=mdp.39015053598960;view=1 up;seq=13*.

GEORGIA

Sherwood, Adiel. *A Gazetteer of the State of Georgia.* 3rd ed. 1837. Reprint, Baltimore: Genealogical Publishing Co., 2009. An earlier (1829) edition is on film 164709 at the Family History Library in Salt Lake City.

INDIANA

Scott, John, and James Scott. *The Indiana Gazetteer or Topographical Dictionary.* 2nd ed. Indianapolis, IN: Douglass and Maguire, 1833. This book is online at *https://babel.hathitrust.org/cgi/pt?id=nyp.33433081818084;view=1up;seq=8*.

MASSACHUSETTS

Nason, Elias. *A Gazetteer of the State of Massachusetts, with Numerous Illustrations on Wood and Steel.* Boston: B. B. Russell, 1874. This book is online at *https://openlibrary.org/books/OL6905654M/A_gazetteer_of_the_state_of_Massachusetts*.

NEW YORK

French, John Homer. *Gazetteer of the State of New York: Embracing a Comprehensive View of the Geography, Geology, and General History of the State, and a Complete History and Description of Every County, City, Town, Village and Locality: With Full Table of Statistics.* Port Washington, NY: Ira J. Friedman, Inc., 1860. This work was reprinted in 1969 and 1980, the latter by Heart of Lakes Publishing, Interlaken, NY. A copy is also online at *https://archive.org/details/gazetteerofstate04fren*.

NORTH CAROLINA

Powell, William S., and Michael Hill. *The North Carolina Gazetteer: A Dictionary of Tar Heel Places and Their History.* 2nd ed. Chapel Hill, NC: University of North Carolina Press, 2010.

OHIO

Jenkins, Warren. *The Ohio Gazetteer and Traveler's Guide.* Rev. ed. Columbus, OH: Isaac N. Whiting, 1939. This book is a revision and update of an earlier edition by John Kilbourn. The URL is too long to include here.

Kilbourn, John. *The Ohio Gazetteer.* 8th ed. Columbus, OH: J. Kilbourn, 1826. This book is available at the Family History Library in Salt Lake City.

PENNSYLVANIA

Gordon, Thomas F. *A Gazetteer of the State of Pennsylvania*. Philadelphia: Thomas Belknap, 1832. This book is online at *https://babel.hathitrust. org/cgi/pt?id=mdp.39015008717863;view=1up;seq=9.*

C. Specialized locality sources
UNITED STATES GENERAL

City Directories of the United States, 1860–1901: Guide to the Microfilm Collection. Woodbridge, CT: Research Publications, 1983. The Family History Library in Salt Lake City has digitized this book. Also, as mentioned in Chapter 3, Ancestry has an extensive collection of U.S. city directories covering the years 1821 to 1989.

Eichholz, Alice, ed., with numerous contributors. *Ancestry's Red Book: American State, County, and Town Sources*. 3rd ed. Salt Lake City: Ancestry Publishing, 2004. The online version is being updated and modified as necessary and is available on the Ancestry Wiki.

Filby, P. William, comp. *A Bibliography of American County Histories*. 1985. Reprint, Baltimore: Genealogical Publishing Co., 2009.

Gannett, Henry. *Boundaries of the United States and of the Several States and Territories*. 3rd ed. Washington, DC: US Geological Survey, 1904. Various publishers have reprinted this book in recent years, and it is readily available.

Hansen, Holly, ed. *The Handybook for Genealogists*. 11th ed. Logan, UT: Everton Publishers, 1999. This edition has some updated features not found in previous editions and is also available on CD. It has been reported that this will be the last edition published.

Kaminkow, Jack, ed. *United States Local Histories in the Library of Congress: A Bibliography*. 5 vols. Baltimore: Magna Carta Book Co., 1976. This work includes: Volume 1, Atlantic States from Maine to New York; Volume 2, Atlantic States from New Jersey to Florida; Volume 3, the Middle West, Alaska, and Hawaii; Volume 4, the West; and Volume 5, Supplement and Index. Volume 5 also corrects errors in the first four volumes.

Kane, Joseph Nathan. *The American Counties*. New York: The Scarecrow Press, 1960. There have been subsequent editions, but they deal with origins of more recent counties.

Kirkham, E. Kay. *The Counties of the United States and Their Genealogical Value: A Verified and Corrected Listing That Shows Parent County, County Seat and Census Information for Each County with Miscellaneous Information*. 3rd ed. Salt Lake City: Deseret Book Co., 1965. This book, though now hard to find, is still useful for the information it provides.

Library of Congress Geography and Map Division, and Michael H. Shelley. *Ward Maps of United States Cities: A Selective Checklist of Pre-1900 Maps in the Library of Congress.* Washington, DC: Library of Congress, 1975. This book is for sale at the U.S. Government Publishing Office, 732 North Capitol St. NW, Washington, DC 20401.

KENTUCKY

Field, Thomas P. *A Guide to Kentucky Place Names.* Special Publication 15, Series XI. Lexington, KY: Kentucky Geological Survey, University of Kentucky, 1961.

Rennick, Robert M. *Kentucky Place Names.* Lexington, KY: University Press of Kentucky, 1984.

MAINE

Chadbourne, Ava Harriet. *Maine Place Names and the Peopling of Its Towns.* Portland, ME: The Bond Wheelwright Co., 1955.

NORTH CAROLINA

Corbitt, David Leroy. *The Formation of North Carolina Counties, 1663–1943.* Raleigh, NC: State Department of Archives and History, 1950.

OHIO

Miller, Larry L. *Ohio Place Names.* Bloomington, IN: Indiana University Press, 1996.

PENNSYLVANIA

Espenshade, A. Howry. *Pennsylvania Place Names.* 1925. Reprint, Baltimore: Genealogical Publishing Co., 2005. This book is also online at *https://archive.org/details/pennsylvaniaplac00espe*.

VIRGINIA

Hummel, Ray O., Jr. *A List of Places Included in Nineteenth Century Virginia Directories.* Virginia State Library Publ. 11. Richmond: Virginia State Library, 1960 and 1981.

These sources are but a sampling of many that are available. There are many more—and getting to be more all the time. I suggest you try entering the name of the state of your interest into your Internet search engine space, followed by the words "localities" and "geography." You might also try entering the names of both the county and the state.

D. Other Internet resources

I also need to mention some other useful Internet resources. One important website, History of the Great Lakes States, relates to the general Great Lakes region and the five states of the Old Northwest Territory: Illinois, Indiana, Michigan, Ohio, and Wisconsin. Its URL is *http://www.envisionthepast.com/*.

As you scroll down the homepage, you will see clickable listings on various topics, including "Biographies and Memoirs," "Documents & Collections," "General History," "Local History," "Maps & Gazetteers," "War & Military," and a number of others.

Let me give an example of the kinds of resources on this site. If you click on "Michigan" under "Maps & Gazetteers," you can scroll down the page that comes up. You will see listed a gazetteer authored by John T. Blois in 1839 entitled *Gazetteer of the State of Michigan, in Three Parts, Containing a General View of the State . . .* This book is available to read on the website—or you can even listen to an audio version (with a computer-generated voice).

Another useful Internet resource is the FamilySearch wiki, already discussed in other contexts. There are lists of geographical resources for every state and, because of the nature of wikis, that information is expanding continuously.

These are a few of the available sources that may be helpful as you seek to learn about the places where your ancestors lived.

E. Local histories

I have not listed local histories in bibliographic form in this chapter because there are so many of them. However, you should note their existence (on town, county, and regional levels) because they contain invaluable information about places that is seldom found in other sources. Chapter 12 discusses local histories in more detail. And, once again, I refer you to a source already mentioned in this chapter: the five volumes of *United States Local Histories in the Library of Congress: A Bibliography*, edited by Jack Kaminkow (Baltimore: Magna Carta Book Co., 1976).

II. GUIDES TO NON-ORIGINAL SOURCES

Sources that help us locate and use non-original source materials pertinent to our family history research are also useful as reference tools. More is said in Chapter 12 about their value and their use, but for our purposes here, we divide them into four major categories:

A. Directories
    1. of newspapers and periodicals
    2. of libraries and societies
    3. telephone and city
B. Bibliographies
C. Indexes
    1. to periodicals
    2. to published genealogies and pedigrees
    3. to multiple source types
D. Textbooks and specialized reference sources

Let us mention a few reference tools in each category.

A. Directories

1. Of newspapers and periodicals

Ayer Directory of Newspapers and Periodicals. Philadelphia: N. W. Ayer and Sons, Inc., annual. Older editions of this directory can be very useful for our purposes. Also, note that there is important additional information about this directory and its current status in Chapter 12.

Carson, Dina C., ed. *Directory of Genealogical and Historical Periodicals in the US and Canada.* Niwot, CO: Iron Gate Publishing, 2002.

Chronicling America. This is an Internet site that can be accessed at *http://chroniclingamerica.loc.gov/*; it is sponsored jointly by the Library of Congress and the National Endowment for the Humanities. This useful site includes a searchable collection of digitized newspapers covering the years between 1789 and 1924. Millions of newspaper pages can be readily accessed and copied. It also includes a user-friendly "U.S. Newspaper Directory, 1690–Present." The directory lists all newspapers (weeklies, dailies, whatever) published in the United States from 1690 to the present. It identifies which titles still exist for specific places and times. It also tells where copies are located and how to access them.

Konrad, J. *A Directory of Family "One-name" Periodicals.* Munroe Falls, OH: Summit Publications, c. 1988. This book is out of print and has limited availability. However, it is available at the Family History Library in Salt Lake City. It was originally part of *A Directory of Genealogical Periodicals* by the same author (*q.v.*).

——. *A Directory of Genealogical Periodicals.* Munroe Falls, OH: Summit Publications, 1975. This book is available at the Family History Library in Salt Lake City.

National Directory of Weekly Newspapers. Washington, DC: National Newspaper Association and Publishers' Auxiliary, 1928 and 1954.

Newspapers.com. This is one of the Ancestry family of websites. It allows both simple and complex searches of thousands of newspapers. More publications are being added on an ongoing basis. A search is made by entering a keyword or a name. The home page claims that, by using this website, you can "Easily View, Print, Save, and Share Your Findings." Articles can be printed and/or downloaded as PDF files. A seven-day free trial is provided, after which there is a subscription fee.

Newspapers in Microform: United States, 1948–1972. Washington, DC: Library of Congress, Catalog Publication Division, 1973.

2. Of libraries and societies

American Library Directory. Medford, NJ: Information Today, Inc., annual. This directory is now available on the Internet. There is a subscription fee, but also a fourteen-day free trial. The directory provides details about more than 35,000 libraries (public, academic, special, and governmental) in the US and Canada. It is at *http:// americanlibrarydirectory.com/.*

Subject Directory of Special Libraries and Information Centers. 5 vols. Detroit: Gale, published at regular intervals since 1974. Of special note is Volume 4, *Social Sciences and Humanities Libraries.* For purposes of this directory, a "special library" is one "built around a special collection limited by subject matter or form." The scope of this limitation includes subject division libraries and departmental collections of educational institutions as well as special collections of public libraries. It also includes libraries of businesses, nonprofit organizations, government agencies, etc.

Meyer, Mary Keysor. *Meyer's Directory of Genealogical Societies in the U.S.A. and Canada.* Mt. Airy, MD: Libra Publications, 1996.

3. Telephone and city directories

These directories give addresses of living persons, including possible relatives, so they can be readily contacted. Any large telephone office or large library will have a good collection of them. Chambers of commerce can also help you locate directories.

Old phone books and especially old city directories can help you find the specific place an ancestor lived and thus add unique insight into your family history in applicable situations. In large cities, knowing exactly where your ancestor lived can facilitate your research.

There are resources available to help you find these old directories. Ancestry has a city directory database on a website called U.S. City Directories, 1822–1995 that can be accessed at *http://search.ancestry.com/search/ db.aspx?dbid=2469.* There is a fee required for use of this site, but the cost can be justified if your research is facilitated. You should note, too, that other kinds of information can also be found in city directories—such as streets, maps, churches (valuable because most Protestants attended whatever church happened to be nearest to where they lived), cemeteries, and historical information. All of these can be useful in your research.

B. Bibliographies

The American Genealogist: Being a Catalogue of Family Histories Published in America From 1771 to Date. 5th ed. 1900. Reprint, Baltimore: Genealogical Publishing Co., 1997. In addition to being in print, this fifth edition has been digitized and is online at *https://archive.org/ details/americangenealog00byuwhit.*

Brigham, Clarence Saunders. *History and Bibliography of American Newspapers, 1690–1820.* 2 vols. and suppl. Worcester, MA: American Antiquarian Society, 1970. This work has been republished and reprinted by several other publishers at various times. It is a revision of a work first issued in eighteen parts in the "Proceedings of the American Antiquarian Society, 1913–1927," as *Bibliography of American Newspapers, 1690–1820.* It includes indexes.

Brown, Stuart E., Jr., Lorraine F. Myers, et al., comps. *Virginia Genealogies.* 3 vols. (Vol. 1: *A Trial List of Printed Books and Pamphlets;* Vol. 2: *A Bibliography;* Vol. 3: *A Bibliography of Printed Virginia Records and of Printed Virginia Local Histories and a Description of Virginia Records*). Berryville, VA: Virginia Book Co., 1967–89.

Cappon, Lester Jesse. *American Genealogical Periodicals: a Bibliography with a Chronological Finding-list.* New York: New York Public Library, 1964.

——. *Virginia Newspapers 1821–1935: A Bibliography with Historical Introduction and Notes.* New York and London: D. Appleton-Century Co., Inc., for Institute for Research in the Social Sciences, University of Virginia, 1936.

Daughters of the American Revolution. *Library Catalogue. Volume One: Family Histories and Genealogies.* Washington, DC: DAR, 1982, *Suppl.* 1983. Note: This work has much less importance now than in the past because the DAR Library Catalog is available online (*http://www.dar.org/library/collections/dar-library-catalog*). This is especially true because of the book's age. However, it is an easy-to-use tool and deserves mention here.

Filby, P. William, comp. *American & British Genealogy & Heraldry: A Selected List of Books.* 3rd ed. Boston: New England Historic Genealogical Society, 1985; *Suppl.,* 1987.

——. *Passenger and Immigration Lists Bibliography 1538–1900.* 2nd ed. Detroit: Gale Research Co., 1988.

Gregory, Winifred, ed. *American Newspapers, 1821–1936: A Union List of Files Available in the United States and Canada.* 1937. Reprint, New York: H. W. Wilson Co., 1967.

——. *Genealogy and Local History: An Archival and Bibliographic Guide.* 2nd rev. ed. Evanston, IL: Genealogical Associates, 1959.

Hamer, Philip May, ed. *Guide to Archives and Manuscripts in the United States.* New Haven, CT: Yale University Press, 1961.

Hoffman, Marian, comp. and ed. *Genealogical & Local History Books in Print.* 5th ed. 4 vols. Baltimore: Genealogical Publishing Co., 1996 and 1997. The four volumes are: (1) *General Reference and World Resources,* (2) *Family History Volume,* (3) *U.S. Sources & Resources A–N,* and (4) *U.S. Sources & Resources N–W.* The editor and compiler of earlier editions was Netti Schreiner-Yantis.

Jarboe, Betty M. *Obituaries: A Guide to Sources.* 2nd ed. rev. Boston: G. K. Hall & Co., 1992.

Johnson, Arta F., ed. *Bibliography and Source Materials for German-American Research, Vol. 1, U.S.A.* Rev. ed. Columbus, OH: the editor, 1982.

Kaminkow, Marion J., ed. *Genealogies in the Library of Congress: A Bibliography.* 5 vols. 1972. Reprint, Baltimore: Genealogical Publishing Co., 2001.

____. *Genealogies in the Library of Congress: A Bibliography. Supplement 1972–1975.* 1977. Reprint, Baltimore: Genealogical Publishing Co., 2001.

____. *Genealogies in the Library of Congress: A Bibliography. Supplement 1976–1986.* 1986. Reprint, Baltimore: Genealogical Publishing Co., 2001.

——. *A Complement to Genealogies in the Library of Congress: A Bibliography.* 1981. Reprint, Baltimore: Genealogical Publishing Co., 2001. This book contains a list of 20,000 genealogies not in the Library of Congress and thus not listed in the author's *Genealogies in the Library of Congress* books. Those genealogies listed in this book are located in twenty-four selected libraries throughout the U.S.

Lancour, Harold, comp. *Bibliography of Ship Passenger Lists, 1538–1825.* 3rd ed. rev. and enl. by Richard J. Wolfe. New York: New York Public Library, 1978.

Meynen, Emil, ed. *Bibliography on the Colonial Germans of North America: Especially the Pennsylvania Germans and Their Descendants.* 1937. Reprint, Baltimore: Genealogical Publishing Co., 1982. Note: This book was originally published in Leipzig, Germany, as *Bibliography of German Settlements in Colonial North America.*

Milden, James Wallace. *The Family in Past Time: A Guide to the Literature.* New York: Garland Publishing, Inc., 1977.

Sanders, Edith Green. *Black Genealogy: An Annotated Bibliography.* Atlanta, GA: Atlanta Public Library, Samuel Williams Special Collection, 1978.

Schweitzer, George K. *Genealogical Source Handbook: A Compendium of Genealogical Sources with Precise Instructions for Obtaining Information from Them.* Knoxville: Genealogical Sources Unlimited, 1981.

Slocum, Robert B., ed. *Dictionaries and Related Works.* 2nd ed. Detroit: Gale Group, 1986.

Sperry, Kip. *A Survey of American Genealogical Periodicals and Periodical Indexes.* Vol. 3 in Gale Genealogy and Local History Series. Detroit: Gale Research Co., 1978.

Toedteberg, Emma, ed. *Catalogue of American Genealogies in the Library of the Long Island Historical Society.* 1935. Reprint, Baltimore: Genealogical Publishing Co., 1969.

U.S. Library of Congress. *American and English Genealogies in the Library of Congress; Preliminary Catalog.* Washington, DC: Government Printing Office, 1910. This work is available online at *http:// archive.org/stream/americanenglishg00usliuoft#page/n7/mode/2up.*

——. *The National Union Catalog of Manuscript Collections [NUCMC], Based on Reports from American Repositories of Manuscripts.* Various places, publishers, and dates of publication. The NUCMC is not an easy tool to use because it is only a catalog. The manuscript materials listed therein are all located in their respective libraries. There were twenty-nine volumes prepared between 1959 and 1993, when NUCMC was discontinued in favor of other programs. Chapter 12 provides additional information about this source.

Virkus, Frederick A. *The Handbook of American Genealogy.* 4 vols. Chicago: Institute of American Genealogy, 1932–43.

Wood, Virginia Steele, comp. *Immigrant Arrivals: A Guide to Published Sources.* Rev. ed. Washington, DC: Library of Congress, Local History & Genealogy Reading Room. Portions of this work were revised in 2001 by Barbara B. Walsh under sponsorship of the Library of Congress Bibliographic Enrichment Advisory Team (BEAT).

C. Indexes

1. To periodicals

Fisher, Carleton E., ed. *Topical Index to the National Genealogical Society Quarterly, Volumes 1–50, 1912–1962.* 1964. Reprint, Washington, DC: National Genealogical Society, 1984. Included in this work are two lists—one of authors (Appendix A) and one of books reviewed (Appendix B).

Jacobus, Donald Lines. *Index to Genealogical Periodicals.* 3 vols. 1932 and 1948. Reprint in 1 vol., Baltimore: Genealogical Publishing Co., 1997.

New England Historical and Genealogical Register: Consolidated Index, Vols. 1–50. 4 vols. (1847–1896). 1908. Reprint, Baltimore: Genealogical Publishing Co., 1972. This work is online at *https:// archive.org/stream/newenglandhistor18wate#page/n7/mode/2up.*

——. *Index (Abridged) to Volumes 51 Through 112, 1897–1958.* Edited by Margaret W. Parsons. Marlborough, MA: M.W. Parsons, 1959.

——. *The New England Historical and Genealogical Register: Index of Persons, Volumes 51–148.* 4 vols. (1897–1993). Edited by Jane Fletcher Fiske. Boston: New England Historic Genealogical Society, 1995.

Periodical Source Index (PERSI). Fort Wayne, IN: Allen County Public Library (ACPL), 1986——. This is the comprehensive index to family history periodicals. In a project lasting more than thirty years, the Genealogy Center at ACPL indexed every article from more than 8,000 genealogy/family history magazines, newsletters, and journals by place, subject, surname, ethnicity, and methodology to generate more than 2.5 million searchable records. In July 2013, the international family history website Find MyPast (*http://www.findmypast.com/*) formed a partnership with ACPL to link the digitized genealogical periodicals and resources to the index and allow online access to the records of both entities. Digitized images of articles indexed in PERSI are being added to the FindMyPast website on an on-going basis as time, resources, and permissions allow. Also, many genealogical societies, with encouragement and support from the Federation of Genealogical Societies (FGS), are working to digitize their publications and provide access through FindMyPast. This is a significant resource.

Rogers, Ellen Stanley, George Ely Russell, et al., eds. *Genealogical Periodical Annual Index.* Vols. 1–40. Bladensburg and Bowie, MD: Heritage Books, 1962–2001. This is not an index to all genealogical periodicals but, rather, to a very limited number. Leslie K. Towle edited a supplement for volumes 31–40 and added *Western Maryland Genealogy* for the final ten years.

Sperry, Kip. *Index to Genealogical Periodical Literature, 1960–1977.* Vol. 9 in Gale Genealogy and Local History Series. Detroit: Gale Research Co., 1979. This is not an index to names in periodical articles. Rather, it is an index to subjects—including research techniques and procedures, genealogical and historical sources and collections, and international family history topics. It also includes published local records by city and county under the state, province, or country; authors and titles are included as well. It excludes personal names, pedigrees, compiled genealogies, and family histories.

Swem, Earl G. *Virginia Historical Index.* 2 vols. in 4. Gloucester, MA: Peter Smith, 1965 reprint.

Trapp, Glenda K. *Kentucky Genealogical Index: An Every Name Index to "Kentucky Ancestors," "Kentucky Genealogist," "Kentucky Pioneer Genealogy & Record," and "The East Kentuckian," All Issues Through 1980.* Evansville, IN: Cook Publications, 1985.

2. To published genealogies and pedigrees

Crowther, George Rodney, III. *Surname Index to Sixty-five Volumes of Colonial and Revolutionary Pedigrees.* Special publication no. 27 of the National Genealogical Society (NGS). Washington, DC: NGS, 1964.

Maussan, William A., and Lewis Edwin Neff. *Mayflower Index: Revised Edition of the Two Volumes of the Mayflower Index Which Was Compiled By the Late William Alexander McAuslan.* Boston: General Society of Mayflower Descendants, 1960.

3. To multiple source types

Biography Index: A Cumulative Index to Biographical Material in Books and Magazines. Vols. 1–16. New York: H. W. Wilson Co., 1949–1990.

Filby, P. William, and Mary K. Meyer, eds. *Passenger and Immigration Lists Index.* 3 vols. Detroit: Gale Research Co., 1981 and annual Supplements. A four-volume cumulation for 1982–85 was published in 1985. Passengers arriving in North America and the West Indies between 1538 and 1900 are listed alphabetically. The lists were compiled from published sources.

Greenlaw, William P. *The Greenlaw Index of the New England Historic Genealogical Society.* 2 vols. Boston: New England Historic Genealogical Society, 1979. This valuable index is available in many libraries; check the library catalog.

Index to American Genealogies and to Genealogical Material Contained in All Works As Town Histories, County Histories, Local Histories, Historical Society Publications, Biographies, Historical Periodicals, and Kindred Works. 5th ed. 1900 and Suppl. of 1908. Compiled and originally published by Joel Munsell's Sons. Reprint, Baltimore: Genealogical Publishing Co., 1967. This vintage online surname index is at *https://babel.hathitrust.org/cgi/pt?id=hvd.32044086446341; view=1up;seq=6.* The 1908 Supplement is online at *https://babel. hathitrust.org/cgi/pt?id=hvd.32044086446366;view=1up;seq=2.*

Newberry Library Genealogical Index. 4 vols. Boston: G. K. Hall, 1960. Because this index is old, many of the call numbers of the listed works have been changed and must be confirmed. You may want to ask a reference librarian for a brief orientation. Index citations refer to pages in books or periodicals on which a name is mentioned, not to entire works on a surname. The nature of cited entries varies considerably. Some are full biographical sketches while others are only a surname on one page of a document. The index is available in print at various libraries and also online at *https://babel.hathitrust.org/cgi/pt?id=mdp.39015082976443; view=1up;seq=11;size=300.*

Passano, Eleanor Phillips. *An Index to Source Records of Maryland: Genealogical, Biographical, Historical.* 1910. Reprint, Baltimore: Genealogical Publishing Co., 1994.

Rider, Fremont, ed. *American Genealogical Index.* 48 vols. Middletown, CT: Godfrey Memorial Library, 1942–52.

————. *American Genealogical-Biographical Index.* Vol. 1——. Middletown, CT: Godfrey Memorial Library, 1952——.This is a surname index to various sources, including published genealogies, the genealogical column of the *Boston Transcript* newspaper, the 1790 U.S. Census, and several volumes of Revolutionary War records. When birth dates are in the records, they are included, as are the names of the states associated with the indexed names. Some of the volumes do not list the names of the sources used. Many of these volumes are available online at the Family History Library in Salt Lake City, branch libraries, and other partner libraries.

Stewart, Robert Armistead. *Index to Printed Virginia Genealogies: Including Key and Bibliography.* 1930. Reprint, Baltimore: Genealogical Publishing Co., 2003.

U.S. Library of Congress. *The Library of Congress Index to Biographies in State and Local Histories.* Baltimore: Magna Carta Book Co., 1979 microfilm publ. This is 31 rolls of 16-mm microfilm of a card index. There are approximately 170,000 cards in the file housed in the Local History and Genealogy Room of the Library of Congress. Several libraries have this microfilm publication.

Webb, Walter. *Biography Index; A Cumulative Index to Biographical Material in Books and Magazines, 1946.* New York: H. W. Wilson Co., 1964.

D. Textbooks and specialized reference sources

I will provide no list here, but rather refer you to the list of texts and specialized reference sources under "Guides to Original Sources" that appears later in this chapter. Virtually every source listed in that section gives extensive guidance on the use of both original and non-original sources of genealogical evidence.

Those who seek background and understanding relating to a particular ethnic group to assist with their research should refer to *Harvard Encyclopedia of Ethnic Groups,* edited by Stephan Thernstrom (Cambridge, MA: The Belknap Press of Harvard University Press, 1980). It contains useful information about virtually every ethnic group and minority from Acadians to Zoroastrians.

III. GUIDES TO ORIGINAL SOURCES

There are some useful resources available to assist us in finding and using the original source materials (records) we need in our research. These fall into five main categories, and some of these duplicate those listed as guides to non-original sources in the previous section because they are guides to both. The five categories are:

    A. Government publications
       1. National government
       2. State government

    B. Non-government local research aids
    C. Textbooks and specialized reference sources
    D. Special publications
    E. Indexes

Let us look at some.

A. Government publications

1. National government

Davidson, Katherine H., and Charlotte M. Ashby, comps. *Preliminary Inventory of the Records of the Bureau of the Census* (Record Group 29, No. 161). Washington, DC: National Archives and Records Service, 1964 (multimedia CD, 2007). This inventory describes the various census records that were in the National Archives on February 1, 1964.

Eales, Anne Bruner, and Robert M. Kvasnicka, eds. *Guide to Genealogical Research in the National Archives of the United States.* 3rd ed. Washington, DC: National Archives and Records Service, 2000. This third edition of the guide supersedes the two previous editions as well as the 1964 publication *Guide to Genealogical Records in the National Archives,* by Meredith B. Colket, Jr., and Frank E. Bridgers. However, quotations I have used in this book from these earlier works are still relevant.

Plante, Trevor K., comp. *Military Service Records in the National Archives of the United States.* Revision (General Information Leaflet 7). Washington, DC: National Archives and Records Service, 2009. More information on locating and using military service records is in Chapters 26 and 27.

Where to Write for Vital Records. Atlanta, GA: U.S. Department of Health and Human Services, Centers for Disease Control & Prevention, 2014. This pamphlet can be accessed online at *https://www.cdc.gov/nchs/w2w.htm.* You can also download a pdf file of the pamphlet by clicking on a link at *https://publications.usa.gov/USAPubs.php?PubID=1139.*

2. State government
GEORGIA

"Genealogical Research in Georgia." Atlanta: Georgia Department of Archives and History, 1966.

NEW JERSEY

Genealogical Research: A Guide to Source Materials in the Archives and History Bureau of the New Jersey State Library and Other State Agencies. Compiled by Rebecca Schlam and Kenneth W. Richards, Trenton: Bureau of Archives and History, New Jersey State Library, 1966.

SOUTH CAROLINA

"Ancestor Hunting in South Carolina." Columbia: South Carolina Department of Archives and History, 1969.

UTAH

Guide to Official Records of Genealogical Value in the State of Utah. Salt Lake City: Utah State Archives and Records Service, 1980. In addition to this 23-page booklet, an exceptional website, *http://archives.state.ut.us*, discusses the records, their content, and their use.

B. Non-government local research aids (state and region)
ARIZONA and NEVADA

Spiros, Joyce V. Hawley. *Genealogical Guide to Arizona and Nevada.* Gallup, NM: Verlene Publishing, 1983.

CALIFORNIA

Sanders, Patricia. *Searching in California: A Reference Guide to Public and Private Records.* Costa Mesa, CA: ISC Publications, 1982.

CONNECTICUT

Kemp, Thomas Jay. *Connecticut Researcher's Handbook.* Vol. 12 in Gale Genealogy and Local History Series. Detroit: Gale Research Co., 1981.

Sperry, Kip. *Connecticut Sources for Family Historians and Genealogists.* Logan, UT: Everton Publishers, 1987.

FLORIDA

Robie, Diane C. *Searching in Florida: A Reference Guide to Public and Private Records.* Costa Mesa, CA: ISC Publications, 1982.

GEORGIA

Davis, Robert Scott, Jr. *Research in Georgia,* 2nd ed. Atlanta: Georgia Genealogical Society, 2012.

Schweitzer, George K. *Georgia Genealogical Research.* Knoxville: G.K. Schweitzer, 1987.

ILLINOIS

Beckstead, Gayle, and Mary Lou Kozub. *Searching in Illinois: A Reference Guide to Public and Private Records.* Costa Mesa, CA: ISC Publications, 1984. This book has special help for people who were adopted.

Szucs, Loretto Dennis. *Chicago and Cook County: A Guide to Research.* Rev. ed. Salt Lake City: Ancestry, 1996. This book describes record types and the major archives and libraries in Chicago and Cook County. Some chapters have bibliographies.

INDIANA

Carty, Mickey Dimon. *Searching in Indiana: A Reference Guide to Public and Private Records*. Costa Mesa, CA: ISC Publications, 1985.

Newhard, Malinda E. E. *A Guide to Genealogical Records in Indiana*. Harland, IN: the author, 1979. A digitized copy of this book is available for use at the Family History Library in Salt Lake City, at branch libraries, and at partner libraries.

KENTUCKY

Hathaway, Beverly West. *Kentucky Genealogical Research Sources*. Salt Lake City: Ancestry, 1974.

MICHIGAN

McGinnis, Carol. *Michigan Genealogy: Sources & Resources*. 2nd ed. Baltimore: Genealogical Publishing Co., 2005. This author has more recently prepared a brief document called *Genealogy at a Glance: Michigan Genealogy Research*, a succinct four-page laminated guide published in 2011 by Genealogical Publishing Co. [See Section IV, "Other Useful Research Guides," later in this chapter for a list of more *Genealogy at a Glance* laminated guides.]

MISSOURI

Preston, Jeannine Tussey, and Joseph A. Preston., eds. *Robert E. Parkin's Guide to Tracing Your Family Tree in Missouri*. Rev. ed. Columbia, MO: Missouri State Genealogical Association, 1997.

NEVADA. See ARIZONA

NEW ENGLAND

Crandall, Ralph, ed. *Genealogical Research in New England*. Baltimore: Genealogical Publishing Co., 1984. This is a collection of essays about research in each of the New England states.

Sperry, Kip. *New England Genealogical Research: A Guide to Sources*. Bowie, MD: Heritage Books, 1988. This is an extensive annotated bibliography of both manuscript and published New England sources; it provides excellent information.

NEW HAMPSHIRE

Towle, Laird C., and Ann N. Brown. *New Hampshire Genealogical Research Guide*. 2nd ed. Bowie, MD: Heritage Books, 1983.

NEW MEXICO

Spiros, Joyce V. Hawley. *Handy Genealogical Guide to New Mexico*. Gallup, NM: Verlene Publishing, 1981.

NORTH CAROLINA

Draughon, Wallace R,. and William P. Johnson. *North Carolina Genealogical Reference—A Research Guide for All Genealogists Both Amateur and Professional.* New ed. Durham, NC: the authors, 1966. A digitized copy of this book is accessible online at the Family History Library, a partner library, or a Family History Center: *https://dcms.lds.org/delivery/ DeliveryManagerServlet?dps_pid=IE1090202.*

Leary, Helen F. M., and Maurice Stirewalt, eds. *North Carolina Research: Genealogy and Local History.* 2nd ed. Raleigh: The North Carolina Genealogical Society, 1996.

OHIO

Bell, Carol Willsey. *Ohio Guide to Genealogical Sources.* 1988. Reprint, Baltimore: Genealogical Publishing Co. 2009.

Sperry, Kip. *Genealogical Research in Ohio.* 2nd ed. 2003. Reprint, Baltimore: Genealogical Publishing Co., 2006.

OKLAHOMA

Blessings, Patrick J. *Oklahoma: Records and Archives.* Tulsa, OK: University of Tulsa Publications, 1978.

PENNSYLVANIA

Iscrupe, William L., and Shirley G.M. Iscrupe, comps. *The Pennsylvania Line: A Research Guide to Pennsylvania Genealogy and Local History.* 4th ed. Laughlintown, PA: Southwest Pennsylvania Genealogical Services, 1990.

SOUTH CAROLINA

Côté, Richard N. *Local and Family History in South Carolina: A Bibliography.* Easley, SC: Southern Historical Press, 1991.

Holcomb, Brent Howard. *A Brief Guide to South Carolina Genealogical Research and Records.* Columbia, SC: the author, 1979.

Schweitzer, George K. *South Carolina Genealogical Research.* Knoxville: the author, 1985.

TENNESSEE

Fulcher, Richard Carlton. *Guide to County Records and Genealogical Resources in Tennessee.* 1987. Reprint, Baltimore: Genealogical Publishing Co., 2009. This is a guide to the records and resources at the Tennessee State Library and Archives in Nashville. It is based primarily on the county records microfilmed by the Family History Library in Salt Lake City.

Schweitzer, George K. *Tennessee Genealogical Research.* Knoxville: the author, 1981.

TEXAS

Kennedy, Imogene Kinard, and Leon Kennedy. *Genealogical Records in Texas.* 1987. Reprint, Baltimore: Genealogical Publishing Co., 2005.

VIRGINIA

"Genealogical Research at the Virginia State Library." An information pamphlet. Richmond, VA: The Virginia State Library, no date.

McGinnis, Carol. *Virginia Genealogy: Sources and Resources.* Baltimore: Genealogical Publishing Co., 2008.

WEST VIRGINIA

McGinnis, Carol. *West Virginia Genealogy: Sources & Resources.* 1988. Reprint, Baltimore: Genealogical Publishing Co., 1998.

Stinson, Helen S. *A Handbook for Genealogical Research in West Virginia.* South Charleston, WV: Kanawha Valley Genealogical Society, 1981.

WYOMING

Spiros, Joyce V. Hawley. *Genealogical Guide to Wyoming.* Gallup, NM: Verlene Publishing, 1982.

The list above includes books and pamphlets relating to research in several—but certainly not all—of the states. I hope you will find this short bibliography helpful. However, there are many other valuable local research aids you should be aware of and use. Do not hesitate to use your Internet search engine to look for resources that can assist you. As with other categories, I again call your attention to the FamilySearch wiki as a good source of information relating to every state.

I also recommend that you look at the state information on Cyndi's List. Starting on Cyndi's homepage (*http://www.cyndislist.com*), click on the "Categories" link. Then, on the "Genealogy Categories" page, click on the letter "U" at the top of the page to take you to "United States." There you will be able to choose the state or any other subject of your interest. It is worth your time to use these resources to learn all you can about the locality of your research interest and the records of that locality.

C. Textbooks and specialized reference sources

Board for Certification of Genealogists. *Genealogy Standards, 50th Anniversary Edition.* Provo, UT: Ancestry, 2014.

Burroughs, Tony. *Black Roots: A Beginners Guide to Tracing the African American Family Tree.* New York: Touchstone, 2001.

Clifford, Karen. *The Complete Beginner's Guide to Genealogy, the Internet, and Your Genealogy Computer Program.* Updated ed. Baltimore: Genealogical Publishing Co., 2011.

Croom, Emily Anne. *The Genealogist's Companion and Sourcebook.* 2nd ed. Cincinnati: Betterway Books, 2003.

Deeben, John P. *Genealogy Tool Kit: Getting Started on Your Family History at the National Archives.* Washington, DC: Foundation for the National Archives, 2012.

Green, Fallon N. *The African American Researcher's Guide to Online Genealogical Sources*. Bloomington, IN: Authorhouse, 2012.

Hendrickson, Nancy. *Unofficial Guide to Ancestry.com: How to Find Your Family History on the #1 Genealogy Website*. Cincinnati: Family Tree Books, 2014.

Jacobson, Judy. *History for Genealogists*. Rev. ed., with 2016 Addendum Incorporating Editorial Corrections to the 2009 Edition, by Denise Larson. Baltimore: Genealogical Publishing Co., 2016.

Johnson, Arta F., ed. *Bibliography & Source Materials for German-American Research, Vol. 1: U.S.A.* [with 1984 update]. Columbus, OH: the editor, 1982 [1984].

Kurzweil, Arthur. *From Generation to Generation: How to Trace Your Jewish Genealogy and Family History*. Rev. ed. New York: HarperCollins, 1994.

Lichtman, Allan J. *Your Family History: How to Use Oral History, Personal Family Archives, and Public Documents to Discover Your Heritage*. New York: Vintage Books, 1978.

Mills, Elizabeth Shown. *Evidence Explained: Citing History Sources from Artifacts to Cyberspace*. 3rd ed. rev. Baltimore: Genealogical Publishing Co., 2017. Also written by this author are a series of short, laminated "QuickSheet" research and citation aids (available from the publisher at http://www.genealogical.com).

——, ed. *Professional Genealogy: A Manual for Researchers, Writers, Editors, Lecturers, and Librarians*. 2001. Reprint, Baltimore: Genealogical Publishing Co., 2010. New edition to be published in 2018.

Morgan, George G. *Advanced Genealogy Research Techniques*. New York: McGraw-Hill/Osborne Media, 2013.

——. *How to Do Everything Genealogy*. 4th ed. New York: McGraw-Hill Education, 2015.

Pfeiffer, Laura Szucs. *Hidden Sources: Family History in Unlikely Places*. Orem, UT: Ancestry, 2000.

Powell, Kimberly. *The Everything Guide to Online Genealogy: Trace Your Roots, Share Your History, and Create Your Family Tree*. 3rd ed. Avon, MA: Adams Media, 2014.

Rising, Marsha Hoffman. *Family History Problem Solver: Tried-and-True Tactics for Tracing Elusive Ancestors*. Cincinnati: Family Tree Books, 2011.

Rose, Christine. *Courthouse Research for Family Historians: Your Guide to Genealogical Treasures*. Hammond, IN: CR Publications, 2004.

Rubincam, Milton, ed. *Genealogical Research: Methods and Sources*. Vol. I. Rev. ed. Washington, DC: The American Society of Genealogists, 1980.

Schaefer, Christina K. *The Center: A Guide to Genealogical Research in the National Capital Area.* Baltimore: Genealogical Publishing Co., 1996.

Schleifer, Jay. *A Student's Guide to Jewish American Genealogy* (Oryx American Family Tree Series). Portsmouth, NH: Greenwood Press, 1996.

Smith, Jessie Carney, ed. *Genealogy: A Research Guide.* Westport, CT: Greenwood Press, 1983.

Smolenyak, Megan. *Who Do You Think You Are?* New York: Penguin Books, 2010.

Stern, Malcolm H., and Dan Rottenberg. *Finding Our Fathers: A Guidebook to Jewish Genealogy.* Baltimore: Genealogical Publishing Co., 1998.

Stryker-Rodda, Kenn, ed. *Genealogical Research: Methods and Sources.* Vol. 2. Rev. ed. Washington, DC: The American Society of Genealogists, 1983.

Szucs, Loretto Dennis, and Sandra Hargreaves Luebking, eds. *The Source: A Guidebook of American Genealogy.* 3rd ed. Salt Lake City: Ancestry Publishing, 2006.

Witcher, Curt. *African American Genealogy: A Bibliography and Guide to Sources.* Fort Wayne, IN: Round Tower Books, 2000.

Yannizze Melnyk, Marcia D. *Family History 101.* Cincinnati: Family Tree Books, 2015.

D. Special publications

DeWitt, Donald L. *Guides to Archives and Manuscript Collections in the United States: An Annotated Bibliography.* Westport, CT: Greenwood Press, 1994. This book lists subject guides and—under regional sections—guides to repositories. It also has a section entitled "Foreign Repositories Holding U.S.-Related Records."

Neagles, James C., and Lila Lee Neagles. *Locating Your Immigrant Ancestor: A Guide to Naturalization Records.* Logan, UT: Everton Publishers, 1975.

Stemmons, John D., ed. *The Cemetery Record Compendium: Comprising a Directory of Cemetery Records and Where They May Be Located.* Logan, UT: Everton Publishers, 1979.

——. *United States Census Compendium: A Directory of Census Records, Tax Lists, Poll Lists, Petitions, Directories, Etc., Which Can Be Used As a Census.* Logan, UT: Everton Publishers, 1973. A digitized version of this work is online at *https://dcms.lds.org/delivery/DeliveryManagerServlet?dps_pid=IE927336.*

——, and Diane Stemmons, comps. *Vital Records Compendium: A Direc-*

tory of Local Records and Where They May Be Located. Salt Lake City: the compilers, 1979.

U.S. Library of Congress. *The National Union Catalog of Manuscript Collections.* (See listing under "Guides to Non-original Sources: Bibliographies"—Section II of this chapter.)

U.S. National Archives Trust Fund Board & National Historical Records Commission. *Directory of Archives and Manuscript Repositories in the United States.* Phoenix, AZ: Oryx Press, 1978.

World Conference on Records, Seminar papers. Salt Lake City: Family History Department of The Church of Jesus Christ of Latter-day Saints, 1969 and 1980. (In 1969, the primary emphasis was on records preservation and genealogy. The 1980 emphasis was on family history.)

E. Indexes

I have not been exhaustive in any of the bibliographic listings in this chapter. However, that is particularly true in this section. What you see here are a few items listed as examples only.

Bowman, Alan P. *Index to the 1850 Census of the State of California.* 1972. Reprint, Baltimore: Genealogical Publishing Co., 1997.

Houston, Martha Lou, comp. *Indexes to the County Wills of South Carolina, 1766–1864.* 1939. Reprint, Baltimore: Genealogical Publishing Co., 1964. This index is based on Works Projects Administration (WPA) inventories; it includes about 12,000 names.

Johnson, William Perry. *Index to North Carolina Wills, 1663–1900.* 3 vols. Raleigh, NC: the author, 1963–68.

Magruder, James Mosby. *Index of Maryland Colonial Wills, 1634–1777, in the Hall of Records, Annapolis, Maryland.* 3 vols. 1933. Reprint in 1 vol., Baltimore: Genealogical Publishing Co., 2012.

Martin, Kim I., et al., comps. *Arkansas Historical Quarterly, Index to Volumes I–LIX (1942–2000).* Little Rock: Arkansas Historical Association, 2005.

McLane, Mrs. Bobby Jones, and Inez H. Cline. *An Index to the Fifth United States Census of Arkansas.* Fort Worth, TX: Arrow Printing Co., 1963.

Metcalf, Frank Johnson, and Max Ellsworth Hoyt, et al. *Index of Revolutionary War Pension Applications.* Rev. ed. Washington, DC: National Genealogical Society, 1976. The index and digitized copies of the application files are available on the Internet on the Ancestry website (*http:// search.ancestry.com/search/db.aspx?dbid=1995*).

New Jersey Index of Wills, Inventories, Etc.: In the Office of the Secretary of State Prior to 1901 [with a new Foreword]. 3 vols. 1912–13. Reprint, Baltimore: Genealogical Publishing Co., 1969. Volume 2 is available online (*http://archive.org/stream/indexofwillsin1279newj#page/n4/mode/1up*).

IV. OTHER USEFUL RESEARCH GUIDES

A. The "At a Glance" guides

This is an interesting category—a small one to be sure—but one that includes some useful research aids that do not fit into any other categories. These are concise four-page guides written by experts and published by Genealogical Publishing Company. These "At a Glance" guides provide succinct instruction relating to specific subjects. At the time of this writing, the available guides pertinent to research in the U.S. include (with year of publication):

1. Specific states/localities

Georgia Genealogy Research, by Michael A. Ports (2017)
Maryland Genealogy Research, by Michael A. Ports (2014).
Massachusetts Genealogy Research, by Denise R. Larson (2015).
Michigan Genealogy Research, by Carol McGinnis (2011).
North Carolina Genealogy Research, Michael A. Ports (2014).
Ohio Genealogy Research, by Michael A. Ports (2015).
Old Southwest Genealogy Research, by Dorothy Williams Potter (2013).
Pennsylvania Genealogy Research, by John T. Humphrey (2012).
Virginia Genealogy Research, by Carol McGinnis (2012).

2. Specific groups of people

African American Genealogy Research, by Michael Hait (2011).
Cherokee Genealogy Research, by Myra Vanderpool Gormley (2012).
Finding Female Ancestors, by Sharon DeBartolo Carmack (2013).
Scots-Irish Genealogy Research, by Brian Mitchell (2014).

3. Specific historical events, subjects, or circumstances

American Cemetery Research, by Sharon DeBartolo Carmack (2012).
Civil War Genealogy Research, by Nancy Hendrickson (2013).
Immigration Research, by Sharon DeBartolo Carmack (2011).
Revolutionary War Genealogy Research, by Craig R. Scott (2011).
War of 1812 Research, by The War of 1812 Preserve the Pensions Fund (2011).

4. Specific record collections and resources

Ancestry.com Research, by George G. Morgan (2013).
Court Records Research, by Wendy Bebout Elliott (2014).
Ellis Island Research, by Sharon DeBartolo Carmack (2011)
Evernote, by Drew Smith (2015).
Family History Library Research, by Carolyn L. Barkley (2012).
FamilySearch.org Research, by George G. Morgan (2014).
Genetic Genealogy Basics, (2016) by Angie Bush (2016).
U.S. Federal Census Records, by Kory L. Meyerink (2012).

Copies of these "At a Glance" research guides are available on the publisher's website (*http://www.genealogical.com*); digital versions of these guides are also available from the publisher. There may be many more of them by the time you read this.

B. NGS "Research in the States" guides

The National Genealogical Society has, through the years, published papers—they call them "Guides"—that relate to family history research in various states of the U.S. At the time of this writing (2016), there are guides available for twenty-three states and one major city: Arkansas, California, Colorado, Florida, Georgia, Illinois, Indiana, Kentucky, Maryland, Michigan, Missouri, Nebraska, New Jersey, North Carolina, Ohio, Oklahoma, Oregon, Pennsylvania, South Carolina, Tennessee, Texas, Virginia, West Virginia, and New York City. These guides are available both in print form and in electronic PDF files. They provide information on history, records, and research facilities. These "Research in the State" guides are available for purchase at *http://ngsgenealogy.org/cs/research_in_the_states*.

C. FamilySearch wiki

I have already referred to this wiki, and more information relating to it can be found in Chapter 10. Suffice it to say here, however, that this unique resource provides excellent information about both the places and the records you will be using in your family history research. For access to the North American portion of this wiki, go to *https://familysearch.org/wiki/en/North_America* and follow the links to the information you seek, or you can use your Internet search engine.

D. US GenWeb Project

One early online resource has persisted and is of some significance. It is the US GenWeb Project. The project site (*http://usgenweb.com/*) was begun in 1996 by a group of dedicated volunteers with the goal of establishing a free link to every county and state in America, as well as to some special national projects. Each state designed its own page, and thus, as the project has developed, every state page is different. The format and the structure of each page and each database are based on the plan of the volunteer who created it. Some state pages are better than others, but, in every case, there are extensive research helps and clickable links available to provide assistance. The various pages include maps and other historical and geographic information. There are also sources and reference aids that are important to the researcher.

As the US GenWeb Project continues, as the accumulated data increase, and as information on the various state sites increases in both quantity and quality, the sites that are part of this project are becoming invaluable resources. Because the state pages have links to all the state family history websites, they provide gateways to the counties and their records. Each county also has a link where you can post queries, if you desire.

Early in your research, you should look at the US GenWeb Project for those states where your research is centered.

V. CONCLUSION

Any source to which you refer for information that will assist with your research can properly be called a reference tool. And, because family history is so closely related to so many different subjects, there are many of these. You will use reference sources dealing with handwriting (calligraphy, chirography, and orthography), with history and geography, with biography, with bibliography itself, with law, with origins of words and names (etymology), with dates and calendar problems (chronology), with heraldry and, of course, with genealogical/family history methodology.

Especially noteworthy is one other work, one that was actually designed and published as a genealogical bibliography. This was, at one time, the most accurate and complete published genealogical bibliography in existence, but it is now quite dated. It is, however, still of some importance:

Filby, P. William. *American & British Genealogy & Heraldry.* 3rd ed. Boston: New England Historic Genealogical Society, 1983. There was also a *1982–1985 Supplement* that was published in 1987.

One additional category of reference sources—those that provide actual secondary genealogical evidence—is discussed in some detail in Chapter 12. This category includes various kinds of biographical works—dictionaries, directories, lists, registers, etc. Though they are reference sources in the usual sense, they do not fit the definition of genealogical reference tools given in the first paragraph of this chapter. They do not usually provide direct assistance in locating records nor facilitate our use of records, but they can provide useful data—some of them better than others—depending on the sources used in their compilation. However, I add this caution: though they are useful, their accuracy is not guaranteed and they should be used with care.

If you will familiarize yourself with the reference tools listed in this chapter, become aware of other similar works, and come to an understanding of their value, their limitations, and their proper use, you will have acquired one of the main prerequisites for becoming a competent family history researcher.

7

Organizing and Evaluating
Your Research Findings

I. THE REASONS AND THE REQUIREMENTS

The steps relating to successful family history research discussed in earlier chapters require us to incorporate four significant processes as part of the record-keeping involvements associated with our research:

1. **Gather** information about possible ancestors and members of their families from the various records created in connection with the recorded events that occurred in their lives.
2. **Compile/organize** that gathered information into a meaningful and usable family-based format.
3. **Analyze/evaluate** that compiled/organized information to determine if it provides sufficient evidence of family relationships/connections—including evidence concerning the nature and details of your ancestors' lives.
4. **Preserve** the documented results of that analysis/evaluation—those things that your evidence has "proved"—in a format that is meaningful and that will be accessible, now and in the future, both to yourself and to others who may be interested.

These processes suggest the need for keeping careful records of your research.

In Chapter 1, we discussed the importance of organizing your research findings into families. This chapter will explore some ways to do this effectively and efficiently. There are options as to how such an objective can be accomplished, but you must be careful about the processes and methods you choose. Some highly recommmended processes come with significant risks. Because you are creating records of considerable importance, remember that the processes involved in the creation and preservation of those records must never be taken lightly.

I hope the information in this chapter will make that task as uncomplicated as possible. That goal will be accomplished if the system you use is (1) simple and easy to understand and (2) not so time-consuming that it takes away, unnecessarily, from your valuable research time. It is easy to become complicated, but complication is not a virtue.

As you extract information from different sources, you must plan to eventually get that information into a meaningful family-based format without losing important details. This includes not only the precious family history information but also the documentation that relates to it.

Your research notes should reflect exactly what was done. They should also tell why it was done and explain how the evidence forms the basis for each conclusion. And if there are unanswered questions about what you found in your research, it should be easy to go back and retrace your steps.

Too many would-be researchers learn neither the purposes nor the processes involved in keeping good records until it is too late. Others never learn—much to the consternation of those who wish to check their work or assume responsibility where they left off. Still others are convinced of the value of good records but never quite make the effort to keep them. They do not understand that good research notes facilitate proper and correct analysis of the information—the potential evidence—found in the records.

There are probably no other areas of family history involvement where one's ability as a researcher will be judged more critically than (1) the records he keeps of his research and (2) his subsequent documentation of his completed records.

Regardless of how thorough your research is and how correct your analysis, if your notes are poorly kept and your work product inadequately documented, your work will never be appreciated by any competent researcher who reviews it. The searches you have made will probably be repeated because of the uncertainty. Then, if the previous work is found to be good, you will be condemned even more for your failure to keep proper records.

In the most practical sense, your research notes must do two things:

1. Keep you, the researcher, continuously and completely in touch with the problem in all its aspects during the research process. In this regard, you must know exactly (1) what you are doing, (2) what you have already done, (3) why you did what you did, and (4) the results of having done it. You should also be able to tell readily, from those notes, what still needs to be done (or done next) and why—and all this after the passage of any length of time.

2. Aid those who follow you to know where your information came from, to check it for completeness and accuracy as they may wish to do, and to continue research where you left off. They should never have to re-do your work because it is not documented satisfactorily.

When a scholar in any subject writes an article for publication, he carefully notes the source of every fact he plans to include and makes sure those facts are accurately quoted and in proper context. As his article appears in its final form, it is well documented, and the information from the various sources is carefully attributed and footnoted. Your family history research and the records you create from that research—though you may not be preparing them for publication—require no less. The process is just as important. The data you have gleaned during your research is of value only to the extent that

- its origin is known;
- it is extracted correctly;
- it is interpreted correctly; and
- it is presented in proper context.

Otherwise, it has no evidentiary value.

Before I leave this section of admonitions, I need to mention two more things that are not necessarily related to each other:

- Keep copies of all records, documents, and correspondence (including e-mail) you accumulate during the research process.
- Identify the purpose of every search you make. (If you do not know why you are searching a particular source, you should re-evaluate.) No search should be made without a purpose, and that purpose should be recorded in your notes so those who look at your notes will know why you did what you did.

Everything possible must be done to prevent <u>needless</u> duplication of effort. There is too much to be done and the expense too great for you to spend time needlessly repeating yourself or others.

II. NOTE-KEEPING METHODS

There are many different ways of keeping research notes in current use. This is good because what pleases me may not work well for you. Each person has his own ideas about what works best. Any system that does the job satisfactorily and has a proper balance between simplicity and completeness is acceptable. An imbalance either way is serious. It is as bad to spend too much time and effort on over-elaborate notes as it is to be too brief. No record-keeping system is good if it takes more time than your research. In addition to doing everything it needs to do, your record-keeping system must be efficient.

Some people become so involved with keeping notes, setting up filing systems, and cross-indexing that they forget their real purpose: correctly identifying and gathering information about their ancestors and their families. Make your notes as complete as necessary, but no more complete than your purposes demand. Use shortcuts if they work, but be careful your shortcuts do not turn out to be booby-traps.

So much can be done nowadays with computers and digital cameras that many people ask whether research notes should still be kept on paper. My answer to this question is that you need to achieve a proper balance. Modern technology should be used where it serves best, but care is needed to keep from going so far in that direction that you defeat your purpose.

Where possible, use digital photography to take pictures of documents, pages of books, tombstones, people, etc. However, because you do not always get good results when taking pictures of documents and pages of books, you might consider one of the portable, hand-held scanners now available, such as the Dacuda PocketScan Wireless. This portable scanner is especially good because you just swipe it over the text or image, and it uses Bluetooth to send a high-resolution image to your smartphone or tablet. Another option is the Flip-Pal Mobile Scanner that saves photo and document copies on a flash drive. I am sure there are others, and there will be more of them at more competitive prices as time passes.

Sometimes, when it is convenient, the researcher will use the word-processing program on his laptop computer to type extracts and/or make abstracts of relevant documents that cannot be readily scanned, photographed, or machine copied. The portability of laptop computers makes this easy, and this technology is a boon for those who type faster and more legibly than they write by hand. However, those who do this must also be careful to proofread what they type and save it properly. These methods of preserving evidence are all good, and you would be foolish not to use them.

A. Computerized research notes

In many cases, computer technology and other technological resources are a great boon to us and help us accomplish our work more efficiently. However, if you decide to use a computer program to keep your research records, you need to weigh both the benefits and the risks. There are some of both.

There are quality computer programs available for preservation of your research notes, and I am positive that there will be more such programs as time passes. I will mention two popular quality programs here: Evernote and ResearchTies:

1. **Evernote** (*https://evernote.com/*): Evernote was not specifically designed for family history, but many have found it readily adaptable to family history use. In fact, Cyndi's List has extensive instructions on how to use Evernote for family history that you may find helpful if you want to use this system (*http://cyndislist.com/evernote/*). Cyndi gives the following endorsement:

> Evernote is a free note-taking software program available on the cloud[1] that will sync your account across several platforms and numerous devices. Your Evernote account stays current and goes with you anywhere you go, any time

---

[1] In Chapter 9, there is an extensive discussion about both the advantages and the concerns relating to the cloud. If you are not familiar with the cloud, you may find it helpful to go to that chapter and read that discussion now.

you need it. I truly believe Evernote was made for genealogical research. Use Evernote to create your own genealogy research notebook. It is the online genealogist's best friend. Evernote is a filing system, an organizational tool, a planner, a storage repository, a collaboration tool, and a powerful search tool for every file, web site, genealogical record, or tidbit that you have ever squirreled away.[2]

The basic version of Evernote is free, as Cyndi mentioned, but most users recommend the Plus version ($34.99/year). One problem with the basic version is that your use of it is limited to just two devices. If that limitation is not a concern to you, you might still want to try it out. It is easy to upgrade should you decide you want to do so.

The Premium version ($69.99/year) may be more than you need.[3] Users also wisely recommend the free Evernote app, which allows access to your files on your mobile devices, and the Evernote Web Clipper browser extension.

Using your Internet search engine, you can also find several Internet articles discussing and explaining the merits and use of Evernote for family history. Also, for the benefit of those interested, Genealogical Publishing Company has a four-page, laminated guide, *Genealogy at a Glance: Evernote,* prepared by Drew Smith, which details the use of Evernote as a method for keeping research notes.

2. **ResearchTies** (*http://researchties.com/*): ResearchTies is a record-keeping program that was specifically designed for family history. For this reason, it is the program I personally prefer. It is certified by FamilySearch and costs $30 per year (2017). The program has been around long enough to have the bugs worked out and to be fine-tuned for efficiency, though small refinements are being made as their value becomes apparent.

The ResearchTies developer, Jill Crandell, a professional genealogist (ICAPGen®) and family history instructor at Brigham Young University, has also provided a complete explanation of the program and its features—as well as a number of tutorials—on the ResearchTies website. For a small fee, she also offers mentoring on the system. The program is designed around "Research planning," "Recording results," and "Document analysis." It is especially good for sharing a research file with multiple users, and the multi-variable search gives you instant access to everything in your research file and also allows easy sharing with non-account holders. The website has ample explanations of program features and operational details.

One feature that is especially valuable, in my opinion, is the ability of ResearchTies to track your research either by person, by family, or by surname. It all depends on the goals/objectives you set for your search. Considering the fact that in many situations, in many different kinds of records, complete and

---

[2] "Evernote for Every Genealogist," *Cyndi's List of Genealogy Sites on the Internet,* Cyndi's List, July 25, 2016, http://www.cyndislist.com/ (accessed November 28, 2016).

[3] The prices given here are accurate as of May 2017.

accurate research requires you to gather information on everyone who has the surname of your ancestor. ResearchTies easily facilitates this approach.

When you define the scope of your search, you can indicate if you are looking for a person, for a family, or for a surname. If you set a surname goal and define a surname search, you can attach all results for that surname to your search. This definitely meets the standard specified in Chapter 3 where it was noted that "in most cases, as you do research relating to your ancestors, it is important that you gather *all* information relating to *all persons of the surname(s) of interest* in your locality of interest."

Neither Evernote nor ResearchTies operates on the hard drive of your computer. Both function directly from what is called "the cloud," as already mentioned, and have the great advantage of being fully accessible on your mobile devices whenever and wherever you need them. You can use your smartphone or tablet to photograph documents and enter them directly into your note files. You can also scan documents and save them in your filing system.

Jill Crandell has offered the following advice relating specifically to ResearchTies, but which also applies to other cloud-based, record-keeping programs:

- For the preservation of digitized documents, users should not rely entirely upon URL hyperlinks because those links can change over time. Websites and record collections on the Internet may also be moved or taken down without notice. Researchers need to download images of all research results to the hard drives of their own computers and save those images in their personal filing systems. After saving a document on his computer hard drive, the researcher should then upload a copy of that document to ResearchTies where it is also preserved on the server [i.e., the cloud]. This process provides electronic security no matter what happens, because there is a duplicate copy of each document in both places. The use of an online service like ResearchTies also provides a way to restore digitized documents should your computer hard drive crash.

- ResearchTies allows the researcher to create PDF and/or Excel reports of his data at any time, which he can also save to his computer hard drive. Downloading is good for security, but it also provides another advantage: If a user wants to end his subscription, he can download the data and move forward with a spreadsheet. If a user chooses to end his subscription, he loses the efficiency of data entry into the ResearchTies logging system as well as the ability to locate specific entries with the multi-variable search engine, but no data is lost.

- In order to prevent both data problems and breaches caused by Internet hackers, ResearchTies employs a reputable programming company and subscribes to quality servers that have back-up systems.

- For long-term data preservation, ResearchTies accounts are fully transferable. For example, when an older subscribing researcher is ready to pass on the records, there is no need to move filing cabinets. He can simply give his account sign-in information to another family member and then notify ResearchTies to update the owner information on the account.[4]

Let me mention now an entirely different issue. For the sake of clarification, I need to mention here that, in addition to note-keeping systems, there are also numerous computerized genealogy/family history software programs available. Though these programs have nothing to do with your research notes, they are essential tools. These programs, their benefits, and selection criteria are discussed in more detail in Chapter 9. Everyone involved in family history should choose and use one of these programs.

B. Research notes on paper

For those who keep their research notes on paper, let me mention four simple "housekeeping" rules that will help prevent their notes from taking too much time as well as ensure their quality and usability:

1. Keep all of your notes on the same size paper *insofar as possible*—preferably standard 8½ x 11 inches. Minimize the use of paper scraps, backs of envelopes, and odd-size papers of all kinds. The actual size of the paper is not important if you can keep everything close to the same size, for filing convenience. However, I know there are things you cannot control, like the size of the paper other people use to write letters and the size of original, photographed, and photocopied documents. Thus, it is important for you to control what you can control.

2. Use acid-free, lined paper. Acid-free paper will not deteriorate with age, and lined paper facilitates neatness.

3. Do not recopy your notes. Make your first version good enough to be your final version. Some people diligently type all of their handwritten notes so they look nice—a procedure that is not worth the time it takes. If you are careful, your original notes will be adequate. Recopying also introduces one more chance for error; surely, we all make enough mistakes without this.

4. Use a pen or a good pencil. Many libraries and records repositories request that pens not be used. Pencils should be sharp (take several with you). The lead should be neither so hard the writing is too light to read nor so soft the writing smears. (A #3 or HB lead is usually best.) Whenever pens are permitted, use one; it will make a better record.

III. RESEARCH LOGS AND NOTES

This section applies primarily to those who keep their research notes on paper. However, many of the principles discussed also apply broadly to all research notes, whether on paper or your computer. Though style and form

---

[4] E-mail from Jill Crandell to the author dated November 26, 2016.

will vary from one person to another, certain characteristics need to be part of every researcher's notes.

Every note-keeping system—manual or electronic—must include a list of all sources searched, including those sources where no information was found. For this discussion, I shall call this list of sources a RESEARCH LOG, though different researchers call it by different names. (In earlier editions of this book, I called it a "research calendar," but I think "research log" is now the preferred term.)

Though this research log is a list of sources searched, it is more than that. Other information is included, but the nature, amount, and arrangement of other information depend on personal preference. The sources you list must be identified sufficiently so anyone can use that identifying information to locate those same sources. To give only a book title or a library classification number falls short of meeting this requirement.

Your list of sources should probably include library classification numbers, but these numbers are not the most important thing. If you include classification numbers or microfilm numbers (which I think is a good idea), always identify the library. You might use the library's initials, such as "FHL" for Family History Library or "LC" for Library of Congress. You might also opt for an abbreviation, such as "Newb" for Newberry Library or "Mid-Con" for Mid-Continent Public Library. Develop your own system based on the libraries you use.

If the source of the information is a digitized record from one of the family history websites, it is necessary to identify both the record source and the website that contained that source.

If your source is an original document you found in a county courthouse or a state archive, that place also needs to be identified on your research log, along with the specific title and identifying information relating to the specific document. Those records, of course, will have no library identification. Though digitized records from the large family history databases may have no numbers to identify them, the website will provide information on how each source should be cited in your records.

When your source of information is a book or a periodical, the source description on your research log should usually be written in footnote form. Each source description should include the following:

- Author, editor, or compiler (as applicable)
- Title
- Edition, if relevant
- Place of publication
- Publisher
- Year of publication
- Page number(s) where applicable

If your source is an original document or a digitized copy of the original record, modify this information to fit the circumstances. There is no right or wrong way so long as you write down sufficient information to completely identify your source. If your source is a personal interview, an unpublished manuscript, a letter, an e-mail message, or some family record in private hands, it is important for you to include people's names and their contact information. (See Figure 1.)

Sidney Orbeck — 138 N. Westside Ave, Haynesburg, Ga.

Surname(s) of interest: Black, Blair, Jackson

Locality of interest: Harrison Co., Va.

Library Call No.	Description of source	Purpose of search	Comments	Date of search	Ms. page
7560 (GS) (film)	Colonial records	Blacks and Blairs were in Harrison Co. before 1795. Looking for any mention.	Found mention of William & Samuel Black, Thynn...	13 Sep 1967	1
	pt 1 - Bk 1-2 (1677-1693)				
	pt 2 - Bk 3-5 (1677-1737)				
	pt 3 - Index, Bks 1-5				
7559 (GS) (film)	Court records (Charlottesville, etc.)	Same	found a few — (see notes)	13 Sep 1967	1-9
	pt 1 - 1677-1697 (indexed)				
	pt 2 - 1697-1714 (")				
	pt 3 - 1714-1737 (")				
	pt 4 - 1748-1750 (")				
	pt 5 - 1750-1767 (")				
	pt 6 - 1767-1797 (")				
Va Hc (GS)	Marriage bonds, 1780-1861 (typescript)	Same	found nothing	19 Sep 1967	Nil
Va Hc6a (GS) (minor?)	Beverly Elliott comp, Virginia Colonial Abstracts (Richmond, 1956)	Same	found entry relating to Samuel Black (see notes)	19 Sep 1967	9
	Records of Blair family in poss. of Mrs. Nellie C. Reynolds, 321 Walton Drive, Chaffee, N.C., 58014	For possible Blair connection.	Some good information but doesn't fit in yet. (cover.)	2 Oct 1967	See own envelope / Extr. 5
(more)					

FIGURE 1—A RESEARCH LOG

When your source is an Internet website, the source citation should always include the date you take the information from that source. This is important because Internet information is frequently updated. According to Purdue University's Online Writing Lab, the following information should be included in the citation of a page from the Internet:

- Author and/or editor names (if stated)
- Article name in quotation marks (if applicable)
- Title of the Website, project, or book in *italics*. [Because your notes are handwritten, titles are <u>underlined</u>.]
- Any version numbers available, including revisions, volumes, or issue numbers
- Publisher information, including publisher's name
- Publication date (if stated)
- Page number(s) (if stated)
- Website URL [address]
- Date you accessed the material[5]

Perfection of form and format in citing sources is not required but (to avoid confusion) you should be reasonably consistent from entry to entry. You should also include sufficient detail that anyone can use your citation to find your source. (See the web citations in this chapter and elsewhere in this book.)

Many family history researchers rely on Elizabeth Shown Mills' book *Evidence Explained*[6] as their guide to citing sources. Most digitized records you access on family history websites have citations attached to them. Make sure those citations include all the necessary elements.

Your sources are not only important on your research log but also when you enter your research results onto your family group forms. Also, whenever you share your research findings, no matter what method of note keeping you use, careful documentation is critical to your credibility.

It is not unusual to search sources in an order different from the order they are listed on your research log because there is not *usually* one correct order of search. The sequence in which you examine various records depends primarily on the purpose(s) of your specific search(es). The purpose of any given search is determined by your analysis of the problem. Writing the dates on which you search the various records enables you to recall your order of search at a future date. That is important because there will be times when information found elsewhere might uncover information that will suggest the need to repeat an earlier search.

---

[5] "Basic Style for Citations of Electronic Sources (Including Online Databases)," *Online Writing Lab.* Purdue University, no date, https://owl.english.purdue.edu/owl/resource/747/08/ (Accessed May 15, 2015).

[6] Elizabeth Shown Mills, *Evidence Explained: Citing History Sources from Artifacts to Cyberspace.* 3rd ed. rev., Baltimore: Genealogical Publishing Co., 2017.

I emphasize again that every source you search must be listed on your research log, whether or not you find any useful information in it. If you did not list a source because of negative results, you would likely search it again unknowingly after the passage of time—and with the same result. Also, those who follow you would probably also search that source again. You must do everything possible to prevent unnecessary duplication, and proper documentation is critical to achieving that purpose.

Another vital function of your research log is to serve as a table of contents to your notes, your document copies, and your research correspondence.

If you have searched a particular record—say, for example, an 1860 census of the place of your interest—and have extracted its relevant contents on pages five through ten of your notes, you simply write "pages 5–10" on your research log, adjacent to your entry for that census. If you searched that census and found nothing relating to your ancestor(s), the notation on your research log should indicate that fact (see Figure 1).

IV. ORGANIZING YOUR RESEARCH NOTES

Research logs need to be limited in some way. Maintaining only one large log for all of your research will soon become unmanageable. There are some options as to what limitations should be used, and different researchers do it in different ways. Some have a separate research log for each family, including the husband, his wife, and their children. Others use a separate log for each individual. These have worked for many researchers, and you should use this family approach if it works for you. Personally, however, because my research approach gathers information on everyone of my ancestral surname, I prefer to make a separate log for each relevant locality (usually one for each county where my ancestors lived), as illustrated in Figure 1.

As I do research in the records of a given county, my notes, document copies, correspondence, photocopies, etc., are all filed with that county's research log. The page numbers assigned to documents, etc., in my note file are listed on the research log, thus making the log a table of contents of my notes for that county. Thus, I have—filed in one place—my research log (as a table of contents) and all relevant notes, document copies, and correspondence relating to my research in that locality. These are kept together in a loose-leaf binder. Manila file folders will also work, but I do not use spiral or solid-bound notebooks because they lack flexibility.

Your name, address, and phone number should be on every page of your notes to help prevent loss. The research date on each page helps you keep track of your research time frame. A typical page heading might look like this:

DATE: _____

RESEARCHER: **Joe Dokes, 111 My St., My Town, My State (809-908-8099)**

SURNAME(S) _____

LOCALITY: _____

This heading is printed on several blank pages at one time so they are readily available when you are taking your notes. The "DATE," "SURNAME," and "LOCALITY" fields are filled in according to your need as research progresses.

Note that the basis of this filing system is the surname you are researching—then the locality. Under every surname, one research log (continued on multiple pages, if necessary) is needed for each locality where the family with that surname lived. As research extends to another locality, I create a new file—each file with a research log and its related note/document file.

To avoid confusion as more surnames and additional locality files for those surnames are added, I use a systematic filing arrangement. My preference is to file alphabetically by surname and then—under each surname file—chronologically by locality from the most recent place to the most remote, front to back in the file.

As a family line is extended, new files are added at the back. In other words, the research logs, notes, and document copies relating to the most recent generations of the family are at the front of the file, and those for the earliest generations are added at the back as the research on a family line extends to earlier generations, locality by locality.

For example, if I do research on the Black family beginning, with the most recent generations, in (a) Maricopa County, Arizona; then trace them to (b) Osage County, Missouri; then to (c) Henrico County, Virginia; and on to (d) James City County, Virginia—extending the family line back in that chronological sequence—the Black family research logs (along with all related notes, documents, and correspondence) are filed in that order—front to back. I also keep a copy of the pedigree for Black and related families at the beginning of the Black family file.

You have probably observed that there is one other issue with this system. That is the issue of multiple surnames in one locality—like Black, Creer, and Jackson in our example. Because I do not want to create duplicate copies of all my records under all three surnames, I use cross-referencing. I first create a primary research log, using any one of these family surnames I choose. For the sake of example, I choose the Black surname and create a research log for Henrico County, Virginia, under the Black surname. I then file all documents, notes, correspondence, etc.—everything—for all three surnames in connection with that log.

Next, I create Creer and Jackson research logs for Henrico County with the usual headings. Then, however, instead of listing all the Henrico County sources again, I simply refer to the log I have already made by writing "SEE BLACK, HENRICO COUNTY, VA" in large letters across the front of both the Creer and the Jackson logs for that county. All documents, notes, correspondence, etc., for these three surnames that relate to Henrico County are filed together behind the Black research log. I can make cross-reference logs for as many surnames as I am researching in the county of my interest, and I can quickly follow them back to the one log and file where everything relating to my research in that county is recorded and filed.

In other locations, your connected families will no doubt be different. In Osage County, Missouri, for example—in a more recent generation—I might have the surnames Black and Harrop, but I would follow the same procedure. The same is true in Maricopa County, Arizona, where the surnames of interest might be Black and Patterson.

In summary, this system sets up all research files alphabetically by surname. Then, under each family surname, the research files for the several localities are arranged in the same sequence in which that family lived in those places—most recent to most remote.

I also need to explain that, in most cases, the reference to a particular source in your actual research notes will be more detailed than your source reference on your research log. The additional information in your notes will include specific volume and page numbers (or other place identifiers) from the source of origin for each entry. For example, on your research log, you will indicate only that the source was the 1860 census of Henrico Co., Virginia, plus the location/source of that record. However, in your manuscript notes, you will record the exact reference (page number, enumeration district, family number, etc.) for every entry where families and individuals with any of these three surnames was found.

The foregoing example of a source reference is typical for most census searches, and similar references might be appropriate for other searches as well. However, be cautious about becoming too general. In the case of the census search, you might also state something like, "Family in area 1836 to abt. 1875." Use as much detail as necessary, and take as much space as you need.

Good notes should also tell the purpose for your search of each source. Some researchers make this notation in their manuscript files while others have a separate column on the research log, as in Figure 1. This notation might be quite specific, like—if the source is death records—"For the death of Charles Black." On the other hand, it might be quite general, like "For all Black, Creer, and Jackson deaths in the county." Remember that you are looking for every record that relates to everyone with your surnames of interest.

It is also critical that your research notes include appropriate notations about any problems with the records. If the record is not legible, if the microfilm was out of focus or is too dim to read because it was under-exposed, if there was water damage to the pages, or if there is *any* problem that affects your research, some explanation is essential. Missing pages (or parts of pages), smudged ink, unreadable handwriting, and damaged pages are all significant problems. Unless your notes specifically identify these problems, those who rely on your notes (and on your research results) will assume the records were perfect.

I add one note of caution and concern at the end of this section on keeping research notes: As you use the wonderful records, resources, and websites now available on the Internet, it is easy to jump quickly from one source to another, copying the information into your family records as you think it might fit, but totally neglecting to document what you have done or to explain the basis for any conclusions you have drawn.

Resist the temptation to follow such a course. Remember the principles discussed thus far in this book. Not only is it essential that you record the sources of the information for every family member you find, you must also explain how the evidence you have found justifies your conclusions and the connections you have made.

V. SPECIAL SEARCHES

A. Area searches

I also note that not all research relates to specific localities. Often, because of incomplete information and lack of success with the various "finding tools," you might find yourself doing what I call an area search in an attempt to locate a particular ancestor. For example, you might search the deed indexes of every county in southwest Virginia for a surname or for a particular individual when definitive clues of his origin have not been forthcoming. Likewise, you might search tax lists for every county in western Kentucky for the same reason.

Such searches are not to be made impulsively because they can be time-consuming. However, there are times when they cannot be avoided if further progress on a line is to be made. These area searches can (and should) be centralized around what appears to be the most probable location and then expanded as necessary until the required information or clue is discovered.

Your research log should be able to meet your needs in such cases. You can make it work by writing something like "Deeds, southwest Virginia counties" under the "Locality" heading. The surname line is filled in as usual; then, as the deed indexes for each county are checked, the proper listings are made both on the log and in your manuscript notes. The same procedure would be followed with the Kentucky tax list search or any other area-type search.

As more and more records are digitized, indexed, and made available on the Internet, these area searches will become much easier. In either case, however, be careful not to jump to conclusions as to the relevance of what you find just because of a person's name. Proof requires more evidence.

B. Preliminary survey

If you are doing a preliminary survey on a particular family and your research is in various compiled sources such as family histories, periodicals, biographical works, and secondary Internet sources, it is appropriate to write "Preliminary Survey" in the "Locality" space at the top of your log. On that same log, you can also keep track of all information, in its varied forms, that you gather from other relatives—including letters, e-mail messages, transcripts of interviews, etc.

Your research logs, all associated notes, document copies, interview transcripts, e-mails, etc., fit quite comfortably into this filing system. An "area search" file can be inserted following the earliest known locality for the surname involved. The log and the notes of your preliminary survey-type search can be filed where they best fit, depending on the timing of the particular survey involved as it relates to other research. These details can all be worked out and adjusted to satisfy your needs and your preferences.

For the benefit of those of you who prefer to base your research note-keeping system on individual families or specific ancestors rather than localities, I refer you to the following FamilySearch Wiki: *https://familysearch.org/wiki/en/Research_Logs*. A link to a printable research log in that format is available there.

VI. EVALUATING THE INFORMATION IN YOUR NOTES

Once you have exhausted all records pertinent to your problems in a given locality, you are ready to examine your findings in depth to determine if you have found evidence pertinent to your research objectives. Because you have been collecting every bit of information on every person of the surname of your interest—not just on those who are your primary objectives—you may have accumulated a large amount of material, including your research notes, various document copies, and perhaps some correspondence. You have undoubtedly already made some superficial analyses, but careful study is now required in order to draw all pertinent data out of your notes. For the novice, this can be especially challenging, and even those with more experience must use great care.

The best way to find out just how much information you have and the value of that information as evidence is to take the information in your notes—item by item—and record it, along with source documentation, on family group worksheets. Much of the information your research has produced will need to be entered on more than one worksheet because it pertains to people both as children and as parents. Also, the information from some sources will relate to several people and multiple family groups.

Be careful that every piece of information is recorded on *every possible worksheet*; this is essential to proper and complete analysis. There are other ways to tabulate data, but this method is usually the best and the safest. Also, let me stress that every time you add information to one of the worksheets, you *must* also record the source of that information on your worksheet.

As you work, keep your family group worksheets in alphabetical order (by names—surname then given name—of husbands) so you can find any sheet quickly. When two or more husbands have the same name (this can happen often when you are dealing with all persons of a single surname in a given locality), arrange them chronologically, eldest first, insofar as you can tell. At some point, as your analysis proceeds, you will likely find you have more than one worksheet that relates to the same family. In these cases, combine the information and the source references onto one worksheet and discard the extra(s). However, take special note of two things:

1. Be *absolutely sure* they relate to the same family. The fact that you would like them to be the same family, or even because you *think* they are the same family, is not enough. As long as there is any question, keep two worksheets. These worksheets can easily be combined later if and when you conclusively prove they are for the same family.

2. On your worksheets, footnote the information from each source very carefully so there will be no doubt as to what information came from what source. This makes it easy to re-check your work should you desire. It also makes it easier to resolve discrepancies in record information. If you know the sources of conflicting evidence, it is usually much easier to decide which is more likely to be correct when considered in light of other evidence and the nature of the conflicting sources.

You may be aware of some researchers who use the family group worksheet as a note-keeping device, taking notes directly from the records onto the forms. Though this may seem to be an efficient system, I oppose it for two reasons:

1. Complete information on record content cannot be easily recorded using this system. This worksheet does not and cannot reflect exactly what the record said—only your initial interpretation of it. This is dangerous until you know how that information relates to other information you have found or may yet find.

2. The nature of such a system tends to produce an excessive number of worksheets, many of which will have no meaning and no value in the final analysis—or at least you do not know their value because of reason number 1.

One means of identifying the sources of your evidence is to record the information from each source with a different color of ink and/or pencil on your worksheet and then make your footnote or source reference note in the same color. However, another—and perhaps better—system is merely to identify both the source of the information and the information from that source with the same number, footnote style.

Once your research findings are recorded on worksheets, you can easily see what has been accomplished in relation to your primary objectives. It will also be clear what you still need to do. In all of this, your chief concern should be for the families of your lineal ancestors, with collateral families having significance primarily because they are essential to complete research and comprehensive analysis. Remember that those families are also your kin and are relevant to the full picture. The information you find on relatives often provides evidence about your direct lines.

Insofar as possible, finished records should be compiled and then, depending on which families show a need for more research, your work will continue following the same research cycle. The research process is continual, just as discussed in Chapter 1. The steps are as follows:

1. Analyze what you already know (from your secondary research—your preliminary survey) to determine what information is needed.

2. Identify your objectives and plan what research you will do as you seek the needed information and evidence.

3. Complete your planned research according to your plan, recording your findings as you go.

4. Organize your research findings onto family group worksheets and then evaluate/analyze them to see if your objectives have been achieved.

5. Start over with step 1—based on what you learned during the previous cycle.

In all your research, remember that without proper analysis there is no sense of direction, and it is easy to get lost in mechanics. Your research should be carefully planned, and you should have a good reason for everything you do.

VII. ONE MORE STEP: THE RESEARCH REPORT

One more step is necessary in the record-keeping process. To help you keep your sense of direction and make meaningful evaluations, you need to prepare periodic research reports. If you are a professional researcher, you must make periodic reports to your clients. And, if you are working on your own family history, you must make those periodic reports to yourself.

As part of your research report, you need to

1. explain the problem(s) on which you have been focusing;

2. tell what research you have done in connection with that problem—what records you have searched—and explain why you searched each record;

3. tell what you found in your search of those records;

4. give your interpretation and evaluation of your research findings as they relate to the problem (in whatever detail is required);

5. outline the status of your research as it now stands as a result of the research you have done;

6. make suggestions for continuing research; and

7. explain why the suggested continuing research is necessary and what you hope to accomplish by it.

Every qualified professional can vouch for the value of the research reports he writes for his clients—not only the value of those reports for his clients but also for himself. After a break of several months, or even years, a careful reading of a good report will bring you up to date. You will know exactly where the research stands and what steps are required to continue. Whether you are a professional researcher or working on your own ancestral lines, your research project is not complete until your report is written.

Each report must cover all research you have completed since your last report and explain the results of that research. If you do this while both the problem and the research are fresh in your mind, you will be grateful later on. Though it is not essential that the points in the above list be numbered or even kept separate, each point must be adequately covered. Also, feel free to number if you find it helpful.

If you have proved a complicated connection, the evidence and the process used to verify that connection should be laid out with precision, step by step, so they can be understood without difficulty. When a long-accepted connection has been disproved by your research, it is doubly important to make a written report of the details and of the evidence involved. Sources and their contents must be explained with particularity—not just in a general way. Others in the family will question your conclusions, as they should, and, if a careful report has not been prepared, the passage of time will dim the details of your proof.

It is difficult for some people to accept new conclusions even when supported by impeccable evidence, so you must be well prepared. Even when all the sources from which your proof was derived are in your notes, it is not the same as having the detailed evidence of your proof and analysis summarized and explained systematically in a report.

Your research reports will become an important part of your permanent files, and no requirement of record keeping is more important. It can also be helpful if your reports are accompanied with visual aids such as small maps, hand-drawn if necessary. Remember, too, that your ancestors can "come alive" in pictures—even pictures of tombstones, houses, churches, etc.

Upon completion of every research report, you will want to enter all new ancestral information into your computerized family history software program and on your "official" online tree,[7] along with the essential documentation. You will want to share your findings directly with members of your family and other interested relatives. Also, you should extend your reach by adding your findings to other major family history websites, such as Ancestry, MyHeritage, FamilySearch, and FindMyPast.

---

[7] The concept of each researcher having an "official" online tree is discussed in Chapter 10. In connection with that discussion, there is also a discussion about the importance of choosing a family history software program capable of communicating with the family history Internet site where you maintain your "official" online tree.

VIII. REMINDER NOTES

As your research progresses from day to day, or from one research trip or computer session to the next, it is easy to forget intricate details of your problem and your research. When you leave the library, the courthouse, or the computer database at the end of the day, your mind is often filled with ideas and possibilities that need to be investigated. However, when you return a week (or a month) later, most of those ideas have been forgotten and can be recalled only as you spend time reviewing the problem. Because of the frailty of the human memory, it is a good idea to drop a brief reminder note into your research file as you conclude each day's research. Do not put your head on your pillow until you have written this brief message to yourself.

Your note can say anything you want it to say, but its purpose is to get you back on track as quickly as possible when you resume your quest. It may be a list of sources that need checking or just a note of "things to do next," with reasons for doing them. Then, when your research is resumed, you need only to read the note and go to work.

Reminder notes must not become a permanent part of your research files because their existence would cause confusion in later years both for yourself and for your successors. Retain each note only until it has served its purpose, and then discard it.

IX. ABSTRACTS AND FORMS

Though Chapter 21 discusses extracts and abstracts (summaries) in some detail, I think it is important to introduce the subject here as part of our discussion on research notes. When you are unable to get a photograph, photocopy, or printout of a relevant document or the digitized image of that document for your notes, it is usually counterproductive and unwise to copy source documents verbatim, either by hand or by typing. This is especially true when you are working with court records—including land and probate records—because there is much verbiage in these documents that contains no relevant family history evidence; it is also very time-consuming. Even photocopies may be impractical if certain records are extensive, unless you are using a computerized record-keeping program like Evernote or ResearchTies. Therefore, efficient research requires that you be able to read a document and pick out the essential details. When doing this, you must always be careful to copy *all* that is important—even including verbatim quotes when *essential* wording is intricate and/or complicated. When there is a question as to value, always include the information in question. It is better to make your abstracts (as we call them) too detailed than too brief. There are also times when unnecessary modifiers and parenthetical phrases can be eliminated without doing harm to a document's meaning or its family history value.

Abbreviations may also be used at times, but be wary lest you are unable to interpret them when they are cold. If you use good judgment, abbreviations can be used to great advantage. Names of people and of places, however, should always be copied *exactly* as they appear in the records in order to facilitate correct analysis.

Some researchers use special forms for abstracting various types of documents. If you find them to be helpful, they can be good. In fact, some family history websites have abstracting forms you can copy and use. A form can serve as a useful guide but it is not mandatory, and most experienced researchers limit its use. One such form (called a "Research Extraction Form") can be either downloaded or completed online at *https://familysearch.org/learn/wiki/en/File:FisherResearch_070511_distributed.pdf*. Once on this page, click on the large red pdf file icon at the top of the page. Abstracts completed online can be easily printed out and added to your research notes.

It is important to mention here that forms for extracting census information are a necessity when you are unable to print copies from digitized images. These census forms save much time. The same is true of any source record with a chart/table format.

X. CARD FILES AND COMPUTER INDEXES

In the past, some researchers maintained card files/indexes of the ancestors they identified, in addition to all of the information kept in their research notes. This has been true especially if they were planning to publish family histories. However, with the present state of available technology, this is not a recommended practice. If you want alphabetical listings of ancestors/family members (with whatever information you keep about each one), your computer word-processing program can instantaneously do whatever you wish it to do in the way of creating alphabetical lists, without regard for the sequence of data entry.

For the serious, and even the casual, family history researcher, computers and family history software programs have substantially eliminated the need for *manual* control of data of the kind that a card file can provide. No one who is interested in family history, no matter your age, should refuse to learn computers; you cannot afford to turn your back on computer technology. With the equipment and programs now available, you can create—in a matter of minutes—virtually any kind of genealogical list you desire to create from the data you enter.

XI. RECORDS RELATING TO CORRESPONDENCE

You also need to keep records of the research you do through correspondence (both what you send and what you receive, both by e-mail and by snail mail). This correspondence should also be listed on your research logs, and copies of all correspondence should be paginated and interfiled with your research notes and document copies. In the past, I have recommended that separate correspondence files be kept. However, with the current state of family history research and the technological resources now available, I no longer make that recommendation.

Other issues relating to correspondence are discussed in the next chapter.

XII. CONCLUDING THOUGHTS

Much more could be said about keeping research notes, but I think enough has been said to help you set up a system that will meet your needs and facilitate your success. The only thing I will add here is that you must *never* destroy any of your notes. If it is a question of space, you might store those files not in current use in bankers' boxes under your bed, but somehow preserve them. If your research records are created on a computer—with a program that operates on the cloud, such as Evernote and ResearchTies—make sure you have adequate back-up not only on your computer hard drive but also on other secure media stored in a safe location remote from the computer. Flash drives can hold a great deal of data. Never trust precious research note files to unsaved computer programs.

Following is a list of essentials for a viable record-keeping system as discussed in this chapter, without regard to the order of their importance:

- Keep your research note-keeping system simple enough so anyone can understand it without extensive explanation.
- Make your research notes sufficiently complete to reflect adequately the research done.
- Do not use a note-keeping system that is so complicated and time-consuming that it detracts from your research.
- If you keep your notes on paper, keep them orderly and on good-quality paper of uniform size, to the extent possible.
- Keep notes that are done well enough the first time so that it is unnecessary to recopy them.
- Create a research log that lists all sources searched, in a footnote-type format. This log should include the sources where nothing is found as well as those containing useful information.
- Include the date of every search.
- Make all source references sufficiently complete that others can use them to locate those same sources.
- Record the purpose of every search.
- Keep your records orderly by limiting your research logs in some way. Do not use one log for everything. Though I recommend locality-based divisions, divisions can also be family based or even individual based, if you prefer.

- Make your research log a "table of contents" to your research notes. It should refer directly to the notes you take, to the document copies you have made, to copies of all correspondence and e-mails, and to anything and everything in your note files.
- Keep your notes in either file folders or loose-leaf binders. Spiral-bound and solid-bound notebooks lack flexibility.
- Put your name, address, and the search date on every page of your notes.
- Keep the overall arrangement of your note files systematic. A good system is to file them alphabetically by surname and, under each surname, chronologically by locality.
- Cross-reference your research logs to each other when you have more than one surname in a locality. Never make identical logs and note files for multiple surnames.
- Keep the appropriate portion of your pedigree at the front of every research file.
- In your notes, identify any relevant conditions or circumstances relating to the records and your research in those records. Do this for every record, in every case.
- Make your note-keeping system, including your research logs, flexible enough to accommodate the filing of all materials and documents in any kind of search, including a research survey and an "area search," as well as your routine research.
- Extract the information from your notes onto family group worksheets for final evaluation to determine if your research objectives are being attained.
- Write detailed periodic reports of your research and the results of that research.
- Use reminder slips during your research, but do not make them a permanent part of your files.
- Keep your research note files on paper, or be sure to keep a copy of all cloud-based records on your computer hard drive, and also keep a backup in a safe place.
- Never throw away any of your research notes.

8

Successful Correspondence

Some people claim that correspondence is no longer necessary to successful family history research—that everything we need can now be found on the Internet. It is true that many things have changed in the last few years but, though the Internet has greatly facilitated our research, there is still a need for correspondence. Some of our letters can be sent by e-mail, and that is a great boon to the work, but correspondence is still a necessary part of much of what we do and is a valuable tool.

It cannot be denied that some things associated with correspondence that were done in the past are no longer required because of technological advances. For example, we no longer make carbon copies of the letters we send (though I checked on the Internet and found out you can still buy carbon paper). Also, electronic communication (e-mail) is virtually instantaneous, and even "snail mail" is sometimes faster than it used to be. In many cases, it is also possible to request copies of documents—and pay for those copies—on the Internet websites of custodial organizations/institutions.

In this chapter, we will discuss various procedures that can help you be more successful with your correspondence, but before doing so, let us discuss briefly how to file our correspondence and the materials accumulated as a result thereof.

You should organize, file, and index your correspondence in much the same way as you do for the notes and document copies acquired through your personal research. However, because the researcher does not rely so heavily on correspondence as in the past, the filing requirements are less complicated. As mentioned in Chapter 7, your correspondence can be accommodated and interfiled with your research notes and tracked on the same research logs. I no longer recommend the keeping of separate correspondence logs.

I. FILING DOCUMENTS ACQUIRED BY CORRESPONDENCE

There are various possibilities for filing the documents you obtain by correspondence. Because you are going to be interfiling them with the research notes and document copies from your personal research, you need a way to do this as effortlessly as possible. First, you need to file the answer to each letter and any documents obtained in connection with that answer with your letter of request to which they relate.

Because documents are of such varied sizes and shapes, it is often difficult to make everything fit in the same file. One way to file odd-sized documents/papers is to fold them individually and place them in envelopes that can be glued to appropriately numbered and titled sheets of file-size paper. However, I recommend this only in extreme cases because the glue will eventually fail. A better solution might be to make an electronic copy, either by scanning or by taking a photograph, and storing it in your properly designated computer files and with an appropriate offline backup. If you do this, your research log must identify each document's location. There are alternatives, but whenever possible, it works best when you can file all the fruits of your research in the same file, both that which comes from your personal research and that which comes from correspondence.

II. ANALYZING YOUR CORRESPONDENCE RESULTS

Organize and evaluate the results of your correspondence with the same care as you use for the findings of your personal research. The best time to do this is immediately upon receipt of the reply. You should record all family data on your family group worksheets and analyze them as soon as possible. This immediate analysis is necessary because it may influence the next step in your research. Research, especially that research done by correspondence, is often a one-step-at-a-time process with the next step being dependent on the results of the previous step.

Of course, you will use the same worksheets to tabulate the results of your correspondence as you use to tabulate the results of your personal searches, whether you are searching in a courthouse or on the Internet. As you do this, remember to document the source of each piece of information.

III. REVIEW OF RESEARCH NOTE REQUIREMENTS

At this point, it may be useful to review the requirements of good research and correspondence notes. There are five essentials of a sound record-keeping system:

1. At the front of each file, include a *worksheet pedigree chart* that shows the relevant portion of your pedigree and includes all known genealogical facts.

2. Initiate a *research log* for your area of focus. (My explanations in Chapter 7 focused on localities—usually the specific county where you are doing research. However, some researchers have logs that relate to specific families and some even to individuals.) On the appropriate research log, list the bibliographic information for all sources searched or to be searched, as well as all correspondence.

3. Maintain a *manuscript note and document file* in connection with each research log. That file should contain your research notes and all document copies, including letters and documents from your correspondence.

4. Create a *family group worksheet* for each family you find in your research, and record on that worksheet all genealogical information that relates to the family listed, including your documentation of the sources from which that information was taken.

5. Write a periodic *research report* explaining what you did, why you did it, what you learned, the significance of what you learned, and what you recommend doing next.

This chapter and the chapter preceding it outline with some exactness how these requirements can be satisfied. Remember, however, that any rule can be altered to fit your personal preferences or circumstances so long as none of these six essentials is neglected. However, insofar as American research is concerned, the steps outlined here have proved workable.

IV. WRITING YOUR LETTER

A. The "Letter" formula

There is much that could be said about letter writing in general, but there are a few guidelines that apply more specifically to family history correspondence. Let us talk first about six such guidelines. The initial letters of the key words in each of the points spell the word *LETTER* and provide a simple formula for better family history correspondence.

1. *LIMIT YOUR REQUEST.* Do not ask for too much. There is no more sure way to destroy the good will of someone whose assistance you need than to make an unreasonable request. If you know something about the records held by a particular public official, you are in a better position to judge what a "reasonable request" might be, thus the importance of understanding something about the records. Should you need additional information, you can always write another letter (or several) once you have secured the good will of your correspondent. Never write a relative asking for "everything you have." The late Archibald F. Bennett told the story of his sister who had shown no interest in the research he was doing until late in her life. Not realizing the extent of the records her brother had compiled, she unthinkingly wrote to him: "Dear Archie, please send me all you have." This was not a reasonable request.

2. *EASY TO ANSWER.* There are several things we can do to make our requests easy to answer:

    a. Ask specific questions. Do not be vague or beat around the bush.

    b. Do not lose your questions in the body of a long letter. Very often, the best procedure is to write your questions on a separate sheet of paper in questionnaire form, leaving space for the answers.

    c. Be careful of sending forms such as pedigree charts and family group record forms. Sometimes these forms can be used to advantage in your correspondence, but they are confusing to the average person. If the person to whom you are writing knows little or nothing about family history, you will likely get a more satisfactory response if you copy any family data you wish to send him in tabular form on a plain sheet of paper. You might then say something like this: "The above information is all I have on this family. Can you make any additions or corrections?" I am not saying you should never use forms in your correspondence; I am merely saying that you should use them wisely and with caution. And *never* send forms to a public official.

3. *TWO COPIES.* You do not have a complete record of your research unless you have a copy in your files of every letter you write. It is a simple matter to print two copies when you send the letter to your computer printer. There are several reasons why this is necessary. Three good reasons include:

    a. If a follow-up letter becomes necessary, it will be much easier to write if you know the specific requests and wording of the original.

    b. As research progresses and you desire information on a particular matter, you will be able to tell, from your letters, if previous attempts have been made to locate the same information. People often make themselves offensive by asking for the same nonexistent information over and over again because they failed to keep copies of their letters. In the same light, you may have located additional facts in the interim that would now make it possible to locate the required information. It is impossible to know this without a copy of the original request.

    c. A third and obvious motive is the necessity for having copies of all correspondence in your research files.

4. *THANKS.* Many, if not most, of those who assist researchers through the mail have no legal obligation to do so. Their help is a favor for which you should show your gratitude. On the other hand, however, do not apologize for your requests.

5. *EXCHANGE.* Never expect to get something for nothing; in this day, it is often difficult to get something for something. To a public official of whom you have asked a favor, a small sum (with an offer to pay any reasonable additional charges) is a necessity. Usually, if you send an

amount somewhere between $10 and $15, depending on what you ask, that is sufficient. If you feel that $15 is not enough, you are probably asking for too much and need to limit your request. If you request copies of specific documents, more money may be required, depending on the cost of making copies. This same principle applies when you seek favors of newspapers, libraries, historical societies, church officials, or other private organizations, except when there are established fees for their services.

When you write to a private individual or a relative, your "fair exchange" is not necessarily monetary unless that person happens to have services for hire as a genealogist or a record searcher. You should always offer to pay the cost of copying valuable materials, but more important is your offer to share information and to make the results of your research available to those who are interested.

Some public officials, as well as private organizations, may return the money you send, but they appreciate your willingness to pay and will be more inclined to help if they do not think you are trying to get something for nothing.

6. *RETURN POSTAGE.* Ethel W. Williams tells of a woman who wrote Abraham Lincoln asking for a bit of advice and his signature for a keepsake. He replied: "When asking strangers for a favor, it is customary to send postage. There's your advice and here's my signature. A. Lincoln."[1] This is excellent advice as it relates to most letters that will pass through the hands of the United States Postal Service.

It is not necessary to offend close relatives with this practice (though that will seldom happen), but all others will appreciate your thoughtfulness and perhaps feel a greater obligation to promptly answer your queries.

When you write to a federal or state agency, it is not necessary to provide for postage, but correspondence addressed to officials of counties or towns—or to newspapers, historical societies, church officials, etc., within the U.S.—should include a stamped envelope that is addressed back to you. The two exceptions are when you allow money for postage in your remittance and when you pay a set fee for the service. Of course, this advice is irrelevant when your letter is sent as an e-mail. You cannot send money in an e-mail, but you can offer to send money to defray any expenses involved.

B. The "4S formula"

In addition to the above rules, which relate especially to family history letters, there are other rules that will add to your effectiveness regardless of

---

[1] Ethel W. Williams, *Know Your Ancestors,* Rutland, VT: Charles E. Tuttle Co., 1960, 271. By permission.

the nature of your request. Among the most important are the ones covered by a formula for clarity disseminated in a U.S. Government (General Services Administration) pamphlet in 1955. It was called "The 4S Formula."[2] The four *S*s in the formula represent *shortness, simplicity, strength,* and *sincerity* (with a list of essential points under each item). The formula goes like this:

1. Shortness

a. Do not unnecessarily repeat the inquiry.
b. Avoid needless words, information.
c. Shorten prepositional phrases.
d. Watch "verbal" nouns, adjectives.
e. Limit qualifying statements.
   I recall an old maxim that says, "Good things, if short, are twice as good." Most things written can be improved much more by deletions than by additions. A stone is polished by breaking off and wearing down the rough edges, not by filling in around them. Busy public officials, especially, do not have time to read lengthy letters. So if you can say something in one or two words, do not use three or four. A good rule of thumb is that, when asking favors, your letters should never be more than one page long, with adequate (even generous) margins on all four edges. A friend of mine says he never writes a letter that he cannot get on half a sheet of 8½" x 11" paper. He has the right idea on brevity but the wrong idea in halving the paper.

2. Simplicity

a. Know your subject.
b. Use short words, sentences, paragraphs.
c. Be compact.
d. Tie thoughts together.
   Letters should be written in a friendly, conversational style. Write as you would talk. Try to write from the other person's point of view, keeping his interests dominant. Also, remember that nothing adds to simplicity more than knowing something about the subject on which you are writing.

3. Strength

a. Use specific words.
b. Use active verbs.
c. Give an answer, then explain.
d. Do not hedge.
   Do not beat around the bush; avoid clichés, stilted language, and word crutches.

---

[2] U.S. General Services Administration, "Pamphlet 58-7468." (Washington, DC: G.S.A, 1955).

4. Sincerity

a. Be human.

b. Admit mistakes.

c. Limit intensives and emphatics.

d. Do not be servile or arrogant.

Try to be yourself and to "put yourself on paper." As was stated under "simplicity," you should write as you speak (your very best speech). When you are corresponding by e-mail, it is a good idea to draft your letter in your word-processing program first. Then, when you have done all the polishing and editing that needs to be done, copy and paste it into your e-mail. Any extra time and effort involved are worth the cost.

C. Objectivity

If I can take all four of the "S" principles and draw from them one idea, perhaps that idea would be the need for objectivity—the ability, in this situation, to look at your own letters and see them as they really are. If you could always do this, many problems would be solved.

I sometimes write things that I think are good at the time I write them, but when I re-read them later, my impression is quite different. The difference in my reaction on these two occasions is the result of objectivity. It is always easier to be objective about something after it has grown cold and I have removed myself from it.

Obviously, it is not practical to let a letter sit for six months before you send it. However, if you can be aware of your natural lack of objectivity when something is first written, you will be able to achieve some of the objectivity you need.

Perhaps a better idea, if your ego can stand it, is to have someone else read and criticize your letters. See if another person can understand what you are trying to say and if you are saying it inoffensively. He will be in a better position to judge this than you are. Also, have him check your spelling, grammar, and punctuation; you may have overlooked something.

Make the first draft of your letter, then print it and have someone check and correct it. When you have done that, make your edits on the computer and then print it out and read it again. Be prepared to rewrite any letter that you would not like to receive personally. Your word-processing software will facilitate whatever corrections you find necessary. Once you feel the letter is ready to send, print out two copies—one to send and one for your manuscript note file.

If you cannot endure criticism, at least let your letters sit overnight before you finalize them. That much time will seldom hurt you, and you can gain a little objectivity overnight if you try.

As already mentioned, this procedure also applies to your e-mail letters. Make those letters as perfect as possible before you copy and paste them to create your e-mail message.

V. APPEARANCE MATTERS

This is not a text on business communications, but a brief summary of some details that make a letter look inviting to the addressee is also in order:

- Leave adequate margins on all four sides. Very few things give a letter a worse appearance than crowding it too close to the edge of the paper. No matter how neatly you write or type or how well you spell, the letter will look sloppy. If you have to crowd your margins to keep the "one-page" rule, break the rule.

- Use short paragraphs and double-space between them. This additional white space on the page makes the letter more attractive and easier to read.

- Keep your left margin straight. Do not wander all over the page.

- Use proper letter form. Any good English text will give you information on proper letter form. If your letters are not business-like, people will think you do not know what you are doing—an image you do not want to convey.

- Type your letters if possible. If you cannot type, write neatly, legibly, and evenly.

VI. TO WHOM DO I WRITE?

One of the researcher's greatest challenges is to know who has custody of the records he needs. This is especially perplexing to the beginner. First, make every possible effort to obtain information from relatives. In the past, I have suggested using newspaper want ads as a way to locate unknown kin, but there are now better ways to do that. Many people do not subscribe to newspapers today, and many subscribers seldom look at the want ads. Today the various family history websites on the Internet (discussed in Chapter 10) are excellent tools for finding relatives who are interested in family history.

For information that is not on the Internet and that relatives do not have (and a significant amount of family history information falls into this category), you must determine who has jurisdiction over those records that might contain the needed information. Record custodians can usually be identified by using proper reference tools. When these fail, you can always write to a probable record custodian and ask about the actual location of the records you need. It is also possible to get phone numbers from the Internet of probable records custodians so you can call and ask. And, of course, the chapters in Part 2 of this book provide information on the location and custody of most important family history sources.

VII. CONCLUSION AND CHECKLIST

Many years ago at a class, I picked up a checklist designed to help letter writers pinpoint trouble spots in their correspondence skills. I do not know the actual origin of this list, but I am taking the liberty of passing it on to you—with some modifications to fit my needs. Each question is worded so that a "no" answer might identify a problem area.

	Yes	No
1. Are most of your letters less than one page long?	____	____
2. Is your average sentence shorter than twenty-two words?	____	____
3. Are your paragraphs short—*always* less than ten lines?	____	____
4. Do you avoid beginning a letter with: "I am doing family history research . . ."	____	____
5. Do you know some good ways to begin letters in a natural and conversational manner?	____	____
6. Can you think of four different words that will take the place of "however"?	____	____
7. Do you know what is wrong with phrases like: "held a meeting," "are in receipt of," "gave consideration to," etc.?	____	____
8. Do you use personal pronouns freely, especially "you"?	____	____
9. Do you use active verbs ("I read your letter" rather than "Your letter has been read")?	____	____
10. When you have a choice, do you use little words (*pay, help,* and *error*) rather than big ones (*remuneration, assistance,* and *inadvertency*)?	____	____
11. Whenever possible, do you refer to people by name and title (Dr. Brown, Mr. Adams) rather than categorically (our researcher, the patron, etc.)?	____	____
12. Compare your letters with your speech. Do you write the way you talk (your most careful talk, of course)?	____	____
13. Do you answer questions before you explain your answers?	____	____
14. Do you resist the use of phrases like: "Attention will be called to the fact," "It is to be noted," "It will be apparent"?	____	____
15. Do you organize your ideas and data before you write your letters?	____	____
16. Have you tried setting off lists of various types into easily read tables?	____	____

17. Do you number and/or indent important points, explanations, etc.?   _____ _____

18. Do you highlight important facts by underlining, using bold-face, or italicizing, or by using separate paragraphs?   _____ _____

19. Do you re-read your letters (including your e-mail messages) before you send them to see if you actually said what you intended to say?[3]   _____ _____

Experience is a marvelous teacher, especially when combined with proper instruction and meaningful guidelines. If you will follow carefully the guidelines given in this chapter, your correspondence should produce satisfying results. And though I have no panacea that guarantees success in every case, I can promise that those who follow sound procedures are more likely to succeed.

---

[3] Instructional handout entitled "The Letter Writer's Checklist," The Genealogical Society of The Church of Jesus Christ of Latter-day Saints, Salt Lake City: no publisher, 1963. Modified and used by permission.

9

Computer Technology and Family History

The 1980s brought the personal computer and, with it, the possibility for a few people to have limited computer technology in their homes. The 1990s saw this technology proliferate, becoming more available, more affordable, and more powerful with much more memory. The 90s also brought the Internet and its ability for instantaneous communication. Since the turn of the century, all progress and possibilities have expanded beyond everything we had even dreamed of before. Smartphones, tablets, and the various Android devices that have come into use since 2005 have put the Internet at the fingertips of most Americans, not just in their homes but practically anywhere they happen to be.

It is almost an understatement to say that we now have ready access to resources beyond comprehension. And though it is hard to comprehend, I believe the future holds surprises beyond anything we can now imagine. After all, most of us never imagined the resources that are now so readily available to us and have become commonplace.

If you were to look at the technological resources listed and discussed in the third edition of *The Researcher's Guide to American Genealogy* in the year 2000, you would immediately observe that the list is very unsophisticated from our current perspective. And I suspect that the innovations yet to come will make our current state of technology also look quite ordinary.

In the third edition, I discussed the miracles of word processing, how to create charts and tables, and how to organize information in a convenient format for both using and sharing. I also discussed how the Internet has facilitated the identification of relatives and enhanced our ability to learn about the holdings of various libraries and archives. I explained how to gain online access to important reference works and research aids. And, finally, I mentioned the ability that computer technology had given us to search files/databases of information compiled by others.

Every one of these processes was exciting to me and miraculous from my perspective at that time—and they still are. It is not my intention to minimize any of them, because they are still important. However, when I consider the incredible resources available today, these tools of the 1990s—as I said earlier—seem quite ordinary. Today most of us are inclined to take these tools for granted because they have become so familiar and commonplace. In fact, very little is said about them in this chapter except as they relate to our discussion of more current resources.

I. CONCEPTS AND DEFINITIONS OF MODERN TECHNOLOGY

This book has two chapters devoted to computer technology. This chapter deals with the whys and hows of family history's wonderful involvement with computer technology. I will begin by seeking to clarify some important computer-related terminology and will then discuss some of the excellent resources that facilitate our research and assist us in getting things right when they are used wisely. The second of these chapters (Chapter 10)—without attempting to be a user manual—discusses some principles for the use of computer technology in family history research and then looks briefly at some of the excellent websites that have essentially come out of nowhere and have so wonderfully transformed the world of family history research.

To begin this discussion, let me clarify some basic, but important, terms. Forgive me if I try to tell you more than you want to know, but this is important:

First, I want to clarify the fundamental computer terms of **software, programs, hardware, and applications**. We hear these terms bandied about everywhere we turn, but sometimes they can be a bit confusing. I will try to be as basic and clear as possible.

The term *software* refers to all *programs* that run on computers and on mobile devices like tablets and smartphones. A computer *program* is nothing more than a collection of instructions executed by a computer to complete a specific task. Though we sometimes use the terms *programs* and *software* interchangeably, there are minor differences. *Software* has a broader definition than *program*, and a *program* is just one type of computer *software*.

There are actually two kinds of computer *software*—*systems software* and *applications software*. *Systems software* encompasses the computer operating system and all those utilities/tools that enable a computer to function. These utilities include the *software* designed to help us analyze, configure, optimize, and maintain our computers. The instructions that are programmed into a computer's *systems software* are what make the computer function. The computer executes these instructions in a *central processing unit* (*CPU*).

Applications software, on the other hand, does our work for us. For example, word processors, spreadsheets, and database management systems are examples of *applications software* (or what are now called apps). Another name for an *application* (or *app)* is *program*.

The physical computer itself and all the support equipment required to operate it (printers, fax machines, modems, etc.) are *hardware*. *Hardware* uses the *systems software* to run the *application software* (*programs*) to perform the specific functions. We sometimes buy *software/programs* on discs and load them into our computer's memory. There are other times when we load these *programs* directly into a computer's memory (a process called *downloading*) from the Internet website of the person or company that distributes it. There is usually a price involved, though many simple *software* programs (*apps*) are free.

Let me repeat, by way of review, that *hardware* can do nothing without *system software* that is programmed to make it run and direct its function. A computer, using this *system software*, runs the *application software* (*programs*) to perform specific functions and/or to solve specific problems.

In addition to these terms that are so essential to your understanding, there are other significant computer-related terms, including the following. (You will observe that there are many abbreviations in common use.)

API (Application Program Interface): Code (in the form of commands, functions, protocols, and objects) put into computer software programs by their developers that allow those programs to communicate with each other in order to perform various tasks using the capabilities of both programs.

Bookmarks/Favorites: A feature on a computer's browser program that conveniently stores the addresses (URLs) of Internet websites so they can be accessed later without the need to either remember or retype them. See **URL**.

Browser (or web browser): A computer software program that allows you to access and browse the Internet. The most common browser programs today are Microsoft Internet Explorer, Mozilla Firefox, and Google Chrome. Netscape Navigator, which was popular a few years ago, has been discontinued.

Clickable link: In technical terms, this is a **Hyperlink** (*q.v.*[1]).

Cookie: A message sent by a website to your computer's browser program that is stored there to facilitate return visits to that website. No information can be retrieved from the originating site that has not been entered. A cookie cannot be used to get your e-mail address or any other data from your hard drive or to gather other sensitive information.

Cursor: The pulsating vertical marker on your computer screen (l) that marks the place on the page where you are working.

Cyberspace: The electronic universe of the Internet.

DNS (Domain Name Service): The three (and sometimes two) letter suffix following the dot (.) at the end of a website address or an e-mail address. The DNS makes it possible to access the desired address on the Internet

---

[1] The letters "*q.v.*" are the abbreviation of the Latin term *quod vide,* which literally means "which see."

without the need to remember and enter the site's unique numerical address, its Internet Protocol or **IP address** (*q.v.*). The DNS suffixes in the United States were once limited mostly to ".com" (for commercial), ".org" (for organization), ".edu" (for educational institution), and ".gov" (for government). Today, however, there are many more DNS suffixes in use— some with three letters and others with two.

Domain name: That part of a website's **URL** (*q.v.*) that is the name unique to the site. In the URL, the domain name follows the **HTTP** (*q.v.*) or **HTTPS** (*q.v.*) and precedes the dot (.) and the **DNS** (*q.v.*).

Download: The process of transferring data (messages, files, programs, etc.) from another computer system to your computer. E-mail messages, for example, are downloaded to your computer from the server of your **ISP** (*q.v.*). Files from other sites can be downloaded to your computer using the **FTP** (*q.v.*) on the Internet. Almost any kind of materials can be downloaded, including application software, data files, graphics, text files, and **GEDCOM** (*q.v.*) files. See also **Upload.**

E-mail (Electronic mail): Messages sent from one computer to another over the Internet through the services of an **ISP** (*q.v.*). The sender and the receiver must both have e-mail addresses and Internet software.

Favorites: See **Bookmarks.**

Flame: An **e-mail** (*q.v.*) message sent to someone to either reprimand or criticize an act that is considered an inappropriate use of e-mail communications or to challenge a view that has been expressed.

Freeware: Computer software that can be used without any payment to the owner/developer. When this software is essential to one's use of a particular Internet site, it can be downloaded from that site. Restrictions and/or limitations are often attached. Continued use usually requires purchase.

FTP (File Transfer Protocol): The electronic protocol/procedure by which messages, files, programs, etc., are downloaded (received) and uploaded (sent) over the Internet to copy a program or file that is on one computer onto another computer.

GEDCOM: (GEnealogical **D**ata **COM**munication): The standard communication protocol developed by the LDS Family History Department that allows people to communicate and share (download and/or upload) genealogical information even though they may use different family history software programs.

Homepage: The opening page (or title page) of an Internet website. It usually tells something about the site, its purpose, and when last updated. It typically has a menu with **hyperlinks** (*q.v.*) to other pages on the site.

HTML (HyperText Markup Language): The primary coding language used to create websites on the Internet. It includes the sequence of characters and other symbols a programmer inserts at various places in a computer-based program to control/dictate how the page will be structured and how it will look when it is displayed.

HTTP (HyperText Transfer Protocol): These letters (or **HTTPS** [*q.v.*]) are the beginning of every website address. They represent a protocol/procedure required by every website address. They are the foundation of data communication for the World Wide Web and have embedded within them the procedures/rules used by "the web" for making files accessible. They run on top of the **TCP/IP** (*q.v.*).

HTTPS (HyperText Transfer Protocol Secure): The "S" at the end of a hypertext abbreviation (see **HTTP**) indicates that the website is secure. That security is achieved by using both the Hypertext Transfer Protocol and a Secure Socket Layer (SSL). **SSL** is a security and authentication protocol that encrypts[2] transferred information.

Hyperlink: The official name for a link that allows you to click your mouse on that link and go directly to a different page or a different website from where you are at the time.

IP address (Internet Protocol address): The unique string of numbers, separated by periods, used to identify any computer or device that uses the Internet. These numbers contain the protocol (or computer language) necessary for that computer or device to use the Internet. See also **TCP/IP**.

ISP (Internet Service Provider): The company that provides you with access to the Internet via their **server(s)** (*q.v.*).

Netiquette: Etiquette on the Internet. It is the informal code of conduct for those who send e-mail. Though many do not comprehend it, it is very important.

Newbie: A person who is new to the Internet and/or to computers in general.

Server: A host computer. An **ISP** (*q.v.*) may have several servers to comprise its network. Those servers are connected to the Internet and deliver Internet service to that ISP's customers. What we refer to as the "cloud" is also a group of several servers. (The cloud is discussed later in this chapter.)

Shareware: A computer program—usually an abbreviated version—available without charge for use on a trial basis. It is expected that the user will buy the full version of the program after the trial period if he desires to continue using it.

TCP/IP (Transmission Control Protocol/Internet Protocol): The communication language (or protocol) of the Internet. Every computer or device with direct access to the Internet has this program (systems software). It is expressed in the computer's or the device's **IP address** (*q.v.*).

Upload: The process of copying a file from your computer to another computer or to a social networking site like Facebook. Upload is the opposite of **download** (*q.v.*).

URL (Uniform Resource Locator): The name given to a complete Internet website address. On the World Wide Web, the URL begins with http:// or

---

[2] Encryption is the process of converting information and data into a form that is not easily understood by unauthorized people. Encrypted language is sometimes called ciphertext.

https://, then often by **www** (*q.v.*) and a dot (.). Next is the **domain name** (*q.v.*), which consists of a word or words (without spaces between them), then another dot (.), followed by a **DNS** (*q.v.*). Any other information at the end of the URL (following slashes, dashes, etc.) relates to some subdivision of the **website** (*q.v.*).

Website: The combination of the **homepage** (*q.v.*) and other related/associated pages belonging to one person or one organization. It usually has one evident purpose. A website can be very limited in its scope, very comprehensive, or somewhere in between.

WWW: (World Wide Web): This is what we know as "the web." It does not constitute the entire Internet but is a major component. It is a visual user interface to the Internet that employs multimedia to bring the Internet to life. One can navigate (or surf) around the web easily and quickly using **hyperlinks** (*q.v.*). Every Internet site on the web has an address or **URL** (*q.v.*) that begins with either "http://" or "https://."

If you have questions about other computer/Internet-related terms, I recommend a website entitled Net Lingo (*http://www.netlingo.com/*).

With the above definitions as background, let us now examine some specific technological resources available for our use as researchers. We will examine each resource individually because of its importance to our research.

II. TECHNOLOGICAL RESOURCES IMPORTANT TO FAMILY HISTORY

The resources discussed here are all important to our work. However, their various natures and the relationship of each to our purposes are such that some require significantly more discussion space than others. These resources are as follows:

A. Family history software programs
B. Internet search engines
C. Social media
D. Wikis
E. Genealogy/family history blogs
F. The cloud
G. DNA
H. Message boards, forums, and special projects
I. Family history websites

We will discuss each one in turn.

A. Family history software programs

As you think about the definitions given at the beginning of this chapter, you need to understand that family history software programs are application software. The primary functions these programs provide are (1) to preserve and (2) manipulate family history records and related items of memorabilia—particularly photographs and documents. You need to choose and use one of the many available programs. They are specially designed to perform the various functions many users desire.

In December 2016, Wikipedia listed and compared twenty such programs (two of them are no longer available). This list was reduced from a list of thirty-eight such programs earlier in the year. The various programs have features, functions, and reports that are innovative and helpful, and each is somewhat different from all the others. With so many options available, it is important that you choose a program that easily performs the functions you want, even though it may have some functions you will never use.

A family history program is more than just a place to preserve your family tree—though that is its primary purpose. When you buy a program, perhaps the most important feature to look for is the program's ability to link/interface directly with the largest and most popular family history websites. You will also want to see how it is organized in relation to your way of looking at things, how easy it is to use, and what "helps" are part of the program.

According to one authority, the most widely used and most functional family history programs—as of March 2017—were, in alphabetical order, *Ancestral Quest, Brother's Keeper, Family Historian, Family Tree Heritage, Family Tree Maker, Heredis, Legacy Family Tree, MyHeritage, RootsMagic, and WinFamily*.[3] Of the ten programs listed, the one considered by that same authority to be the best—and upon which she chose to bestow her gold award—was *Legacy Family Tree*. At the time of this writing, only three of the family history programs on this list were certified by FamilySearch. These are *Ancestral Quest, Legacy Family Tree*, and *RootsMagic*. You may find it helpful to read the pros and cons of all ten programs and view comparison charts, which you can do on the website noted in footnote 3.

You will also be interested to note that in December of 2015, *Family Tree Magazine*, after analyzing several family history programs, cited *RootsMagic* as the only program its staff felt had no major drawbacks.[4]

It is good to read the critiques, but it is also good to seek input from those who have used the programs. Find out what it is that they like and do not like about the programs they are using.

B. Internet search engines

Every computer with access to the Internet has the potential to connect with many search engines. A search engine is a web-based computer program

---

[3] Renee Shipley, "The Best Genealogy Software of 2017: Linking the Past with the Future," Top Ten Reviews.com. TechMediaNetworks, Inc., DBA as Purch, March 3, 2017, http://www.top tenreviews.com/software/home/best-genealogy-software/ (accessed May 24, 2017).

[4] "Genealogy Software for Windows," *Family Tree Magazine*, December 9, 2015, http://www. familytreemagazine. com/Article/windows_genealogy_software (accessed January 4, 2017).

designed specifically to help the user quickly find the specific information he seeks. Search engines provide the platform from which Internet searches are made.

A search engine does not search the web directly, but is a server or collection of servers that indexes Internet websites, stores the results, and then produces lists of website pages, in order of relevancy, to match the search queries made by users. These indexes are created by what is called "spidering" software that continuously crawls through Internet websites collecting data. Then, based on each search request, a relevancy formula (called an algorithm) determines the sequence of the relevant web pages on the resulting list that will appear on the searcher's computer screen. Some major search engines, listed alphabetically, are Alta Vista, Dog Pile, Duck Duck Go Search, Google, Lycos, MSN, and Yahoo.

Somewhere near the top of every Internet page is a search engine space where you can type keywords or key terms relating to the information you hope to find. That space is a rectangular box in which the word "Search" usually appears. One search engine is set as a default on your computer. However, you can easily opt to use other search engines and even to change your default.

After keying in the keywords or phrases you want to find, you click on "Search" or press the "Enter" key, and the search engine does its magic. It searches for web pages containing those keywords and terms and then displays its findings in order of perceived priority, based on the algorithms of the specific search engine. Someone might tell you he "Googled" a particular subject. This is his way of saying he searched for information relating to that subject on the Google search engine. Google, I should mention, is a very popular and useful search engine with many features that are helpful to the family history researcher.

Because different search engines work differently, it is a good idea to make most of your searches on more than one search engine. I also recommend that one of those search engines be Google because of its special design features.

Search engines make finding Internet-based sources relating to your ancestors easy if you use them wisely. To facilitate the most efficient use of a search engine, there are some things—call them tricks if you will—that some search engines, especially Google, use:

1. **Boolean logic.** Boolean logic is named for a nineteenth-century mathematician named George Boole. Based on this man's logic, every value is essentially either TRUE or FALSE. This logic is employed in a search engine by your use of the simple words **AND** and **OR**. The **AND** makes sure that both (or all) requested terms appear in every search result. For example, if I search for *Cox* **AND** *genealogy*, the results will include every web page where **both** of these words appear, regardless of where either one is located on the page. No pages will be listed in the search results except those where both terms are found. On a search engine that allows quotation marks to be used, I can also combine my Boolean logic

search by using quotation marks, such as *"Jehu Cox"* **AND** *Indiana* **AND** *genealogy*. With this search, results will show only those pages containing all three of my search terms.

Note that the use of **OR**, as in *Cox* **OR** *Cocks*, produces a result that includes every page where **either one or both** of my search terms is present. On the other hand, if my search terms are *Cox* **AND** *Cocks*, the results will include only those pages where **both** appear. I can also use quotation marks and include the search terms like *"family history"* **OR** *genealogy*. I can also add a locality to my search, such as *Cox* **OR** *Cocks genealogy* **OR** *"family history"* **AND** *"Knox County, Kentucky"*. A search like this one, utilizing both **AND** and **OR**, as well as quotation marks, facilitates a very precise search yet also allows for differing wording on the web pages.

2. **Punctuation and symbols**

   a. **Quotation marks:** Quotation marks (" ") can be used on some search engines, particularly Google. If you have a specific phrase or name you are seeking, quotation marks can be helpful. You can use a term like *"will indexes"*; the name of a place, such as *"Lincoln, Lancaster, Nebraska"*; or a specific name, like *"Jehu Cox"*. When quotation marks are used, the search engine returns only those results that contain the quoted phrase. Without the quotation marks, the search engine will look for each search word individually, and your search result will be quite different from the results of the quotation mark search. This means you must not use quotation marks unless you are looking for a very specific phrase—something, perhaps, like the title of a book or a specific place. Using quotation marks at the wrong time could cause you to mistakenly miss some significant search results. If the search engine recognizes quotation marks, you may find it helpful to almost always put names in quotes (like "Jehu Cox").

   b. **Minus sign:** The minus sign (–) is also a useful tool. If a search brings up a large quantity of sites with a common word you would like to exclude from your search results, that word can be eliminated from your search by adding it to the search query after a minus sign. For example, when I am searching for people with the surname *Greenwood*, I can add *–Lee* to my search query to remove the many results relating to the celebrity. Depending on my results, I may do subsequent searches with other common, unwanted names (or other words) preceded by the minus sign.

   c. **Wildcards (placeholders):** Wildcard operators in search engines allow us to make quite specific searches while considering usage and spelling variations at the same time. The wildcard (or placeholder for unknown words or terms) used on search engines is *always* an asterisk (*). It can be used in place of no words, one word, or multiple words, all at the same time. As an example, let us take my name. Instead of doing three separate searches for *Val Greenwood*, for *Val D. Greenwood*, and for *Val David Greenwood*, all three possibilities are covered by searching for *Val * Greenwood*.

You will soon discover that this type of search will also bring up results that have several words between Val and Greenwood, like *"Val Lankford's team at Greenwood King Properties."* This fact demonstrates the value of narrowing your searches by adding additional, strategic keywords.

d. **Number ranges:** Many search engines allow us to limit a search by including a number range—which in the case of family history searches includes a search within a specific date range. If I want to limit my search to a range of years, I can include that date range in my search engine query. For example, if I am interested in searching for Jehu Cox only between the years 1820 to 1840, I can add that date range to my search engine query. I do this by adding two dots (periods) between the two years of the desired search range, as *1820..1840*. This is a feature you may want to use in your search for records of a particular kind during a given time period and in a specific place (as *"tax lists" "Franklin County, Kentucky" 1810..1825*).

e. **Search operators:** I need also to mention those useful words that search engines call "search operators" that can be used for Google searches. These words can be added to the beginning of a search query to help narrow the results. Some operators are:

1) **site:** Use this search operator to limit your search to a specific website—usually a very large site that would not get much attention in a normal search engine query. For example: *site:Rootsweb. com* "Jehu Cox".

2) **related:** Use this operator to find sites similar to a site you already know about. For example: *related:FamilySearch.org "Jehu Cox"*.

3) **link:** Use this Google operator to find sites that have links to the site listed. For example: *link:myheritage.com "Jehu Cox"*.

4) **allinanchor:** With this operator, Google lets you search text that is used to create hyperlinks both within and between websites—text that is called anchor text. For example: *allinanchor:"Jehu Cox"*.

There are also other search operators. Go to *http://www.googleguide. com/advanced_operators_reference.html* for a list and explanations.

f. **The Google "Advanced Search" page.**[5] In your use of the Google search engine, you should be aware of a web page named "Google Advanced Search" (*google.com/advanced_search*). Your use of this page can simplify most of the search procedures we have talked about

---

[5] The information in this section comes from the web page "Advanced Search" *Google*, https://www.google.com/advanced_search (accessed December 20, 2016

thus far. You can fill in blanks on the page to customize your search to do just about anything you want to do in the way of searching. By filling in the designated blank boxes and then narrowing your search appropriately, your potential for making successful searches is very good.

You can choose to search for pages with:

All these words:
This exact word or phrase:
Any of these words:
None of these words:
Numbers ranging from: to:

When you have filled in the above blanks according to your desires, you can then further narrow your search results by:

Language: There are many options here.

Region: The regions listed are essentially countries—one of which is the United States (but not individual states).

Last update: You can choose to search pages that were last updated anytime, in the past 24 hours, in the past week, in the past month, or in the past year.

Site or domain: You have the option here, if you desire, to search one specific site (like wikipedia.org) or limit your results to one domain (like .edu, .org, or .gov).

Terms appearing: You have the option to search for terms based on where they appear on the page. Thus, you can opt to search for words in the page's title, in the page's text, in the page's URL, or in links to the page.

SafeSearch: The SafeSearch program allows you, if you choose, to display only the most relevant results or filter any explicit results from your search product. In fact, you can instruct SafeSearch to filter out sexually explicit content.

File type: You have the option to look for files in any format or in a specific format of your preference, including Adobe Acrobat PDF (.pdf), Adobe Postscript (.PS), Autodesk DEF. (.def.), Google Earth KUL (.kill), Google Earth KHZ (.kHz), Microsoft Excel (.axles), Microsoft PowerPoint (.pot), Microsoft Word (.doc), Rich Text Format (.rtf), or Shockwave Flash (.swift).

Usage rights: You can choose here to look for results based on what legal rights are required. The first option is not to filter by license at all (to just search). The other options allow searches for materials you are (a) free to use or share; (b) free to use or share, even commercially; (c) free to use, share, or modify; or (d) free to use, share, or modify, even commercially.

Using the Google Advanced Search page gives you amazing control over your Internet searches if you construct your search queries carefully. And, for additional assistance with your searches, the Advanced Search page also has links to some helpful tools. These include "Find pages that are similar to, or link to, a URL," "Search pages you've visited," "Use operators in the search box," and "Customize your search settings." As you explore this site, take time to click on these options and learn about the help they offer, and then employ those that fit the needs of your specific research.

g. Keyword helps for search engines

1) **Use specific keywords.** A search will be more successful when you add specific, narrowing keywords. You might profitably add a keyword like *died* after an ancestor's name if that is the object of your search. In fact, if you are looking for death information on an ancestor, you might profitably make multiple searches—one more search using *death*, another using *dead*, a fourth using *buried*, and a fifth using *burial*. You might even consider an additional search using the keyword *obituary*. If this seems cumbersome, another possibility is to do this in one search using the Boolean OR—*died* **OR** *death* **OR** *dead* **OR** *buried* **OR** *burial*. You will have more success when you narrow your searches by adding specific keywords to produce specific results. You need to be specific, innovative, and unafraid to experiment.

2) **Places as keywords.** Keywords in your search should include places whenever possible—both narrow and broad. One search might include the name of the state where a sought-after event took place while another search might narrow that search to the county, and still another might zero in on the specific town or city. Much depends on what you already know and the nature of what you are trying to learn.

3) **Clues from previous searches.** Additional sources of information, and sometimes even additional searches, might be suggested by the results of your previous search. For example, the name of a library or historical society within the county or town of your search might appear in several of your search results. Such an institution might well have information about local residents, including your ancestor. Also, if the name of a local church appears in your search results,

consider that the records of that church might be an additional source of information.

4) **More than one search engine.** Though Google is a search engine you should always use, it is wise to utilize more than one search engine; each one uses a different program, which can produce different results.

5) **The five Ws.** One researcher, as part of his presentation at the 2016 RootsTech conference, suggested that search queries should be built around the five W questions: Who, What, Where, When, and Why. He suggested that you first write a sentence about the specific information you are seeking and then take the main words from that sentence to determine the keywords of your query.[6] For example, you might write, "I want to know if Robert Atkins was living in Gainesville, Cooke County, Texas, in 1886." From that, you might pick the keywords for your search engine query as *"Robert Atkins"* AND *"Gainesville, Texas"* AND *1886*.

6) **Capitals not required.** In making search engine queries it does not matter whether you use capital letters or lowercase letters or any mixture of them—even for proper nouns. The search engine cannot tell the difference.

7) **"Stop words" ignored.** Your search engine queries need not include what are called "stop words." Stop words are the more common words in the language that are believed to have no significance by themselves; they are mostly adjectives and prepositions. If you include them, the search engine ignores them unless they are included in a phrase within quotation marks. There are two different lists of stop words at http://xpo6.com/list-of-english-stop-words/.

8) **Abbreviated place names as keywords.** When you include place names in your search engine queries, you should find comfort in the fact that most search engines will give you results that include abbreviations and other alternate spellings automatically with your place queries.

9) **Intuitive search engines.** Search engines are designed to be intuitive, thus recognizing misspelled and mistyped words (and abbreviated place names as noted in item 8) in your queries. When you misspell words in your search queries, the search engine usually detects the misspellings and corrects them, working much like the spell checker on your word-processing program.

C. Social media

Social media are difficult to define because there is so much variation in the nature of the various websites within the category. A good basic definition is

---

[6] Barry J. Ewell, Presentation at RootsTech Conference in Salt Lake City on 6 February 2016 entitled "Using Google."

that they are websites for networking with other users in online communities to share information and ideas. This sharing can include personal messages, videos, pictures, and practically anything else that is shareable.

The September 2015 issue of *Family Tree* magazine listed what its staff considered the five most important social media websites relating to family history. The list included Facebook, Family.me, Flickr, Pinterest, and WeRelate.[7] That year, 2015, was the sixteenth year in a row that the magazine had published its list of the 101 best family history websites. The list has changed over the years, and will change in the future.

Let us look at the five social media sites on the 2015 list. They are listed here in alphabetical order:

1. **Facebook** (*https://www.facebook.com*). Facebook is a social-networking site where relatives and family members can connect to share information, research results, and copies of photographs and documents. Also, every family history site you can think of has a Facebook page, as does every family history software program.

   A blog post in the December 18, 2016, *FamilySearch User Newsletter* made the following observations about Facebook and family history:

   > You already know that Facebook is a great place to share news and photos and to connect with old friends. However, did you know that Facebook can also be a great place to connect with your ancestors—or at least to find the answers you need to connect your ancestors to your family tree? With FamilySearch's Facebook groups, you can interact with other people tracing their families who lived in the same areas as your family and perhaps even break through your brick wall or help others break through theirs.
   >
   > FamilySearch's [Facebook] overview page, called "Genealogy Help on Facebook," is a great starting point. Mostly organized by location, it contains links to a variety of Facebook groups covering everything from Iowa to Thailand to genetics. Some groups included on the site are run through FamilySearch and some aren't, but all offer opportunities to expand your genealogy knowledge—and success![8]

2. **Family.me** (*https://www.family.me/*). Family.me has the stated goal of promoting collaboration among family members. It combines online family trees with social networking for the simple stated purpose of bringing relatives together.

---

[7] David A. Fryxell, "Best Social Media Genealogy Websites of 2015," *Family Tree Magazine,* 21 July 2015, http://www.familytreemagazine.com/article/best-social-media-genealogy-websites-2015 (accessed October 10, 2016). Note that this category was not included in the 2016 version of "best" websites.

[8] Leslie Albrecht Huber, "Finding Your Ancestors on Facebook, *Family History User Newsletter,* FamilySearch, August 16, 2016, https://mail.google.com/mail/u/0/#inbox/15911e3b30db10a1 (accessed December 18, 2016). As this article indicates, FamilySearch has a Facebook wiki at https://familysearch.org/wiki/en/Genealogy_Help_on_Facebook where there are hyperlinks to many Facebook regional research groups, all of which are sponsored by FamilySearch.

3. **Flickr** (*https://www.flickr.com/*). Flickr is a site where people share photographs and where they can find and download pictures from a variety of sources, such as the National Archives, the Smithsonian, and other significant sources.

4. **Pinterest** (*https://www.pinterest.com/*). Pinterest has a format similar to a scrapbook where images can be shared and borrowed. It allows you to share family photographs, copies of documents, interesting thoughts, maps, and just about anything else you want.

5. **WeRelate** (*http://www.werelate.org/*). WeRelate is sponsored by the Foundation for On-line Genealogy and the Allen County Public Library (ACPL). It is actually a wiki—one of the world's largest family history wikis—where users have posted pages on some 2.75 million people (2016). There is a discussion about wikis later in this chapter.

Yet another important social media website that I need to mention is **My-Heritage** (*https://www.myheritage.com/*). Details concerning MyHeritage are in Chapter 10, but I need to say here that this website was designed to function as a social media site. This approach differs from other major family history sites that function on the cloud, as I will discuss later. The MyHeritage developers believe their social media design to be faster and more efficient.

D. Wikis

"Wiki" is a Hawaiian word meaning "quick." The Honolulu airport gave the name "WikiWiki" to their shuttle buses. On the Internet, the term "WikiWikiWeb"—shortened in common usage to just "wiki"—is used to describe websites that are open for input and discussion by their users. To become an authorized wiki participant, a person is required to register with the wiki involved. Having registered, he can contribute new information, and he can delete and/or edit information provided by others. Most people are familiar with the popular Wikipedia website because it frequently comes out near the top of many search engine queries. Though Wikipedia is often a good place to start one's research on many subjects, it is seldom the best place to finish that research.

There are three types of family history wikis:

- **Family tree wikis:** those that relate specifically to pedigrees and lineages
- **Reference wikis:** those that provide useful background and pertinent "how to" information that is helpful to research
- **Specific topic wikis:** those that relate to precise subjects

Many wikis are moderated, which means the site owner must approve all content before it can appear on the wiki. The top wikis also request that those who provide content also provide source citations for their content.

The best thing about a wiki is that anyone with relevant information can publish that information on the wiki and make it available to everyone else.

And, sadly, that is also the worst thing about a wiki. There is the benefit of a wonderfully broad contributor base, but there is also very limited authority control, and contributors need not be experts. Remember that opinions are not facts, and the repeated assertion of those opinions does not make them any more accurate. We know that from our family history research.

Some of the more popular wikis in each of our three categories include the following:

1. **Family tree wikis**

   - **Family Tree** on the FamilySearch website (*https://familysearch. org/*) is the largest and most widely used family tree wiki. Its use is free, and as of May 2016, there were about 1.1 billion records on this wiki.[9] The fact that this program is a wiki is the reason I do not recommend that you make Family Tree the place to maintain your personal official tree. Keep a copy of your tree there, of course, but realize that it is vulnerable and other people can make changes at any time. There is much more information about Family Tree and the FamilySearch website in Chapter 10.

   - **WikiTree** (*https://www.wikitree.com/*) is a popular, fast-growing, and free wiki with more than 12,866,621 profiles included, edited by 387,678 genealogists/contributors in 2016.[10]

   - **WeRelate** (*http://www.werelate.org/*) is another large and significant family tree wiki. It had more than 2,750,000 people on its pages in 2016. Note that we mentioned this site earlier in the chapter when we discussed its function as a social media site.

   - **Familypedia** (*http://familypedia.wikia.com*) claimed in 2016 to be working on 216,200 articles and 331,436 other pages,[11] including many family historical accounts. The focus of this wiki is to capture the details of the lives of our ancestors and to provide information about the historical and social context in which they lived.

   - Other family tree wikis include **Ancient Faces** (*http://www.ancient-faces.com/*) and **Genealogy Today** (*http://wiki.genealogytoday. com/*).

2. **Reference ("how to") wikis**

   - The **FamilySearch wiki** (*https://familysearch.org/wiki/*) is one of the most important wikis in the reference category. Information from this wiki has been included in many places in this book, and there is also a more detailed explanation about it in our discussion of the Fami-

---

[9] "Online records," FamilySearch.org, July 21, 2016, https://familysearch.org/wiki/en/Family Search.org (accessed December 24, 2016).

[10] "WikiTree [Homepage]," WikiTree, https://www.wikitree.com/ (accessed December 24, 2016).

[11] "Welcome to Familypedia!" Familypedia, http://familypedia.wikia.com/wiki/Family_History_ and_Genealogy_Wiki (accessed December 24, 2016).

lySearch website in Chapter 10. As of July 2016, there were 84,966 articles on the English FamilySearch wiki,[12] most of them written by the Family History Library staff.

- The **Ancestry family history wiki** (*http://www.ancestry.com/wiki/*) is also significant. Included on this wiki are two books published by Ancestry: *The Source* and *Red Book*. There are also other significant Ancestry materials as well as articles written by site users. The approximately 8,500 articles (in 2015) are available for general use.

- The **Encyclopedia of Genealogy** (*http://eogen.com/*) is another useful wiki, created by many contributing genealogists as a guide to research procedures. There is an alphabetical index to subjects.

3. **Specific topic wikis**

Here I will give just three examples:

- **Our Archives (U.S. National Archives Wiki for Researchers)** (*http://www.ourarchives.wikispaces.net/*) is a valuable subscription-only wiki. You can subscribe by clicking on "Participate" on the right side of the homepage. You will receive further instruction after entering a username, a password, and your e-mail address.

- **Build a Better GEDCOM** (*http://bettergedcom.wikispaces.com/*) is another popular wiki that provides information about working with GEDCOM files.

- **TNG (The Next Generation) Wiki** (*http://tng.lythgoes.net/wiki/*) is a community effort to organize extended help files for the latest version of the TNG website.[13]

E. Genealogy/family history blogs

The word "blog," now so common in our computer jargon, is short for weblog. A blog can best be described as a personal online journal that is frequently updated and intended for wide-ranging public consumption. A typical blog is a single-page website where entries reflecting the purpose of the blog's host are posted frequently; the most recent entry is posted at the top of the page. Comments and feedback from blog readers are usually (but not always) welcome, and the blog's author is called a blogger. Many blogs use RSS[14] (a content distribution tool) to "publish" or distribute some of their content. An RSS feed delivers each new blog entry (or a notice of that new entry) to subscribers' e-mail accounts.

---

[12] "FamilySearch Wiki: Featured Articles," FamilySearch, July 18, 2016, https://familysearch. org/wiki/en/ FamilySearch_Wiki:Featured_Articles (accessed February 6, 2017).

[13] The TNG (The Next Generation) website (http://lythgoes.net/genealogy/software.php) is an innovative and intuitive site where a subscriber (for $32.99 in 2016) can create his own family history website without the limitations common to most websites as they relate to format, additions, deletions, and edits.

[14] RSS stands for Really Simple Syndication.

Here is a list of a few popular family history blogs:

Ancestry Insider
Boston 1775
Climbing My Family Tree
Creative Genealogy
Dear Myrtle's Genealogy Blog
Eastman's Online Genealogy
　　Newsletter
GeneaBloggers
Genealogy Blog
Genealogy Gems

Genealogy Guys
Genea-musings
The Genealogue
The Genetic Genealogist
The Practical Archivist
Think Genealogy
YouTube (There are hundreds of family history video presentations here.)

You can locate most blogs by entering the blog's name into the search box of an Internet search engine. Put the name in quotation marks.

F. The cloud

The term "cloud" is now in common usage in the technology world. Though the expression is common, there is, in fact, no real cloud. That which we have come to call the cloud is nothing more than Internet-based computing. The files involved are not located on your computer hard drive but rather on a remote server (or group of servers) where you create, store, and access your files. You have direct access to those cloud-based files on any and all of your electronic devices that have Internet access (desktop, laptop, tablet, and smartphone).

As stated, files maintained on the cloud are not on your computer hard drive, though you can create a copy there of any part of the file—or of all the file if you desire. Not only can you create files on the cloud, you can copy photographs and documents into your cloud files. The cloud allows you to work directly on the remote server(s)—wherever you are and on whatever device you are using, all with instantaneous backup. Using your cloud app, you can also take pictures on your mobile device and they will be on the cloud.

The cloud, in essence, synchronizes your computer files across multiple devices. Everything you put on the cloud is backed up automatically as you create it, and the cloud's very nature makes it easy for you to allow anyone you choose to have access to it, use it, and edit it—or not. Sometimes this collaboration is good and sometimes bad, but it is a significant advantage to be able to share a large file with a relative in this very simple way.

There is also an advantage in not taking up space with large files on your computer hard drive, and this off-site storage is relatively inexpensive. Many cloud programs provide a basic level of storage (usually around five gigabytes [GB]) at no cost, and even most of the premium accounts have reasonable fees.

There are some so-called cloud services that are exceptions to what I have just explained. These exceptions are technically not cloud programs but rather computer backup programs that are established on the remote servers. They back up designated files that are on your computer hard drive and then—with the proper apps—allow access to those back-up files on your mobile devices as well as on the computers and devices of anyone else you authorize.

Some of the clouds popular with family history researchers include the following:

- Amazon Cloud Drive (*https://www.amazon.com/clouddrive*)—unlimited photo storage plus 5 GB for videos and files for $59.99/year (2017). There is a three-month free trial period, and it is free to those with an Amazon Prime membership.
- Backblaze (*https://www.backblaze.com/cloud-backup.html*)—automatically backs up files on your hard drive for $5/month (2017)—unlimited files and file size. This program is not a true cloud but online backup of computer files. There is a 15-day free trial period.
- Dropbox (*https://www.dropbox.com*)—$8.25/month for individuals for 1 TB (1,000 GB) of space (2017). Dropbox offers a 30-day free trial.
- Evernote Basic (*https://evernote.com/basic*)—is free (2017) and allows 60 MB of new uploads/month. (Note that Evernote Plus [*https://evernote .com/plus*] for $34.99/year [2017] allows 1 GB new uploads/month. Evernote Premium [*https://evernote.com/premium*] costs $69.99/year [2017] and allows unlimited uploads.) There is further discussion relating to Evernote as a program for keeping research notes in Chapter 7.
- Google Drive (*https://www.google.com/drive/*)—is popular because it is free for the first 15 GB of storage as part of your Google account; 100 GBs of storage are available for $1.99/month and 1 TB for $9.99/month (2017).
- iCloud (*https://www.icloud.com/*) —5 GB of storage is free. iCloud uses reliable cloud technology and can be used with either Apple or Windows computers, but peripheral devices must be Apple products.
- Mozy Home (*http://mozy.com/*)—2 GB of storage is free, a 50 GB account is $5.99/month, and a 125 GB account is $9.99/month (2017).
- One Drive (*https://onedrive.live.com/about/en-us/plans/*)—5 GB of storage is free, and 50 GB account is $1.99/month (2017).
- pCloud (*https://www.pcloud.com*)—20 GB of storage is free, a 500 GB account is $47.88/year, and a 2 TB account is $95.88/year (2017). Copies of your encrypted files are maintained on five servers; pCloud provides online storage for all of your photos, documents, and research related documents and makes them accessible whenever and wherever you need them. It has apps for every type of device with Internet access.
- ResearchTies (*http://researchties.com/*)—not a cloud program *per se*, but a program that operates on the cloud for keeping research notes and records. It has 10 GB storage space and costs $30/year (2016). Chapter 7 has additional information.

- SugarSync (*https://www.sugarsync.com*)—100 GB of storage for $7.49/ month, 250 GB for $9.99/month, and 500 GB for $18.95/month (2017).

I want to make just one observation about Dropbox. The program has been widely used and is useful on any computer, but there is some apprehension about its use for family history because it was designed primarily for file sharing and not for long-term file storage, which must be an important consideration.

Also, though Mozy and Backblaze are not true clouds but computer backup programs, that difference is minimized to some extent by apps that allow online access to the backed-up files on your mobile devices. In fact, this may be an advantage in many cases because the files operate on your own computer hard drive. It is not exactly like working directly on the cloud but, with the available apps, most advantages of the cloud are present.

It is noteworthy that both the Ancestry and FamilySearch websites are cloud-based resources and, with the right apps, can—like other cloud-based programs—be accessed on any mobile device with an Internet connection.

To be fair in my coverage of cloud technology, I need to make it clear that there are both positive and negative arguments relating to use of the cloud. In addition to the things already mentioned, it is worth noting that when you work on the cloud, an instantaneous off-site backup is made of everything you do. You are fully protected from a crash of your computer hard drive and the consequent loss of files.

On the negative side, you should also understand that there are some questions about cloud security. How you respond to these concerns is a personal matter. However, those who believe the cloud is the final answer to all of their record-keeping problems need to know that there are potential issues. Based on a report from the Cloud Security Alliance, one website published a list of nine security concerns relating to cloud technology. I have listed three of those concerns here because (in my opinion) they are the ones most relevant to family history usage. The concerns listed are not necessarily in order of importance:

- *Data breach:* If a multi-tenant cloud service database is not designed properly, a flaw in the application of one client could give an attacker access to the data of every client of that service.
- *Data loss:* A hacker could delete data out of spite or just for recreation. Also, a careless service provider, a fire, or a natural disaster (such as flood or earthquake) might cause information loss. Remember, also, that we are talking about the Internet, which is notoriously insecure.
- *Shared technology vulnerabilities:* Cloud service providers share their infrastructure, platforms, and applications as they accommodate many clients on the same servers. The very nature of these services suggests that an important element can be easily compromised and expose the files of all clients to the possibility of compromise and breach if the

designer failed to ensure that system components have reliable isolation features.[15]

In addition to these potential security risks—which may, in fact, be remote with the current state of technology and the care taken by competent service suppliers—I believe there is one other, more serious, risk that every family history researcher needs to recognize and make plans to address if he chooses to work on the cloud. That risk arises from the fact that most cloud technology operates and is accessible based on the payment of subscription fees. That being true, consider what might happen to your records when you are no longer subscribed (or even when your account might accidentally lapse). In essence, every account on the cloud has a built-in divorce; your account on the cloud will end at some point in one way or another.

With that in mind, also remember that none of us is going to live forever. After you are gone—or, even after you become old and forgetful—you will want your family to have access to your records. What will become of your cloud files? Where will those files be then? Will they survive the "divorce"?

If you determine to maintain your records on the cloud, I suggest that you make sure that whatever is on your cloud is also on your computer hard drive. And, at the risk of sounding distrustful, I also suggest that you keep all of your family history note files in some other safe place—perhaps on a flash drive that is stored offsite.

If you use cloud technology to keep your family history records, you should do so with a full understanding of both the benefits and the concerns. I have talked about the concerns because you need to be aware of them as you proceed. They are real, but so are the benefits.

As you use cloud technology, do so in a way that maximizes the benefits and minimizes the concerns. I also want to make it clear that, aside from the benefit of accessing your files anywhere, anytime, and on any mobile device with Internet access, the most important benefit might be the ability the cloud gives you to work seamlessly with others in a cooperative effort.

As long as you maintain your working files and copies of source documents so they cannot be lost, as we discussed in Chapter 7, you may feel comfortable and secure in your use of cloud technology.

A discussion of many of the clouds used for family history, plus a glossary of cloud-related terms, prepared by Thomas MacEntee is available at *https:// familytreewebinars.com/pdf/webinar-6556.pdf*. Note, however, that this discussion was prepared in 2012 and, like everything else, is becoming outdated.

To learn more about specific clouds and their apps, you can also go to the websites of those clouds you want to consider and read their explanations.

---

[15] Charles Babcock, "9 Worst Cloud Security Threats," *Information Week.* March 3, 2014. http://www.informationweek.com/cloud/infrastructure-as-a-service/9-worst-cloud-security-threats/d/d-id/1114085 (accessed December 26, 2016). You can go to the article if you are interested in the other six concerns.

If you decide to sign up for a cloud program, you can do it on the cloud's website. The URLs for those clouds most used for family history were listed earlier in this section.

G. DNA

DNA (deoxyribonucleic acid) is a code of the genetic material in the cells in all life forms. Your DNA determines who you are and the nature of your physical characteristics. It is inside the nucleus of nearly every cell of every person and serves as the control center of the cell. It consists of twenty-three pairs of chromosomes, which are arranged in long (relatively speaking) strings of DNA. These strings are arranged in pairs like double twisted ladders called a double helix, and one chromosome from each of the twenty-three pairs was inherited from each of your parents. The two chromosomes of each pair (except for the X and Y sex chromosomes) contain the same genes.

Each rung of the "ladder" is made up of a pair of interlocking units called bases. These bases are identified by the four letters of the DNA alphabet: A, T, G, and C. A always pairs with T, and G always pairs with C. A person's approximately 20,000 genes written in the DNA alphabet provide directions to his cells about how to function and what traits to manifest. The DNA itself is composed of chemical building blocks containing primarily phosphate and sugar.

All of the information in a person's DNA is known as his genome, which might be likened to a complete DNA instruction manual. The phenomenal amount of information contained in a genome includes information about every protein a person's body will ever synthesize—about 30,000 of them.

A typical human cell contains about two meters of DNA. To write out the sequence of one small human gene in the four-letter DNA alphabet (that is the A, T, G, and C alphabet) would take a fourth of a page of text. And to write out the complete sequence of all the base units in a human's genome, we are told, would require more than a thousand books.[16]

So, what does all of this have to do with your family history? It is important because it is possible to use DNA to trace your origin and the origins of your ancestors. This is true because of three kinds of DNA markers:

1. The paired chromosomes of the genome—the genetic markers known as *autosomes*—half of which you received from your father and half from your mother

2. The *Y chromosome* a male child received from his father

3. The *Mitochondrial DNA (mtDNA)* passed to every child from his or her mother

---

[16] See B. Alberts, A. Johnson, J. Lewis, et al., "The Structure and Function of DNA," *Molecular Biology of the Cell*. 4th ed., Garland Science, 2002, https://www.ncbi.nlm.nih.gov/books/NBK26821/ (accessed October 13, 2016).

With the exception of the Y chromosome and the mtDNA, all other chromosomes that mothers and fathers pass on to their children are combinations of the chromosomes of those parents—one of each from each parent. However, a father's Y chromosome is handed down unchanged to his sons, his X chromosome is handed down unchanged to his daughters, and one of a mother's X chromosomes and her mtDNA are passed unaltered to each of her children, both sons and daughters.

Each person receives only half of each of his parents' chromosomes and the attached DNA, and no two individuals, except identical twins, have all of the same DNA. Identical twins have identical DNA because they came from the same egg that was fertilized by the same sperm. Every child that is born (and this includes you and me when we were born) gets half of each of his parents DNA, while the other half is lost. Our brothers and sisters, if we have any, will each have different assortments of our parents' chromosomes and DNA. This reality shows the importance of having DNA tests for many people—and usually for the oldest people first because much of the DNA record is lost with each new generation.

The Y chromosome can be used to determine the origins of paternal (male) ancestors, and mtDNA markers can be used to identify the origins of maternal (female) ancestors. A perfect match found to another person's mtDNA test results indicates a shared recent female ancestor. It might also identify a link—perhaps distant—to a specific geographic region.

Autosomal DNA tests are used to make matches of both males and females and are the most widely used tests today. In addition to identifying close relatives, they can help you learn to which of over 200 populations you have the greatest similarity and what proportions of your ancestry come from various continental groups. This capability—and every other identifying capability—will become better as more people complete DNA testing.

Genealogical DNA tests are available today from four providers:

- 23andMe (*https://www.23andme.com/*)
- Ancestry DNA (*https://www.ancestry.com/dna/*)
- Family Tree DNA (https://www.familytreedna.com/)
- Living DNA (*https://www.livingdna.com/*)
- MyHeritage DNA (*https://www.myheritage.com/dna/277523481*)

There will, no doubt, be other providers who will become involved as time passes. If you look at the wiki website of the International Society of Genetic Genealogy (*https://isogg.org/wiki/List_of_DNA_testing_companies*), you will get a feel for what the future might hold in this area. This society also has a chart (online at *https://isogg.org/wiki/Autosomal_DNA_testing_comparison_chart*) that compares the features and benefits of the major DNA testing providers and of their respective tests. This may be helpful as you look at the pros and cons of DNA testing.

As of this writing, only Family Tree DNA and Living DNA (which is British) provide the Y chromosome and the mtDNA tests. Though some others have provided these tests in the past, the tests of all other organizations presently check only for autosomal DNA matches—matches in the twenty-two pairs of each person's numbered non-sex chromosomes. (The sex chromosomes are X and Y for a male, and two X's for a female). Autosomal tests are better suited for fishing expeditions than the Y chromosome and mtDNA tests.

If you opt for the mtDNA or the Y chromosome tests, order the full sequence test for mtDNA and the 67-marker test for the Y chromosome. Though these tests are more expensive, they provide the best coverage for the price. They have the potential of providing much more information than the more limited tests.

Also, as you consider whether you should have a DNA test, remember that a specific connection can be made only with others who have also had a test completed by the same testing organization. So, naturally, as more people have tests, there is a better chance of obtaining meaningful matches. The ideal situation, of course, would be for everyone to have a DNA test, thus guaranteeing useful results. Remember that the closer the relative, the better the match.

If everyone had a DNA test performed by the same testing organization, the result could be wonderful. Unfortunately, it is not likely that this will ever happen short of government mandate because DNA testing is a profit-making business. Not only do the testing companies not want to merge their businesses, it seems unlikely they will ever agree to share test results with each other. We can only dream of such a result. Nevertheless, in spite of these limitations, many people are getting positive results from their DNA tests.

Incidentally, DNA testing is painless; most samples are obtained with either a saliva sample or a cheek swab. And there are often special promotions that offer tests at reduced prices.

H. Message boards, forums, and special projects

A. Message boards and forums. Message boards and forums are similar kinds of websites. Both are sites where people ask questions seeking help in finding their ancestors. Message boards relate primarily to surnames and people, while forums relate mostly to "how to" issues and places. In the process of asking and answering questions, of course, the users engage in online conversations where they can, hopefully, further the family history research of both themselves and others.

Message boards have become very popular on the Internet since the 1990s. You can find a message board for just about any surname. In the days before the Internet, we called them queries and put them in newspaper columns and genealogy magazines, but this whole phenomenon is much bigger now. Ancestry, for example, has an important message board site at *https://www.boards.ancestry.com/surname.aspx?* that claims to have more than 25 million posts on more than 198,000 boards.

The website known as Genealogy.com has a feature it calls "GenForum" with more than 14,000 online forums (2017). These include forums for locations, genealogy topics, and surnames (*http://www.genealogy.com/forum/*).

RootsWeb (*http://boards.rootsweb.com/*), a website now owned by Ancestry, provides an alternate way to get to those same 25 million posts on more than 198,000 boards that are on the Ancestry site. RootsWeb's website lists them as "Uncategorized Mailing Lists." Though the URL is much too long to include here, you can get to the site quite easily by entering the search term, "uncategorized genealogy mailing lists" in your Internet search engine. I should also mention that you can use the "Site:" search operator as part of a search engine query to limit your search to the RootsWeb site, as explained earlier in this chapter.

Another useful resource is the Cyndi's List page entitled "Queries & Message Boards—General Resources" (*http://cyndislist.com/queries/general*). Here you will find a clickable list of numerous message boards and forums, many of them relating to research and families in the United States. Among the resources listed by Cyndi are "Family Tree Circles" (*http://www.family-treecircles.com/*) and "Genealogy Senses Forum" (*http://genealogy-senses.proboards.com/*). The "Site:" search operator can also be used to search a message board—any message board—for your ancestors.

B. Special projects. From the very beginning of the Internet, there have been projects of various kinds seeking to further the work of genealogists and family history researchers. Many of these have gone by the wayside or have been absorbed by other sites as procedures and facilities have been enhanced. If you were to look at the third edition of this book and try to find all of the websites cited there, you would find that many (perhaps most) of them no longer exist, perhaps because they have become irrelevant or, perhaps, for other reasons. Also, as noted, you will see that some others have become affiliates of larger, more prominent sites.

One important special project is the USGenWeb Project (*http://usgenweb.com/*). This project was begun in 1996 by a group of dedicated volunteers with the goal of establishing a free link to every county and state in America as well as to some special national projects. The project is still going forward, entirely with the work of volunteers. There is additional information on the GenWeb Project in Chapter 6.

I. Family history websites

This is the subject and focus of the next chapter of this book.

III. CONCLUSION

In this chapter, I have introduced various definitions and resources as they relate to family history and modern technology. These are fundamental to your involvement in meaningful family history research today. In Chapter 10, I will discuss some basic principles that will apply as you utilize the various family history websites and the numerous resources available on the Internet. I will also discuss some basic details of research on some of the more significant websites as we consider the resources you will be using as you continue your quest to become a successful family history researcher.

10

Family History on the Internet

Much has happened in the world of technology since the third edition of this book, and most of what has happened has been positive. Technological advances that relate to family history have come very rapidly and in ways that most of us never dreamed were possible. In my opinion, the greatest technological advances of recent years, as they relate to family history research, are the following:

- The digitizing of records and placing the digitized images of those records in databases on Internet websites.
- The indexing of those digitized records to create clickable links between the index entries and the specific digitized images in the records to which they relate. It is worth observing, however, that though much indexing has been done, the indexing of important digitized record collections is still in its infancy. It is an ongoing process, and there is still a very long way to go.

I have used two words here that I need to define before we go further; it is important that you understand their meaning as they are critical to the understanding of significant family history resources. The words of concern are *digitize* and *database*. To digitize means to convert a simple image—a printed page, a picture, or an image from a roll of microfilm or sheet of microfiche—into a picture that can be displayed and read on a computer screen. This picture/image is a digitized image.

A computer database is an accumulated work containing a large amount of data—such as a book or a roll of microfilm—that has been converted into digitized images in computer-readable form for quick access. Once converted, any and every specific, individual, computer-based picture (digitized image) from that converted work can be observed on a computer screen. For the family history researcher, the work involved might consist of birth records from a particular state, a book of wills from a county courthouse, or some other record containing valuable family history information. When such a database has been indexed, links between the index and the images on the database allow direct immediate access to any entry on any page of that database.

I. SIGNIFICANT STEPS AND A CURRENT PERSPECTIVE

Because countless indexing projects have been completed, and many more are ongoing, many billions (with a "B") of names already appear in the indexes to those records on various family history websites. And the digitized record containing any and every name in the index can be readily retrieved on your computer screen with the simple click of your computer mouse.

When you use an index on one of these family history websites to search for an ancestor, every name from the indexed database, with its associated identifiers, that in some way matches your search criteria is displayed on your computer screen. The names on this list of possible matches are prioritized so that the best and the most probable matches are located closest to the top of the list. When you determine that an entry on the list might be the person you seek, you can click your mouse and go directly to the digitized image of that specific entry. It is exciting when your quest is rewarded with a viable connection, and it is even more exciting—looking at the issue from a broader perspective—to realize that the number of both digitized records and indexes to those records is rapidly growing.

The exact extent of the records on these amazing websites is unclear due to the diverse nature of the documents involved. Because of that diversity, there is no agreement on what actually constitutes a record.[1] Though no one can authoritatively tell us how many records there are, it is a very large number. At the time of this writing in 2016, four major family history sites (I have listed them alphabetically) claimed to have the following numbers of records:

Ancestry.com	More than 16 billion records, with 1 million records added daily.
FamilySearch.org	5.39 billion searchable names in historical records.
FindMyPast.com	More than 2.9 billion historical records. In March 2016 a FindMyPast subsidiary site named *Mocavo* was integrated into this site. (At the time of this writing, this site's emphasis was not on U.S. records, but many more U.S. records were being added—850 million records in 2015. In 2016, FindMyPast claimed

---

[1] I do not say this to be critical but merely to point out that this is a very difficult question because of the nature and variety of the documents involved.

to have "the largest exclusive collection of U.S. marriage records anywhere online.")

MyHeritage.com   More than 7 billion records (7,187,880,490 in January 2017).

Though these are currently the major family history websites, there are many others. And, no matter how records are counted or what the term "record" actually means in this context, there are numerous websites—and many of them are very significant.

Though it seems obvious, I also emphasize that many important—even critical—records are not available on any of these websites. We know that with the passage of time, many more significant digitized records from many more places are going to be available. However, it is not realistic to think that there will ever be a time when every record required by our research will be digitized and indexed. Although we wish blanket coverage were possible, such is not a reasonable expectation; there are just too many records.

A few other sites with notable record collections as of this writing include:

AmericanAncestors.org   This is the website of the New England Historic Genealogical Society. It claims to have more than 1 billion records, including a large collection of early American records and published genealogical journals and magazines. The site also has links to, and partnerships with, other major sites with large collections.

Archives.com   This site claims to have more than 4.8 billion photos, newspapers, and vital records.

CyndisList.com/categories   This site has a significant collection of records, as well as links to other major sites with large collections.

FamilyHistory.com   This site belongs to Ancestry and claims to have 26,000 family history databases.

FamilyLink.com   This site belongs to MyHeritage and claims to have more than a billion family tree records.

Fold3.com   This site belongs to Ancestry and specializes in military records. It claims to have nearly 475 million records.

Genealogy.com   This site has no original documents but claims to have "hundreds of articles, thousands of Family Tree Maker trees, hundreds of thousands of forums and millions of posts."

Genealogybank.com   This site claims to have the largest collection of newspaper obituaries online, with more than 2 billion digitized and indexed newspaper records.

MooseRoots.com	This site claims to have more than a billion records, primarily census records, vital records (birth, marriage/divorce, and death), immigration records, and military collections. Site use is free.
Newspapers.com	This site belongs to Ancestry and claims to have digitized images of 4,400 newspapers with 216 million pages.
Rootsweb (Rootsweb. ancestry.com)	This site belongs to Ancestry and has extensive collections, some of which can be used without a paid subscription. Most of the collections at Rootsweb represent the research of others rather than original sources, but the site also claims to have millions of original source documents.

This list is short when you consider the vast number of websites now devoted exclusively to family history, as well as those catering in various ways to the interests of family history researchers.

In September 2016, *Family Tree Magazine* published its seventeenth annual list of what staff members consider the 101 best genealogy websites. The 2016 list is divided into fifteen categories:

1. Best Big Genealogy Websites
2. Best Websites for Exploring Your Ancestors' Lives
3. Best US Genealogy Websites
4. Best Websites for Sharing Your Genealogy
5. Best Websites for Putting Ancestors on the Map
6. Best Genealogy Library Websites
7. Best Websites for Finding Ancestors in Old Newspapers
8. Best African-American Genealogy Websites
9. Best Cemetery and Directory Sites for Genealogy
10. Best Tech Tools for Genealogy in 2016
11. Best Immigrant Ancestors Websites
12. Best British and Irish Genealogy Websites
13. Best International Genealogy Websites
14. Best Genetic Genealogy Websites
15. Best Genealogy News and Help Websites.[2]

Over the seventeen years these lists have been published, the number of categories, the categories themselves, and many of the listed websites have

---

[2] David A. Fryxell, "101 Best Websites for Genealogy in 2016," *Family Tree Magazine*, 17, no. 6, 2016, http://www.familytreemagazine.com/article/101-best-websites-2016 (accessed December 3, 2016).

changed. Such will also surely be true in the future. You will want to look at the most current list of "Best" genealogy/family history websites at *http://www.familytreemagazine.com* whenever you happen to be reading this book. It is certain that some categories and websites will be different.

For your information, here are the twelve websites on the 2016 "Best US Genealogy Websites" list. They are listed here alphabetically:

Access Genealogy (*https://www.accessgenealogy.com/*)
American Ancestors (*https://www.americanancestors.org/index.aspx*)
American Battle Monuments Commission (*https://www.abmc.gov/*)
BYU Idaho Family History (*http://abish.byui.edu/specialcollections/*)
Civil War Soldiers & Sailors System (*https://www.nps.gov/civilwar/*
    soldiers-and-sailors-database.htm)
CSI: Dixie (*https://csidixie.org/*)
Daughters of the American Revolution (*http://www.dar.org/*)
Fold3 (*https://www.fold3.com/*)
HeritageQuest Online (*http://www.heritagequestonline.com/*)
National Archives and Records Administration (*https://www.archives.gov/*)
Nationwide Gravesite Locator (*http://gravelocator.cem.va.gov/*)
USGenWeb (*http://usgenweb.org/*)[3]

You should also be aware of a Google-sponsored site called Family History Websites, compiled and maintained by Kip Sperry of the Brigham Young University family history faculty (now retired). This site's URL is *https://sites.google.com/site/familyhistoryinternetsites/*. As of December 2016, there were 259 clickable websites listed in thirteen categories on this site, each category relating in some way to family history. Note, however, that many of the sites are listed in multiple categories because of the nature of the groupings. Also, note that the site has some bias toward LDS family history resources, which is not a bad thing because of the quality of so many of those resources. The categories are as follows:

1. Blogs and Newsletters—21 sites
2. Brigham Young University—11 sites
3. FamilySearch—10 sites
4. Forums and Message Boards—8 sites
5. General—36 sites
6. Libraries and Archives—18 sites
7. Link Collections—14 sites
8. Maps—11 sites
9. Miscellaneous—19 sites

---

[3] David A. Fryxell, "Best US Genealogy Websites in 2016," *Family Tree Magazine*, 17, no. 6, 2016, http://www.familytreemagazine.com/article/best-us-genealogy-websites-2016 (accessed September 20, 2016).

10. Records—60 sites
11. Societies and Organizations—15 sites
12. Technology and Forms—26 sites
13. Tips—10 sites

There is a temptation, and indeed a tendency—because there are so many available resources—to want to explore most, if not all, of them. And, you may ask, "Why not?" There is always the possibility of finding something important on one site that is not on another. Moreover, there is always the chance you can connect with other people who are interested in some of your lines.

My primary concern here is that you understand how to use these websites to the extent of their potential while, at the same time, recognizing that some of them have significant limitations, and every one of them has some limitations.

II. KEEPING ON TRACK

Because there are so many important websites and because you want to take advantage of those that are relevant to your research, you are faced with three important issues:

- How can you effectively correlate your research between multiple family history sites?
- How can you keep focused and keep everything in proper perspective as you seek to take advantage of all relevant resources?
- How can you keep from going in too many directions at once and being overwhelmed with irrelevant matters?

There are steps you can take—and need to take—to maintain control and keep on track as you involve yourself with the many and varied family history websites. I recommend that you take the following actions as you proceed:

A. Establish an "official" *online* tree on one of the major family history websites.

B. Establish an "official" *offline* tree on a quality family history software program.

C. Decide on your focus—the person or the family where you want to begin research.

D. Complete your preliminary survey relating to that focus.

E. Identify your research objectives—use a "T" chart to zero in.

F. Carefully consider the origin of all information/evidence as you do your research.

G. Keep complete records of your research activities and findings, and carefully document all of your research results.

Let us carefully examine each of these steps.

A. Establish an "official" *online* tree

You need to create your own "official" online family tree on just one family history website. That official tree (at least in 2016) should be on one of the four top sites listed earlier. Many family history websites will ask you to create your family tree, and you usually need to do so before you can do meaningful research on those sites. However, although this may be necessary, it is important that you choose just one website for your "official" tree. The tree you create on that site will be the one where you will maintain the results of your latest personal research and all additions and changes you make as your research progresses. You want others to view this tree, but you cannot allow them the kind of access to that tree that allows them to change it.

Yes, you want others to look at your tree, make comments, offer suggestions, and collaborate with you concerning it, but you do not want—and you cannot allow—anyone but yourself to edit or make additions to your official tree. Although you do research on other sites and will have family trees on those sites, this one will be your "official" family tree. With regard to this important issue, there are two points I need to stress:

1. The fact that you choose one website for your "official" tree should never deter you from using the resources found elsewhere. Your "official" tree just provides a home base for you to preserve your conclusions free from the threat of unsanctioned alterations, yet where others can see it and communicate with you concerning it.

2. The Family Tree program on the FamilySearch website is not a safe place for your "official" tree because trees established on that site are open to edits, additions, and deletions by others. The fact that the Family Tree program is a wiki has some benefits, but it is not an appropriate place for your official online tree. You need your "official" online tree to be somewhere else.

B. Establish an "official" *offline* tree

It is also important for you to set up an "official" offline family tree on a quality family history software program. There are many such programs; as discussed in Chapter 9, Wikipedia listed and compared twenty such programs in December 2016.

These software programs have features and reports that are clever and well designed. However, the one feature you must have on the program you choose is the ability to synchronize it with your official online tree so that your changes, additions, and updates at either location are also made at the other location. Note that the Family Tree Maker and RootsMagic programs can be synchronized with Ancestry.[4] The RootsMagic, Family Historian, and Family Tree Builder programs can be synchronized with MyHeritage. RootsMagic, Legacy, and Ancestral Quest can be synchronized with FamilySearch. And Family Historian and RootsMagic can be synchronized with FindMyPast. This may be a good time to go back and review the discussion of family history software programs in Chapter 9.

C. Decide on your focus

Next, you must decide which ancestor or family on which to focus as you commence research, just as we discussed in Chapter 3. You cannot efficiently focus on all of your ancestral lines at the same time. It is folly to try to do so, and it can also be a bit overwhelming.

D. Complete your preliminary survey

Your next step is to complete the preliminary survey relating to those ancestors on whom you have chosen to focus (see Chapter 3). The major family history websites can facilitate your preliminary survey, especially helping you locate other individuals with the same family lines, learning what information they have, and—where possible—joining forces with them in future research efforts.

E. Identify your research objectives

Once you have identified your focus and your preliminary survey is completed, you must analyze your problem and determine appropriate research objectives. I recommend that you use a "T" chart (see Chapter 3) to help with this process. It is important to set clear and logical research objectives and to know what you are looking for—what information you are seeking and what issue(s) you are trying to resolve. As part of this process, you must learn about the available records, a task that can also be facilitated by your use of the fam-

---

[4] In December 2015, Ancestry announced that it would no longer be selling and supporting Family Tree Maker software. Because of the resulting outcry from subscribers, Ancestry now offers two alternatives for compatible family history software programs. One alternative is still Family Tree Maker. It is now available through a company called Software MacKiev, which produces both the Mac and Windows versions. An updated version of FTM became available on March 1, 2016.

The second alternative is RootsMagic. As of June 2017, the RootsMagic program was fully integrated with Ancestry Hints and Ancestry Records. The program offers new features "such as color coding, Problem Alerts, Shareable CD's, running straight off of a flash drive, FamilySearch integration, DataClean, multi-provider WebHints, Mac and Windows versions with a single license, . . . [a]nd . . . is able to directly import any Family Tree Maker file." RootsMagic also provided a free upgrade to all owners of the RootsMagic 7 program and agreed to sell the upgraded RootsMagic program to Family Tree Maker users for the price of an upgrade. ("Family Tree Maker Users Have a New Home," RootsMagic, http://www.rootsmagic.com/ftm/ [accessed July 3, 2017].)

ily history websites and their wikis.[5] The chapters in Part 2 of this book are also a resource for those seeking to understand the content and availability of various kinds of records.

Remember, also, that even with your research focus on a specific ancestor or family, you will be searching many records in the localities where that ancestor lived for everyone with your ancestor's surname. Complete research demands that you do so.

F. Consider the source of every piece of information

When you find information about an ancestor or an ancestral family on the Internet, you need to make sure you understand the exact nature of what you have found. That is, you must distinguish clearly between the results of other people's research on one hand and the information found in original documents on the other hand.

As you encounter information provided by others, take note of how well documented it is. You want to know the sources of their information. And you want to know how well reasoned their conclusions are. Also, when their information comes from original documents, you must determine whether the evidence provided is primary or secondary and whether it is direct or indirect (circumstantial).[6] Likewise, when there are discrepancies between the information found in different sources, you must determine the proper value and weight to give each piece of conflicting information in an effort to resolve those discrepancies.

Some pedigrees that other people have posted on the Internet may extend beyond what is on your personal tree, and some may show ancestors that are different from those that appear on your tree. If someone has done careful, thorough research in quality sources and his conclusions are well documented and thoughtfully reasoned, you can put some trust in those conclusions. However, if your own pedigree connections are carefully documented and the reasons for your conclusions are clear, be very careful as you weigh the evidence.

You must examine conflicting connections judiciously for any evidence you may not have discovered and/or conclusions based on superior reasoning. However, you must never make any change to your official tree without sufficient proof that the change is appropriate and justified. On the other hand, when someone else's answer proves to be based on better evidence than what you have previously accepted, by all means accept it and go forward. It may open up new vistas for you.

G. Keep complete records and document your results

I cannot emphasize too strongly the importance of keeping careful records of all your research, whether that research was in records found online or in

---

[5] There is additional explanation and discussion about wikis in Chapter 9.

[6] See Chapter 4.

records found elsewhere. Careful documentation is critical. Use your research log to list every source you search. Prepare and maintain your research log as a table of contents for your research notes, your correspondence, and your document copies. Carefully follow the procedures outlined in Chapter 7. I am sorry to report that when people are researching in computerized indexes and databases, there is a tendency for them to jump quickly from one source to another and not adequately document their research. Proper documentation is critical.

III. MAJOR FAMILY HISTORY WEBSITES

It is important that you have some understanding of the exceptional family history websites that exist. There is insufficient space here to discuss all of them—or even a few of them—in great detail, nor would it be wise to do so because they are all undergoing constant change. However, you should take the time necessary to explore them. What follows here is only a brief introduction to the four largest sites that were listed earlier in this chapter—Ancestry, FamilySearch, FindMyPast, and MyHeritage.

Though I believe this discussion will be helpful, I undertake it with some misgivings because I believe that, in a very few years, these websites will all be sufficiently redesigned so that the only thing about them that will be the same as it is today is the data they contain—and that will be expanded significantly.

Each of these websites has its own internal tutorials. Each also has usage and navigation helps to assist you in taking full advantage of its resources.

Even if such were possible, this book is not intended to be a user manual for family history websites. You will need to explore these sites on your own, based on your own needs and circumstances—perhaps taking some guidance from what is presented here. My hope is that this material will still have relevance after the passage of much time.

A. Ancestry (*https://www.ancestry.com/*)

Ancestry is the largest, best-known, and most-visited family history website. Full membership on this site has a subscription price. However, trial memberships are offered, and free, limited-use memberships are available. Also note that all LDS Family History Centers, the National Archives and Regional National Archives, and many local libraries have the Ancestry Library Edition and provide cost-free access. You may want to check for these resources in your area before you pay for an Ancestry membership. It is important to note that the United States is Ancestry's largest area of records content.

Using the Ancestry Library Edition is a viable option, but there are limitations not experienced by those who have personal memberships that allow each person to enter his personal tree and use that tree as a working base. However, if your research is well planned and your objectives are clear, the

Library Edition works quite satisfactorily. You have full access to the vast collection of Ancestry records and their related indexes. Remember, also, that many of Ancestry's features are also available to use free of charge on your own computer or portable electronic device.

If you are not sure of what you would like to do, you may want to set up a free Ancestry account first and try using the free data collections at home before you decide. Whichever type of personal account you choose—free or subscription—you need to add your family tree (pedigree) to that account, either by entering the information yourself or by importing a GEDCOM file[7] from the family history software program you are using. You will make that choice on the page where you opt to create your tree. You are also free to edit any information on your tree at any time and as you need to do so. Many people choose Ancestry as the location of their "official" online tree because you can set up your tree so that others can examine it but can make no alterations.

Family trees created on free Ancestry accounts or on the library edition do not automatically seek to find matches with the family trees of others on the website as do those trees created on subscription memberships. That feature is one of the main values of a paid-subscription membership. Although not having that access will limit your preliminary survey capability and many of your other options, there are still meaningful things you can do.

Once your tree is set up, take time to explore the site. Click on the various items listed in the drop-down menus on the homepage. There are vast numbers of indexed databases on this site, including many that are available to free account users. And, though Ancestry gives free users only limited access to some records, it also allows full access to some others—including the 1880 and 1940 U.S. census schedules.

Each time you open your Ancestry account, go directly to your tree. There you will see leaf icons beside some of the names. A leaf icon by a person's name indicates that Ancestry has one or more "clues" relating to that person. To see those clues, click on the leaf. These clues relate to information the Ancestry program has found in the website's databases about that person. With experience, you will likely find you want to ignore many of these clues because they provide no new information.

In most cases, it is best to limit your clue looking to only those clues relating to the individuals who are your current point of focus. Because there are often multiple clues associated with many persons on your tree, much time can be consumed looking at all of them, and it is easy to get overwhelmed and/or sidetracked.

---

[7] GEDCOM is an acronym for *Genealogical Data Communication.* The GEDCOM program was developed by The Church of Jesus Christ of Latter-day Saints as a medium for transferring genealogical data from one file to another. Most family history software programs accommodate GEDCOM to both import and export genealogical data—though some do so better than others.

Your first use of the Ancestry website will likely involve some of the "preliminary survey" steps discussed in Chapter 3. This is a use you will employ many times. You can look for other relatives by choosing "Public Member Trees" on your homepage "Search" menu. The database you access through the Public Member Trees page contains the family trees of those Ancestry subscribers who have elected to make their trees visible to other subscribers. You may contact these people for more information and/or to coordinate research efforts. Remember, however, that there is no guarantee of accuracy in member trees.

1. Research on Ancestry

There are three kinds of searches you can make on the Ancestry site:

- Global searches
- Category searches
- Database searches

Let us look briefly at each one:

a. Global searches: A global search is essentially a scattergun shot. You can do a global search either (a) for a particular ancestor, (b) for all people with a specific surname in a specific location and time period, or (c) for some combination of the other two. The nature and scope of your search depend on the search criteria you select. These search criteria are the data you enter in the blank spaces provided on the form where you define your search. Each search will look at all records on the website that relate in some way to those persons who match your search criteria in some way.

A global search is initiated from your homepage by clicking on the "search" option on the menu line at the top of the page and then selecting "All Collections." If you are searching for a specific person, enter his first and last names in the spaces provided, and then enter a place where he might have lived and a birth year (which can be estimated). The program allows you to specify variations in the names and the date ranges according to your desires.

You can also narrow the focus of your search by adding additional information, such as names of other family members, other life events, the person's sex, and various keywords (things that relate to religion, occupation, social or fraternal affiliations, etc.). Once you have keyed in all desired information, your clicking of "Search" will reveal a list of all records on the website that are roughly within the scope of your search criteria.

A list of the names of potential matches, with some identifying data, will appear, with the names the program deems most likely to be a match listed first. You can examine a copy of the extracted record or the database image for any entry on that list by clicking on the entry.

You can also do a global search for every person of a particular surname found in the records of the same locality, within whatever time
frame you desire. The procedure is the same as already described, except you enter nothing in the "First & Middle Names" field when you set
your search parameters. You can enter time and place limits, according
to your desires, in the designated spaces. Again, you can enter as much
or as little information as you desire.

When you click on "Search," a list of names will appear, with the best
matches nearest the top. There is usually no value in looking beyond a
page or two of these results—in many cases, no more than just a few
entries are relevant. You can gauge relevance based on what you see in
the list of search results.

A global search is a good way to become acquainted with the records
available on the Ancestry website, and it may actually turn up useful
information.

b. Category searches: A category search is one in which you search for
an ancestor or for members of an ancestral family in records of a speci-
fied category. The largest categories are listed on the "Search" menu.
At the time of this writing, the specific record categories listed on the
"Search" menu included "Census & Voter Lists"; "Birth, Marriage &
Death"; "Immigration & Travel"; and "Military."

Other record catagories, such as "Newspapers & Publications"; "Pictures"; "Stories, Memories & Histories"; "Maps, Atlases & Gazetteers";
"Schools, Directories & Church Histories"; "Wills, Probates, Land,
Tax & Criminal"; "Reference, Dictionaries & Almanacs"; and "Family
Trees," will appear when you choose the "Card Catalog" option. Category searches can (and should) be limited by date range and geographic
area.

c. Database searches: Global and category searches notwithstanding,
the key to your most efficient use of Ancestry is the database search.
Searches of the site's major databases are initiated from the "Card Catalog" menu under the "Search" menu. A search can be made in any specific database(s) you choose—not just the broad categories listed under
"Category Search." Your choice of records will depend on the research
objectives you set.

For example, if your ancestor was born somewhere in the state of
Ohio sometime around 1840 to 1845, you may want to search the 1850
Ohio federal census in an attempt to find him in the household of his parents. The indexed database of that census makes the search much easier
than having to search page by page through the entire state of Ohio,
as you would have done in the past. Once you click on "1850 United
States Federal Census" on the list of databases, options are presented
that allow you to search the entire state of Ohio or any county within
the state. Once you have chosen your limiting options and clicked on

"search," a list of possible matches appears on the computer screen. As with the other search types, the possible matches are prioritized in order of their likelihood of being the person you seek. From any entry on that list, your mouse click will take you directly to the digitized image of the actual census page where the listed individual appears. You can also use this option to search for everyone with your ancestor's surname in the state or in any county in the state as they are enumerated in the census, but I will say more about that later.

The "Card Catalog" page on Ancestry has two blank boxes on the left—one labeled "Title" and the other labeled "Keyword(s)." You can initiate a search by making an entry in either box or with entries in both boxes. In the "Title" box, you might enter the name of a type of record, such as "obituary," or perhaps the name of a place—usually a state. When I entered "Utah" in the "Title" box in June 2017, I got a list with the titles of eighty-four different digitized Utah records that are on the Ancestry site.

On the left side of the page, you can also limit your search by ten-year periods. On the right side, you can limit your record options, should you choose to do so, by marking the specific record or records you want to search. This feature facilitates access to those records that relate to the specific research objectives you have set.

Each search you initiate from the "Card Catalog" page allows you to limit that search in almost any way you choose. You can zero in on those time periods, localities, and records appropriate for the ancestor(s) you are seeking.

A useful aid to help you search for people by their names is the wildcard. The Ancestry site (and many other sites) use the question mark (?) and the asterisk (*) as internal wildcards in names. You can use a question mark to stand for one letter in a name or an asterisk to stand for any number of letters from 0 to 5. A wildcard may be employed at either the beginning or the end of a name—but not both—and also in the middle of a name. You can also use more than one wildcard in the same name. However, you must always have at least three other letters. For example, if you were looking for variations of Smith, one possible way you could enter it is Sm?th*. Or, perhaps, S*th*. The program also allows you to set search parameters underneath each entry to indicate how precise you want your matches to be.

Note: Let me emphasize once more the importance of compiling complete families as you do your research, which also requires that you gather information on everyone of your surname of interest, a practice that is one of your best guarantees of accuracy. I also stress the importance of proving your pedigree connections according to the requirements of the Genealogical Proof Standard (GPS) as discussed in Chapter 4.

2. Other features of Ancestry

Many more features of Ancestry deserve your attention. One other item on the top-of-the-page menu line that needs mention is "DNA." With this option, you can elect to order a kit for an autosomal DNA test. In June 2017, the test cost $99, though discounts are frequently offered. (See the discussion on DNA in Chapter 9.) There is also a "Help" option on the homepage menu that gives access to a "Support Center," "Community," "Message Boards," and "Hire an Expert."

a. The **Support Center** offers help in multiple categories, including help with account problems, issues relating to your family tree (such as how to download or upload a GEDCOM file), and problems associated with research (such as how to do various kinds of searches); you can also get help with issues about the use of Ancestry on your mobile device. In addition, it has articles on various relevant subjects as well as access to a community support group.

b. **Community** facilitates your contact with Ancestry's support community and provides an interface with other Ancestry users. You can ask questions, give answers and tips, start and/or join discussions, and offer solutions to the problems of other researchers. There are also more than 198,000 **Message Boards** with more than 25 million posts (2017).

c. **Hire an Expert** facilitates hiring a professional genealogist for those who desire to do so. As of 2017, there were biographies and photos on the site of thirty professional researchers with more than 150 years of combined research experience.

d. In addition to the many options accessible from the top-of-the-page menus, there is also an **Extras** category. This option duplicates some other menu items and offers other services of interest as well. You may like to look at "Ancestry Academy," which offers video courses on various aspects of research. There is an additional fee to join the Academy, but those who join have access to everything offered.

3. Ancestry wiki

Ancestry also has a significant wiki that can be accessed at *http://www.ancestry. com/wiki/*. There are three categories of content on the Ancestry wiki:

a. Ancestry publications (two of them):

1) Eichholz, Alice, ed. [with numerous contributors]. *Red Book: American State, County, and Town Sources.* 3rd ed. Salt Lake City: Ancestry Publishing, 2004.

2) Szucs, Loretto Dennis, and Sandra Hargreaves Luebking, eds. *The Source: A Guidebook to American Genealogy.* 3rd ed. Salt Lake City: Ancestry Publishing, 2006.

b. Other content from Ancestry.com.

c. Content generated and edited by Ancestry users.

4. Outside resources relating to Ancestry

There are some useful outside resources to facilitate your use of Ancestry. com. These (at the time of this writing) include the following:

a. *48 Ancestry.com Search Tips.* This free booklet is available online in a pdf file at *http://ftu.familytreemagazine.com/free-ancestry-search-tips/*. The booklet itself lists no compiler except Family Tree University, and no date or place of publication is stated. At the beginning of this little book, there is a "Quick Start Guide" and a chart illustrating the differences between public family trees and private family trees on the Ancestry website. The greater part of the booklet, however, comprises two articles:

    1) A four-page piece by David A. Fryxell entitled "10 Easy Ways to Use Ancestry.com."

    2) A ten-page article by Nancy Hendrickson called "Card Catalog Crash Course."

b. Hendrickson, Nancy, *Unofficial Guide to Ancestry.com: How to Find Your Family History on the #1 Genealogy Website.* Cincinnati: Family Tree Books, 2014. This detailed book explains all facets of the Ancestry website, but it is already somewhat dated.

c. Morgan, George G., *Genealogy at a Glance: Ancestry.com Research.* Baltimore: Genealogical Publishing Co., 2013.

It is unclear if these resources will be updated periodically to keep pace with changes on the website.

B. FamilySearch (*https://familysearch.org*)

FamilySearch is the only major non-commercial family history website. I use the words "non-commercial" because there is no charge for use of this website. It is owned and operated by the Family History Department of The Church of Jesus Christ of Latter-day Saints (LDS) and demonstrates the Church's commitment to

- the discovery and preservation of family history;
- the gathering of records associated with family history research; and
- making those records freely available to anyone who wants to use them.

No expense is spared in this effort. However, there is a place on the website where a person who wishes to make a financial donation or become a volunteer to further family history work is invited to do so.

The three primary contributing factors in the development of this website are (1) the Church's long history in records preservation, (2) its leadership and involvement in record indexing, and (3) its working partnerships with several major commercial family history websites in order to facilitate their success.

1. The indexing of records

Hundreds of thousands of volunteers are working—at many levels of involvement, at various speeds, at varying skill levels, and in many languages—to index significant digitized records and make the contents of those records readily accessible for research.

This indexing effort is remarkable, but as remarkable as it is, it would take many generations, at the present rate, to index and publish just those records now in the Church's Granite Mountain Records Vault. Also, in addition to those records, there are many more records that are currently being filmed with cameras using digital technology—at the rate of 35 million images every month in 2015. And the pace of filming/digitizing these valuable records is steadily increasing.

In addition to the excellent resources provided on its website, FamilySearch—in order to expedite the process of making searchable records available—has formed partnerships with several commercial family history sites (including Ancestry.com, FindMyPast.com, MyHeritage.com, AmericanAncestors.org, and Geneanet.org). FamilySearch provides these partner sites with digitized records, and the partner sites then hire commercial companies to index them. As the indexing of a record is completed, the computerized index and the associated digitized database are added to the partner site.

Once a partner site has created an index, that partner has exclusive rights to its use in order to recover its investment. However, after the time required for investment recovery, the index also becomes available on FamilySearch. Depending on the nature of the specific agreement with the partner site relating to a specific digitized record, that record is sometimes available, in the interim, on FamilySearch—but without the index.

FamilySearch's motivation for entering these partnerships is to promote and ensure the success of the partner sites, the work of which benefits everyone involved in family history work. These partnership agreements also allow members of the LDS Church free membership on the partner sites if they have accounts on FamilySearch.[8] Members of the Church who wish to have memberships on these partner websites must obtain those memberships through their FamilySearch account. Otherwise, their memberships will not be partner memberships and will require payment of the subscription price.

FamilySearch wants as many people as possible to participate in the indexing of records. On the menu at the top of the FamilySearch homepage is an item entitled "Indexing." All interested persons are invited to click on this menu item and volunteer to do indexing. The "Indexing" menu option offers four choices:

- **Overview.** If you choose this option, you will be able to take a "Test Drive" of the indexing process with an interactive guided tour. In con-

---

[8] Also, note that these websites have entered into partnerships with other organizations, including the National Archives. The partnering websites are available without charge at the National Archives in Washington and at the Regional National Archives.

nection with your "Test Drive," you can also choose to "Get Started." If you select this option, you can learn the basics and start indexing immediately. You can also opt to "Find a Project" from the many projects available.

- **Web Indexing.** If you choose this option, you'll see a list of suggested batches of records for you to start indexing.
- **Find a Project.** This option allows you to immediately choose an actual indexing project and go to work. This result is the same result as if you chose "Find a Project" under "Overview."
- **Help Resources.** This option provides help to indexers. Here you will find relevant tips, tutorials, and mentoring. Indexers can return here whenever necessary.

Once you have signed up and the indexing program has been downloaded onto your computer, there will be an indexing icon on your computer desktop to provide easy access every time you return. The more people who get involved, the more indexed records there will be available online.

2. The FamilySearch homepage

The homepage features large icon menu options presently running across the middle of the page. Clicking on these will take you to a great variety of records and other valuable resources. I introduced you to some of these resources in earlier chapters. As you scroll up and down the page, you will also observe other useful features.

a. Your FamilySearch account

In the upper right corner is the option to either "Sign In" (if you already have a FamilySearch account) or sign up for a "Free Account." Because every FamilySearch account is free, the "Free Account" option takes you to a page where you can key in the information needed to create your account, including a username, password, and contact name. Your contact name is a unique public name used to identify your contributions to FamilySearch.

Once subscribed, you can click on your name at the top of the page to manage the various account options as they relate to you.

b. The Family Tree program

Back in the middle of the page is the "Family Tree" option, which takes you to the tree you will enter on the site; you can get to the same page by clicking on the "Family Tree" tab at the top of the page. Family Tree is a significant tool. It not only allows you to display your pedigree, it also allows you to display it in different ways that are beneficial for different purposes. These include (1) the usual landscape format, (2) a portrait format (if pictures are present), (3) a fan format showing four generations beyond the person in the middle as well as that person's children, or (4) a descendency format that displays the descendants of whichever ancestor you choose and for whatever number of generations you choose.

Family Tree also allows you to put any person on your pedigree in a central position on the computer screen and view that person's progeny as well as his forebears.

You can do many things in each of these pedigree formats. In the landscape format, there is a clickable space below each couple that allows you to display a list of all of their children who are in the program. You can also add children as appropriate.

The size of your computer screen permits only a few generations to be displayed at one time, but if you click on the arrow following a person's name, the pedigree for that person is extended. Also, plus (+) and minus (–) signs in the upper left corner of the page enable you to make everything on the page either larger or smaller for easier display and navigation. To see more of your pedigree, you can make everything smaller.

Clicking on a person's name in any pedigree format brings up that individual's "Person" card. Essential information about that person is on this card, including his birth and death dates. There are also places you can click to see the sources of the information relating to that person.

I have already mentioned that the Family Tree program on FamilySearch is not the best place for your personal "official" online tree because anyone who wants to can make changes.

c. The Help Center

You will notice the "Get Help" option in the drop-down menu or tab (depending on what device you are using) in the top right corner of the page. Here you can receive assistance with all aspects of the website—especially helpful for those just getting started or encountering challenges.

The "Help Center" option also brings up a link to the "Learning Center, where you will find tabs labeled "All," "Articles," "Lessons," and "Wiki." Select the tab you want and then search for content in the search box provided. If you click on "Lessons," you can access family history lessons of all kinds—on slides, audio, and video. There are hundreds of these lessons.

d. The "Search" options

There are several options available when you click on the "Search" tab:

1) The "Records" option

After clicking on "Records" on the "Search" menu, you can search indexed databases by entering an ancestor's name (sometimes you will want to enter just a surname) and other vital information about that person—as much or as little as you wish (sometimes none). It is a good idea to be more general in your initial searches and then become more specific once you have more information. Remember, also, the importance of gathering information on every person with your ancestor's surname in those localities where your ancestor lived.

When you enter the name, you can use the "?" and "*" wildcards mentioned in the Ancestry discussion. After entering the desired information under the heading "Search Historical Records," which you will see at the top of the page, you can choose how closely you want your result to match what you have entered. It is not usually a good idea to choose "Match all terms exactly," though that may be best in some situations.

The searches you make here are essentially the same as the universal searches described in the discussion of the Ancestry website. The parameters of each search can be as broad or as narrow as you choose, and search tips are available on the lower part of the page.

You can also choose to "Research by Location" by clicking on the United States and then on the state of interest from the list that appears. You can then select the specific record(s) you want from the list that appears. This type of search is what we described in our Ancestry discussion as a database search. If you have planned your research and have chosen your objectives carefully, this is the type of search you will make most frequently because you will know both what you are looking for and where to look for it.

This type of search, as it is set up, will examine only indexed records. If there is a camera icon on this list in front of the record's name, you will be able to call up a digitized image of the entries in that record. Note, however, that in some cases, the record of interest may actually be located on a partner website, and a fee will be required to access it unless you have a subscription to that site.

Another option under "Search" gives you the ability to search a specific record collection.

2) The "Family Tree" option

Choosing this option takes you to a page where you can search for your deceased ancestors by name or ID. You can refine your search further by indicating place and year of birth, christening, death, burial, and/or marriage. You can also add the name of your ancestor's spouse, father, and/or mother to narrow down the search results even more.

3) The "Genealogies" option

If you choose the "Genealogies" option on the "Search" menu, you can enter an ancestor's name information to gain access to genealogical information submitted over the years by patrons of the Family History Department to the following other resource files:

- Guild of One-Name Studies
- Community Trees
- Oral Genealogies
- Pedigree Resource File
- Ancestral File
- International Genealogical Index (IGI)[9]

The accuracy of the information in these files will vary, and any information you find there should be verified. The records in all six of these files are accessible from this one search menu. You will want to use this source during your preliminary survey.

4) The "Catalog" option

This option on the "Search" menu takes you to the FamilySearch Catalog (formerly called the Family History Library Catalog). This catalog includes listings and descriptions of the genealogical resources of the following:

- FamilySearch.org
- The Family History Library in Salt Lake City
- Selected Family History Centers
- Selected other libraries (called partner libraries[10]) with significant genealogical collections

You can do a catalog search by place, surname, title, author, subject, keyword, call number, or microfilm/fiche number. You can also do a combined surname and keyword search when you need to limit the number of results.

5) The "Books" option

This option features a collection of more than 325,000 (in 2017) digitized and indexed family history and genealogy books in important family history libraries—the partner libraries. In addition to family histories, there are county and local histories, genealogical periodicals, textbooks, various gazetteers, and some medieval histories and pedigrees. To do either a simple search or an advanced search, enter your keyword(s) at the top of the page.

Many of the digitized books listed on this site can be accessed and read online, but those with copyright restrictions are accessible only when you are present at the Family History Library, a Family History Center, or a partner library.

---

[9] These sources are discussed in Chapter 3; the evidence here is secondary, and you will want to use them during your preliminary survey.

[10] A current list of partner libraries is available on the Family History Research Wiki. You can find it by keying in "partner libraries" in the "Search by place or topic" space on the wiki home page.

On this "Books" page, you can also learn about the partner libraries and gain access to each library's collections catalog by clicking on the library's name.

6) The "Wiki" option

The Family History Research Wiki option takes you to a treasure trove of information to assist with your research. Navigation in the wiki can be complicated, and the process of accessing some of the wiki resources is tricky. Though FamilySearch employees created most of the wiki content, other users are welcome both to add to and edit wiki content if they have pertinent information.

Your best access to materials on this wiki is through use of the search box at the top or the middle of the main wiki page (which appears when you click on the "Wiki" option). In that box, keying in your search terms will generate a list from which you can choose whatever best identifies what you want. When you click on the item of your choice, you will get a list of all wiki pages that include the words in the selected item. From that list, you can choose what you want to see. If this sounds complicated, just follow the instructions on the wiki homepage; it is not as complicated as it sounds.

As you use the wiki, clickable subheadings take you to pages that are gateways to broader subjects and resources. The wiki contains much valuable information,[11] but I find it particularly useful in providing information about the places where my ancestors lived, as discussed in Chapter 3. Note that the Research Wiki can also be accessed from the "Get Help" tab.

e. Other FamilySearch features

1) The "App Gallery," etc.

At the bottom of the page, you will see a number of links that can be clicked on. I will not list them or say more about them except to mention the "App Gallery." It provides a listing—with information on each—of the assorted and diverse apps available to help you "find, connect, organize, and explore your family" on the Internet. I believe there are more apps than you will need, but you will have to decide which ones will be helpful to you—which ones will facilitate your research and its associated functions.

2) Training materials

There are also instructional materials on the FamilySearch website that relate to its use, providing both explanations and practice. These materials cover both skills and website components. In fact, there is instruction to help you master the use of Family Tree without worrying about messing up your own pedigree.

---

[11] In June 2017, there were 85,283 articles on the Family History Research Wiki.

Your best access to these lesson materials is through the wiki homepage. Key in the word "training" in the search box, and then click. If you are interested in training on a specific subject, you can make your search term more specific. On the page that appears, look at the options presented, then choose whatever interests you. I suggest that you experiment with different search terms relating to various subjects.

There are two publications that contain detailed instructions on the use of FamilySearch that you might find helpful. However, even at the time of this writing, revisions on the website have already made these publications outdated. I have no information on plans to update either one. They are as follows:

Morgan, George G. *Genealogy at a Glance: FamilySearch.org Research*. Baltimore: Genealogical Publishing Co., 2014.

McCullough, Dana. *Unofficial Guide to FamilySearch.org: How to Find Your Family History on the* Largest *Free Genealogy Website*. Cincinnati, OH: Family Tree Books, 2015.

C. FindMyPast *(http://www.findmypast.com/)*

The FindMyPast website began as an outgrowth of a small, organized group of professional genealogists and heir hunters in Great Britain in 1965 when they formed an association they called Title Research. This was long before the world had even thought about personal computers. The first major project of the Title Research organization was undertaken in 2001. That project created a computerized version of the birth, marriage, and death records in the General Register Office of England & Wales. This record was for the use of members only. In 2003, however, the fledgling organization put their product on the Internet with the title *1837online.com*. It was an instant sensation, and the organization subsequently generated projects to put the 1861 and 1891 British censuses online as well. The success of these projects led the group to change its name from Title Research to FindMyPast in 2006.

At the time of this writing, FindMyPast is a subsidiary of the Scottish Publisher DC Thomson. FindMyPast headquarters are in Cambridge, Massachusetts; its corporate office in Wilmington, Delaware; and its principal business office in Venice, California. The primary emphasis of this website is still on British records, but there are also records from other countries—especially countries with British ties—including 850 million U.S. records.

FindMyPast has partnerships with a number of organizations, including FamilySearch, the New York Genealogical and Biographical Society, and the New England Historic Genealogical Society. Just as with Ancestry, all LDS Family History Centers, the National Archives and Regional National Archives, and many local libraries have the FindMyPast Library Edition and provide cost-free access. In 2015, the site boasted that they had some 18 million registered users. This figure included those registered on other sites belonging to the company's family. Other company sites include Genes Reunited and the British Newspaper Archives. New records are being added at a remarkable rate.

The FindMyPast website is quite self-explanatory and relatively easy to use. When you first enter the site, you need to subscribe. A member of The Church of Jesus Christ of Latter-day Saints, who is subscribed to Family Search.org, can receive a free subscription because of the partnership arrangement between the two sites. Those partner subscriptions must be completed on the FamilySearch site.

I also need to mention that, for those who would like to access the records on the FindMyPast site but do not wish to buy a yearly subscription, there is a "pay-as-you-go" option available for purchasing copies of records. There were three different pay-as-you-go packages at the time of this writing: 60 credits for $10.95, 300 credits for $37.95, and 900 credits for $82.95. Each record view costs between five and sixty credits, depending on the record. Unused credits expire ninety days after purchase, but expired credits are reinstated to the user's account if he purchases more credits or subscribes to the site within three months of the expiration. I should also note that at the time of this writing, the subscription fee on FindMyPast had been greatly reduced and was much lower than subscriptions for the other major commercial sites. It is unclear how long this subscription price sale will be available.

Once subscribed to FindMyPast, you can enter your personal information and then enter your family tree or download a GEDCOM file of it. FindMyPast is set up to examine your family tree and then survey the databases on the site for information that might relate to the people on your tree—and then give you hints (suggestions) about where to find records relating to those people. An orange circle that appears next to a name with a number inside of it shows that hints are available, as well as the number of those hints. When your research is focused on a particular ancestor and his family, do not neglect to click on the orange circle to find the hints relating to him. I do not recommend spending time looking at hints on those lines where you are not currently working because they can only distract you from the work at hand.

You have the option on FindMyPast of either keeping your family tree private or making it available for others to see. You exercise this option by going to the "Settings" symbol in your Family Tree and either ticking or un-ticking the "Public tree" box. In my opinion, you should make your tree public so that others can see it; they will be able to see it but will not be able to make changes. And information relating to living persons will not be displayed.

You can initiate a global search for any person from the FindMyPast homepage by typing in the requested identifiers in the spaces provided. As on the other websites, the breadth or narrowness of your search depends on how much information you enter. Searches, as they relate to the hints you have received, can be easily made by clicking on those orange hint circles. More focused searches can be made by clicking on the "Search" menu at the top of the page. The scope of your search will depend on how much information you enter, the specific record types you select, and the other options you choose. When you identify a record you want to see, you can elect to see either a transcript or a digitized copy of the actual record, or both, just as on the other sites. If you find a record that relates to someone on your tree, the program gives you the option of attaching that record to the desired person with just a click of your mouse.

It is also important to note, as mentioned in Chapter 6, that digitized images of articles indexed in the Periodical Source Index (PERSI) are being added to the FindMyPast website on an on-going basis as time, resources, and permissions allow. Many genealogical societies, with encouragement and support from the Federation of Genealogical Societies (FGS), are also working to digitize their publications and provide access to those articles through FindMyPast.

Every record you choose to examine on FindMyPast is tracked, and you will bring up a list of those records when you click on the "My Records" menu option at the top of the homepage. You have the option of saving whatever documents you find relevant to your research objectives.

Of special note is the fact that FindMyPast has all of the available U.S. census records for those tracing their American forebears. The site also has many U.S. birth, marriage, divorce, and death records; immigration and travel records; newspaper articles; and some other important American records. However, most records on this site still (in 2017) relate to Great Britain. It is significant, however, that FindMyPast has an excellent blog with helpful instruction on research procedures, reading old handwriting, and other helpful information.

D. MyHeritage *(https://www.myheritage.com/)*

MyHeritage is functionally different from the other three sites because it was designed as a social media website, as was explained in Chapter 9. You will see the difference as you use the site. You will also be able to detect the social media aspects in the description of the site that follows. Some of these social media characteristics are very innovative and provide clear advantages to site users. However, some people find other site features annoying, depending on their personal preferences.

1. Establishing your account and getting started

Signing up for MyHeritage and getting your family tree on the website is accomplished in essentially the same way as on the other sites. You should also note that—just as with Ancestry and FindMyPast—all LDS Family History Centers and many local libraries have the MyHeritage Library Edition and provide cost-free access to their patrons. The National Archives and Records Administration is not a partner site for MyHeritage.

As with the other sites, you can either manually enter your family tree or download a GEDCOM file. You should experience no problems with these basic procedures. However, I was disappointed with my attempt to have separate family trees for my paternal and maternal lines, with me at the beginning and including both my father and my mother on both trees. Once the two GEDCOM files were downloaded, the website quickly combined the people on both trees and created two identical trees. This was obviously something I did not want to happen, and it left me with only one reasonable option—I deleted one of my trees. If you want to have more than one tree on the site, your trees must have no overlapping or matching data.

Once you have established your MyHeritage tree, several options are presented. First, you will encounter a "Welcome" message that invites you to turn your personal pages into a family history website for you and members of your family—a place where you (and they) can share family news, including birthdays, anniversaries, and photos. Not everyone wants this kind of personal involvement, but the fact that the site is set up that way will not inhibit the research efforts of those who are more left-brained and desire just to do research.

2. Dealing with "matches"

On the sides of the MyHeritage homepage are some items of interest. One item tells how many matches there are with your family tree and the historical collections on the MyHeritage website, and how many historical collections are the sources of those matches. It also tells the number of both pending (old matches that you have not yet looked at) and new "smart matches."

Smart matches are proposed matches of people on your lines with people on the lines of other site members. Most of these matches are obviously correct—100 percent correct or close to it. (In each case, the percentage of likelihood is shown.) However, there are some cases where additional research will be required to determine whether the suggested match is sound.

In those few cases where the site indicates that further research is needed, you must be very careful. You must not declare it to be a good match until you have done your research. You need to, at least, complete a good preliminary survey on the individual or the family involved to see what has already been done and if there are any obvious conflicts or reasons to question either the identity of the individual or the family connection. The primary value of these "smart matches" is that they can put you in contact with other people with the same ancestral lines. This feature provides one of the best tools of any of the websites to help you find other relatives.

Let me add one more note of caution at this point: Because you can get overwhelmed by the number of matches presented for your consideration, it is not usually wise to pursue all of them at once. It is best to look only at those potential matches that relate to those specific ancestors you are actually working on at the time. I emphasize again, as I have before, that you cannot work on every ancestral line at the same time—not even during the preliminary survey stage—and it is foolish to try.

3. Involving others, if you wish

There is a list on the homepage of close family members whom you may wish to invite to share your MyHeritage family website. If you decide to go that route, you need to enter the e-mail address for each person you wish to include.

There is also a list on the homepage of upcoming events (such as birthdays and anniversaries) relating to your close relatives. You can add other such events to the list if you want. Also, there is a place on this homepage to publish your own family news for the benefit of those who join your site. Again, your involvement in these activities is optional. You can also add photos, and that is always a good idea.

Though it is not essential for you to add other people, including close family members, to your site if you do not choose to do so, it may be a good idea to add at least those you want to involve in your research. Some of them may be enthused and become useful allies in your research efforts. But you need to be very selective about those whose names you add to this list and what privileges you extend to them.

4. Main menu options

Across the top of the MyHeritage homepage are six items on a drop-down menu. Some of these are things I have already mentioned because they came into play in other places. The six menu options are "Home," "Family Tree," "Discoveries," "DNA" (new on MyHeritage in 2016), "Photos," and "Research."

a. The "Home" option

Under "Home," you will see "Family Events," "Family Statistics," "Invite Family," "Site Members," and "Site Account." The options offered to you here relate specifically to your website, its content, and its setup. Before you have gone too far in the development of the website and the creation of your MyHeritage account, I suggest that you visit the "Site Account" page at the end of your menu line. Take time to look at the various available menu options. The settings you choose from that menu will determine both how your MyHeritage account is set up and how the website functions. You need to be in control.

b. The "Discoveries" option

"Discoveries" on the menu line offers you three choices: "Matches by People," "Matches by Source," and "Discoveries." The people matches relate to the people on your tree and those people in the various family trees on the MyHeritage site. All "new information" (i.e., information not on your tree) is noted. The source matches show "new information" that relates to people on your tree that is found on other websites. Because the source matches are listed only by the names of the websites, it is necessary to open the link to determine if that information is of any value to you.

The information contained in both of these types of matches is secondary evidence based on other people's research. It may be accurate— or not. The source option would be easier to evaluate as to its present value to your research if you did not have to open the link to determine which people and which lines it relates to. When you choose to click on a link under either option, you will be shown, in each case, the number of suggested matches between your tree and the listed source or website.

In most cases, I do not recommend that you go down that list and look at every suggested match. You can spend a lot of time looking at information you already know. However, as those matches relate to the lines you are working on, there are two potential benefits: (1) You have potential contact with others who are interested in, and working on, the same lines, and (2) the new information you discover may prove to be true and open up new horizons for you.

The best time to look at these matches is during your preliminary survey stage. Once you have done all of that, it is usually more efficient—once you have established specific research objectives—to go to the "Research" menu and search those records that relate more directly to your objectives.

Insofar as the "Instant Discoveries" option is concerned, you may be able to get some ideas for research, but most of these suggested connections are going to require quite a bit of research. Thus, whatever time you spend here is best concentrated on those families that are your current point of focus.

c. The "Research" option

I suggest that you concentrate your efforts primarily on the options available under this "Research" menu. The available options under the "Research" menu include "Birth, Marriage & Death"; "Census & Voter Lists"; "Family Trees"; "Newspapers"; "Immigration & Travel"; "Collection Catalog," and "Hire a Researcher." With each choice, except the last one, you will be able to enter name, date, and place information for the person or family you are researching. This information can be as specific or as general as you choose. That decision depends on the nature of the search you wish to make. If you choose the "Collection Catalog" option, you will bring up a random list of specific records that extends for several pages. This may not be the best place to start.

With each option you select on the "Research" menu, you can choose the specific databases (i.e., records) you want to search—based on the person or the family where your research is focused and on your specific research objectives as they relate to that person or family.

In an earlier version of MyHeritage, the "Research" menu included an option to "Search all records." They called this "SuperSearch," and it was essentially the MyHeritage equivalent of the global search option on other sites. Though this option is no longer listed under the "Research" menu, you will find it under the alternative "Research" menu at the bottom of the page.

d. Other observations about MyHeritage

This is a very sophisticated website, and there are some amazing things here—including many interesting "bells and whistles." There are many helpful resources, but you must stay in control of your own research approach. If you permit it, this site can quickly take you in more directions than you will be able to deal with at one time.

I believe it is a good idea to explore the options that the site offers and become acquainted with how they work. Your research efforts, however, should focus on the steps outlined early in this chapter, and your main efforts should concentrate on a very limited number of ancestral lines at one time—those family lines that were in the same locality at the same time.

I should also mention that, once you subscribe to the MyHeritage website, you will receive many e-mails relating to the site; there will be messages every day to tell you of the "Smart Matches" in the databases that relate to your tree. You will also get e-mail messages on "Record Matches" and "Calendar Events." Do not let these e-mails distract you. Just focus your attention on the lines you are presently working on and your current research objectives. Otherwise, you may be trying to go in too many directions at once.

In fairness, I should say that you will also get e-mails from every site where you register, but there seem to be a lot more coming from MyHeritage. Some people like this feature.

IV. ENHANCING YOUR SEARCH RESULTS ON THESE MAJOR SITES

With the above major websites, there are some other useful search options available. And, although the sites are not exactly alike, they are similar in many respects. If you have made a census search, for example, and have not found the person whom you should have found, you may want to try another tactic. You might try leaving the spaces blank where you enter the given name and the surname of the person you are seeking (but failed to find). Instead, with Ancestry, go further down the page and click on "Show more options." This will give you the option to enter the name of another family member. You can enter the name of a parent, a sibling, a spouse, or a child of the person you have been unable to find. It all depends on what you actually know. This approach just gives the computer another way to view your problem—just in case there was some sort of glitch with the name of the person you are seeking. If you have no results when making a search with one name, try another if you know one, but you usually should not make a search for more than one of these names at a time.

With FamilySearch, your options are slightly different. You can enter the name of a parent, a spouse, or "other person." This last option could be a sibling. But, again, do not make these searches by entering more than one name at a time.

With FindMyPast, your option is to enter the name of another "household member." Depending on your results—or lack of results—you can make as many searches as you want of the names of other known family members.

On the MyHeritage site, you can add the name of a relative (i.e., a family member) and the specific type of relationship.

This is also a good place to call your attention to an article in the March/April 2016 edition of *Family Tree Magazine* that discusses and compares the three large commercial websites, Ancestry, FindMyPast, and MyHeritage.[12] The article compares several aspects of these three websites, including "Historical records," "Trees," "Unique features," "Subscription prices," and "Site info and help," It also looks at search procedures on the three sites and compares their "Historical record content," their "User-submitted trees," and their "Search technologies." There is also a comparison of how each site handles "Social networking with relatives," "Mobile apps," and "DNA research tools." You may it helpful to look at this interesting article.[13]

V. OTHER IMPORTANT WEBSITES

There are many important websites and there is much that could be said, but you should understand that the more that is said here, the more information will be included that will be outdated very quickly. However, there are two other websites I believe deserve mention as part of this discussion:

- The Family History Guide
- Puzzilla

A. The Family History Guide (*http://www.thefhguide.com/*)[14]

I mentioned this website in Chapter 1. It is an amazing free website, and I believe it has the potential of revolutionizing the way people learn and do family history research. The site—in its second release in November 2016—is designed around the FamilySearch website, but it also has links to significant content from all four of the major websites we have just discussed (Ancestry, FamilySearch, FindMyPast, and MyHeritage).

---

[12] FamilySearch was not included in the discussion because it is a nonprofit, noncommercial site.

[13] Sunny Jane Morton, "Insider Tips for Ancestry.com, FindMyPast and MyHeritage," *Family Tree Magazine*, March/April, 2016, 33–40.

[14] The unusual capitalization of words in this section is intentional, done at the request of the site developer, to reflect usage on the website.

The Family History Guide is a significant resource for all family history researchers. And most of the research you do on those major websites is facilitated by accessing their databases through The Family History Guide website. One of the more important features of The Family History Guide is the Introduction section. This section has links for those who are new to computers or to family history. This Introduction also provides a useful overview of the site.

The Family History Guide features what its developers call "Projects"; there are nine of these. Included within these Projects are "over 1,200 goals, step-by-step instructions, links to over 2,500 articles and videos from Family Search, Ancestry, FindMyPast, MyHeritage, and more![15] The nine Projects are as follows:

Project 1—Family Tree. Helps users create and manage their family trees online with FamilySearch.

Project 2—Memories. Discusses the gathering, preserving, and utilizing of photos and documents relating to ancestors and family members.

Project 3—Descendants. Focuses on tracing the descendants of your ancestors, including the use of Puzzilla, which is discussed below.

Project 4—Discover. Deals primarily with the basics of organizing, planning, and doing your family history research.

Project 5—Indexing. Provides help for those who avail themselves of the opportunity to do record indexing.

Project 6—Help. Provides help for those doing their own research and shows how the user can give help to others.

Project 7—Technology. Relates to the use of various electronic media for family history work.

Project 8—DNA. Explains DNA testing for ethnicity and ancestral research.

Project 9—Countries/Ethnic. Provides research tools and instructions for sixty countries and five ethnic groups.

Each project is supported by various goals. After you choose a goal, you choose an activity within the scope of that goal in order to draw upon the specially designed project resources. These resources include the following:

- Links to documents and videos
- Page number icons that guide you in your selection of a document
- Video icons that guide you in your selection of a video
- Tips and PDG files that add further information
- The Vault, which contains links to additional articles and websites that are not included in the main part of the site

Your topic Choices are links to resources on other websites.

---

[15] This quotation is from an advertising flier circulated by the site developer.

In connection with these projects, there is also a Project Tracker that facilitates monitoring of both your projects and your goals. It also facilitates access to various training plans using the materials on the website.

Other special features on the website include the following:

- **Children.** Provides links to family history activities that are designed for children
- **Training.** Contains courses, tools, and tips for those who teach family history skills
- **LDS.** Relates to issues relevant to members of The Church of Jesus Christ of Latter-day Saints associated with preparing and submitting the records of their ancestors for vicarious temple ordinances
- **Content Review.** Provides a place for site users to give feedback on the Projects, Goals, and Choices in The Family History Guide

As you can see, the primary purpose behind The Family History Guide—accomplished very well—is to teach. There are training course outlines for those who teach others as well as training materials for those who want to learn more about the processes of family history research on their own.

The website boasts of the following unique features:

- Over 1,200 Goals for learning, supported by over 2,300 flexible Choices
- Step-by-step instructions to make learning easier
- Links to over 2,400 videos and articles from FamilySearch, Ancestry, and more
- QUIKLinks that take you directly to a given record collection or other link on the sites of FamilySearch, Ancestry, MyHeritage, or FindMyPast without having to navigate through menus to find it—all with the click of your mouse
- Project Tracker sheets and Training materials for self-study and/or group instruction
- Family history resources for children and for those with LDS interests

I have already mentioned, but I note again, that although there are no records or databases on The Family History Guide site itself, the fourth item on the above list indicates that there are "QUIKLinks" to the records on the databases of the Ancestry, FamilySearch, FindMyPast, and MyHeritage websites. Tutorial videos on the site show you how to proceed with whatever research you are doing.

There is significant value in this website as a tool to facilitate your Internet research. In fact, many of the Internet references I have provided in other chapters of this book can be more easily accessed through the hyperlinks on this website. It is also significant that updates and improvements are being made to the site on a regular basis. If they find a useful resource or see a better way to achieve the site's objectives, there will be updates made on the site. There is a continual process of site enhancement.

I should also mention that, though use of The Family History Guide is free, financial contributions are welcome; there is a link on the site where donations can be made.

B. Puzzilla (*https://puzzilla.org/*)

Puzzilla is a tool used by family history researchers for descendancy research. They use it to identify the descendants of their ancestors—collateral relatives or cousins. To use it, you must have a FamilySearch account with your own family tree on the Family Tree section of that site. Puzzilla correlates with your personal tree in the Family Tree section of FamilySearch as it looks at the digitized records on the FamilySearch website.

You need to understand that Puzzilla's primary purpose is to help LDS Church members who are seeking relatives for whom they can perform ordinances in the temple. However, it is also a useful tool for others who are seeking additional information on their distant cousins. With Puzzilla, you can find additional information that relates to those distant cousins and identify even more of your collateral relatives.

I cannot go into detail here, and it would probably be confusing for me to do so. The tutorial video on the website provides all the instruction necessary to make Puzzilla work for you, and it is an excellent tool to use when research is bogged down on your direct-line ancestral families.

Using the interface between your Family Tree pedigree and the digitized databases on the FamilySearch site, research for your distant cousins can often be quite fruitful. It is important, however, that you be very careful—just as you must be careful in all of your research—about jumping to unsupported conclusions and creating erroneous connections. You need to understand that every hint that Puzzilla produces will not generate a valid connection.

There are two versions of the Puzzilla program, both of which are available on the program website. One version is free, and it is good. The other version, the premium version, however, has some impressive features that make it much more useful.

The premium Puzzilla version ($39.95/year in 2017) offers a 30-day free trial that will allow you to become quite familiar with the program and do quite a bit of work while you are working in the trial mode.

Note, also, that the premium version is available for free use at all Family History Centers connected with the Family History Library in Salt Lake City. At any Family History Center, you will be able to bring up your personal tree by signing in with the user name and password of your FamilySearch account.

An impressive Puzzilla premium feature that is new in 2017 relates to the expedited way the site allows you to look at its "hints" and "super hints." Using this feature, you can search through all of the descendants of whatever direct ancestor you choose in systematic order, looking at ten hints at a time. This is a helpful timesaver because only a small percentage of the hints will actually lead to new information; this feature just streamlines the process for you. You will be able to find valid hints much quicker than ever before. The premium version also provides source documentation for all of the clues it provides.

There are ways to do descendant research on other sites as well, but at present (2017), Puzzilla is, in my opinion, the most efficient.

V. CONCLUSION

At the conclusion of these two chapters on computer technology and Internet resources, it is important that we keep a practical perspective by quoting the following:

Guidelines for Use of Computer Technology in Genealogical Research Recommended by the National Genealogical Society

Mindful that computers are tools, genealogists and family historians

- accept that computer technology has not changed the principles of genealogical research, only some of the procedures;
- learn the capabilities and limits of their computing equipment and software;
- do not accept uncritically the ability of software to format, number, import, modify, check, chart or report their data, and therefore carefully evaluate any resulting product;
- treat compiled sources examined on-line in the same way as other compiled sources, being aware of their potential weaknesses as well as their usefulness as guides to original sources;
- accept digitized images or enhancements of an original record as a satisfactory substitute for the original only when there is reasonable assurance that the image accurately reproduces the unaltered original;
- cite sources for data obtained on-line or from digitized media with the same care that is appropriate for sources on paper and other media, and enter data into a digitized database only when its source can remain associated with it;
- always cite the sources for information or data posted on-line or sent to others, naming the author of a digitized file as its immediate source, while crediting original sources cited within the file;
- preserve the integrity of their own databases by evaluating the reliability of downloaded data before incorporating it into their own files;
- include, whenever sharing digital data they have altered, a description of the alteration; and

- treat people on-line as courteously and civilly as they would treat them face-to-face. [16]

These standards are an excellent reminder of the importance of our task and our need to resist the temptation to take shortcuts or to expect more from technology than technology is capable of delivering. As wonderful and helpful as technology is, research is still research, and facts are still facts. You and I have the duty to be faithful to both research and facts. After all, these are our ancestors we are dealing with, and we owe it to them to get it right.

---

[16] "Guidelines for Use of Computer Technology in Genealogical Research," *References for Researching,* National Genealogical Society, https://www.ngsgenealogy.org/cs/standards_for_use_of_technology (accessed January 4, 2017). © 2000, 2001, 2002, 2016 by National Genealogical Society. Permission is granted to copy or publish this material provided it is reproduced in its entirety, including this notice.

11

Family History: Going Beyond Genealogy

I. THE WHAT AND WHY OF FAMILY HISTORY

After all that has been said about the significance of making correct connections and putting together complete families, there are still other important matters that will be a boon to your family history. In recent years, as already discussed, many genealogists have caught a new vision. They have become not just genealogists but also family history researchers. That probably sounds strange, but I have a feeling that many who have thought they were involved in family history in the past now have a new concept of what family history is.

Family history, as you and I look at it today, is a "marriage" of sorts between history and genealogy—what seemed like a most unlikely union in years past. However, even to cite such a marriage is overly simplistic. Family history also includes other fields of study, such as demography, geography, psychology, sociology, and literature.

While the goal of the genealogist has traditionally been to identify and link past generations of ancestors into pedigrees, the goal of the family history researcher is to do all of that as well as to understand something of the lives and times of individuals, couples, and families.

Members of The Church of Jesus Christ of Latter-day Saints often quote a scripture in connection with their interest in ancestral connections. I will not quote it here, but the scripture is in Malachi 4:5–6 in the Old Testament. It speaks of turning "the hearts of the children" to "their fathers." That is an interesting concept—and an interesting process. To complete this heart-turning process, it is essential for us to know more about them than just names, dates, places, and relationships. We must know *them* (the people involved) and the things they experienced. We must know something of the things that mattered to them most. We must feel something of the things they felt. For example, I can turn my heart much more readily to the great-grandmother who bore fourteen children if I can relate to what she must have felt of tragedy in her life as she buried five of those children before they reached age six. It also gives me a greater appreciation for her as I begin to comprehend the difficulty of her family's pioneer existence in a two-room log cabin on the frontier.

One thing that has happened to the field of history in this unlikely union mentioned earlier is that the historian has discovered he can enrich his understanding of the past by seeing it from the perspective of those most affected by its events. He has also discovered that families and individuals had a greater impact on historical events than was previously thought possible. Likewise, the effect of events on individuals, families, and communities may be more important than the events themselves.

> [Historians] saw that they could enrich our understanding of history by recounting how most people lived and worked, by analyzing the options that were open to them, and by finding out what values and expectations they shared. Historians also took a fresh approach to historical change, portraying human events as moving from the bottom up rather than from the top down. No longer were the common folk seen only as those who endured the deeds and misdeeds of history's movers and shakers. In the words of Gertrude Himmelfarb, "The victims of history have become its principle agents and actors."[1]

Recall how Alex Haley captured the fancy of our entire nation in the late 1970s with his story of *Roots*. Though there has been some disagreement about the quality of Mr. Haley's research and the accuracy of some of his conclusions, we cannot ignore his impact. Mr. Haley did more to generate more interest in more people in their family trees than have all of the world's great genealogists combined.

I am not sure we understand all of the reasons for the success of *Roots* but, regardless of that, its message struck America very close to home, perhaps pricking our collective consciences because of how little most of us know about our own ancestors.

Allan J. Lichtman quoted the anthropologist David Schneider as saying the following at a symposium on kin and communities:

> The most rootless yearn for roots; the most mobile bemoan their placeless fate; the most isolated yearn for kin and community, for these represent the basic things that make life worth living for many people.[2]

---

[1] Allan J. Lichtman, *Your Family History* (New York: Vintage Books, 1978), 5.

[2] Ibid., 11

Our understanding of our ancestral roots enhances our understanding of ourselves. Professor Lichtman explains:

> Psychologists in clinical practice have suggested that the person who understands the patterns of thinking and feeling that emerge over generations of family history is likely to function better as a secure, responsible, self-directed person.

He cited a case in point:

> As a part of their psychiatric training at Georgetown University Medical School, many students of Dr. Murray Bowen, a pioneer in family therapy and himself a family historian, have explored their own family histories. After many years of working with families, Dr. Bowen observed that "it became increasingly impossible to see a single person without seeing his total family sitting like phantoms alongside him." Although Thomas Wolfe may have correctly noted that you can't go home again, each of us takes a large chunk of home along with us wherever we go.[3]

The challenge I give to the genealogist is to reach beyond the vital statistics to a new world of understanding, both of his ancestors and of himself. I challenge him to preserve those details of his family in a written form that will bring understanding to many others and truly enable their hearts—along with his own—to turn to their fathers. Someone has said that there is little point in digging up an ancestor if you are not going to make him live. If that is true—and I believe it is—our challenge has not been met satisfactorily until we feel a bit of what he felt, shared vicariously in his joys and heartaches, shed a tear with him in his sorrow, laughed at the humor in his life, and felt a sense of pride in his accomplishments.

II. SOURCES

The sources of much family history data are mainly those found in the home. They include various family documents, material objects (artifacts), photographs, and the evidence derived from oral interviews. In addition, however, much family history information is also found—but often overlooked—in the traditional sources of genealogical evidence, especially original records.

A. In the home

The homes of our relatives, and even our own homes, may contain documents and material objects of great importance to our families' histories. Professor Lichtman gives us the following lists of home sources, including both documents and material objects:[4]

---

[3] Ibid., 11–12

[4] Ibid., 86–87.

HOME SOURCES

Family documents	*Material objects*
The family Bible	Books and magazines
Letters	Toys and games
Telegrams	Athletic equipment
Post cards	Records
Diaries	Tape recordings
Journals	Guns
Appointment calendars	Knives
Ledgers	Souvenirs
Account books	Maps
Bills	Ornaments
Canceled checks	Trophies
Bankbooks	Medals
Bank statements	Posters
Credit cards	Buttons
Employment records	Jewelry
Tax records	Clocks and watches
Social Security card	Coins and stamps
Identification cards	Bottles and cans
Driver's licenses	Boxes and containers
Hunting and fishing licenses	Bottle tops
Wills	Instruments
Deeds	Appliances
Bills of sale	Machinery
Insurance policies	Locks
Stocks and bonds	Metalwork
School records	Tools
School assignments	Furniture
Military records	Clothing
Medical records	Needlework
Prescriptions	Quilts
Church records	China
Citizenship papers	Silverware
Passports	Plates
Marriage licenses	Mugs
Birth certificates	Glassware
Baptismal certificates	Bowls and pitchers
Confirmation certificates	Mirrors
Court records	Knick-knacks
Yearbooks	Candlesticks
Scrapbooks	Rugs
Clippings	Painting
Awards and citations	Sculpture
Calling cards	Plaques

Greeting cards and invitations	Religious objects
Recipe files	Photographs
Baby books	Albums
Family histories and genealogies	Home movies
Memoirs	Houses and apartments
Poetry	Factories, offices, and stores
	Cemeteries

With regard to our use of material objects in family history, Lichtman wrote:

> Material objects . . . are more difficult to use than written documents. Nevertheless, when thoughtfully approached, many seemingly commonplace objects can add to your knowledge of family history. Items like quilts and samplers may actually record such events as births and marriages. More than just supplying information, the things people owned and used often remind us of skills, habits, and styles of life that have now disappeared. A set of surveyor's tools or a roll-top desk might evoke the life of an ancestor, lending us a little of his physical presence that otherwise might seem so remote. When shown to a relative, objects might trigger a flood of reminiscences about an earlier time. If you locate your great uncle's tools and place them before him, he will probably respond with stories from his working days. If you show your grandfather the chalice that he brought with him from Russia, he may better recall his life in the old country. . . . Not all objects have a story behind them, but attics, basements, and closets are filled with objects stored for sentimental or other reasons, and often they can reveal much about the people who owned and used them.[5]

Once found, precious documents and artifacts should be properly preserved. If you have questions about proper methods for preserving documents and heirlooms, check with qualified experts, such as curators of museums and historical societies. Professor Lichtman gives some basic guidelines:

> Check all storage places for fire hazards, possible water leaks, and excessive vibrations. Try to retain moderate and stable temperature and humidity. A temperature between 60 and 70 degrees Fahrenheit and humidity between 40 and 60 percent are appropriate for most items. Keep strong light off your possessions, and try to protect them from dust, dirt, and pollution. Watch for signs of insects and other pests; if necessary, call on the services of a professional exterminator. Don't pile up fragile documents or stuff them in drawers. Don't put Scotch tape on items, mount them on ordinary paper or wood, lean them against one another, or clean them with common household products. In some cases, you may even want to purchase transparencies for covering documents or acquire cabinets, shelving, racks, boxes, and containers especially designed for specific types of items. If you don't use such storage facilities, make sure to properly line drawers, shelves, and boxes. If you must transport them, pack them with great care. Always remember, when unsure what to do, seek the aid of qualified experts.[6]

---

[5] Ibid., 95–96.

[6] Ibid., 102–103.

B. Photographs

In her presentation at the World Conference on Records in 1980, May Davis Hill suggested that "photographs are more than mere illustrations of what some person looked like. . . . Photographs," she said, "provide expanded information seldom available from other sources."[7] She suggested that we train ourselves to examine every detail of a picture and not just the features that are observable by superficial observation. This practice, she claimed, will enable us actually to enter people's homes and glimpse details of their lives. Each photograph should be considered as an original document of family history with potentially valuable information about the subjects. One major advantage of these pictures, especially of snapshots, is that most families have so many of them, often spanning extended periods of time and many significant family transitions. They chronicle change and are primarily remembrances of "events" more than of daily life in the family. They show us what our ancestors looked like, but they also tell us much more.

Mrs. Hill suggested two things to help us sharpen our observations of photographs so we can extract important details:

- Train the eye to see every detail.
- Cultivate the habit of curiosity about historical facts.

Concerning the matter of training the eye to see details, she says:

> The eye becomes lazy when not often used for exploratory purposes. If family photographs have been in one place for a long time, one ceases to see them. Changing them about can bring out features and relationships never before perceived. If you wish to see more in a familiar image, put it in a place where you write or are otherwise mentally active. Leave it there while you work, but not long enough for the images to settle in your mind as they would in a permanent arrangement. The eye unconsciously examines the image before it while the mind is active. Facts that have lain hidden can pop into consciousness under such circumstances.[8]

Concerning the habit of curiosity, Mrs. Hill points out that this can help us with undated photographs. She suggests careful observation of such details as clothing styles and hairstyles:

> If there is a tennis court, for example, take into account the fact that tennis was introduced in this country on Long Island in 1874. It would take a few years to spread elsewhere. Obviously a knowledge of costume is useful, and a certain amount of knowledge of the history of photography helps with dating as well. Like tintypes and Herbert Hoover's round collar, some things persist beyond the time of their greatest prevalence, however, particularly among the aged. For instance, many women who were widowed in the Civil

---

[7] May Davis Hill, "The Story Behind Your Photographs," Paper No. 353, *World Conference on Records.* Vol. 2 (Salt Lake City, 1980), 36.

[8] Ibid., 13.

War continued to wear the styles of that time—the center-parted hair and the full skirt bordered with braid—until the 1890s. The tendency continued well into the twentieth century.[9]

Put your old photograph collections in the order you want to ultimately keep them, and then number them. This will allow you to put them in different arrangements for study and comparison with one another and then to return them easily to the preferred arrangement. Consider not only photograph collections that may have come into your hands but also those in possession of other—especially older—relatives. Get copies of those that are significant to you—a very simple process with modern technology. Put properly identified and dated pictures on Ancestry, FamilySearch, and MyHeritage, and get copies of meaningful pictures others have posted. You will also want to save meaningful photographs on your own family history software program. You may even find some pictures of relatives on Facebook that you will want to copy and preserve.

There are always lessons in old photographs. As you sort through the unidentified and undated pictures of your forebears, you learn the value of carefully identifying and dating your own photographs for the benefit of posterity.

> Generally, the more you know about a picture, the more valuable it becomes as source material for family history. Where was the picture taken? What was going on at the time? Was someone present who isn't in the picture? Why was the picture taken? Was it taken by an amateur or a professional? Was the picture posed or spontaneous? Be careful to distinguish between posed formal photographs and spontaneous snapshots. The photographer often controls the pose of a formal photograph and may even select the objects that appear in the picture. Yet formal photographs posed by the family itself may reveal much more about the family life than a snapshot would. Whereas much information can be teased from the analysis of a formal photograph, the effect of snapshots is cumulative.[10]

Photographs tell us more about their subjects than do any other historical documents.

C. Conventional genealogical sources

The thing most significant about conventional sources is that the family history researcher can take the same sources he used as a genealogist and look a little deeper than he might have looked before. He can go beyond the names, dates, places, and relationships to unearth and extract the priceless information that tells of people's lives and circumstances. There are many clues and insights relating to the realities with which our ancestors lived.

The property bequeathed and devised by a person's will tells us much about that person. We learn whether he was rich or poor, and we also learn the nature

---

[9] Ibid., 136.

[10] Lichtman, 113–114.

of his personal goods and treasures. His will can provide information about all aspects of family life. It can disclose his occupation and the tools he used in practicing his trade. It can tell us of his religious affiliation, much of his lifestyle and personal tastes, his political preferences, his favorite charities, and his feelings about family members.

In addition to wills, other documents relating to the administration of a person's estate may also have significant value. Consider, for example, what you might learn about an ancestor's way of life from a detailed inventory of his personal property. In days gone by, inventories were not as general (or unspecific) as they are today. An inventory today might merely list "household furnishings," while the same document a century or two ago listed household items in minute detail, even to counting the knives, forks, spoons, and pewter mugs.

The census schedules also have much valuable personal information about the individuals enumerated. Note the headings of the various columns and you will see that we are told much about education and literacy; about wealth, property, and consequent social status; about health matters; and even whether the person was gainfully employed and the nature of his employment. Birthplaces of family members also tell much about the family's mobility.

Passenger lists in more recent years give "personal descriptions" of the immigrants; military records and some land entry records often do the same. How valuable that is!

Details of military service can be found in service and pension records. Pension applications can also give details of family wanderings. Church records—if one is willing to leave behind the registers of christenings, marriages, and burials—tell of financial contributions, special services rendered, and even of disciplinary actions.

I should also mention that local histories, though they may not specifically mention our ancestors, can often provide insights into their lives and the events and circumstances that affected and molded those lives, as they tell of events that affected entire communities.

III. HISTORICAL CONSIDERATIONS

As you look at the lives of your ancestors, try to understand the "causes" of what you perceive. Consider why these people did what they did and the effect of their choices. The answers to these questions are priceless. For example, you might consider (but do not limit yourself to) the following list of inquiries. This list is designed to trigger your curiosity and facilitate your investigation:

1. Why was the family living where it was? What factors caused them to choose that particular area in preference to another? Was it a matter of matching job skills with available employment? Or were some other factors involved?

2. What was the Americanization process like for your immigrant ancestor? This is an especially critical inquiry if your ancestor spoke no (or little) English or was part of a racial minority. What struggles did the family members have because of language/racial barriers? How did they deal with these obstacles? How did their standard of living suffer (if it did) because of these problems so common to immigrants? Did the family change their surname (or its spelling)? Why? Did the American dream go sour? Why did they come to America at all?

3. What was the home like where the ancestral family lived? How different was their home from your own? What "modern conveniences" did the home have to offer? Central heating? Modern plumbing and bathroom facilities? Ample kitchen cupboard space? Closet and storage space? (Such amenities were considered significant luxuries.) Was there a basement? An attic?

4. Who lived in the home? Were there other persons living there besides members of the immediate family? Who were they? Perhaps grandparents or cousins, or maybe employees, apprentices, or boarders? How long were they there? What influence did their presence have on the family?

5. What were the circumstances of daily family life? Consider such things as sleeping accommodations or even seating arrangements at the dinner table. Our children, who today feel deprived if they do not have private bedrooms, would be greatly surprised at some of the arrangements in the homes of their ancestors, with large families sharing restricted quarters. What were the household furnishings like? What about the household tasks and the tools used to perform those tasks? What chores were assigned to the children? What fuel was used for heating and cooking? How was it obtained? How stored? What about food preservation methods and insect control methods before the days of refrigeration and modem insecticides? What about varmint control?

6. What were your ancestors' courtships like? How did they meet? How long did the courtship last? What did they do on dates? How similar or dissimilar was their courtship from courtships of today? Why?

7. Are there any unique sayings or expressions that were used by the family or by family members? Some of these are priceless. I remember fondly an expression my father used as I was growing up to describe someone of small stature: "He'd have to stand on a brick to kick a duck!"

8. What traditions became part of the family? Were family members independent and self-sufficient? Did scrupulous honesty prevail in all things? Was the family raised on a tradition of hard work? What was the sexual morality? How important was service to others? Did the family have and read good literature? What books were part of the family "library"? Were there traditions of going to certain places or doing certain things on certain holidays?

9. What was the size of the family? What benefits and/or problems did the family size carry with it?

10. What were the nature and quality of intra-family relationships? Did the brothers and sisters get along well together? Were some of them best friends? Were there any rivalries among the children, and, if so, what were they like and what were they about? What was the nature of family discipline? Did father rule with an iron hand, or did he "spare the rod and spoil the child"? Were children permitted to speak when not spoken to?

11. What were the family's social status and financial condition? Were they considered well-to-do? What did that mean? How would their circumstances compare to your own? Were they (or were they not) considered "important" people in the community? Why? How did they get along with their neighbors? How did others perceive them?

12. What was the extent of the family's involvement in civic affairs? What differences did such participation (or lack of it) make? Were there any special interests involved?

13. Did the family have pets? If so, what were they? How important were they to the family members? How did they feel about having animals in the house? Did everyone feel the same way about these things? How were any differences resolved?

14. What circumstances surrounded deaths in the family? How did the family members deal with death and its realities? How intimate was the family with death? Did they bury any young children? Teenagers? Was the breadwinner snatched away in his prime, leaving a destitute widow and a young family? If so, how did they cope? Or were family deaths confined to elderly grandparents whose lives had essentially been fulfilled? What were the causes of death the family dealt with? The circumstances associated with death (and often the illness preceding death) can give significant insight.

15. How was medical care handled? Were folk remedies used freely and extensively? Did they have access to good medical doctors? Did any family members have serious health problems? Allergies? Problems relating to hearing and/or vision? If so, how did these affect their lives?

16. What did the family do about religion? Were there any important family religious observances? Were there any unique traditions or practices associated with religious holidays? Did they study the scriptures as a family? Did they attend church regularly? Together? What church? What effect did this have on their lives? Were they called on to suffer or sacrifice for their religious beliefs? What do you know of their personal feelings about, and their relationships with, Deity? Did they pray regularly—as individuals and/or as a family?

17. What foods did they eat? How was their diet different from yours? What were their favorite foods? How was their food prepared? What methods did they use for food preservation?

18. How did the scientific events of the day affect the family? What, for example, was the effect of the electric light, the telephone, the automobile, the radio, the telegraph, etc., on the family? Did they read a newspaper regularly—daily or weekly?

19. Did they have a modern bathroom? Was the family able to afford these advantages? Were they quick to accept the "newfangled"? Or were some of these things troubling to them?

20. How did your ancestors travel, and how mobile were they? If they moved, what was the distance involved and how long did it take? What was the reason for the move and who else moved with them? What were conditions like along the way? How did they make the move? What did they do at night along the way? Was security or safety a problem or concern?

21. What educational opportunities were available? What was the highest level of education achieved? What were the schools like? How large were the student bodies? How many students in their classes? How many grades in each class?

22. What did they do for entertainment? Was most entertainment family centered, church centered, school centered, community centered? How important was so-called "entertainment"?

23. How did the major historical events of the day affect the family? Such things as wars and economic depressions are of particular interest. There is great potential for a major effect. Did any family member serve in the military? In actual combat? Was there an injury and, if so, was it serious and/or permanent? Was any family member reported as missing in action, killed in action? Was any family member a prisoner of war? Where? How long?

24. Did the "family fortune" survive bad economic times? Was there any loss of social status with the loss of economic status?

25. Did your ancestor or any family member have any special talent? What was the talent? How widely was it recognized? Did this prove to be valuable or significant for the family? If so, how?

26. What was the family's political affiliation? How extensive was family or individual involvement in political matters? What effect did this have on the family?

The whole idea behind the foregoing questions is to give you a fresh approach to understanding your ancestors by viewing them in the context of the events of their daily lives, examining why they did what they did. You can appreciate them much more—turn your heart to them, if you will—if you can understand how they were like you and how they were different. Such a view is made possible only by inquiring into the intricacies and intimate details of their lives.

Asking all of these questions about the lives of your ancestors also suggests another important thing you need to do: That is, you need to answer those same questions—those that are relevant—as they relate to your own life. Write down the question and your answer and preserve them for your posterity. Can you even imagine how much they will value that information and the insight it will give them into your life? If you have children, I am confident they do not know your answers to many of those questions.

IV. AFRICAN AMERICAN FAMILY HISTORY AND THE FREEDMEN'S BUREAU RECORDS

This discussion on compiling complete families in our genealogical research cannot conclude without calling attention to a significant project relating to one of the most important records to come forth in our time, the historic Freedmen's Bureau records. I also need to point out what those marvelous records mean to the African American community.

This project, sponsored and funded by The Church of Jesus Christ of Latter-day Saints and the Family History Library, has resulted in a digitized and indexed database that has been given to the newly constructed Smithsonian National Museum of African American History and Culture in Washington, DC. Both the database and the index are also now online, where they can be used free of charge, at *http://www.discoverfreedmen.org/* and at *https://familysearch.org*.

The Freedmen's Bureau was organized under the authority of a congressional act in 1865 in an effort to assist the freed slaves. These records were created in an attempt to bring families back together that had been splintered by slavery and to help bridge the gap between slavery and freedom. The records are of various types, including marriage registers, hospital patient registers, educational records, census schedules, labor contracts, collections of letters, apprenticeship and indenture papers, and many other kinds of handwritten documents. It has been estimated that these Freedmen's Bureau records contain the names of 1.8 million of the 4 million people who were enslaved.

Because of the diversity of the documents and the challenges of reading mid-nineteenth-century handwriting, the indexing of these records was a significant accomplishment, a task accomplished through the combined efforts of more than 25,000 volunteers throughout the United States and Canada. Key volunteers for the project included the nationwide chapters of the Afro-American Genealogical Society partnered with local congregations of the LDS Church.

Using the index and the digitized database, the Smithsonian's Transcription Center is now (2017) working to create a word-by-word transcription of every document in the collection in order to make these amazing records even more accessible to those who can benefit from them.

V. WRITING FAMILY HISTORY

As you gain new insights into your family history, it will be important to preserve the information you learn. However, having said this, I need to back up and put your gathering of data into a proper perspective. If you are going to write family history, there are certain steps that must be followed, as with any research. It is unwise to jump in without proper preparation.

A. Choose your focus

If you are going to succeed in writing meaningful family history, decide beforehand what type of work you wish to do. Because there are a variety of possibilities, you must decide what your focus will be before you embark. For example, you may wish to write a life sketch of a specific ancestor, or perhaps a historical "portrait" of a couple.

Another possibility is to compile the history of a specific couple and their children, what we call a nuclear family. This project may not be significantly different in content from the historical portrait of the husband and wife. The approach, however, may be very different. In the couple portrait, you would zero in on the couple—keeping your focus on them—with the children coming and going.

A more ambitious project is the history of an extended family. You might consider doing a history of one of your two sets of grandparents and their descendants. However, you might like to get a little experience with a less-demanding project first.

Another interesting possibility is to write your autobiography.

B. Decide what questions you will ask

We talked about possible inquiries in Section III, above. The questions you ask, however, will depend on your subject and the particular focus you choose. Your questions should be designed to help you to discover events as well as learn the causes of those events—to try to find out why people did what they did. If you are dealing with living relatives, you may ask questions either in person, in a mail questionnaire, or in an e-mail message.

Much depends on the accessibility of your source. If your source is also the subject of what you are writing, your approach will differ somewhat from your approach if your source is another family member—such as a surviving sibling, spouse, or child. And, even if your subject is still living, you should ask questions of some—perhaps several—other "witnesses."

Make a preliminary list of questions ahead of time—a list you can add to later as you think of other things and as new avenues of inquiry open up. In fact, if you are doing an oral interview, you will add questions during the interview as new lines of inquiry become apparent. The same is true as you work with records and documents. One unexpected bit of information can open up whole new vistas for exploration.

If you do an oral interview, you must, of course, make use of the proper recording equipment. In the past, I suggested you use a good portable tape recorder or video camera. Tape recorders are still okay, if that is all you have available. However, in recent years there has been a proliferation of more sophisticated digital voice recorders with many hours of recording time available. Most of these, with their large storage capacity, free you from the problems associated with tape. Plus, what you record can be downloaded to your computer. There are many different types, models, and brands available in many price ranges. Whatever equipment you use, it is important to have a microphone of reasonable quality. I recommend you do some tests before you start recording to make sure you are going to get the desired results.

Try to conduct yourself so the interviewee can forget about the recorder's presence. Just start the machine and let it run without concern about pauses or gaps. If you use a tape recorder, you will have to turn over and change tapes from time to time, but there should be no other direct interaction with the machine.

In the third edition of this book, I referred readers to the Appendix of Allan J. Lichtman's book *Your Family History* for a suggested list of questions for a mail questionnaire. Because the book was published in 1978, it has limited availability today (though used copies are still available on Amazon.com). I could have copied those questions here, but I chose not to do so because they do not fit everyone's situation and because they occupied eight and one-half pages of Dr. Lichtman's book. I have no other specific reference to give, but I suggest, rather, that you first create a relationship with the person and then, in your back-and-forth communications, send him a few questions at a time. If you have e-mail correspondence with the individual, that can work well.

There are some specific things you need to know but, after that, open-ended questions are best. If you are looking for good questions to ask, you can get some helpful ideas from various sources by entering the statement "family history questions to ask relatives" in the search box of an Internet search engine. You will get many references to websites that can help you with personal interviews, telephone interviews, e-mail interviews, or interviews conducted by mail. (When I entered the above query and clicked my mouse, the result was a list of about 1,300,000 results in 0.79 seconds. Your result will be similar, but it is not necessary to look at all of them. In fact, many of them will not be relevant to what you are doing.)

With all of this, there is one essential fact to remember: Regardless of how you conduct an interview, it is critical for you to be well prepared ahead of time.

Also, note that when doing an interview about someone who is dead, some of the questions you pose will have to be answered—if they can be answered at all—by information found in records and documents, in photographs, or perhaps in family artifacts. However, even in this case, it is important to decide beforehand on the questions to be asked in order to give cohesiveness and direction to your research.

C. Collect your data and materials (do your research)

Oral sources, where available, are possibly the most important, but as already shown, your research must certainly not be limited to such, even if your subject is living.

Nothing of much importance will happen unless you do your research. However, remember that research could go on "forever" and you still will not have the answer to every question. At some point, you must stop collecting information and start organizing it so you can write.

D. Correlate your findings with historical context

It is important that what you write presents a complete understanding of your subject(s). In order for your understanding to be complete, you must take the information gathered and correlate it to events outside the family (both locally and in the larger society). National and world events might have a significant impact. You will understand your subject more completely if you can see the events of his life in the broader context.

Many local histories have been written. Those histories of the localities where your subjects lived are invaluable as a means of enhancing your understanding of your ancestors and their lives. Note that insights and perspectives gained from such histories may also open up new avenues of investigation.

E. Create—write your story

Do not be intimidated by the task of writing. Do not feel the pressure to create a great classic or a work of considerable proportions. It is much better to plan something modest and simple and to complete it than it is to plan something grand and glorious and never quite get it off the ground.

Be selective in what you write. You cannot write everything. One Pulitzer Prize-winning author said the secret of his success was in knowing what to leave out. Be fair to your subjects by presenting their lives objectively and truthfully without trying to say too much. In writing whatever it is you decide to write, consider your audience and their interests.

You do not have to write a book, nor do you—in the traditional sense—have to "publish" what you produce. It may just be a sensitive, specialized little history you wish to share with only your closest relatives.

VI. OBJECTIVITY

Before concluding this discussion, I want to offer a few thoughts on objectivity—a quality of extreme significance to the family history researcher. Sometimes we are so determined to be objective and unbiased that our very determination carries biases with it. The cold, detached presentation of facts may itself be biased because of its failure to be sensitive to important realities. James B. Allen made an excellent statement to illustrate this point. I quote that statement here to conclude this chapter:

[G]enuine objectivity recognizes that truth can be distorted by a mere presentation of a multitude of facts. The documents you have, for example, may well reveal an embarrassing incident in an individual's life—but does objectivity demand that you tell it? Was the incident such a minor variation in the person's total life that merely telling it gives undue emphasis to it, and leaves a misleading impression of his character? Will it really make any difference if some such stories are left out? Or, if your integrity demands that you deal with it, are you capable of putting it into words that will not distort the reader's view of your subject's over-all personality, or otherwise leave a wrong impression? If not, should you be writing this person's history at all? . . .

The biographer's task, then, is complicated—especially when it comes to keeping problems in proper perspective as he deals with them.[11]

I sincerely hope your pursuit of genealogy, with all of its family history details, will be rewarding. I hope your heart will be truly turned to your fathers. And I hope you come to understand both yourself and your forebears better because of that pursuit.

---

[11] James B. Allen, "Writing Mormon Biographies," Paper No. 16, *World Conference on Records.* Vol. 2 (Salt Lake City, 1980), 3.

Part 2

Records and Their Use

12

Compiled Sources and Newspapers

I. FAMILY HISTORY AND COMPILED SOURCES

The term "compiled sources" encompasses a wide variety of materials. The thing that distinguishes these sources is that they bring together (i.e., compile) into one place information gathered from more than one other place. I have classified these compiled sources into eight categories:

A. Family histories and genealogies

B. Local histories

C. Compiled lists (dictionaries, directories, registers, etc.)

D. Biographical works

E. Genealogical and historical periodicals

F. Guide to published records

G. Compendium genealogies

H. Special manuscript collections

Compiled sources are of relatively recent origin. They have grown up almost simultaneously with genealogical interest. This parallel growth has occurred because research results can be compiled only after people do research.

Compiled sources are often referred to as "printed secondary sources" because they contain secondary evidence. The term "secondary" is not necessarily a mark of inferiority or unreliability; it merely indicates a greater potential for error because the information they contain has been brought together from other places. Errors are not always present in these compilations, but there is a significant risk because errors are so easily made.

Some compiled sources represent extensive research and bring together much valuable information from many different places. When they are well documented and are based on sound research and evaluation, their value is beyond measure.

The resources listed in this chapter do not include publications of single-source materials such as published censuses, church records, wills, military records, etc. The exclusion of these materials is intentional because of the vast area they cover. However, there is information relating to several of these types of publications in the chapters pertaining to the records themselves. Indexes, bibliographies, and reference tools of all kinds are also excluded because they were included in Chapter 6.

Let us examine each of the categories of compiled sources listed above.

A. Family histories and genealogies

This is one of the largest and fastest-growing categories of compiled sources. These are the chief objects of our earlier reference to sources that bring together, in one place, valuable data from many different sources. Because of this "bringing together," they are very useful, but we cannot rely on the accuracy of what we find in such works until such has been proven. Too many compilers fail to follow proper scientific procedures, and many of the connections they present are nothing more than guesses and wishful thinking. The late Donald Lines Jacobus discussed four reasons why the compilers of these records have not adhered more carefully to proper research methods:

> There are several reasons why scientific methods have been unpopular with many genealogical students and writers. First in responsibility is that all-too-human trait of *laziness*. It is much easier to make a "likely guess" than to collect data with infinite labor and attention to detail. Second, comes the factor of sheer *ignorance*. Many compilers of family histories quite evidently have no knowledge of the existence of documentary archives, and assume that the only way the early generations of their family can be put together is by accepting what little is to be found in print and guessing at connections.
>
> A third and very important factor is that of *expense*. Many amateur genealogists and compilers cannot afford the cost of thorough research in documentary sources. With this factor, the present writer has an understanding sympathy. Yet it is an old maxim that "whatever is worth doing at all is worth doing well," and one may be entitled to ask whether it never occurs to the perpetrators of the worst genealogical atrocities to give consideration to this maxim. And it may be observed that, despite the lack of funds to compile a worthwhile genealogy, the compilers nearly always seem able to raise the funds to publish their productions.
>
> For the professional genealogist, as for the amateur, there are valid excuses for failure to take advantage of the opportunities for original research. The professional, dependent upon his work for a livelihood, is restricted by the limitations of cost set by his client, and these limitations frequently do not permit as thorough a search as should be made. Errors made by professionals very often are due to the fact that, to keep within authorized limits of expense, they were forced to rely to a greater extent than they desired on printed sources of information. No one is responsible for this situation, for a large number of those who employ the services of genealogists are not people of large wealth.

A final reason for the unpopularity of scientific methods in genealogy is *the romantic temperament of some of those who pursue genealogy as an avocation or hobby.* To people of that type, scientific methods are a bore. It irritates them to be told that a line of descent, innocently accepted from an unmeritorious printed source, is incorrect. They like that ancestral line, and intend to keep it. Denial or question of its accuracy seems to them purely destructive and negative. With people of this temperament, genealogy is not a serious study; it is a mere diversion, and they derive more pleasure from the exercise of their imaginative talent than they could from grubbing for facts. They believe what they want to believe, regardless of facts and scornful of evidence. Let us concede, without argument, that "genealogists" of this type are entitled to their opinions; just as those who believe that the earth is flat are entitled to that opinion. It is entirely natural that these temperamental enthusiasts should oppose scientific methods, and that with the uninformed their opinions may have weight. [Emphasis added.][1]

It is difficult to evaluate genealogies and family histories, but we can make a reasonable evaluation of a family history work by answering the following questions as they relate to a specific work:

- Are the conclusions presented by the work well documented? Many such works merely state "facts" with no indication of their sources.
- What kinds of sources are included in the work's documentation? Are they original records (or digitized copies or photocopies of such) or are they non-original materials? It can make a significant difference.
- Does the work explain in sufficient detail—that can be completely understood and re-examined—the research and analysis that form the basis for acceptance of difficult problems and connections?

Yes, there are some good things written that are poorly documented, but they are the exception. And the sad thing about such works is that those using them have no clue concerning either the completeness of the research or the accuracy of the analysis.

Though the proportion of good family histories and genealogies is low, even those of inferior quality can provide useful clues for our research. Any information we have to work with is better than no information at all and can save time in research. The thing we need to remember is that just because something is "in the book" does not make it true. Far too many genealogical authors fall into those categories described by Mr. Jacobus for us to accept unquestioningly everything we read.

I believe that better-informed, better-trained genealogists and family history researchers are producing a higher quality product today than was produced in Mr. Jacobus's day. Better access to records—especially on the Internet— has had a significant effect, but we are still far from perfect. It is unfortunate

---

[1] Donald Lines Jacobus, "Is Genealogy an Exact Science? *The American Genealogist,* Vol. X (October 1933), 68–69. Used by permission.

that so many of us are willing to base a significant family connection on one piece of circumstantial evidence.

In concluding this section, it is important to note that some useful guides to available published family histories (also listed in Chapter 6) are available:

> Kaminkow, Marion J., ed. *Genealogies in the Library of Congress: A Bibliography.* 5 vols. 1972, 1977. Reprint, Baltimore: Genealogical Publishing Co., 2001.
>
> ____. *Genealogies in the Library of Congress: A Bibliography. Supplement 1972–1975.* 1977. Reprint, Baltimore: Genealogical Publishing Co., 2001.
>
> ____. *Genealogies in the Library of Congress: A Bibliography. Supplement 1976–1986.* 1986. Reprint, Baltimore: Genealogical Publishing Co., 2001.
>
> ____. *A Complement to Genealogies in the Library of Congress: A Bibliography.* 1981. Reprint, Baltimore: Genealogical Publishing Co., 2001. This book consists of a list of 20,000 genealogies not in the Library of Congress and thus not listed in the author's *Genealogies in the Library of Congress* books. The listed genealogies are located in twenty-four selected libraries throughout the U.S.

B. Local histories

In this category, we have town, county, regional, and state histories. Many of these were written in the 1800s and early 1900s, but many more are still being written. In the eastern states and some of the midwestern states, compiling such histories has been a popular project. Note, however, that there is a great variation in the quality and reliability of the resulting works. In several states, published histories exist for every county (as in New York and Iowa), and in some other states, the number of published town histories is remarkable.

Regional histories are those relating to more than one county. An example of such a work is John Thomas Scharf's *History of Western Maryland* [with a *"New, Every-Name Index"* by Helen Long]. 3 vols. 1882. Reprint, Baltimore: Genealogical Publishing Co., 2003. This work, which covers Frederick, Washington, Allegany, Garrett, Montgomery, and Carroll counties, is online at *https://archive.org/details/historyofwestern21scha*.

An important feature of many local histories is a biographical section (often in a separate volume) with short biographical sketches of prominent citizens and early settlers in the locality. Some of these are quite authentic because the families provided the information; others contain many errors for the same reason. Those books that specialized in biographical sketches accompanied with pictures of the persons named therein have been called "mug books" because anyone could get his "mug" in the book if he paid the required fee, and no one could if he did not.

Though your ancestors may not have been eulogized in such books, you can often find information about them in sketches of other family members or of their in-laws. For example, there is no biographical sketch of William Jasper Kerr in the published history of Jefferson County, Iowa, but the sketch of his son-in-law, John Workman, says that his (John's) wife, Amanda J. Kerr, was born in White County, Tennessee on October 14, 1825. This is very useful information considering that you previously knew only that William Jasper Kerr came from somewhere in Tennessee—no county being known.

These histories, exclusive of any biographical materials—whether they be for town, county, region, or state—provide information on the settlement patterns of the locality and on the origins of settlers. They tell of religion, economics, education, and social conditions that might affect both research procedures and direction. They tell of geography and terrain, of watercourses, and of their effects upon settlement and population. Events not only molded the lives of the people, they were sometimes controlled or influenced significantly by those people. And even the nature of records kept was dictated by historical context. No family history researcher knows all he should about research in any given area until he knows something of that area's history.

Helpful guides to county histories include:

Filby, P. William, comp. *A Bibliography of American County Histories.* 1985. Reprint, Baltimore: Genealogical Publishing Co., 2009.

Kaminkow, Marion J., ed. *United States Local Histories in the Library of Congress: A Bibliography,* 5 vols. Baltimore: Magna Carta Book Co., 1975–76. This work includes: Volume 1, Atlantic States from Maine to New York; Volume 2, Atlantic States from New Jersey to Florida; Volume 3, the Middle West, Alaska, and Hawaii; Volume 4, the West; and Volume 5, Supplement and Index. Volume 5 also corrects errors in the first four volumes.

Access to local histories is usually available through libraries in the areas concerned, but many are available at the Family History Library in Salt Lake City. Many more have been digitized and are on the Internet. To find them, key in the name of the place and the words "local history" or "county history" into your Internet search engine. Try separate searches for the names of both county and town/city.

C. Compiled lists (dictionaries, directories, registers, etc.)

Many different, though related, types of materials are included under this heading. Any lists—pioneers, early settlers, soldiers, patriots, immigrants, petitioners, etc., etc.—compiled from several (usually original) sources with some data or information on the listed persons—fall into this category. Some are quite comprehensive in their general coverage, others are comprehensive in their coverage of specifics, and still others are not comprehensive in any way. The purposes for which different lists were compiled were quite different. A few of the important works of this type will reveal the nature of these very useful tools:

Bancroft, Hubert Howe. *California Pioneer Register and Index, 1542–1848.* 1884–90. Reprint, Baltimore: Genealogical Publishing Co., 2005. This reprint is a compilation of biographical sketches extracted from the first five volumes of the author's seven-volume *History of California.*

Coulter, Ellis M., and A. B. Saye. *A List of the Early Settlers of Georgia.* 1949 and 1967. Reprint, Baltimore: Genealogical Publishing Co., 2006.

Coulter, Willa M. *Some Families of Revolutionary War Patriots from Virginia, Maryland, Pennsylvania, South Carolina and Kentucky.* Baltimore: Genealogical Publishing Co., 1993.

Farmer, John. *A Genealogical Register of the First Settlers of New England* (with additions and corrections by Samuel G. Drake). 1829 and 1947. Reprint, Baltimore: Genealogical Publishing Co., 2009.

Heitman, Francis B. *Historical Register and Dictionary of the United States Army, from Its Organization, September 29, 1789, to March 2, 1903.* 2 vols. 1903. Reprint, Urbana, IL: University of Illinois Press, 1993.

Hinman, Royal R. *A Catalogue of the Names of the First Puritan Settlers of the Colony of Connecticut.* 1846. Reprint, Baltimore: Genealogical Publishing Co., 2011.

Holmes, Frank R., comp. *Directory of the Ancestral Heads of New England Families, 1620–1700.* 1923. Reprint, Baltimore: Genealogical Publishing Co., 2008.

Kaminkow, Jack, and Marion Kaminkow. *A List of Emigrants from England to America, 1718–1759.* 1981. Reprint, Baltimore: Genealogical Publishing Co., 1989.

Noyes, Sybil, Charles T. Libby, and Walter G. Davis. *Genealogical Dictionary of Maine and New Hampshire.* 5 parts. 1928–39. Reprint, Baltimore: Genealogical Publishing Co., 2002, with all five parts in one.

Pope, Charles Henry. *The Pioneers of Massachusetts: A Descriptive List, Drawn from Records of the Colonies, Towns and Churches, and Other Contemporaneous Documents.* 1900. Reprint, Baltimore: Genealogical Publishing Co., 2002.

———. *The Pioneers of Maine and New Hampshire, 1623–1660: A Descriptive List Drawn from the Records of the Colonies, Towns, Churches, Courts, and Other Contemporary Sources.* 1908. Reprint, Baltimore: Genealogical Publishing Co., 2009.

Savage, James. *A Genealogical Dictionary of the First Settlers of New England, Showing Three Generations of Those Who Came Before 1692 on the Basis of Farmer's Register.* 4 vols. 1860–62. Reprint, Baltimore: Genealogical Publishing Co., 2008.

Skordas, Gust. *The Early Settlers of Maryland: An Index to Names of Immigrants, Compiled from Records of Land Patents, 1633–1680, in the Hall of Records, Annapolis, Maryland.* 1968. Reprint, Baltimore: Genealogical Publishing Co., 2009.

These lists are usually quite reliable (though often incomplete) because they are based on data found in original records. However, due to the secondary nature of the evidence they contain, they do have errors. Generally, however, accuracy is somewhat greater than family histories and genealogies because of the experience of their compilers and the nature of their sources. They do not usually contain information sufficient to prove a genealogical connection, but they are helpful as we seek to locate families.

D. Biographical works

Almost every library contains several useful biographical works. We ought to investigate those in our local libraries for relevant information on our American ancestral lines. Of course, most of these deal with persons who have achieved some degree of prominence in one field or another. Even those dealing with specific geographic areas have information only on prominent citizens. Because of this, the average genealogist will often pass them by because of his belief that his ancestors were just "common folks." This is a point well taken if the assumption is true. However, there is a "multiplier factor" in this type of source that makes it more useful than it might ordinarily be. Though our direct ancestors may not have been included, descendants of those ancestors—on lines other than our own—may have achieved prominence and were included. Because some of the ancestry of these persons is the same as ours, the value is practically the same. This is illustrated in the case of Robert Lowe.[2]

Robert was known to be the son of William Lowe who was killed by outlaws when he first came into Kentucky. The birthplace of William Lowe was unknown, nor was it known where he came from. Neither Robert nor any of his descendants achieved sufficient prominence to put their names in any biographical work, but Robert Andrew Lowe, a son of Robert's brother James, did achieve sufficient prominence to be listed in *Who's Who in America*. In his short biographical sketch, it told that his father, James, was born in Laurens County, South Carolina—a breakthrough on the problem.

The possibility that our ancestors had prominent descendants on lines other than our own should never be overlooked. And biographical works often pro-

---

[2] Though this is a real case, the names used are not the actual names of those involved.

vide the needed clues, just as in the Lowe example. Do not overlook in-laws either. We can get the same kind of good data out of these sources as we did from the Iowa county history in the Kerr example discussed earlier in this chapter.

A good bibliography of some important American biographical sources is Robert B. Slocum's *Biographical Dictionaries and Related Works*, 2nd ed. (Detroit: Gale Research Co., 1986). A few of the early American sources listed in Slocum's work include:

Allen, William. *The American Biographical Dictionary: Containing an Account of the Lives, Characters and Writing of the Most Eminent Persons Deceased in America from Its First Settlement.* 3rd ed. Boston: J. P. Jewett, 1857. This work was originally published in 1809 as *An American Biographical and Historical Dictionary.*

American Biography, a New Cyclopedia. New York: The American Historical Society, Inc., 1916.

Appleton's Cyclopaedia of American Biography. 7 vols. New York: D. Appleton, various editions, 1887–1900. A new, enlarged edition was published from 1915 to 1931 as *The Cyclopaedia of American Biography* by Press Association Compilers.

Brown, John H., ed. *The Cyclopaedia of American Biographies.* 7 vols. Boston: Cyclopaedia Publishing Co., 1903. This work was also published in 1904 in ten volumes under the title *The Twentieth Century Biographical Dictionary of Notable Americans.*

Drake, Samuel F. *Dictionary of American Biography, Including Men of the Time; Containing Nearly Ten Thousand Notices of Persons . . .* Boston: Houghton and Osgood, 1879.

Hall, Henry. *America's Successful Men of Affairs. An Encyclopedia of Contemporaneous Biography.* 2 vols. New York: New York Tribune, 1895–96.

Herringshaw, Thomas W., ed. and comp. *Herringshaw's National Library of American Biography.* 5 vols. Chicago: American Publishers' Association, 1904–14.

Leonard, John W., ed. *Men and Women of America: A Biographical Dictionary of Contemporaries.* New York: L. R. Hamersly, 1908.

The National Cyclopaedia of American Biography. New York: James T. White Co., 1893–19--.

Officers of the Army and Navy (Regular and Volunteer) Who Served in the Civil War. Philadelphia: L. R. Hamersly, 1894.

Rogers, Augustus C., ed. *Sketches of Representative Men, North and South.* New York: Atlantic Publishing Co., 1872.

Rosenbloom, Joseph R. *A Biographical Dictionary of Early American Jews: Colonial Times Through 1800.* Lexington, KY: University of Kentucky Press, c. 1960.

True, Ransom B., ed. *Biographical Dictionary of Early Virginia, 1607–1660.* Richmond, VA: Association for the Preservation of Virginia Antiquities, 1980.

United States Congress, *Biographical Dictionary of the American Congress, 1774–1961. . .* Rev. ed. Washington, DC: U.S. Government Printing Office, 1961.

Wakelyn, Jon L. *Biographical Dictionary of the Confederacy.* Westport, CT: Greenwood Press, c. 1977.

Who Was Who in America, Historical Volume, 1607–1896. Chicago: A. N. Marquis Co., 1963.

Who's Who in America. A Biographical Dictionary of Notable Living Men and Women. Chicago: A. N. Marquis Co., 1899 –1900—. Indexes are available.

The significant differences between this type of source and the compiled lists discussed earlier are that most of these were usually current or semi-current biography at the time of their publication, and their purpose was always biographical rather than either historical or genealogical. Some well-known sources of more recent American biography are as follows:

> *The American Catholic Who's Who*
> *American Men of Science*
> *Celebrity Register*
> *Contemporary Authors*
> *Current Biography*
> *Dictionary of American Biography*
> *Dictionary of American Scholars*
> *Leaders in Education*
> *Who's Who African-American*
> *Who's Who in American Art*
> *Who's Who in American Jewry*
> *Who's Who in American Junior Colleges*
> *Who's Who in Commerce and Industry*
> *Who's Who in Genealogy*
> *Who's Who in Labor*
> *Who's Who in Our American Government*
> *Who's Who in the Central States*
> *Who's Who in the East*
> *Who's Who in the Northwest*
> *Who's Who in the South*
> *Who's Who in the West*
> *Who's Who of American Women*

There are many, many more—some of them for specific states, regions, counties, and even cities. Most information in these sources was provided by the subjects themselves and is usually quite reliable.

E. Genealogical and historical periodicals

This area is much larger and more comprehensive in scope than is usually suspected by the beginning family history researcher. It runs the gamut from the scholarly journal to the mimeographed, one-man, low-budget publication of a specific family. There are literally hundreds of publications—monthlies, bi-monthlies, quarterlies, semi-annuals, and annuals—each making its own contribution to family history and the science of genealogy. Governmental units, libraries, historical societies, genealogical societies, patriotic and hereditary societies, families, and private individuals all play an important role. Some of these periodicals are excellent, some are good, and some are bad. All, however, were or are published with good intent.

Many periodicals are published on a very restricted basis and copies are almost impossible for the average person to obtain—in fact, something of significant interest to us might well be published without our ever knowing of its existence unless someone makes a specific effort to inform us or we come across it accidentally. Very few libraries, if any, have all such publications, though several subscribe to all of the most reputable ones. Many have extensive holdings. The New York Public Library receives some 600 genealogical periodicals annually and the Family History Library in Salt Lake City subscribes to most of the same ones. Almost every library subscribes to at least a few periodicals—usually some of the most important ones.

Bearing in mind the inaccessibility of genealogical periodicals, note that Genealogical Publishing Company has made a significant—though little known—effort to resolve that problem by reprinting and indexing articles from several key journals, most articles selected by Gary Boyd Roberts. The fruits of this project include seventy-five volumes, most averaging about 1,000 pages. There are twenty volumes from *The William and Mary Quarterly*, *Tyler's Quarterly Historical and Genealogical Magazine* (1853–1935), and *Virginia Magazine of History and Biography*. Sixteen of those twenty volumes contain about 2,000 articles on the principal families in those articles. The remaining volumes from these twenty volumes cover various published records: vital records, military records, land records, wills, and tax (and related) records.

Those states covered by articles in the other volumes include Maine, New Hampshire, Connecticut, Rhode Island, Massachusetts, New York, Pennsylvania, New Jersey, Maryland, Kentucky, West Virginia, and Ohio, as well the New England region. Most volumes also contain compiled genealogies, though some (Ohio in particular) also contain extensive published source documents. The project was essentially designed to glean the most important genealogical content from the complete run of each periodical. There are also other multi-volume works included (mostly biographical) that are not periodicals.

You will find the volumes of this large collection of publications containing articles from key genealogical periodicals on the Genealogical Publishing Company website, *http://www.genealogical.com*.

Following is a list of a few current, available genealogical and historical periodicals published in the United States with the names of sponsoring organization and contact addresses:

A.P.G. Quarterly, Association of Professional Genealogists, P.O. Box 535, Wheat Ridge, CO 80034-0535.

The American Genealogist (an independent publication with no organizational sponsor), P.O. Box 11, Barrington, RI 02806-0011.

The Augustan Omnibus, Augustan Society, Inc., P.O. Box 771267, Orlando, FL 32877-1267.

Avotaynu, The International Review of Jewish Genealogy, Avotaynu, Inc., 794 Edgewood Avenue, New Haven, CT 06515.

Bluegrass, Kentucky Genealogical Society, P.O. Box 153, Frankfort, KY 40602.

Branches and Twigs, Genealogical Society of Vermont, P.O. Box 14, Randolph, VT 05060-0014.

The Bulletin: Genealogical Forum of Oregon, Inc., 2505 S.E. 11th Avenue, Suite B-18, Portland, OR 97202-1061.

Central Illinois Genealogical Quarterly, Decatur Genealogical Society, P.O. Box 1548, Decatur, IL 62525-1548.

The Connecticut Nutmegger : Connecticut Genealogical Society, P.O. Box 435, Glastonbury, CT 06033-0435.

Crossroads (formerly *The Genealogical Journal*), Utah Genealogical Association, P.O. Box 1144, Salt Lake City, UT 84110.

Delaware Genealogical Society Journal: Delaware Genealogical Society, 505 N. Market Street, Wilmington, DE 19801-3091.

Detroit Society for Genealogical Research Magazine, Detroit Society for Genealogical Research, Detroit Public Library, c/o Burton Historical Collection, 5201 Woodward Avenue, Detroit, MI 48202-4007.

Eastman's Online Genealogy Newsletter: The Daily Online Genealogy Newsletter. This informative online blog is sponsored by MyHeritage and updated daily by Dick Eastman. It has both a free edition and a paid edition. It is at *https://blog.eogn.com/.*

Family Tree Magazine, F+W Media, Inc., 10151 Carver Road #200, Cincinnati, OH 45242. This magazine is available both in hard copy and online. Online subscriptions are available at *http://www.familytree magazine.com/.*

FGS Voice (online publication), Federation of Genealogical Societies, subscriptions available at *https://fgs.org/cpage.php?pt=71.*

Filson Club Historical Quarterly, The Filson Historical Society, 1310 S. Third Street, Louisville, KY 40208.

The Genealogist, American Society of Genealogists; Joseph C. Anderson II, Secretary, 5337 Del Roy Drive, Dallas TX 75229-3016.

The Genealogical Magazine of New Jersey, The Genealogical Society of New Jersey, P.O. Box 1476, Trenton, NJ 08607-1476.

Georgia Genealogical Society Quarterly, Georgia Genealogical Society, P.O. Box 550247, Atlanta, GA 30355-2747.

Hawkeye Heritage, Iowa Genealogical Society, 628 E. Grand Avenue, Des Moines, IA 50309-1924. This bi-monthly publication is available either electronically or in paper.

The Hoosier Genealogist: Connections, Indiana Historical Society, 450 West Ohio Street, Indianapolis, Indiana, 46202.

Idaho Genealogical Society Quarterly, Idaho Genealogical Society, Inc. P.O. Box 1854, Boise, ID 83701-1854.

Illinois State Genealogical Society Quarterly, Illinois State Genealogical Society, P.O. Box 10195, Springfield, IL 62791-0195.

Internet Genealogy, Moorshead Magazines Ltd., P.O. Box 194, Niagara Falls, NY 14304.

Journal of the Afro-American Historical and Genealogical Society, Afro-American Historical and Genealogical Society, P.O. Box 73067; Washington, DC 20056-3067.

Kentucky Ancestors, Kentucky Historical Society, 100 W. Broadway Street, Frankfort, KY 40601.

Maryland Genealogical Society Journal, Maryland Genealogical Society, 201 West Monument Street, Baltimore, MD 21201.

The Mayflower Descendant: a Quarterly Magazine of Pilgrim Genealogy and History, New England Historic Genealogical Society, 101 Newbury Street, Boston, MA 02116 (formerly published by Massachusetts Society of Mayflower Descendants—not published 1926–1929, 1936, 1938–1984).

Mayflower Quarterly, General Society of Mayflower Descendants, 4 Winslow Street, Plymouth, MA 02360.

Morasha, Jewish Genealogical Society of Illinois, P.O. Box 515, Northbrook, IL 60065-0515.

National Genealogical Society Quarterly, National Genealogical Society, 3108 Columbia Pike, Suite 300, Arlington, VA 22204-4370.

New England Historical and Genealogical Register, New England Historic Genealogical Society, 101 Newbury Street, Boston, MA 02116.

New York Genealogical and Biographical Record, The New York Genealogical and Biographical Society, 36 West 44th Street, Suite 711, New York, NY 10036-8105.

North Carolina Genealogical Society Journal, North Carolina Genealogical Society, P.O. Box 30815, Raleigh, NC 27622-0815.

Ohio Records and Pioneer Families, Ohio Genealogical Society, 611 State Route 97 West, Bellville OH 44813-8813.

Oregon Genealogical Society Quarterly, Oregon Genealogical Society, 955 Oak Street, Eugene, OR 97401.

Pennsylvania Genealogical Magazine (called *Publications of the Genealogical Society of Pennsylvania* from 1895 until 1947), Genealogical Society of Pennsylvania, 2207 Chestnut Street, Philadelphia, PA 19103.

St. Louis Genealogical Society Quarterly, St. Louis Genealogical Society, #4 Sunnen Drive, Suite 140, St. Louis, MO 63143.

Southern Genealogist's Exchange Quarterly, The Southern Genealogist's Exchange Society, 6215 Sauterne Drive, Jacksonville, FL 32210.

Stirpes, Texas State Genealogical Society, P.O. Box 7308, Tyler, TX 75711-7308.

The Tree Searcher, Kansas Genealogical Society, Box 103, Dodge City, KS 67801.

Tree Shaker, Kentucky Genealogical Society, Ashland, KY 41105-1544.

Vermont Genealogy, Genealogical Society of Vermont, P.O. Box 14, Randolph, VT 05060-0014.

Tree Talks, Central New York Genealogical Society, P.O. Box 104, Colvin Station, Syracuse, NY 13205-0104.

The Virginia Genealogist, (published from 1957 through 2006). Copies of most issues are available at the Family History Library in Salt Lake City and at the New England Historic Genealogical Society in Boston.

Virginia Magazine of History and Biography, Virginia Historical Society, 428 North Boulevard, Richmond, VA 23220.

The William and Mary Quarterly, Omohundro Institute of Early American History and Culture, Earl Gregg Swem Library, 400 Landrum Drive, Williamsburg, VA 23185 (website: *http://oieahc.wm.edu/*)

Your Genealogy Today (formerly *Family Chronicle*), Moorshead Magazines Ltd., P.O. Box 194, Niagara Falls, NY 14304.

Of course, there are many more genealogical periodicals than are listed here. There are also some excellent past periodicals that are no longer being published. In virtually every case, back issues have been preserved and are available for research. There are also many indexes to facilitate their access and use.

In keeping with the times in which we live, many of these periodicals provide access to current issues on the Internet—some having both paper and electronic editions. Information relating to (and sometimes direct access) can be gained by searching for the name of the periodical or the sponsoring organization in your Internet search engine. In many instances, however, current and more recent issues are available only to members of the societies that publish them.

A few of the most widely circulated of these periodicals are listed in the *Gale Directory of Publications and Broadcast Media*[3] (formerly *Ayer Directory of Publications*). This directory contains detailed entries that include addresses, phone numbers, fax numbers, e-mail addresses, and website URLs. It is often useful to refer to this directory under the periodical's place of publication to determine when publication started. However, the *Standard Periodical Directory* (Lexington, NY: Oxbridge Publishing Co.) and *Ulrich's International Periodicals Directory* (New York: R. R. Bowker) have easier-to-use, more complete lists of genealogical periodicals and give the same information. The *Standard Periodical Directory* lists publications by category, has the same information at *Gale,* and lists about 59,000 publications. *Ulrich's,* as its title suggests, is international in scope and is available to subscribers online at *https://ulrichsweb.serialssolutions.com/login/.*

Biennially, over a period of twenty years, Mary Keysor Meyer produced updated versions of *Meyer's Directory of Genealogical Societies in the U.S.A. and Canada.*[4] Also of note is Kip Sperry's *A Survey of American Genealogical Periodicals and Periodical Indexes,*[5] published in 1978. The works of both Meyer and Sperry are excellent, but they are now quite outdated. One of the most significant problems with these works is the ever-changing nature of nonprofit organizations—especially their address changes.

Between the covers of these many periodicals is a wealth of genealogical and historical information. All types of information are included—genealogies, family histories, family sketches, biographical sketches, indexes to otherwise unindexed records, locality histories, information from valuable private record collections, copies of lost records, genealogical queries with useful data, procedural instructions on the use of various record types, guides to record use, research standards, etc.—and most of this information lies hidden and undetected because of limited circulation, lack of indexes, and lack of knowledge of existing indexes.

There are some useful periodical indexes. (Some of the general ones are listed in Chapter 6 under "Guides to Non-original Sources.") Among them are Jacobus's *Index to Genealogical Periodicals,* the *Genealogical Periodical Annual (GPA) Index,* Swem's *Virginia Historical Index,* and Munsell's *Index to American Genealogies.*

Some periodicals also have excellent special indexes of their own. These include the *Pennsylvania Magazine of History and Biography,* the *National Genealogical Society Quarterly,* and the *New England Historical and Genealogical Register.* There are many others. Indexes to state publications are also

[3] *Gale Directory of Publications and Broadcast Media* (Detroit, MI: Gale Research, 1869 –).

[4] Mary Keysor Meyer, ed., *Meyer's Directory of Genealogical Societies in the U.S.A. and Canada,* 11 biennial editions (Mt. Airy, MD: Libra Publications, 1976–1996).

[5] Kip Sperry, *A Survey of American Genealogical Periodicals and Periodical Indexes* (Detroit: Gale Research Co., 1978). This is Volume 3 in the Gale Genealogy and Local History Series.

frequently found in state libraries and state historical societies. For example, the *Maryland Historical Magazine* is card indexed at the Maryland Historical Society.

Certainly, periodicals should be used when their use is feasible, but this is a good thing that can be overdone. It is unwise to spend hours searching haphazardly through periodical literature for information on our ancestors if we do not know what we are looking for or where to look. Also, notwithstanding the great genealogical value of these periodicals, there is not significant value for everyone. Also, remember that the evidence they contain is secondary, and the possibility of error must always be considered.

F. Guide to published records

This is a unique category because there is only one book that fits here. I list it here by itself because this book on published records—published source documents as well as compilations—does not fit in any other category, and it is too valuable to leave out. The book is:

> Meyerink, Kory, ed. *Printed Sources: A Guide to Published Genealogical Records*. Provo, Utah: Ancestry Publishing, 1998.

The chapters in this work were written by several different specialists. The chapters include "General Reference"; "Instructional Materials"; "Geographic Tools: Maps, Atlases and Gazetteers"; "Ethnic Sources"; "Bibliographies and Catalogs"; "Published Indexes"; "Vital & Cemetery Records"; "Church Sources"; "Censuses and Tax Lists"; "Published Probate Records"; "Printed Land Records"; "Court and Legal Records"; "Military Sources"; "Immigration Sources"; "Documentary Sources"; "Family Histories and Genealogies"; "County & Local Histories"; "Biographies"; "Genealogical Periodicals"; "and "Medieval Genealogy."

The book was designed as a companion volume to *The Source*,[6] and it serves well. It has one major fault, however—the same fault as the third edition of *The Researcher's Guide*—it has not been updated since its publication in 1998 and is out-of-date. Though there is still significant value, an update would be welcome.

G. Compendium genealogies

A compendium is a work that treats a broad subject in brief form. These are usually comprehensive treatises of a broad scope but with only abstracts of information. One compiler of a compendium genealogy said it was his objective "to compress the lineages contained in thousands of individual family

---

[6] Loretto Dennis Szucs, and Sandra Hargreaves Luebking, eds., *The Source: A Guidebook of American Genealogy.* 3rd ed. Salt Lake City: Ancestry Publishing, 2006).

genealogies into a single volume."[7] Genealogical compendia are notoriously inaccurate because the data presented therein are generally from sources other than original records—usually from family histories or family members. They are useful but should be used with great care. Some of the most widely known compendia in American genealogy are as follows:

> d'Angeville, Count Howard H., and Arthur Adams. *Living Descendants of Blood Royal in America*. 5 vols. London: World Nobility and Peerage, 1959–80.
>
> Hardy, Stella Pickett. *Colonial Families of the Southern States of America*. 2nd ed. 1958. Reprint, Baltimore: Genealogical Publishing Co., 2007.
>
> Mackenzie, George Norbury, ed. *Colonial Families of the United States of America*. 7 vols. 1907–20. Reprint, Baltimore: Genealogical Publishing Co., 2007.
>
> Munsell, Joel's sons. *American Ancestry: Giving the Name and Descent, in the Male Line, of Americans Whose Ancestors Settled in the United States Previous to the Declaration of Independence, A.D. 1776*. 12 vols. 1887–99. Reprint, Baltimore: Genealogical Publishing Co., 1998, in 4 vols.
>
> Pittman, Hannah D. *Americans of Gentle Birth and Their Ancestors: A Genealogical Encyclopedia, Embracing Many Authenticated Lineages and Biographical Sketches of the Founders of the Colonies and Their Descendants Found in All Parts of the United States*. 2 vols. 1903–7. Reprint, Baltimore: Genealogical Publishing Co., 1970.
>
> Virkus, Frederick A., ed. *The Compendium of American Genealogy. The Standard Genealogical Encyclopedia of the First Families of America*. 7 vols. 1925–42. Reprint, Baltimore: Genealogical Publishing Co., 2012.

H. Special manuscript collections

Some people expend significant time, effort, and expense gathering data and materials for publication (or just for the joy of gathering) that, for one reason or another, are never published. Many of these collections have found their way into libraries, historical societies, and archives. Many more lie hidden away in private and family records. The obvious disadvantage of these types of records, even those in libraries and archives, is that they are hard to locate even when we know they exist. Some have been microfilmed and this helps, but it does not completely solve the problem.

In the past, the best guides to such materials—those records hidden away in unexpected places—were the continuing series of the *National Union Cata-*

---

[7] Frederick A. Virkus, ed., *Compendium of American Genealogy*. Vol. 1. (1925; repr., Baltimore: Genealogical Publishing Co., 2012), 5.

log of Manuscript Collections (NUCMC), prepared in twenty-nine volumes by the Library of Congress with assistance from the Council on Library Resources between 1959 and 1993.[8]

These volumes contain descriptions of more than 72,000 collections in more than 1,400 different repositories with more than a million index references to topical subjects and personal, family, corporate, and geographic names. Though all *NUCMC* printed volumes are currently out of print, many libraries have these volumes, either on their shelves or on microfilm. Microfilm copies are still available for purchase from the Library of Congress.

The publisher, Chadwyck-Healey, has made *NUCMC* cataloging available in its online publication, *ArchivesUSA™*. Also, under the authorship of Harriet Ostroff, Chadwyck-Healey published, in two volumes, an *Index to Personal Names in the National Union Catalog of Manuscript Collections, 1959–1984* (Alexandria: 1988).

In addition, Chadwyck-Healey has established an online *Archive Finder* (*http://archives.chadwyck.com/marketing/index.jsp*) to provide easy electronic access to this resource. I quote below the description of the online *ArchivesUSA™* website and *Archive Finder* on that site. (Note that *National Inventory of Documentary Sources [NIDS] UK/Ireland*—which is not part of our discussion—is also included in this important resource.)

> *ArchivesUSA* is a current directory of over 5,600 repositories and more than 175,000 collections of primary source material across the United States. *NIDS UK/Ireland* is a major reference work that reproduces on microfiche the finding aids to thousands of archive and manuscript collections in libraries and record offices, museums and private collections throughout the UK and Ireland. Used together in *Archive Finder*, researchers are able to read descriptions of a repository's holdings to determine whether a collection contains material useful to their work as well as find the information they need to contact the repository directly.
>
> Repository records provide detailed information including phone and fax numbers, hours of service, materials solicited, email and home page URLs when available. Each collection record links to its corresponding repository record, simplifying the research process.
>
> *Archive Finder* integrates the following information into comprehensive collection records:
>
> - The entire collection of *NUCMC* from 1959 to 2009. The *National Union Catalog of Manuscript Collections* (*NUCMC*) includes information gathered and indexed by the Library of Congress, covering

---

[8] Library of Congress, *National Union Catalog of Manuscript Collections* (1959–61; 1962; 1959–62 Index: 1963–64; 1965; Index 1963–65; 1966, Index 1963–66; 1967, Index 1967; —), Vol. 1 publ. Ann Arbor, MI: J. W. Edwards, 1962; Vols. 2–3 publ. Hamden, CT: Shoe String Press, 1964; remaining vols. publ. Washington, DC: Library of Congress, 1965–1993.

115,000 collections. Only *Archive Finder* makes all of the historical *NUCMC* fully searchable in electronic form.

- Names and detailed subject indexing of 72,000 collections whose finding aids have been published separately in ProQuest UMI's microfiche series, *National Inventory of Documentary Sources in the United States* (*NIDS*).

- Names and detailed subject indexing of over 47,000 collections whose finding aids have been published separately in ProQuest UMI's microfiche series, *National Inventory of Documentary Sources in the United Kingdom and Ireland* (*NIDS UK/Ireland*).

- Collection descriptions submitted directly to us from repositories.

- A growing number of more than 6,000 links to online finding aids.

Detailed indexing of collections allows powerful searching across eight combinable fields. Users can zero in on material relevant to their research.[9]

As you will note from the above-quoted description, repositories with archival collections not included in *NUCMC* are invited to submit descriptions of their collections for inclusion in this resource. I do not know the extent of their response.

Many family and personal records fall into this manuscript category, but mainly it comprises compilations and collections of original documents of various kinds. If we use *NUCMC* to seek family history data, there are a number of approaches that can be rewarding:

- Search under the heading "genealogy."
- Search for our surnames of interest.
- Search under the specific localities where our ancestral family lived.
- In those localities where our family lived, look for lawyers' papers—especially in counties where the records were burned.
- If our ancestor was in the military and we know the service regiment, look for papers of commanding officers.

Of special interest to the user of *NUCMC* is the geographical guide published in the 1981 volume. It shows which repositories had reported and when they did so. In addition to the regular yearly indexes, an index to repositories was compiled every few years and a cumulative index every four or five years.

Why did *NUCMC* cease? The reason given is that other programs came along that apparently better fulfilled the needs of researchers. The first of these was Research Libraries Information Network (RLIN), which assumed the "necessary" functions of *NUCMC* in 1993. The next program, superseding RLIN in 2007, was Online Computer Library Center (OCLC). OCLC is

---

[9] "About Archive Finder," *Archive Finder,* http://archives.chadwyck.com/marketing/about.jsp (accessed January 5, 2017).

the sponsor of WorldCat, which I have mentioned in previous chapters. World Cat is an online international library catalog that itemizes the collections of research libraries. Both of these successor programs have focused primarily on research library collections and the international nature of their influence rather than on manuscript collections. Thus, though NUCMC ceased, it is still relevant because of the work of the publisher Chadwyck-Healey and *ArchivesUSA™*.

II. NEWSPAPERS

Another useful, though far from trustworthy, printed family history source is the local newspaper of the geographical area where our ancestors lived. Important family history information can be obtained from obituaries, marriage and engagement stories and announcements, birth announcements, probate court proceedings, legal notices, notes of thanks, news items, etc. All of these can be useful. I have known of several situations where the only information that could be found about a person's birthplace was in his obituary.

Generally, weekly newspapers are a better source because they usually provide more detailed information about events than do the larger dailies, though there are exceptions. Also, when we use newspapers, especially older ones, remember that journalism has not always had the "objective reporting of facts" as its stated objective.

Following are some examples of marriage notices and obituaries from early newspapers.

—Marriages—

Raleigh Register and North Carolina Gazette—Tuesday, June 10, 1834:

In this City, on Thursday evening last, by the Rev. Mr. Dowd, Mr. Thomas J. Johnson to Miss Ann Maria Walton.

In this county, on the 29th ultimo, Mr. John M'Cullars to Miss Aley Ann Warren, eldest daughter of Nathaniel Warren, Esq.

In Orange county, on the 8th ultimo, Col. Jehu Ward to Miss Martha M'Callian, daughter of John M'Callian, Esq.

In Person county, on the 14th ultimo Mr. Irby Sanders to Miss Sarah Briggs. Also on the 15th Mr. John H. Jones to Miss Rebecca Winstead.

In Franklin county, on the 14th ultimo, Mr. Thomas Debnam to Miss Priscilla Macon, daughter of Nathaniel Macon, Esq.

At Oxford, on the 27th ultimo, Capt. Samuel B. Meacham to Miss Martha Curran.

In Chowan county, by Rev. John Avery. Mr. Robert T. Paine to Miss Lavinia Benbury.

—Deaths—

Virginia Argus (Richmond) —Wednesday, August 6, 1806:

DIED—On Friday evening Mrs. AMBLEM of this city of the most elevated standing in the city, and beloved by all who knew her.

On Sunday morning, Mrs. FRANCES GAUTIER an old and respectable inhabitant of this city.

On the 28th of July last in Goochland county, at their dwelling house, Mr. WILLIAM POWERS and his wife JUDITH, within a few hours of each other; he lay sick 19 days with a dysentery which he bore with christian fortitude; she was taken with a shock of the dead Palsy which carried her off in about twenty-six hours; in her health before she was taken ill, she often declared there would not be two days difference in their deaths. They lived 57 years together in a well-spent life of conjugal affection, and by their care and industry had raised a plentiful fortune, together with a numerous family; and like Theodocius and Constance, were both buried in one grave, and as they were lovely and pleasant in their lives, in their deaths they were not divided.

Note from the above examples that details in early newspapers are often sketchy, even for persons of "the most elevated standing." Sometimes, however, these newspaper accounts provide useful data for identifying ancestors and especially for distinguishing them from other persons of the same name. One of the most difficult identity problems in research is that of contemporaneous people with the same names. Any information that helps distinguish one from another is invaluable.

It is often difficult to locate old newspapers that might be of value to our research, but there are some useful aids available. In the past, we have referred readers to the following valuable reference works:

Brigham, Clarence Saunders. *History and Bibliography of American Newspapers, 1690–1820.* 2 vols. Reprint, Westport, CT: Greenwood Press, 1976.

Gregory Gerould, Winifred, ed. *American Newspapers 1821–1936: A Union List of Files Available in the United States and Canada.* 1937. Reprint, New York: Kraus Reprint Corp., 1967.

Milner, Anita Cheek. *Newspaper Indexes: A Location and Subject Guide for Researchers.* 3 vols. Metuchen, NJ: Scarecrow Press, 1977–82.

The first two of these reference works cover newspapers published in the United States after 1690 and tell the locations (specific libraries, historical societies, newspaper offices, etc.) of existing copies. They tell how often each paper was published (weekly, daily, etc.), what copies have survived, and the time covered by the publication. Many libraries have copies of these works. The third reference is not a guide to the newspapers themselves but a guide to newspaper indexes.

There are three issues involved when we seek to use old newspapers in our family history research:

- whether a newspaper was published in the time and place of interest;
- whether copies of a previously published paper still exist; and
- the location of extant (still existing) copies.

Modern computer technology has dealt with (and is continuing to deal with) these issues. One important project is the "Chronicling America" project of the Library of Congress, in which many historic newspapers from all states, between the years 1836 and 1922, have been digitized and fully indexed. This resource is available at *http://chroniclingamerica.loc.gov/newspapers/*.

Another valuable Internet source of old indexed newspapers is Newspapers.com (*https://www.newspapers.com/*), where there are more than 5,200 accessible, indexed newspapers (2017). All newspapers on this site are also available for browsing. Access to the site is by subscription; however, a seven-day free trial is available. If you have a specific, limited time period involved, you might find browsing to be worthwhile because the indexing was accomplished by optical character recognition (OCR) and is far from perfect. Unfortunately, old newspapers do not scan well.

I should also mention a website named Newspaper Archive (*https://newspaperarchive.com/*). This site claims to be the world's largest newspaper archive, with newspapers covering more than 400 years for 50 states and 22 countries. The collection covers more than 7,854 and counting newspaper titles (2017). This is also a subscription site, but there are different subscriber levels. There is also a fourteen-day free trial, and the site has some significant search features that greatly facilitate the finding of pertinent newspaper stories.

One other important newspaper source is Ancestry. Ancestry has an indexed "Historical Newspapers Collection" (*http://search.ancestry.com/search/group/histnews*) available to Ancestry subscribers.

I also call attention to the *Gale Directory of Publications and Broadcast Media* (formerly *Ayer's Directory*)[10] mentioned earlier in this chapter in connection with genealogical periodicals. This directory, first published in 1869, has had many different titles and has been published sometimes annually and sometimes at other intervals. Today the directory is available both in print and in electronic format, but not every library has it in its reference collection. The current edition is especially valuable if the newspaper you seek is still in publication, as many older newspapers are. In such cases, the directory is a useful guide to the newspaper's current address and archive. The date the paper began publication is also indicated—and whether it had weekly or daily circulation.

If we are unaware of any specific newspaper in the locality where our ancestors lived, we should certainly consult *Gale* for possibilities. If there are no newspapers being published (or none were published during the relevant time period) in the town where they lived, get the names of nearby towns from a map and see if any of those towns had newspapers that might interest you.

The Library of Congress has digitized some of the earliest editions of the *Ayers* directories, and these early editions are available online at *http://loc.*

---

[10] *Gale Directory of Publications and Broadcast Media* (Detroit: Gale Research, 1869—).

gov/rr/news/news_research_tools/ayersdirectory.html. This is a useful tool to learn what newspapers were being published in those periods, beginning in 1869.

Though I do not recommend using newspaper want ads as a method for finding unknown relatives, current newspapers, especially weeklies, can still be used to good advantage because we often have relatives living in places where our ancestors lived many years ago. Though our direct ancestors moved away, some of their siblings may have stayed behind. It is, in fact, possible that a sizable branch of our family is still living in the area. Sometimes a kind letter and a small remittance to the editor of the local weekly will put our inquiry in his news columns where it can be seen.

III. LIMITATIONS OF COMPILED SOURCES

This chapter has already discussed limitations as they relate to the various categories of compiled sources, but it seems appropriate now to establish them more clearly in our minds by summarizing briefly some of the major problems presented by these materials. It is important to understand these problem areas. However, at the same time, we ought not to become so obsessed with the negatives that we overlook the good points.

Consider the following issues:

A. Accessibility and availability

Because of limited publication and shortage of indexes, we cannot always take full advantage of many compiled sources. We are often unaware of many items that could be useful; others, of which we are aware, are difficult to find.

B. Reliability

When it comes to credibility gaps, it is hard to compete with most compiled sources. High-quality, reliable compiled sources do exist and we are grateful for them, but they are the exception. Typically, the reliability gap is wide because of the frequent absence of scientific research methods in their production. In fact, all printed sources should be approached with due caution. In them, we frequently find families that are inaccurate and pedigree connections that lack verification. Hence, they often fail to contain even good circumstantial evidence. Also, because of their distance—not necessarily speaking of time but of the number of generations removed—from any original records, clerical errors are also possible. In research, the effect of any kind of error can be serious. Note, however, that compiled sources often provide helpful clues and give us starting places for our research.

C. Completeness

The most incomplete compiled sources are, no doubt, family histories and compendium genealogies. Other sources are generally limited in their nature and scope and we do not expect them to be complete in quite the same way. We often find that family histories have been compiled by persons with limited qualifications and without thorough research. They are frequently full of information gaps that might have been filled if the research had been better. There are not only incomplete families but also incomplete information on many family members.

D. Documentation

If stated "facts" lack documentation, they mean nothing. Many compiled sources indicate that one thing or another is true but they provide no documentation and give no explanation about what evidence supports it or tell why it is believed to be true. Footnotes and/or complete source references are essential in credible compiled sources, and, without them, there is no way to determine authenticity. Also, even when complete and detailed source references are given, if the information was obtained from other compiled sources, it cannot be accepted as fact unless substantiated by better evidence. Merely finding something stated in two or three different family histories does not make it true. These books often go on and on quoting each other, accepting something as fact merely because "it's in the book." However, to borrow a popular trite saying, "It ain't necessarily so."

I have seen books with some (usually not extensive) documentation that, when the sources are carefully examined, have no correlation between those sources and their alleged product. This is nothing more than sloppiness and can usually be traced to poor methods of record keeping, but it adds up to poor research methods. Many other writers omit all documentation. Both approaches create a problem, and I am not sure which is worse.

E. Our dilemma

We will, no doubt, encounter other problems in our use of compiled sources, but those noted above are the main ones. William Bradford Brown (1806–1846) made a sobering summary of the situation as he observed it when he wrote the following in the *Pilgrim News Letter*:

> When I enter a genealogical room and see the many workers industriously copying from the printed records, I have a feeling almost of dismay, realizing that each one is perhaps adding to the already hopeless tangle of twisted pedigrees.[11]

This is the dilemma presented by compiled sources, and the thing that makes this dilemma so serious is the fact that so many uninformed, would-be family history researchers never progress beyond the compiled sources in that "genealogical room" of which Mr. Brown wrote—whether they consult those books in a library or online. Their research begins and ends in compiled

---

[11] As quoted by Donald L. Jacobus in *Genealogy as Pastime and Profession*, 2nd ed. rev. (Baltimore: Genealogical Publishing Co., 1968), 61. Used by permission.

sources. Mr. Jacobus explained the problem further when he said that most family histories are written

> in blissful ignorance of record sources, only scratching the surface of the research, full of erroneous deductions and inconsistencies, bearing evidence of rank amateurishness. . . . Too often. . . [these authors] are satisfied to follow what is found in print on the early generations, in total ignorance of its trustworthiness, and to reconcile all difficulties they encounter by assumptions and guesses. In view of this situation, it is remarkable that so many good family histories have been written, and that the average one is even as good as it is.[12]

In addition to what has already been said, there is one other point to be observed—a point that is now a reality because of the Internet and the many amazing family history resources available there. The compiled genealogical/family history information on the Internet is no better than what is in the compiled sources we have been discussing. In fact, much of that information came from those same unsubstantiated sources. The fact it is on the Internet does not improve its quality. Please proceed with due caution, verifying the documentation on those online pedigrees. No family history or genealogy is better than the research that produced it.

IV. FINAL OBSERVATION

This discussion on compiled sources generated some criticism in early editions of this book. It was duly pointed out to me that what I had written was an attack on the work of good genealogists. My critics advised me that "Mr. [Milton] Rubincam and Mr. [John] Coddington [*et al.*] produced many valuable works, and that I had belittled their efforts and insulted their work"!

If I have insulted good genealogists, I apologize. However, I seriously doubt that good genealogists took offense. The estimable Milton Rubincam, who so graciously reviewed the original manuscript of the first edition of *The Researcher's Guide* and voluntarily wrote the Introduction, offered no criticism and indicated no need for softening the blow. Mr. Rubincam and Mr. Coddington, who are both now deceased—and many others—shared my concerns and employed appropriate methods in their research.

I am pleased to observe that many good works are being compiled. We should utilize them and recognize their value. However, there is another, more current, issue with the genealogical information now being proliferated on the Internet. Many people have great concern about the flood of questionable genealogies being published on the Internet and with the willingness of so many people to accept them as fact, regardless of the source. None of this "work product" is better than the research that produced it, and, in far too many cases, that research has been shallow and incomplete. In many cases, it is highly suspect and does not represent sound practice. Please proceed with caution.

---

[12] Jacobus, 64–65.

13

Vital Records

V ital records, as we will consider them in this chapter, are primarily civil (or non-church) records of births, marriages, and deaths. They can be an important source of genealogical evidence. We will also consider certificates of divorce, but not divorce decrees—which are court records. These vital records do not have a place in every American pedigree problem because they are a relatively recent source in most areas of the country. However, where they apply, their use is essential, and research is not complete until they have been explored.

I. BEGINNING AND BACKGROUND

A. The colonial period

The American system of keeping vital records is unique in many ways when compared with the systems used by other countries, even though the roots of at least part of the American system began on foreign soil. The primary roots, however, lie in America herself.

Because the early settlers in most of those colonies that later became the United States of America were predominantly British, they followed British customs. Beginning in 1538, shortly after the separation of the English church from the church in Rome, it became a requirement for Church of England ministers to keep a record of christenings (baptisms), marriages, and burials in the registers of their parish churches. This was nearly seventy years before the first permanent British colony was established on American soil, and the practice was continued in the English churches established in the early colonies, being implemented and facilitated by colonial statute.

The first known law in the colonies to this effect was passed by the Grand Assembly of Virginia in 1632. That law required the minister or warden from each parish to appear in court once a year, on June 1, and present a record of christenings, marriages, and burials for the preceding year.[1] These were the traditional events recorded by the church, but, in effect, they provided a record of births, marriages, and deaths.

A statute passed by the General Court of the Massachusetts Bay Colony in 1639 required town clerks of that colony to make a record of the actual births and deaths rather than christenings and burials. This act was also different because it placed the burden for keeping these records upon governmental rather than church officials. Connecticut, Old Colony (New Plymouth), and other colonies soon adopted this same pattern.

B. The system grows—slowly

As time passed, legal machinery was effected to help collect and preserve these records. The early laws were repeatedly strengthened to better accomplish this task. Again, the Massachusetts Bay Colony provides a good example of these strengthening procedures. In 1644, that colony added a penalty to its registration laws for those persons who failed to report vital events to their town clerks, and in 1692, the colony went so far as to establish registration fees. This 1692 act, the most comprehensive vital registration law of the period, empowered town clerks to collect three pence for each birth or death registered and to assess fines upon those who failed to report. The act also allowed—but did not require—the clerks to issue birth certificates.[2]

None of these early laws was ever very effective. Even much later than the colonial period already discussed, problems plagued those responsible for keeping the records. The main problem was incomplete coverage. Though many towns and cities had legislation, not one state had anything close to complete registration coverage before the mid-nineteenth century.

The most significant reason that those early laws were ineffective was the lack of concern for property rights (the only reason given for such legislation to exist)[3] by a population swelled with recent immigrants, many of whom settled only temporarily awaiting their chance to move west. The population was so unsettled that enforcement of these laws was next to impossible.

C. The turning point

A better reason than protection of property rights was needed to induce compliance. And a better reason was finally provided by a group of medical men and statisticians who saw the importance of knowing about births and deaths—especially deaths, by cause—as a means of fighting disease and con-

---

[1] National Office of Vital Statistics, *Vital Statistics of the United States 1951* (Washington, DC: U.S. Public Health Service, 1954), Vol. I, 3.

[2] Ibid., Vol. I, 3.

[3] It is not hard to understand why concern for property rights did not provide sufficient motivation for people to record vital events. It was likely as difficult for them to see that connection as it is for us.

trolling epidemics. This held true in both Britain and America. Regarding the situation in Britain, Sir Arthur Newsholme wrote:

> Panic was a large factor in securing repentance and good works when cholera threatened; as it, likewise, was in an earlier century when plaque became epidemic; and in both instances the desire for complete and accurate information as to the extent of the invasion led England to the call for accurate vital statistics. It may truly be said that the early adoption of accurate registers of births and deaths was hastened by fears of cholera, and by the intelligent realisation that one must know the localisation as well as the number of the enemy to be fought.[4]

English-speaking peoples were considerably slower to develop vital registration than were many other peoples of the world, and the entire world was relatively slow. By 1833, only one-tenth of the world's population lived in the areas covered by regular vital registration. Some jurisdictions with earlier vital registration were Austria, Bavaria, Belgium, Denmark, Finland, France, Norway, Prussia, Saxony, Sweden (some of which had vital registration systems operated by their churches), and five U.S. cities (6 percent of the U.S. population)—Baltimore, Boston, New Orleans, New York, and Philadelphia.[5]

Though these five U.S. cities were the forerunners in the development of American vital registration, and though some of them had health departments and kept statistics of death by cause, complete records are not available for any of them from this early period because their laws were largely ineffective. In Baltimore, for example, it was not until 1875 that death certificates were actually *required* by statute.

England and Wales had no vital registration until July 1837 (Act of 1836) when a central registry office was established with responsibility for recording all births, marriages, and deaths in the country—most likely in response to the cholera epidemic, which took 42,000 lives in Great Britain and Ireland during 1831 and 1832. The Act of 1836 is regarded by many as the turning point in the development of vital registration in both England and the United States. Vital records began to improve consistently from that time. And the chief motivation behind these improved records was the gathering of facts needed to facilitate war against disease and poor sanitary conditions.

In the U.S., vital records have never been kept on a national level as they are in Britain, but rather their keeping has been largely a state responsibility. When America's founders framed the Constitution in 1787, they created a republic in which all rights and duties not expressly given to the federal government automatically belonged to the individual states. Because hardly anyone saw the need for vital registration in 1787, each state has developed its own system of vital registration. This development, however, did not come

---

[4] Sir Arthur Newsholme, *Evolution of Preventive Medicine* (Baltimore: Williams and Wilkins, 1927), 113. Used by permission.

[5] National Office of Vital Statistics, Vol. I, 4.

without the prodding and direction of federal agencies and other interested organizations.

The one man with perhaps the greatest influence on the early development of American vital records was Lemuel Shattuck of Massachusetts. Shattuck was inspired by England's Act of 1836 and made it the model for the statute adopted by Massachusetts in 1842 and strengthened in 1844. The 1844 legislation was the first in America to require centralized state filing of records and to use standard forms. The American Statistical Association, which Shattuck founded, was the pressure group that worked to secure this legislation.[6] New Jersey was not far behind, making registration of births, marriages, and deaths mandatory on a statewide basis in 1848.

D. Vital registration and the census

Shattuck's accomplishments in Massachusetts were not the end of his influence upon vital records. Because of his work in designing the 1845 census of Boston, he was called to Washington in 1849 to help plan the 1850 federal census. This census bore the marks of his genius and foresight and of his interest in vital records. That census inaugurated the most significant innovations in the history of the federal census.

It is not my purpose here to discuss the census in detail—that is done in Chapters 14 and 15—but some of Shattuck's census innovations related to vital records. The 1850 census included an attempt to collect vital statistics data by enumeration. He apparently was not convinced that such a system would work, but felt that if it produced any information, it would be of more value than what was being done otherwise at the time.

An additional column was added to the population schedules of the 1850 census asking: "Married within the year?" Also added was a mortality schedule to gather data on persons who died during the census year (June 1, 1849, to June 1, 1850).

In the 1860 census, a column was added to the population schedules to report the month of birth for each child born within the census year (June 1, 1959, to June 1, 1860). These birth and death statistics, as collected in connection with the decennial[7] censuses, were published by the federal government up to and including 1900.[8]

This method proved to be quite unsatisfactory, and Shattuck's fears concerning the effectiveness of the system were confirmed. However, for lack of something better, the program continued. Perhaps the biggest shortcoming was the fact that these enumerations covered only the twelve months immediately preceding the census date—only one year out of every ten.

---

[6] Ibid., Vol. I, 5.

[7] Every ten years.

[8] Ibid., Vol. I, 5.

A second problem was getting people to report events accurately, especially deaths. Memories were apparently very short. It is estimated that the 1850, 1860, and 1870 counts of deaths fell short by 40 percent of the actual number that should have been reported.[9] With the census of 1880, the census law was amended to withdraw mortality schedules from the censuses of those cities and states that had begun official registration of deaths. In those jurisdictions, death information was secured from the actual death records.[10]

The census as a tool for collecting vital records was not abandoned until the 1910 census when registration within the several states had developed sufficiently to provide better national statistics than the censuses could ever produce.[11] Nothing is known of the location of any 1900 mortality schedules except that they were probably destroyed prior to World War I, and those for 1890 were destroyed by fire on March 22, 1896.[12]

In defense of these vital records by enumeration (if they need defense), it must be said that the only other choice was to have practically no vital records at all.[13]

E. Organization and standardization

Registration was working well in a handful of large U.S. cities as early as the mid-1800s, but the records in the rest of the country were very poor. This situation prompted the American Medical Association to adopt a resolution in 1855 calling for all members to petition their state legislatures to establish vital statistics offices. In 1879, an act of Congress created the National Board of Health, which began almost immediately to publish health statistics for those cities that could provide them. That their main emphasis was directed toward uniformity of registration is not difficult to appreciate. At the beginning, when there were just twenty-four cities participating in the program, fourteen separate forms were used. The differences among these forms were so significant that comparison of data was next to impossible.[14]

The effect of this new National Board of Health was extraordinary. By March of 1880, in only its second year, weekly information was being received from about ninety cities. Also in 1880, the board called a meeting of all state and local registration officials (which proved to be the beginning of an annual convention) and, among other things, discussed collection procedures, standard forms, and uniform legislation from state to state.[15]

---

[9] Ibid., Vol. I, 7.

[10] Katherine H. Davidson, and Charlotte M. Ashby, comps., *Preliminary Inventory of the Records of the Bureau of the Census* (Washington, DC: The National Archives, 1964), 110.

[11] National Office of Vital Statistics, Vol. I, 7.

[12] Information provided by the National Archives in letter of February 1970.

[13] Mortality schedules are discussed in more detail in Chapter 14 in connection with census records.

[14] National Office of Vital Statistics, Vol. I, 7.

[15] Ibid., Vol. I, 7.

The 1900 census on mortality was operated quite differently from those of earlier years. The legislative adjustment that effected this change also put the National Board of Health's Committee on Vital Statistics in charge of the mortality schedules. Prior to the taking of that census, the Census Office carried on extensive correspondence with the states and with those cities with populations over 5,000. The office collected extensive data on registration procedures and then published its findings for the benefit of all registration personnel. It recommended a death certificate form and suggested that all areas adopt it before January 1, 1900. Eighteen states and the District of Columbia adopted the form either wholly or with slight modifications, and seventy-one major cities in the remaining states followed suit. Because of this, it is believed that the 1900 mortality census was 90 percent complete.[16] It is unfortunate that we do not have it.

Various interested organizations continued to have a significant effect on the local registration of births and deaths even though they had no direct control. By 1910, registration was considered complete enough that it was no longer necessary to collect vital information as part of the census. These organizations and their progeny under the Census Office (later the Bureau of the Census) have continued their efforts. Thus, since 1933 every state has had a model (uniform) law—or a modification thereof—and is in a national registration area that assures sameness from state to state, both in procedures and in forms. The last states to adopt statewide birth and death registration (Georgia and New Mexico) did so in 1919, but they were close on the heels of a half-dozen others.

Useful death records generally developed slightly earlier than good birth records, primarily because of the motivation behind the registration movement—the war against disease. And, of the three kinds of vital records being considered here, marriage records have been the slowest to develop. Although marriage records in most localities are often found for periods earlier than birth or death records, the rate of development of marriage records did not keep pace.

Marriages still have not reached the point of statewide registration in all states, nor has a standard form been accepted by all states. However, all states now keep good marriage records at some jurisdictional level.

II. USING VITAL RECORDS FOR FAMILY HISTORY

The utility of American vital records as a source of genealogical evidence is questioned by many in light of the foregoing historical data. These records, in most states, are considered too modern. In some respects, this is true, but there is sufficient value in them that they should not be passed over lightly. Death records, especially, contain information of exceptional genealogical value even though most of the records are of relatively recent vintage.

---

[16] Ibid., Vol. I, 7.

FIGURE I—IMPORTANT DATES IN THE HISTORY OF BIRTH AND DEATH REGISTRATION: UNITED STATES

AREA	RECORDS ON FILE FOR ENTIRE AREA		ADMITTED TO REGISTRATION AREA*	
	DEATHS	BIRTHS	DEATHS	BIRTHS
Alabama	1908	1908	1925	1927
Arizona	1909	1909	1926	1926
Arkansas	1914	1914	1927	1927
California	1905	1905	1906	1919
Colorado	1907	1907	1906	1928
Connecticut	1897	1897	1890	1915
Delaware	1881	1881	1890	1921
District of Columbia	1855	1871	1880	1915
Florida	1899	1899	1919	1924
Georgia	1919	1919	1922	1928
Idaho	1911	1911	1922	1926
Illinois	1916	1916	1918	1922
Indiana	1900	1907	1900	1917
Iowa	1880	1880	1923	1924
Kansas	1911	1911	1914	1917
Kentucky	1911	1911	1911	1917
Louisiana	1914	1914	1918	1927
Maine	1892	1892	1900	1915
Maryland	1898	1898	1906	1916
Massachusetts	1841	1841	1880	1915
Michigan	1867	1867	1900	1915
Minnesota	1900	1900	1910	1915
Mississippi	1912	1912	1919	1921
Missouri	1910	1910	1911	1927
Montana	1907	1907	1910	1922
Nebraska	1905	1905	1920	1920
Nevada	1911	1911	1929	1929
New Hampshire	1850	1850	1890	1915
New Jersey	1848	1848	1880	1921
New Mexico	1919	1919	1929	1929
New York	1880	1880	1890	1915
North Carolina	1913	1913	1910	1917
North Dakota	1908	1908	1924	1924
Ohio	1909	1909	1909	1917
Oklahoma	1908	1908	1928	1928
Oregon	1903	1903	1918	1919
Pennsylvania	1906	1906	1906	1915
Rhode Island	1852	1852	1890	1915
South Carolina	1915	1915	1916	1919
South Dakota	1905	1905	1906	1932
Tennessee	1914	1914	1917	1927
Texas	1903	1903	1933	1933
Utah	1905	1905	1910	1917
Vermont	1857	1857	1890	1915
Virginia	1912	1912	1913	1917
Washington	1907	1907	1908	1917
West Virginia	1917	1917	1925	1925
Wisconsin	1907	1907	1908	1917
Wyoming	1909	1909	1922	1922
Alaska	1913	1913	1950	1950
Hawaii	1896	1896	1917	1929
Puerto Rico	1931	1931	1932	1943
Virgin Islands	1919	1919	1924	1924

[Courtesy of Department of Health, Education and Welfare, U.S. Public Health Service, National Center for Vital Statistics. From *Vital Statistics of the United States 1950* (1954), Vol. 1, p. 13.]

*A state was admitted to the registration area when it was felt that its level of registration had reached 90 per cent.

The death certificate form calls not only for information on the person's death but also on his birth (date and place) and on his parentage. As an example, if an 82-year-old person died in 1915, his death certificate might well provide valuable information about his family (time and place) for an event that transpired in 1833. Of course, some certificates lack some of this information because of a lack of knowledge on the part of informants, and not all informants provided accurate information. Errors in birth information are not uncommon. I have a death certificate for one of my ancestors giving a fictitious name for her father because the informant, a son-in-law, apparently did not choose to disclose that the decedent was born out of wedlock. Those who have willfully given erroneous information create some serious problems for family history researchers—as do those who ignorantly give erroneous information.

The information on a death certificate can help us verify information from family sources, too. I once worked on a problem where the female ancestor had never been positively identified, even though her name, approximate age, and place of birth were all apparently known. This problem was during the census period, but a search of the appropriate census schedules failed to show any person of that identity, even though there were several families of the correct surname in the correct area. A death certificate was secured for this woman's son, which showed the maiden surname of his mother (the person for whom we had been searching) as something entirely different from what the family thought it was. Further investigation proved the information on the death certificate was correct, and the ancestor was then properly identified and the pedigree extended.

Dates and places can also be verified through vital records. Whenever there are vital records available in connection with the persons on our pedigree beyond the immediate generation, those records should be secured and analyzed for any value they might have in preparing an accurate family history. These records must not be overlooked—not even when we think we already have all necessary information on the person involved. Dates and places passed down in the family are often the victims of copying errors and poor memories.

III. SECURING COPIES OF THE RECORDS

A. Since statewide registration

It is a relatively easy matter to locate and secure copies of those vital records kept since the instigation of statewide registration in the several states. Much has been written about this and many books have been published with lists of essential data. Such a list could be given here, too, but data in lists of this kind becomes quickly outdated (especially the prices), so I shall forbear. Rather, I refer to the booklet (already mentioned in Chapter 6) published by the Department of Health and Human Services, *Where to Write for Vital*

Records. As explained in Chapter 6, this booklet is online at *https://www.cdc. gov/nchs/w2w/index.htm.* Or, if you prefer, a pdf copy of the booklet can be downloaded at *https://publications.usa.gov/USAPubs.php?PubID=1139.* The booklet includes information on registration areas (usually the states, but also some large cities), the cost of copies, addresses of record custodians, and brief remarks. The remarks relate primarily to completeness and to the time period covered by the records.

Another book I recommend is Thomas Jay Kemp's *International Vital Records Handbook.* The most recent version is the seventh edition, published in 2017.[17] It contains the latest forms and information for each state and gives useful details about records created before statewide vital records registration. The book contains the application forms required for obtaining copies of the certificates. I should also mention that this book is international in scope.

B. Before statewide registration

Locating vital records in any state or registration area prior to the adoption of statewide registration laws is usually a more difficult task than finding later records. There were many differences in custom and practice, even within the same state. Some places kept records very early; others kept no records at all until legislation required it. It is fortunate that many of these records have been microfilmed and are now being digitized and indexed to give us easier access.

The most exhaustive attempt to compile a list of available early vital records in the United States was made by the federal government's Historical Records Survey program. These surveys were completed as Works Projects Administration (WPA) projects in the late 1930s and early 1940s. All forty-eight of the states then in the U.S. participated in the Historical Records Survey program. (Alaska and Hawaii were not included because they were not yet states.) Though all of the states participated, the projects of eight states did not include vital records inventories. Those states were Connecticut, Delaware, Maine, Maryland, Ohio, Pennsylvania, South Carolina, and Vermont.

Each state where the vital records were inventoried published an inventory or a guide to vital statistics records available for its counties, cities, and towns and told where and how the records were filed. A *WPA List of Vital Records* was issued in 1943 showing the vital records inventories published for each of those forty states. Though I have used that source in the past, I am no longer able to locate a copy, and the Internet has been of no assistance in doing so.

Copies of these inventories have been available at various larger libraries and historical societies, especially in the states concerned, but they are

---

[17] Thomas Jay Kemp, *International Vital Records Handbook, 7th ed. (Baltimore: Genealogical Publishing Co., 2017).*

U.S. STANDARD CERTIFICATE OF LIVE BIRTH

LOCAL FILE NO.   BIRTH NUMBER:

C H I L D	1. CHILD'S NAME (First, Middle, Last, Suffix)	2. TIME OF BIRTH (24 hr)	3. SEX	4. DATE OF BIRTH (Mo/Day/Yr)

5. FACILITY NAME (If not institution, give street and number)	6. CITY, TOWN, OR LOCATION OF BIRTH	7. COUNTY OF BIRTH

M O T H E R	8a. MOTHER'S CURRENT LEGAL NAME (First, Middle, Last, Suffix)	8b. DATE OF BIRTH (Mo/Day/Yr)

8c. MOTHER'S NAME PRIOR TO FIRST MARRIAGE (First, Middle, Last, Suffix)	8d. BIRTHPLACE (State, Territory, or Foreign Country)

9a. RESIDENCE OF MOTHER-STATE	9b. COUNTY	9c. CITY, TOWN, OR LOCATION

9d. STREET AND NUMBER	9e. APT. NO.	9f. ZIP CODE	9g. INSIDE CITY LIMITS? ☐ Yes ☐ No

F A T H E R	10a. FATHER'S CURRENT LEGAL NAME (First, Middle, Last, Suffix)	10b. DATE OF BIRTH (Mo/Day/Yr)	10c. BIRTHPLACE (State, Territory, or Foreign Country)

CERTIFIER	11. CERTIFIER'S NAME _____ TITLE: ☐ MD ☐ DO ☐ HOSPITAL ADMIN. ☐ CNM/CM ☐ OTHER MIDWIFE ☐ OTHER (Specify)_____	12. DATE CERTIFIED ___/___/___ MM DD YYYY	13. DATE FILED BY REGISTRAR ___/___/___ MM DD YYYY

INFORMATION FOR ADMINISTRATIVE USE

M O T H E R	14. MOTHER'S MAILING ADDRESS ☐ Same as residence, or State City, Town, or Location

Street & Number   Apartment No.:   Zip Code

15. MOTHER MARRIED? (At birth, conception, or any time between) ☐ Yes ☐ No IF NO, HAS PATERNITY ACKNOWLEDGEMENT BEEN SIGNED IN THE HOSPITAL? ☐ Yes ☐ No	16. SOCIAL SECURITY NUMBER REQUESTED FOR CHILD? ☐ Yes ☐ No	17. FACILITY ID. (NPI)

18. MOTHER'S SOCIAL SECURITY NUMBER	19. FATHER'S SOCIAL SECURITY NUMBER

INFORMATION FOR MEDICAL AND HEALTH PURPOSES ONLY

M O T H E R	20. MOTHER'S EDUCATION (Check the box that best describes the highest degree or level of school completed at the time of delivery) ☐ 8th grade or less ☐ 9th - 12th grade, no diploma ☐ High school graduate or GED completed ☐ Some college credit but no degree ☐ Associate degree (e.g., AA, AS) ☐ Bachelor's degree (e.g., BA, AB, BS) ☐ Master's degree (e.g., MA, MS, MEng, MEd, MSW, MBA) ☐ Doctorate (e.g., PhD, EdD) or Professional degree (e.g., MD, DDS, DVM, LLB, JD)	21. MOTHER OF HISPANIC ORIGIN? (Check the box that best describes whether the mother is Spanish/Hispanic/Latina. Check the 'No' box if mother is not Spanish/Hispanic/Latina) ☐ No, not Spanish/Hispanic/Latina ☐ Yes, Mexican, Mexican American, Chicana ☐ Yes, Puerto Rican ☐ Yes, Cuban ☐ Yes, other Spanish/Hispanic/Latina (Specify)_____	22. MOTHER'S RACE (Check one or more races to indicate what the mother considers herself to be) ☐ White ☐ Black or African American ☐ American Indian or Alaska Native (Name of the enrolled or principal tribe)____ ☐ Asian Indian ☐ Chinese ☐ Filipino ☐ Japanese ☐ Korean ☐ Vietnamese ☐ Other Asian (Specify)____ ☐ Native Hawaiian ☐ Guamanian or Chamorro ☐ Samoan ☐ Other Pacific Islander (Specify)____ ☐ Other (Specify)____

F A T H E R	23. FATHER'S EDUCATION (Check the box that best describes the highest degree or level of school completed at the time of delivery) ☐ 8th grade or less ☐ 9th - 12th grade, no diploma ☐ High school graduate or GED completed ☐ Some college credit but no degree ☐ Associate degree (e.g., AA, AS) ☐ Bachelor's degree (e.g., BA, AB, BS) ☐ Master's degree (e.g., MA, MS, MEng, MEd, MSW, MBA) ☐ Doctorate (e.g., PhD, EdD) or Professional degree (e.g., MD, DDS, DVM, LLB, JD)	24. FATHER OF HISPANIC ORIGIN? (Check the box that best describes whether the father is Spanish/Hispanic/Latino. Check the 'No' box if father is not Spanish/Hispanic/Latino) ☐ No, not Spanish/Hispanic/Latino ☐ Yes, Mexican, Mexican American, Chicano ☐ Yes, Puerto Rican ☐ Yes, Cuban ☐ Yes, other Spanish/Hispanic/Latino (Specify)_____	25. FATHER'S RACE (Check one or more races to indicate what the father considers himself to be) ☐ White ☐ Black or African American ☐ American Indian or Alaska Native (Name of the enrolled or principal tribe)____ ☐ Asian Indian ☐ Chinese ☐ Filipino ☐ Japanese ☐ Korean ☐ Vietnamese ☐ Other Asian (Specify)____ ☐ Native Hawaiian ☐ Guamanian or Chamorro ☐ Samoan ☐ Other Pacific Islander (Specify)____ ☐ Other (Specify)____

Mother's Name Mother's Medical Record No.

26. PLACE WHERE BIRTH OCCURRED (Check one) ☐ Hospital ☐ Freestanding birthing center ☐ Home Birth: Planned to deliver at home? ☐ Yes ☐ No ☐ Clinic/Doctor's office ☐ Other (Specify)_____	27. ATTENDANT'S NAME, TITLE, AND NPI NAME _____ NPI:____ TITLE: ☐ MD ☐ DO ☐ CNM/CM ☐ OTHER MIDWIFE ☐ OTHER (Specify)_____	28. MOTHER TRANSFERRED FOR MATERNAL MEDICAL OR FETAL INDICATIONS FOR DELIVERY? ☐ Yes ☐ No IF YES, ENTER NAME OF FACILITY MOTHER TRANSFERRED FROM _____

REV. 11/2003

FIGURE 2—STANDARD CERTIFICATE OF BIRTH
(Certificates with this format are in use in many states.)

MOTHER	29a. DATE OF FIRST PRENATAL CARE VISIT ___/___/___ MM DD YYYY ☐ No Prenatal Care	29b. DATE OF LAST PRENATAL CARE VISIT ___/___/___ MM DD YYYY	30. TOTAL NUMBER OF PRENATAL VISITS FOR THIS PREGNANCY _____ (If none, enter x0".)

31. MOTHER'S HEIGHT _____ (feet/inches)	32. MOTHER'S PREPREGNANCY WEIGHT _____ (pounds)	33. MOTHER'S WEIGHT AT DELIVERY _____ (pounds)	34. DID MOTHER GET WIC FOOD FOR HERSELF DURING THIS PREGNANCY? ☐ Yes ☐ No

35. NUMBER OF PREVIOUS LIVE BIRTHS (Do not include this child)		36. NUMBER OF OTHER PREGNANCY OUTCOMES (spontaneous or induced losses or ectopic pregnancies)	37. CIGARETTE SMOKING BEFORE AND DURING PREGNANCY For each time period, enter either the number of cigarettes or the number of packs of cigarettes smoked. IF NONE, ENTER x0".	38. PRINCIPAL SOURCE OF PAYMENT FOR THIS DELIVERY
35a. Now Living Number _____ ☐ None	35b. Now Dead Number _____ ☐ None	36a. Other Outcomes Number _____ ☐ None	Average number of cigarettes or packs of cigarettes smoked per day. # of cigarettes # of packs Three Months Before Pregnancy _____ OR _____ First Three Months of Pregnancy _____ OR _____ Second Three Months of Pregnancy _____ OR _____ Third Trimester of Pregnancy _____ OR _____	☐ Private Insurance ☐ Medicaid ☐ Self-pay ☐ Other (Specify) _____

35c. DATE OF LAST LIVE BIRTH ___/___ MM YYYY	36b. DATE OF LAST OTHER PREGNANCY OUTCOME ___/___ MM YYYY	39. DATE LAST NORMAL MENSES BEGAN ___/___/___ MM DD YYYY	40. MOTHER'S MEDICAL RECORD NUMBER

MEDICAL AND HEALTH INFORMATION	41. RISK FACTORS IN THIS PREGNANCY (Check all that apply) Diabetes ☐ Prepregnancy (Diagnosis prior to this pregnancy) ☐ Gestational (Diagnosis in this pregnancy) Hypertension ☐ Prepregnancy (Chronic) ☐ Gestational (PIH, preeclampsia) ☐ Eclampsia ☐ Previous preterm birth ☐ Other previous poor pregnancy outcome (Includes perinatal death, small-for-gestational age/intrauterine growth restricted birth) ☐ Pregnancy resulted from infertility treatment–If yes, check all that apply ☐ Fertility-enhancing drugs, Artificial insemination or Intrauterine insemination ☐ Assisted reproductive technology (e.g., in vitro fertilization (IVF), gamete intrafallopian transfer (GIFT)) ☐ Mother had a previous cesarean delivery If yes, how many _____ ☐ None of the above 42. INFECTIONS PRESENT AND/OR TREATED DURING THIS PREGNANCY (Check all that apply) ☐ Gonorrhea ☐ Syphilis ☐ Chlamydia ☐ Hepatitis B ☐ Hepatitis C ☐ None of the above	43. OBSTETRIC PROCEDURES (Check all that apply) ☐ Cervical cerclage ☐ Tocolysis External cephalic version: ☐ Successful ☐ Failed ☐ None of the above 44. ONSET OF LABOR (Check all that apply) ☐ Premature Rupture of the Membranes (prolonged, 312 hrs.) ☐ Precipitous Labor (<3 hrs.) ☐ Prolonged Labor (3 20 hrs.) ☐ None of the above 45. CHARACTERISTICS OF LABOR AND DELIVERY (Check all that apply) ☐ Induction of labor ☐ Augmentation of labor ☐ Non-vertex presentation ☐ Steroids (glucocorticoids) for fetal lung maturation received by the mother prior to delivery ☐ Antibiotics received by the mother during labor ☐ Clinical chorioamnionitis diagnosed during labor or maternal temperature ≥38°C (100.4°F) ☐ Moderate/heavy meconium staining of the amniotic fluid ☐ Fetal intolerance of labor such that one or more of the following actions was taken: in-utero resuscitative measures, further fetal assessment, or operative delivery ☐ Epidural or spinal anesthesia during labor ☐ None of the above	46. METHOD OF DELIVERY A. Was delivery with forceps attempted but unsuccessful? ☐ Yes ☐ No B. Was delivery with vacuum extraction attempted but unsuccessful? ☐ Yes ☐ No C. Fetal presentation at birth ☐ Cephalic ☐ Breech ☐ Other D. Final route and method of delivery (Check one) ☐ Vaginal/Spontaneous ☐ Vaginal/Forceps ☐ Vaginal/Vacuum ☐ Cesarean If cesarean, was a trial of labor attempted? ☐ Yes ☐ No 47. MATERNAL MORBIDITY (Check all that apply) (Complications associated with labor and delivery) ☐ Maternal transfusion ☐ Third or fourth degree perineal laceration ☐ Ruptured uterus ☐ Unplanned hysterectomy ☐ Admission to intensive care unit ☐ Unplanned operating room procedure following delivery ☐ None of the above

NEWBORN INFORMATION

NEWBORN	48. NEWBORN MEDICAL RECORD NUMBER 49. BIRTHWEIGHT (grams preferred, specify unit) _____ 9 grams 9 lb/oz 50. OBSTETRIC ESTIMATE OF GESTATION _____ (completed weeks) 51. APGAR SCORE Score at 5 minutes: _____ If 5 minute score is less than 6, Score at 10 minutes: _____ 52. PLURALITY - Single, Twin, Triplet, etc. (Specify) _____ 53. IF NOT SINGLE BIRTH - Born First, Second, Third, etc. (Specify) _____	54. ABNORMAL CONDITIONS OF THE NEWBORN (Check all that apply) ☐ Assisted ventilation required immediately following delivery ☐ Assisted ventilation required for more than six hours ☐ NICU admission ☐ Newborn given surfactant replacement therapy ☐ Antibiotics received by the newborn for suspected neonatal sepsis ☐ Seizure or serious neurologic dysfunction ☐ Significant birth injury (skeletal fracture(s), peripheral nerve injury, and/or soft tissue/solid organ hemorrhage which requires intervention) 9 None of the above	55. CONGENITAL ANOMALIES OF THE NEWBORN (Check all that apply) ☐ Anencephaly ☐ Meningomyelocele/Spina bifida ☐ Cyanotic congenital heart disease ☐ Congenital diaphragmatic hernia ☐ Omphalocele ☐ Gastroschisis ☐ Limb reduction defect (excluding congenital amputation and dwarfing syndromes) ☐ Cleft Lip with or without Cleft Palate ☐ Cleft Palate alone ☐ Down Syndrome ☐ Karyotype confirmed ☐ Karyotype pending ☐ Suspected chromosomal disorder ☐ Karyotype confirmed ☐ Karyotype pending ☐ Hypospadias ☐ None of the anomalies listed above

56. WAS INFANT TRANSFERRED WITHIN 24 HOURS OF DELIVERY? 9 Yes 9 No IF YES, NAME OF FACILITY INFANT TRANSFERRED TO. _____	57. IS INFANT LIVING AT TIME OF REPORT? ☐ Yes ☐ No ☐ Infant transferred, status unknown	58. IS THE INFANT BEING BREASTFED AT DISCHARGE? ☐ Yes ☐ No

Mother's Name ___ *Mother's Medical Record No.* ___

FIGURE 2—STANDARD CERTIFICATE OF BIRTH—*continued*
(Certificates with this format are in use in many states.)

U.S. STANDARD CERTIFICATE OF DEATH

LOCAL FILE NO.   STATE FILE NO.

1. DECEDENT'S LEGAL NAME (Include AKA's if any) (First, Middle, Last) | 2. SEX | 3. SOCIAL SECURITY NUMBER

4a. AGE-Last Birthday (Years) | 4b. UNDER 1 YEAR — Months / Days | 4c. UNDER 1 DAY — Hours / Minutes | 5. DATE OF BIRTH (Mo/Day/Yr) | 6. BIRTHPLACE (City and State or Foreign Country)

7a. RESIDENCE-STATE | 7b. COUNTY | 7c. CITY OR TOWN

7d. STREET AND NUMBER | 7e. APT. NO. | 7f. ZIP CODE | 7g. INSIDE CITY LIMITS? □ Yes □ No

8. EVER IN US ARMED FORCES? □ Yes □ No | 9. MARITAL STATUS AT TIME OF DEATH □ Married □ Married, but separated □ Widowed □ Divorced □ Never Married □ Unknown | 10. SURVIVING SPOUSE'S NAME (If wife, give name prior to first marriage)

11. FATHER'S NAME (First, Middle, Last) | 12. MOTHER'S NAME PRIOR TO FIRST MARRIAGE (First, Middle, Last)

13a. INFORMANT'S NAME | 13b. RELATIONSHIP TO DECEDENT | 13c. MAILING ADDRESS (Street and Number, City, State, Zip Code)

14. PLACE OF DEATH (Check only one — see instructions)

IF DEATH OCCURRED IN A HOSPITAL □ Inpatient □ Emergency Room/Outpatient □ Dead on Arrival | IF DEATH OCCURRED SOMEWHERE OTHER THAN A HOSPITAL □ Hospice facility □ Nursing home/Long term care facility □ Decedent's home □ Other (Specify)

15. FACILITY NAME (If not institution, give street & number) | 16. CITY OR TOWN, STATE, AND ZIP CODE | 17. COUNTY OF DEATH

18. METHOD OF DISPOSITION □ Burial □ Cremation □ Donation □ Entombment □ Removal from State □ Other (Specify) | 19. PLACE OF DISPOSITION (Name of cemetery, crematory, other place)

20. LOCATION-CITY, TOWN, AND STATE | 21. NAME AND COMPLETE ADDRESS OF FUNERAL FACILITY

22. SIGNATURE OF FUNERAL SERVICE LICENSEE OR OTHER AGENT | 23. LICENSE NUMBER (Of Licensee)

ITEMS 24-28 MUST BE COMPLETED BY PERSON WHO PRONOUNCES OR CERTIFIES DEATH | 24. DATE PRONOUNCED DEAD (Mo/Day/Yr) | 25. TIME PRONOUNCED DEAD

26. SIGNATURE OF PERSON PRONOUNCING DEATH (Only when applicable) | 27. LICENSE NUMBER | 28. DATE SIGNED (Mo/Day/Yr)

29. ACTUAL OR PRESUMED DATE OF DEATH (Mo/Day/Yr) (Spell Month) | 30. ACTUAL OR PRESUMED TIME OF DEATH | 31. WAS MEDICAL EXAMINER OR CORONER CONTACTED? □ Yes □ No

CAUSE OF DEATH (See instructions and examples)

32. PART I. Enter the chain of events—diseases, injuries, or complications—that directly caused the death. DO NOT enter terminal events such as cardiac arrest, respiratory arrest, or ventricular fibrillation without showing the etiology. DO NOT ABBREVIATE. Enter only one cause on a line. Add additional lines if necessary. | Approximate interval Onset to death

IMMEDIATE CAUSE (Final disease or condition resulting in death) —→ a. _____

Due to (or as a consequence of)

Sequentially list conditions, if any, leading to the cause listed on line a. Enter the UNDERLYING CAUSE (disease or injury that initiated the events resulting in death) LAST b. _____

Due to (or as a consequence of)

c. _____

Due to (or as a consequence of)

d. _____

PART II. Enter other significant conditions contributing to death but not resulting in the underlying cause given in PART I | 33. WAS AN AUTOPSY PERFORMED? □ Yes □ No
34. WERE AUTOPSY FINDINGS AVAILABLE TO COMPLETE THE CAUSE OF DEATH? □ Yes □ No

35. DID TOBACCO USE CONTRIBUTE TO DEATH? □ Yes □ Probably □ No □ Unknown | 36. IF FEMALE □ Not pregnant within past year □ Pregnant at time of death □ Not pregnant, but pregnant within 42 days of death □ Not pregnant, but pregnant 43 days to 1 year before death □ Unknown if pregnant within the past year | 37. MANNER OF DEATH □ Natural □ Homicide □ Accident □ Pending Investigation □ Suicide □ Could not be determined

38. DATE OF INJURY (Mo/Day/Yr) (Spell Month) | 39. TIME OF INJURY | 40. PLACE OF INJURY (e.g. Decedent's home; construction site; restaurant; wooded area) | 41. INJURY AT WORK? □ Yes □ No

42. LOCATION OF INJURY State _____ City or Town _____
Street & Number _____ Apartment No. _____ Zip Code _____

43. DESCRIBE HOW INJURY OCCURRED | 44. IF TRANSPORTATION INJURY, SPECIFY □ Driver/Operator □ Passenger □ Pedestrian □ Other (Specify)

45. CERTIFIER (Check only one)
□ Certifying physician-To the best of my knowledge, death occurred due to the cause(s) and manner stated.
□ Pronouncing & Certifying physician-To the best of my knowledge, death occurred at the time, date, and place, and due to the cause(s) and manner stated.
□ Medical Examiner/Coroner-On the basis of examination, and/or investigation, in my opinion, death occurred at the time, date, and place, and due to the cause(s) and manner stated.

Signature of certifier _____

46. NAME, ADDRESS, AND ZIP CODE OF PERSON COMPLETING CAUSE OF DEATH (Item 32)

47. TITLE OF CERTIFIER | 48. LICENSE NUMBER | 49. DATE CERTIFIED (Mo/Day/Yr) | 50. FOR REGISTRAR ONLY- DATE FILED (Mo/Day/Yr)

51. DECEDENT'S EDUCATION-Check the box that best describes the highest degree or level of school completed at the time of death.
□ 8th grade or less
□ 9th - 12th grade, no diploma
□ High school graduate or GED completed
□ Some college credit, but no degree
□ Associate degree (e.g. AA, AS)
□ Bachelor's degree (e.g. BA, AB, BS)
□ Master's degree (e.g. MA, MS, MEng, MEd, MSW, MBA)
□ Doctorate (e.g. PhD, EdD) or Professional degree (e.g. MD, DDS, DVM, LLB, JD) | 52. DECEDENT OF HISPANIC ORIGIN? Check the box that best describes whether the decedent is Spanish/Hispanic/Latino. Check the 'No' box if decedent is not Spanish/Hispanic/Latino.
□ No, not Spanish/Hispanic/Latino
□ Yes, Mexican, Mexican American, Chicano
□ Yes, Puerto Rican
□ Yes, Cuban
□ Yes, other Spanish/Hispanic/Latino (Specify) _____ | 53. DECEDENT'S RACE (Check one or more races to indicate what the decedent considered himself or herself to be)
□ White
□ Black or African American
□ American Indian or Alaska Native (Name of the enrolled or principal tribe) _____
□ Asian Indian
□ Chinese
□ Filipino
□ Japanese
□ Korean
□ Vietnamese
□ Other Asian (Specify) _____
□ Native Hawaiian
□ Guamanian or Chamorro
□ Samoan
□ Other Pacific Islander (Specify) _____
□ Other (Specify) _____

54. DECEDENT'S USUAL OCCUPATION (Indicate type of work done during most of working life. DO NOT USE RETIRED).

55. KIND OF BUSINESS/INDUSTRY

NAME OF DECEDENT For use by physician or institution
To Be Completed/Verified By: FUNERAL DIRECTOR
To Be Completed By MEDICAL CERTIFIER
To Be Completed By FUNERAL DIRECTOR

FIGURE 3—STANDARD CERTIFICATE OF DEATH

TYPE/PRINT IN PERMANENT BLACK INK FOR INSTRUCTIONS SEE HANDBOOK

U.S. STANDARD
LICENSE AND CERTIFICATE OF MARRIAGE

LICENSE NUMBER · STATE FILE NUMBER

DEPARTMENT OF HEALTH AND HUMAN SERVICES - PUBLIC HEALTH SERVICE · NATIONAL CENTER FOR HEALTH STATISTICS - 1989 REVISION

GROOM

1. GROOM'S NAME (First, Middle, Last)
2. AGE LAST BIRTHDAY
3a. RESIDENCE—CITY, TOWN, OR LOCATION
3b. COUNTY
3c. STATE
4. BIRTHPLACE (State or Foreign Country)
5. DATE OF BIRTH (Month, Day, Year)
6a. FATHER'S NAME (First, Middle, Last)
6b. BIRTHPLACE (State or Foreign Country)
7a. MOTHER'S NAME (First, Middle, Maiden Surname)
7b. BIRTHPLACE (State or Foreign Country)

BRIDE

8a. BRIDE'S NAME (First, Middle, Last)
8b. MAIDEN SURNAME (If different)
9. AGE LAST BIRTHDAY
10a. RESIDENCE—CITY, TOWN, OR LOCATION
10b. COUNTY
10c. STATE
11. BIRTHPLACE (State or Foreign Country)
12. DATE OF BIRTH (Month, Day, Year)
13a. FATHER'S NAME (First, Middle, Last)
13b. BIRTHPLACE (State or Foreign Country)
14a. MOTHER'S NAME (First, Middle, Maiden Surname)
14b. BIRTHPLACE (State or Foreign Country)

SIGNATURES

WE HEREBY CERTIFY THAT THE INFORMATION PROVIDED IS CORRECT TO THE BEST OF OUR KNOWLEDGE AND BELIEF AND THAT WE ARE FREE TO MARRY UNDER THE LAWS OF THIS STATE.

15. GROOM'S SIGNATURE
16. BRIDE'S SIGNATURE

LICENSE TO MARRY

This License Authorizes the Marriage in This State of the Parties Named Above By Any Person Duly Authorized to Perform a Marriage Ceremony Under the Laws of the State of _____ .

17. EXPIRATION DATE (Month, Day, Year)
18. SUBSCRIBED TO AND SWORN TO BEFORE ME ON: (Month, Day, Year)
19. SIGNATURE OF ISSUING OFFICIAL
20. TITLE OF ISSUING OFFICIAL

CEREMONY

21. I CERTIFY THAT THE ABOVE NAMED PERSONS WERE MARRIED ON: (Month, Day, Year)
22a. WHERE MARRIED—CITY, TOWN, OR LOCATION
22b. COUNTY
23a. SIGNATURE OF PERSON PERFORMING CEREMONY
23b. NAME (Type/Print)
23c. TITLE
23d. ADDRESS OF PERSON PERFORMING CEREMONY (Street and Number or Rural Route Number, City or Town, State, Zip Code)
24a. SIGNATURE OF WITNESS TO CEREMONY
24b. SIGNATURE OF WITNESS TO CEREMONY

LOCAL OFFICIAL

25. SIGNATURE OF LOCAL OFFICIAL MAKING RETURN TO STATE HEALTH DEPARTMENT
26. DATE FILED BY LOCAL OFFICIAL (Month, Day, Year)

CONFIDENTIAL INFORMATION. THE INFORMATION BELOW WILL NOT APPEAR ON CERTIFIED COPIES OF THE RECORD.

	27. NUMBER OF THIS MARRIAGE— First, Second, etc. (Specify below)	28. IF PREVIOUSLY MARRIED, LAST MARRIAGE ENDED		29. RACE—American Indian, Black, White, etc. (Specify below)	30. EDUCATION (Specify only highest grade completed)	
		By Death, Divorce, Dissolution, or Annulment (Specify below)	Date (Month, Day, Year)		Elementary/Secondary (0-12)	College (1-4 or 5+)
GROOM	27a.	28a.	28b.	29a.	30a.	
BRIDE	27b.	28c.	28d.	29b.	30b.	

PHS-T-004
REV. 1/89

FIGURE 4—STANDARD CERTIFICATE OF MARRIAGE

becoming more difficult to find. A list of these inventories, including guides to inventories of church records (which we discuss in Chapter 24), follows:

ALABAMA:	"Guide to Public Vital Statistics Records in Alabama: Preliminary Edition." March 1942.
	"Guide to Vital Statistics Records in Alabama: Church Archives." May 1942.
ARIZONA:	"Guide to Public Vital Statistics Records in Arizona." August 1941.
ARKANSAS:	"Guide to Vital Statistical Records in Arkansas."
	Vol. I, Public Archives. c. 1942.
	Vol. II, Church Archives. c. 1942.
CALIFORNIA:	"Guide to Church Vital Records in California: Alameda and San Francisco Counties; Six Denominations." May 1942.
	"Guide to Public Vital Statistics Records in California."
	Vol. I, Birth Records. June 1941.
	Vol. II, Death Records. July 1941.
COLORADO:	"Guide to Vital Statistics Records in Colorado."
	Vol. I, Public Archives. 1942.
	Vol. II, Church Archives. 1942.
FLORIDA:	"Guide to Public Vital Statistics Records in Florida." February 1941.
	"Guide to Supplementary Vital Statistics from Church Records in Florida: Preliminary Edition."
	Vol. I, Aluchu. June 1942.
	Vol. II, Gilchrist. June 1942.
	Vol. III, Orange. June 1942.
GEORGIA:	"Guide to Public Vital Statistics Records in Georgia." June 1941.
IDAHO:	"Guide to Public Vital Statistics Records in Idaho: State and County." March 1942.
ILLINOIS:	"Guide to Public Vital Statistics Records in Illinois." May 1941.
INDIANA:	"Guide to Public Vital Statistics Records in Indiana." July 1941.
IOWA:	"Guide to Public Vital Statistics Records in Iowa." October 1941.

KANSAS:	"Guide to Public Vital Statistics Records in Kansas." March 1942.
KENTUCKY:	"Guide to Public Vital Statistics Records in Kentucky." February 1942.
LOUISIANA:	"Guide to Public Vital Statistics Records in Louisiana." December 1942.
	"Guide to Vital Statistics Records in Church Archives in Louisiana."
	Vol. I, Protestant and Jewish Church. December 1942.
	Vol. II, Roman Catholic Church. December 1942.
MASSACHUSETTS:	"Guide to Public Vital Statistics Records in Massachusetts." 1942.
MICHIGAN:	"Vital Statistics Holdings by Government Agencies in Michigan."
	Birth Records. 1941.
	Marriage Records. 1941.
	Death Records. July 1942.
	Divorce Records. May 1942.
	"Guide to Church Vital Statistics Records in Michigan: Wayne County." April 1942.
MINNESOTA:	"Guide to Public Vital Statistics Records in Minnesota." 1941.
	"Guide to Church Vital Statistics Records in Minnesota." April 1942.
MISSISSIPPI:	"Guide to Vital Statistics Records in Mississippi."
	Vol. I, Public Archives. April 1942.
	Vol. II, Church Archives. July 1942.
MISSOURI:	"Guide to Public Vital Statistics Records in Missouri." July 1941.
	"Guide to Vital Statistics: Church Records in Missouri." April 1942.
MONTANA:	"Guide to Public Vital Statistics Records in Montana." March 1941.
	"Inventory of the Vital Statistics Records of Churches and Religious Organizations in Montana. Preliminary Edition." July 1942.
NEBRASKA:	"Guide to Public Vital Statistics Records in Nebraska." September 1941.
NEVADA:	"Guide to Public Vital Statistics Records in Nevada." December 1941.

NEW HAMPSHIRE: "Guide to Church Vital Statistics Records in New Hampshire. Preliminary Edition." May 1942.

"Guide to Public Vital Statistics Records in New Hampshire." 1942.

NEW JERSEY: "Guide to Vital Statistics Records in New Jersey."

Vol. I, Public Archives. 1942.

Vol. II, Church Archives. 1942.

"Guide to Naturalization Records in New Jersey." December 1941.

NEW MEXICO: "Guide to Public Vital Statistics Records in New Mexico." March 1942.

NEW YORK: "Guide to Public Vital Statistics Records in New York State (Inclusive of New York City)."

Vol. I, Birth Records. January 1942.

Vol. II, Marriage Records. August 1942.

Vol. III, Death Records. 1942.

"Guide to Vital Statistics Records in Churches in New York State (Exclusive of New York City)."

Vol. I. May 1942.

Vol. II. June 1942.

"Guide to Vital Statistics Records in the City of New York: Churches."

Borough of the Bronx. April 1942. Borough of Brooklyn. 1942.

Borough of Manhattan. 1942. Borough of Queens. May 1942.

Borough of Richmond (Staten Island). 1942.

NORTH CAROLINA: "Guide to Vital Statistics Records in North Carolina."

Vol. I, Public Vital Statistics. June 1942.

NORTH DAKOTA: "Guide to Public Vital Statistics Records in North Dakota." August 1941.

"Guide to Church Vital Statistics Records in North Dakota." March 1942.

OKLAHOMA: "Guide to Public Vital Statistics Records in Oklahoma." June 1941.

OREGON: "Guide to Public Vital Statistics Records in Oregon." April 1942.

RHODE ISLAND: "Summary of Legislation Concerning Vital Statistics in Rhode Island." July 1937.

"Guide to Public Vital Statistics Records: Births, Marriages, Deaths in the State of Rhode Island and Providence Plantations." June 1941.

SOUTH DAKOTA: "Guide to Public Vital Statistics Records in South Dakota." January 1942.

TENNESSEE: "Guide to Public Vital Statistics Records in Tennessee." June 1941.

"Guide to Church Vital Statistics Records in Tennessee." August 1942.

TEXAS: "Guide to Public Vital Statistics Records in Texas." June 1941.

UTAH: "Census of Weber County (Exclusive of Green River Precinct), Provisional State of Deseret, 1850." October 1937.

"Guide to Public Vital Statistics Records in Utah." November 1941.

VIRGINIA: "Index to Marriage Notices in the *Southern Churchman,* 1835–1941."
Vol. A–K. May 1942.
Vol. L–Z. May 1942.

"Guide to the Manuscript Collections of the Virginia Baptist Historical Society. Supplement No. 1, Index to the Obituary Notices in the *Religious Herald,* Richmond, Virginia, 1828–1938."
Vol. I, A–L. August 1941.
Vol. II, M–Z. September 1941.

WASHINGTON: "Guide to Public Vital Statistics Records in Washington." June 1941.

"Guide to Church Vital Statistics Records in Washington. Preliminary Edition." February 1942.

WEST VIRGINIA: "Inventory of Public Vital Statistics Records in West Virginia: Births, Deaths, and Marriages." March 1941.

"Guide to Church Vital Statistics Records in West Virginia." February 1942.

WISCONSIN: "Guide to Public Vital Statistics Records in Wisconsin." September 1941.

"Guide to Church Vital Statistics Records in Wisconsin." September 1941.

"Outline of Vital Statistics Laws in Wisconsin." September 1941.

WYOMING: "Guide to Public Vital Statistics Records in
                                Wyoming." June 1941.
                                "Guide to Vital Statistics Records in Wyo-
                                ming: Church Archives. Preliminary Edi-
                                tion." March 1942.

As I do not know where all of these guides are currently available, I suggest
that a letter to the county clerk or other appropriate jurisdictional authority in
the locality of your interest will usually provide a quick answer as to what, if
any, vital records are available for times prior to statewide registration. The
booklet *Where to Write for Vital Records* offers some very brief information
on this subject, as does Kemp's *International Vital Records Handbook*.

It might also be appropriate to mention that, though these inventories were
up to date in 1942, etc., many changes in the interim have outdated much of
what they say.

C. Other helps

In the foregoing historical discussion, I mentioned that registration of
births and deaths in large cities usually predated statewide registration by several years. In New Orleans, for example, there are birth records from 1790 and
death records from 1803, while there was not statewide registration in Louisiana until July 1914. Four large cities that had vital registration before the
states in which they are located are still self-contained registration districts.
They are as follows:

Baltimore, Maryland—records from 1875.

Boston, Massachusetts—records from 1639.

New Orleans, Louisiana—birth records from 1790, death records from
    1803.

New York, New York:

    The Bronx Borough—records from 1898. (The Bronx records from
        1866 to 1897 are in Manhattan Borough at the Municipal Archives,
        31 Chambers St., New York, NY 10007.)

    Brooklyn Borough—death records from 1847; others from 1866 (at
        Municipal Archives, Manhattan).

    Manhattan Borough—records from 1847 at the Municipal Archives,
        also some death records from 1795.

    Queens Borough—became a separate district after the beginning of
        statewide registration.

    Richmond Borough (Staten Island)—became a separate district after the
        beginning of statewide registration.

Several other cities that were originally in this category have since ceased
to function as separate entities and are now part of their state registration ar-

eas. In most cases, however, the records from those early periods are still on file in the cities concerned. Of special note are Philadelphia from 1860 and Pittsburgh from 1870 (including Allegheny City [now a part of Pittsburgh] from 1882 to 1905). There was state registration in Pennsylvania from 1885, but records in the present Bureau of Vital Statistics date from 1906. The New York State cities of Albany, Buffalo, and Yonkers also had their own registration offices prior to 1914 when they joined the state system.

In many states, you have the option of securing copies of vital certificates from either the state vital records office or a local official; in other states, you can get them only from the state office.

There are also a few states that have had their early vital records (from various sources) collected and indexed in their state libraries and/or archives and (sometimes) even published. Many of those early vital records are also now digitized and indexed, and are available on one or more of the family history Internet websites. If your ancestors lived in one of these states, you may get some real help from these digitized records. Those records on the following list that are not yet available in indexed digitized databases will likely soon be. Take note of the following collections; I have indicated those collections available in indexed digitized form at the time of this writing:

CONNECTICUT: The Barbour Collection. This index, prepared by Lucius Barnes Barbour, the Connecticut Examiner of Public Records from 1911 to 1934, contains vital data and other information found in early Connecticut town records up through the mid-1800s. There are entries for many towns well into the 1860s, with coverage of 137 towns on 14,333 typewritten pages. This collection is held by the Connecticut State Library, 231 Capitol Avenue, Hartford, CT 06106. It has also been published by Genealogical Publishing Company (GPC) in fifty-five volumes between 1994 and 2002 under the title *The Barbour Collection of Connecticut Town Vital Records*. A list of the volumes, showing the towns included in each, is on the GPC website (*http://www.genealogical. com*). The entries are alphabetical under each town.

Also, note that Ancestry has the Barbour Collection in a searchable digitized database at *http://search.ancestry.com/search/db. aspx?dbid=1034*.

The Hale Collection. This index to more than one million gravestone inscriptions from more than two thousand Connecticut graveyards extends well into the 1900s. It is the result of a WPA project directed by Charles R. Hale during the mid-1930s. The Connecticut State Library in Hartford holds this collection of bound volumes. These records, and other more recent Connecticut cemetery tombstone inscriptions, are now being transcribed onto a website at *http:// hale-collection.com/*. A Facebook page, "Hale Collection of Connecticut Cemetery Inscriptions," is updated on a continuing basis, to show what cemeteries are being added to the website.

Ancestry also has the Hale Collection available in a searchable digitized database at *http://search.ancestry.com/search/db.aspx?dbid=2900.*

Genealogies of Connecticut Families. This book is not a collection of vital records but is a significant source of genealogical information about more than 75,000 persons in Connecticut families from more than 400 articles taken from *The New England Historical and Genealogical Register.* There is also an introduction by Gary Boyd Roberts.[18]

DELAWARE: Birth records, 1861–1913, with a card index for the same period; death records, 1855–1910, with a card index to records from very early to 1888; a card index to baptisms, 1759–1890; and a card index of marriages, 1730–1850. These records are at the Delaware Public Archives, 121 Martin Luther King Jr. Blvd., North, Dover, DE 19901. Most of these were collected by Clerks of the Peace in the counties.

Ancestry has the following vital records indexes for Delaware:

---

[18] *Genealogies of Connecticut Families* (3 vols.) copied from articles in *The New England Historical and Genealogical Record.* 1983 (Reprint, Baltimore: Genealogical Publishing Co., 2006).

- Birth Records, 1800–1908 (*http://search. ancestry.com/search/db.aspx?dbid=1672*)
- Marriage Records, 1744–1912 (*http://search. ancestry.com/search/db.aspx?dbid=1508*)
- Marriage Records, 1806–1933 (*http://search. ancestry.com/search/db.aspx?dbid=1673*)
- Death Records, 1811–1933 (*http://search. ancestry.com/search/db.aspx?dbid=1674*)

FamilySearch also has several Delaware database collections, including the following. They are indexed and can be accessed at no charge:

- Births and Christenings, 1710–1896 (*https:// familysearch.org/search/collection/1674747*)
- State Birth Records, 1861–1922 (*https://fam ily search.org/search/collection/1534607*)
- Marriages, 1713–1919 (*https://familysearch. org/search/collection/1674782*)
- Marriage Records, 1913–1954 (*https://family search.org/search/collection/1609795*)
- Death Records, 1855–1961 (*https://family search.org/search/collection/1520546*)
- Deaths and Burials, 1815–1955 (*https://family search.org/search/collection/1674781*)
- Vital Record Index Cards, 1680–1934 (*https:// familysearch.org/search/collection/1922410*)
- Vital Records, 1650–1974 (*https://familysearch. org/search/collection/1447341*)
- Wilmington Vital Records, 1847–1954 (*https:// familysearch.org/search/collection/1921755*)

MAINE:

Vital records index, early to 1892. These records are for only eighty towns, and the records of only seventeen have been published under authority of the Maine Historical Society.

Ancestry has an indexed database of Maine birth records for 1621–1922 (*http://search. ancestry.com/search/db.aspx?dbid=1960*).

FamilySearch also has many Maine vital records online, including those listed below. Because many of these records are indexes that may contain transcription errors, always consult the original record to confirm what you find in the index:

- Births and Christenings, 1739–1900 (*https:// familysearch.org/search/collection/1674856*)

- Marriages, 1771–1907 (*https://familysearch. org/search/collection/1674915*)
- Marriage Index, 1892–1966, 1977–1996 (*https://familysearch.org/search/collection/ 2077670*)
- Deaths and Burials, 1841–1910 (*https://family search.org/search/collection/1674914*)
- Death Index, 1960–1996 (*https://family search.org/search/collection/2046945*)
- Vital Records, 1670–1907 (*https://family search.org/search/collection/1803978*)

MARYLAND:

There are indexes in the Hall of Records, Annapolis, for births, 1801–1877, and deaths, 1865–1880, for Anne Arundel County and some during the 1600s in Charles, Kent, Somerset, and Talbot counties.

There are also card indexes to pre-Revolutionary marriages in Charles, Kent, and Somerset counties; to later marriages in Anne Arundel, Caroline, Cecil, Dorchester, Frederick, and Prince George's counties; and a separate index for Baltimore County marriages.

Ancestry has the following vital record databases for Maryland:

- Marriages, 1655–1850 (*http://search.ancestry. com/search/db.aspx?dbid=7846*)
- Marriages, 1667–1899 (*http://search.ancestry. com/search/db.aspx?dbid=4729*)
- *Names in Stone, Maryland*, Vol. 1 (*http:// search.ancestry.com/search/db.aspx?dbid= 49053*)
- *Names in Stone, Maryland*, Vol. 2 (*http:// search.ancestry.com/search/db.aspx? dbid=49265*)

FamilySearch has online databases of the following Maryland vital records:

- Births and Christenings, 1650–1995 (*https:// familysearch.org/search/collection/1674912*)
- Marriages, 1666–1970 (*https://familysearch. org/search/collection/1675199*)
- Deaths and Burials, 1877–1992 (*https://family search.org/search/collection/1675198*)

MASSACHUSETTS:

Church, cemetery, and town meeting records for more than 200 towns, from early to 1850, have been collected and published, mostly by the New England Historic Genealogical Society, Franklin P. Rice, and the Essex Institute. Many more are still in the towns themselves. In addition, the Massachusetts Archives, 220 Morrissey Blvd., Boston, MA 02125, has vital records for the years 1841–1925, plus indexes to these records. All information from the 1841–1910 Birth, Marriage & Death indexes is in a searchable database.

Ancestry has searchable databases for the following Massachusetts vital records (accessible at *http://search.ancestry.com/search/db.aspx?dbid=2495*):

- Town birth records, 1620–1850
- Town marriage records, 1620–1850
- Town death records, 1620–1850
- Death index, 1970–2003
- Marriages, 1633–1850

NEW HAMPSHIRE: Town records—many extending to the 1850s, 1860s, and later—have been transcribed and indexed in a special collection at the New Hampshire State House, 107 N. Main St, Concord, NH 03303. There is a complete card index to surnames.

FamilySearch has New Hampshire "Town Clerk, Vital and Town Records, 1636–1947," available online. These records are not indexed; however, they are arranged by record type within each town in each county. Unfortunately, many of the images are difficult to read.

RHODE ISLAND: The Arnold Collection of Rhode Island Vital Records, covering 1636–1850, is published in twenty-one volumes and available at the New England Historic Genealogical Society, 99-101 Newbury St., Boston, MA 02116. It is available for a fee on the society's website (*https://www.americanancestors.org/*). The Arnold Collection volumes have all been digitized and are available on FamilySearch.

For a description of the contents of each volume and for access to those volumes on

FamilySearch, go to *https://onerhodeisland family.com/free-rhode-island-resources/ free-r-i-vital-records/*. If this URL is too cumbersome, enter "Arnold's Rhode Island Vital Records" in your Internet search engine.

Ancestry has indexed digitized databases for the following Rhode Island records:

- Births, 1636–1930 (*http://search.ancestry. com/search/db.aspx?dbid=4262*)
- Deaths, 1630–1930 (*http://search.ancestry. com/search/db.aspx?dbid=4264*)
- Marriages, 1851–1920 (*http://search.ancestry .com/search/db.aspx?dbid=4263*)

FamilySearch has an indexed database to the following:

- Births and Christenings, 1600–1914 (*https:// familysearch.org/search/collection/1675525*)

VERMONT: The Vermont State Archives and Records Administration, 1078 U.S. Route 2, Middlesex, Montpelier, VT 05633 has vital records going back to 1909. Vital Records 1720–1908 are in an indexed Ancestry database at *search.ancestry.com/search/ db.aspx?dbid=4661*. Ancestry also has Vermont birth, marriage, and death databases 1909–2008. Vermont birth, marriage, and death records 1760–2008 are available through *https://familysearch.org*.

VIRGINIA: Birth and death records, 1853–1896, arranged chronologically, were kept in the towns and cities. They are on noncirculating microfilms at the Library of Virginia, 800 East Broad St., Richmond, VA 23219. They are also on microfilm at the Family History Library in Salt Lake City. The FamilySearch website has name indexes of Virginia Deaths and Burials, 1853–1912 (*https://familysearch.org/search/collec tion/1708697*) and Virginia Births and Christenings, 1584–1917 (*https://family search.org/search/collection/1708660*), but without access to images of actual birth and death records.

Marriage records from 1785 to 1940 are also on microfilm at The Library of Virginia and the Family History Library. A guide to these records is available,[19] and an index is also available on FamilySearch (*https://family search.org/search/collection/1708698*), but there is no access to images of the actual marriage records.

It is interesting to note that, of the states in the above list, all except Delaware, Maryland, and Virginia are in New England. New England, as a whole, was a leader in the keeping of vital records. However, as good as these collections are, none of them is complete.

The South and the Mid-Atlantic states were generally much less record-conscious than was New England. And the further south you go, as a rule, the more deficient are the vital records.

D. Marriage and divorce records

1. Marriage records: A marriage record is most often found in the county where the license was issued, usually in the jurisdiction of the county clerk or county recorder, based on the legal requirements of the individual states. However, in New York and the New England states, they were kept in the towns. The early records consist mostly of records of licenses and bonds. Many of these early records have been published in books and various periodicals, but the quality of many of those published marriage records is often deficient.

One such publication of importance to those with early New England ancestry is Clarence Almon Torrey's *New England Marriages Prior to 1700*.[20] Torrey's monumental work was originally a manuscript index in twelve handwritten volumes. It included some 37,000 marriages from about 100,000 references in about 2,000 sources. This amazing alphabetical listing is available on both microfilm and photocopy at the New England Historic Genealogical Society Library in Boston. Also, as noted in footnote 20, a revised edition has been published by Genealogical Publishing Co. and is available from that company. In addition to this, this work has now been digitized and indexed and is available on Ancestry at *http://search.ancestry.com/search/db.aspx?dbid=3824*. Note, however, that because of the book's organization and format, it is a good idea to go there and not to rely solely on the digitized Ancestry record.

Torrey's work includes many marriages that took place in England for people who later came to New England. Nearly every married couple that lived in New England before 1700 is included, along with the marriage date of the

---

[19] John Vogt and T. William Kethley, *Marriage Records in the Virginia State Library: A Researcher's Guide* (Athens, GA: Iberian Publishing Co., Inc., 1988).

[20] Clarence Almon Torrey, *New England Marriages Prior to 1700*, rev. ed. (1985; reprint, Baltimore: Genealogical Publishing Co., 2004).

couple or the birth year of the oldest child. It includes maiden names for 70 percent of the women, birth and death years of both spouses, notations about earlier or later marriages of either spouse, and places of residence. Listings in the book are alphabetical by husbands' names. The Barbour Collection (Connecticut) was apparently not used by Torrey as an input source.

Another book related closely to Torrey's work is a supplement to it called *Third Supplement to Torrey's New England Marriages Prior to 1700*, prepared by Melinde Lutz Sanborn and published in 2005.[21] As the title indicates, this book was actually Mrs. Sanborn's third supplement, but it includes everything that was in the first two.

The first supplement included additions, corrections, and deletions found in the major genealogical periodicals in the three decades following Torrey's death in 1962, while the second one concentrated on (1) periodicals published 1991 to 1995, (2) the unpublished works of leading New England genealogists, (3) English marriages of colonial immigrants, and (4) two important immigration study projects—the *Great Migration* project[22] and the *Mayflower Families Through Five Generations* project.[23]

As noted, Mrs. Sanborn's *Third Supplement* incorporated everything from the first two supplements. It then added information from major genealogical periodicals published from 1962 through the spring of 2003, plus new entries provided by leading genealogists from their personal unpublished research work and from various websites. Because many of the entries in this work come from multi-generational studies—often running five or six generations, well into the 18th century—it includes many post 17th-century marriages and provides significant leads to later generations.

Marriage records are, for the most part, available quite early in many areas of the U.S., with such well-known exceptions as South Carolina, which did not have official marriage records until 1911. However, it should be noted that most early marriage records contain very little detailed genealogical data.

One substitute for original marriage records that is of interest to the researcher is the newspaper notice or marriage announcement. There were also

---

[21] Melinde Lutz Sanborn, *Third Supplement to Torrey's New England Marriages Prior to 1700* (2003; reprint, Baltimore: Genealogical Publishing Co., 2005).

[22] *The Great Migration* project is an ongoing project, the purpose of which is to compile both genealogical and biographical accounts of every New England settler between 1620 and 1640. This includes about twenty thousand men, women, and children who came from England to New England. The project website is at http://greatmigration.org/.

[23] *The Mayflower Families Through Five Generations* project is an ongoing project of the General Society of Mayflower Descendants to trace the first four to six generations of descendants for every *Mayflower* passenger and publish the results. New volumes are published regularly as the project progresses. By 2016, some twenty-five volumes had been published. They are well documented and they represent the best genealogical information available today on these families. More information is available at the project website, http://mayflowerhistory.com/mayflower5g/.

lists published in many newspapers of marriage licenses recently issued. Newspaper announcements, especially, can provide interesting and significant details.

Not surprisingly, there are often errors in marriage records, and you should be alert to that possibility. The parties themselves sometimes falsified the data they gave to the record keeper. Some people fudged on their ages; some falsified other information. Also, some county clerks, unfortunately, followed the questionable practice (in the name of efficiency) of recording the marriage date at the time the license was issued instead of waiting for the certificate to be returned. There are also spelling errors in these records, as in all other records we use.

In addition to possible errors, you should be aware that some of these records might be wholly or partially unreadable for one reason or another. Some of those on microfilm have been poorly filmed. In other cases, record keepers had illegible handwriting. There are also cases where records have been damaged and/or have faded with the passage of time or because of neglect and/or exposure to weather and elements.

Though they are not actually vital records, there are other possible sources of marriage information. These include widows' pension applications, family Bibles, and census records, all of which are discussed elsewhere in this book.

2. Common-law marriages: While on the subject of marriage, I want to comment briefly on the subject of common-law marriages. They are widely misunderstood and many relationships that people have called common-law marriages are not marriages at all but rather unlawful cohabitations. A common-law marriage *is* a legal marriage, and its existence is based mainly on three factors: legality, eligibility, and intent.

The *legality* of such a marriage depends on state law. Note that, in order for a common-law marriage to exist, common-law marriages must be recognized as legal marriages in the state where the couple lived. Many states (and the District of Columbia) now recognize common-law marriages, and many others have recognized them at some time in the past. Common-law marriages are not favored in most places because the difficulty of proving intent is burdensome—especially after one party is deceased. Keep in mind that the existence of a legal marriage does not usually become an issue until one of the parties is deceased. For this reason (and many others), some states that previously accepted such marriages no longer do so.

Those jurisdictions that currently recognize common-law marriages are Alabama (recognized because it is not prohibited by statute), Colorado, District of Columbia, Iowa, Kansas, Montana, New Hampshire (recognized at death of one party, with some limitations), Oklahoma, Rhode Island (recognized because it is not prohibited by statute), South Carolina, Texas, and Utah (only when based on judicial recognition).

Some states that have recognized common-law marriages in the past but no longer do so are Florida (before 1968), Georgia (before 1997), Idaho (before 1996), Indiana (before 1958), Michigan (before 1957), Minnesota (before 1941), Mississippi (before 1956), Montana (before 1978), Nevada (before 1943), Ohio (before October 10, 1991), Pennsylvania (before 2005), and South Dakota (before 1959).

The *eligibility* of both parties is critical; they must be eligible to enter into a legal marriage. There is no marriage if either has a living, undivorced spouse or if there are other impediments, such as age or a too-close relationship between the parties.

The *intent* of both parties to be married to each other is also essential. Some indications of intent include consummation, cohabitation, and a reputation in the community that they are married to each other. Joint bank accounts and joint ownership of property are also considered as good indicators of intent.

When a common-law marriage exists, it is of the same validity in the eyes of the law as any other marriage, and is usually recognized (i.e., given full faith and credit) even in states that do not permit or recognize the formation of such marriages within their own boundaries. Note also that, just like other marriages, a common-law marriage can be dissolved only by a legal divorce or by death. There is no common-law divorce.

Remember that when there was a common-law marriage, there is no record. Nevertheless, if the common-law marriage is alleged after one or both of the parties is deceased, there may be some very useful court records created in order to establish spousal inheritance rights.

3. Divorce records: Divorce records follow much the same pattern as marriage records but are not generally as early. Most of the records are in the counties where the divorces were granted, but many states now have central filing of official divorce records. In many cases, certificates of divorce are issued. However, the court records relating to a divorce often provide much more information. There is more information about these court records, their location, and their use in Chapter 22.

E. Obtaining copies of the records

You need to understand that, in most states, the marriage license does not have to be issued in the same county where the marriage takes place—only in a county within the same state. The license and certificate are returned by the officiator to the county of issue after the marriage has been performed. This can make it a bit tricky to locate marriage records in many cases. Just knowing this fact can help answer many questions.

How you get copies of the records you need depends on several factors. As we have discussed, these are high-priority records for digitizing and indexing on the various family history websites. In cases where the records are available on one of the family history websites, you should definitely access and use them. The number and extent of these will increase as time goes by merely because of their value and the nature of the evidence they provide. Marriages, after all, are the very basis and foundation of those families whose histories you are seeking to establish.

There are also many situations where the custodians of these records have made them available online, sometimes with indexes to facilitate access. Also, many older records are in state historical societies and/or state archives—again, sometimes with indexes.

There are other situations where you can apply for and pay online for copies of the records you want and have the requested copies mailed to you. And sometimes, for an additional fee, you can have these copies sent to you by some expedited method.

There are also still some situations where it will be necessary to write a letter of request to the office where the records are maintained. We will talk about such letters in the next sub-section.

As you deal with these records, you need to understand that certified copies of these more recent official records are available only to persons to whom the records relate or to that person's nearest family members—and only after providing proof of identity. However, you need not worry about certified copies when you are getting records for family history purposes. Those reasons for which certified copies are needed are legal reasons, and uncertified copies of official vital records contain the same information as certified copies. They lack only the state's (or other custodian's) seal of certification.

In most situations, you can obtain the desired records very easily. However, growing concerns in many states about identity theft have led to the restriction of some records. You may find that to be a problem in some states—especially with birth and death records—but there is little concern about identity theft with marriage and divorce records.

F. Writing for records

In a case where you need to write for a copy of a vital record certificate, you should be as brief as possible, not only as a matter of winning goodwill but also as a matter of practicality. In the first place, busy public officials do not have time to read long letters. In the second place, your specific requests and desires may be overlooked in the body of a long letter. And, in the third place, time is too precious to spend it writing verbiage that may only be confusing.

In such letters, you need to tell your relationship to the person about whom you are inquiring.

Insofar as possible, send the correct amount of money with your request. Personal checks, cashier's checks, and money orders are often accepted. Do not send cash. It is impossible to prove that cash was sent, and it is more difficult to keep a good record of it. Earlier in this chapter, I gave information about the government publication called *Where to Write for Vital Records*. This booklet is online at *https://www.cdc.gov/nchs/w2w/index.htm*. It can also be downloaded at *https://publications.usa.gov/USAPubs.php?PubID=1139*.

Your Internet search engine can often be used to find information about obtaining copies of vital records certificates from your specific state of interest. On some sites, you can print out copies of the necessary application forms for the records you want. And, in many cases—as was stated in the previous subsection—you can request on an Internet website for the record to be mailed, or even faxed, to you. Also, when you make a request online, you can usually pay the required fees with your credit card.

When requesting a copy of a certificate, you need to provide all the information you can that relates to the event. Otherwise, the record may not be found. It is not necessary to give information about a person's *death* when you are requesting his *birth* certificate as some people do, but if you desire a death certificate, the date of death is needed. (There are a few exceptions to this rule depending on the filing system used in the state. Most states file their records chronologically, but some have special indexes.)

The specific place of death within the state is not always important, but it may help registration officials determine if they are sending the certificate for the right person, especially if the name is common.

Correct names are important. You will appreciate this when you write for the death certificate of someone you know died on a certain date in a certain place, and the certificate is not found. The certificate may be there, but the name you gave for the decedent was incorrect. This can happen with women because of forgotten or unknown remarriages. Any attempt to secure the death certificate of a married woman under her maiden surname will be disappointing.

A request for a birth certificate must usually include the names of parents, but parents' names are not quite so important when requesting a copy of the death record or marriage record. They can be helpful, however, if other important information is unknown. Ages on death certificates fall into this same "helpful" category. Even if you do not have all pertinent names and dates, it is still worthwhile to try to obtain a copy of the record. If the record is found, it will have even greater value for you. Remember that vital records custodians must have some information to work with—and more is better, so long as it is relevant to your request.

The following letter is a typical request for a death certificate. Remember, however, that this example is given only as a suggestion and is not an exact fit for every situation:

123 Any Street
Haysbury, GA 30000
September 30, 2017

Minnesota Department of Health
Central Cashiering—Vital Records
P.O. Box 64499
St. Paul, MN 55164-0499

Gentlemen:

Please send me a copy of the death certificate of my great-grandmother Martha Black, who died on or about June 7, 1928, in Cloverton, Pine County, Minnesota, at about age 59. Her father was Mendon Marshall, and her husband was Braxton Black.

A money order for thirteen dollars ($13) is enclosed to cover your fee. Thank you for your help.

Sincerely,

(signed) Sidney Orbeck

The dates on which the several states began keeping vital records are shown in Figure 1, earlier in this chapter.

IV. TOWN MEETING RECORDS

In most of New England, vital records information was recorded in town meeting records. Typical of these are the ones of Chester, Vermont, some of which are shown below. Note that births and marriages were generally recorded more faithfully than were deaths. Also, note that it was quite common to record the births of all the children in a family at the same time, often several years after the actual dates of some of those births:

Jacob Chase of Chesterfield and Olive Wilson of Chester were Joined in Marriage Feb^{ry} 1st, 1792 by Daniel Heald Jus' Peace

October Y' 3: 1792 then personally came before me the subscriber at my dwelling house in Chester John Chandler and Anna Tarlick Both of Chester and Said John Chandler Did then and there Say the following words / viz/ I take this wooman to be my weded wife and then Said Ann Tarlick Said Likewise I take this man to be my weded husband but nither of them took eatch other by the hand.

Daniel Heald Just. Peace

Polly Ston Dafter of John Ston June by Lucy his wife born September ye 30 1773

Rhoda Ston Dafter of John Ston Juner by Lucy his wife born October 8th 1774

Sally Ston Dafter of John Ston Juner by Lucy his wife born Jany 4th 1777

Lucy Ston Dafter of John Ston June by Lucy his wife born Jany 4th 1779

John and Betsy Ston Son and Dafter of John Ston Juner by Lucy his wife born Sept 4th 1783

John Ston Son of John Ston June by Lucy his wife born July 28th 1784

Earl and Betsy Ston Son and Dafter of John Ston Juner by Lucy his wife born April 13th 1786

Ivanna Ston Dafter of John Ston Junr by Lucy his wife born June 2th 1788

Ivanna Ston Dafter of John Ston Junr by Lucy his wife born June 2th 1790 [24]

Calvon Here and Abner Here Sons of William Here by Merean his wife May 22 1788

Abner Here Departed this Life May 23 1788

Calven Here Departed this Life August 6 1788

Thomas Riggs Here Son of William Here by Merean his wife born July 13 1789

Aber^n Here Son of William Here by Merean his wife born June 29 1791

Stephen Here Son of William Here by Merean his wife born March 22–1796

Some town meeting records have been published, others have been microfilmed, and some have been digitized and are now searchable on various family history websites in indexed databases. Many, however, are still available only at the town hall.

V. RECORD PROBLEMS

The main problems and limitations in the use of vital records by the family history researcher are the following:

A. Limitation of time

The greatest problem with vital records, of course, is the time limitation. They are wonderful records, but they are of no value for the periods not covered. However, we often imagine greater limitations than actually exist. As already discussed, many gaps can be bridged through efficient use of even relatively recent records.

B. Lack of needed information

Another limitation is the need we frequently have for quite detailed information in order to secure the desired records. Too often, the vital records office, because of the filing system employed, will require the very information from you that you are trying to obtain. Below is a list of information that is always necessary, regardless of the filing system used:

1. Name at the time of the event.
2. Place of the event (at least the state). An older person often went to live with a child in another state, and it may be difficult to find this information.

---

[24] This family was recorded in the Chester town meeting records in 1798.

3. Date of the event. In every state, it is necessary to have at least an approximate death date; some require it to be exact.

4. Names of the parents, in the case of a birth record. For a marriage or death certificate, those names are also helpful. (In any case, the name of one parent is better than the names of neither.)

Without names, places, and dates, you lack the essential identifying data required for finding the record. The need for complete identifying data is even more acute if the name is common.

C. The reliability question

There is always a reliability issue when you use vital records. On a marriage record, the age of a party or the name of a parent may be deliberately falsified for one reason or another. These same items of information might also be unintentionally misstated with just as serious an effect. With a death certificate, you are at the mercy of the informant. If his connection to the deceased was close, the information may be accurate, but often, even those close to a person actually knew little about him. The date and place of birth and the names of parents as given on the death certificate of an elderly person are strictly secondary evidence. Also, consider that even members of the immediate family who could otherwise furnish reliable data do not think as clearly as they should when confronted with the shock of the loved one's death and the pressure of the situation. (Note that this is also one reason why obituary notices are often inaccurate or incomplete.)

D. Early forms

The forms used by some states before they entered the national registration areas left much to be desired (especially death records). Many of them called for only limited family history information. The early Texas death certificates, for example, asked only for the country of birth (and "U.S.A." gives little assistance in research). Such was the case as late as 1927.

E. Handwriting

Handwriting is sometimes a problem. If you have trouble reading the prescriptions written by your family doctor, you can understand why a birth or death certificate filled in, at least partially, by that same doctor might also be hard to read. In more recent years, these certificates are usually typewritten (and even computer generated in more recent years), and death certificates are generally the responsibility of the funeral director, but these practices are both of relatively recent origin. Thus, some old handwritten certificates hold many secrets, undecipherable by even the most adept.

One plus is that most registration offices do not attempt to interpret the records. All copies they provide are photocopies. This gives you the opportunity to puzzle over the actual handwriting and study it to your heart's content in your effort to arrive at a correct interpretation. You do not have to accept anyone else's say-so, and you may have useful clues in what you already know that will facilitate your interpretation.

F. Other legibility problems

Other issues are also often responsible for illegibility. Acts of God, such as floods and fires, take their toll. Mildew, insects, poor ink, and inferior grades of paper can render a record (or portions thereof) unreadable after a time and thus limit its evidentiary value. The record collections that have most often become victims of improper care are those kept on the local (town or county) level. Elected public officials too often have no idea about the value of the records in their stewardship. And, among vital records, marriage records and those birth and death records dating before statewide registration have suffered most. Overheated attics and musty basements have too long been used as repositories for the oldest and most valuable records.

Many states have passed legislation requiring that old records be brought into places where they can be properly preserved. This is a step forward, and it should be encouraged by every family history researcher and every genealogical organization.

G. Restrictive legislation

Another problem is that some states are enacting laws designed to restrict access to their vital records. The availability of vital records is based on state law, and thus varies somewhat from state to state. In many jurisdictions, there is a 100-year restriction on birth records and a 50-year restriction on death records, but exceptions are often made when a record is requested for genealogical information. There are other states, such as Texas, where these restrictions are for 75 years and 25 years, respectively.

An example of an interesting state statute relating to vital records is Connecticut Statute Chapter 93 Registrars of Vital Statistics, Sec. 7-51a, which limits access to death and marriage certificates for 50 years and limits access to birth certificates for 100 years, but then gives unlimited access "[d]uring all normal business hours, [to] members of genealogical societies incorporated or authorized by the Secretary of the State to do business or conduct affairs in this state."

Being aware of laws like this one can assist you immeasurably as you seek to secure copies of ancestral records.

In many states, marriage records have fewer restrictions and are considered public records. California, however, has an interesting statute that allows the couple obtaining a marriage license to check a box on the application to make the record private and unavailable to anyone.

VI. FINAL OBSERVATIONS

Many vital records are now digitized and available on one or more of the family history websites discussed in Chapter 10. That is where your search for vital records in appropriate time periods should begin. FamilySearch, Ancestry, MyHeritage, FindMyPast, Archives.com, AmericanAncestors.org, and several other websites should be considered as you seek the record of a specific vital event. If the record you seek is not found on one of these websites, use an Internet search engine to go to the vital records information of the specific state to see if the record is available online or can be ordered online. Your last resort is to write a letter, as suggested earlier .

It is plain that vital records are not without fault as a family history source, but the perfect source does not exist. If you overlook vital records when they are available, you are not doing the best research you can do—even if extra effort is required to obtain them. In the interest of putting together complete and accurate family history records, your research must also be complete and accurate.

14

Census Returns

There is probably no other single group of records that contains more information about individuals and families who lived in the United States during the 1800s than do the U.S. federal census population schedules. These census records are also of great value for the 1900s, but not as much as in the 1800s because there are many other good records available in the 1900s. Census records have always been a boon to the family history researcher, but they are now even more valuable and more useful because all available census records are now digitized and indexed. Even though those indexes are far from perfect, if you use them wisely they are of critical importance. In fact, no research on an American family history problem that is centered in any time period since the beginning of the census is complete until all pertinent census schedules have been consulted.

I. WHAT IS THE CENSUS?

The year of the first United States census was 1790. It was taken because of a provision in the U.S. Constitution, which was signed in 1787, declaring that

> Representatives and direct Taxes shall be apportioned among the several states which may be included with this Union, according to their respective Numbers. . . . The actual Enumeration shall be made within three Years after the first Meeting of the Congress of the United States, and within every subsequent Term of ten Years, in such Manner as they shall by Law direct.[1]

It is a unique historical phenomenon for a government to prescribe the necessity and the method for taking a census in its originating document but, due to the very nature of this new government, the census was an administrative necessity. Because of the purpose for which the census was taken—counting

---

[1] U. S. Constitution, Art. 1, Sec. 2.

the population—the resulting censuses have been called census population schedules.

The first census essentially did just what it was charged to do—it counted the population. After naming the head of each household, it simply counted the number of people in the household in three age categories: "Free white males of 16 years and upward . . . ," "Free white males under 16 years," and "Free white females . . ." It also counted "All other free persons" and the number of "Slaves" belonging to each household. Through several decades of these censuses, this basic pattern remained unchanged, except that the age groupings became more numerous and thus more specific.

Since 1790, the federal census has been taken every ten years, just as the Constitution mandated. Because of the every-ten-year requirement, they are called decennial censuses. Early on, these censuses contained a minimal amount of family history data. However, notwithstanding that fact, when properly used they are invaluable aids as we work to create a complete family history picture. They are also helpful as we seek to locate and identify specific persons and families.

By carefully studying Charts 1, 2, and 3 in this chapter, you can gain an excellent knowledge of the various censuses, their content, and their potential value. As you observe Charts 1 and 2, you will quickly note that there is no summary included of the census schedules for the years 1880 and later.

That omission of those census schedules from the charts was intentional because too much information tended to make the charts too complicated. Instead, if you will go to Chapter 15, under the subsection E of section "I. Benefits and Uses," there is a careful analysis and comparison of the 1880, 1900, 1910, 1920, 1930, and 1940 censuses. The time you spend studying the charts in this chapter and that analytical comparison of the more recent available census schedules in Chapter 15 will be well spent. Also, your study of the reproductions of the census forms in this chapter should also prove to be beneficial.

When the censuses before 1830 were taken, the government provided no printed forms for use by census takers, though a list of the information to be gathered—the essential characteristics of a form—was specified in each census statute. Because of this, there is little uniformity in the appearance of the forms that were used for the 1790, 1800, 1810, and 1820 censuses. We presume that those who took the census, the marshals' assistants, provided their own paper, but we are not sure of that in every case.

The only exception to this no-form situation is the 1790 census of Massachusetts, where the state provided a printed form. The remaining 1790 enumerations were taken on paper ranging in length from four inches to three feet, and some were taken "in merchants' account books, journals, or ledgers; others were bound with old newspapers, wrapping paper, or wallpaper."[2]

The census records that enumerated the American people were called population schedules.

The most significant changes in the census population schedule format came in 1850. The entire format of the 1850 census was altered from what had been used in previous years. Lemuel Shattuck of Massachusetts, probably America's greatest crusader in the vital registration and the public health movement (see Chapter 13), was likely the person most responsible for these innovations.

Shattuck prepared a census for Boston in 1845 that so impressed federal officials, they invited him to Washington in 1849 to help with plans for the 1850 federal census. He was, it appears, almost solely responsible for the changes that were made. The main change in this census—and this was major—was to make the individual, rather than the household, the primary census unit. Instead of describing an entire household on a single line as in the earlier censuses, one line was used to record information about each person.

As explained in Chapter 13, Shattuck, apparently against his own better judgment, also introduced the practice of using the census to collect data on births, marriages, and deaths. The Shattuck-designed 1850 forms provided a column that asked if a husband and wife were "Married within the year?" There was also a column added in 1870 to record the month of birth for each child born during the census year.

Beginning in 1850, other census schedules—non-population schedules—were added; these are of some significance to us. Of particular interest to the family history researcher are (1) mortality schedules,[3] (2) slave schedules, (3) agricultural schedules, (4) manufacturing schedules, and (5) social statistics schedules. The mortality schedule was never quite the success hoped for, yet this method of collecting national vital statistics continued through the 1900 census.[4] These different schedules are discussed later in this chapter.

---

[2] Katherine H. Davidson and Charlotte M. Ashby, comps., *Preliminary Inventory of the Records of the Bureau of the Census* (Washington, DC: The National Archives, 1964, 99).

[3] For more information on vital statistics by enumeration, see Chapter 13.

[4] National Office of Vital Statistics, *Vital Statistics of the United States* (Washington, DC: U.S. Public Health Service, 1954), Vol. 1, 6. Note that the 1900 mortality schedules were destroyed in compliance with an act of Congress after statistical summaries were completed.

CHART 1—CENSUS CONTENT CHART (1790-1840)

CONTENT	1790	1800	1810	1820	1830	1840
Names of heads of families only	X	X	X	X	X	X
Number of free white males under 16 in family.	X					
Number of free white males 16 and over in family.	X					
Number of free white females in family (no age breakdown).	X					
Number of free white males and females (separately) in family, in age groups: under 10, 10-15, 16-25, 26-44, 45 and over.		X	X	X		
Number of free white males and females (separately) in family, in 5 year age groups under 20 years of age.					X	X
Number of free white males and females (separately) in family, in 10 year age groups, ages 20-99.					X	X
Number of free white males and females (separately) in family, 100 years of age and over.					X	X
Number of free white males in family ages 16-18.			X			
Number of all other free persons (including colored).	X	X(a)	X(a)	(a) X(b)	X(c)	X(c)
Number of slaves.	X	X	X	X(d)	X(e)	X(e)
Number of foreigners not naturalized.				X	X	
Number of deaf and dumb (white and colored enumerated separately).					X(f)	X(f)
Number of blind (white and colored enumerated separately).					X	X
Number of insane or idiotic (white and colored enumerated separately).						X(g)
Civil division of place of residence.	X	X	X	X	X	X
Number of persons engaged in agriculture.				X		X
Number of persons engaged in commerce.				X		X
Number of persons engaged in manufacturer. [sic]				X		X(h)
Number of persons empoyed in mining.						X
Number of persons employed in navigation of the ocean.						X
Number of persons employed in the learned professions and engineers.						X
Names and ages of pensioners for Revolutionary or Military Service.						X
Number of white males over 21 years of age who cannot read and write.						X
Total number of persons in household.					X	X

General note: All of the above catagories which refer to "number of persons" have to do with each household individually.

(a) Except Indians, not taxed.
(b) Free colored persons in age groups (under 14, 14-25, 26-44, 45 and over) by sex.
(c) Frce colored persons in age groups (under 10, 10-23, 24-35, 36-54, 55-99, 100 and over) by sex.
(d) In age groups (under 14, 14-25, 26-44, 45 and over) by sex.
(e) In age groups (under 10, 10-23, 24-35, 36-54, 55-99, 100 and over) by sex.
(f) Whites only are in age groups (under 14, 14-24, 25 and over). Colored not divided by age.
(g) Those in public charge and those in private charge are separately listed.
(h) and the trades.

CHART 2 - CENSUS CONTENT (1850 - 1870)

CONTENT	1850	1860	1870
Name of every person whose usual place of abode on the census date was in this household. *(1)*	x	x	x
Dwelling houses are numbered in order of enumerator's visit.	x	x	x
Families are numbered in order of enumerator's visit.	x	x	x
Enumeration districts listed at tops of pages.	x	x	x
Post office addresses at tops of pages.		x	x
Age of every person at last birthday prior to census date. *(1)*	x		x
Sex of every person.	x	x	x
Color or race of every person. *(2)*	x	x	x
Profession, occupation, or trade of every person. *(3)*	x	x	x
Value of real estate owned by person.		x	x
Value of personal property owned by person.		x	x
Place of birth (state, territory, or country) of each person.	x	x	x
Place of birth (state, territory, or country) of each person's father and mother.	x	x	x
If person was married within the census year. *(1)*	x	x	x
If person attended school within the census year. *(1)*	x	x	x
If person could not read or write.	x	x	x
If person was deaf and dumb, blind, insane, or idiodic. *(4)*	x	x	x
If person was a pauper or a convict. *(4)*	x	x	
Month of birth if born within year prioor to census date.			x
If person's father/mother were of foreign birth. *(5)*			x
If person was a male citizen of the U.S. age 21 and over.			x

NOTES:

(1) The census date was June 1 in all three of these censuses.

(2) In 1850 and 1860, this included white, black, and Mulatto. In 1870 it added Chinese and Indian.

(3) In 1850, this included only males over 15; in 1860 it included everyone over 15; in 1870 it included everyone.

(4) The correct word was to be written in the column.

(5) There are separate columns for the father and the mother. The answer was "Yes" or "No."

CHART 3—IMPORTANT CENSUS DATA

STATE	BECAME A TERRITORY	BECAME A STATE	FIRST AVAILABLE CENSUS	PERTINENT COMMENTS	MISSING CENSUSES								
					1790	1800	1810	1820	1830	1840	1850	1860	1870
Alabama	1817	1819	1830	Before creation of the State of Miss. in 1817 Ala. formed the E. half of the Miss. Terr. It had been a part of Ga. until 1802. That part of the state S. of the 31st parallel was in Spanish W. Fla. until 1812.			All (as part of the Miss. Terr.)	All. (Census of some counties is in *Alabama Historical Quarterly* [Fall 1944, Vol. 6].)					
Alaska	1912	1959	1900	Those censuses before territorial status were taken while Alaska was still a district.									
Arizona	1863	1912	1870 (1850 and 1860 are in N.M. Terr.)	Ariz. was in N.M. Terr. 1850-63. A portion in the S. was added by the Gadsden Prchs. in 1852 while still in N.M. Terr.									
Arkansas	1819	1836	1830	Ark. was in the La. Prchs. of 1803 and was part of the Mo. Terr. 1812-19 when Mo. first applied for statehood. The Ark. Terr. included the Indian lands in Okla.				All					
California		1850	1850	Spain controlled Calif. before 1822. From 1822 to 1848 it was owned by Mexico.							San Francisco, Santa Clara, and Contra Costa cos.		
Colorado	1861	1876	1870 (1860 Census of Arapahoe Co. in Kan. Terr.)	The area now comprising Colo. included about 50 million acres previously assigned to Utah and Kan., about 10 million from the N.M. Terr. The Terr. of Jefferson was voted by the residents in 1859 but was never recognized by Congress.								Little River County	

CHART 3—(continued)

STATE	BECAME A TERRITORY	BECAME A STATE	FIRST AVAILABLE CENSUS	PERTINENT COMMENTS	MISSING CENSUSES								
					1790	1800	1810	1820	1830	1840	1850	1860	1870
Connecticut		1788	1790	One of the original 13 states. Fifth to ratify the Constitution.									
Delaware		1787	1800	One of the original 13 states. First to ratify the Constitution.	All (reconstructed)								
District of Columbia	1790	Became seat of govt. in 1800.	1800 (Part of 1790 is in Montgomery and Prince George's counties, Maryland.)	Land area was taken from both Va. and Md. to form the district.		Incomplete	All (including Alexandria Co., now in Va.)						
Florida	1822	1845	1830	Fla., which early included parts of S. Miss. and Ala., had at various times belonged to Spain and Britain, was ceded to U.S. by Spain in 1819.								Hernando County	
Georgia		1788	1820	One of the original 13 states. Fourth to ratify the Constitution.	All (reconstructed)	All except Oglethorpe County	All	Franklin, Rabun, and Twiggs cos.					
Hawaii	1900	1959	1900	Ruled by native monarchs until 1893, was then a republic until 1898, then ceded itself to U.S.									
Idaho	1863	1890	1870 (Part is in Utah census.)	Originally a part of the Oregon Terr., 1848-53; Wash. Terr., 1853-63; became Idaho Terr. in 1863 including small parts of Mont. and Wyo. W. of the divide.									Kootenai County

CHART 3—(continued)

STATE	BECAME A TERRITORY	BECAME A STATE	FIRST AVAILABLE CENSUS	PERTINENT COMMENTS	MISSING CENSUSES								
					1790	1800	1810	1820	1830	1840	1850	1860	1970
Illinois	1809	1818	1820	Ill. was part of the N.W. Terr. (1787), became part of Ind. Terr. (1800), thus remained until 1809. Original Ill. Terr. included area of present Wisc. and E. part of Minn.		All (as part of the Ind. Terr.)	All except Randolph County						
Indiana	1800	1816	1820	Became part of the N.W. Terr. (1787). The Ind. Terr., as set up in 1800 incuded Ill., Wisc., W. Mich., E. Minn., with E. Mich. being added in 1803.		All	All	Daviess County	*				
Iowa	1838	1846	1840	Iowa was part of the La. Prchs. (1803). Was in Mo. Terr. 1812-21, unorganized territory 1821-34, Mich. Terr. 1834-36, Wisc. Terr. 1836-38.									
Kansas	1854	1861	1860	Kan. was part of the La. Prchs. (1803). Was in Mo. Terr. 1812-21, unorganized territory (Indian) 1821-54.									Arapahoe County
Kentucky		1792	1810	Very early the Ky. area was considered part of Augusta Co., Va. Later (1584) part of Virginia Co. Pre-settlement Ky. called Fincastle Co., Va. During time of early settlement it was called Kentucky Co., Va. (c. 1775-76). In 1776 it was divided into 3 counties—Fayette, Jefferson and Lincoln. Further divided into 9 counties in 1790. The early settlers called it Transylvania.	All. (Tax lists have been substituted.)	All. (Tax lists have been substituted.)							

*Wabash County, Indiana, for 1830 was originally reported missing. However, the county was not created until 1832 (from Cass and Grant counties).

CHART 3—(continued)

STATE	BECAME A TERRITORY	BECAME A STATE	FIRST AVAILABLE CENSUS	PERTINENT COMMENTS	MISSING CENSUSES								
					1790	1800	1810	1820	1830	1840	1850	1860	1870
Louisiana	1805	1812	1810	Part of the La. Prchs. (1803). S. part of prchs. lands became Orleans Terr. in 1804. La. was the major portion of this territory.			St. Landry and W. Baton Rouge p'sh. and some areas no longer in state.					Bienville Parish	
Maine		1820	1790 (in Mass.)	This territory was annexed by Mass. in 1693 as York(shire) Co. and remained part of Mass. until 1820. In 1760 the one county was divided to form three.		Part of York Co.							
Maryland		1788	1790	One of the original 13 states. Seventh to ratify the Constitution.	Allegany, Calvert, and Somerset counties	All of Baltimore Co. except the City of Baltimore			Montgomery, Prince George's, St. Mary's, Queen Anne's, and Somerset counties				
Massachusetts		1788	1790	One of the original 13 states. Sixth to ratify the Constitution. Included Maine until 1820.		Part of Suffolk County	All						
Michigan	1805	1837	1820	Part of the N.W. Terr. (1787). In 1800 the W. part of lower Mich. and E. part of upper Mich. became part of Ind. Terr. In 1802 all of state was in Ind. Terr. and thus remained until 1805 when									

CHART 3—(continued)

STATE	BECAME A TERRITORY	BECAME A STATE	FIRST AVAILABLE CENSUS	PERTINENT COMMENTS	MISSING CENSUSES								
					1790	1800	1810	1820	1830	1840	1850	1860	1870
Michigan (continued)				Mich. Terr. was created. Jurisdiction extended W. to the Miss. River, including Wisc. and E. Minn. (1818-36).									
Minnesota	1849	1858	1850 (There was also a special enumeration in 1857.)	In 1787 E. part of area became part of N.W. Terr. W. part was in La. Prchs. of 1803. In 1800 E. part was in Ind. Terr.; 1818 in Mich. Terr.; 1836 in Wisc. Terr. Thus remained until 1849. Wisc. Terr. also included the W. part of the state. The Minn. Terr. (1849) extended W. to the Mo. River including much of what later became the Dakota Territory.									All originals missing except the counties alphabetically from Stearns to Wright. (State Hist. Soc. and Nat'l Archives have copies of missing schedules.)
Mississippi	1798	1817	1820	Originally claimed by Ga. Remained loyal to the Crown during Revolutionary War, but was taken over by Spain 1789-91. Held by Spain until 1798. All of the state S. of 31st parallel was in Spanish W. Fla. until 1812. In 1817 Ala. was separated from the Miss. Territory.		All	All (including Alabama)		Pike County			Hancock, Sunflower, and Washington counties	
Missouri	1812	1821	1830	N. part of the La. Prchs. was made Mo. Terr. in 1812. Originally this territory included Ark., Iowa, Kan., Neb., and Okla.			All (in La. Terr.)	All					
Montana	1864	1889	1860 (in Neb. Terr. and Wash. Terr.)	Extreme N.W. part of state was in Ore. Terr. 1846-53, Wash. Terr. 1853-63, Idaho Terr. 1863-64. Most of state part of La. Prchs. (1803).									

CHART 3—(continued)

STATE	BECAME A TERRITORY	BECAME A STATE	FIRST AVAILABLE CENSUS	PERTINENT COMMENTS	MISSING CENSUSES								
					1790	1800	1810	1820	1830	1840	1850	1860	1870
Montana (continued)				In La. Terr. 1805-12, Mo. Terr. 1812-54, Neb. Terr. 1854-61, Dakota Terr. 1861-64.									
Nebraska	1854	1864	1860	Originally part of La. Prchs. (1803). Part of Mo. Terr. 1812-20 (no settlers until 1823), unorganized territory 1820-34. In 1834 part of area was placed under jurisdiction of Ark., part under Mich., and part under Mo. When Neb. Terr. was created it included parts of Colo., Mont., Wyo., and N. and S. Dakota (N. from the 40th parallel to Canada and W. from Mo. River to continental divide). Area was reduced to present size of state in 1861 with creation of Colo. and Dakota Terr.									
Nevada	1861	1864	1860 (in Utah Terr.)	Land ceded to U.S. by Mexico 1848. From 1850 to 1861 it was part of Utah Terr., except S. tip of state which was in N.M. Terr. 1850-63, before Ariz. Terr. was organized.									
New Hampshire		1788	1790	One of the original 13 states. Ninth to ratify the Constitution.		Parts of Rockingham and Strafford counties		Grafton Co.; parts of Rockingham and Strafford counties					
New Jersey		1787	1830	One of the original 13 states. Third to ratify the Constitution.	All	All	All	All					

CHART 3—(continued)

STATE	BECAME A TERRITORY	BECAME A STATE	FIRST AVAILABLE CENSUS	PERTINENT COMMENTS	MISSING CENSUSES								
					1790	1800	1810	1820	1830	1840	1850	1860	1870
New Mexico	1850	1912	1850	Land ceded to U.S. by Mexico in 1848, except for strip of land which Texas had claimed E. of the Rio Grande. When territory was created in 1850 it included Ariz. and part of Colo. (A small area in S.W. corner and a larger area now in Ariz. were added by Gadsden Prchs., 1852.)									
New York		1788	1790	One of the original 13 states. Eleventh to ratify the Constitution.			Courtland County						
North Carolina		1789	1790	One of the original 13 states. Twelfth to ratify the Constitution. Included Tennessee until 1796.	Caswell, Granville, and Orange counties		Craven, Green, New Hanover and Wake counties	Currituck, Franklin, Martin, Montgomery, Randolph, and Wake counties					
North Dakota	1861	1889	1860 (as the Dakota Terr.)	Area was originally part of the La. Prchs. (1803). Later when Minn. Terr. formed in 1849 it included all of the area of N.D. as far W. as the Mo. River, but was left in unorganized territory in 1859 when Minn. was cut to its present boundaries. As Dakota Terr. was organized in 1861 it included both Dakotas									

CHART 3—(continued)

STATE	BECAME A TERRITORY	BECAME A STATE	FIRST AVAILABLE CENSUS	PERTINENT COMMENTS	MISSING CENSUSES								
					1790	1800	1810	1820	1830	1840	1850	1860	1870
North Dakota (continued)				and most of Wyo. and Mont. In 1864 Wyo. and Mont. separated to form Mont. Terr. A movement to divide the Dakotas began in early 1870s but was not legislated until 1889 when both became states.									
Ohio	1799	1803	1820	Ohio was originally part of the N.W. Terr. (1787) and was the first state carved out of this area. It began to function as a state in 1802.		All	All	Franklin and Wood counties					
Oklahoma	1890	1907	1890 (partial)	Okla. became part of the Ark. Terr. in 1819 but the relevant history dates from 1866 when the Indian tribes ceded the W. portion of their domain to the U.S. Land was not opened for white settlement until 1889. The Indian Terr. (about the E. ⅓ of the present state) was not officially organized but remained under the jurisdiction of Ark. until statehood.									
Oregon	1848	1859	1850	Original Oregon Terr. embraced all of Wash. and Idaho, British Columbia to 54°40', and Mont. and Wyo. W. of the continental divide until cut to present size to become a state.									

CHART 3—(continued)

STATE	BECAME A TERRITORY	BECAME A STATE	FIRST AVAILABLE CENSUS	PERTINENT COMMENTS	MISSING CENSUSES								
					1790	1800	1810	1820	1830	1840	1850	1860	1870
Pennsylvania		1787	1790	One of the original 13 states. Second to ratify the Constitution.		Part of Westmoreland County	Parts of Bedford, Cumberland and Philadelphia counties						
Rhode Island		1790	1790	One of the original 13 states, Thirteenth to ratify the Constitution.									
*South Carolina		1788	1790	One of the original 13 states, Eighth to ratify the Constitution.		Richland County							
South Dakota	1861	1889	1860 (as the Dakota Terr.)	Originally part of the La. Prchs. (1803). When Minn. Terr. was formed (1849) it included all of the area of S. Dak. E. of the Mo. River, but this area was later left unorganized (1859) when Minn. was cut back to its present size. When the Dak. Terr. was created in 1861 it included both Dakotas and most of Mont. and Wyo. In 1864 Mont. and Wyo. separated to form the Mont. Terr. and in the early 1870s a movement to form two Dakotas began, but no legislation to this effect was passed until 1889 when both were								

*It was previously reported that the censuses for Clarendon County, South Carolina, for 1820-1850 were missing. However, the present-day Clarendon County was not created until 1855 (from Sumter District). The old Clarendon County (created in 1785 from Camden) became defunct in 1800.

CHART 3—(continued)

STATE	BECAME A TERRITORY	BECAME A STATE	FIRST AVAILABLE CENSUS	PERTINENT COMMENTS	MISSING CENSUSES								
					1790	1800	1810	1820	1830	1840	1850	1860	1870
South Dakota (continued)				made states. Before the area E. of Mo. River was in Minn. Terr. it had been in the Wisc. Terr. (1836-49).									
Tennessee		1796	1820 (one county in 1810)	Tenn. was originally a part of N.C. In the early settlement period it was called Washington Co., N.C. The State of Franklin was formed in an effort to separate from N.C. but it was never recognized.		All. (Part reconstructed from tax lists.)	All missing except Rutherford County. Grainger County published.	Anderson, Bledsoe, Blount, Campbell, Carter, Claiborne, Cocke, Grainger, Greene, Hamilton, Hawkins, Jefferson, Knox, McMinn, Marion, Monroe, Morgan, Rhea, Roane, Sevier, Sullivan, and Washington counties					

CHART 3—(continued)

STATE	BECAME A TERRITORY	BECAME A STATE	FIRST AVAILABLE CENSUS	PERTINENT COMMENTS	MISSING CENSUSES								
					1790	1800	1810	1820	1830	1840	1850	1860	1870
Texas		1845	1850	Texas belonged to Spain before 1822. In 1822 Mexico became sovereign. It belonged to Mexico until an independent republic was set up in 1836 by the settlers.								Blanco, Coleman, Concho, Duval, Edwards, Hardeman, Kimble, Knox, LaSalle, McCullock, McMullen, Tarrant, Taylor, Wichita, Wilbarger, and Wilson cos.	Archer, Baylor, Concho, Edwards, Hardeman, Knox, Taylor, Wichita, and Wilbarger counties
Utah	1850	1896	1850	Original territory included all of Nevada except S. tip. It also included W. Colo. and S.W. Wyo. (as far N. as the present Utah-Idaho border).									
Vermont		1791	1790	Prevented from being one of the original states by claims made on her territory by N.H. and N.Y. Fourteenth state.									
Virginia		1788	1810	One of the original 13 states. Tenth to ratify the Constitution. Included W.Va. until 1863; Ky. until 1792. Alexandria Co. was in the Dist. of Col. in the censuses of 1820, 1830 and 1840. The 1810 of Alexandria Co. is missing.	All. (Tax lists have beeen substituted.)	All	Cabell, Grayson, Greenbrier, Halifax, Hardy, Henry, James City, King Wm., Lee, Louisa, Mecklenburg, Nansemond, Northampton, Orange, Patrick, Pittsylvania, Russell, and Tazewell cos.						

CHART 3—(continued)

STATE	BECAME A TERRITORY	BECAME A STATE	FIRST AVAILABLE CENSUS	PERTINENT COMMENTS	MISSING CENSUSES								
					1790	1800	1810	1820	1830	1840	1850	1860	1870
Washington	1853	1889	1860	In Ore. Terr. 1848-53. What later became Idaho Terr., with small sections of Mont. and Wyo., was included in Wash. Terr. from 1853-63.									
West Virginia		1863	1810 (in Va.)	Separated itself from Va. and was admitted to the Union during the Civil War.	All (part of Va.)	All (part of Va.)	Cabell, Greenbrier, and Hardy counties (in Va.)						
Wisconsin	1836	1848	1820 (in Mich. Terr.)	Was part of the N.W. Terr. (1787). In Ind. Terr. 1800-09, in Ill. Terr. 1809-18, in Mich. Terr. 1818-36. In the beginning the Wisc. Terr. extended W. as far as Mo. River and included what later became the Minn. Terr. and much of the Dakota Terr.		All (as part of Indiana Terr.)	All (as part of Illinois Terr.)						
Wyoming	1868	1890	1860 (in Neb. Terr.)	The area was mainly in the La. Prchs. (1803). Later it was in Neb. Terr., 1854-61, Dakota Terr. 1861-64, Mont. Terr. 1864-68. The extreme W. part was in the Ore. Terr. 1848-53, Wash. Terr. 1853-63, Idaho Terr. 1863-68; and the S.W. corner was in Utah Terr. 1850-68.									

FIRST CENSUS OF THE UNITED STATES 1790

HEADS OF FAMILIES _____

(STATE)

_____

(COUNTY)

NAME OF HEAD OF FAMILY	Free white males of 16 years and upward, including heads of families.	Free white males under 16 years.	Free white females including heads of families.	All other free persons.	Slaves.
Town, City					

FIGURE 1 — THE 1790 FEDERAL CENSUS

CENSUS OF 1800

SCHEDULE OF THE WHOLE NUMBER OF PERSONS WITHIN THE DIVISION ALLOTTED TO..............

Name of county, parish, township, town or city, where the family resides.	Names of heads of families.	Free white males:					Free white females:					All other free persons, except Indians not taxed	Slaves
		Under 10 years of age	Of 10 and under 16	Of 16 and under 26, including heads of families	Of 26 and under 45, including heads of families	Of 45 and upwards, including heads of families	Under 10 years of age	Of 10 and under 16	Of 16 and under 26, including heads of families	Of 26 and under 45, including heads of families	Of 45 and upwards, including heads of families		

FIGURE 2 — THE 1800 FEDERAL CENSUS
(Note that the same schedule form was also used for the 1810 census.)

CENSUS OF 1820

SCHEDULE OF THE WHOLE NUMBER OF PERSONS WITHIN THE DIVISION ALLOTTED TO.............

Name of county, parish, township, town or city, where the family resides.

Names of heads of families.

Free white males:
Under 10 years of age
Of 10 and under 16
Between 16 and 18
Of 16 and under 26, including heads of families
Of 26 and under 45, including heads of families
Of 45 and upwards, including heads of families

Free white females:
Under 10 years of age
Of 10 and under 16
Of 16 and under 26, including heads of families
Of 26 and under 45, including heads of families
Of 45 and upwards, including heads of families

Foreigners not naturalized

Number of persons engaged in:
Agriculture
Commerce
Manufacture

Slaves:
Males:
Under 14 years
Of 14 and under 26
Of 26 and under 45
Of 45 and upwards
Females:
Under 14 years
Of 14 and under 26
Of 26 and under 45
Of 45 and upwards

Free colored persons:
Males:
Under 14 years
Of 14 and under 26
Of 26 and under 45
Of 45 and upwards
Females:
Under 14 years
Of 14 and under 26
Of 26 and under 45
Of 45 and upwards

All other persons, except Indians not taxed

FIGURE 3 — THE 1820 FEDERAL CENSUS

NOTE: In addition to the columns shown on this reproduction of the 1820 census form provided by the Census Bureau, there was also a column which showed, for those engaged in manufacturing, the "nature of manufacturing."

Department of Commerce
Bureau of the Census
CENSUS OF 1830.

SCHEDULE of the whole number of persons within the Division allotted to .... by the Marshal of the
District (or Territory) of ....

White persons included in the foregoing
Aliens—foreigners not Naturalized
Who are blind
Who are deaf and dumb, of 25 and upwards
Who are deaf and dumb, of 14 and under 25
Who are deaf and dumb, under 14 years of age

Total

Slaves

Females:
Of 100 and upwards
Of 55 and under 100
Of 36 and under 55
Of 24 and under 36
Of 10 and under 24
Under 10 years of age

Males:
Of 100 and upwards
Of 55 and under 100
Of 36 and under 55
Of 24 and under 36
Of 10 and under 24
Under 10 years of age

Free white persons, including heads of families

Females:
Of 100 and upwards
Of 90 and under 100
Of 80 and under 90
Of 70 and under 80
Of 60 and under 70
Of 50 and under 60
Of 40 and under 50
Of 30 and under 40
Of 20 and under 30
Of 15 and under 20
Of 10 and under 15
Of 5 and under 10
Under 5 years of age

Males:
Of 100 and upwards
Of 90 and under 100
Of 80 and under 90
Of 70 and under 80
Of 60 and under 70
Of 50 and under 60
Of 40 and under 50
Of 30 and under 40
Of 20 and under 30
Of 15 and under 20
Of 10 and under 15
Of 5 and under 10
Under 5 years of age

Names of heads of families

Name of county, city, ward, town, township, parish, precinct, hundred, or district

FIGURE 4 — THE 1830 FEDERAL CENSUS

NOTE: This reproduction of the 1830 census form provided by the Census Bureau fails to show that this census also enumerated in each household "free colored persons" within the same sex and age categories as it did slaves. This census also gives the same information as for "white persons included in the foregoing" on slaves and free colored persons who were deaf and dumb and blind. On this part of the form slaves and free colored persons were counted together.

FIGURE 5 — THE 1840 FEDERAL CENSUS

Department of Commerce
Bureau of the Census
CENSUS OF 1840.

SCHEDULE of the whole number of persons within the Division allotted to .... by the Marshal of the ....
District (or Territory) of ....

Names of heads of families

Name of county, city, ward, town, township, parish, precinct, hundred, or district

Free white persons, including heads of families

Males: Under 5 years of age / Of 5 and under 10 / Of 10 and under 15 / Of 15 and under 20 / Of 20 and under 30 / Of 30 and under 40 / Of 40 and under 50 / Of 50 and under 60 / Of 60 and under 70 / Of 70 and under 80 / Of 80 and under 90 / Of 90 and under 100 / Of 100 and upwards

Females: Under 5 years of age / Of 5 and under 10 / Of 10 and under 15 / Of 15 and under 20 / Of 20 and under 30 / Of 30 and under 40 / Of 40 and under 50 / Of 50 and under 60 / Of 60 and under 70 / Of 70 and under 80 / Of 80 and under 90 / Of 90 and under 100 / Of 100 and upwards

Slaves

Males: Under 10 years of age / Of 10 and under 24 / Of 24 and under 36 / Of 36 and under 55 / Of 55 and under 100 / Of 100 and upwards

Females: Under 10 years of age / Of 10 and under 24 / Of 24 and under 36 / Of 36 and under 55 / Of 55 and under 100 / Of 100 and upwards

Total

Number of persons in each family engaged in

Pensioners for Revolutionary or military services, included in the foregoing

Name   Age

NOTE: The 1840 census contains extensive information not included on this reproduction of the form provided by the Census Bureau. The same information, by sex and age, is included for free colored persons as for slaves. The unnamed "number of persons engaged in . . ." columns included mining; agriculture; commerce; manufacturing and trades; navigation of the ocean; navigation of canals, lakes, and rivers; and learned professions and engineers. There are also columns giving the number (among those already enumerated) of deaf and dumb, blind, and insane and idiots, for both white and black—and whether the insane and idiots were at public or private charge. With regard to education, it enumerated the number of scholars in universities and colleges, academies and grammar schools, and primary and common schools. The number of scholars at public charge was also stated, as was the number of white males over 21 in each household who could not read and write.

DEPARTMENT OF COMMERCE
BUREAU OF THE CENSUS
WASHINGTON

SCHEDULE 1.–Free Inhabitants in ...., in the County of ...., State of ....,

enumerated by me, on the .... day of ...., 1850.

Ass't Marshal

Dwelling-houses numbered in the order of visitation.	Families numbered in the order of visitation.	The name of every person whose usual place of abode on the first day of June, 1850, was in this family.	Description			Profession, Occupation, or Trade of each male person over 15 years of age.	Value of Real Estate owned.	Place of Birth, naming the State, Territory, or Country.	Married within the year.	Attended school within the year.	Persons over 20 years of age who cannot read and write.	Whether deaf and dumb, blind, insane, idiotic, pauper, or convict.
			Age	Sex	Color—White, black or mulatto.							
1	2	3	4	5	6	7	8	9	10	11	12	13

FIGURE 6 — THE 1850 FEDERAL CENSUS

Page No. _____

SCHEDULE 1.—Free Inhabitants in _____ in the County of _____

State of _____ enumerated by me, on the _____ day of _____, 1860.

Post Office _____   , Ass't Marshal.

Dwelling Houses—numbered in the order of visitation.	Families numbered in the order of visitation.	The name of every person whose usual place of abode on the first day of June, 1860, was in this family.	DESCRIPTION.			Profession, Occupation, or Trade of each person, male and female, over 15 years of age.	VALUE OF ESTATE OWNED.		Place of Birth, Naming the State, Territory, or Country.	Married within the year.	Attended School within the year.	Persons over 20 years of age who can not read and write.	Whether deaf and dumb, blind, insane, idiotic, pauper, or convict.
			Age.	Sex.	Color, White, Black, or Mulatto.		Value of Real Estate.	Value of Personal Estate.					
1	2	3	4	5	6	7	8	9	10	11	12	13	14
1													
2													
3													
4													
5													
6													
7													
8													
9													
10													
11													
12													
13													
14													
15													
16													
17													

FIGURE 7—THE 1860 FEDERAL CENSUS

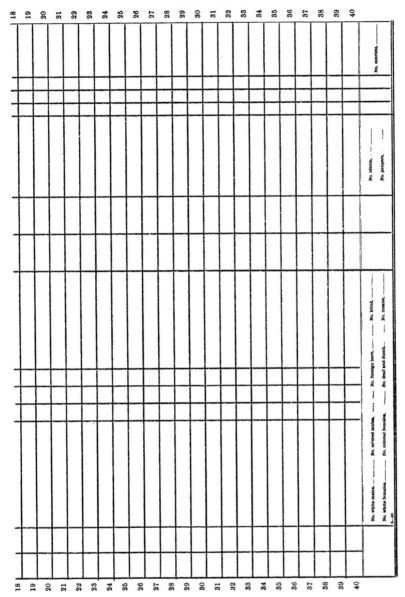

FIGURE 7—THE 1860 FEDERAL CENSUS—*continued*

FIGURE 8—THE 1870 FEDERAL CENSUS

[7-296]

Page No. .... Supervisor's Dist. No. .... Enumeration Dist. No.	Note A.—The Census Year begins June 1, 1879, and ends May 31, 1880. Note B.—All persons will be included in the Enumeration who were living on the 1st day of June, 1880. No others will. Children BORN SINCE June 1, 1880 will be OMITTED. Members of Families who have DIED SINCE June 1, 1880, will be INCLUDED. Note C.—Questions Nos. 13, 14, 22 and 23 are not to be asked in respect to persons under 10 years of age.

SCHEDULE 1.—Inhabitants in ...., in the County of ...., State of ....

enumerated by me on the .... day of June, 1880.

.... *Enumerator.*

	In Cities: Name of Street.	In Cities: House Number.	Dwelling houses numbered in order of visitation.	Families numbered in order of visitation.	The Name of each Person whose place of abode, on 1st day of June, 1880, was in this family.	Personal Description: Color—White, W.; Black, B.; Mulatto, Mu.; Chinese, C.; Indian, I.	Personal Description: Sex—Male, M.; Female, F.	Personal Description: Age at last birthday prior to June 1, 1880. If under 1 year, give months in fractions, thus: 3/12.	If born within the Census year, give the month.	Relationship of each person to the head of this family—whether wife, son, daughter, servant, boarder, or other.	Civil Condition: Single, /.	Civil Condition: Married, /.	Civil Condition: Widowed, /. Divorced, D.	Married during Census year, /.	Occupation: Profession, Occupation or Trade of each person, male or female.	Occupation: Number of months this person has been unemployed during the Census year.	Health: Is the person [on the day of the Enumerator's visit] sick or temporarily disabled, so as to be unable to attend to ordinary business or duties? If so, what is the sickness or disability?	Health: Blind, /.	Health: Deaf and Dumb, /.	Health: Idiotic, /.	Health: Insane, /.	Health: Maimed, Crippled, Bedridden, or otherwise disabled, /.	Education: Attended school within the Census year, /.	Education: Cannot read, /.	Education: Cannot write, /.	Nativity: Place of Birth of this person, naming State or Territory of United States, or the Country, if of foreign birth.	Nativity: Place of Birth of the Father of this person, naming the State or Territory of United States, or the Country, if of foreign birth.	Nativity: Place of Birth of the Mother of this person, naming the State or Territory of United States, or the Country, if of foreign birth.
			1	2	3	4	5	6	7	8	9	10	11	12	13	14	15	16	17	18	19	20	21	22	23	24	25	26
1																												
2																												
3																												
4																												
5																												
6																												
7																												
8																												
9																												
10																												
11																												
12																												
13																												
14																												
15																												
16																												
17																												
18																												
19																												
20																												
21																												
22																												
23																												
24																												
25																												
26																												
27																												
28																												
29																												
30																												
31																												
32																												
33																												
34																												
35																												
36																												
37																												
38																												
39																												
40																												
41																												
42																												
43																												
44																												
45																												
46																												
47																												
48																												
49																												
50																												

NOTE D.—In making entries in columns 9, 10, 11, 12, 16 to 23, an affirmative mark only will be used—thus /, except in the case of divorced persons, column 11, when the letter "D" is to be used.
NOTE E.—Question No. 12 will only be asked in cases where an affirmative answer has been given either to question 10 or to question 11.
NOTE F.—Question No. 14 will only be asked in cases when a gainful occupation has been reported in column 13.
NOTE G.—In column 7 an abbreviation in the name of the month may be used, as Jan., Apr., Dec.

FIGURE 9—THE 1880 FEDERAL CENSUS

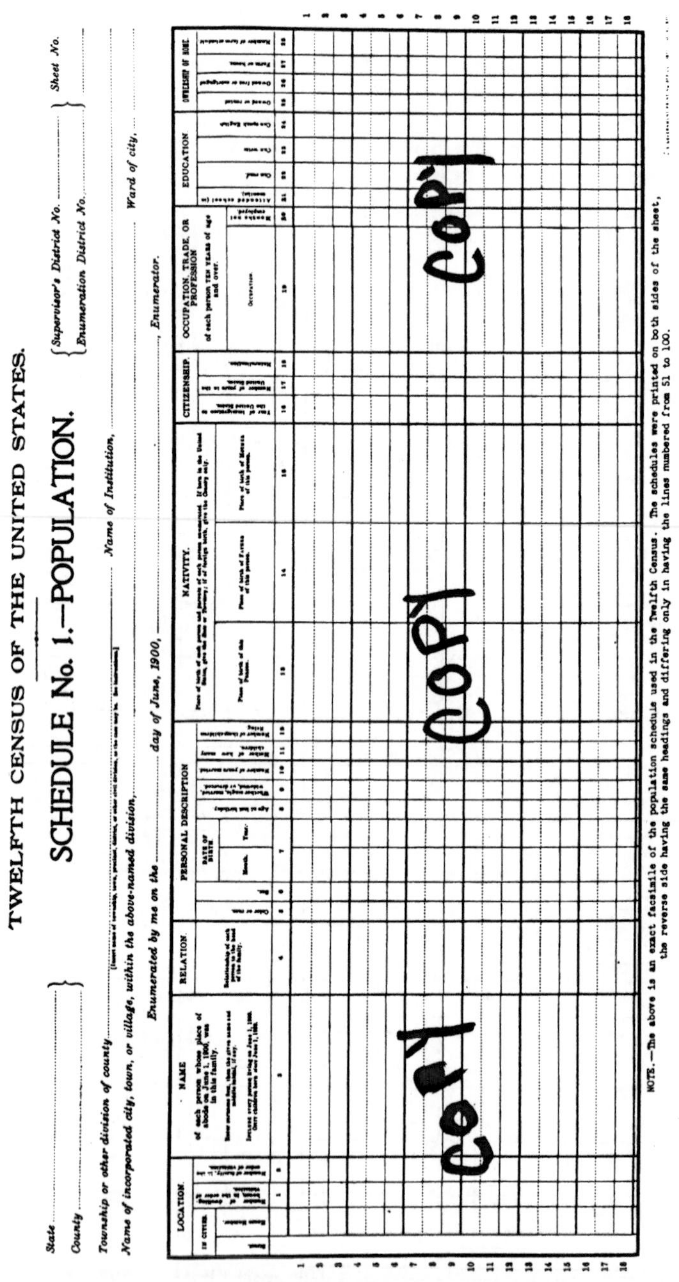
7—224

TWELFTH CENSUS OF THE UNITED STATES.

SCHEDULE No. 1.—POPULATION.

State .... *County* ....

Supervisor's District No. .... *Enumeration District No.* .... *Sheet No.* ....

Township or other division of county .... *Name of Institution,* ....

Name of incorporated city, town, or village, within the above-named division, ... *Ward of city,* ....

Enumerated by me on the .... *day of June, 1900,* ...., *Enumerator.*

LOCATION				NAME	RELATION	PERSONAL DESCRIPTION								NATIVITY			CITIZENSHIP			OCCUPATION, TRADE, OR PROFESSION		EDUCATION				OWNERSHIP OF HOME			
		1	2	3	4	5	6	7		8	9	10	11	12	13	14	15	16	17	18	19	20	21	22	23	24	25	26	27	28

NOTE.—The above is an exact facsimile of the population schedule used in the Twelfth Census. The schedules were printed on both sides of the sheet, the reverse side having the same headings and differing only in having the lines numbered from 51 to 100.

FIGURE 10—THE 1900 FEDERAL CENSUS

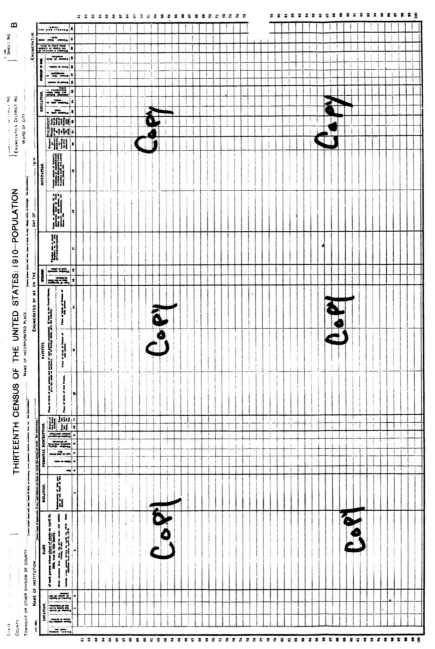

FIGURE 11—THE 1910 FEDERAL CENSUS

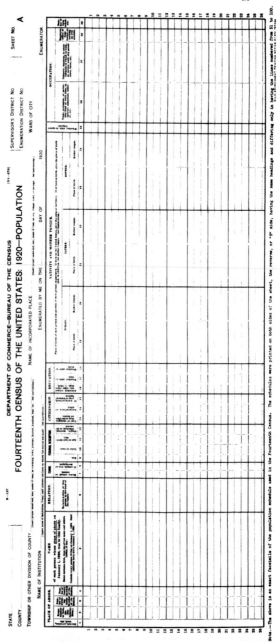

FIGURE 12 — THE 1920 FEDERAL CENSUS

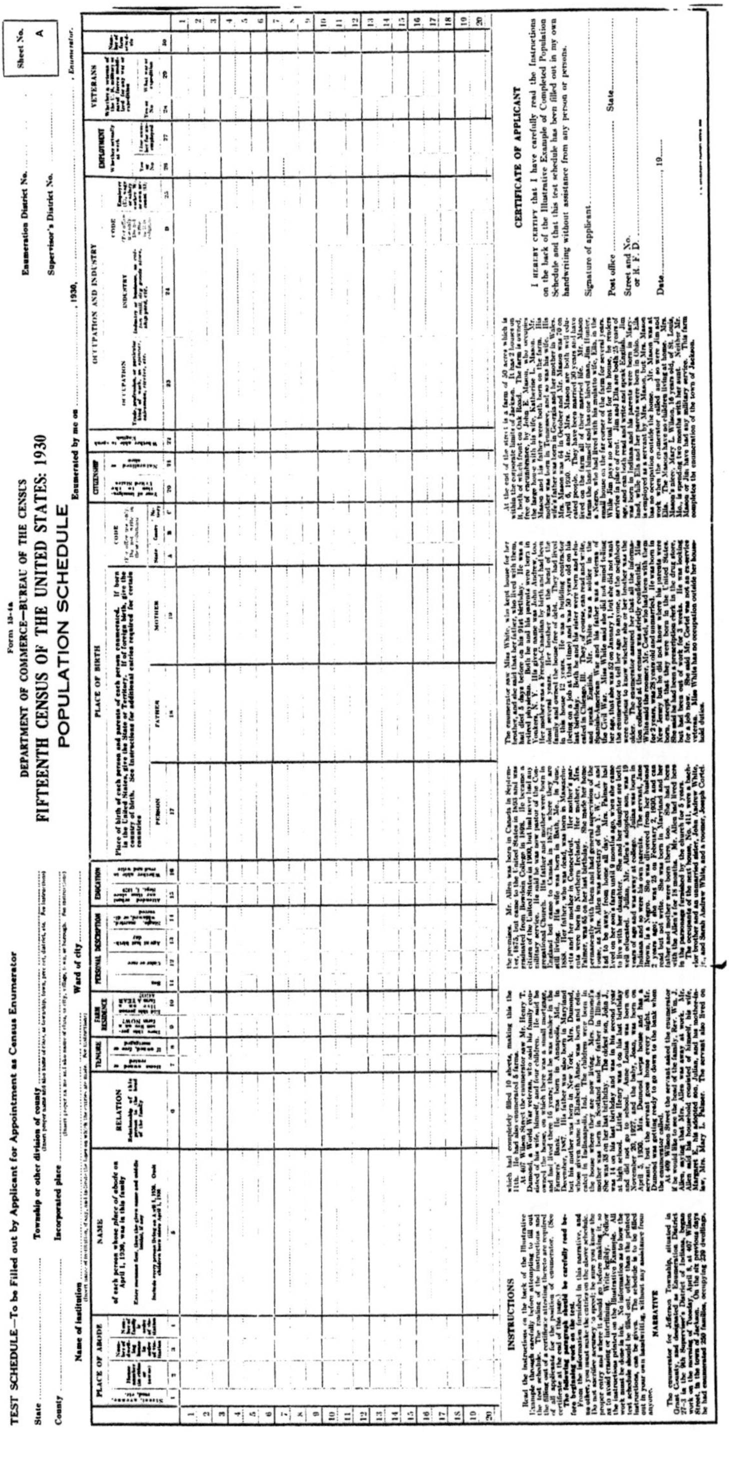

FIGURE 13—THE 1930 FEDERAL CENSUS

1940 Federal Census

SHEET NO.

ENUMERATION DISTRICT NO.

SUPERVISOR'S DISTRICT NO.

STATE

COUNTY

TOWNSHIP OR OTHER DIVISION OF COUNTY   .1940

INCORPORATED PLACE   .ENUMERATOR

WARD OF CITY

ENUMERATED BY ME ON

UNINCORPORATED PLACE

INSTITUTION

BLOCK NO.

LOCATION — Street, Avenue, road, etc. — House Number

HOUSEHOLD DATA — No. of Household in order of visitation — Home owned (O) or rented (R) — Value if owned or Monthly rental if rented — Farm? (Yes or No)

NAME — Name of each person whose usual place of residence on April 1, 1940, was in this household.

BE SURE TO INCLUDE:
1. Persons temporarily absent from household. Write "Ab" after names of such persons.
2. Children under 1 year of age. Write "Infant" if child has not been given a first name. Enter ⊗ after name of person furnishing information.

RELATION — Relationship of this person to the head of the household, as wife, daughter, father, mother-in-law, grandson, lodger, lodger's wife, servant, hired hand, etc.

PERSONAL DESCRIPTION — Sex — Color or Race — Age at Last Birthday — Marital Status

EDUCATION — Attended school or college at any time since March 1, 1940 — Highest grade of school completed

PLACE OF BIRTH — If born in U.S. give state, territory or possession. If foreign born, give country in which birthplace was situated on Jan. 1, 1937. Distinguish: Canada-French from Canada-English and Irish Free State from Northern Ireland.

CITIZENSHIP — Citizenship of the foreign born

RESIDENCE, APRIL 1, 1935 — In what place did this person live on April 1, 1935? For a person who lived in a different place, enter city or town, county, and State. — City, town, or village having 2,500 or more inhabitants. If less, enter "R." — County — State (or Territory or foreign country) — On a Farm? (Y or N)

PERSONS 14 YEARS OLD AND OVER — EMPLOYMENT STATUS

Was this person AT WORK for pay or profit in private or nonemergency Govt. work during week of March 24–30, 1940? (Y or N)

If not, was he at work on, or assigned to, public EMERGENCY WORK (WPA, NYA, CCC, etc.) during week of March 24–30? (Y or N)

Was this person SEEKING WORK? (Y or N)

If not seeking work, did he HAVE A JOB, business, etc.? (Y or N)

If neither at work nor assigned to public emergency work ("No" in cols. 21 & 22) — Indicate whether engaged in home housework (H), in school (S), unable to work (U), or other (Ot)

OCCUPATION, INDUSTRY, AND CLASS OF WORKER — For a person at work, assigned to public emergency work, or with a job ("Yes" in col. 21, 22, or 24), enter present occupation, industry, and class of worker. For a person seeking work ("Yes" in col. 23): (a) if he has previous work experience, enter last occupation, industry, and class of worker; or (b) if he does not have previous work experience, enter "New worker" in Col. 28, and leave Col. 29–30 blank.

OCCUPATION — Trade, profession, or particular kind of work, as — Frame spinner / Salesman / Laborer / Rivet heater / Music teacher

INDUSTRY — Industry or business, as — Cotton mill / Retail grocery / Farm / Shipyard / Public school

Class of Worker

If at private or nonemergency Govt. work. "Yes" in col. 21 — Number of hours worked during week of March 24–30, 1940.

If seeking work or assigned to public emergency work. "Yes" in col. 22 or 23 — Duration of unemployment up to March 30, 1940 — in weeks.

INCOME IN 1939 (12 months ending Dec. 31, 1939) — Number of weeks worked in 1939 (Equivalent full-time weeks) — Amount of money, wages or salary received (including commissions) — Did this person receive income of $50 or more from sources other than money wages or salary? (Y or N)

Number of Farm Schedule

Line No.

National Archives and Records Administration   NARA's web site is http://www.archives.gov   NA 14129 (6-09)

FIGURE 14—THE 1940 FEDERAL CENSUS

SUPPLEMENTARY QUESTIONS		FOR PERSONS OF ALL AGES					FOR PERSONS 14 YEARS OLD AND OVER									FOR ALL WOMEN WHO ARE OR HAVE BEEN MARRIED		

For Persons Enumerated on Lines 14 and 29.

Col. 5 VALUE OF HOME, IF OWNED:

Where owner's household occupies only a part of a structure, estimate value of portion occupied by owner's household. Thus the value of the unit occupied by the owner of a two-family house might be approximately one-half the total value of the structure.

Col. 10 COLOR OR RACE:

White	W	Neg	
Negro	Neg	In	
Indian	In	Ch	
Chinese	Ch	Jp	
Japanese	Jp	Fi	
Filipino	Fi	Hin	
Hindu	Hin	Kor	
Korean	Kor		

Other races, spell out in full.

Col. 11 AGE AT LAST BIRTHDAY:

Enter age of children born on or after April 1, 1939, as follows. Born in:

April 1939	11/12
May 1939	10/12
June 1939	9/12
July 1939	8/12
August 1939	7/12
September 1939	6/12
October 1939	5/12
November 1939	4/12
December 1939	3/12
January 1940	2/12
February 1940	1/12
March 1940	0/12

(Do not include children born on or after April 1, 1940.)

Col. 14 HIGHEST GRADE OF SCHOOL COMPLETED:

None	0
Elementary school, 1st – 8th	1, 2, 3, 4, 5, 6, 7, 8
High school, 1st – 4th year	H-1, H-2, H-3, H-4
College, 1st – 4th year	C-1, C-2, C-3, C-4
College, 5th or subsequent year	C-5

Col. 16 CITIZENSHIP OF THE FOREIGN BORN:

Naturalized	Na
Having first papers	Pa
Alien	Al
American citizen born abroad	Am Cit

Cols. 30 and 47 CLASS OF WORKER:

Wage or salary worker in private work	PW
Wage or salary worker in Gov't work	GW
Employer	E
Working on own account	OA
Unpaid family worker	NP

Col. 41 WAR OR MILITARY SERVICE:

World War	W
Spanish-American War, Philippine Insurrection or Boxer Rebellion	S
Spanish-American War & World War	SW
Regular establishment (Army, Navy or Marine Corps) Peace-Time Service only	R
Other war or expedition	Ot

Col. 21 WAS THIS PERSON AT WORK?

Enter "Yes" for persons at work for pay or profit in private or nonemergency Government work. Include unpaid family workers – that is, related members of the family working without money wages or salary on work (other then household or incidental chores) which contributed to the family income.

Col. 24 DID THIS PERSON HAVE A JOB?

Enter "Yes" for a person (not seeking work) who had a job, business, or professional enterprise, but did not work during week of March 24–30 for any of the following reasons: Vacation, temporary illness, industrial dispute, layoff not exceeding 4 weeks with instructions to return to work at a specific date, layoff due to temporarily bad weather conditions.

SYMBOLS AND EXPLANATORY NOTES

National Archives and Records Administration

NARA's web site is http://www.archives.gov

NA 14129 (6-09)

FIGURE 14 *continued*—THE 1940 FEDERAL CENSUS, SECOND PAGE

II. WHERE ARE THE CENSUS POPULATION SCHEDULES?

A. 1790 through 1940

The 1790 census—as much of it as still exists—has been available in indexed and published form for many years, with copies available in many libraries throughout the U.S. Though some 1790 schedules were destroyed and are thus unavailable, contemporaneous tax lists have been used in their place and have proven to be useful substitutes—though not so complete. Some of these tax list compilations were published as "reconstructed censuses."

In 1966, the National Genealogical Society in Washington, DC, undertook a project of transcribing and indexing the 1850 census. They began with Tennessee as a pilot project, hoping eventually to cover all states and territories. The project was finally abandoned in 1968—before Tennessee was completed—because of its great cost (even with volunteer labor). It would be sad if that was the end of the story. Today there are indexes to not only the entire 1850 census but to all available census records.

The available census schedules have all been converted to digitized databases, and indexes to them are available on the Ancestry website and on a few other sites. The FamilySearch website has some of the indexes with clickable links to the digitized databases on Ancestry, but unless you are an Ancestry subscriber, there is a charge for accessing that site. The exception to this is in those libraries with Ancestry subscriptions.

It is amazing that you can not only access the specific information contained in the census record but also, with the click of your mouse, you can bring up a digitized image of the actual census record listing the person (1850 and later) or the household (prior to 1850) you found in the index. You are free to search for a specific person or for everyone of a specific surname. And there are other search options as well.

The search options are intriguing. There is some flexibility based on the search options you choose. For example, you can search for a specific person or you can even search for all males (or for all females) within whatever age range you desire (from exact to plus or minus ten years), without regard for surname, in whatever county you choose—and then personally examine the digitized images of every entry identified, if you desire.

This can be a helpful approach if you have been unable to find the person you seek in the index when he should have been there. There are various reasons why a person may not be found in the index. Perhaps those who made the index misread and mis-indexed his name. Or perhaps the census taker spelled the name differently than you spell it. Your advantage over the indexers is significant because you know exactly what name you are looking for, while indexers had to decipher every name and make their best interpretation.

All original U.S. census records—except those no longer in existence—are at the National Archives in Washington, DC. For many years, they were available there for public searching. However, heavy constant use had a wearing effect, and, as usage continued to increase, the pre-1890 schedules became heavily damaged. Older schedules also deteriorated because of age. Though efforts were made to keep the original volumes repaired, it eventually became necessary to withdraw them from public use and replace them with copies.

Between 1936 and 1940, the Census Bureau microfilmed the 1840 through 1880 schedules and retired the originals. The 1800 through 1830 and the 1900 through 1940 schedules have also been microfilmed, mostly from the original schedules. Copies of these microfilms were used to create those digitized records now on the various family history websites. Because some of the original 1860 and 1880 schedules were damaged and pages in others were torn and/or faded, the damaged parts were removed and replaced by photocopies in the bound original volumes.[5]

Neither the original census schedules nor microfilm copies of those censuses taken within the last seventy-two years (the current official restriction period) are open to public use. Based on the current restriction schedule, the 1950 census will become available in 2022.

In the past, a basic census search was a major project, especially in larger counties, because of the time-consuming process of searching entry by entry and page by page. However, that has all changed since the records have been digitized and indexed on the various family history websites.

B. Missing census schedules

Parts of the early census schedules are missing for various reasons, and the earliest censuses have suffered the most extensive losses. Some have claimed that the loss of the missing 1790, 1800, and 1810 schedules was caused by the fire in Washington, DC, set by the British during their siege of that city in the War of 1812. However, these reports are based on speculation rather than fact. Under the provisions of the various Census Acts between 1790 and 1820, the court clerks deposited the population schedules in the U.S. District Courts for preservation. It was not until a congressional resolution of May 28, 1830, that the District Court clerks were requested to forward the census schedules for the first four censuses to the U.S. Secretary of State.[6] The actual reasons for the loss of these early records are unknown.

In 1849, the responsibility for the census was shifted from the State Department to the Interior Department. When the latter department was created, the records were transferred to the new department, but no inventories of transferred materials have been found.

The earliest inventories of census holdings that have been located were made in 1865 and 1870. A comparison of these inventories with later inventories suggests that many of the missing schedules, including seventeen volumes of 1790–1820 censuses, were lost prior to an inventory taken in 1895.

---

[5] Davidson and Ashby, 93–101.

[6] Ibid., 94.

Extensive efforts have been made to locate missing schedules, but most attempts have been futile. One of the few records found was the 1830 census for the Western District of Missouri.

It was apparently customary in earlier times for both the State and Interior departments to lend census schedules to agency officials and congressional representatives upon request, and it is possible that some of the losses resulted from this practice.

The location of the inventory of 1895 is now unknown, but a comparison has more recently been made between the inventories of 1870 and 1903, revealing many discrepancies—some of which were apparently due to the binding and rebinding of records. There is no good explanation for how or when the missing early schedules were actually lost,[7] except that they were *not* casualties of the War of 1812.

Congress prescribed the process for getting census schedules into the hands of the federal government after they were taken. As mentioned, the 1790–1820 schedules were sent to Washington pursuant to the congressional resolution of 1830. In 1830 and 1840, the marshals who took the census were required to make two copies, one to be sent to the clerk of the District Court and the other to Washington, DC. In 1850–70, the assistants were to turn over their original enumerations to the clerks of the County Courts. Then two copies "duly compared and corrected" were to be sent to the marshals of the District Courts. The marshals were then required to send one copy to the Secretary of the Interior and the other to the secretary of the state or territory to which that census district belonged.

Census schedules missing from the National Archives collection, up through 1870, are identified on Chart 3 in this chapter. Because of Congress's requirement for duplicate copies, schedules not in the National Archives are reported to be in state custody.

There are no missing population schedules in any census after 1870, according to a 1968 letter from Milton D. Swenson, chief of the Personal Census Service Branch of the Census Bureau, with one major exception—all of the 1890 census, except some relatively small segments.[8]

C. The 1890 census

Only small portions of the 1890 schedules exist. A fire in the Commerce Department (another new department) building on January 21, 1921, is to blame. Though not all of the schedules were consumed in the blaze, most were so badly damaged that Congress authorized their disposal. Those who would blame Congress for the destruction of a large portion of this census are in error, for there is little that can be done with a pile of ashes. Because those ashes were once a census, they could not be destroyed without congressional approval.

---

[7] Ibid., 94–95.

[8] Letter from Milton D. Swenson, dated March 11, 1968.

Fragmentary 1890 schedules for some states do exist (many of them singed around the edges). A card index to the names on those schedules has been prepared by the National Archives, but that is of little importance now because the surviving records are on an indexed database on many family history websites, including Ancestry and FamilySearch. The surviving records are for Alabama, the District of Columbia, Georgia, Illinois, Minnesota, New Jersey, New York, North Carolina, Ohio, South Dakota, and Texas.

Contents of these 1890 schedules include the following:

ALABAMA:	Perry County (Perryville Beat No. 11 and Severe Beat No. 8)
DIST OF COLUM:	Q, R, S, 13th, 14th, 15th, Corcoran and Riggs Streets, and Johnson Avenue
GEORGIA:	Muscogee County (Columbus)
ILLINOIS:	McDonough County (Mound Township)
MINNESOTA:	Wright County (Rockford)
NEW JERSEY:	Hudson County (Jersey City)
NEW YORK:	Westchester County (Eastchester) and Suffolk County (Brookhaven Township)
NORTH CAROLINA:	Gaston County (South Point and River Bend Townships) and Cleveland County (Township No. 2)
OHIO:	Hamilton County (Cincinnati) and Clinton County (Wayne Township)
SOUTH DAKOTA:	Union County (Jefferson Township)
TEXAS:	Ellis County (J.P. No. 6, Mountain Peak and Ovilla Precinct), Hood County (Precinct No. 5), Rusk County (No. 6 and J.P. No. 7), Trinity County (Trinity Town and Precinct No. 2), and Kaufman County (Kaufman).[9]

The 1890 census was the only one (until 1970) to use what is called a "family schedule"—a separate page (actually one sheet on both sides) for each household. On the two sides of that page, there was room to enumerate ten household members. The name of each person was entered at the top of a column on the page, with other information about that person in the column below. If there were more than ten persons in a household, two sheets of paper were used. A copy of this form is shown in Figure 13.

There were also some Civil War Union Army Veterans' Schedules, prepared in connection with the 1890 census, that are still intact and available; they are discussed later in this chapter.

---

[9] National Archives, *Federal Population Censuses, 1790–1890* (Washington, DC: National Archives, 1966), 145.

FAMILY SCHEDULE—1 TO 10 PERSONS.

Supervisor's District No. _____	Eleventh Census of the United States
Enumeration District No. _____	SCHEDULE No. 1
	POPULATION AND SOCIAL STATISTICS

Name of city, town, township, precinct, district, beat, or } _____ ; County: _____ State: _____
other minor civil division

Street and No.: _____ ; Ward: _____ Name of Institution: _____

Enumerated by me on the _____ day of June, 1890

Enumerator _____

A.—Number of Dwelling-house in the order of visitation	B.—Number of families in this dwelling-house	C.—Number of persons in this dwelling-house	D.—Number of Family in the order of visitation	E.—No. of Persons in this family	

INQUIRIES.		1	2	3	4	5
1	Christian name, in full, and initial of middle name.					
	Surname.					
2	Whether a soldier, sailor, or marine during the civil war (U.S. or Conf.) or widow of such person.					
3	Relationship to head of family.					
4	Whether white, black, mulatto, quadroon, octoroon, Chinese, Japanese, or Indian.					
5	Sex.					
6	Age at nearest birthday. If under one year, give age in months.					
7	Whether single, married, widowed, or divorced.					
8	Whether married during the census year (June 1, 1889, to May 31, 1890.					
9	Mother of how many children, and number of these children living.					
10	Place of birth.					
11	Place of birth of Father.					
12	Place of birth of Mother.					
13	Number of years in the United States.					
14	Whether naturalized.					
15	Whether naturalization papers have been taken out.					
16	Profession, trade, or occupation.					
17	Months unemployed during the census year (June 1, 1889, to May 31, 1890).					
18	Attendance at school (in months) during the census year (June 1, 1889 to May 31, 1890)					
19	Able to Read.					
20	Able to Write.					
21	Able to speak English. If not, the language or dialect spoken.					
22	Whether suffering from acute or chronic disease, with name of disease and length of time afflicted.					
23	Whether defective in mind, sight, hearing, or speech, or whether crippled, maimed, or deformed with name or defect.					
24	Whether a prisoner, convict, homeless child, or pauper.					
25	Supplemental schedule and page.					

TO ENUMERATORS.—See inquiries numbered 26 to 30, inclusive, on the second page of this schedule. These inquiries must be made concerning each family and each farm visited.

FIGURE 15—THE 1890 FEDERAL CENSUS

SCHEDULE NO. 1.—POPULATION AND SOCIAL STATISTICS.

	INQUIRIES.	6	7	8	9	10
1	Christian name, in full, and initial of middle name.					
	Surname.					
2	Whether a soldier, sailor, or marine during the civil war (U.S. or Conf.) or widow of such person.					
3	Relationship to head of family.					
4	Whether white, black, mulatto, quadroon, octoroon, Chinese, Japanese, or Indian.					
5	Sex.					
6	Age at nearest birthday. If under one year, give age in months.					
7	Whether single, married, widowed, or divorced.					
8	Whether married during the census year (June 1, 1889, to May 31, 1890.					
9	Mother of how many children, and number of these children living.					
10	Place of birth.					
11	Place of birth of Father.					
12	Place of birth of Mother.					
13	Number of years in the United States.					
14	Whether naturalized.					
15	Whether naturalization papers have been taken out.					
16	Profession, trade, or occupation.					
17	Months unemployed during the census year (June 1, 1889, to May 31, 1890).					
18	Attendance at school (in months) during the census year (June 1, 1889 to May 31, 1890)					
19	Able to Read.					
20	Able to Write.					
21	Able to speak English. If not, the language or dialect spoken.					
22	Whether suffering from acute or chronic disease, with name of disease and length of time afflicted.					
23	Whether defective in mind, sight, hearing, or speech, or whether crippled, maimed, or deformed with name or defect.					
24	Whether a prisoner, convict, homeless child, or pauper.					
25	Supplemental schedule and page.					
26	Is the house you live in hired, or is it owned by the head or a member of the family?					
27	If owned by head or member of family, is the house free from mortgage incumbrance?					
28	If the head of the family is a farmer, is the farm which he cultivates hired, or is it owned by him or by a member of his family?					
29	If owned by head or member of family, is the farm free from mortgage incumbrance?					
30	If the home or farm is owned by head or member of family, and mortgaged, give the post-office address of owner.					

TO ENUMERATORS.—The inquiries numbered 26 to 30, inclusive, must be made concerning each family and each farm visited.

FIGURE 15 *continued*—THE 1890 FEDERAL CENSUS, SECOND PAGE

D. Recent census schedules—confidential

Recent census schedules (those less than seventy-two years old) are restricted to protect the privacy of living persons. However, under special circumstances, personal information can be furnished by the Bureau of the Census from these restricted schedules for genealogical and other proper purposes (based on a provision in the various Census Acts [Sect. 32 of 1909 Act; Sect. 33 of 1919 Act; and Sect. 18 of 1929 Act]). The Census Bureau will furnish information, under certain circumstances, as proof of age. If a person makes an application for information relating to himself, this is not considered to constitute publication. It has also been ruled that this personal application releases the Census Bureau from the confidential restrictions of the law.[10] A copy of the application form and the instructions for completing that form are found at Figures 16–17. Copies of both can be obtained on the Internet at *https://www2.census.gov/library/publications/2013/demo/BC-600.pdf.* These applications must be printed, signed, and mailed with the proper fee to U.S. Census Bureau, P.O. Box 1545, Jeffersonville, IN 47131.

There are circumstances where one can obtain information from recent census schedules relating to other persons. The requirement for obtaining copies of these records is that the requester must be either

1. the person to whom that information relates;
2. the parent or guardian of a minor child (with written request);
3. the parent or guardian of a mentally incompetent person (with written request by legal guardian, supported by certified copy of court order of appointment);
4. the legal representative of the person (with certified copy of appropriate court order appointing him);
5. the surviving spouse (with certified copy of death certificate);
6. an immediate family member of a deceased person (parent, sibling, or child with certified copy of death certificate);
7. a beneficiary of a will or of insurance (with certified copy of death certificate and proof of beneficiary status).

The exact address of the person's residence at the time of the census and the name of the head of the household must be given. If possible, the names of other family members should be given to remove all identity questions. Those who make such requests must be at least eighteen years old. For a reasonable fee, on a per individual family member basis, a full schedule of the family can be provided if requirements are satisfied for the release of each individual's census data.

The reasons for the restriction on access to recent censuses are explained in a letter sent to the LDS Genealogical Society (now the Family History De-

---

[10] Davidson and Ashby, 96–99.

U.S. DEPARTMENT OF COMMERCE
Economics and Statistics Administration
U.S. CENSUS BUREAU

FORM BC-600
(4-10-2013)

APPLICATION FOR SEARCH OF CENSUS RECORDS

IMPORTANT INFORMATION

PLEASE READ AND FOLLOW CAREFULLY

This application is for use in requesting a search of census records.* Copies of these census records often are accepted as evidence of age, citizenship, and place of birth for employment, social security benefits, insurance, and other purposes.

If the applicant is located, an official transcript will be provided including the following information:

Personal Census Information	Available for census year(s)
• Census year	1910–2010
• County where taken	1910–1980
• State where taken	1910–2010
• Name	1910–2010
• Relationship to head of household	1910–2010
• Name of person in whose household you were counted	1910–2010
• Age at the time of the census	1910–1950, 1970–2010
• Date of birth	
Year and quarter	1960
Month and year	1970–1980
Year	1990
Month/day/year	2000–2010
• Place of birth	1910–1950
• Citizenship if requested or if foreign born	1910–1950
• Occupation (if requested)	1910–1950

The U.S. Census Bureau's records are arranged according to the address at the time of the census. Censuses are taken primarily for statistical, not legal, purposes. Attention is called to the possibility that the information shown in the census record may not agree with that given in your application. The record must be copied exactly as it appears on the census form. The U.S. Census Bureau CANNOT make changes even though it realizes that enumerators may have been misinformed or made mistakes in writing down the data they collected. Those agencies that accept census transcripts as evidence of age, relationship, or place of birth usually overlook minor spelling differences but would be reluctant to consider a record that was changed years later at an applicant's request.

If you authorize the U.S. Census Bureau to send your record to someone other than yourself, you must provide the name and address, including ZIP Code, of the other person/agency.

Birth certificates, including delayed birth certificates, are not issued by the U.S. Census Bureau. You can obtain the birth certificate from the Health Department or the Department of Vital Statistics of the state in which the applicant was born.

The average time it should take you to fill out the BC-600, "Application for Search of Census Records", including the time spent reading instructions is 12 minutes.

Send comments regarding this burden estimate or any other aspect of this collection of information, including suggestions for reducing this burden, to: Paperwork Project 0607–0117, U.S. Census Bureau, 4600 Silver Hill Road, AMSD-3K138, Washington, D.C. 20233-1500. You may e-mail comments to Paperwork@census.gov; use "Paperwork Project 0607-0117" as the subject.

Respondents are not required to respond to any information collection unless it displays a valid approval number from the Office of Management and Budget. This 8-digit number appears in the top right corner of page 3 of this form.

* Information from 1940 and earlier censuses is public information and is available from the National Archives.

The completed application should be mailed to the U.S. Census Bureau, P.O. Box 1545, Jeffersonville, IN 47131, together with a money order or check payable to "Commerce-Census."

FIGURE 16—INSTRUCTIONS, APPLICATION FOR SEARCH OF CENSUS RECORDS

INSTRUCTIONS FOR COMPLETING THIS FORM
PRINT OR TYPE INFORMATION EXCEPT SIGNATURE
PLEASE FOLLOW NUMBERED INSTRUCTIONS

DETACH HERE

1. Purpose

The purpose for which the information is desired must be shown so that a determination may be made under 13 U.S.C. 8(a) that the record is required for proper use. For proof of age, most agencies require documents closest to date of birth; therefore we suggest you complete information for the EARLIEST CENSUS AFTER DATE OF BIRTH.

2. Signature

Each application requires a signature. The signature should be the same as that shown on the line captioned "full name of person whose census record is requested." When the application is for a census record concerning another person, the requester must sign the application, and the authority of the requester must be furnished as stated in instruction 3 below. If signed by marking (X), please indicate the name of the person whose mark it is and have witnesses sign as instructed. IF SIGNATURE IS PRINTED, please indicate that is the usual signature.

3. Confidential information given to other than person to whom it relates

(a) Census information is confidential and ordinarily will not be furnished to another person unless the person to whom it relates authorizes this in the space provided or if there is other proper authorization as indicated in 3(b), 3(c), and 3(d).

(b) Minor children – Information regarding a child who has at this time not reached the legal age of 18 may be obtained upon the written request of either parent or guardian.

(c) Mentally incompetent persons – Information regarding persons who are mentally incompetent may be obtained upon the written request of the legal representative, supported by a certified copy of the court order naming such legal representative.

(d) **Deceased persons – If the record requested relates to a deceased person, the application MUST be signed by (1) a blood relative in the immediate family (parent, brother, sister, or child), (2) the surviving wife or husband, (3) the administrator or executor of the estate, or (4) a beneficiary by will, or insurance. IN ALL CASES INVOLVING DECEASED PERSONS, a certified copy of the death certificate MUST be furnished, and the relationship to the deceased MUST be stated on the application. Legal representatives MUST also furnish a certified copy of the court order naming such legal representatives; and beneficiaries MUST furnish legal evidence of such beneficiary interest.**

4. Fee required

The $65.00 fee is for a search of one census for one person only. The time required to complete a search depends upon the number of cases on hand at the particular time and the difficulty encountered in searching a particular case. The normal

processing time is 3 to 4 weeks. The fee covers return postage of your search results by regular mail. You do not need to include a return envelope for normal processing. For an additional fee of $20 the search can be completed in one business day after we receive it. If you want your search results returned to you by express mail you must include a self-addressed, prepaid express mail envelope with your application. You may also submit your application by express mail for faster service.

No more than one census will be searched and the results furnished for one fee. Should it be necessary to search more than one census to find the record, you will be notified to send another fee before another search is made. Tax monies are not available to furnish the information. **If a search has been made, the fee cannot be returned even if the information is not found.**

5. Full schedules

The full schedule is the complete one-line entry of personal data recorded for that individual ONLY. The names of other persons will not be listed. If the applicant specifies "full schedule," the Census Bureau will furnish, in addition to the regular transcript, whatever other information appears on the named person's record in the original schedule, but only for THAT PERSON. In this case the information is typed on a facsimile of the original census schedule and verified as a true copy. There is an additional charge of $10.00 for EACH full schedule requested.

The Census Bureau also will provide "full schedule" information for those other members of the same household for whom authorizations are furnished. (See Instruction 3 for authorization requirements). A fee of $10.00 is required for each person listed on the full schedule.

LIMITATIONS – Certain information, such as place of birth, citizenship, and occupation, is available only for census years 1910 through 1950. Full schedule information is not available for census years 1970, 1980, 1990, 2000, and 2010.

6. Census years 1910–1920–1930–1940–1950– 1960–1970–1980–1990–2000–2010

The potential of finding an individual census record is increased when the respondent provides thorough and accurate address information FOR THE DAY THESE CENSUSES WERE TAKEN. If residing in a city AT THE TIME THESE CENSUSES WERE TAKEN, it is necessary to furnish the house number, the name of the street, city, county, state, and the name of the parent or other head of household with whom residing at the time of the census. If residing in a rural area, it is VERY IMPORTANT to furnish the township, district, precinct or beat, AND the direction and number of miles from the nearest town.

1990, 2000, and 2010 Request – It is VERY IMPORTANT to provide a house number and street name or rural route and box number. Always include a ZIP Code.

7. Locator Map (optional)

Box 7 is provided for a sketch of the area where the applicant lived at the time of the requested census.

DO NOT RETURN WITH APPLICATION

IF YOU NEED HELP FILLING OUT THIS APPLICATION, PLEASE CALL 812–218–3046, MONDAY THROUGH FRIDAY 7:00 A.M. THROUGH 4:30 P.M. EASTERN TIME

FORM BC-600 (4-10-2013)

DETACH HERE

FIGURE 16—*continued*

OMB No. 0607-0117

FORM **BC-600**
(4-10-2013)

U.S. DEPARTMENT OF COMMERCE
Economics and Statistics Administration
U.S. CENSUS BUREAU

APPLICATION FOR SEARCH OF CENSUS RECORDS

RETURN TO: U.S. Census Bureau, P.O. Box 1545, Jeffersonville, IN 47131

DO NOT USE THIS SPACE – OFFICIAL USE ONLY
Case number

NAME OF APPLICANT

1. Purpose for which record is to be used *(See Instruction 1)*
   - [ ] Passport (date required) _____
   - [ ] Proof of age
   - [ ] Genealogy
   - [ ] Other – *Please specify*

I certify that information furnished about anyone other than the applicant will not be used to the detriment of such person or persons by me or by anyone else with my permission.

2. Signature – Do not print *(Read instruction 2 carefully before signing)*

PRESENT MAILING ADDRESS
Number and street

City _____ State _____ ZIP Code _____

Telephone number (Include area code)

IF SIGNED BY MARK (X), TWO WITNESSES MUST SIGN HERE

Signature _____ Signature _____

NOTICE – Intentionally falsifying this application may result in a fine of up to $250,000 or up to 5 years of imprisonment, or both (title 18, U.S. Code, section 1001).

	(Fee)
$	
[ ] Money Order	
[ ] Check	
[ ] Other	

Papers received (itemize) _____ Returned _____

Received by _____ Date _____

Returned by _____ Date _____

3. If the census information **is to be sent to someone other than the person whose record is requested**, give the name and address, including ZIP Code, of the other person or agency.

This authorizes the U.S. Census Bureau to send the record to: *(See instruction 3)*

4. **FEE REQUIRED:** *(See instructions 4 and 5)* A check or money order **(DO NOT SEND CASH)** payable to "Commerce-Census" must be sent with the application. Checks will be processed by electronic fund transfer. This fee covers the cost of a search of no more than one census year for one person only.

5. Fee required . . . . $ 65.00
   ___ extra copies @ $2.00 $ ___
   ___ full schedules @ $10.00 $ ___
   ___ expedited fee @ $20.00 $ ___
   TOTAL amount enclosed $ ___

FULL NAME OF PERSON WHOSE CENSUS RECORD IS REQUESTED	First name	Middle name	Present last name	Maiden name *(If any)*	Nicknames

Date of birth *(If unknown, estimate)*	Place of birth *(City, county, State)*	Race	Sex

Full name of father *(Stepfather, guardian, etc.)* _____ Nicknames

Full maiden name of mother *(Stepmother, etc.)* _____ Nicknames

First marriage *(Name of husband or wife of applicant)* _____ Year married *(Approximate)* | Second marriage *(Name of husband or wife of applicant)* _____ Year married *(Approximate)*

Names of brothers and sisters

Name and relationship of all other persons living in household *(Aunts, uncles, grandparents, lodgers, etc.)*

PLEASE COMPLETE REVERSE SIDE

FIGURE 17—APPLICATION FOR SEARCH OF CENSUS RECORDS

6.

GIVE PLACE OF RESIDENCE FOR APPROPRIATE CENSUS DATE *(SEE INSTRUCTIONS 1 AND 6)*

Census date	Number and street *(Read instruction 6 first)*	City, town, township *(Read instruction 6 first)*	County and State	Name of person with whom living *(Head of household)*	Relationship of head of household
April 15, 1910 *(See instruction 6)*					
Jan. 1, 1920 *(See instruction 6)*					
April 1, 1930 *(See instruction 6)*					
April 1, 1940 *(See instruction 6)*					
April 1, 1950 *(See instruction 6)*					
April 1, 1960 *(See instruction 6)*					
April 1, 1970 *(See instruction 6)*					
April 1, 1980 *(See instruction 6)*					
April 1, 1990 *(See instruction 6)*		ZIP Code			
April 1, 2000 *(See instruction 6)*		ZIP Code			
April 1, 2010 *(See instruction 6)*		ZIP Code			

7. LOCATOR MAP (Optional)
PLEASE DRAW A MAP OF WHERE THE APPLICANT LIVED, SHOWING ANY PHYSICAL FEATURES, LANDMARKS, INTERSECTING ROADS, CLOSEST TOWNS, ETC., THAT MAY AID IN LOCATING THE APPLICANT FOR THE CENSUS YEAR REQUESTED.

HAVE YOU SIGNED THE APPLICATION AND ENCLOSED THE CORRECT FEES?

FORM BC-600 (4-10-2013)

FIGURE 17—*continued*

partment) dated January 12, 1960, by the Personal Census Service Branch.[11] The letter explained:

> On the occasion of each decennial census enumeration, assurances have been given that the information collected regarding any individual will not be disclosed and that it will be combined with similar information for other individuals to provide statistical totals. Presidential Proclamations have been issued prior to decennial censuses assuring the American people that the information given to the census enumerator would be confidential. Repudiation of this pledge would seriously reduce public confidence and would lead to doubts as to whether future legislation might make personal information available within a short period of time.
>
> The insurance of confidentiality of the information is an important element in securing reliable information from the public. We regularly receive information which the respondent would be unwilling to give to other agencies. If the confidence which people have in Census operations were to be shaken, the problems of getting reliable information and the cost of the censuses would be substantially increased. At the present time, there are approximately thirty million persons who were living at the time of the Census of 1900. Most of these people were living in the United States at that time and, presumably, were included in that census. Some of them no doubt were living in institutions at the time of the census; others were living in unusual family arrangements which they may prefer not to be disclosed. The possibility that such facts would be revealed, even after a substantial period of years, might be a source of embarrassment to some families. In future enumerations, knowledge that this might occur could result in the withholding of correct information.

III. SPECIAL CENSUS INDEXES

A. The Soundex indexes

During the 1930s, under the sponsorship of the Works Projects Administration (WPA), as part of a Federal Works Project, names and other pertinent data on persons enumerated in the censuses were copied onto file cards. The following censuses were included in the project:

1880—only households with children 10 and younger

1900

1910—part only—21 states[12]

---

[11] As previously stated, the current restriction is now seventy-two years rather than the seventy-five years indicated in the letter, and all census schedules through 1940 are now unrestricted and available for research. All of these have also been digitized and indexed.

[12] States with the 1910 Soundex are Alabama (cities separate), Arkansas, California, Florida, Georgia (cities separate), Illinois, Kansas, Kentucky, Louisiana (cities separate), Michigan, Mississippi, Missouri, North Carolina, Ohio, Oklahoma, Pennsylvania (Philadelphia County separate), South Carolina, Tennessee (cities separate), Texas, Virginia, and West Virginia.

1920

1930—part only—12 states, 2 of those partial[13]

For each one of these censuses separately, the cards for heads of households were filed under each state using a system where similar-sounding names beginning with the same letter of the alphabet were interfiled in a logical order based on a numerical coding system called Soundex indexing. The name of every household member was entered on the card for the head of each household.

Soundex indexing has been a boon to research in these census records but, because indexed digitized database records are now available for all of these census schedules on various family history websites, the value of the Soundex has been significantly minimized. However, because of spelling errors and name variations in the census records, there are cases where the Soundex can still be a useful tool in helping to locate specific census records.

An innovative researcher can still usually locate the census records he needs without consulting the Soundex by skillfully using the database indexes. It is true that errors made by the indexers' misreading of entries are a potential problem with the database indexes, but those who prepared the Soundex indexes made those same kinds of errors. A Soundex card is not always accurate, and we know that the indexers missed some names. Thus, when you find a Soundex card for the family you seek, it is still necessary for you to go to the census record and look at the record for the family.

With the 1880 Soundex, if a child was listed in the census in a household where he was not a child of the head of that household, a separate index card was created for him, in addition to his listing on the household card.

The Soundex indexes are available on microfilm at various research libraries, including the Family History Library in Salt Lake City, and also are searchable on microfilm at the National Archives in Washington, DC, and at the regional National Archives (see Chapter 5). Personal use of the Soundex is helpful because it enables you to "look around" for your family and also to pick up other families of the same surname in the same locality and anywhere else in the same state.

I will not explain here how to use the Soundex because detailed instructions are at the beginning of each microfilm. They explain how to encode the surname you wish to find and how to look for that code number under the proper state.

---

[13] The twelve states with the 1930 Soundex are all in the South: Alabama, Arkansas, Florida, Georgia, Kentucky (Bell, Floyd, Harlan, Kenton, Muhlenberg, Perry, and Pike counties only), Louisiana, Mississippi, North Carolina, South Carolina, Tennessee, Virginia, and West Virginia (Fayette, Harrison, Kanawha, Logan, McDowell, Mercer, and Raleigh counties only).

The Soundex index for the 1910 census of twenty-one of the states is called a Miracode index. It uses the Soundex codes but lists the visitation numbers assigned by the enumerator as its basis rather than page and line numbers. Rolls 28–40 of Microfilm Publication T1224, *Census Enumeration District Descriptions,* contain the enumeration district numbers of specific places on the census films. These Miracode cards are typewritten; all other Soundex cards are handwritten.

Those searching the 1880 Soundex of Illinois should be aware that an error occurred when it was microfilmed. All cards for Soundex codes O-200 through O-240 were skipped. All information from those skipped cards has since been photocopied and published in a book entitled *The 1880 Illinois Census Index: Soundex Code O-200–O-240, the Code That Was Not Filmed.*[14]

The 1920 Soundex is the most complete of the Soundexes. In addition to all of the states, it includes the territories of Alaska, Hawaii, the Canal Zone, Puerto Rico, Guam, American Samoa, and the Virgin Islands. It contains approximately 107 million names and has essentially the same format used in 1910, plus additional information. On each 1920 Soundex "family card" is the name of the head of the household; the volume number, enumeration district number, and sheet number; the line number; color, age, and birthplace; citizenship; county and city; and street and house number. Everyone living in the household was listed on this "family card." If the household was too large for one card, an additional card was used. The card lists name, relationship to head of household, age, birthplace, and citizenship for each household member. But it is still essential to go to the digitized census record.

The additional cards made for non-family members in the 1920 Soundex have the name of the individual; the volume number, enumeration district number, sheet number; line number; color, age, and birthplace; citizenship; county and city; with whom enumerated and relationship to that person. Note that in 1910, there were several boxes from which to select the correct relationship, but in 1920, the relationship was written in. There was also a "Remarks" space on the 1920 card.

B. The 1910 street index

There was a cross-index to streets prepared for thirty-nine of the nation's largest cities in connection with the 1910 census. The index was created by the Bureau of the Census to assist in finding personal data needed by government agencies and requested by individuals. This index, filmed and made available on microfiche through a special Archives Gift Fund from the Federation of Genealogical Societies, is on fifty microfiche as part of National Archives Record Group 29 in the records of the Bureau of the Census (Microfilm Publication M1283). It enables the user to determine the enumeration district and the corresponding volume in which a specific address is located.

---

[14] Nancy Gubb Franklin, comp., *The 1880 Illinois Census Index: Soundex Code 0-200–0-240, the Code That Was Not Filmed* (Evanston, IL: the compiler, 1981).

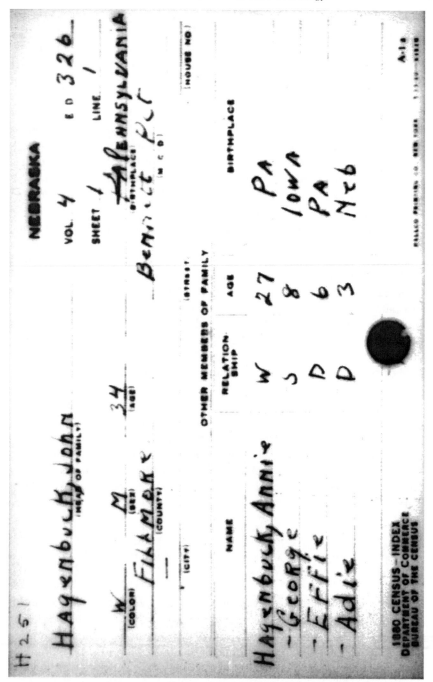

FIGURE 18—A CARD FROM THE 1880 SOUNDEX

Some ask why we need a street index when we have indexed databases for all of the available censuses. It is true that we seldom need this type of index but, unfortunately, because of mistakes made by both census takers and indexers, we are sometimes unable to find the entry we seek. In those situations, we can resort to these street indexes. First, however, it is necessary to use a city directory to find a street address. Then, with that address, you can go to the appropriate street index to zero in on your evasive ancestor.

The cities, the fiche numbers, and the streets (as applicable) are shown in the following table prepared by the Federation of Genealogical Societies and published in their May/June 1984 *Newsletter:*[15]

FICHE	CITY	STREETS
1	Akron, Ohio	All streets
	Atlanta, Georgia	All streets
2	Baltimore	A St. through Haubert St.
3	Baltimore	Haw St. through Sycamore Ave.
4	Baltimore	T Alley through 42nd St. North
5	Canton, Ohio	All streets
	Charlotte, North Carolina	All streets
6	Chicago	A St. through Curtis St.
7	Chicago	Curtis St. through Ingraham Ave.
8	Chicago	Institute Pl. through Ogden Ave.
9	Chicago	Ogden Ave. through Wabash Ave.
10	Chicago	Wabash Ave. through 38th Pl. East
11	Chicago	38th Pl. East through 87th St. West
12	Chicago	78th St. West through 138th St. East
13	Cleveland, Ohio	Abbey Ave. through Woodbridge St. West
14	Cleveland, Ohio	Woodbridge Ct. SW through West 125th St.
15	Dayton, Ohio	All streets
16	Denver, Colorado	All streets
17	Detroit, Michigan	All streets
18	District of Columbia	All streets
19	Elizabeth, New Jersey	All streets
	Erie, Pennsylvania	All streets
	Ft. Wayne, Indiana	All streets
	Gary, Indiana	All streets
20	Grand Rapids, Michigan	All streets
21	Indianapolis, Indiana	All streets
22	Kansas City, Kansas	All streets
	Long Beach, California	All streets
23	Los Angeles (and L.A. County), California	A St. through Oxford Ave. South
24	Los Angeles (and L.A. County), California	Oxford Way through 134th St.
25	Newark, New Jersey	All streets

---

[15] Used by permission of the Federation of Genealogical Societies.

26	New York City (Brooklyn)	A St. through Ivy St.
27	New York City (Brooklyn)	J St. through Westminster Rd.
28	New York City (Brooklyn)	Westminster Rd. through East 109th St.
29	New York City (Manhattan & the Bronx)	Abbott St. through Patterson Ave.
30	New York City (Manhattan & the Bronx)	Paul Ave. through West 38th St.
31	New York City (Manhattan & the Bronx)	West 39th St. through 13th Ave.
32	New York City (Richmond [Staten Island])	Abbotsford Ave. through Elwood Pl.
33	New York City (Richmond [Staten Island])	Ely St. through Mystic Ct.
34	New York City (Richmond [Staten Island])	Nahant St. through Willowbrook Park
35	New York City (Richmond [Staten Island])	Willowbrook Rd. through 18th St.

(NOTE: There is no street index for the Queens Borough of New York City.)

36	Oklahoma City	All streets
	Omaha, Nebraska	All streets
	Paterson, New Jersey	All streets
37	Peoria, Illinois	All streets
38	Philadelphia	A St. through Dingler's Ct.
39	Philadelphia	Discount Pl. through Landsdowne St.
40	Philadelphia	Larch St. through Pennsgrove St.
41	Philadelphia	Pennsylvania Ave. through Walnut Ln.
42	Philadelphia	Walnut Ln. East through 95th St. South
43	Phoenix, Arizona	All streets
	Reading, Pennsylvania	All streets
	Richmond, Virginia	All streets
44	San Antonio, Texas	All streets
	San Diego, California	All streets
45	San Francisco, California	A St. through Washburn St.
46	San Francisco, California	Washington St. through 49th Ave. South
47	Seattle, Washington	A St. through 73rd East St.
48	Seattle, Washington	73rd North St. through 89th St. North
49	South Bend, Indiana	All streets
	Tampa, Florida	All streets
	Tulsa, Oklahoma	All streets
50	Wichita, Kansas	All streets
	Youngstown, Ohio	All streets

Also, note that there is an outline of the 1910 boundaries of each of the 329 enumeration districts in the United States on rolls 28 through 40 of Microfilm Publication T1224. The title is *Census Enumeration District Descriptions*.

IV. MILITARY SERVICE INFORMATION IN THE CENSUS

Two censuses—1840 and 1890—included valuable information about persons who had performed military service. The 1840 census included an enumeration of Revolutionary War pensioners of the federal government, and the 1890 census included a special enumeration of surviving Union Civil War veterans and deceased veterans' widows.

A. 1840 Census of Pensioners

The government published all of this pensioner information under the title *A Census of Pensioners for Revolutionary or Military Services* (Washington, DC, 1841), and the LDS Family History Library prepared an index to that publication. Both the government's list and this index have been published by the Genealogical Publishing Company.[16] Just as a note of caution, however, there appear to be some omissions in the 1840 census of pensioners. There also appear to be some men listed as pensioners who were not.

B. The 1890 special enumeration

The 1890 special enumeration, entitled "Surviving Soldiers, Sailors, and Marines, and Widows, etc.," is incomplete. Enumerations for fourteen states and territories, alphabetically from Alabama through Kansas (and part of Kentucky), do not exist.

> The schedules are arranged by state or territory, thereunder by county, and thereunder by minor subdivision. Each entry shows the name of a Union veteran of the Civil War; name of widow, if appropriate; veteran's rank, company, regiment or vessel; dates of enlistment and discharge and length of service in years, months, and days; post office address; nature of any disability; and remarks.[17]

The meaning of the "etc." in the title is not clear, but in Allegheny County, Pennsylvania, Ambrose C. Niven is listed as "heir" in connection with William Johnson who served as a "landsman" on the U.S.S. *Lancaster*. These 1890 schedules have been digitized and indexed; they can be accessed at *https://familysearch.org/search/collection/1877095*.

Both of these military service enumerations are useful tools because they can lead you to other important records, but the 1890 veterans' schedules (the remaining portion) are more inclusive and have more useful features than the 1840 pensioners' census.

---

[16] *A Census of Pensioners for Revolutionary or Military Services, 1840.* [Published with] *A General Index to a Census of Pensioners,* 2 vols. in 1, 1841 and 1965 (Reprint, Baltimore: Genealogical Publishing Co., 2005).

[17] Anne Bruner Eales and Robert M. Kvasnicka, eds., *Guide to Genealogical Research in the National Archives of the United States,* 3rd ed. (Washington, DC: National Archives, 2000), 28.

C. Other census records relating to veterans

There are also some special Civil War veterans' schedules (both Confederate and Union) for the Dakota Territory taken in 1885. Those schedules that relate to counties now in South Dakota have been indexed (typewritten) and are online at *http://history.sd.gov/archives/data/civilwar/*.

In addition, there is also veterans' information in the population schedules of 1900, 1910, 1930, and 1940. There is information in the 1900 and 1910 censuses concerning Civil War veterans (both Union and Confederate) and their widows. In 1930, the census identified American veterans according to the wars in which they served. In 1940, a supplementary schedule gathered information concerning a limited number of veterans, wives of veterans, widows of veterans, and children (under age 18) of veterans. There is more information about these records in Chapter 15.

V. COLONIAL CENSUSES, SPECIAL ENUMERATIONS, AND STATE CENSUSES

In addition to the federal decennial population schedules, which we have discussed, a few limited censuses were taken during the colonial period, and most states have taken their own censuses at various times for various reasons. The federal government has also taken special censuses in a few of the states between the regular enumerations. Most censuses taken during the colonial period have been published.

The nature and extent of the various colonial and state censuses is itself a complete study and is not discussed in this book. For the present, you should be aware of the little U.S. government pamphlet *State Censuses; an Annotated Bibliography of Censuses of Population Taken After the Year 1790 by States and Territories in the United States,* by Henry J. Dubester (Washington, DC, 1948). This booklet is out of print but can be found in some libraries and government document repositories. A more recent (but certainly not current) listing is a little catalog entitled *U.S. and Special Censuses* (Salt Lake City: Ancestry Publishing, 1985).

Some of the state censuses are now available on the Internet in indexed databases. Ancestry has many, and many more will no doubt be added as time progresses. Other online state census records can be located by entering the name of your state of interest and the words "state census" in your Internet search engine space.

The following are some of the special enumerations taken by the federal government in various states:

1857:   **MINNESOTA TERRITORY.** This is in the National Archives in five printed volumes, and is on an indexed database at FamilySearch (*https://familysearch.org/search/collection/1503055*).

1864:   **ARIZONA TERRITORY.** The Secretary of State in Phoenix has the originals, the National Archives has copies, and Ancestry has a searchable database (*http://search.ancestry.com/search/db.aspx?dbid=3121*).

1866: **ARIZONA TERRITORY.** Photostats are in the National Archives.

1867: **ARIZONA TERRITORY** (Mohave, Pima, and Yuma counties only). Photostats are in the National Archives.

1869: **ARIZONA TERRITORY** (Yavapai County only). Photostats are in the National Archives.

1880: **SPECIAL CENSUS OF INDIANS NOT TAXED**, within the jurisdiction of the United States. These schedules show the tribe's name; the Indian Reservation; the Agency; the nearest post office; the number in each household and a description of the dwelling; the Indian name, with its English translation, of every person in the family; each person's relationship to the head of the family; his marital and tribal status; his description; his occupation; health; education; ownership of property; and means of subsistence. This census is available on Ancestry in a searchable database: *search.ancestry.com/search/db.aspx?dbid=2973*. These records include the following four volumes:

- Standing Rock Agency: Standing Rock Reservation (Dakota Territory)
- Tulalip Agency: Swinhomish, Muckleshoot, and Lummi Reservations, and Indians not on a reservation (Washington)
- Tulalip Agency: Tulalip and Port Madison Reservations (Washington Territory)
- Yakama Agency: Yakama Reservation (Washington Territory)

Four additional volumes of this special census are also in the National Archives (Microfilm catalog no. M1791):

- Vols. I and II: Indians near Fort Simcoe and at Tulalip (Washington Territory)
- Vol. III: Indians near Fort Yates (Dakota Territory)
- Vol. IV: Indians in California (Round Valley Reservation)

1885: **COLORADO, DAKOTA TERRITORY, FLORIDA, NEBRASKA, and NEW MEXICO TERRITORY.** This census was taken by the states and territories on a federal option, with the promise of partial reimbursement. The schedules are similar to those of 1880, and photostats of all except Dakota Territory are in the National Archives. They are also available there on microfilm. The Dakota census, with several counties missing, is located at various sites in North and South Dakota. Filmed copies of the South Dakota schedules are in the National Archives and the schedules for what is now North Dakota have been published in a volume called *Collections of the State Historical Society of North Dakota*, Vol. 4 [1913], pp. 338–448. There is a general index.[18] The North Dakota counties of Boreham,

---

[18] *Guide to Genealogical Research in the National Archives*, rev. ed. (Washington, DC: The National Archives, 1983), 35.

DeSmet, Flannery, Hettinger, Sheridan, and Stevens are missing. Internet availability of digitized databases, with indexes, of this 1885 census is as follows:

- Colorado: *http://search.ancestry.com/search/db.aspx?dbid=6837*
- South Dakota part of territory: *http://search.ancestry.com/search/db.aspx?dbid=6247*
- Florida: *https://familysearch.org/search/collection/1457854*
- Nebraska: *http://search.ancestry.com/search/db.aspx?dbid=6585*
- New Mexico Territory: *http://search.ancestry.com/search/db.aspx?dbid=1976*

1907:   **OKLAHOMA** (Seminole County only)

VI. IMPORTANT NON-POPULATION CENSUS SCHEDULES

At the outset of this discussion about non-population census schedules, I need to explain that in 1918 and 1919 (before creation of the National Archives), these schedules, with the exception of the 1885 mortality schedules (because these were still in the states), were removed from federal custody and each state was given the option to acquire those schedules relating to itself. This is explained by Davidson and Ashby:

> The 1850–80 non-population schedules [including schedules of mortality, industry, manufacturing, agriculture, business, and social statistics], which were seldom used by the Census Bureau, were authorized for disposal (65th Cong., 2d sess., H. Doc. 921). When the Daughters of the American Revolution and other organizations objected to the destruction of these records, the 1,349 volumes of these schedules were transferred in 1918–19 by the Census Bureau to state libraries and historical societies or, in cases where state officials declined to receive them, to the DAR Library in Washington.[19]

Let us look now at a few specifics relating to some of the more important non-population schedules.

A. Mortality schedules

Beginning with the 1850 census—the first census that gathered details about every person in every household—those in charge of the process conceived the idea that a certain amount of useful vital (birth, marriage, death) information could be collected through the census medium (see Chapter 13). This was the beginning of mortality schedules. In compliance with an act of Congress, the designers devised a separate schedule that would be used to collect information about those persons who died during the twelve months immediately prior to the census date—what was called the census year (see Glossary of Terms at the end of this chapter)—and about the reasons for those

---

[19] Davidson and Ashby, 96.

deaths. Most of the mortality schedules for 1850, 1860, 1870, 1880, and the limited census of 1885 still exist.

The mortality schedules turned over to the DAR were for the states of Arizona, Colorado, Georgia, Kentucky, Louisiana, Tennessee, and the District of Columbia. Most, but not all, of these were indexed by the DAR and some have been transcribed. In 1980, those original schedules still in DAR custody were sent to the National Archives.

Nearly all of the available mortality schedules are in indexed databases on Ancestry. Some are also on FamilySearch. The schedules for the limited census of 1885 (Colorado Territory, Florida, Nebraska, New Mexico Territory, and Dakota Territory, excluding the area now in North Dakota) were microfilmed with the population schedules for their respective states. The following list shows the availability of indexed searchable databases of the mortality schedules for the various states in 2016:

ALABAMA:	Ancestry has 1850, 1860, 1870, and 1880 schedules.
ARIZONA:	Ancestry has 1860, 1870, and 1880 schedules.
ARKANSAS:	Ancestry has 1850, 1860, 1870, and 1880 schedules.
CALIFORNIA:	Ancestry has 1860, 1870, and 1880 schedules.
COLORADO:	Ancestry has 1850, 1860, 1870, 1880, and 1885 schedules.
CONNECTICUT:	Ancestry has 1850, 1860, 1870, and 1880 schedules.
DELAWARE:	Ancestry has 1850, 1860, 1870, and 1880 schedules.
DIST OF COLUM:	Ancestry has 1850, 1860, 1870, and 1880 schedules.
FLORIDA:	Ancestry has 1850, 1860, 1870, and 1880 schedules.
GEORGIA:	Ancestry has 1850, 1860, 1870, and 1880 schedules.
IDAHO:	Ancestry has 1870 and 1880 schedules.
ILLINOIS:	Ancestry and FamilySearch both have 1850 schedules. Only Ancestry has 1860, 1870, and 1880 schedules.
INDIANA:	Ancestry and FamilySearch both have 1850, 1860, 1870, and 1880 schedules.
IOWA:	Ancestry and FamilySearch both have 1850, 1860, 1870, and 1880 schedules.
KANSAS:	Ancestry has 1860, 1870, and 1880 schedules.

KENTUCKY:	Ancestry and FamilySearch both have 1850, 1860, 1870, and 1880 schedules.
LOUISIANA:	Ancestry and FamilySearch both have 1850, 1860, 1870, and 1880 schedules.
MAINE:	Ancestry and FamilySearch both have 1850, 1860, 1870, and 1880 schedules.
MARYLAND:	Ancestry and FamilySearch both have 1850, 1860, 1870, and 1880 schedules.
MASSACHUSETTS:	Ancestry and FamilySearch both have 1850, 1860, 1870, and 1880 schedules.
MICHIGAN:	Ancestry and FamilySearch both have 1850, 1860, 1870, and 1880 schedules.
MINNESOTA:	Ancestry and FamilySearch both have 1850, 1860, 1870, and 1880 schedules.
MISSISSIPPI:	Ancestry and FamilySearch both have 1850 schedules. Only Ancestry has 1860, 1870, and 1880 schedules.
MISSOURI:	Ancestry and FamilySearch both have 1850, 1860, 1870, and 1880 schedules.
MONTANA:	Ancestry has 1860, 1870, and 1880 schedules.
NEBRASKA:	Ancestry has 1860, 1870, 1880, and 1885 schedules.
NEVADA:	Ancestry has 1860 and 1880 schedules. (NOTE: Humboldt and St. Mary's counties are missing in 1860, and the 1870 schedules are lost.)
NEW HAMPSHIRE:	Ancestry and FamilySearch both have 1850, 1860, 1870, and 1880 schedules.
NEW JERSEY:	Ancestry and FamilySearch both have 1850, 1860, 1870, and 1880 schedules.
NEW MEXICO:	In 2016, no mortality schedules for New Mexico are on indexed databases. (NOTE: It is reported that microfilm copies of the 1850, 1860, and 1880 mortality schedules are available at the New Mexico State Records Center and Archives, 1205 Camino Carlos Rey, Santa Fe, NM 87507. The 1885 schedules are on microfilm at the National Archives, including the Regional National Archives.)
NEW YORK:	Ancestry and FamilySearch both have 1850 schedules. Only Ancestry has 1860, 1870, and 1880 schedules.

NORTH CAROLINA:	Ancestry and FamilySearch both have 1850, 1860, 1870, and 1880 schedules.
NORTH DAKOTA:	Ancestry and FamilySearch both have 1850, 1860, and 1880 schedules. Only Ancestry has 1885 schedules.
OHIO:	Ancestry and FamilySearch both have 1850, 1860, 1870, and 1880 schedules.
OKLAHOMA:	Ancestry has 1860 schedules as part of Arkansas Indian Lands.
OREGON:	Ancestry has 1850, 1860, 1870, and 1880 schedules.
PENNSYLVANIA:	Ancestry and FamilySearch both have 1850, 1860, 1870, and 1880 schedules.
RHODE ISLAND:	Ancestry and FamilySearch both have 1850, 1860, 1870, and 1880 schedules.
SOUTH CAROLINA:	Ancestry and FamilySearch both have 1850 schedules. Only Ancestry has 1860, 1870, and 1880 schedules.
SOUTH DAKOTA:	Ancestry has 1850, 1860, and 1880 schedules. (NOTE: 1870 schedules are lost.)
TENNESSEE:	Ancestry and FamilySearch both have 1850, 1860, 1870, and 1880 schedules.
TEXAS:	Ancestry and FamilySearch both have 1850, 1860, 1870, and 1880 schedules.
UTAH:	Ancestry and FamilySearch both have 1850, 1860, 1870, and 1880 schedules.
VERMONT:	Ancestry has 1850, 1860, 1870, and 1880 schedules.
VIRGINIA:	Ancestry and FamilySearch both have 1850, 1860, 1870, and 1880 schedules.
WASHINGTON:	Ancestry has 1850, 1860, 1870, and 1880 schedules. (NOTE: Washington was in Oregon Territory in 1850.)
WEST VIRGINIA:	Ancestry and FamilySearch both have 1850, 1860, 1870, and 1880 schedules. (NOTE: West Virginia was in Virginia in 1850 and 1860.)
WISCONSIN:	Ancestry has 1850, 1860, 1870, and 1880 schedules.
WYOMING:	Ancestry and FamilySearch both have 1850, 1860, 1870, and 1880 schedules.

SCHEDULE 3.—Persons who Died during the Year ending 1st June, 1850, in *the Town of* _____ *in the*
County of *Hancock,*   State of *Maine* , enumerated by me, _____

NAME OF EVERY PERSON WHO DIED during the Year ending 1st June, 1850, whose usual Place of Abode at the Time of his Death was in this Family.	DESCRIPTION.					PLACE OF BIRTH. Naming the State, Territory, or County.	The Month in which the Person died.	PROFESSION, OCCUPATION, OR TRADE.	DISEASE, OR CAUSE OF DEATH.	Number of DAYS ILL.
	Age.	Sex.	White, Colored, or Mulatto.	Free or Slave.	Married or widowed.					
1	2	3	4	5	6	7	8	9	10	11

FIGURE 19—A PAGE FROM A MORTALITY SCHEDULE, 1850 CENSUS

Though the reporting of deaths in the census mortality schedules was incomplete, these schedules comprise a valuable resource that must not be overlooked. In using them, however, be aware of their limited coverage. They represent deaths for only one year out of every ten. The fact that there were four mortality schedules covering deaths over a thirty-one year period (1849–80) means that a maximum of only 13 percent of the deaths during those years would be listed on these schedules.

Unfortunately, the 13 percent figure is actually quite optimistic. The Public Health Service says the actual count fell far short of this, based on its estimate that only about 60 percent of the actual deaths within those twelve-month periods were reported in the mortality schedules for 1850, 1860, and 1870.[20] If that is true, then fewer than 8 percent of the actual deaths for this thirty-one-year period are reported in the mortality schedules. However, we can be encouraged—but only slightly—because that 8 percent figure is probably low since the 1880 schedules had a somewhat higher rate of completeness.

As you use the mortality schedules, you will see that their form and format were changed slightly from one census to the next. However, the nature of the information reported changed very little. Their content is as follows:

> The information usually shown in the schedules includes the name of the person [who died], his age, sex, state of birth, month of death and cause of death. The 1880 [and 1885] Mortality Schedules include also the state of birth of each parent of the deceased person, but the names of the parents are not given. The schedules are set up by county, but, where indexed, are indexed by the state as a whole.[21]

The 1850 and 1860 mortality schedules have particular significance for blacks because of the absence of family and personal data in the slave schedules for those years. The value of these two schedules lies in the fact that the same critical vital data were given on the mortality schedule for a slave who died during the census year as for any other person who died.

For those interested, the National Archives and the Regional National Archives have all of the census mortality schedules on microfilm. The National Archives Microfilm Rental Program, which once flourished, was discontinued in 2009, thus these films must be used at the Archives. The DAR library and the LDS Family History Library also have extensive microfilm holdings. The latter used to make films available to researchers at Family History Centers and FamilySearch Centers but discontinued that service in September 2017 because of the extensive records that are now digitized.

Many other libraries have microfilms of mortality schedules relating to their own geographic areas. However, if you understand how to work around the potential problems with the indexes, your most efficient use of these re-

---

[20] National Office of Vital Statistics, Vol. 1, 7.

[21] "Federal Mortality Schedules in the NSDAR Library, Washington, DC" (unpublished instruction sheet from NSDAR, 1967).

cords will be with the indexed databases on the Ancestry and FamilySearch Internet sites, as cited above.

The mortality schedules were never quite the success hoped for, yet this method of collecting national vital statistics continued through the 1900 census.[22] Unfortunately, the 1900 mortality schedules were destroyed by congressional order.

B. Slave schedules

Census enumerations prior to 1870 also included slave schedules. The slave schedules relating to the 1850 and 1860 censuses are indexed. Note, however, that these indexes and the schedules contain the names of slave owners and not the names of slaves.[23] The schedules list the age, gender, and color of each slave—sometimes listing them in what appear to be family groups. Both the 1850 and 1860 censuses had slave schedules for Alabama, Arkansas, Delaware, District of Columbia, Florida, Georgia, Kentucky, Louisiana, Maryland, Mississippi, Missouri, North Carolina, South Carolina, Tennessee, Texas, Utah Territory, and Virginia. There are slave schedules for the state of New Jersey for 1850 only.

The FamilySearch website has the 1850 slave schedules in indexed digitized format: *https://familysearch.org/search/collection/1420440*. Ancestry has them at *http://search.ancestry.com/search/db.aspx?dbid=8055*. Ancestry also has an indexed digitized database of the 1860 schedules: *http://search. ancestry.com/search/db.aspx?dbid=7668*. These 1860 records on Ancestry can also be accessed from FamilySearch at *https://familysearch.org/wiki/en/ United_States_Census_Slave_Schedules*. However, there is a price for access unless you are an Ancestry subscriber.

C. Agricultural schedules

All 1850 through 1910 censuses included agricultural schedules.[24] However, the schedules for 1900 and 1910 were destroyed by congressional action in 1919. These agricultural schedules contain information on every farm with annual produce worth $100 or more and include the name of the owner or tenant, and the kind and value of the acreage, machinery, livestock, and produce in considerable detail. Earlier schedules that have survived are in scattered locations. The National Archives has microfilm copies of many of the 1850–1880 agricultural schedules, but not for all states or for all years. There is a listing of these and other non-population schedules available on microfilm from the National Archives, by state, at *https://www.archives.gov/ research/census/nonpopulation#mpubs*. The table is organized alphabetically

---

[22] National Office of Vital Statistics, *Vital Statistics of the United States 1950* (Washington, DC: U.S. Public Health Service, 1954), Vol. 1, 6.

[23] The lone exception, insofar as I have observed, to listing names of slaves is the slave schedule for Utah (actually for Utah County, Utah) completed in 1851.

[24] The 1840 census reported only the number of persons engaged in agriculture.

according to state but, for some reason, there are no states in this alphabetical listing before the District of Columbia. The same incomplete table is in *The Source: A Guidebook of American Genealogy* by Loretto Dennis Szucs and Sandra Hargreaves Luebking (Ancestry Publishing, 2006).[25]

Ancestry has indexed databases to a few of these agricultural schedules (in 2016). These include schedules for the states of Alabama, California, Connecticut, Georgia, Illinois, Iowa, Kansas, Maine, Massachusetts, Michigan, Minnesota, Nebraska, New York, North Carolina, Ohio, South Carolina, Tennessee, Texas, Virginia, and Washington. I anticipate there will be more as time goes forward.

There are other websites that may also have some of these agricultural schedules. You can use your Internet search engine to look for those pertinent to your research. The Pennsylvania Historical & Museum Commission, for example, has online digitized images of the 1850 and 1880 Pennsylvania agricultural schedules, but these are (in 2016) available only to citizens of Pennsylvania.

For agricultural schedules not found online, check the online catalogs for the various state archives, libraries, and historical societies to see what they might have; those are the most likely repositories.

Though agricultural schedules have been little used by genealogists in the past, they have taken on new life as researchers have become more interested in the historical side of their families. As they seek to understand more about their ancestors' lives, they have found a significant source of information about the lives of these people who lived in our early, agriculturally oriented society.

D. Manufacturing/industrial schedules

These schedules were known by different titles at different times. The first schedules were generated in connection with the 1810 census, but the results were meager and inconsistent because no instructions were given to the enumerators. However, the schedules for 1820 and for 1850 through 1870 can be very helpful, especially in rural areas where many farmers had sideline businesses to bolster their income. Businesses listed on these schedules included all mining, fishery, mercantile, manufacturing, and trading businesses that produced at least $500 worth of product. Farmers often operated such businesses as sawmills, blacksmith shops, flour or feed grain mills, tanneries, cooper (barrel making) shops, and cheese making operations.

The 1820 manufacturing enumeration

> records 14 items relating to the nature and the names of articles manufactured, including market value of articles annually manufactured; kind, quantity, and cost of raw materials annually consumed; number of men, women,

---

[25] *The Source* is on the Ancestry Wiki at *https://www.ancestry.com/wiki/index.php?title=The_Source:_A_Guidebook_to_American_Genealogy.*

boys, and girls employed; quantity and kinds of machinery; amount of capital invested; amount paid annually in wages; amount of contingent expenses; and general observations. The surviving schedules are on microfilm as *Records of the 1820 Census of Manufacturers, M279, 27 rolls.*[26]

The 1850, 1860, and 1870 industrial schedules include

the name of the company or owner, kind of business; amount of capital invested; and quantity and value of materials, labor, machinery, and products.[27]

Many farmers were listed on both the agricultural and manufacturing/industrial schedules, thus providing even more insight into their lives and the lives of family members.

E. Social statistics schedules

I also need to mention the social statistics schedules prepared in connection with the 1850, 1860, 1870, and 1880 censuses. These schedules have no information about specific individuals but rather provide contemporaneous snapshots of the communities (the counties, cities, towns, and villages, depending on local circumstances) in which our ancestors lived. For each political subdivision, these schedules tell the total value of all real estate; amount of annual taxes collected; number of schools, teachers, and students; number and types of libraries and how many books; information about newspapers, including name, type, and circulation; church denominations, how many people each church could seat, and value of church property. They also tell the number of paupers—both native and foreign-born—and the cost of supporting them, and the number of persons in prison—both native and foreign-born. They report also the average wages paid to farmhands, day laborers, carpenters, and female domestic servants.

These social statistics schedules can never be indexed because they contain no names of individuals, but if you can locate those schedules relevant to the places your ancestors lived and will take time to study them, they can help you better understand your ancestors and the environment in which they lived. They are not always easy to find, but most of those that still exist are located in the archives or other official repositories of the individual states.

The same chart referred to earlier in connection with other non-population schedules also has information on the location of the social statistics schedules. Note once again, however, that none of the states whose names are in the first part of the alphabet (all before the District of Columbia) are listed on the chart. Also, note that the Family History Library in Salt Lake City has microfilm copies of the social statistics schedules for 1850 through 1880 for Alabama and the 1870 schedules for Tennessee. You can find the microfilm numbers in the library's online FamilySearch catalog.

---

[26] Eales and Kvasnicka, 42.

[27] Ibid., 42.

F. Defective, dependent, and delinquent classes

It should also be mentioned that the 1880 census included a supplementary schedule that provides additional information on six different situations: (1) Insane Inhabitants, (2) Idiots, (3) Deaf-Mutes, (4) Blind Inhabitants, (5) Homeless Children (in institutions), (6) Inhabitants in Prison, and (7) Paupers and Indigent Inhabitants.

> Prior to the 1880 census, the only inquiries about mental and physical defects were part of the population schedules. Individuals in institutions are listed in the regular population schedule.
>
> In 1880 those who were blind, deaf, idiotic, insane, or permanently disabled were recorded in the population schedules, with further information about their condition on supplemental schedules of dependent classes, which are extant for some states among the nonpopulation schedules.[28]

VII. GLOSSARY OF CENSUS TERMS

Chapter 15 is devoted exclusively to helping you use the census; but, before embarking on that adventure, I would like to help you become familiar with some common census terms. The following list is adapted from a list published in the previously cited inventory of the records of the Census Bureau by Davidson and Ashby.[29] I have already used some of these terms in this chapter, and I believe this list will enhance your understanding of census records.

ABSTRACT: The summary or aggregate of census results submitted by the assistant to the marshal or by the marshal to Washington.

ASSISTANT: The local census taker, 1790–1870.

CENSUS BUREAU: The Census Office, established 1902.

CENSUS DAY: The day set by law for the decennial enumeration to begin and the day for which certain census statistics were supposed to be taken. The census days were as follows:

1st–4th censuses, 1790–1820	First Monday in August
5th–12th censuses, 1830–1900	June 1
13th census, 1910	April 15
14th census, 1920	January 1
15th–23rd censuses, 1930–2010	April 1

In researching the census, it is always important to note and compare the actual date of enumeration with the census day. That time discrepancy can explain many inconsistencies.

CENSUS OFFICE: The temporary office set up for each decennial census before the permanent office, the Census Bureau, was established in 1902.

---

[28] Ibid., 41.

[29] Davidson and Ashby, 139–141.

CENSUS YEAR: The twelve-month period immediately preceding the census day for which certain census inquiries are made. This term was first used in the seventh census act (1850).

CIVIL DIVISION: An area over which a state or local government has jurisdiction and which, beginning with the tenth census (1880), was one of the bases for establishing enumerators' subdivisions.

DECENNIAL CENSUS: The population enumeration required by the Constitution to be taken every ten years beginning in 1790.

DISTRICT: The enumeration area, often coterminous with a state or territory, over which a U.S. Marshal had jurisdiction, 1790–1870; also, the smaller area assigned to a supervisor of the census beginning in 1880.

DIVISION: That portion of a district that was assigned to an assistant for taking the censuses, 1790–1840.

ENUMERATION: The population census required by the Constitution.

FAMILY SCHEDULE: The population schedules used only in 1890. [NOTE: Family Schedules became the standard in later censuses when most of the enumeration was completed by mail—mostly 1970 and later.]

INTERDECENNIAL PERIOD: The time between decennial censuses.

MARSHAL: The judicial official who supervised the taking of the census in his judicial district, 1790–1870.

RECORDS: The term often used by the Census Office and the Census Bureau for all the census documentation except original schedules and published reports.

REGISTRATION AREA: A city in which an official registration of deaths or other vital statistics is maintained. Beginning with the tenth (1880) census, the Superintendent of the Census was authorized to obtain from such official records the statistics so maintained.

REPORTS: The term used for published census results.

RETURNS: A term often used interchangeably with schedules or completed questionnaires. Apparently the word *returns,* as used in the first census act, was interpreted by some assistants to mean abstracts or totals obtained from the schedules and by other assistants to mean the schedules themselves.

SCHEDULE: A completed census questionnaire.

SCHEDULE FORM: A blank census questionnaire.

SUBDIVISION: An enumeration area, the boundaries of which either are the limits of known civil divisions or are natural boundaries. The term was first used in the seventh (1850) census act.

15

Using Census Records in Your Research

We know from experience that a student can memorize all of the essential facts about a genealogical source but still not know how to use it. It is with this thought in mind that the present chapter was prepared. My sole purpose here is to help bridge the gap between theory and practice. My method of seeking this objective will be to discuss the various benefits and limitations of census records as a family history source. I will also provide examples of how census schedules can be used to solve some specific types of problems.

I. BENEFITS AND USES

A. 1790

For many years, one of the greatest benefits of the 1790 census schedules has been the fact that they are readily accessible because they are published and completely indexed. Those published indexes are available in many libraries, and the census records themselves, when you wish to examine them, are available on National Archives microfilms—state by state—as pdf files. There is no charge for accessing them at *https://archive.org/details/1790_census*.

With regard to benefit and use, let us suppose you know your ancestor lived somewhere in Pennsylvania and was in the proper age range to be the head of a family in 1790. By searching the index to the Pennsylvania 1790 census, you might discover his county of residence. Even if your ancestor's name proved to be common and you find nine or ten people with the same name in various counties, the census is still useful because it at least limits the search to those few counties. Otherwise, the entire twenty-one counties of 1790 Pennsylvania might need to be considered.

If your ancestor's surname was common (at least 100 persons in the entire 1790 census), the geographic distribution of that surname, by state, is given in a special publication.[1]

The 1790 census has proven to be a useful "finding tool." Even those published tax lists used to replace the lost schedules in Delaware, Virginia, Kentucky (then part of Virginia), Georgia, and the three missing counties of North Carolina (Caswell, Granville, and Orange) are useful in this function.

B. 1800–1840

Because there are now indexed digital databases available on the Internet for all of these censuses, they can serve the same "finding tool" function as the 1790 census. Before the advent of the indexed databases, it was usually necessary to know the county of residence on the years of the census enumerations. Now, however, the indexes and digitized records greatly facilitate access to these records; you can limit your search to an exact place, or you can make it geographically as broad as you wish. These census schedules are now a useful finding tool as well as a source of useful information about family/household configuration and makeup.

Many people believe there is little value in using these early censuses. "Even after I find my family," they ask, "what do I have?" The truth is that when you trace a family through all of these early censuses, you learn much. They contain useful clues about movements in and out of an area, about births of children, about marriages, about deaths, and about younger family members coming of age and themselves becoming heads of families. You can get these kinds of clues, however, only if you search *all pertinent available schedules* and if you search for *all persons in the geographic area who bear the surname of interest*. Information thus obtained can also be a guide to the existence of other useful records relating to your family, such as wills, deeds, marriage records, etc.

Many of the schedule forms for those censuses before 1830 were hand drawn by the enumerators and were not always on the same size paper. Because of this process, some columns (especially those relating to slaves and "free persons of color") were not always included.

C. 1850–1870

The great value of these schedules lies in the fact that they provide information on every person living in every household. The implied relationships between the members of a household provide some of the best circumstantial evidence available for the eventual proving of family connections. You cannot always safely assume what the relationship is between two persons living in

---

[1] United States Census Bureau, *A Century of Population Growth From the First Census of the United States to the Twelfth, 1790–1900*, 1909 (Reprint, Baltimore: Genealogical Publishing Co., 2012).

the same household, but you at least have some basic information with which to work. An elderly person living with a family may prove to be a parent of either the husband or the wife. (Though the person's surname will *often* suggest which one, all you really have is circumstantial evidence.) Just as with the earlier censuses, it is important that you check every census pertinent to your problem and extract all information for every household where anyone with your surname is listed. By doing this you will come to better understand the family, its movements, marriages, deaths, etc. In addition, you will often find clues to suggest the use of other records. Though you may not see the necessity of getting all information relating to everyone of your surname of interest, I promise you that it is important. Nearly every family history researcher has seen cases where important clues and even family connections were passed over unnoticed when this procedure was neglected.

The movement of a family from one area to another and the length of time the family lived in a certain locality can often be told from studying the census enumerations. The names of states where the children in a household were born, as they relate to those children's ages, are most helpful in this regard.

Whether you can expect to find land deeds for a family can often be told by whether the census shows that the person was a landowner. This is true because the census should tell the value of real estate owned. The listed value of real estate (and of personal property in the 1860 and 1870 schedules) can be an indicator of the social prestige and economic status of the family. Those who had extensive possessions were also more likely to leave wills when they died and were more likely to be written about in local histories. These censuses also tell whether children attended school and whether members of the family could read and write.

Because these censuses are now all indexed, digitized, and readily accessible, they are easy to search and are a significant finding tool. Not only do they contain detailed family-oriented information on the families you seek in your research, they are easy to use. They are not foolproof, however, and you need to remember the potential problems associated with indexes and make compensation for them.

You also need to make sure you get the information on every household where there are persons with your surname of interest. Otherwise, your census research is incomplete. On the various family history websites, you can check the indexes very quickly and then go directly to the proper pages of the digitized records. Once you locate the specific household you seek, you need to make another search of that same locality using only the surname to pick up everyone with surname(s) you seek.

If you have trouble finding a specific person, in the place where he should have been, you can even make a search for all males in that place within an appropriate age range. You then have the advantage over the indexer because you know exactly the name you are looking for and do not have to guess on what a hard-to-read name might be.

D. 1880

The 1880 census is listed here in a category by itself because it has some rather distinct differences from, and advantages over, earlier censuses. However, everything we have said about using the earlier schedules also applies to this one. In years past, this census had an advantage because of its partial index (to only those households with children 10 and under) but, in that regard, the playing field is now level. The remaining advantages (or differences) of the 1880 census are as follows:

- The statement of the relationship of every person in a household to the head of the household makes family information found here much more authoritative than the circumstantial evidence on relationships in the 1850, 1860, and 1870 schedules.
- The state (or country) of birth for the father and mother of each person is stated in this census.

Though the above-listed advantages are significant, to each I add a word of caution: They can be deceptive and work to your disadvantage if not properly understood. Consider:

- All relationships given are to the head of the household only and not to other members of the household. There is no way to tell if the head of the house has been married more than once and whether those listed as his children are also his wife's children.
- The places of birth listed for a person's father and mother are not necessarily correct. Some people did not even manage to get their own states of birth recorded correctly. You have no way to know who provided the information to the census taker.

Sometimes the states of birth listed for the parents of the children in the household can provide clues to help you see if the father has been married more than once and which of his children belong to which marriage. For example, if the state of birth of the child's mother differs from the state of birth listed for the wife in the census, you have an obvious clue (circumstantial evidence) to the possibility of another marriage. But, of course, this is not a foolproof formula. Also, if a man had more than one wife and they were both (or all) born in the same state, there is no clue.

E. Similarities and differences, 1880–1940

These census schedules for the years 1900 through 1940 are a great boon to the family history researcher who is looking for connections in more recent times. They provide a significant amount of information about both families and individual family members. All are similar in many ways to the 1880 schedules—most differences being quite insignificant. There are, however, some important similarities and differences as they relate to various issues.

The following list explores those similarities and differences relating to the information called for in the census columns:

1. **NAME:** In all of these censuses, **1880 through 1940**, every person whose usual place of residence was in a household was to be enumerated by name in that household. Names listed did not have to be (and usually were not) complete (as in first name, middle name, and last name). Nicknames were often listed; inaccurate spellings are common.

2. **AGE:** An age is stated for every person in every one of these censuses. The **1880** census gives the month of birth for a child who was born within the year. The **1900** census gives the month and year of birth for everyone. The **1910, 1920, 1930, and 1940** censuses give only age at last birthday, though some enumerators in **1920** listed the ages of children under 10 in years and months (e.g.: 6 7/12 or 5 3/12).

3. **COLOR OR RACE:** All of these censuses reported the color or race of every person. The number of races in the **1880 through 1920** censuses was five. The most significant changes were made in **1930 and were continued in 1940**, with the option to add other races on a case-by-case basis. Enumerators were given special instructions for reporting the race of interracial persons. A person with both white and black lineage was to be recorded as black, no matter the fraction of that lineage. (The term "mulatto" was no longer used.) If a person had mixed black and American Indian lineage, he was listed as black, unless considered predominantly American Indian within the community. Those with both white and American Indian lineage were listed as Indian, unless the percentage of Indian blood was small and he was accepted as white in the community. Essentially, every person whose lineage was both white and some other race was reported as the other race. Those with minority interracial lineages were reported with the race of their father. Mexican was listed as a race in 1930 for the first and only time. Enumerators wrote "W" for white, "Neg" for black, "Mex" for Mexican, "In" for American Indian, "Ch" for Chinese, "Jp" for Japanese, "Fil" for Filipino, "Hin" for Hindu, and "Kor" for Korean. All other races were to be written out in full.[2]

4. **BIRTHPLACE:** The requirement with **all six** of these censuses was to record the name of the state of birth, if born in the U.S., and the name of the country, if born elsewhere. This practice was followed very well. However, a few enumerators went beyond the requirement, recording the county if the person was born in the same state as the enumeration.

---

[2] See "History, 1930" United States Census Bureau, https://www.census.gov/history/www/through_the_decades/index_of_questions/1930_1.html (accessed July 24, 2017).

5. **IMMIGRATION AND CITIZENSHIP:** The **1880** census has no information on immigration or naturalization. The **1900** census tells how long an immigrant has been in the U.S. and whether naturalized. The **1910** census tells the year of immigration, how many years in the U.S., and whether naturalized. The **1920** census gives the year of immigration, whether the immigrant had been naturalized or was an alien, and year of naturalization. The **1930** census tells the person's native language, year of immigration, current status (naturalized, first papers, or alien), and whether the person spoke English. The **1940** census tells the citizenship of all persons who were foreign born.

6. **LANGUAGE:** The **1880** census asks no questions about language. The **1900, 1910, and 1920** censuses tell whether each person spoke English. The **1910** census identifies the language spoken. The **1920 and 1930** censuses identify the "mother tongue" for each person, and the **1920** also tells the "mother tongue" for each person's father and mother. The only question about language in the **1940** census was on the Supplemental Schedule (see item 15 below). The person was asked the "Language spoken in the home in earliest childhood."

7. **FARM AND HOME OWNERSHIP:** The **1880** census has no information about farm or home ownership. The **1900, 1910, and 1920** all tell whether a farm or home is owned or rented and whether owned property is mortgaged or free of mortgage. The **1930** schedules also tell whether the home is owned or rented. It tells the value of the home, if owned, or the cost of monthly rent; it also asks if the household owns a radio and if it resides on a farm. A farm schedule cross-reference is given. There is no information about mortgages. The **1940** census has no information relating to this except to ask if the household lives on a farm.

8. **OCCUPATION:** The **1880** schedules merely ask for "profession, occupation or trade of each person, male or female." The **1900** census similarly asks for "occupation, trade, or profession of each person 10 years of age and over." The **1910 and 1920** censuses have information on the following issues relating to occupation: "Trade or profession of, or particular kind of work done by this person," "general nature of industry, business, or establishment in which this person works," and "whether [the person is] an employer, employee, or working on own account." In **1930**, the census asked about the person's "occupation" and "industry." It also asked whether the person was "actually employed." In the **1940** census, "usual occupation, industry, and class of worker" are not asked of everyone but only of (a more or less random) 5 percent of individuals on a "Supplemental Schedule" (see item 15 below). If the supplemental person happened to be a farmer, there is a cross-reference to the farm schedule.

9. **MARITAL STATUS:** The **1880** census tells if the person was married and if the marriage of a couple took place within the census year. The **1900 and 1910** both tell the number of years of the present marriage. The **1880, 1900, 1910, 1920, 1930, and 1940** censuses all give each person's marital status (single, married, widowed, or divorced). In the **1910 and 1920** censuses, married persons were identified as being in their first marriage ("M1") or in a second or subsequent marriage ("M2").

10. **SOCIAL SECURITY:** The Supplemental Schedule (see item 15 below) of the **1940** census asked three questions relating to the recently implemented Social Security Act.

 a. "Does this person have a Federal Social Security number? Answer 'yes' or 'no' for every person 14 years of age or older."

 b. "Were deductions for Federal old-age insurance or railroad retirement made from this person's wages or salary in 1939? Answer 'yes' or 'no' for every person 14 years of age or older." (Note that deductions for Federal old-age insurance were made from wages and salaries [$3,000 or less] received in non-government employment [except for agriculture, railroads, charitable and nonprofit organizations, employment as sailors, and domestic service]).

 c. "If so, were deductions made from (1) all, (2) one-half or more, and (3) part, but less than half, of wages, or salary?"

11. **A WOMAN'S CHILDREN:** The **1900 and 1910** censuses both tell how many children a mother has borne and how many of those children were living at the time of the census. The **1880 and 1920** schedules do not have this kind of information. There is also information on the **1940** Supplemental Schedule (see item 15 below). There the following questions were asked "For all women who are or have been married":

 a. "Has this woman been married more than once (yes or no)?"

 b. "Age at first marriage?"

 c. "Number of children ever born (do not include stillbirths)?"

12. **MENTAL AND PHYSICAL HEALTH:** The **1880** census has "health" columns telling whether a person is "blind," "deaf and dumb," "idiotic," "insane," or "maimed, crippled, bedridden, or otherwise disabled." The **1900** census tells whether a person is "deaf and dumb" and whether "blind." The **1910, 1920, 1930, and 1940** schedules have no information on physical or mental disabilities.

13. **WAR VETERANS:** The **1900 and 1910** censuses both tell if the person is a Civil War veteran (Union or Confederate) or the widow of such a veteran. The **1930** census identified American veterans according to the war in which they served—"WW" for World War I, "Sp" for the Spanish-American War, "Civ" for the Civil War, "Phil" for the Philippine insurrection, "Box" for the Boxer rebellion, and "Mex" for the

Mexican expedition. The **1880 and 1920** censuses have no information relating to service, veterans, or survivors of veterans. The **1940** census gathered veteran information only for those on the Supplemental Schedule (see item 15 below). It asked:

    a. "Is this person a veteran of the United States military forces; or the wife, widow, or under 18-year-old child of a veteran? If so, enter 'Yes.'"

    b. "If child, is veteran-father dead? (Yes or No)"

    c. "War or military service [with one-letter designation for area of service]."

14. INCOME: Of these six censuses, only the **1940** census asked anything about income: It asked three questions about "Income in 1939 (12 months ending Dec. 31, 1939)":

    a. "Amount of money, wages, or salary received?"

    b. "Did this person receive income of $50 or more from sources other than money wages or salary? (Y or N)"

    c. "Number of Farm Schedule?"

15. SUPPLEMENTAL SCHEDULE (1940 CENSUS ONLY): The supplemental questions referred to in several places above were asked of persons whose names were on two designated lines on each page of the census schedule (about a 5 percent sample).

As with the earlier censuses, the reliability of the stated information on any particular issue depended on many unknown and uncontrollable variables.

II. LIMITATIONS OF THE CENSUS AS A FAMILY HISTORY SOURCE

As valuable as the census records are as a source of family history information, there are still some significant shortcomings. We have already discussed some of these, but a listing of some of the limitations may be helpful.

A. Not designed for family history purposes

The problem here is the fact that none of the records we rely on in our research were designed with family history in mind. Each one of them came into existence for another purpose, and we use them because they are all we have. We have to adapt and make do with what exists.

B. Limitation of time

The very fact that there was no general census taken of the families in America until 1790 is a limiting factor. Other records must be used for earlier periods. Also, in connection with this problem, I might also note the very nature of census development—the earlier schedules do not contain nearly as much family history information or personal data as do the later schedules.

C. Incompleteness

At the taking of every American census there have been families missed due to a built-in "error factor"—the length of time allowed for the process. The act providing for the 1790 census allowed nine months for the marshals to complete their job. This same length of time was allowed for all censuses until 1850 when the time was cut to five months. In 1870, it was reduced to one month. Whenever an enumeration was conducted over a period of time—even if it was only two or three days—some families were missed completely and others were enumerated more than once.

Also, the U.S. has never made use of "prior schedules," that is, schedules left at the residence in advance of the enumeration to be completed by the head of the family. Such schedules are used in nearly every European country and may or may not add to the validity of the census results, but they make it possible to take the entire census in a very short period (even one day). In 1970 and later enumerations, the U.S. census used a form that was mailed to families, but this was the first move in that direction.

Another problem was that some families, especially in "low-class," multiple-dwelling units (those created from the division of large, old, single-family homes), were inadvertently bypassed because the enumerator (or the assistant) did not find them. And there were others missed also. Every genealogist has searched for a family that "should have been there"—it was there in both earlier and later enumerations—but it was not to be found.

Under the issue of *incompleteness,* I also include those schedules for entire counties and even entire states that have been lost or destroyed.

D. Indifferent and incompetent enumerators (or assistants)

In some instances, incompleteness can be explained under this heading, but a census can be incomplete in spite of a conscientious census taker, so we give him the benefit of the doubt. Unfortunately, however, there have been census takers who took the job only for what they could get out of it or because it was assigned to them by legislative act. Many of these persons were not well qualified and did not fulfill the obligation satisfactorily. Many census schedules reflect this because the instructions the census takers received (or should have received) were not carefully followed.

Some schedules list the members of a household by initials only. A few list no places of birth. Sometimes families were not home when the census taker made his visit and neighbors were asked to give the information, or, if he was personally acquainted with the family, the assistant would complete the schedules from the best of his own knowledge. There were also times when young children in the family provided the "facts" for the census enumeration if no one else was at home. I have observed cases where even the racial designation of a person or of a family is in error.

Some census takers went so far as to expand the population. Apparently reimbursed according to the number of families enumerated, they listed some families twice in different parts of their schedules, often with slight variations in the information.

Before I go on, let me emphasize that most of those who were commissioned to take the census did a good job, and the censuses they took represent their best and most conscientious effort. Some were even overzealous, going well beyond the requirements made of them. A good case in point is provided by those who listed counties of birth and not just states and countries.

E. Incorrect information given by family members

Family members often gave incorrect information to the enumerator or assistant, which resulted in inconsistencies in the records. In the early censuses, we have no way to know who provided the information that appears on the census record. Anyone who has read very many censuses is aware of this problem. It manifests itself in almost every family that is traced through all available censuses.

Inconsistent ages illustrate the problem best, but names and places of birth also have some tendency to change from one census to the next. There may be many different reasons for these differences, and you have no way to know the reason in any given case. This is why you must not stop after searching just one census, even if you believe the family to be complete. With this kind of problem, the effect is the same whether or not the error was intentional. You definitely need evidence from other sources.

F. Legibility

Too often, census schedules are difficult to read, and there are many reasons for this. Careless handwriting, unfamiliar abbreviations, poor spelling, the workings of time on poor-quality inks—these are all familiar problems. The 1880 census, taken on such poor-quality paper that it has been unable to withstand the ravages of time, was one of the first withdrawn from public use. (The originals are now in various non-federal repositories throughout the country as indicated on pages 130 and 131 of Katherine H. Davidson and Charlotte M. Ashby, *Preliminary Inventory of the Records of the Bureau of the Census* [Washington, DC: National Archives, 1964].)

There are additional problems in reading microfilmed copies of the census schedules. On some, the photography was of poor quality—under-exposure, over-exposure, etc. Others present special photography problems, such as faded writing that simply does not photograph well. Another problem was found in the photographing of double pages of bound volumes on single frames— because one page in the two-page frame usually stood higher than the other, it was impossible to get both into proper focus at the same time except near the center of the large volumes.

This latter problem was solved, however, in the refilming of the 1850, 1860, and 1870 censuses on single-page frames by the National Archives. The difference is remarkable! They are much more readable, not just because everything is in focus, but also because the images are larger and the photography is generally better. The later censuses were initially microfilmed on single-page frames. Though most are quite readable, there are, unfortunately, some films of inferior quality.

Another problem with microfilms is that most film operators were paid according to their production and thus worked very rapidly. At a hurried pace, it is easy to turn two pages inadvertently at one time. Because this has been known to happen, you should be alert to the possibility.

If you wonder why I talk about microfilm images when the census records are now all available on digital databases, the answer is that they were digitized from the microfilm copies.

G. You must know something about the place of residence

Before we had indexes, it was generally necessary to know at least the county in which a family lived in order to find that family in the census. This problem was especially acute in large cities where a census may include many volumes. It was almost essential to know the ward (or other geographic subdivision) where your family lived in order to complete a reasonably satisfactory search. Without that information, a simple census search could take many days.

With the indexed census databases, it is not usually necessary for you to know exactly where your ancestors lived in order to search for them in census records, but it is still a fact that the more you know, the better are your chances for success. If you know the county, that knowledge enables you to narrow your search results and be more successful in reaching your research objectives. If, for some reason, your index search does not come up with the family(ies) you hoped to find, then it may be necessary to resort to the methods of the past. If your ancestor(s) lived in one of those thirty-nine cities included in the 1910 street indexes, that fact might help expedite your search. (See the discussion and listing in Chapter 14.)

Remember the general rule that you begin your searches on the family history websites with very broad criteria and then narrow your searches by becoming more specific once you have more information.

G. Spelling problems

How a name might be spelled is always an issue, but I hope it is not an issue that will hinder your efforts or diminish your success. The important thing is that you be ever aware of the possibility and make the necessary allowances in your research. Do not hesitate to try different spelling variations or use wildcards in your searches on the family history websites.

III. WHEN SHOULD THE CENSUS BE SEARCHED?

As previously stated, there is no absolute rule about the sequence of searches. It all depends on the nature of your specific problem, your analysis of that problem, and your research objectives. The census schedules for the relevant time periods must always be searched in all cases, whether early or late.

By its very nature, a census search will usually be one of the first searches on a pedigree problem when your problem falls within the right time frame. And, because of this, there will be times when it will be necessary to go back to the same census again later when further research has revealed additional clues—such as maiden surnames on female lines. You should never hesitate to re-look at a census when the need is indicated. On the other hand, however, you should be certain you are getting all you can on your first time through. Failure to do so is a very serious (and common) error. It is good, however, that the indexed databases make these subsequent searches much easier.

IV. EXAMPLES OF CENSUS USE

A. Example No. 1

(Note that this case is fictitious. It is presented here for purposes of illustration.)

Frank James Shears was, according to family records, born in Missouri sometime around 1857. This is all we know of him until his marriage. He died in Arkansas in 1920. We do not know the names of his parents or anything else about them. We also know nothing of any brothers or sisters.

SOLUTION: There are a couple of ways to approach this problem, and you will probably want to use both of them in order to get all of the evidence you can. The question you consider is which to do first. One way is to go directly to the online census index for Missouri to see if the name of Frank Shears comes up. The other alternative is to get the 1920 death certificate first to see if you can zero in on a specific county where he was born and also get the names of his parents. It is probably wise to get the death certificate first so you will have a little more information before you go to the census.

You would write to the state Vital Records office, Arkansas Department of Health, in Little Rock, Arkansas, for the death certificate of Frank James Shears. This certificate should tell the date and place of his birth and the names of his parents. (This information would be secondary evidence because of the time element.)

The death certificate (giving his death as December 2, 1920, at Rumly, Searcy County, Arkansas) is secured. It gives the following information:

Date of birth:	15 April 1856
State of birth:	Missouri
Father's full name:	Findley Shears
Mother's maiden name:	Unknown

This information helps but still does not tell where in Missouri the birth took place. However, an obituary in the local newspaper says that Frank J. Shears was born in Fulton, Missouri.

Once you have learned from a quick Internet search that Fulton, Missouri, is in Callaway County (founded in 1820), you have sufficient information for a meaningful search of the 1860 census of Callaway County. Even if the death certificate had not given his father's name, this census could still be searched, but the father's name gives us one more piece of information to work with.

You should begin by making a search of the index on one of the Internet websites for a 4-year-old (plus or minus) child named Frank James Shears in Callaway County—and also look for all families named Shears (or Sheers, Shares, Shires, etc.). It does help, however, to know the father's name in case there is more than one young child named Frank Shears.

The search of the 1860 census of Callaway County, Missouri, finds the following family:

Findlay Sheers	28	Wagon maker	born Ky
Hulda "	29	housewife	" Mo
William "	6		" "
Frank "	4		" "
Alice A. "	2		" "
Jno. F. "	3/12		" "

All other Sheers families found in this census—when a surname search for the Shears name is completed—should be copied into your research notes. At this point, you do not know how (or even if) any of them are related to this family, but the chances are good that there is some relationship.

These results, of course, suggest the need to look at other censuses. Undoubtedly, this couple was young enough to have more children after 1860, which indicates the necessity for also searching both the 1870 and 1880 schedules of Callaway County, if the family did not move away in the intervening years. If the family did move, it is important to determine their destination and then search those censuses for the place of their destination.

From the results of our 1860 census search, it is apparent that you also need to search the 1850 census. Because the eldest child of this couple was only 6 years old, it appears quite likely that Findlay and Hulda were not married until after 1850 and should both be in the households of their parents in 1850. However, because you do not know Hulda's maiden surname, the search for her and her family will have to wait. This is one of those situations where a later, second search of the census will be necessary after you have more information.

The 1850 census of Callaway County, Missouri, revealed the following family:

Francis Sheers	48	farmer	born Ky
Sarah "	41	housewife	" "
Findlay "	17	farm hand	" "
Sarah "	14		" "
William "	12		" Mo
Martha "	7		" "
Alice A. "	5		" "
Jno. F. "	3		" "

(This same family—minus Findlay and some of the other older children—was also found in the 1860 census, but it wasn't possible to know who they were then because Findlay was no longer in the household. This is why it was wise to have extracted all families of the surname as part of your 1860 census search.)

This 1850 census was very useful. It told a great deal about the "Sheers" family, including the approximate time of their migration from Kentucky to Missouri. As a result, the 1840 census index was searched and showed the Francis Shears family in Callaway County:

Francis Shears	1 male 30–40	1 female 30–40
	1 male 5–10	1 female 5–10
	2 males under 5	1 female under 5

In comparing the 1840 and 1850 censuses, it becomes obvious that there is much that the 1850 census does not tell about this family:

- Where is the female in the 1850 census who was between 5 and 10 in the 1840 census? Did she die? Did she marry? Or was she not a member of the family? It's impossible to say at this point.

- Where is the other male in the 1850 census who was under 5 in 1840? William is the only one in 1850 who would have been in the proper age group.

- There may have been children of relatives living with the family in 1840—or maybe even some unrelated children—who were gone from the home by 1850.

- What about the irregular gap between the ages of William (12) and Martha (7) in 1850? Such a gap suggests three possibilities:

  1) One or more children born during this period may have died, perhaps the one unaccounted-for male from the 1840 census.

  2) There may have been no children born to this couple during this period. That situation would not be too strange, and it is also a possibility to consider.

  3) Francis Sheers' wife may have died during this period, and he may not have remarried for three or four years and, hence, had no children during this period. (She would have died following the 1840 census.) If this is the case, Sarah (in the 1850 census) is Findlay Shears' stepmother and not his mother.

There is no evidence to prove any one of these three possibilities now, so, though the census is invaluable in supplying some evidence to help resolve the problems, it does not provide all of the evidence needed. Further evidence from other sources must be obtained.

As part of the process of doing complete research, it will be vital that you search all available census records in which Findlay Shears and his son Frank James can be found. These include 1870, 1880, 1900, 1910, and 1920. It will also be a good idea to search the 1830 Callaway County census to see what can be learned from it.

It is hoped that other research will reveal the Kentucky origin of Findlay Shears, and the 1820 census of the appropriate Kentucky county can also be searched. A further extension of the pedigree and the identification of other localities will also give reason and opportunity to search the earlier census schedules (1810, 1800, and 1790).

As was noted earlier, no research on an American family history problem after the beginning of the census is complete until all pertinent censuses have been searched. As part of that research, you should gather all information in the census records in the localities where this family lived for every person who bears the family name. Once the proper places are identified, these searches can be made quickly utilizing the indexed census databases.

B. Example No. 2

Family tradition suggests that the ancestor being sought—the father of William Jasper Kerr—is named Joseph Kerr. William Jasper (born 1781) died on January 10, 1846, in Jefferson County, Iowa. His wife, Jemima, died there in 1842. William Jasper Kerr was supposedly born in North Carolina, but family tradition suggests that he lived in Tennessee before coming to Iowa.

In a history of Jefferson County, Iowa, is a biography of one John Workman (born 1819 in Kentucky), an early resident of Jefferson County. His biography says that in 1840 he married Amanda J. Kerr, who was *born in White County, Tennessee,* on October 14, 1825. According to family records, this Amanda J. Kerr was the daughter of William Jasper Kerr. This biography gives you a place to look for the Kerr family in Tennessee.

The first step is to use the indexed census databases to search and compare censuses in Jefferson County, Iowa, with those of White County, Tennessee, to see if there is any correlation. The results of this search were as follows:

WHITE COUNTY, TENNESSEE—1820

| Joseph Carr | 3 males under 10
1 male 26–45 | 2 females 16–26 |
| William Kerr | 2 males under 10
1 male 26–45 | 1 female 26–45 |

(NOTE: Our William Jasper Kerr would have been 39.)

WHITE COUNTY, TENNESSEE—1830

| Joseph Kerr, Jr. | 2 males 10–15
1 male 20–30
2 males 30–40
1 male 50–60 | 1 female 5–10
1 female 15–20
1 female 30–40 |
| William Kerr | 1 male 5–10
1 male 30–40
1 male 50–60 | 3 females under 5
1 female 20–30 |

William Kerr, Sr.	2 males under 5	1 female under 5
	1 male 5–10	1 female 5–10
	1 male 10–15	1 female 15–20
	1 male 15–20	1 female 40–50
	1 male 40–50	
	1 male 60–70	

(NOTE: William Jasper Kerr would have been 49. William Kerr, Sr., is the only one with a male of that age in his household. The older man living in that household might be either his father or his father-in-law.)

WHITE COUNTY, TENNESSEE—1840

Levi J. Kerr	2 males under 5	1 female 15–20
	1 male 15–20	
	1 male 20–30	
William Kerr	3 males under 5	No females
	1 male 5–10	
	1 male 15–20	
	1 male 40–50	
	1 male 60–70	

(NOTE: William Jasper Kerr would have been 59. The William who fits seems to be gone.)

JEFFERSON COUNTY, IOWA—1840 (This is the first census of Jefferson County, which was created in 1839 from Indian lands.)

Henry Kuerr (?)	2 males 5–10	2 females 5–10
	2 males 20–30	2 females 20–30
William Kerr	1 male 5–10	1 female 5–10
	2 males 10–15	1 female 10–15
	1 male 15–20	1 female 20–30
	1 male 20–30	1 female 40–50
	1 male 50–60	

(NOTE: William Jasper Kerr would have been age 59 in 1840, and when this family is carefully compared with the family of William Kerr, Sr., in the 1830 census of White County, Tennessee, you can see a close—though not perfect—correlation.)

| Archibald Kerr | 1 male 20–30 | 1 female under 5 |
| | | 1 female 20–30 |

(NOTE: William Jasper had a son Archibald whom this fits.)

Based on these censuses, the move from White County, Tennessee, to Jefferson County, Iowa, seems likely, and this could be the family you seek. However, nothing can be proven by these census records alone; additional evidence is required. What you do have here is the fact that there is no conflicting evidence in the census records to show that such a move did not occur. That is a good start.

Further evidence needed to help solve the original problem was found in a Revolutionary War pension file for a veteran (a spy) named Joseph Kerr who applied for and received a pension while living in *White County, Tennessee,* in 1833. He was born in 1760 in Chester County, Pennsylvania (according to his pension application), and came to North Carolina with his parents as a child. His military service was in North Carolina. This might well be the man sought, but more evidence is needed to prove it. It is also possible that he is the older man in William Kerr, Sr.'s, household in the 1830 census of White County, Tennessee, but as of now, there is no proof.

These early census schedules, even though they do not list the names of individual family members, have provided valuable evidence. This evidence should be considered carefully, along with other evidence, but it cannot stand alone. It is purely circumstantial and is insufficient to establish proof by itself.

C. Example No. 3

George Andrew Crossman and his wife, Lucy, came to the little mining town of Park City, Utah, in the 1880s. Here they resided as faithful members of the Roman Catholic Church, prospered, saw children grow up and marry, and then they died. They came from somewhere in New York State—just where was not certain, though in more recent years the children consistently said it was "Haminville" (or "Hammondville," or some other town with a similar name). Though this seemed like good information, a problem arose when no such a place in New York State could be identified, though the best available gazetteers for New York State were used, including those published during the proper time period. This made it impossible to trace the family in earlier periods because New York is quite a big place.

Since the Crossmans migrated to Utah in the 1880s and the children were quite young at the time, the answer to locating the family in New York obviously lay in the use of the partial index to the 1880 census. The surname Crossman was encoded according to the Soundex formula (see Chapter 13) as C625 and was easily located in the New York index—not at any place the name of which even remotely resembled "Haminville"—but *at Crown Point in Essex County* (on lower Lake Champlain). The family was enumerated as follows:

Crossman,	George A.	27	Miner	born N.Y.
"	Lucy E. (wife)	21	Keeping house	" "
"	Emma E. (dau.)	4		" "
"	Cora A. (dau.)	3		" "
"	Henry G. (son)	1		" "
Bennett,	Newell R. (boarder)	21	Laborer	" "

The family was located on p. 4, Supervisor's District 7, Enumeration District 44. This was an easy solution to an otherwise difficult problem.

Today, I would have handled this problem in a different manner. I would have gone to Ancestry.com and used the indexed digitized database of the 1880 census on one of the family history websites, but the result would have been the same.

V. CONCLUSION

Census schedules can help us solve many genealogical problems, but they can also present problems if they are not wisely used and properly interpreted. They must be read scrupulously because the overlooking or misreading of important data may have disastrous and far-reaching results because everyone will assume you did a good job. No one ever really checks on you. Perhaps we should all be checked on more often than we are—and this ought especially to include checking on ourselves. I like the motto of the Royal Society of London: *"Nullus in verba:* we take no man's word for anything."

A guide to help us minimize human error and mine the census for all its potential is found in the following rules:

- Note the heading on each column in each census schedule you use. Know what information you can expect to find in that column and the value of that information to your research.

- Always consider the possibility that the enumeration of a family may be split between two pages, and may even begin with the listing of the head of the family on the bottom line of a page—and perhaps with no repetition of the surname at the top of the next page. Be sure to look at every line.

- Look for and extract every family (the complete household) with the surname of your ancestor, as well as every household (regardless of the family head's surname) where a person of your ancestor's surname is listed. There are forms available for extracting census information, but it is often best to print each page or make a photocopy of each page where a family or individual of your surname appears. This is much faster. It also assures that you get everything and that it is correct. (Be prepared to do what needs to be done.) These families can be identified quickly and easily if you search the index to the census database with the given name space left blank. And do not hesitate to search for various spelling variations.

- In hard cases, you should consider several families before and several families after your ancestor. Check these families for similar migration patterns using the birthplaces of children, similar occupations, and similar naming patterns. Remember that relatives often moved together and lived near each other. If your ancestor owned no land, you might be able to identify the area of the county where he lived through the land records of his neighbors. This information can also help you locate nearby cemeteries and churches.

- Find your ancestor and the members of his family in every census during their lives, always considering the rules stated above.

- Your census research can be greatly enhanced by the use of maps. Detailed maps of the area of interest can provide a perspective on your problems available in no other way. We have talked about maps before, and there are lots of good maps on the Internet. These maps are helpful even when you use indexed databases. You need to relate the locality information at the top of the census schedules to maps for the locality.

- If your ancestor lived near a county or state boundary, extend your research into the neighboring jurisdiction. Close neighbors often lived on both sides of these arbitrary divisions.

- Do not limit your census research to the population schedules only. Utilize every relevant, available census schedule for the year and the area where your ancestor lived.

- Do not be afraid to repeat a census search of a particular locality when new evidence is found. This is especially true when other research identifies additional ancestral families in the area—such as the family of your ancestor's wife whose surname you have just learned.

As a final note, let me also make some observations about the use of census indexes. Though they are important and marvelous tools if wisely used, indexes may become more of a bane than a boon to the family history researcher. Things you would almost certainly pick up reading through the census entry by entry can be overlooked when you rely solely on the indexes. Thus, if you fail to find the family you seek in the index—even after searching for obvious spelling variations—despite evidence to suggest they should be there, do not hesitate to search the record.

Before you make a page-by-page search, however, I offer some suggestions that will help you get more mileage from those indexes. Essentially all of these suggestions should be prefaced with the reminder that you should not be afraid to *use some imagination* when the entries you seek do not readily appear. Also, if you decide to search the census page by page, do not be in too big of a hurry; take time to do it right and to consider the following issues as you do so:

- Consider every possible spelling variation.

- Consider that the indexer may have misread the name and mistaken one letter for another. If the indexer can misinterpret names, so can you. Capital *T*'s and *S*'s could be interchanged easily, as could *J*'s and *I*'s, as well as small *n*'s and *u*'s, or *a*'s, *u*'s, and *o*'s, etc. Even whole names can be misread. I have seen *James* mistaken for *Francis* and *Newland* for *Nesdand*.

- Consider possible phonetic spellings and silent letters, either dropped or added. *H*'s and *E*'s, in particular, are commonly dropped and added. Letters may be doubled, or letters normally doubled may appear singly.

- Consider that the sound of a vowel could have been misunderstood by the census taker, both at the beginning of the name and in the middle. Remember, for example, the Angle/Engle/Ingle and the Matlick/Matlock/Matlack examples in Chapter 2.

- Consider the possibility of typographical errors in indexing as well, such as transpositions of letters and adjacent keys on the keyboard being struck. Could we possibly find *Ranold* instead of *Arnold*? Or perhaps *Amith* or *Smirh* instead of *Smith*?

- Consider how you might best use the wildcards * and ? in your searches of the indexes on the various family history websites, as discussed in Chapter 10.

It is very important to your research success that you not only use the census records, but that you use them correctly, thoroughly, and with some imagination.

16

Understanding Probate Records
and Legal Terminology

I. DEFINITION AND BACKGROUND
OF PROBATE RECORDS

All records relating to the disposition of an estate after its owner's
death are referred to as probate records. These are many and varied in
both content and value, but they fall basically into two main classes:

- TESTATE
- INTESTATE

If a person died leaving a valid will, we say he died testate; if he had no
valid will, he died intestate. In most localities in America, these records comprise, as a group, one of the most useful family history resources in existence.

Historically, since the first permanent settlement, there has never been a
time in North America when people did not make wills or when the estates
of those who failed to do so were not handled by a court appointed for that
purpose to ensure that the rightful heirs—the legal heirs—became the heirs
in fact. In those colonies set up by British grant or dominion, English law
and custom were meticulously followed. Thus, the right of probate was never
challenged.

Statutory probate law in America developed as a state, rather than a federal,
function. As a result, the laws differ somewhat from state to state. In general,
however, especially insofar as wills are concerned, anyone was free to make
a will if he was of sound mind, of legal age, and free from restraint. And, of
course, anyone was free not to make a will and thus die intestate if he chose to
do so or if he procrastinated until it was too late. It can also be correctly stated
that persons not of legal age, not of sound mind, and under the force of restraint (any or all of the above) could also make wills—but not legal ones. If a

will was successfully challenged on any of these points, it was not a valid will and its provisions could not be carried out. Instead, the maker was deemed to have died intestate.

II. CONTENT AND GENEALOGICAL VALUE

Some of our ancestors died leaving no property or property of little value and hence there is no record of probate. If we seek these persons in our research, then probate records will have no direct value for us. Most persons who have lived to adulthood in America, however, have left some type of estate to be administered and, in the resulting records, our research can achieve varying degrees of success. In fact, we cannot completely write off the value of probate records even for those who died without property. They are often mentioned in the probate records of others—sometimes as witnesses; sometimes as beneficiaries; and sometimes as executors, administrators, or trustees—and sometimes just as innocent third parties (such as the persons from whom something being bequeathed was acquired or as owners of adjoining land).

The very nature of probate records recommends them as an invaluable family history source. Though they were not created for family history purposes, they exist because of relationships—both family and social—between various persons. When a man makes a will, it is because he wants those he loves—generally his family—to have the substance and benefits of his worldly estate after he dies. Also, the laws governing intestate estates are based on the same premise—that members of a deceased person's family are his rightful beneficiaries. Thus, the great value of probate records lies in their content, and those explicit statements of relationship between those persons who made wills and the persons named therein stand as powerful (though incomplete) evidence in the family history "court."

Because more people are involved than just those who made wills (the testators) and those who died without so doing (the intestates), the true value of probates is multiplied far beyond what one might ordinarily expect. Every person named therein and every relationship stated therein increases the value of these records. A probate record is a family-oriented source, and families—complete families—after all, are the very essence of family history research.

In colonial and frontier America, the proportionate number of persons who left wills was greater than we often imagine. This is because our American forebears were a land-and-property-minded people. Land was inexpensive—sometimes free—and even those of humble circumstances could be landowners. Thus, the proportionate number of wills is likely to be higher in rural and agrarian communities than in the larger cities and industrial areas where large numbers of people lived in rented accommodations and owned nothing of sufficient value to warrant the making of a will.

Due to these issues, the family history researcher depends heavily on probate records. This is especially true for those earlier periods when the population was nearly all rural and practically everyone owned land. It is even more true in those time periods and those localities where few other records were being kept. And, not coincidentally, probate records meet the challenge very well.

III. THE LIMITATIONS OF PROBATE RECORDS

I will say more about record problems later, particularly as they concern individual record types; however, at this point I need to mention a few problems of a general nature. Though probate records are good, they are not a perfect source, and the following points illustrate how and why they fall short of that mark:

- It is obvious that not everyone left a will and, as I have already said, for some persons it is impossible to find any kind of probate record. And there would undoubtedly be many more wills if everyone who had intended to make one had done so.

- There are many cases where all of a person's children or other persons one would expect to be named are not actually named in those records relating to the probate of his estate. And even the surviving spouse is not named in every case. In a will, a person *usually* names his spouse and his living children, as these are the natural objects of his benevolence and the ones who normally have legal claim on his estate. If one or more of his children died leaving children of their own, he *may* name them (his grandchildren) as they too are his issue and appropriate objects of his bounty. If he had died intestate, they would have been legal heirs.

  Note my use of the words *usually* and *may* in the above paragraph. What is *usual* is never a sure thing, and what *may* be is even less certain. In fact, there are many wills wherein no one is named specifically but only by relationship—"my wife," "all my children," etc. And there are other times when people are named but relationships are neither stated nor apparent from the context.

- In intestacy, our problem is usually even more difficult because, in so many cases, until quite recent years, there are no statements in many of the surviving probate documents that give the names and relationships of beneficiaries.

- To find places of residence of next-of-kin stated, either in a will or in the proceedings of the court, is rare in early probate records. However, in the state of New York, when a petition for probate or administration was filed with the court, that petition required a list of all possible heirs (regardless of whether they were named in the will), plus their addresses. This practice dates back to about 1790. This requirement also became common in other states but not generally that early.

- To find the maiden surname of a man's wife or of his daughters-in-law in his probate records is almost unheard of, though we often find names of sons-in-law and brothers-in-law.

- Only occasionally can a person's date of death be found in the records of the Probate Court. However, any lack of that date is usually not serious because the date the will was made and the date that probate was granted establish an approximate time of death that is usually sufficient for identification.

- Not knowing a person's domicile at the time of his death is often a barrier to finding probate records for that person. He may live in one place for most of his life and then disappear about the time we expected he would have died. Because we can find no probate record, we erroneously assume there is no such record. What may be just as likely is that he moved in his old age to another place to live with one of his children. He would then die in that place, his estate would be administered, and the whole matter would be recorded there. Because there are few master probate indexes on a state level, it is usually necessary to know the county of a person's residence at the time of death in order to find his probate record. However, as more probate records are digitized and indexed, the problem of the late mover should become less critical.

    Note, also, that this problem is minimized in cases where real property (land) is owned in the former place because there should be an ancillary administration relating to that property. However, there is no ancillary administration unless the real property is in another state.

- Though probate records are usually indexed within each jurisdiction (mainly county), most of those indexes are to testators (the persons who made the wills) and intestates only and not to the beneficiaries or heirs. There are but few exceptions. Again, the digitizing and indexing of records that is now taking place will greatly help with this problem—but only if everyone named in these documents is included in the index. And all of this is going to take time.

Remember that probate records were not devised and created as a source for family history research. Rather, they were created as a legal vehicle for settling estates in the most equitable manner, legally dispersing the deceased person's earthly possessions, in an equitable manner, to those nearest and dearest to him. Though no records were created with family history as their prime objective, we must make the most of what is available, and probate records are among the best.

IV. LEGAL TERMINOLOGY

Though it may appear otherwise, my purpose here is not to write a legal dictionary. It is my hope, however, that I can help you gain an understanding of a certain amount of common legal terminology. Such an understanding will help you better understand probate records as a source of evidence relating to your forebears. And you will also be better able to understand other court records.

The various types of probate records are not included in this list but will be discussed in Chapters 17 and 18. As you study the following list, note the frequent use of the Latin abbreviation *q.v.* It is used to refer you to another definition; it literally means "which see."

ABUTTALS: The lands, roads, streams, etc., to which a piece of land is abutted (also called *buttals*). Sometimes the term is used to designate end boundaries as opposed to side boundaries, which are called *sidings*.

ACCOUCHEMENT: Childbirth.

ADMINISTRATION: Administration is a process, not a record. It involves the method of setting legal machinery to work in a particular probate case, as well as the modes of operation within the legal process until the estate is settled. This is necessary because the laws of descent and distribution are not self-implemented. They must be carried out by people within the scope of established legal machinery. The term applies to both testate cases and intestacies since the term *execution* (*q.v.*) is not in common use in this sense. Administration normally involves the collection, management, and distribution of an estate (*q.v.*) by the proper legal processes. (Based on this definition, I could have more accurately entitled this chapter "Understanding records relating to the administration of estates.")

ADMINISTRATION *CUM TESTAMENTO ANNEXO* (*C.T.A.*): (Administration with will annexed)—An administration of an estate (*q.v.*) granted by the proper court when the decedent (*q.v.*) left a valid will and (1) failed to name an executor (*q.v.*), (2) named an incapable person as executor, or (3) the named executor refused to act. Such administrations are carried out according to the terms of the will, as if by the executor.

ADMINISTRATION *DE BONIS NON* (*D.B.N.*): (Administration of the goods not administered)—Administration of any goods (*q.v.*) of a deceased person not already administered by a former administrator (*q.v.*). It relates to an administration started by one administrator but finished by another.

ADMINISTRATION *DE BONIS NON CUM TESTAMENTO ANNEXO*: Administration granted by the court when the executor (*q.v.*) of a will died before completing the administration of the estate (*q.v.*).

ADMINISTRATION WITH WILL ANNEXED: See ADMINISTRATION *CUM TESTAMENTO ANNEXO*.

ADMINISTRATOR: A person appointed by the proper court to administer a deceased person's estate (*q.v.*). He performs essentially the same duties as an executor (*q.v.*), but he is appointed by the court rather than by the deceased. He is bound to settle the estate strictly according to state statute unless appointed with the will annexed. (See ADMINISTRATION *CUM TESTAMENTO ANNEXO*.) He must give security by entering into a bond (*q.v.*) with sureties. See SURETY.

ADMINISTRATRIX: A woman who administers an estate (*q.v.*).

AFFINITY: A relationship (or rather a connection) through marriage rather than by blood. See CONSANGUINITY.

AGNATION: Kinship or relationship on the father's side, or by male descent. See also ENATION.

ANCILLARY ADMINISTRATION: An administration of property located in a state other than the state of domicile (*q.v.*) at death. It is a subordinate administration and is an indication that the main administration took place in another state (the record will usually tell you where).

APPURTENANCE: Something that is a subordinate part of something else. In a land deed, the term might refer to a right of way (*q.v.*) or other easement (*q.v.*). It usually refers to a legal right or privilege belonging to the land or to equipment needed for an activity associated with the land.

ASSIGNMENT: The transfer of a person's interest in property to another party or, more specifically, the document by which this is accomplished. The parties are known as the *assignor* (the one who makes the assignment) and the *assignee* (the one to whom it is made).

ATTEST: To bear witness to something, such as the execution (*q.v.*) of a will and thus to affirm formally with one's signature that the document was properly authenticated and is thus genuine.

ATTORNEY: An agent or substitute, or anyone authorized to act in another's stead. An *attorney in fact* is anyone appointed to act in behalf of another person's interests in private, business, or legal matters. Such authority is given by a document called a *power of attorney* or *letter of attorney* (see Chapter 20). An *attorney at law* is a lawyer who counsels and/or represents another person in legal matters.

BENEFICIARY: A person who receives benefit from a trust (*q.v.*) or from a life insurance policy. Those receiving property or goods by a will are also called beneficiaries. See also HEIR.

BEQUEATH: To give personal property (*q.v.*) by will. Distinguishable from *devise* (*q.v.*), which relates to real property (*q.v.*).

BEQUEST: A gift of personal property (*q.v.*) made by a will. It is also the personal property thus bequeathed (see BEQUEATH).

BODILY HEIRS: See HEIRS OF THE BODY.

BOND: A document guaranteeing that the person entrusted with responsibility related to someone else's property will perform faithfully. One person, called a surety (*q.v.*), pays the bond premium to guarantee performance by the person who is the responsible party.

BY THESE PRESENTS: See PRESENTS.

CHATTEL: A broad term for personal property (*q.v.*). It can include both animate and inanimate properties. All interests in real property (*q.v.*) *less than a freehold estate* (*q.v.*)—such as a lease—are also considered chattel. Until after the Civil War, the word chattel was also used as a euphemism for *slaves*.

COMMON LAW: That system of law that originated in England and was carried to her colonies. It is based on the authority of usage, custom, and court decrees rather than on statutory enactments. In the United States, it may also include parliamentary English law inherited and perpetuated in the colonies, unless repugnant to the U.S. Constitution or overruled by statute or by court action.

COMMUNITY PROPERTY: Property owned in common by the marital community of a husband and his wife as a marital partnership. It exists only in states where Spanish property law predominates, and all property acquired by either spouse during the marriage is community property. Separate property can also become community property through usage. Community property states are Arizona, California, Idaho, Louisiana, Nevada, New Mexico, Texas, and Washington.

CONSANGUINITY: Blood relationship, either lineal or collateral. See also AFFINITY.

CONSIDERATION: The price or motive, etc. (something for something), required in every contract.

CONVEYANCE: Another word for a land deed. It is the legal document by which title to real property (*q.v.*) is transferred.

CORPOREAL PROPERTY: Any property that can be seen and handled, as opposed to INCORPOREAL PROPERTY that exists only in contemplation. For example, a house is corporeal but the contemplated annual rents are incorporeal. Some incorporeal property such as easements (*q.v.*) can be inherited and is an appurtenance (*q.v.*) to the land.

COTENANCY: Joint ownership to land and/or personal property (*q.v.*). There are four types: (1) tenancy by the entirety, (2) joint tenancy, (3) tenancy in common, and (4) community property (*q.v.*). The first three types are associated with ownership of property as defined under English common law (*q.v.*):

1. *Tenancy by the entirety.* This is joint ownership of land by husband and wife with the right of survivorship. Today it is usually considered that the joint acts of both parties during their lives are essential to terminate the cotenancy, but historically the husband was deemed to have full control and the subject property could even be foreclosed to satisfy his private debts. Many states no longer recognize tenancy by the entirety in real property (*q.v.*), and most others no longer allow it unless created by specific language.

   This type of ownership probably had its origin in the premise of the archaic common law (*q.v.*) notion that a man and his wife were one person, and that one was the man. Historically, because of this, the main effect of tenancy by the entirety was that the husband had

full control, and the wife had no protection for her portion of ownership. Often wives who owned separate property were forced to deed
that land jointly to their husbands and themselves in a tenancy by
the entirety, the resulting effect of which was to divest them of their
property.

2. *Joint tenancy.* Joint tenancy is much like tenancy by the entirety but
is not limited to husbands and wives or to two owners, and it can be
terminated by the individual act (partition or sale) of any party. Each
owner has exactly the same rights and interest arising out of the same
instrument. The most important feature is the right of survivorship.

3. *Tenancy in common.* This is merely concurrent ownership by separate
titles of undivided portions of the same property. There is no right of
survivorship and each portion is held by fee simple (*q.v.*) title by its
owner and is freely transferable to others. Any party may terminate
the cotenancy. The shares owned by individual tenants need not be
equal.

COURT OF PROBATE: Any court having jurisdiction over the probate
(*q.v.*) of wills, the granting of administration (*q.v.*), the supervision of
the administration, and settlement of estates (*q.v.*) of decedents (*q.v.*). In
some states, these courts have names other than Probate Court, such as
Court of the Ordinary, Orphans' Court, Circuit Court, Superior Court,
Surrogate Court, District Court, County Court, etc. Each state has its
own system and its own laws.

CURTESY: The life estate to which a man is entitled under the common
law (*q.v.*), upon the death of his wife, in all lands she possessed in fee
simple (*q.v.*). Curtesy has been called the husband's version of dower
(*q.v.*), but curtesy was much more favorable to husbands than dower was
to wives. It is a husband's common law entitlement to a life estate (*q.v.*)
in the real property (*q.v.*) of his wife. For curtesy to apply, the couple
must have a living child capable of inheriting the mother's estate. Due to
a husband's superior status under the common law, he acquired a legal
right to the use and profits of his wife's real property at the time of their
marriage. Then, when a child was born to the couple who was capable
of inheriting that property, the husband (by common law) acquired a life
estate in the property. This right of the husband during his wife's life,
which was created by the birth of their first child, was called *curtesy initiate*. When the wife died, curtesy initiate became *curtesy consummate*.

Curtesy and dower rights have both been abolished in most states and
replaced by statutory inheritance laws for asset and property distribution. An important factor in abolishing dower and curtesy is their inherent gender discrimination. Joint tenancy (see COTENANCY) is now
widely used for possession and distribution of marital property.

CURTILAGE: The enclosed space of ground and buildings immediately
surrounding a dwelling house (*q.v.*) or that is habitually used for family

and domestic purposes. Barns, chicken houses, and gardens are considered as curtilage if located near the house.

DECEDENT: A deceased person, especially one who has died recently—either testate (*q.v.*) or intestate (*q.v.*).

DEGREE OF RELATIONSHIP: A term that differs in its meaning from *relationship*. Though these terms are sometimes used interchangeably, degree of relationship is actually a legal term and does not state a specific relationship (i.e., cousin, brother, second cousin once removed, etc.) of one person to another. Degree simply means step and represents the dis-

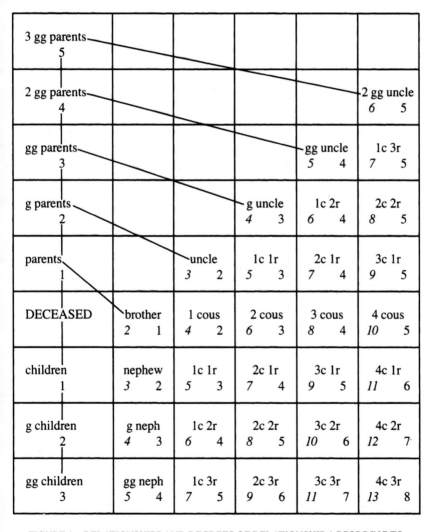

FIGURE 1—RELATIONSHIPS AND DEGREES OF RELATIONSHIP ACCORDING TO *CIVIL LAW* AND CANON LAW

tance between two persons who are related by blood. Under canon law (used in most states) two persons descending from a common ancestor, but not one from the other (brothers, cousins, etc.), have collateral consanguinity (*q.v.*) and a degree of relationship of the same number as the number of generations the furthest is removed from their closest common ancestor. For example, an uncle and nephew are related in the second degree because the nephew is two generations from the common ancestor (his grandfather and his uncle's father). Two brothers are related in the first degree, and first cousins are related in the second degree, and so on. In lineal relationships (direct line), each generation is a degree. This means that both a man's parents and his children are related to him in the first degree. (Figure 1 shows degrees of relationship under both civil law and canon law. Those for the *civil law are in italics* and are on the left.) Utah law prohibits marriage of persons whose consanguinity is less than the fifth degree under civil law. Using the chart, can you identify what marriages are prohibited?

DELIVERED: See SEALED AND DELIVERED.

DESCENT AND DISTRIBUTION: The area of statutory law relating to the transfer of a decedent's (see DECEDENT) property, both real and personal, to the proper persons (his heirs [*q.v.*] and next of kin [*q.v.*]) when he failed to leave a valid will. In addition to distribution of such property, it also relates to the rights and liabilities of these persons.

DEVISE: To pass on or convey real property (*q.v.*) by will. When used as a noun, it is the property so given. See also BEQUEATH.

DEVISEE: The person to whom real property (*q.v.*) is passed on or conveyed by a will. See DEVISE.

DEVISOR: A testator (*q.v.*) who disposes of real property (*q.v.*) by his will. Broadly interpreted, it is anyone who makes a will.

DOMICILE: The place of one's permanent home, and to which, if he is absent, he intends to return. The place of the decedent's (see DECEDENT) domicile at the time of his death is where his estate (*q.v.*) will be administered. There may also be ancillary administrations (*q.v.*) in other states where he owned real property (*q.v.*) when he died.

DONEE: A person to whom lands are given in tail. See TAIL, ESTATE IN.

DONOR: The person who conveys lands or tenements (*q.v.*) to another in tail. See TAIL, ESTATE IN.

DOWER: The lands and tenements (*q.v.*) to which a widow has a life estate (*q.v.*) after her husband's death, for the support of herself and her children. Under common law (*q.v.*), this was one third (in value) of all real property (*q.v.*) her husband owned in fee simple (*q.v.*) at any time during their marriage. There is no dower in community property states, and the laws of most other states today provide for the surviving widow in other ways.

DWELLING HOUSE: The house where a person resides with his family, including the curtilage (*q.v.*).

EASEMENT: A non-possessory right that a real property (*q.v.*) owner has (without profit) to use adjacent land, such as a watercourse or a right-of-way over that adjacent land.

EFFECTS: Personal property (*q.v.*) of any kind. On occasion, the context of a document will make this also include real property (*q.v.*).

ENATION: Kinship or relationship on the mother's side, or by female descent. See also AGNATION.

ENDOWMENT: Assigning (see ASSIGNMENT) or setting off the widow's dower (*q.v.*) by the administrator (*q.v.*) or executor (*q.v.*).

ENFEOFF: To bestow a freehold title in real property (*q.v.*) in exchange for pledged service. (See FREEHOLD ESTATE.)

ENTAIL: To limit succession of a title to real property (*q.v.*) by creating an estate in tail. See TAIL, ESTATE IN.

ESCHEAT: The reversion of property to the state (or, in feudal law, to the lord) when there are no qualified heirs (see HEIR) and no will. See also FEUDAL SYSTEM.

ESTATE: The sum total or aggregate of a person's property. An estate is not a legal entity so it cannot sue or be sued, although the term may have been used in court records for the sake of convenience. A person might also be referred to as having an estate in certain lands. Estate also is used to refer to the nature of a person's title to real property (e.g., fee simple [*q.v.*] estate, life estate [*q.v.*], etc.).

ESTATE TAIL: See TAIL, ESTATE IN.

ET UXOR: A Latin term meaning "and his wife," often used in indexing and abstracting—often written simply as *et ux.*

EXECUTION: Usually means *making* or *completing*. (The testator [*q.v.*] executes the will.) It can also mean *performing* or *carrying out* (in which case the executor [*q.v.*] would execute the will). However, the term is seldom used in this latter sense—the term *administration* (*q.v.*) usually being preferred. Technically, a document is executed when it is sealed and delivered (*q.v.*).

EXECUTOR: A person named by the testator (*q.v.*) in his will to see that its provisions are carried out after his (the testator's) death. The three-word term *custodian and administrator* was sometimes used. If more than one person is named, they are called *coexecutors* or *joint executors*. In modern practice, the more frequently used and preferred term is *personal representative.*

EXECUTRESS: See EXECUTRIX.

EXECUTRIX: A woman named in a will to administer it; also *executress.*

FAST ESTATE: See REAL PROPERTY.

FEE: See FEE SIMPLE.

FEE SIMPLE: In American law, an estate (*q.v.*) in land with the potential of lasting forever. The owner is entitled to the property to do with it as he wishes. He can convey it, devise (*q.v.*) it, or let it descend to his heirs after he dies. It is total ownership, although it may be subject to easements and restrictions. It is often designated by only the word *fee* or by *fee simple absolute*. (There are also defeasible fee estates, but these are less common. Such estates are terminated automatically upon the occurrence or non-occurrence of a specified event or condition. The failure of the specified event or condition leaves the fee absolute. For example, a man may leave certain property to his wife in fee simple, but with the provision that if she remarries, the property is to go to his son. Her failure to remarry leaves her fee simple title absolute.) A fee simple title can be taken for non-payment of taxes and is also subject to purchase under eminent domain for public use.

FEE TAIL: See TAIL, ESTATE IN.

FEUDAL SYSTEM: A system where the sovereign owns all the land and subsequently grants his rights in that land to other persons whom we might call tenants-in-chief. These men in turn grant rights to the land to others, and this chain of subordination (subinfeudation) might go on and on. Feudalism means the land is not owned by the person who appears to be its owner but is held by him from someone else. Those who hold the land have tenure (*q.v.*) in it and the types and forms of tenure vary, but most involve some type of service to the lord. Military service was important in early centuries. Also, payments of money, called quit rents (*q.v.*), were often involved.

Colonial grants in America were feudal grants, and land tenure in colonial America existed in a watered-down form. Feudalism, however, was done away with by the various states once they gained independence. (Its existence makes little difference to colonial land records because subinfeudation was not allowed once the property was in private hands.)

FIDUCIARY: A person who has taken upon himself a position of trust, responsibility, or confidence in another's behalf. An attorney (*q.v.*), an executor (*q.v.*), a guardian (*q.v.*), and a trustee (*q.v.*) are all fiduciaries.

FIEF: Something over which one has rights or executes (see EXECUTION) control. The term *fief* is seen only occasionally in early American (especially colonial) records and never in more recent records. Originally, the term related to land (the feud) held under feudal law on condition of rendering service to the proprietor. See FEUDAL SYSTEM.

FIXTURE: A chattel (*q.v.*) attached to the land and usually becoming part of the realty (*q.v.*) because of its attachment. A house is an appurtenance (*q.v.*) to the land, and the cupboards built into the house are fixtures.

FOLIO: A leaf. In old records, it was customary to number leaves rather than pages; hence, a folio would be both sides of a leaf or two pages.

Sometimes we find several pages numbered together in what is called a folio.

FREEHOLD ESTATE: An estate in land held for an undeterminable duration. There are four types: (1) fee simple absolute (see FEE SIMPLE), (2) defeasible fee (see FEE SIMPLE), (3) fee tail (see TAIL, ESTATE IN), and (4) life estate (*q.v.*).

GOODS: A term used to describe personal property (*q.v.*) but with varying definitions from place to place. Normally goods do not include animals or a leasehold (*q.v.*) title to real property (*q.v.*).

GOODS AND CHATTELS: The most comprehensive, all-inclusive, description of personal property (*q.v.*).

GUARDIAN: A person who has the vested right as well as the responsibility to manage the rights and property of another person, as of a minor child or a person incapable of managing his own affairs for some reason (insane, spendthrift, habitual drunkard, incompetent, etc.). A *testamentary guardian* is a guardian named in the will of the child's parent. Otherwise, the guardian is chosen by the election of the child or by the court.

GUARDIAN *AD LITEM*: (for the suit)—A guardian appointed by the court to represent the interests of a minor child or incompetent person in a specific lawsuit only.

HEIR: A person who inherits or succeeds to the possession of property, through legal means, after the death of another, usually his parent or ancestor. The term is generally applicable to cases of intestacy, but it is frequently used, in a popular sense, to designate any successor to a decedent's (see DECEDENT) property, either by will or by operation of probate law.

HEIRS AND ASSIGNS: These were "magic" words under common law (*q.v.*). They were essential in any conveyance (*q.v.*) granting a fee simple (*q.v.*) title. Though they are no longer necessary for that purpose in a deed or will, they are still often used. Typical wording would state that title to the subject property was transferred to a named person (or persons) and to his (or their) "heirs and assigns forever."

HEIRS OF THE BODY: All lineal descendants of a decedent (*q.v.*). It excludes any surviving spouse, adopted children, or collateral relatives. The use of the term makes no distinction as to whether a child was legitimate or was born out of wedlock. Though an adopted child has inheritance rights, he is not included within the meaning of this term. "Bodily heirs" is an equivalent term.

HEREDITAMENT: Something capable of being inherited—real (*q.v.*), personal (*q.v.*), corporeal (*q.v.*), or incorporeal (*q.v.*). See LANDS, TENEMENTS, AND HEREDITAMENTS.

INCORPOREAL PROPERTY: Personal property without physical substance. It has value but lacks physical substance. A lease, a mortgage, an easement, or some other property rights are examples. See also CORPOREAL PROPERTY.

INDENTURE: An agreement in which two (or more) parties are bound by reciprocal obligations toward each other and signed by both parties. Most deeds are not of this nature (though they may use this language) but rather are *deeds poll*, signed by only one of the parties, the grantor. Typically, we think of the indentured servant who agreed to labor for a certain number of years in return for some reciprocal benefit given by the other party, such as boat fare from Europe to America and room and board during the time of the indenture.

INFANT: Any person not of full legal age; a minor. Do not be confused into thinking of only babes in arms.

INSTRUMENT: See LEGAL INSTRUMENT.

INTERMARRIAGE: A term used in early legal documents to indicate that the marriage contract is a reciprocal and mutual arrangement by which each party was "married" to the other party. It does not suggest that the parties are related to each other or that they were of different ethnic backgrounds.

INTESTATE: As a noun, it is the person who died without a valid will; it is the opposite of testator (*q.v.*). It is also an adjective referring to the status of such a deceased person. In intestacy, the court, under the provisions of state statutes, provides for the distribution and disposition of the estate to the lawful heirs. A person who makes a will also dies intestate if, for some reason, that will is not valid. A person with a valid will can also die intestate as to part of his property.

ISSUE: All lineal descendants of a common ancestor are his issue—not his children only. The term is narrower than heirs, which includes spouses, ancestors, and collaterals (siblings, cousins, aunts, and uncles). See HEIR.

ITEM: It means *also* or *likewise*. You will see this word marking the beginnings of new paragraphs or divisions in a will.

JOINT TENANCY: One of three types of cotenancy (*q.v.*).

LANDS, TENEMENTS, AND HEREDITAMENTS: The most comprehensive description of real property (*q.v.*). It is the real property equivalent of "goods and chattels" (*q.v.*). This verbiage is frequently found in land deeds and wills and is a good example of the legal propensity to use three words when one would have been sufficient.

LATE: Defunct; living recently but now deceased.

LEASEHOLD: An estate (*q.v.*) in real property (*q.v.*) held under a lease. A leasehold title is usually considered a chattel (*q.v.*) or personal property (*q.v.*).

LEGACY: *Legacy* and *bequest* (*q.v.*) are equivalent terms. A legacy amounts to a gift of personal property (*q.v.*) by a will. It is often limited to money.

LEGAL INSTRUMENT: A formally executed written document that is legally enforceable.

LEGATEE: A person to whom a legacy (*q.v.*) is bequeathed. However, the term is often used to describe anyone receiving property by will, whether real property (*q.v.*) or personal property (*q.v.*).

LEGATOR: A person who makes a will and leaves legacies (see LEGACY). It is a relatively obscure and seldom-used term.

LIFE ESTATE: An estate (*q.v.*) lasting only during the life of the person holding it or for the duration of someone else's life. (This latter type is called a life estate *per autre vie.*) Widows were often given life estates in the wills of their husbands. Dower (*q.v.*) estates and curtesy (*q.v.*) estates were life estates.

LITIGATION: A judicial contest or lawsuit.

MESSUAGE: A dwelling house (*q.v.*), along with all of its outbuildings (*q.v.*) and curtilage (*q.v.*).

METES AND BOUNDS: Refers specifically to the boundary lines and limits of a piece of land. They are defined by reference to natural and/or artificial monuments such as trees, roads, ditches, rivers, etc. This method of describing land boundaries was used exclusively before the passage of the Land Act of 1785 and the introduction of the Rectangular Survey system (*q.v.*). In states not affected by that law, this method of describing land continues in use. However, the tools used by surveyors have changed dramatically, and technological improvements assure much greater accuracy. It is also used in connection with the Rectangular Survey (*q.v.*) system to describe a tract of land once a starting point is located within the system, but compass directions are used in the descriptions in place of geographical features. See also ABUTTALS.

MINOR: See INFANT.

MOIETY: Half (of anything). The term *moiety* generally refers to a half interest in real property (*q.v.*).

MONEY: A medium of commerce and exchange. Money during the colonial period of America was mainly English or based on the English system of pounds (£), shillings (s), and pence (d). There are 20 shillings in a pound and 12 pence in a shilling. Sometimes dollars are mentioned, but any similarity of these to our present dollar is purely coincidental (theirs bought much more). For a period in Virginia, tobacco was used as legal currency because of the scarcity of precious metals, and the Dutch in New Netherland used beaver pelts (called simply "beavers") and wampum (shell beads) as media of exchange. See also PROCLAMATION MONEY.

MOVABLE ESTATE: Personal property (*q.v.*).

MOVABLES: Not quite equivalent to movable estate (*q.v.*). These are personal property (*q.v.*) items belonging to a person that are in his control and can be moved about from place to place. They include inanimate objects, vegetable products, and animals in the possession, power, and use of the owner.

NATURAL AFFECTION: Affection existing naturally between near relatives and usually regarded as good and legal consideration (*q.v.*) in a conveyance (*q.v.*). In some deeds, "love and affection"—which has the same meaning—are named as the consideration.

NATURAL HEIRS: Has the same legal meaning as "heirs of the body" (*q.v.*).

NEXT-OF-KIN: A term used in the law of descent and distribution to identify the closest living blood relatives of the deceased. It is often used exclusively to identify those who would share in the estate (*q.v.*) under the relevant statutes.

ORDINARY: A judicial officer in some states (Georgia and formerly South Carolina and Texas) with power invested, by statute, relating to wills and other probate (*q.v.*) matters.

ORPHAN: A minor or infant (*q.v.*) whose parents are deceased.

OUTBUILDINGS: Sheds and other buildings, the use of which is associated with the house but are separate from the dwelling house (*q.v.*). These buildings are part of the messuage (*q.v.*).

PARTITION: The dividing of real property (*q.v.*) among all cotenants (see COTENANCY) according to their respective rights, regardless of the nature of their cotenancy. In the case of tenancy in common (*q.v.*), the court may require that partition be made by sale of the property.

PARTURITION: Giving birth to a child.

PER STIRPES: A Latin term meaning "by branch." It is used in the law of descent and distribution of estates (*q.v.*) to describe a method of dividing an intestate estate so a group of grandchildren of the decedent (*q.v.*) whose parent is also deceased take the share to which their parent would have been entitled if he were living—acting as a group and not as individuals. Today the term *by representation* is the term used more commonly. A *per stirpes* distribution is quite different from a *per capita* distribution, where each heir takes an equal share of the estate.

PERSONAL ESTATE: Personal property (*q.v.*).

PERSONAL PROPERTY: It is the same as goods and chattels (*q.v.*) and movables (*q.v.*). Personal property can be either corporeal property (*q.v.*) or incorporeal property (*q.v.*).

PERSONAL REPRESENTATIVE: The modern term used in wills instead of executor (*q.v.*) and executrix (*q.v.*). It is also used in connection with the administration of intestate (*q.v.*) estates instead of administrator (*q.v.*) and administratrix (*q.v.*).

PERSONALTY: see PERSONAL PROPERTY.

PLEADINGS: The written statements of the parties to a legal suit or action in which each presents, alternately, either his allegations or claims for relief on one side or his defense against those allegations or claims on the other side. The most common pleadings are the declaration, complaint, bill, or information of the plaintiff (the person bringing the action) and the answer of the defendant (the person against whom the action is brought).

PRESENTS: Literally means *this document* or *this instrument.* In legal documents, the term "by these presents" refers to the instrument in which the phrase itself occurs.

PROBATE: A term that means *prove,* especially the act of establishing the validity of a will that was produced before the proper court as the "last will and testament" of a certain deceased person. In American law, however, we find the word *probate* used as an inclusive term to describe all matters over which a court of probate (*q.v.*) has jurisdiction.

PROBATE COURT: See COURT OF PROBATE.

PROCLAMATION MONEY: Referring to uniform coin values that were established in the American colonies by royal proclamation in 1704. Where reference is made in early deeds or other conveyances (see CONVEYANCE) to the consideration being in "proclamation money" (or "proc. money"), this is what is involved. The proclamation was not enforced and was effectively ignored.

PROGENY: The descendants of a common ancestor; his issue (*q.v.*).

PROTHONOTARY: The chief or principal clerk who officiates in some courts. The title was used quite widely in earlier years but appears to be used today only in the courts of Pennsylvania and Delaware.

QUIT RENT: A rent paid by the tenant of a freehold estate (*q.v.*) discharging him from any other obligation or rents, usually just a nominal sum. Under the feudal system (*q.v.*), this was a payment made to one's feudal superior in lieu of services that might otherwise have been required.

REAL ESTATE: See REAL PROPERTY.

REAL PROPERTY: Property comprised of land and its appurtenances (*q.v.*), as distinguished from personal property (*q.v.*). The term applies to lands, tenements, and hereditaments (*q.v.*). It also encompasses both appurtenances (*q.v.*) and fixtures (*q.v.*). The term *fast estate* is sometimes used.

REALTY: See REAL PROPERTY.

RECTANGULAR SURVEY: A system of land survey adopted in the United States with the Northwest Ordinance of 1785. The law required public lands to be surveyed and described in terms of subdivision, section, township, and range before settlement. See also METES AND BOUNDS.

REGISTER OF WILLS: A county officer in some states who records and preserves all wills admitted to probate (*q.v.*), issues letters testamentary (*q.v.*) or letters of administration (*q.v.*), receives and files all accounts of executors (*q.v.*) and administrators (*q.v.*), and acts generally as clerk of the court of probate (*q.v.*).

RELATIONSHIP: See DEGREE OF RELATIONSHIP.

RELICT: The surviving spouse, either husband or wife, when the other spouse has died. The distinction is slight, but the term relates to the relict of the united pair and not of the deceased person.

RIGHT OF WAY: The right of one party, established by law, contract, grant, or usage for legal passage over the real property (*q.v.*) of another.

SEAL: A legal term used to denote document authentication. This usage is a carryover from the historical usage of a wax seal, carrying the imprint of the drawer's signet ring as a means of authenticating the document. This was especially important in times when most people could not write. However, as education became more widespread, wax seals lost much of their former significance, and the signatures on documents became more important than seals.

SEALED AND DELIVERED: Words describing the usual formula for attesting (see ATTEST) a document. These words, followed by the signatures of witnesses, indicate the document was effectively sealed (see SEAL) and the transaction was complete. Sometimes written: *signed, sealed, and delivered*. (Most states today have abolished the use of seals for legal purposes.)

SEIZED: The word used to express the seizin (*q.v.*) or an owner's actual possession of a freehold (*q.v.*) or fee simple (*q.v.*) title to property (sometimes spelled *seised*).

SEIZIN: The possession of a freehold (*q.v.*) or fee simple (*q.v.*) estate (*q.v.*) in land by possessing a proper legal title thereto (often spelled *seisin*).

SEPARATE EXAMINATION: The questioning by a court official of a married woman after she signed a deed or other instrument. The questioning, to establish her accord with the document, was conducted out of the husband's hearing to determine if she acted of her own free will and not under her husband's duress.

SIDINGS: The early designation in a deed of the property adjoining the subject land on its sides, when measured by metes and bounds (*q.v.*), as distinguished from the property adjoining on the ends, which were referred to as abuttals (*q.v.*). In actual usage, all adjoining properties were commonly referred to as abuttals.

SIGNED, SEALED, AND DELIVERED: See SEALED AND DELIVERED.

STIRPES: Latin term for the person from whom a family is descended. See *PER STIRPES*.

SURETY: A person who gives security, by means of a bond, to make himself responsible for another person's performance of a duty or responsibility should that other person default.

SURROGATE: In some states, a judicial officer with jurisdiction over probate matters, guardianships, etc. (New York and New Jersey).

TAIL, ESTATE IN: An estate (*q.v.*) in real property (*q.v.*) that does not descend to heirs (*q.v.*) of the donee (*q.v.*) generally but to only one line of his lawful issue, continuing in that direct line for as long as that posterity continues in regular order. When an owner in that direct line dies without issue, the estate is terminated. Estates in tail are illegal today in most jurisdictions because of the problems and confusion they create with land titles. (There is further explanation in Chapter 20.)

TENANCY BY THE ENTIRETY: One of three types of cotenancy (*q.v.*).

TENANCY IN COMMON: One of three types of cotenancy (*q.v.*).

TENANT: Strictly speaking, this is any person who possesses lands or tenements (*q.v.*) by any right or title, either in fee simple (*q.v.*), freehold (*q.v.*), leasehold (*q.v.*) for life, for years, at will, or otherwise. Usually, however, the term is used in a more restrictive sense to include only those who hold or are in possession of the lands or tenements (*q.v.*) that belong to other persons (called landlords), the term of tenancy usually being fixed by lease.

TENEMENTS: Refers literally to anything held by a tenant (*q.v.*) in tenure (*q.v.*), but the term is often applied only to houses and other buildings. See LANDS, TENEMENTS, AND HEREDITAMENTS.

TENURE: Occupancy or tenancy of any kind.

TESTAMENTARY: Pertaining to a will.

TESTAMENTARY GUARDIAN: See GUARDIAN.

TESTATE: The status of one who dies leaving a valid will. It is the opposite of intestate (*q.v.*). To die with a valid will is to die testate.

TESTATOR: A man who leaves a valid will in force at his death.

TESTATRIX: A woman who dies leaving a valid will.

THESE PRESENTS: See PRESENTS.

TO WIT: Namely; *videlicet* (*viz.*).

TRACT: A lot, piece, or parcel of real property (*q.v.*) of any size.

TRUST: The legal right or title to property held by one person (the trustee [*q.v*]) for the benefit of another (the trust beneficiary [*q.v.*]). The beneficiary holds an equitable title.

TRUSTEE: The person who holds and administers a trust (*q.v.*) estate. He holds legal title to property in behalf of the trust beneficiary (*q.v.*).

UXOR: Latin word for wife. See *ET UXOR*.

VALID: Legally binding.

VIDELICET: Abbreviated *viz.*; Latin term for *namely* or *to wit*.

VOID: Having no legally binding effect; invalid.

WILL CONTEST: Any kind of litigated controversy (see LITIGATION) concerning the eligibility of an alleged will to be admitted for probate (*q.v.*). It is not related to the validity of the will's contents (see Chapter 17) but to other issues.

YOUNGER CHILDREN: A term used in English conveyances and somewhat applicable in colonial America with reference to land settlements. It pertains to all children who are not entitled to the rights of the eldest son, who was the person who held the right to succeed to the estate (*q.v.*) of his ancestor under laws of primogeniture. The term included daughters who were older than that son.

V. IMPORTANT DETAILS

What I am writing here is with the assumption that the more you know about those legal processes that created the probate records that we use in our research (within limits of course), the more value those records will have for you. Based on this assumption, let me explain a few details about probate law and the probate process.

A. The Philosophy of Probate

The general rule is that all rights and property a person owns or is entitled to when he dies may be disposed of by a will, subject to the payment of just debts and other legitimate obligations. A competent testator, subject to certain restrictions, can dispose of his property in any way he desires.[1] He can leave it to his widow, to his children, to other relatives; or he can leave it to strangers—or even to his faithful dog or his favorite charity. Because the right and power to make a will are statutory and not natural (or absolute) rights, any restrictions that exist must be prescribed by state statute. And, based on that fact, various restrictions have been put in place to protect the rights of spouses and children.

Historically, under the common law, a married woman was considered incompetent to make a will of real property (even with her husband's consent) unless she had previously entered into an antenuptial contract or agreement (see Chapter 18) to preserve that right. A woman could, however, make a will (or testament) of personal property with her husband's consent. A widow or an unmarried woman was free from such restraints.

In more recent years, following the adoption of Married Women's Property Statutes, women generally have had the same probate rights as men. However, when those statutes were new, some courts failed to interpret them as they were intended.

---

[1] Under the English common law, when a man died, one-third of his estate went to his wife (dower), one-third to his issue, and one-third he could dispose of as he wished.

The above statements are the basic rules, but there are a few exceptions:

- Under common law, the widow's dower was usually preserved for her. It took precedence over any devise of realty in her husband's will unless she elected to accept the provisions of the will in lieu of dower or unless she had already forfeited her right to claim dower by a prenuptial agreement. In a few states, the widow could claim both dower and devised property.

- There are some states (Arizona, California, Idaho, Louisiana, Nevada, New Mexico, Texas, Washington) where property acquired by either husband or wife during their marriage is regarded as community property, the equal property of both—as a marital community—and neither husband nor wife can devise the interest of the other. (Community property law comes from Spanish property law and not from English common law. There are also some variations of these laws from one state to another.)

- Posthumous children (those born after the death of their father) who are not provided for in the will usually take of their father's estate as though he (their father) died intestate.

- In some states, if the parent has no children at the time the will is drawn and children were later born to him, the will is deemed to be revoked unless it includes provisions for such children.

- Living children who are not provided for by the will are usually allowed to take of the estate as if he died intestate, unless it appears their omission was intentional.

- Several states will invalidate a will when the testator leaves his property to charity, at the exclusion of his wife and children, unless the will was made at least a specified time (often more than one year) before the testator's death.

- Some states do not allow a will made in favor of a mistress and illegitimate children at the exclusion of the testator's wife and legal children.

- In Louisiana, the probate process is called "succession."

- In some cases, state law reserves certain portions of the deceased's estate, called "legitime," to his descendants who are under 24 or incapacitated. These descendants are called "forced heirs." If there is one forced heir, he is entitled to 25 percent of the estate. The rest will pass by inheritance laws or may be willed to others; if there are two forced heirs, one-half is disposable.

B. Legal Requirements

I mentioned earlier that a valid will could generally be made by any person (1) of sound mind and (2) of legal age who was also (3) free from restraint. Let us look briefly at each of these requirements:

1. Of sound mind: There is no absolute rule as to what the phrase "of sound mind" means, but in general, it does not require perfect mental sanity. Often a person may not be completely sane on all subjects yet have the capacity to make a will. The following quotation, though somewhat dated, provides a good definition. When considering records relating to people from past generations, old is often best.

> If the testator is able, without prompting, to summon before his mind, on the same occasion, and hold there for a reasonable time the nature of the business about which he is engaged, the persons who might naturally be the objects of his bounty and his relations to them, the kind and extent of the property to be disposed of, and the scope and effect of the disposition which he is about to make, he will be considered to have sufficient mental capacity to make a valid will. . . .
>
> It is not necessary that the testator know the number and the condition of his relatives, or that he should be able to give an intelligent reason for giving or withholding from any of them; nor that he should remember the names of absent relatives; nor that he should know the precise legal effect of the provisions which he makes in the will.[2]

The claim that a would-be testator was not of sound mind is one of the most common reasons for challenging the validity of a will. However, it is very difficult to establish.

2. Of legal age: Legal age is much easier to define than mental soundness. The age when a person becomes legally competent age-wise to make a will varies from state to state. In more than half of the states, it is now legal to make a will by age 18 (some earlier), but historically this has not been so. The most common "legal age" for making a will has been 21, though a few states have allowed persons younger than this to make wills (actually testaments) of their personal property.

3. Free from restraint: In order for a will to become void because of restraint or undue influence, such restraint must destroy the free will of the testator.

> Mere solicitations, however importunate, do not of themselves constitute undue influence, neither does honest persuasion, appeals to affection or gratitude, or to the ties of kindred, or for pity for future destitution; neither do fair and flattery speeches when not accompanied by fraud. To be sufficient the influence must amount to coercion or fraud, and must have overcome the free agency, or free will, of the testator.[3]

Those acts constituting undue influence or restraint may vary with each case. Often undue influence constitutes fraud, as has been suggested. This is a little easier to define and to deal with. A will becomes invalid if one of the following applies:

- The testator was fraudulently induced to sign a will that he believed to be another.

---

[2] Charles E. Chadman, ed., *Chadman's Cyclopedia of Law* (Chicago: American Correspondence School of Law, 1912), Vol. VII, 34–35. (I have chosen to use an old source because genealogy generally deals with old records. In this matter, however, time has wrought few changes.)

[3] Ibid., 50–51.

- The testator was deceived as to the content of the will he signed.
- A legacy was given to a person who fraudulently assumed a character not his real one.
- There have been any fraudulent impositions on the testator. (Only fraud by a beneficiary gives grounds for contest.)[4]

Whenever fraud is claimed, it must be proven.

There is a legal mechanism provided for the settlement of probate matters (whether there is a will or not). And, because of the required legal procedures, probate matters cannot be settled apart from that mechanism. Thus, when the researcher knows more about the nature and function of that legal mechanism, the records created as part of that process are a more valuable tool in the process of locating and identifying ancestors. In most states, probate law is of English origin with some statutory modifications. However, a few states settled by the French and Spanish—notably in the South and West—have statutes somewhat colored by French and Spanish law. In Louisiana, probate law is of French-Roman origin and has only gradually yielded to outside influences.

Whenever you use probate records, it is helpful to understand the basics of probate custom and law in the state where your problem is centered. Successful research may depend on that understanding.

---

[4] Ibid., 46–47.

17

What about Wills?

The word *will* has multiple definitions, but as a noun it is a wish or a desire; it can even be a command. In legal practice, which is our concern here, a will is the declaration of a person's wishes or desires—even his command—concerning the final disposition of his property after he dies. If properly executed, the provisions of that will become mandatory once his death occurs. The form of a will has no legal significance so long as it is properly executed.

A will, when it operates to pass on personal property only, is more properly called a *testament*, and sometimes, when it operates to pass on real property, is called a *devise*. However, the popular name for an instrument embracing both real and personal property is *last will and testament*. Nevertheless, for the sake of our discussion, we will just call them *wills*.

There have been many different approaches to wills. Some wills are even humorous (though they may not have seemed so to the families of those who made them). One that seems to be a favorite of lawyers reads, in part:

> To my wife, I leave her lover, and the knowledge that I wasn't the fool she thought I was. To my son I leave the pleasure of earning a living. For twenty-five years, he thought that pleasure was mine. He was mistaken. To my daughter, I leave one hundred thousand dollars. She will need it. The only good piece of business her husband ever did was to marry her. To my valet, I leave the clothes he has been stealing from me. To my partner, I leave the suggestion that he take some other clever man in with him at once if he expects to do any more business.[1]

Some wills are very long—others short. What is believed to be the longest will on record was made in Great Britain in 1919 and admitted to probate on

---

[1] Joe McCarthy, "To My Wife, I Leave Her Lover," *This Week Magazine* (September 26, 1965), 12. By permission.

2 November 1925 at Somerset House, the home of the British Principal Probate Registry, in London. It filled four bound volumes and contained 95,940 words—2,216 pages.[2] What is believed to be the world's shortest valid will was dated 19 January 1967 in Langen, Hesse, Germany. It simply said, "Vse zene" (the Czech for "All to wife").[3]

I. KINDS OF WILLS

Though a will is a specific kind of document, there are different kinds of wills in addition to what we think of as common everyday wills:

CONJOINT WILL: See JOINT WILL.

HOLOGRAPHIC WILL: A will that is written, dated, and signed all in the testator's own handwriting. There are differences in the statutes from state to state, but such wills do not generally require witnesses. They are sometimes—especially in Louisiana—called *olographic wills.*

JOINT WILL: A will made by two or more persons together and signed by both (or all). Such wills are usually executed to make testamentary disposition of joint property or of separately owned property to be treated as a common fund. Joint wills are sometimes called *conjoint wills.* They were especially popular with the Dutch in New Netherland because they protected their children from the orphan masters.

NUNCUPATIVE WILL: A will declared or dictated orally by the testator. Such wills can usually dispose only of personal property (in limited amount) and are valid only for persons in their last sickness, persons overtaken with sudden illness, or soldiers and sailors in combat. They are valid only if given before sufficient witnesses (numbers vary—usually two or three) and if they are reduced to writing within a limited time (usually six to twelve days). No special form is required in a nuncupative will, but it must appear that the testator intended his words to amount to his will and that he desired the persons present to bear witness that what he said was intended to be his will. Some states do not allow them.

The nuncupative will of Joseph Killgore was recorded in court as follows:

> Memorandum. That on the Thirtieth Day of April last past, we the Declarants being at the House of Joseph Killgore late of York dec[d]. when the Said Joseph was Sick on his Bed, when he had with him M[r]. John Frost writing his Will, and to our best discerning the Said Joseph was of Sound and disposing Mind and gave express Directions to the Said Frost with respect to the Disposition

---

[2] "Last will and testament of Frederica Evelyn Stilwell Cook," Wikipedia, 3 October 2016. https://en.wikipedia.org/wiki/Last_will_and_testament_of_Frederica_Evelyn_Stilwell_Cook (accessed October 26, 2016).

[3] Will of Karl Tausch noted in *The Guinness Book of World Records*, by Norris and Ross McWhirter. ©1968 by Sterling Publishing Co., Inc., New York 10016. By permission.

of his real Estate, but as to his personal, he then Said that it was his Will that (it being so Small) It was not worth while to put it into his Will, But that John Should have his moveable Estate except a Coat and Jacket to a grandson and Son of his Daughter, and the Said Joseph then and there declared that the above was his Will relating to his personal Estate, and desired the Declarants to bear Witness to it accordingly, or Words to that Effect.

In Witness whereof we have hereunto Set our Hands this fifteenth Day of May Anno Domini 1764.

John Frost
Gilbert Warren
her
Jane X Hasty
mark

York ss. York May 15, 1764.

Messrs. John Frost Gilbert Warren and M^{rs}. Jane Hasty the above Declarants personnally appearinge Severally made Oath the Truth of the above to which they have Subscribed,

Before. Danl. Moulton, Jus. Peac

York ss. At a Court of Probate held at New York May 15, 1764

The above Instrument being presented to me under Oath as the nuncupative Will of Joseph Killgore above named dec^d. I do hereby approve and allow the Same, and do commit the administration of the personal Estate of the Said Dec^d. above mentioned to his Son John Killgore to be administered according to the Direction of the Said Will.

Jer. Moulton. Judge

OLEOGRAPHIC WILL: See HOLOGRAPHIC WILL.

UNOFFICIOUS WILL: A will made in disregard to natural obligations of inheritance.

UNSOLEMN WILL: A will in which no executor is named. It will require the court to appoint an administrator *cum testamento annexo.*

While we are discussing wills, we need to talk also about codicils. A CODICIL is not a special kind of will, yet it deserves mention here because it is a supplement or an addition to a will that may explain or modify, add to or subtract from, qualify or alter, restrain or revoke provisions of the will itself. It is made with the same solemnity as the will and thus becomes part of the will. And wherever there are differences, it supersedes the will. There is no limit to the number of codicils that can be added to a will if they are properly executed. The late P. T. Barnum left a fifty-three-page will with eight codicils.[4]

Zachariah Gilson added the following codicil to his will. It is quite typical:

I Zachariah Gilson of Westminster in the County of Windham & State of Vermont do this 19th day of June in the year of our Lord Christ make and

---

[4] McCarthy, 12.

publish this codicil to my last Will and Testament in manner following that is to say, I give to my beloved Annah Gilson, the whole of her wearing apparel of every description for her to dispose of at her own election. I also give unto my daughter Uceba Bewster the sum of ten dollars to be paid in one year after my decease and furthermore I give unto my youngest daughter Lois Gilson - the sum of twenty four dollars to be paid within two years after my decease. And it is my desire that this my present Codicil be annexed to and made a part of my last Will and Testament to all intents and purposes. In Witness where of I have hereunto set my hand and seal the day and year above written.

Signed, sealed published and declared by the above named Zachariah Gilson as a codicil to be annexed to his last Will and Testament in presence of

John Sessions ⎤
Hannah Foster ⎬   (signed) Zachariah Gilson
Sally White ⎦

II. PROVING (PROBATING) THE WILL

Let us now take a simplified look at the steps taken by a typical will as it goes through the administration processes—from the time it is made until the estate is settled.

1. The first step is the making and proper execution of the document. When a person wants his estate divided in a different manner from that provided for by statutes, he must make a will. Stepchildren for whom a person may wish to provide ordinarily have no rights as heirs when there is no will. Also, there are cases where some children may have already received their portions. There are other cases where the testator may not wish to leave equal inheritances to all of his children but rather to show favoritism to one or more for some reason. Or, a specific piece of real estate or specific items of personal property may be reserved for a particular child. There are many different situations that might motivate a person to make a will.

When a will is created, all formalities that the law requires must be followed in order for it to be valid. Generally, this means that the will must be in writing, it must be signed, it must be acknowledged before competent and qualified witnesses who must so attest with their signatures—and in a few states, it must be sealed. (Use of the seal, which was such a commonplace thing in earlier years, has now been generally abandoned.) Those who serve as witnesses cannot be named as beneficiaries in the will.

A typical, modest, and relatively short will was made by Skinner Stone in 1764:

> In the Name of God Amen.
> I Skinner Stone of Berwick in the County of York & Province of the Massachusetts Bay in New England yeoman, being of sound mind and Memory tho weak in Body, expecting shortly to put off this Body, do commit the Same to the Earth to be buried with decent Burial at the Discretion of my

Execut^x hoping for a glorious Resurrection to Immortality, and my Soul into the Hands of God who gave it. Begging ye Pardon of all my Sins and the Salvation of my Soul thro the Merits and Mediation of the Lord Jesus Christ and with Respect to what worldly Estate God hath been pleas'd to bless me with I dispose of it in manner and Form following Viz^t

Imp^r I give and bequeath unto my beloved Wife Judith Item. the whole of my Estate real and personal for her Use & Improvem^t and for her to dispose of by Sale if She see Cause therefor, Provided she take Care for and be at the Charge of the Education & Support of Such of my Children as are here named viz' William Gabriel Jude Abigail & Patience till they come of age, or Shall be otherwise So disposed of at the Discretion of my Said Wife as not to Stand in Need of any assistance from her, excepting what of my Estate is otherwise disposed of as hereafter mentioned.

Item. I give to my beloved Son Jonathan Stone five Shillings lawful money to be paid by my Executrix.

Item. Such part of my Estate as may remain undisposed of at the Decease of my Said Wife Jude, I give and bequeath to my five children above named viz' William Gabriel Jude Abigail and Patience to be equally divided amongst them.

And I do hereby constitute and appoint my Said Wife Jude Stone the Sole Executrix of this my last Will & Testament And do hereby revoke and disannul all former Wills and Testaments whatsoever, and do confirm and declare this & this only to be my last Will and Testament.

In Witness whereof I have hereunto Set my Hand & Seal this 20th Day of March in the Year of our Lord One thousand Sevene Hundred and Sixty four.

Signed Sealed & delivered by ye said	his
Skinner Stone to be his last Will &	Skinner X Stone
Testam^t in presence of	mark
John Morse, Paul Stone	

After a will is made and is appropriately executed, a codicil may be added at any time before the testator's death—or a new will can be drawn if such is desired. Any new will that is properly executed automatically voids its predecessor; so, quite strictly speaking, the *last* will and testament is the only one that has legal effect. No special language is required in a will to invalidate the earlier will.

2. The second step is the death of the testator. If there is any action that can be taken prior to the testator's death, then the instrument is not a will, regardless of how it is worded or what its maker may have called it. The only exceptions to this would be either a document that was a combination of a will and something else[5] or a conditional will, the effectiveness of which depends upon the occurrence of some uncertain event or condition.

The rights of devisees and beneficiaries under a valid will become vested property rights immediately upon the death of the testator—but not one min-

---

[5] In such a case, the will segment of that combination document must meet the prerequisites of a will.

ute before. Those vested rights, however, do not become possessory until certain other steps are taken.

3. The next step is that the will must be presented for probate before the proper judicial authority to show it is what it claims to be—i.e., the last will and testament of the decedent. The executor or some other interested person must present the will upon his own oath before the proper court. (In each state, there are special courts that are responsible for the probating of wills, but these courts are not called by the same name in every state. There is more information about these courts, with their names and jurisdictions, later in this chapter.)

The will is ordinarily brought before the proper court to be probated by the filing of a written application or petition for probate. In more recent years, these applications have proven to be invaluable family history documents as they must include names of all of the testator's next-of-kin, their relationship or degree of relationship to him (with ages of minors), and post office addresses.

4. The next step is for the court to admit the will to probate. Usually a time is set for a hearing, and notice of that fact is published (sometimes directly to all interested parties and sometimes in a newspaper, or both, depending on state statute). If no one comes forward to contest the will at the hearing, it is considered that there is no contest and the will is ordinarily admitted to probate on the testimony of one of the witnesses whose signature attested its validity. Even in the case of contest, the testimony of only one witness is sufficient if that witness can verify due execution. Should all subscribing witnesses be deceased or incompetent or beyond reach of the court, the will can still be proven by other witnesses with only slightly more difficulty.

In more recent years, the probate laws of most states have provided the means for wills to be "self-proving" because of the legal requirements under which wills are witnessed and executed. Thus, the appearance of a witness is not required.

Having passed all of the necessary requirements, the will is admitted to probate and letters testamentary (legal authorization to proceed with the administration) are granted to the executor by the court.

5. Upon admission to probate and upon payment of a recording fee, the will is recorded (registered) by the court. In the modern probate court, this is usually accomplished by a photographic process, but historically wills were recorded by a clerk copying them verbatim in longhand into a will book—called a "Register"—kept by the court. It has not always been a legal requirement in most states that a will be thus recorded, but the advantages have generally been sufficient that most wills presented for probate were recorded.

In most states, before the era of photographic registration/recording, the original of every will submitted for probate was filed by the court in a special separate file (called a "dossier" or "probate packet") along with all other papers relating to the same probate case. This is in addition to the recorded or registered copy. Even wills that were never admitted to probate can usually be found in the probate packet or estate file.

In connection with the recording (registering) process, each will is, at the same time, usually included in the will index (by the testator's name). Most courts maintain a direct index—that is, an index to testators only. It is rare—but not unknown—for reverse indexes to be created. A reverse index is an index to the wills' beneficiaries. These indexes, when available, are of extraordinary value as a research tool.

As a side note, I think it is important to observe that, with the extensive digitizing and indexing of records now being accomplished by various family history websites, wills should have a high priority because of their family-based format and contents. Though it may be difficult and time-consuming to index the names and relationships of all persons named in a will, that procedure would create a resource of significant value to family history researchers. Though I see no evidence of this now, I hope the usefulness of this procedure will be understood and that this course will be chosen and followed as these valuable records are digitized and indexed.

6. Unless a will specifies to the contrary, the executor's proper performance must be guaranteed by a surety who posts a fiduciary bond. The executor then, with court authorization, proceeds to pay the just obligations of the deceased and have this action approved by the court. There is usually a "notice to creditors" published, and creditors file their claims against the estate.

The executor is bound to adhere unconditionally to the will's directions. Once probate has been granted by the court, the only permissible variations from the will's provisions are to settle all just debts and estate obligations and to set off the widow's dower (where applicable).

During the administration process, an inventory is taken and an appraisal made of the property. In more recent times, this appraisal is usually accomplished by appraisers, but that was not always the case. There may also be a sale (often by public auction) as part of the administration process to provide cash to settle obligations to creditors. And, as creditors are satisfied, they sign releases or receipts.

7. After the estate obligations are discharged and the court has given approval, the specific provisions of the will are carried out as stipulated.

Many states also require that a *decree of distribution* (or similarly titled document) be completed by the executor, through the court's authority, to show how the distribution to beneficiaries was completed. This document, issued and recorded by the court, is the final document in the probate proceedings and is often (again depending upon state statute) recorded both in the probate court and (when land is involved) with local land records.

In the probate court, this decree of distribution signifies that the executor has completed his job; and in the recorder's office (land records)—in those states requiring it—this gives notice to the world that title to real property has legally passed. These documents generally do not go back a long way historically, but they are valuable as far as they go. The beneficiaries may have signed receipts also.

If the executor happened to die before his responsibility was discharged (and this may have been either before or after the death of the testator), or if he renounced his right, the court would have appointed another person in his place to carry out the provisions of the will as if he (the replacement) had been named executor himself. This replacement person is called the administrator (*de bonis non*) *cum testamento annexo* (with will annexed). Such an appointment is made by court order and is registered in the court along with the petition by which that appointment was requested.

Other records that could have been created as the administration process was carried out include petitions for dower, petitions and accounts relating to the support of orphans and the appointment of guardians (discussed in the next chapter), powers of attorney, etc.

III. THE CONTESTED WILL

One family history benefit of probate records is the fact that people try to get everything they think they have coming and often a little bit more, if they think they can. If the will does not give a person what he feels is due to him, or if he is omitted completely, he will probably look for grounds to contest it—usually that the testator was not of sound mind, that the will was made under restraint or undue influence, that it was not properly executed, or that some essential statutory requirement was not met by the will's provisions. The following 1966 news story from a Salt Lake City newspaper illustrates a typical case:

> KANSAS COURT HEARS UTAHN'S 'WILL' CASE
>
> Phillipsburg, Kan.—The case of a Salt Lake City man who is contesting his uncle's will was continuing Thursday before District Judge William B. Ryan. George T. Hansen Jr., president of the Hyland Oil Corp. of Salt Lake City, is seeking to have the will of the late Dane G. Hansen, who left a fortune estimated at $9 million, declared invalid.
>
> The Salt Lake City man was left $10,000 under terms of the will. The elder Hansen left $1 million for a family trust fund and the remainder of his estate to a foundation for charitable, educational and scientific purposes.
>
> The younger Hansen alleges his uncle was not competent when the will was signed. Hansen died Jan. 6, 1965, and his will was admitted to probate Feb. 12, 1965. He was 82 when he died of cancer.
>
> Hansen was a bachelor and accumulated his wealth as an oil producer and a highway and bridge contractor.
>
> Two witnesses to the will signing testified Tuesday that Hansen was mentally competent when he signed the document Nov. 2, 1964. A third witness, Dr. A. E. Cooper of the Norton County Hospital staff, was expected to testify Wednesday.[6]

---

[6] *Deseret News* (March 25, 1966), 12C. By permission.

Note that not everyone has the legal right to contest a will: only those who have an interest in the estate, and only then if they would receive more through laws of intestate succession than through the will.

When a will is contested, a lawsuit ensues with the executor as the defendant. (He is, of course, the natural defender.) Some states require that all interested parties must be made parties to such a suit, either plaintiff or defendant, including also the husbands of female heirs. Thus, the names of all these persons will be in the complaint because they are indispensable parties.

The documents resulting from such a suit can be a virtual gold mine of family history evidence. When Philip Ryon died in Clark County, Kentucky, in the 1850s, some of his children contested his will. Philip had been twice married and left families by both marriages. However, when he died at a "good old age," his will left everything to the second wife and her children. The first wife's descendants contested the will and presented their arguments and evidence, thus providing a skeletal record of Philip Ryon's descendants. The contention was that Philip, in his old age, was not of sound mind and that he acted under undue influence from family members (and they won their case).

Though relatively few wills are ever contested, if a will of your ancestor has been contested, it is important for you to know about it. The existence of the contest and the records arising therefrom are usually quite easy to ascertain.

The procedure differs somewhat from state to state. In some states, contested wills are registered as if there had been no contest, and a notation of the contest is in the book of registered wills. This notation might be included after the recording of the will itself, where information about probate is usually given, and there is often a direct reference to the location of the record of the contest. Some other states do not record contested wills unless the contest fails and the will proceeds to probate. These differences are based on the probate laws of the various states and on whether such lawsuits can be handled in the court with probate jurisdiction or somewhere else.

There are also other procedures followed, especially in more recent times, but you can easily learn if a will has been contested. Sometimes there is a notation in the will index, and in other places, a special register of will contests is kept by the court clerk.

You should be aware that in nearly every state, the clerk of the court keeps a special, indexed book, called a probate docket, with a separate page for each case. Every document filed with, or created by, the court relating to the case is listed on that page. Thus, by looking at the page in the docket book relating to any probate case, you can tell immediately if the will was contested and be guided to the proper documents. This process is controlled by state law, and there are slight variations.

In most, but not all, states, a will contest is tried in the court of original probate jurisdiction, but judgments by that court can be appealed to a higher court. Such appeals are rare, but they do happen. Ordinarily, however, there will be no more information in the appellate court record than from the trial court record because no new facts are added to a case on appeal.

Though the record of the trial court is sent up to the appellate court with the appeal and becomes part of that court's record, it also remains in the trial court. There will also be an opinion written by an appellate court judge that might be of interest and historical value, but it will provide no additional family history information.

On occasion, other records (such as land records) offer clues relating to probate contests. For example, a deed may state that the grantor received the land he is selling because of such and such suit in probate court. Never ignore such a clue.

Even family traditions might tell of circumstances that make a lawsuit probable; do not overlook them. A man who has married more than once and died leaving families by all of his wives could easily create such a condition if there were hard feelings between the families and/or apparent inequities in his will. (There is further discussion about courts and their records in Chapter 22.)

IV. THE VALUE OF WILLS

Having discussed the legal details involved in probating a will, let us look now at the value of the records and what they mean to us as researchers.

A. Relationships

As mentioned earlier, the most significant quality of wills is the fact that they usually identify specific relationships—direct statements of relationship between people by someone who knows. Nothing is more critical in our research than information on how people are related to each other, and this is direct evidence from a primary source! Names, dates, and places mean little unless these relationships are established. Most other records are of lesser value in this critical area.

B. Time period

I have also mentioned this before, but again I stress that we can often find wills and other probate records for people who lived during periods and in places where there are few other records. Also, most of these are reasonably accessible and are becoming more accessible as the records are being digitized and indexed on major family history websites.

C. Less obvious values

In addition to the more obvious values of wills, let us look at some values that are often less apparent:

- A will often gives clues to former places of residence. Consider, for example, the will of Samuel Wheelwright (Vol. I, p. 69, York County,

Massachusetts) wherein he names the place where he previously held land:

> Item. I do give and bequeath unto Hester my beloved Wife . . . all the rent which was dew to me from my land at Crofts in the County of Lincoln in England until the time it was sold by Mr. Ed^w Loyde.

- When a name is common, legacies mentioned in a will can sometimes be traced to prove relationships. For example, if there are three contemporaries named Samuel Black living in the same locality, wills can often help prove (or disprove) parentage. You may find a William Black giving 200 acres of a certain description to his son Samuel. Once this information is known, your task is to locate the conveyance whereby one of the three Samuels disposed of that identical parcel of land. Then, if you can positively identify the Samuel who sells this land, you will know whether he is your Samuel and thus William's son (or not).

- A will may also give you an idea about the existence of other records. A man may mention his religious affiliation in his will, thus leading to church records—often the specific parish or congregation. A man's profession is very often indicated in his will, either directly or indirectly. If he owned land, that mention is a clue to search land records. If he has extensive property, financial means, or social prominence (usually quite obvious in his will), published sources may be available that tell something about him. Previous military or naval service is also frequently mentioned in a will.

- Records of a will's probate may also provide information on when the testator's death occurred—sometimes the exact date. There are occasions where that information is essential for identification.

- Those persons named as executors, those who signed as subscribing witnesses, or those bound as sureties for bonds are often relatives. A careful study of records relating to those individuals may lead to more information about our ancestors.

V. RECORD PROBLEMS

Chapter 16 discussed some general problems with probate records as a family history source. Let us look now at some specific problems relating to wills and consider a few examples without rehashing what has already been said. Of course, not every will has problems, and not all problems are manifested in the same way from one will to the next. Following are some of the more common problems.

A. Incomplete listings of family members

A man may omit the names of one, some, or all of his children from his will, and he may neglect to tell his wife's name since he has only one and her identity is "observable." If his children are previously deceased, especially if they died young, they may not be named. A child who died as an adult may still be named in his parent's will if he left a spouse and children to receive his portion. Also, if a person died intestate, the children of that deceased child were heirs to their parent's portion.

Children who had already received their inheritance are sometimes left unmentioned, and a child who was disowned might also go unnamed. Thankfully, however, neither of these two circumstances always caused an omission. Statutes differ, but most states do not allow a child to be omitted unless the intent of the parent to do so is expressed in the will. Exceptions to this are those cases where (1) the entire estate was left to the testator's other spouse and (2) clear evidence shows that the child was provided for outside the will.

Statutes protect a person's children from being negligently overlooked. They safeguard the rights of children born after the will was executed, and they protect the rights of children mistakenly believed to be dead. Most statutes that protect the overlooked or pretermitted child, as such is called, typically provide for the child to take of the estate as if the parent had died intestate. Because of such statutes, there are often records in the Probate Court, in connection with the settlement of the estate, that help us fill the gaps.

B. Inconclusive relationships

This problem is better illustrated than described, so let us consider the will of Francis Champernoun as an example (York County, Massachusetts, Vol. I, p. 55, probated December 25, 1687). (I used this same example in Chapter 2.)

> I give and bequeath & confirm unto my Son in Law Humphrey Elliot & Elizabeth his now wife . . . the other part of my sd Island . . .
>
> Item. I give and bequeath unto my Son in Law Robert Cutt my daughter in Law Bridget Leriven my daughter in Law Mary Cutt and my daughter in Law Sarah Cutt . . . all that part of three hundred acres of land belonging unto me lying between broken Neck and the land formerly belonging unto . . .

Based on this evidence alone, it is unclear how all of these persons are related and the connections are thus left to speculation. It seems quite unlikely that they are all the children-in-law of the testator, especially in view of the surnames of the females. Perhaps some (or all) were stepchildren. More research is needed.

C. No relationships

Again, let us go to an example to illustrate the problem. This one is from the will of Jeremiah Willcox (Pasquotank County, North Carolina, Vol. 34, p. 44, probated in July Court 1754):

> I give and bequeath to my son Stephen Three hundred acres of land . . .
>
> . . . [Some other land is to be sold to a certain party] and if not I leave it to my Two Daughters Sarah and Ruth . . .

I give to *Elizabeth Wakefield Living in Virginia* Two Cows and one calf
Called Blossom & Pyde and all the Rest of my Cattle to be Equally Devided
Between my wife and my Three Children . . .

I Leave my Loving wife Elizabeth all the Remainder of my house hold
goods. . . . [Emphasis added; see Figure 4, Chapter 2.]

The question here is about "Elizabeth Wakefield Living in Virginia" to
whom Jeremiah gave livestock. He did not tell us who she is. It does not appear that she is his child because he seems to have had only three children,
Stephen, Sarah, and Ruth. More evidence is needed.

We also see many cases where a spouse and children are mentioned and
provided for but are not named.

D. Wife and children not related

If a man has married more than once, that fact is not usually something
he mentioned in his will. This means that the named wife may or may not be
the mother of some or all of the named children—and you have no way to
tell without more evidence. Also, if you know she is the mother of only some
of the children, it is difficult to tell which ones. In this kind of situation, it is
often impossible to identify even the existence of a problem based only on the
information in the will.

E. Other problems

You will encounter other common difficulties as you use wills in your research. These problems include spelling, nicknames, handwriting, and legal
jargon. Most of these, however, can be solved by the conscientious researcher.
There are no general solutions other than those already given. Each problem
is unique and must be studied and solved (if possible) on its own merits. Evidence from other sources is essential.

VI. FINDING AND USING WILLS

A. Original and registered wills

Most wills in the United States are registered and filed in the counties where
they were probated (at the testator's place of domicile). There are, however,
a few states with non-county probate jurisdictions. Also, though the name of
the responsible court may be different, each court's duties relating to probate
matters are the same.

The present name of the relevant courts and the applicable court jurisdiction in each state are as follows:

ALABAMA: Probate Court in the county.

ALASKA: Superior Court in specified areas within four
                                judicial districts. (Judicial districts are unre-

lated to the state's boroughs [county equivalent]. Probate jurisdiction prior to statehood [3 January 1959] was in the District Court. The Family History Library in Salt Lake City has an index to these pre-statehood records.)

ARIZONA: Superior Court in the county.

ARKANSAS: Circuit Court in the county. (There are twenty-three circuits, each with several divisions that do not necessarily correlate to county boundaries. There is at least one county seat in each county [some counties have two] and a courthouse in each county seat.)

CALIFORNIA: Superior Court of California in the county.

COLORADO: District Court in the county—except Denver County, including Denver City, which has a Probate Court. (Excluding the Second Judicial District, which is the city and county of Denver, there are twenty-one judicial districts.)

CONNECTICUT: Probate Court in the district. (The state is divided into fifty-four Probate Court districts, with most large towns, and many smaller towns, having their own probate districts. Many of these districts cross county boundaries. The "Probate Court Directory" has current court locations with addresses, phone numbers, and fax numbers.)

When the original Connecticut counties were formed in 1666, probate jurisdiction was in the County Court. (All extant original county and early district probate files are at the State Library, where there is a complete index from 1641. There is a microfilm copy of both the files and the index at the LDS Family History Library. There is also a "Probate District Guide" in the State Library showing which probate district or court covered each of the towns or cities.)

DELAWARE: Court of Chancery in the county. (Although this court has probate jurisdiction, all probate records—and card indexes to them—are in the Hall of Records, Dover.)

DIST. OF COLUMB.: Probate Division of the Superior Court of the District. (There are some transcripts in the National Archives, 1801–88, but originals more than ten years old are available at Probate Systems Office, Probate Division, 515 5th Street, NW, Washington, DC 20001.)

FLORIDA: Probate Division of Circuit Court in the county. (There are twenty judicial circuits.)

GEORGIA: County Probate Court.

HAWAII: Circuit Court. (There are four circuits for the six inhabited islands: [1] Oahu; [2] Maui, Molokai, and Lanai; [3] Hawaii; and [4] Kauai.)

IDAHO: Magistrate Division of the District Court in the county. (There are seven judicial districts in the state with a District Court in each county.)

ILLINOIS: Probate Division of Circuit Court in the county. (There is a Circuit Court in each county and twenty-four judicial circuits in the state.)

INDIANA: County Probate Court has jurisdiction in St. Joseph County. The Superior Court (in the county) has jurisdiction in Allen, Madison, Hendricks, and Vandenburgh counties. The Circuit Court (in the county) has jurisdiction in all other counties. However, the Superior Court and the Circuit Court have concurrent jurisdiction in Bartholomew, Elkhart, Grant, Johnson, Lake, LaPorte, and Porter counties.

IOWA: District Court in the county, sitting in probate. (There are eight judicial districts in the state and a District Court in each county.)

KANSAS: District Court in the county. (There are thirty-one judicial districts in the state and a District Court in each county.)

KENTUCKY: District Court in the county. (There are fifty-nine judicial districts in the state and a District Court in each county.)

LOUISIANA: District Court in the parish (county equivalent). In Orleans Parish, the Civil District Court. (There are forty-two judicial districts in the state outside of Orleans Parish and a District Court in each parish.)

MAINE: County Probate Court.

MARYLAND: Register of Wills in the Orphans' Court in Baltimore City and in every county except Harford and Montgomery, where Circuit Court judges are the Orphans' Court judges. (All Maryland probates—in fact all official records—prior to 1788 are at the Hall of Records, Annapolis, as per state statute. Many other records since that time are also filed there for safekeeping, at the discretion of county officials.)

MASSACHUSETTS: Probate and Family Court in the county.

MICHIGAN: Probate Court in the county or district. (There is one court in each county, except for ten counties that have consolidated to create five Probate Court districts. Those combined counties are [1] Charlevoix and Emmet, [2] Alger and Schoolcraft, [3] Clare and Gladwin, [4] Mackinac and Luce, and [5] Mecosta-Osceola. The two counties involved in each case share one probate judge because their populations are small. However, each county may have a separate probate register, and files unique to a county are in an office located in that county.)

MINNESOTA: District Court in the county. There are ten districts in the state and a District Court in each county (except Hennepin, Anoka, and Ramsey counties, where there are Probate Courts).

MISSISSIPPI: Chancery Court in the county. (There are twenty districts in the state and a Chancery Court in each county.)

MISSOURI: Probate Division of the Circuit Court in the county. (There are forty-five circuits in the state and a Circuit Court in each county.)

MONTANA: District Court in the county. (There are twenty districts in the state and a District Court in each county.)

NEBRASKA: County Court. (There are ninety-three County Courts in twelve judicial districts.)

NEVADA: County Probate Commissioner in the District Court. (There are nine judicial districts and a District Court in each county.)

NEW HAMPSHIRE: Circuit Court Probate Division in the county. (There are ten divisions, one in each county. Probate records before 1771 were kept in the provincial capital; those between 1735 and 1771 have been published. Transcripts of these early records are in the State Archives Room in the Library of the New Hampshire Historical Society, 30 Park St,. Concord, NH 03301.)

NEW JERSEY: Surrogate's Court in the county. All New Jersey original wills and inventories up through 1952 are on file at the New Jersey State Archives. (Thirteen volumes of will abstracts, 1670–1817, have been published and are completely indexed.) Current jurisdiction is in the County Surrogate Court, and copies of records since 1901 are available from the county Surrogate Court or from the Clerk of the Superior Court, Records Information Center, P.O. Box 967, Trenton, New Jersey 08625-0967. Also, many New Jersey probate records have been digitized and indexed on the Ancestry.com website.

NEW MEXICO: County Probate Court has jurisdiction over uncontested estate cases. (There are thirteen judicial districts and thirteen counties. Contested cases go to District Court for trial.)

NEW YORK: Surrogate's Court in the county. (Historically [until about 1846], the County Clerk had custody of probate records in counties with less than 40,000 population. Today every county has a Surrogate's Court.)

NORTH CAROLINA: Superior Court in the county. (All records prior to 1760 were kept on a colony-wide basis, and some as late as 1780 were recorded by the Secretary of the Province.)

NORTH DAKOTA: District Court in the county. (There are eight districts in the state and a court in each county.)

OHIO: Probate Division of Court of Common Pleas in the county.

OKLAHOMA: District Court in the county. (There are twenty-six districts in the state and a District Court in each county.)

OREGON: County Court in Gilliam, Grant, Harney, Malheur, Sherman, and Wheeler counties; Circuit Court in all other counties.

PENNSYLVANIA: Register of Wills in the County Court of Common Pleas.

RHODE ISLAND: Every city or town has its own Probate Court.

SOUTH CAROLINA: Probate Court in the county. (Until 1785, all estate administrations were at Charleston.)

SOUTH DAKOTA: Circuit Court in the county. (There are eight circuits in the state and a Circuit Court in each county.)

TENNESSEE: Probate Court in Shelby County, Probate Division in the Chancery Court in Davidson County, and Chancery Court in all other counties. In Dyer County, the Probate Court and the Chancery Court have concurrent jurisdiction.

TEXAS: County Court as a general rule, but some larger counties have Probate Courts.

UTAH: District Court in the county. (There are eight districts in the state and a District Court in each county.)

VERMONT: Probate Division of District Court. (The districts in the north are the same as the counties, but the five southern counties of Bennington, Orange, Rutland, Windham, and Windsor each have two districts per county. A copy of each will is also recorded in the town clerk's office in the town where real property devised in the will is situated.)

VIRGINIA: Circuit Court in the counties and independent cities (see Chapter 22 for information on independent cities).

WASHINGTON: County Superior Court.

WEST VIRGINIA: County Court.

WISCONSIN: Circuit Court in the county. (There are ten administrative districts for the Circuit Courts. Each of sixty-six counties has its own Circuit Court, while three Circuit Courts serve two counties each: Buffalo and Pepin counties share a circuit, as do Florence and Forest counties, and Shawano and Menominee counties.)

WYOMING: District Court in the county. (There are nine districts in the state and a District Court in each county.)[7]

---

[7] The source of this information in earlier editions was *Martindale-Hubbell Law Dictionary*, 120th ed. (Summit, NJ: Martindale-Hubbell, Inc., 1988), Vol. VIII (by permission) as well as correspondence with various court officials. In this edition, that information has been updated using court websites of the individual states and by other correspondence.

Except where indicated otherwise (with very few exceptions), the courts listed above have custody of the probate records of their respective states. The main exceptions are states like Delaware, New Jersey, North Carolina, and South Carolina where older records have been, or are being, transferred from the courthouses to state archives and libraries for safekeeping.

As mentioned earlier, in addition to the recording of probate records in those courts with probate jurisdiction, some states also require that certified copies of decrees of distribution, affidavits of heirship, probate decrees, and even wills be registered with the custodians of land records and recorded by them as proof of title whenever land is devised.

Some archives and some family history libraries, such as the Family History Library in Salt Lake City, are also interested in these records and are working for their preservation. The Family History Library has had an energetic microfilming program in the counties of several states, and recorded probate records (with their indexes) have always been considered an "essential" source. That library has also cooperated with a number of the states' archives and other agencies in microfilming projects. Copies of many records already filmed have also been purchased.

These microfilm acquisition programs, as shown by my past-tense verbs, are now outdated. The library is working to collect these records at a rapid and ever-accelerating pace but is digitizing rather than microfilming. They do not claim to have all, or even most, of the available probate records, but they are gathering them, and the collection is significant. Not only are they accumulating these records, but they are also giving them high priority in their indexing program.

I have not identified indexed records on the above list because such identification would soon be outdated. I suggest, instead, that you enter the name of the locality of your interest, plus "probate records" or "wills" in your search engine space. Such a search will reveal immediately if those records have been indexed. If they are not indexed when you first look, you can come back later and try again. The pace of indexing makes more of these records available every week on one website or another.

B. Published wills and abstracted wills

I indicated earlier that some probate records have been published and are available in book form in various places. The quality of these publications varies considerably, so no generalized comment about quality is appropriate. These publications have been helpful in the past because they have made information available that would otherwise be difficult to access. However, with all the records that have been microfilmed and are now being digitized, as well as those records being digitized from original will books, these published works have less value for us than they have had in the past. If the originals, films, or indexed digitized copies are available, they are the records you should use.

In the past, various people and organizations undertook to make typescript abstracts (abbreviated extracts with only "essential" data) of wills and publish those abstracts. Though some are quite accurate, you should use them with extreme caution because there is no good way to judge their accuracy.

A few years ago while doing research on a problem in Woodford County, Kentucky, I had occasion to use some typescript will abstracts, which proved quite interesting—and frightening. With this particular problem, I also gained access to microfilms of the county's registered wills so I was able to make a comparison. In the abstract of the will of George Blackburn, Sr., in 1817, the following beneficiaries were listed:

1. Wife Prudence
2. Son-in-law William White
3. Daughter Mildred White
4. Son Churchill J.
5. Son Jonathan
6. Daughter Harrett
7. Daughter Margaret Kinkade
8. Daughter Maria
9. Son Edward
10. M. B. George
11. Daughter Nancy Bartlett

From the microfilm copy of the registered will, I extracted the names of the following beneficiaries.

1. Wife Prudence
2. Son-in-law William White
3. Daughter Mildred White
4. Son Jonathan
5. Son Churchwill J.
6. Son George Blackburn, Jr.
7. Daughter Margaret Kinkiad
8. Son Edward M.
9. Daughter Nancy Bartlett
10. Son William B.
11. Daughter Elizabeth Peart
12. Daughter Mary Holloway

It is interesting to compare the two lists. The discrepancies between the two provide a good illustration of why we should use the originals or the records on digitized databases. First, note that some of George Blackburn's children were missed in the abstract: the son William B. and the daughters Elizabeth Peart and Mary Holloway. Also, we have no idea who M.B. George is, and the two persons named in the abstract as "Daughter Harrett" and "Daughter Maria" were not daughters at all but listed in the will as slaves bequeathed by George to his wife Prudence. There were also some minor spelling variations.

C. Indexes

Three kinds of indexes need to be mentioned here:

1. Direct will indexes—those prepared and continuously updated in the will registers by court personnel when the wills were probated and put on record in the court. These are indexes to testators, those persons who made the wills.
2. Reverse will indexes—these are indexes to the beneficiaries named in the wills. They are not common.
3. Database indexes—those indexes prepared from digitized computer databases.

Let us examine the use and value of each of these.

1. Direct will indexes

If you are looking for a will on microfilm in a county courthouse or on a county or state website, you will normally utilize this kind of index. You must know the jurisdiction to use this index. It is an index to testators only—those persons who made the wills. There were varying approaches used by different jurisdictions in preparing these "direct" indexes, but you can understand most of them quite easily because they are generally in some type of alphabetical arrangement—usually not strictly alphabetical because entries were added as wills were probated.

2. Reverse will indexes

Though such are not common, reverse indexes (to beneficiaries) will occasionally be found. (Most of those I have seen are in North Carolina.) These should never be overlooked. Where they exist, they are very valuable to family history research. Consider an example of a reverse index and how it can be used to help solve a pedigree problem—especially the problem of identifying female ancestors:

You know the wife of Simon Hendricks is named Mahala, and that is about all you know concerning her identity. A reverse probate index, during the proper time period and in the locality where the family lived, shows that a Mahala Hendricks was named in the will of one Shadrack Plant. Upon finding the will, you discover that Plant's will named "my daughter Mahala Hendricks," and the time period involved seems to be agreeable. This may or may not be your Mahala. It is certainly a lead to pursue, but it is not a slam-dunk. You need to consider evidence in other available records to prove whether this is a valid connection. The significance of this circumstantial evidence depends on how many Mahala Hendrickses there are who could be this person.

Following is an extract of a portion of a page from the reverse index to wills in the Superior Court of Guilford County, North Carolina:

Name of Devisees	from	Name of Devisors	Date when Probated		Record of Wills	
					Book No.	Page
Cobb Susan		Cobb John	Aug	1846	C	252
John		"				
Christian		"				
Clapp Delilath		Hoffman Cathrine	Aug	1846	C	253
Clapp John R.		Clapp George	Aug	1846	C	254
Barbaɪa H.		"				
Jacob		"				
Clapp Eve		Clapp Jacob	Nov	1846	C	256
Joshua		"				
Cobble Mary		Coble Abraham	Feb	1847	C	263
Roddy		"				
Louisa		"				
Cathrine		"				
Letitia		"				
Adaline		"				
Caulk Elizabeth		Caulk Hannah	Feb	1847	C	265
Hannah		"				
Clendenin Jenny		Donnell Robert	May	1847	C	274
Betsy Ann		"				
Cox Isaac		Mendenhall Moses	Aug	1847	C	277
Rachel		"				
Cain Andrew		"				
Sarah		"				

3. Database will indexes

If the will you want is part of a digitized record and is on one of the family history websites, this third kind of index comes into play. These have become increasingly relevant in recent years, but they are still somewhat of a disappointment as I indicated earlier.

You will recall, from our discussion of these websites in Chapter 10, that when you enter a search name in the proper place on the website, along with relevant dates and places, the program generates a long list of people who are potential matches. Based on what you know, you can decide which of these looks promising, click on any (or all) of them—one at a time—and go directly to the digitized records (in this case, the wills) in which those names appear. You can do this with a click of your computer mouse. Though this is good, it appears that in most wills that have been indexed, only the names of those persons who made the wills—the testators—have been included. These are direct indexes, the same as the indexes listed under number one, above.

The main benefit of these is that I can search an extended geographic area all at one time. My disappointment is that these will indexes do not include every name of every beneficiary named in every will. That would be a marvelous benefit to the family history researcher.

Also, as you use these indexes, remember my warnings about spelling issues. It is essential that you use wildcards and variant spelling possibilities to cover all bases.

VII. HELP WITH A DIFFICULT PROBLEM

All agree that one of the most difficult problems in American family history research is to find the specific place of an ancestor's origin in the Old World. There are a few situations where this can be accomplished through probate records. An example will illustrate what I mean:

Your immigrant ancestor dies and leaves a will in America. In that will, he says something similar to what Francis Champernoun said in his will, proved in 1687 in York County, Massachusetts (now Maine):

> To my grandson Champernoun Elliot, son of Humphrey Elliot all ye lands of
> Right belonging unto me or that may belong unto me either in Old England
> or in New England not by me already disposed of.

The fact of significance here is that a man died in America leaving land in "Old England." Such property could not pass through probate in an American court but would have to be probated by an ancillary proceeding in England. But where in England was the property? Though the will does not say, and though English probate jurisdictions before 1858 are quite complicated, this still might not be too difficult. The Prerogative Court of Canterbury (PCC) in London claimed probate jurisdiction over the English estates of most persons who died outside the country, regardless of where in England their property was located, and the record of this probate may be there. Since the probate records of the PCC are all available, it might not be too difficult to determine where this land was located and perhaps Francis Champernoun's place of origin.

The LDS Family History Library has these English probate records on microfilm along with calendars (indexes) and act books (minute books). In addition, the Ancestry website has digitized copies of all the wills in this collection, along with their associated indexes.

Note, also, that abstracts of all PCC records with American references are in a book compiled by Peter Wilson Coldham entitled *American Wills & Administrations in the Prerogative Court of Canterbury, 1610– 1857* (Baltimore: Genealogical Publishing Co., 1989).[8]

---

[8] The above case is used here as an example only. It illustrates the possibility that exists in such cases. The truth of this matter is that much is already known about this Francis Champernoun, including his birth in Darlington, Devonshire, England, in 1714.

18

The Intestate, Miscellaneous Probate Records, and Guardianships

I. THE INTESTATE AND THE PROBATE PROCESS

The process of settling an estate is somewhat different when the decedent left no valid will behind at his death from the process followed when there is a will. In effect, when the intestate dies, the state legislature has already made his will for him; statutory law dictates completely the formula for settling his estate and distributing his property among his heirs.

Too often we think that those records relating to the settling of intestate estates have little value (and sometimes this may be true), but there are frequently occasions when the intestacy generates records of equal or greater value than the probate and administration of a will. Especially if the estate is large, people who claim to be relatives seem to come out of nowhere. It is interesting how people who were never heard of before come forward to claim inheritance rights in the estate. However, before any one of them can collect a cent, he must first prove the validity of his claim, and such proof must be recorded in Probate Court. A case came into court a few years ago in Pennsylvania when a woman died intestate leaving an estate valued at more than $17,000,000. Before final settlement was reached more than sixteen years later, 26,000 persons claimed to be relatives and more than 2,000 hearings were held in Probate Court, resulting in 115,000 pages of testimony.[1] Though this case is extreme, the principle applies in estates of even much smaller size.

---

[1] Joe McCarthy, "To My Wife, I Leave Her Lover," *This Week Magazine*, September 26, 1965, 14.

Petition for Administration.   Republican Job Printing House, Columbus, Wis.

State of Wisconsin, Columbia County.

In the Matter of the Estate

Samuel Stahl   deceased.

To the County Court of Said County:

The petition of *Mary E. Grover, Wm E. Stahl and Winfield S. Stahl* of the *Residences as hereinafter stated*, in the County of ____ and State of ____ respectfully represents:

That *Samuel Stahl* died at the *Village* of *Lodi* in the County of *Columbia* and State of *Wisconsin* on the *9th* day of *February*, 1904, intestate as petitioners believe, and being at that time an inhabitant of said County of *Columbia* residing at the *Village* of *Lodi aforesaid*.

That said deceased left personal estate to be administered within this State, the value of which does not exceed *Thirty five hundred* dollars, and real estate within this State, consisting of his homestead, worth about *Fifteen hundred* dollars, the annual rents and profits of which do not exceed *one hundred* dollars, as petitioners believe ; and that said deceased left *no* debts known to your petitioners amounting to about ____

That said deceased left surviving *him* next of kin and heirs at law as follows, viz.: *No widow. Children as follows: Benjamin F. Stahl of Portland Oregon; Harriet Jane Tuttleman of Bancroft Iowa; Mary E. Grover of Portland Iowa, P.O. Burt Iowa; Joseph C. Stahl, of Marysville, Washington; Almira A. Davidson of Marysville, Washington; William E. Stahl of Burt Iowa, Winfield S. Stahl of Bancroft, Iowa; and Grand children as follows: Guy F. Streeter of West Bend, Minn.; John Burt Streeter of Lake Arthur, La.; Lou Streeter of Pocahontas, Iowa; Winfield S. Streeter of Lake Arthur, La.; Wesley Streeter of Winnebago City, Minn.; George Streeter of Lake Arthur La.; Eugenia Streeter of Pocahontas, Iowa; Leo Streeter of Winnebago City, Iowa, Claire Streeter of Pocahontas, Iowa; the last three named are minors, and are children of Catherine Streeter deceased, and Samuel Barnett of Waupun, Wis, son of Sabin Barnett and Louisa A. Barnett deceased.*

That your petitioners *are children* of said deceased. Wherefore, your petitioners pray that administration of the estate of said deceased be granted unto *Winfield S. Stahl of Bancroft Iowa*, or some other suitable person.

Dated *February 10th* 1904.

Mary E. Grover
Wm E. Stahl
Winfield S. Stahl

STATE OF WISCONSIN,
COLUMBIA COUNTY. ss.

Mary E. Grover, Wm E. Stahl and Winfield S. Stahl being duly sworn, on oath say that *they are* the petitioners above named; that *they have heard read* the above and foregoing petition, and know the contents thereof, and that the same is true to *their* own knowledge, excepting as to matters therein stated on information and belief, and as to those matters *they* believe it to be true.

Subscribed and sworn to before me this *10th* ____

S. D. Waters
Notary Public

Mary E. Grover
Wm E. Stahl
Winfield S. Stahl

FIGURE 1—A PETITION FOR PROBATE

(This is a very informative document. Compare it with the Assignment of Real Estate illustrated in Figure 2. They relate to the same estate.)

Assignment of Real Estate

At a .... term of the County Court in and for the County of Columbia in the State of Wisconsin, held at the Probate Office in the City of Portage, on the ....*3rd*.......... Tuesday of *November* ....A. D. 191*9*..., being the *18th day of said month, and on the 4th day of said term, to wit, on Nov. 21st 1919.*......... Present, ...*Hon A. P. Kellogg*....County Judge.

IN THE MATTER OF THE ESTATE

OF

Samuel Stahl .... Deceased.

Whereas *Samuel Stahl* ....of *Lodi* .... in said County, died intestate on the .....*7th*.... day of *Feb* .....19*04*, and *his*.... estate has been fully and finally settled by and under proper proceedings in this Court, all .....*his*...... debts and the expenses of administration paid, and.....*his*......personal estate fully accounted for and assigned to the persons entitled thereto: whereby the real estate owned by said deceased at the time of......*his*........death can now be assigned in accordance with law.

And Whereas, It has been established to the satisfaction of this Court, that said deceased left ..*him*...surviving ......*no widow*.......... ....and..*seven*.......... and only ..*seven*..child.*ren*...........viz: *Benjamin F. Stahl, Harriet Jane Tallman, Mary E. Grover, Joseph E. Stahl, Almina A. Davidson, William E. Stahl and Winfield S. Stahl; nine grandchildren, children of a deceased daughter Cathrin Streator, to wit, Guy F. Streator, John Burt Streator, Lewis S. Streator, Winfield S. Streator, Wesley Streator, Geo S. Streator, M. Jean Streator, Leo Streator and Ralph C. Streator; one grand child, child of a deceased daughter Louise A. Burnett, to wit: David Burnett; that said Benjamin F. Stahl died during the administration of said estate, and before settlement of the account of administrator, leaving him surviving, on love at law his widow Mary E. Stahl, and seven children to wit: Janette Louise Roberts; Lizzie Hay Roberts, John J. Stahl, Loyal C. Stahl, Mary B. Robinson, Lilian A. Robit* who ..*are the*....heir s and only heirs at law and entitled to said real estate.

It is Therefore Ordered, Adjudged and Decreed, That all the real estate owned by said deceased at the time of.....*his*.......death be and the same is assigned to said*Harriet Jane Tallman, Mary E. Grover, Joseph E. Stahl, Almina A. Davidson, William E. Stahl and Winfield S. Stahl children, to each one ninth third; To Guy F. Streator, John Burt Streator, Lewis S. Streator, Winfield S. Streator, Wesley Streator, Geo S. Streator, M. Jean Streator, Leo Streator and Ralph C. Streator, to each the undivided one eighth ninth third; To David Burnett the undivided one ninth third; To Janette Louise Roberts, Lizzie Hay Roberts, John F. Stahl, Loyal C. Stahl, Mary B. Robinson, Lilian A. Robit, and Benjamin F. Stahl, the undivided one ninth third; subject to dower if* .....in common and undivided, share and share alike, to have and to hold the same to *him and their* heirs and assigns forever, but subject *to the dower and homestead rights therein of* ....

widow of said deceased.

By the Court *A. P. Kellogg*

....

County Judge.

Dated Nov. 21 1919.

FIGURE 2—DECREE OF DISTRIBUTION (ASSIGNMENT OF REAL ESTATE)

(This document relates to the same estate as the Petition in Figure 1. Note that circumstances have changed somewhat during the nearly sixteen years between the two documents.)

In most jurisdictions, records of intestate administrations are separated from the wills. There are, however, some courts where all probate records are recorded together in the same books. In these, it is not unusual to find master probate indexes listing all documents on file for each probate case. Where such indexes exist, they can save much time and energy. Their existence signals the fact that all probate records are in the same registers in the Probate Court. However, whether or not recorded versions of such documents exist, the original documents (if still extant) are in the court's probate (or estate) files. Each file (or probate packet, as it is often called) contains all of the records relating to one probate case. And this includes those cases where wills were declared void and were thus never granted probate.

Just as we surveyed the steps involved in the process of probating a will, let us also take a simplified, systematic look at the process of administering an intestate estate:

1. There is, of course, no case until after the person dies, and for the case to be intestate, the person who died must have left no valid will. No court can acquire jurisdiction without proof of death.

2. Probate proceedings are usually set in motion by a petition for probate being filed in the proper court. The person filing the petition must show, with this filing, the fact and the nature of his interest in the estate. This petition, usually called a petition (or application) for letters of administration, also tells (1) that the death has taken place (in recent times, a death certificate has been required), (2) the decedent died intestate, and (3) property lying within that court's jurisdiction (and sometimes additional property) was left to be administered. The approximate value of the property must be stated and—in more recent years—the names and relationships of potential heirs must also be stated. Probate jurisdiction lies within the state where the decedent had domicile at the time of death.

   Persons most often claiming the right of administrator are the surviving spouse and other next-of-kin. A surviving wife often claimed her right to administration as a co-administratrix with another next-of-kin. If there are several next-of-kin in the same degree of relationship who make claim to the right to administer the estate, the court selects the one it considers most suitable.

   In appointing an administrator, the court usually follows certain guidelines, including (a) that a sole administration is preferred to a joint one, (b) that males are preferred to females (at least historically), (c) that residents are preferred to non-residents, (d) that unmarried women are preferred to married women, (e) that whole-blood relatives are preferred to those of half-blood, (f) that those more interested in the estate are preferred to those less interested, etc. Persons who have no valid interest in the estate cannot be appointed as administrators. If there are no relatives claiming the right of administration, creditors usually will have claim.

3. When the court receives a petition, a hearing is set and notice is given to all interested parties, either by direct notice or by publication, or both, depending upon state statute. The hearing is to establish proof of the claims made in the petition.

4. When the proof of claims is established, administration is granted and letters of administration (see the list of terms later in this chapter) are issued. The administrator now has authorization to proceed. The administrator, once appointed, must give bond, with sureties, for faithful performance of his administration[2] according to statutory requirements, before the actual letters of administration are issued.

    (In some states, the minimum size of an estate requiring administration is set by statute, and in other states, there is no statutory limitation, though there must usually be sufficient assets to justify an administration grant. This is why we find no trace of probate records for many of our ancestors. Also, many people held property in ways that avoided probate, such as husbands and wives holding title to property as joint tenants.)

5. Once the above details are taken care of, the administrator can begin his task. This first requires publishing the required notices to creditors and paying the decedent's just debts and obligations.

6. An important duty that comes early in the administration process is making an inventory of estate assets and filing it with the court. Failure to make an inventory is generally considered a breach of the administrator's bond. Today, in most states, the court will appoint appraisers to ascertain the true value of the estate.

7. The administrator must then distribute the personal property, the real property, and the monies of the estate according to statutory requirements. In some cases, there will be a sale of estate assets to pay debts and other obligations. There may also be valuable assets that none of the heirs has need of or use for.

8. The administrator keeps an accurate record of everything he does as part of his administration because he must make a periodic accounting thereof to the court, usually on an annual basis (if his job takes that long).

9. At the termination of his trust, the administrator makes a final account. This final account (or settlement, as it is sometimes called) must be accepted by those parties interested in the estate and may be disputed by them for appropriate reasons.

10. In some states, especially in more recent years (so do not expect to find these in very many old records), a decree of distribution is prepared by the administrator and issued by the court at the completion of the administration. As with the testate estate, this document provides proof

---

[2] See definitions of terms in Chapter 16.

of title. It finally and officially vests the title to the decedent's property in his heirs. It is often (again depending on state law) recorded in the local land records when real estate is involved, as well as being filed in the Probate Court. This document is called by various names in different places. Such titles as *decree of distribution, decree of heirship, probate decree, assignment of real estate, order of distribution, probate assignment, certificate of devise,* and other titles, are used in different states.

The value of these records lies in the fact that they show how the estate was divided and who got what. These are often a better source of family history evidence than wills because they always name names, and they cannot omit living legal heirs.

11. Creditors and heirs sign releases or receipts as they receive their inheritances. These are also filed with the court.

12. Should the administrator be relieved of his duties before completing them, by death or for any other reason (perhaps even at his own request), the court will choose a successor. This person is called an administrator *de bonis non.* His job is to complete the work begun by the first administrator.

Other records that often arose as part of the administration process include petitions for (and assignments of) dower or curtesy, petitions, accounts, documents relating to orphans and guardianship issues (discussed later in this chapter), powers of attorney, etc.

II. MISCELLANEOUS PROBATE RECORDS

There are many other kinds of probate documents besides wills, as our discussion has already indicated, some dealing with testate estates, some with intestate estates, and some with both. We want to look now in more detail at some of the more important documents. Before doing so, however, let me say that many of these records are of significant value to us. The originals of these records for each case—like original wills, for example—are usually found in the estate files and are listed in the court's probate docket.

Estate files are seldom microfilmed or digitized because (1) they are voluminous and (2) they include folded loose papers that are time-consuming to handle. However, they are generally easy to locate and their use can be rewarding. Keep in mind that these are original records—while recorded wills probated before the advent of photocopying are not.

Here are some of the documents you will encounter:

ACCOUNT (or ACCOMPT): The administrator of an estate or a guardian is sometimes required by statute to make a periodic (often yearly) accounting of his administration or guardianship. And, at the end of his trust, he must submit a final account. (See also SETTLEMENT.) These accounts are a record of the activities associated with his specific fiduciary duties. The following is a typical account of an administration from mid-eighteenth-century New England:

> The account of Elizabeth Hodsdon of her admin[ion] of the **Estate** of her late Husband John Hooper the third late of Berwick in **the** County of York dec[d] Intestate. The Said Accomptant chargeth herself with y[e] person[l] Estate of S[d] as p[r] Invent[y] £21"13"—And prayeth an Allowance of the following Articles of Charge viz[t]

To paid for Letters of Admin[ion] Inventory & c	£—"12"—
To a Tourney to exhibit y[e] Inventory and give Bond for Admin[ion]	—"10"—
To so much due to y[e] appriz[rs] for their services	—" 9"—
To p[d] for Swearing Apprizers	—" 1" 2
To so much for 3 Bondsmen to y[e] Admin[x] 1 Day themselves & Horses and Expense each 4/	—"12"—
To p[d] Doct[or] Parsons for Visits & Medicins p[r] Rec[t]	—"12"—
To p[d] Hall Jackson £ 17,17. N. Hampsh[r] old Ten[r]	—"17"10
To Eben[er] Thomson to get a War[t] of Apprizem[t]	—" 3"—
To D[o] to a Scribe for drawing this acco[t]	" 1" 4
To Sundries allowed y[e] Widow as necessarye for Life	14"08"10
To Admin[x] time attending the Apprizers 1 Day	—" 2"—
Probate Fees on this acco[t]	—" 6"—
Due to Marg[t] Norson for nursing y[e] Admin[x] in y[e] lifetime of the Said Intestate	3"—"—
	£ 21"15" 2

Errors excepted   Eliz[a] (her mark) Hodsdon

York Ss. At a Court of Probate held at York July 12, 1763.

Elizabeth Hodsdon above named made Oath that the above account is just and true. Ordered that She be allowed twenty one pounds fifteen Shillings and two pence out of the Said Estate in full discharge thereof.

ADMINISTRATION BOND: A bond (*q.v.*) posted by the person selected as administrator of an estate to ensure that his administration will be accomplished satisfactorily. Such a bond requires sureties. See also TESTAMENTARY BOND.

ANTENUPTIAL CONTRACT: Though an antenuptial (or prenuptial) contract or agreement is not a probate document, such a document can have substantial effect on the probate proceedings whenever it exists. It is a contract made between a man and a woman who are about to marry; wherein certain property rights of one or both are secured and delineated. These contracts are usually made by persons who have been previously married and who want to preserve their properties and wealth, when they eventually die, to the issue of their previous unions rather than to each other. Such contracts take precedence over laws of descent and distribution. They have been quite common, especially in states with community property laws and with the Dutch in New Netherland.[3] Other names are *marriage settlement* and *prenuptial agreement.* A similar contract made after the marriage is called a *postnuptial contract (q.v.).*

ASSIGNMENT OF DOWER: This is the document by which a widow's dower in her late husband's property is assigned to her as part of the administration. There are many different terms used to describe this document in various states, but they all boil down to the same thing. It may be called a *dower division,* the *setting off of the dower,* and sometimes merely the *widow's dower.* Ordinarily, there is not a lot of family history information in this kind of record, but occasionally there will be an accompanying *petition (q.v.)* or a *plat* (a map of the land) showing the division of the estate among the heirs. The assignment of Mercy Cloutman's dower provides a typical example:

> York Ss. Lebanon June 20, 1763.
> We the Subscribers being appointed by the hon^ble Jeremiah Moulton Esqr Judge of Probate for Said County to divide and set-off to Mercy Cloutman Widow of John Cloutman late of Said Lebanon dec^d Intestate one third part of the real Estate of the Dec^d We have attended that Service, and have Set off to the Said Mercy one third part of the Said Estate on the following Manner, Eight Acres of Land in the Lot originally granted to John Cartice, jun^r in Said Township. N. Seven in the first Range of the Home Lots which Lot ye Said Cloutman purchased of one Samuel Rounds beginning at the highway leading between the first and Second Range of Lots and extending Eastwardly the wedth of the Lot thirty two Rods which contains Eight Acres and is bounded Northerly by a Lot granted to Richd Cutt Esqr and Southerly by a Lot granted to Crisp. Bradbury and is Forty Rods in Breadth. As Witness our Hands.
>
> > Joseph Farnam
> > Philip Doe (his mark)
> > Paul Farnam
>
> York Ss. At a Court of Probate held at York July 11, 1763
>
> The within Instrument being presented to me under Oath for my Approbation. I do hereby approve and allow of the Same as the Division of the Widow's Dower in the Estate of John Cloutman Dec^d And do order that ye Same be assigned to her accordingly—
>
> > Jer^a Moulton Judge

---

[3] There is an example of an antenuptial contract in Chapter 20.

BOND: This instrument, often referred to as a *fiduciary* or *probate bond*, is filed in the Probate Court to guarantee that the person entrusted with the care of others' property faithfully performs his specified duties. A sum of money is affixed as a penalty, binding the bondsman to pay that sum if the prescribed duties are not performed. If the obligation is properly discharged, the penalty is void. In probate matters, the administrator appointed by the court to settle the intestate estate and the executor of the testate estate (unless expressly excused from the bonding obligation by the testator in the will) must both be bonded. In earlier times, the bondsmen (sureties) for a bond of this type were often relatives of the administrator or the executor, thus providing another research clue in difficult cases.

CAVEAT: Latin for "Let him beware," a caveat is the means for an interested party to give formal notice to the court to suspend a proceeding until he can be heard. Caveat power is often used to temporarily prevent a will from being probated or letters of administration from being granted. In such a case, the caveat is usually a precursor to an attack on the validity of the will or administration. Some states require a caveat to be submitted to initiate a will contest.

DECREE OF DISTRIBUTION: As mentioned earlier, the decree of distribution is the final instrument issued in the administration of an estate. By it, the heirs receive their actual title to the property of the deceased. In earlier periods, in some localities, this was sometimes called a *division*. Other names have also been applied, as previously mentioned. The following decree of distribution was made in Nevada County, California, in 1904:

> In the Matter of the Estate of William D. Woods, deceased.
> Decree of Distribution of Estate.
>
> W.J. Woods, the Executor of the will of Wm. D. Woods, deceased having on the 21st day of July 1904 filed in this Court his final a/c and petition, setting forth among other matters that his accounts are ready to be finally settled, and said estate is in a condition to be closed, and that a portion of said estate remains to be divided among the devisees of said deceased, said matter coming on regularly to be heard this 1st day of August 1904 at 10 o'clock AM the said executor appearing by his counsel, Chas. W. Kitts, Esq. this Court proceeded to hear said final account and said petition for distribution; and it appearing that said executor has collected the sum of $50 and has expended the sum of $431.50 as such; that he has paid the legacies provided in said will to M.B. Townsend, E.M. Shaw and the heirs of J.A. Holman, deceased; that he waives his commissions as executor; waives repayment of the sums he has paid exceeding the amount collected by him and has settled on his own account with Chas. W. Kitts, as his attorney, and that said account is in all respects just and true. It is hereby ordered that the same be and the same is hereby settled, allowed and confirmed.

This court proceeded to the hearing of the petition, and it appearing to the satisfaction of this court that the residue of said estate, consisting of the property hereinafter particularly described, is now ready for distribution, and that said estate is now in a condition to be closed. That the whole of said estate is separate property. [California is a community-property state.] That the said William D. Woods, died testate, in the county of Nevada, Cala., on the 22nd day of Feby 1904 leaving him surviving, his son, W.J. Woods, a resident of Grass Valley, Cala., his daughter Matilda B. Townsend of said City of Grass Valley, his Daughter E.M. Shaw a resident of Bakersfield all of the age of majority and S.A. Holman, Jr., A.J. Holman, L.E. Holman, M.W. Holman and W.H. Holman, children of his deceased daughter, Julia A. Holman deceased. That since the rendition of his said final account nothing has come into the hands of said executor, and nothing has been expended by said executor as necessary expenses of administration; and that the estimated expenses of closing said estate will amount to the sum of nothing. That the said W.J. Woods is entitled to the whole of the residue after paying to said Matilda B. Townsend, E.M. Shaw legacies of $100 each, and to the heirs of said Julia A. Holman a legacy of $100, all of which have been paid.

Now on this, the 1st day of Aug 1904, on motion of Chas. W. Kitts Esq., counsel for said executor it is hereby ordered, adjudged and decreed, that the residue of said estate of William D. Woods, deceased, hereinafter particularly described, and now remaining in the hands of said executor and any other property not now known or discovered, which may belong to the said estate, or in which the said estate may have an interest, be the same is hereby distributed as follows, to wit: The "Woods Ranch" consisting of the W ½ of N.W. ¼ of Section 27 and the south east quarter of the north east quarter of Section 28 Tp 16 N.R. 8 E.M.D.M. containing 89 ac and being the whole of said legal sub divisions, save such portions as have been conveyed by said testator.

All that portion of lot 3 in Blk 15 in the City of Grass Valley, Nevada Co., Cala., as per map of said City of Grass Valley, made by Saml Bethell in 1872, fronting 50 ft on Carpenter Street, bounded south by Perdue's lot and thence extending back easterly 100 ft.

That part of lot 3 in block 15 aforesaid, bounded north by Main Street; east by west lines of lots of Pattison, Clemo & Wesley and Carpenter St.; on south by Grass Valley Townsite.

Lot 6 in Sec 27 Tp 16 NR 8 EMDM.

Done in open Court, this 1st day of Aug 1904.

F.T. Nilon, Judge

Filed August 1st 1904
  F.L. Arbogast, Clerk
By A.J. Hosking, Deputy Clerk.
State of California,
              ss.
County of Nevada.

DEED OF PARTITION: See PARTITION in Chapter 20.

DEPOSITION: A deposition is not strictly a type of probate record but belongs to all types of court proceedings. It is a statement of a witness, made under oath, responding to certain questions. It is not taken in open court but reduced to writing and intended for use in a court action. In a case where a will is being contested, the depositions of friends, neighbors, family, etc., on the mental soundness of the testator (or some other issue) may be taken and presented to the court (and is sometimes admissible as evidence). A deposition is taken in response to questions posed by an opponent.

DISCHARGE: See RELEASE.

DISCLAIMER: See RENUNCIATION.

DISTRIBUTION: The payment or division to those entitled to benefit from the decedent's estate, after payment of debts and liabilities. It follows the settlement (*q.v.*) and is frequently called a *final distribution*. See also DECREE OF DISTRIBUTION.

DIVISION: See DECREE OF DISTRIBUTION.

DOWER: See ASSIGNMENT OF DOWER.

FINAL ACCOUNT: See SETTLEMENT.

FINAL DISTRIBUTION: See DISTRIBUTION.

FINAL SETTLEMENT: See SETTLEMENT.

INVENTORY: An inventory is a detailed list of all the goods and properties of the deceased, usually made by the administrator, by the executor of the estate, or by others appointed. The inventory gives a glimpse into the personal life of the decedent—his occupation, his wealth or lack of it, and the nature of the times and circumstances in which he lived. In the absence of other probate records the inventory can also give some indication of the approximate time of death—a must in many cases. The inventory of William Gowen's estate in 1763 tells his occupation and also indicates that he was not a man of affluence:

> A true Inventory of the Estate of William Gowen late of **Kittery** in ye County of York Mariner dec^d taken by us the Subscribers October 8th 1763. Shown to Abigail Gowen Widow and Admin^x of Said dec^ds Estate vizt.

To 1 feather Bed & Furniture	£6"10"—
One Ditto and Furniture	6"10"—
To 1 Desk 40/. a Trunk 10/. a Chest 6/.	2"16"—
A round Table 13/. two Small Ditto 6/.	—"19"—
2 Small old Chests 2/. a Spinning Wheel & Real 4/.	—" 6"—

12 old Chairs 10/. 2 old Bibles & Sunday Small Books 10/.	1"—"—
2 old Tramells grate from Toaster and Spit	—"12"—
a Small pʳ old handjrons fireslice & Tongs	—" 9"—
Ironing Box & Heaters 6/. old narrow ax 1/6.	—" 7" 6
a Coffee Mill 5/. three old pewter Dishes 6/.	—"11"—
12 old pewter Plates 6/. 2 old Basons 2/6.	—" 8" 6
4 pewter Porringes 3/6. old earthen Ware 6/.	—" 9" 6
Some old glass Bottles and Caps	—" 5"—
2 Small looking Glasses 5/. 1 Dᵒ 3/. 5 old Candlesticks 2/.	—"10"—
a marking Iron & Hammer 1/6.	—" 1" 6
a warming pan 12/. Six old maps 3/.	—"15"—
4 old casks 4/. Some old Knives & Forks 1/.	—" 5"—
2 old Razors 1/. old Cutlash 8ᵈ	—" 1" 8
two potts and Tea Kettle and frying pan 14/.	—"14"—
old Skimmer and flesh Forks 1/. 3 old Tubbs 2/4.	—" 3" 4

£ 23"14"—

James Gowen
Japhet Emery
Joseph Goold

York Ss. Decʳ 31, 1763.

Abigail Gowen within named made Oath that yᵉ Severˡ articles mentioned in the within Inventory are all yᵉ Estate belonging to yᵉ Said Decᵈ that has come to her hands, and that if any thing more here after appear, She will give it into yᵉ Regᵉʳ office. The apprizers being Sworn.

Jer: Moulton Judge

LETTERS OF ADMINISTRATION: This is the document (singular) issued by the Probate Court to appoint the administrator of an intestate estate and authorize him to function in that responsibility. The following example is a document commonly referred to as an "administration" but is actually a combination of letters of administration and estate *inventory*. It also mentions a bond for £80, but this document itself is not a bond:

> Letters of Administration granted to Elizabeth Littlefield on the Estate of Nathan Littlefield deceased she produceing in Court An Inventory of the said Estate and John Barrett was bound in Eighty pounds bond To our soveraigne Lord the King his Heires and successors that she the Said Elizabeth Littlefield shall administer according to Law.

	£	S	d
Imprimis[4] Wearing cloaths	3	00	00
Ip. Bed and bedding	04	00	00
Ip. Some household goods	01	00	00
Ip. 2 guns 2 pistols: 1 sword and amunition	03	00	00
Ip. 2 oxen and Two Steeres	12	00	00
Ip. 1 Cow and Calfe	03	00	00
Ip. 2 yearling	02	00	00
Ip. 1 Heyfor 2 year old	01	10	00
Ip. 1 Horse	02	00	00
Ip. 1 sow and 9 pigs	03	00	00
Ip. 3 yds Searge	01	10	00
Ip. Board and Shingle nayles	01	10	00
Ip. Sheeps Wool	00	10	00
Ip. to one quart pt of a p^r of Logging wheels	00	10	00
Ip. to Steel traps	01	00	00
	40	10	00

The prmisses abovesd were apprized th 13th of March 1688 by us here subscribed

> Jona[th] Hamonds
> Sam[ll] Wheelwright

LETTERS TESTAMENTARY: An executor named in a will has no legal authority, even though named in the will and the testator is deceased, until authorized by the Probate Court. The court's authorization—letters testamentary—is equivalent to the letters of administration (*q.v.*) issued by the court to the administrator of an intestate estate.

MARRIAGE SETTLEMENT: See ANTENUPTIAL CONTRACT.

PETITION: An application made, in writing, to the court for an exercise of judicial power in a matter that is not the subject of a suit. The would-be administrator or executor petitions the Probate Court to grant him letters of administration (*q.v.*) or letters testamentary (*q.v.*).

POSTNUPTIAL CONTRACT: A written agreement made by a couple after their marriage concerning the inheritance of property of one or both. It takes precedence over statutes of descent and distribution. See also ANTENUPTIAL CONTRACT.

PRENUPTIAL AGREEMENT: See ANTENUPTIAL CONTRACT.

RECEIPT: A receipt is merely a written acknowledgment that money, goods, or property has been received. In some states, it is not unusual to find receipts recorded in the Probate Court. Such receipts give the acknowledgment of creditors, heirs, or beneficiaries that they have received payment or property and that they discharge the executor or administrator from further responsibility in their behalf. An example of a receipt, from the records of Cumberland County, Massachusetts (now Maine), follows:

---

[4] *Imprimis* is a Latin term meaning *first or in the first place.*

Know all men by these presents that we Samuel Whitmore and Mary his Wife of Gorham in the County of Cumberland do acknowledge to have rec[d] in full of Joel Whitney of Gorham in the County aforesaid Three pounds twelve Shillings in full for our Part & Portion in the Estate of Abel Whitney late of Gorham deceas'd We do hereby acquit exonerate and discharge the Said Joel his Executors and admin[rs] from every part and parcel thereof. In Witness whereof we have hereunto Set our Hands and Seals y[e] 28th Day of January Anno Domini 1765.

Ammos Whitney ⎤
Zebulon Whitney ⎦

⎰ Sam[ll] Whitmore
⎱ Mary Whitmore

RELEASE: There are many kinds of releases but two are significant here. The first is accomplished when an heir releases his expectancy interest to the source of that interest. The second conveys one person's rights or interest to someone else who has an interest in the same estate. As an example of the first, children might release certain rights in their deceased father's estate to their widowed mother. This document is sometimes called a *discharge*. It might also be recorded in the land records since it acts more as a conveyance than a devise. Both types of release require fair consideration. An example used in Chapter 2, and repeated here, illustrates the second type:

Know all men by these Presents that we William Bryer Shipwright Richard Bryer Weaver Andrew Haley husbandman and Mary his Wife Caleb Hutchins Caulker and Sarah his Wife Joseph Hutchins Weaver and Elizabeth his Wife William Wilson Weaver and Eadah his Wife John Haley Husbandman & Hephzib[a] his Wife all of Kittery in the County of York in the Province of the Massachusetts Bay in New England and William Tapley Taylor of New Hampshire & R [*sic*] his Wife Do forever acquit exonerate and discharge our Father in Law Benjamin Hammond of Kittery & Province afors[d] and our Mother Sarah Hammond lately call'd Sarah Bryer from the Demands of us or our or either of our Heirs in and unto any part of the Cattle or Household Goods or moveable Estate of our hon[d] Father William Bryer late of Kittery afores[d] de[cd] and We the Subscribers that have receiv'd of our Mother Sarah Hammond any part of the moveable Estate above mentioned We do hereby promise to return the Same to our Mother Sarah Hammond on her Demand. Furthermore we the Subscribers Do by these Presents promise and engage to let our Mother above named have and improve one third part according as the Law directs of the Land or Lands that was the Estate of our Father William Bryer as aforesaid during her natural Life.

In Witness whereof we have hereunto Set our Hands and Seals this 31" Day of January Anno Domini 1738/ 9.

Sam[l]. Haley ⎤
her   ⎬
Elizabeth X Dill ⎦
mark

Andrew Haly
Caleb Hutchins
Joseph X Hutchins

William Willson
John Haley   his
William Bryer   X
                     mark

Witnesses for Wm. Tapley ⎫	his
Andrew Haley ⎬	William X Tapley
Caleb Hutchins. ⎭	mark

RENUNCIATION: A renunciation, sometimes called a *disclaimer*, is a refusal to accept a testamentary transfer or a transfer made by will. Under the common law, an heir (one who took property by inheritance from an intestate) was unable to renounce.

SALE BILL: A sale bill is a record made of the goods and properties sold at public sale by the executor or administrator of the estate. The record is usually quite complete, listing the specific items sold, the buyers, and the prices. Relatives often buy many of the articles offered at such sales, and a thorough study of the record may provide useful clues to identities; however, one cannot expect to find conclusive proof of relationship in a sale bill by itself. A sale bill might also give insight concerning an ancestor's lifestyle and material circumstances. Following is a sale bill for the estate of Newton Brent in 1795 from the records of Lancaster County, Virginia:

November 3d 1795. Memodum of goods sold belonging to the estate of Newton Brent decd.

Item	To	£		s		d
1 tenant Saw	To Wm Gibson	£0	.	12	.	0
7 walnut chairs	William Kirk	0	.	9	.	0
1 gun	James Pollard	1	.	5	.	0
1 do	John Thrall	0	.	3	.	0
1 sword	Thomas James	0	.	3	.	0
1 whip saw	Capt. Gibson	1	.	3	.	6
3 planes	Thomas Lawson	0	.	4	.	0
1 small box of tools	Thomas Short	0	.	4	.	0
parcel planes	Tarpley George	0	.	4	.	3
1 bead plane	John Flowers	0	.	1	.	0
1 red bull	Wm Eustace	2	.	10	.	0
1 pied cow & calf	Wm Eustace	1	.	14	.	0
1 cow & calf w horns	Capt Gibson	1	.	15	.	0
1 cow & calf	John Hunt	1	.	15	.	0
1 cow	Wm Eustace	2	.	0	.	0
1 Heifer	Vincent Brent	1	.	8	.	6
1 small bull	Wm Eustace	1	.	3	.	0
1 do do	John Thrall	1	.	8	.	6

1 do do	............Henry Palmer	....	1 . 6 . 0
5 first choice sheep	..........Thoˢ Jaines	....	1 . 16 . 0
5 2nd do do	.... do do	....	1 . 3 . 6
5 3rd do do	..........Vinson Brent	....	0 . 16 . 6

£24 . 4 . 9

At a court held for Lancaster county on the 21st day of February 1797 This account of the sale of part of the estate of Newton Brent decd was returned and ordered to be recorded—

Teste. Henry Towles cl. curia

SETTLEMENT: The settlement (or *final settlement*) is the instrument that itemizes payment of estate expenses, showing how the monies were disbursed to settle the decedent's financial obligations. It also indicates the total assets and the individual shares of those left to benefit. All that remains is the final distribution to the heirs or beneficiaries. As noted, this is frequently called the *final account*.

TESTAMENTARY BOND: This is a bond (*q.v.*) posted with the court by the executor of a will guaranteeing a proper administration of the estate. Such a bond requires sureties. See also ADMINISTRATION BOND.

WARRANT: A warrant is a court order. In probate cases, some states require a warrant to precede nearly every action of the case. A warrant may be issued prior to the assignment of the dower (*q.v.*), prior to the taking of the inventory (*q.v.*), prior to the settlement (*q.v.*), prior to the distribution (*q.v.*), or prior to almost any other action in which the court has interest. Family history-wise, the warrant seldom gives more (and often gives less) information than the record of the proceeding that it ordered.

III. GUARDIANSHIPS

A. Court Jurisdiction

Guardianships are closely related to probate records and to the probate or administration process. The reason for this, as you can understand, is that when the decedent is survived by minor children, such children are not capable under the law of managing their own persons or properties. Hence, a guardian must be appointed. In some courts, the records arising out of guardianship matters are kept in the probate files, while in other courts these records are filed elsewhere. However, regardless of this, in most states, the two processes are within the jurisdiction of the same courts.

The following list shows the courts where guardianship matters are controlled in the several states. As you use this list, be aware that the jurisdiction in most states is in the county of the child's residence, and not the guardian's. This generally makes the records easier to locate and use.

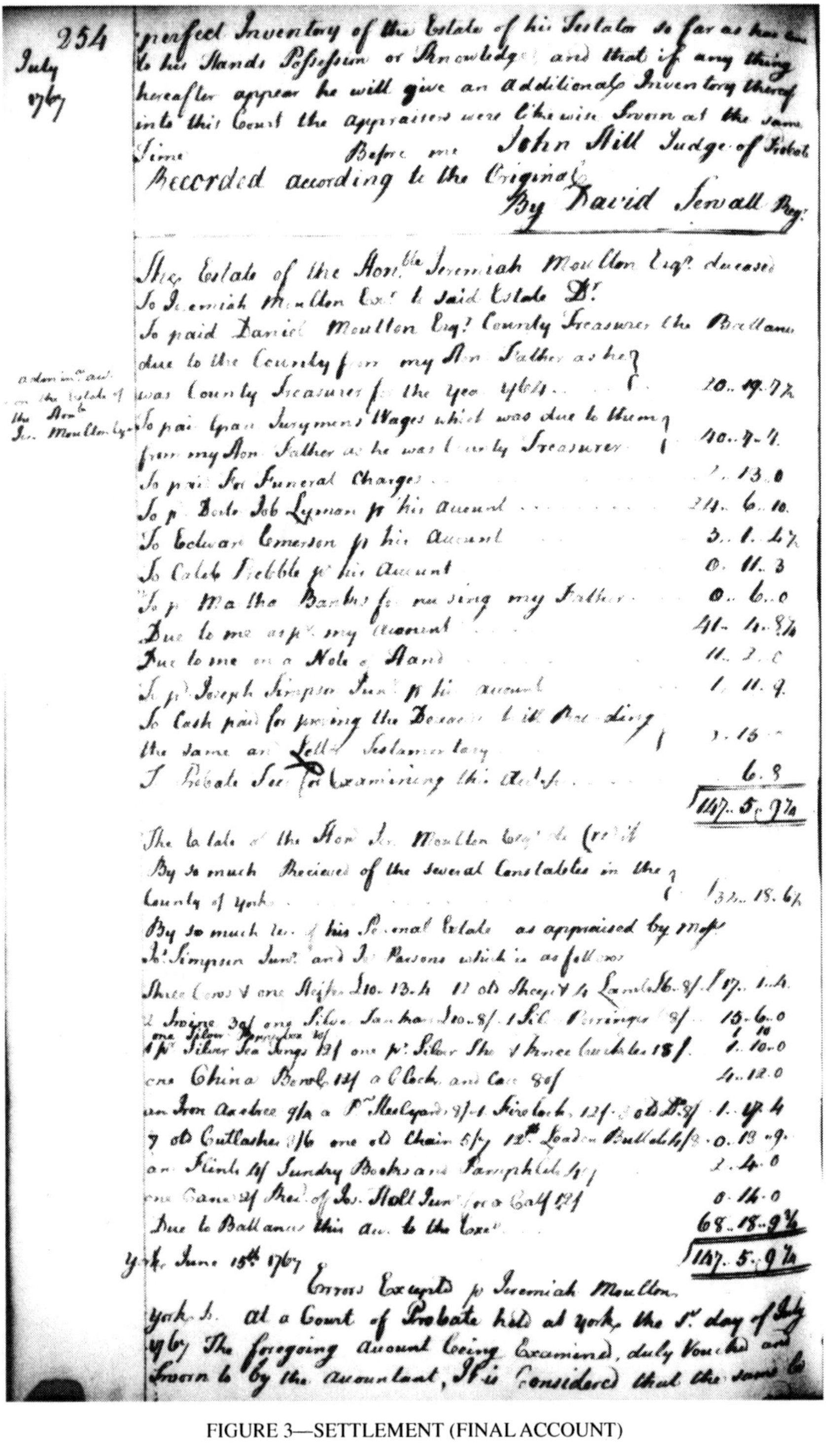

254 July 1767

perfect Inventory of the Estate of his Testator so far as has come to his Hands Possession or Knowledge, and that if any thing hereafter appear he will give an Additional Inventory thereof into this Court the appraisers were likewise Sworn at the same Time Before me John Hill Judge of Probate

Recorded according to the Original

By David Sewall Reg.

The Estate of the Hon.ble Jeremiah Moulton Esq.r deceased To Jeremiah Moulton Ex.r to said Estate D.r

To paid Daniel Moulton Esq.r County Treasurer the Ballance due to the County from my Hon. Father as he was County Treasurer for the year 1764	20.. 19.. 7½
To paid Grand Jurymens Wages which was due to them from my Hon. Father as he was County Treasurer	40.. 7.. 4
To paid for Funeral Charges	7.. 13.. 0
To p.d Doct.r Job Lyman p his Account	24.. 6.. 10
To Edward Emerson p his Account	3.. 1.. 4½
To Caleb Preble p his Account	0.. 11.. 3
To p.d Martha Banks for nursing my Father	0.. 6.. 0
Due to me as p.r my Account	41.. 4.. 8½
Due to me on a Note of Hand	11.. 2.. 0
To p.d Joseph Simpson Jun.r p his account	1.. 11.. 9
To Cash paid for proving the Deceased Will Recording the same and Letter Testamentary	1.. 15.. 0
To Probate Fee for Examining this Acc.t	6.. 8
	147.. 5.. 9½

The Estate of the Hon. Jer. Moulton Esq.r C.r

By so much Recieved of the several Constables in the County of York	32.. 18.. 6½
By so much ... of his Personal Estate as appraised by Mess.rs Jo.s Simpson Jun.r and Jo. Parsons which is as follows	
Three Cows & one Heifer £10.. 13.. 4 11 old Sheep & 4 Lambs £6.. 8/	17.. 1.. 4
2 Swine 30/ one Silver Tankard £10.. 8/ 1 Silver Porringer 8/ (one Silver Porringer 40/)	13.. 6.. 0 (10)
1 p.r Silver Tea Tongs 12/ one p.r Silver Shoe & Knee Buckles 18/	1.. 10.. 0
one China Bowl 12/ a Clock and Case 80/	4.. 12.. 0
an Iron Andiron 9/4 a p.r Steelyards 8/ 1 Firelock 12/ 3 old ... 8/	1.. 17.. 4
7 old Cutlashes 3/6 one old Chain 5/7 12 lb Leaden Bullets 4/8	0.. 13.. 9
an Flint 1/ Sundry Books and Pamphlets 4/	2.. 4.. 0
one Cane 2/ Share of Jo.s Hall Jun.r for a Calf 12/	0.. 14.. 0
Due to Ballance this Acc. to the Exec.r	68.. 18.. 9½
	147.. 5.. 9½

York June 15th 1767

Errors Excepted p Jeremiah Moulton

York ss. At a Court of Probate held at York the 5.th day of July 1767 The foregoing account being Examined, duly Vouched and Sworn to by the accountant, It is Considered that the same be

FIGURE 3—SETTLEMENT (FINAL ACCOUNT)

ALABAMA:	Probate Court in the county (but administration of guardianships may be removed to the County Chancery Court).
ALASKA:	Superior Court in specified areas in four judicial districts. (Judicial districts are unrelated to the state's boroughs [county equivalent].
ARIZONA:	Superior Court in the county.
ARKANSAS:	Circuit Court in the county.
CALIFORNIA:	Superior Court in the county.
COLORADO:	District Court in the county. (The Juvenile Court has jurisdiction in Denver.)
CONNECTICUT:	Probate Court in the district (see Chapter 17). Appeals can be made to the Superior Court.
DELAWARE:	Family Court in the county (for minors); County Chancery Court (for all others).
DIST. OF COLUMB.:	Probate Division of the Superior Court of the District.
FLORIDA:	Circuit Court in the county.
GEORGIA:	County Probate Court.
HAWAII:	Family Court Division of the Circuit Court. There are four circuits for the six inhabited islands: (1) Oahu; (2) Maui, Molokai, and Lanai; (3) Hawaii; and (4) Kauai.
IDAHO:	District Court, Magistrate's Division, in the county.
ILLINOIS:	Circuit Court in the county for testamentary guardians and Juvenile Court in the county for all other minors.
INDIANA:	The court having probate jurisdiction in the county (see Chapter 17).
IOWA:	District Court in the county, sitting in probate.
KANSAS:	District Court in the county.
KENTUCKY:	District Court in the county.
LOUISIANA:	District Court in the parish (county equivalent) and, in Orleans Parish, the Civil District Court. (Guardianship is called *tutorship*.)
MAINE:	County Probate Court.
MARYLAND:	Orphans' Court in Baltimore City and in every county except Harford and Montgomery. In these two, Circuit Court judges sit as Orphans' Court judges.

MASSACHUSETTS:	Probate and Family Court in the county.
MICHIGAN:	County Probate Court (see Chapter 17).
MINNESOTA:	Probate Division of the District Court in the county (except Hennepin, Anoka, and Ramsey counties, where there are Probate Courts).
MISSISSIPPI:	County Chancery Court.
MISSOURI:	Probate Division of the Circuit Court in the county.
MONTANA:	District Court in the county.
NEBRASKA:	County Court.
NEVADA:	County Guardianship Commissioner in District Court.
NEW HAMPSHIRE:	Circuit Court Probate Division in the county.
NEW JERSEY:	Surrogate's Court (which is clerk of the Superior Court) in the county. (In cases of dispute, the County Court must order the Surrogate to act, and in cases of incompetency, the County Court and the Superior Court have jurisdiction.)
NEW MEXICO:	County Probate Court.
NEW YORK:	Family Court or Surrogate's Court in the county.
NORTH CAROLINA:	Family Court, District Court Division, in the county.
NORTH DAKOTA:	District Court in the county.
OHIO:	Probate Division of Court of Common Pleas in the county.
OKLAHOMA:	District Court in the county.
OREGON:	County Court in Gilliam, Grant, Harney, Malheur, Sherman, and Wheeler counties; Circuit Court in all other counties.
PENNSYLVANIA:	Register of Wills in County Court of Common Pleas.
RHODE ISLAND:	Probate Court of the city or town.
SOUTH CAROLINA:	Probate Court in the county.
SOUTH DAKOTA:	Circuit Court in the county.
TENNESSEE:	Probate Court in Shelby County; Probate Division in the Chancery Court in Davidson County; and Chancery Court in all other counties. In Dyer County, the Probate Court and the Chancery Court have concurrent jurisdiction.

TEXAS:	Generally in County Court, but some larger counties have Probate Courts.
UTAH:	District Court in the county.
VERMONT:	Family Division of the District Court (see Chapter 17).
VIRGINIA:	Circuit Court in the counties and independent cities (see Chapter 22).
WASHINGTON:	County Superior Court
WEST VIRGINIA:	Family Court of the county.
WISCONSIN:	Circuit Court of the county.
WYOMING:	District Court in the county.[5]

When guardianship records are kept under the jurisdiction of the court of probate, they are more likely to be indexed and easier to use, but this is not always the case. You will find vast differences in the accessibility of these records, which seems to have little to do with the nature of the jurisdictions that keep them.

B. The value of guardianship records

There are different situations in which guardianship records may have been kept. First, be aware that it is not always necessary for the parents to be deceased for guardianship records to exist. There are many instances where children are left legacies (often by a grandparent or other relative) and their own natural parents are appointed as special guardians of the property and the rights that such a legacy may involve. In some states, however, statutes prohibit natural parents from acting as guardians in such situations; other states allow them to be co-guardians.

You may also find a guardian *ad litem* being appointed to represent a minor child or an incompetent person in a specific lawsuit, but seldom is there significant family history value in such an appointment in and of itself. The records of the lawsuit itself, however, may have some value.

Another type of situation that suggests the need to investigate guardianship records is where a young person comes of age, marries, and secures property in a locality, but there is no indication in other records of his being connected to anyone in an earlier generation. The reason for this lack of connection may be that his parents died when he was young. You should never hesitate to check guardianship records when you find a situation like this; they may hold the answer to your problem.

---

[5] The source of this information in earlier editions was *Martindale-Hubbell Law Dictionary*, 120th ed. (Summit, NJ: Martindale-Hubbell, Inc., 1988), Vol. V (used with permission) as well as correspondence with various court officials. In this edition, that information has been updated using court websites relating to the individual states.

There are several kinds of records and varying kinds and amounts of information these records can give you if you are alert to the possibilities. The records involved include petitions, appointments, bonds, inventories, and accounts. Once the guardian is appointed, he must be bonded and must then make an inventory. Throughout the term of the guardianship, he must periodically (usually annually) make an accounting to the court regarding his activities in relation to his charge. Then, as the guardianship terminates by the coming of age, marriage, or death of the child, a final account (or settlement) must be filed with the court.

The information found in these records will vary, but a number of things are quite consistent. For one thing, there is usually a difference in how the guardian is chosen depending upon the age of the child. The general rule has been that if the child is under 14, the court has full authority to name his guardian (giving preference to relatives). However, if he is 14 or older, the child is usually allowed to nominate his own guardian, subject to court approval. Sometimes just this small detail can give you a general idea of the child's age. If the guardian was named in the parent's will (what is called a *testamentary guardian*), the matter is settled, but it will be noted in the record of the appointment.

The final account filed at the termination of the guardianship is sometimes even more useful in determining the child's age because this accounting usually occurred when the child reached legal age. The necessity for the bonding of the guardian was also often waived by the testator when he named his child(ren)'s guardian by will.

Other information often found in guardianship records will include the names of the natural parent(s), the name of the guardian and frequently a relationship, and the name(s) of the child(ren). Descriptions of real property are sometimes given in these records and can be useful identification aids.

Following is a document naming one Samuel Jefferds as guardian of Bartholomew Jefferds, the son of yet another Samuel:

> Jeremiah Moulton Esqr Judge of the Probate of Wills & c. for and within the County of York within the Province of the Massachusetts Bay.
>
> To Samuel Jefferds of Wells in Said County yeoman Greeting. Trusting in your love and Fidelity I do by these presents, pursuant to the Power & authority to me granted in and by an Act of the General Assembly of the Said Province nominate & appoint you *to be Guardian unto Bartholomew Jefferds a Minor and Son of Samuel Jefferds late of Wells afores^d Clerk dec^d who has chosen you to the Said Trust*, with full Power & authority to ask demand Sue for recover receive & take into your Custody all & Singular Such part & portion of Estate as recrues to him in Right of his S^d Father or which by any other way or Means whatsoever doth of Right appertain or belong to him; and to manage employ & improve the Same for his best profit & advantage; and to render a plain & true Acco^t of your Guardianship upon Oath, so far as the Law will charge you therewith when you Shall be lawfully required, and

pay & deliver Such & so much of the Said Estate as shall be remaining upon your Acco^t the Same being first examined & allowed by the Judge of Probates for the time being unto the Said Minor when he Shall arrive at full age or otherwise as the Said Judge or Judges by his or their Decree or Sentence pursuant to Law Shall limit & appoint.

In Testimony whereof I have hereunto Set my Hand & Seal of the Said Court of Probate. Dated at York the fifth Day of April Anno Domini 1763.

Jer: Moulton

[Emphasis added.]

The above is an interesting document because it is not clear if this appointment is based on a testamentary designation by the boy's father. Everything depends on the antecedent of "who has chosen you . . ." If this clause refers back to "Samuel Jefferds late of Wells afores^d Clerk dec^d," then Samuel the guardian is a testamentary guardian. However, if it refers to "Bartholomew Jefferds," then it tells us that Bartholomew was 14 or older and thus chose his own guardian, subject to court approval. Sometimes the language used in documents can be confusing, and you must be careful not to make assumptions until you have more evidence.

The Family History Library in Salt Lake City has some guardianship records for some localities on microfilm, but those holdings are limited. Also, these records are not high on the priority list of records to be digitized and indexed. You must never assume such records do not exist because they are not in one of the website indexes or the Family History Library—even in areas for which the library has extensive collections of other records. When you have the telltale clues, research at the county courthouse—in person or by correspondence—may become necessary and will be worth the effort required.

Apprenticeship records are also important and useful. Very often, you will find apprenticeship records for orphans, especially in earlier time periods.

IV. CONCLUSION

At the conclusion of this discussion, let me re-emphasize that in most American localities, the records discussed in this chapter and the chapter immediately preceding it comprise, collectively, one of our most important source categories of family history evidence because they deal with families and family connections. In addition, their value is enhanced because they exist in places and for time periods for which few other records are available.

As a family history researcher, you must gain a thorough understanding of all those records that relate to the probate and administration of peoples' estates and then use those records knowledgeably.

19

Government Land: Colonial and American

I. BACKGROUND

To begin this discussion of land records, let me first say that it is rare to find complete basic genealogical data in them. Land records are not the type of source usually filled with names, birth dates, birthplaces, names of parents, etc.—information that identifies and sets one person apart from all others. Certainly some of this information can be found in some land records, but it is most uncommon to find all essential family history evidence in land records by themselves. Though land records are far from being a perfect source, if you consider them as a whole, they comprise one of the most important sources for American family history research. There are three reasons for this:

1. As was said in the discussion of probate records, the early American was land-minded. Land was inexpensive and readily available—which was not true in the countries from which most immigrants came—so most people owned land. Hence, in early America and, in fact, until well into the nineteenth century, the great majority of males who lived to maturity—except in the larger cities—can be found in the land records. Nowhere in the modern world has this been true to the extent that it has been in North America. And any record type that includes a large part of the population must be considered important.

2. Land records exist from the very beginning of the first permanent settlements in America, and they are frequently one of the few sources of identifying evidence in existence for early settlement periods. The very existence of these records at a time when there were few other records makes them valuable far beyond what their ordinary content might suggest.

3. The third factor is unique to those land records resulting from private land transactions. This is discussed in more detail in Chapter 20 but,

basically, it is that the older the records, the more family history information (especially concerning relationships) they contain. This pattern is essentially opposite to the pattern followed by most sources of family history information!

Though there are many different kinds of land records arising out of many different situations, the main situations that generated land records have been as follows:

- When a government conveys land to individuals
- When individuals deal in land—one person conveying it to another

Considering these two types of situations, land transfers in America have gone through five important phases (overlapping somewhat in time):

1. In the beginning, all land was claimed by the British Crown. Because of this, the first phase was for the Crown to make grants to the colonies. Such grants (or charters) were made between 1606 (Virginia) and 1732 (Georgia).

2. The second phase was for the colonies to transfer that land to the individual colonists or settlers. This phase, of course, lasted only through the colonial period, so the time period was from about 1607 until the Revolutionary War. The various methods employed in accomplishing these transfers and the resulting records are discussed later.

3. The third phase began when the United States became a sovereign nation after winning independence from Mother England. It involved the transfer of land from the individual states and from various foreign powers to the federal government. This phase began in 1780, when New York and Connecticut ceded certain western lands to which they held claim to the federal government. It ended in 1867 with the purchase of Alaska from Russia. This phase made the federal government (we the people) a landowner, thus creating *public land* (or *the public domain*). The entire nation was not a part of this public domain, however. The thirteen original states plus Kentucky, Maine, Tennessee, Texas, Vermont, and, later, West Virginia retained state ownership and control of the ungranted public lands within their boundaries. These nineteen states are *state-land states*.

4. The transfer of the land from the federal government to private individuals was the fourth phase. This was accomplished by various means, as will be discussed later in this chapter. It began with the Land Ordinance of 1785 and ended, for all practical purposes, with the Taylor Grazing Act of 1934.

5. The fifth phase is probably the most significant to the family history researcher. It involves all land transactions between individual parties. These transactions are under the jurisdiction of the county (most common) or of some other local government entity. This phase began as soon as individuals began to hold land (see phase two) and still continues.

This chapter looks at the details of phases two and four and discusses the value of those records created when a governmental entity transfers land to private parties. Chapter 20 discusses phase five.

II. LAND FROM THE COLONIAL GOVERNMENT

A. The land-grant process

When a government, under English common law, conveyed land to an individual it was called a land grant, and a record was made of the transaction. Title to land thus conveyed was transferred by issuance of a patent or letters patent. During the colonial period, the individual colonies—either by authority from the Crown or by the authority they held under their colonial charters—could make such grants to their settlers. A transfer of this kind was actually a state deed of real estate from the government to the individual and in each case was for a specified tract of land and not for land in general. A small consideration was usually involved, sometimes in a commodity or cash in the form of a *quit rent*.[1] Quit rents were not imposed in New England (except in early Maine and New Hampshire) nor in Dutch New York, and all quit rents were eliminated during the Revolutionary War.

Several records resulted from early colonial land grants. Let us examine the grant process and the records it generated:

1. The first step in the land-grant process was the filing of an ENTRY (sometimes called a *petition* or *application*) by the person seeking the grant. The entry was filed with the colonial governor. Though some of these colonial land entries were recorded, many of them were probably never considered of sufficient importance to make a permanent record because the entry had nothing to do with actual title to the land.

2. Upon approval of the entry, a WARRANT was issued for the land. A warrant was an order, and in cases where land was involved, it was an order directing that the lands to be granted be "laid-out." It was sometimes issued directly to the applicant by authority of the governor or of the Crown. It was surrendered by the applicant at the office of the local land jurisdiction where the warrant was to be carried out. This procedure was not followed in all colonies but, in those where it was followed, most of the warrants were recorded and preserved at the office where they were surrendered. The entryman (applicant) ordinarily had the right to specify the land he wanted to have "laid out."

3. Next, the chosen land was surveyed and measured to meet the requirements of the entry and warrant, and then a PLAT (sometimes called a

---

[1] A quit rent was a small fee paid as a rent for a special purpose. In its true usage under feudal law, it was paid on property by a freeholder in lieu of feudal services. In America, some colonies set up quit rent systems as a means of buying tenure on proprietary grants. Having such rents due did not prevent one from having a freehold title—as good a title to land as was had by anyone else.

survey) of the land was made. This is a map of the tract, often show-ing its location in relation to natural landmarks and lands held by oth-ers. The plat had an accompanying written description that included its metes and bounds. Many plat (or survey) books and other records of the plats have been preserved, but not every colony followed the same procedure.

The land descriptions were very specific, but quite different from the Rectangular Survey system descriptions used later on in the public do-main. The following description is from a plat for fifty acres made in behalf of William Smith in Giles County, Virginia, and is typical:

> 50 acres . . . assigned to him . . . in the county of Giles on the South side of East River and bounded as followeth, To wit, Beginning at a beech on the bank of the River running thence 54° W 54 poles[2] to 4 Spanish oaks on the top of a hill S 66° E 34 poles to two white oaks on the side of a hill S. 31° E 28 poles to two white oaks East 20 poles to two white oaks N 31° E 36 poles to a Sugar tree and Spruce Pine on a cleft of rocks N 14° W 39 poles to down the clefts and crossing the River to a large Sedar tree thence up the River with the meanders thereof and binding thereon 129 poles to the beginning variation three degrees East.

4. Some colonies also issued LICENSES to land-grant applicants. A li-cense, in this sense, was a document granting permission for the ap-plicant to take up certain lands—usually a specifically described and surveyed tract. The colonies that used land licenses often preserved lists of the licensees in conjunction with the land descriptions.

5. After this paperwork, the grant was essentially complete. The grantee was now ready to take possession of his land, and the PATENT could be issued and recorded. Title to the land was secured through the pat-ent. Everything done previously had fulfillment in the issuance and re-cording of the patent. The patent itself was sometimes nothing more than a brief statement of confirmation; it was documentary evidence of title to the land, and it is probably the land-grant document most often preserved.

Technically speaking, there is no one document type that can be called a land grant. A grant was not a document so much as it was a process, and it of-ten involved several documents, as already noted. However, it is not unusual to find documents that are called "grants." Typical of these is the "grant," in 1643, to Francis Littlefield from Sir Ferdinando Gorges, Lord Proprietor of Maine, long before the entire colony was annexed by the Massachusetts Bay Colony. You will note that, in form, this document is essentially a deed to Littlefield from Gorges's agent and deputy governor. It is actually a patent:

> To all to whome theise presents shall come greeting know yee that I Thomas Gorges Deputy Governor of the province of Mayne by vertue of Authority

---

[2] A pole is equivalent to a rod (16½ feet or 5½ yards).

from Sr fferdinando Gorges Knight Lord Proprietor of the said province for
divers good causes & considerations me thereunto moveing have In the be-
halfe of the said fferdinando Gorges given granted & confirmed & by theise
pnts do give grant & confirme unto ffrancis Littlefield of Wells in the county
of Somersett the elder ffifty Acres of Land scituate Lying & being in Wells
aforesaid actioning the land of Edmond Littlefield on the Easter side thereof
containing twenty poles in breadth towards the sea & soe up into the Mayne
Land till ffifty acres be compleated wth all the Marsh twenty pole likewise
in breadth and eight acres or thereabouts to be ground lyeing betweene the
said land & the Sea wall to contayne taken in Egunquick Marsh to have & to
hould the aforesaid land & all & singular the primises wth the appurtenances
unto the said ffrancis Littlefield his heirs & assignes for ever to the only use
& behoofe of the said ffrancis Littlefield his heires & assignes for ever more,
yeilding & paying for the prmises yearely unto the said Sir fferdinando Gorges his heires & assignes two shillings & six pence on the Nine & twentieth
day of September And I the said Thomas Gorges doe hereby depute Edmund
Littlefield to be my lawful attorney in the behalf of the Said sʳ fferdinando
Gorges to enter into the prmises or into pte thereof in name of the whole & to
take possesion therof & after seisin & possesion so taken to deliver possesion
& seisin of the prmises unto the said ffrancis Littlefield in witness whereof I
the said Thomas Gorges have hereunto sett my hand & seale the ffoureteenth
Day of July Anno Dmi 1643.

Tho Gorges Deputi Govrnor

Sealed Signed & Delivered
In the presence of
Roger Guarde
George Puddinton

Veareable & quyet possession taken
& given to ffrancis Littlefield of all
pts & prtlls of land & marshs with the
apurtenances mentioned in the Deed

By me Edmund Littlefield

B. Headright grants

One special type of grant was known as a HEADRIGHT GRANT. It was
not unlike other grants except in the consideration (price) involved. Some of
the colonies, in order to attract settlers, granted land to those who paid the
price of passage for settlers to come to that colony from the Old World. One
man, upon paying the passage for several other persons (often as his indentured servants), would thus be granted a certain amount of land (initially fifty
acres) "per head"—hence the term *headright grant.*

Some records of these headright grants have been published in various
forms. One of the best-known examples is Mrs. Nell M. Nugent's abstracts
of the Virginia land grants between 1623 and 1732 under the title *Cavaliers
and Pioneers: Abstracts of Virginia Land Patents,* 3 vols. (Vol. 1: *1623–1666,*
1934. Reprint, Baltimore: Genealogical Publishing Co., 2004; Vol. 2: *1666–
1695* [Richmond: Virginia State Library, 1977]; Vol. 3: *1695–1732* [Rich-
mond: Virginia State Library, 1979].) Four additional volumes in this series
(1732–1776) are available at the Virginia Genealogical Society. Though the

text of the first three volumes is also available online, the URL is much too long to print here. However, it can be quite easily located by entering "Virginia land grants Nugent" into your Internet search engine. There is a comprehensive index at the end of these online abstracts, which lists every name found in the records, including the names of those persons whose passage was paid by the grantee. The location of the land is told in each case.

C. Non-grant transfers

Not all lands passing from the colonies to individual owners were because of grants. Another means of transfer was cash sale, and such sales became increasingly popular during the eighteenth century. Persons and companies with considerable capital often bought expansive tracts at bargain prices and then leased the land to others. Many of these owners never personally set foot in the colonies but were content to sit back in England and collect rent from their tenants. Also, in those colonies established under proprietary grants (Delaware, Maryland, Pennsylvania, the Carolinas, and early Maine and New Hampshire), the lord proprietors collected rents annually through their agents or deputies, and RENT ROLLS were religiously maintained—one copy in the county and a duplicate copy for the lord proprietor.

During the Revolutionary War, most states seized the proprietary and crown lands and sold them along with confiscated Loyalist properties.[3]

D. Value of land grants and related records

There is considerable family history value in the records discussed here— much more than just historical interest. All of them contain valuable names, dates, and places that help us put wandering ancestors in specific places at specific times and provide other useful clues essential to family history investigation—even clues relating to connections between individuals and families. This being true, do you think there might be a family connection between Francis Littlefield and Edmund Littlefield in the land grant (patent) we just looked at?

III. AFTER THE REVOLUTION

A. Initial legislation

After the War for Independence, the states continued to grant their previously ungranted lands just as was done earlier in their parent colonies. There is little difference in the land-grant records of the colonies before the war and of the states after the war.

The main differences in land-grant records after the war were more apparent elsewhere. Those differences were due to the formation of what came to be known as the public domain, where the federal government was the land-

---

[3] There is more information about Loyalists and records relating to them in Chapter 26, "Military Records: Colonial Wars and the American Revolution."

owner. When the federal government became a landowner, that fact generated a completely different kind of record—a record documenting the transfer of land from the federal government (all of us) to private individuals (one of us).

The enactment of the Land Ordinance of 1785 marked the start of this new type of record. The primary objectives of this legislation were (1) to get the land settled quickly and (2) to form new states. Below are the provisions of this significant legislation:

- All land should be purchased from the native tribes prior to settlement.
- All land should be surveyed and laid out in townships and sections (Rectangular Survey System, based on meridians and base lines) prior to settlement.
- The first tracts surveyed would be drawn by lot for military bounties that had been promised earlier.
- The remaining tracts would be offered for sale at public auction in township and section-size units.

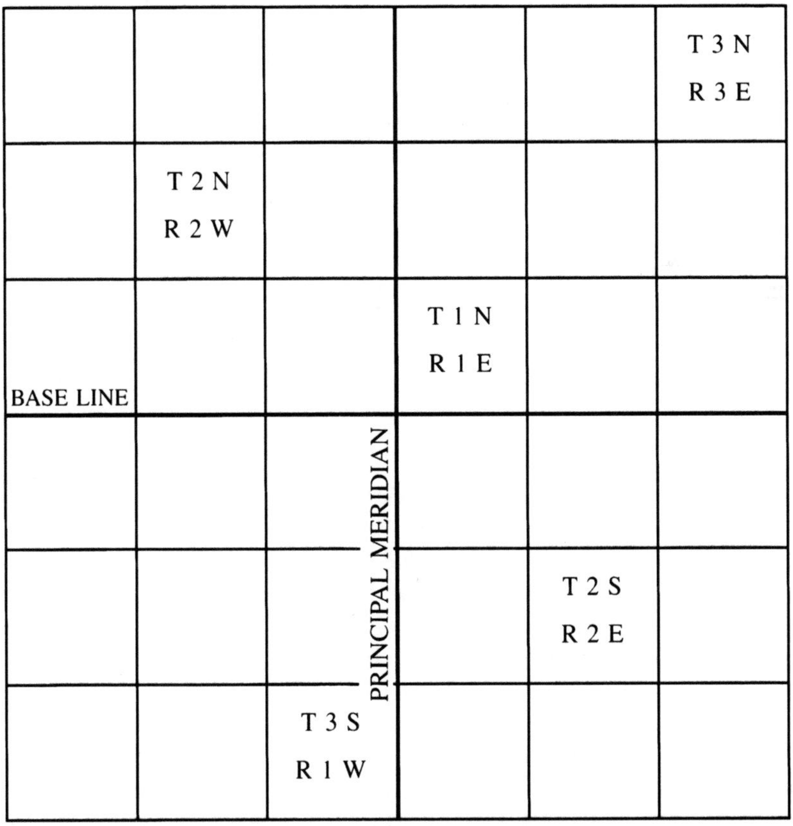

FIGURE 1—NUMBERING TOWNSHIPS AND RANGES FROM THE BASE LINE
AND PRINCIPAL MERIDIAN

6	5	4	3	2	1
7	8	9	10	11	12
18	17	16	15	14	13
19	20	21	22	23	24
30	29	28	27	26	25
31	32	33	34	35	36

FIGURE 2—NUMBERING AND DIVIDING THE SECTIONS OF A TOWNSHIP

- Some lands (specifically identified) would be set aside for educational purposes.
- Absolute (or fee simple) title would be transferred with all lands.

Another law, the Northwest Ordinance in 1787, specifically provided that if a land holder died intestate, his widow would receive one-third of the land (in fee simple) and the remainder would descend to his children in equal portions. It also provided that wills and deeds had to be duly proved and recorded within one year or they would be invalid. This 1787 ordinance also made both resident and nonresident landowners subject to taxation, but provided a tax exemption for government-owned land.

Before 1800, the large size of land tracts (townships and sections) available for purchase put the cost of land so high that it was too expensive for those without military warrants to obtain it. In that year, the Harrison Land Act reduced tract sizes and allowed purchases to be made on credit. These changes made it possible for individual settlers to own land.

B. Rectangular Survey system

Because many have asked what the Rectangular Survey system involves, I will explain it as simply as I can. The public land system that Congress adopted specified that two lines should run through every territory that was to be surveyed—a *base line* that runs east and west and a *meridian line* that runs north and south—these lines intersecting each other at right angles. All land in the surveyed territory was divided into townships and surveyed from the beginning point where this base line and meridian line intersected. Each township was six miles square (thirty-six square miles) and subdivided into thirty-six sections with each section having 640 acres (one square mile). Townships were numbered with reference to the base line and the meridian line—first either north or south from the base line and then either east or west from the meridian line. Going north or south, the numbering was referred to as townships, and going east or west, the numbering was referred to as ranges. For example, a township that lay four townships south of the base line and three ranges west of the meridian line would be described as Township 4 south, Range 3 west (written as T 4 S R 3 W).

The sections could also be divided by running lines through their centers, both north and south and east and west, to create half sections and quarter sections. Quarter sections were also divisible, but that was not part of the original survey. Figures 1 and 2 illustrate the system.

IV. HISTORY OF LAND ENTRIES IN THE PUBLIC DOMAIN

A. Bounty land warrants—federal and state

Early in the American Revolution, the Continental Congress authorized each private and noncommissioned officer to receive a bounty of fifty dollars, fifty acres of land, and a new suit of clothes for his military service. This type of land grant to the military veteran was called a *bounty land warrant*. It was a grant in return for military service.

In addition to the promises made by the Continental Congress, some states also pledged bounty land for their Revolutionary veterans and preserved tracts in their western territories to make good on those pledges. A good example of this was the area known as the Western Reserve in what is now northeastern Ohio. This was a large area owned by Connecticut and reserved by that state in 1786 for grants to her veterans. At the time, she ceded the rest of her western land holdings to the federal government.

Federal bounty land warrants were also issued to those who served in later wars—the War of 1812, the Indian wars, and the Mexican War.

B. Bounty land in the public domain

After the Revolution, the first legislation by the federal government for military bounty land was passed in 1812 as an incentive for volunteer service in the War of 1812. The lands involved were in special districts located in Arkansas, Illinois, and Missouri, and the grants were not transferable. Only the veteran who served and who was awarded the grant could claim it.

Four very important acts were also passed between 1847 and 1856. The Act of 1847 provided bounty land for those who had served for at least one year in the Mexican War. The Act of 1850 extended this bounty to War of 1812 veterans and veterans of the Indian wars. The Act of 1852 extended benefits to officers as well as enlisted men and, for the first time, made all benefits assignable (which meant they could be sold or given away). The Act of 1855 (amended in 1856) included every soldier (or his heirs) who had served at least fourteen days in any war since, and including, the Revolutionary War.

These four acts (1847, 1850, 1852, and 1855) were unique because they offered bounty land as a reward to soldiers who had already served, rather than as an incentive for enlistment as previous legislation had done. All four acts provided that a warrant for a quarter section (160 acres) of land, *located on any part of the surveyed public domain*, would be granted to each person who qualified. *Scrip* (a certificate) was issued to those who qualified and could be exchanged for title at any public land office or could be (and usually was) sold to someone else.[4]

More is said about bounty land warrants in Chapter 26 as part of our discussion about veterans' benefits in connection with colonial wars and the Revolutionary War.

C. Land sales by the federal government

Following passage of the Northwest Ordinance of 1785, the federal government sold land in very large parcels—townships (23,040 acres) and sections (640 acres)—for a minimum of $1 per acre, payable within one year. A new ordinance in 1796 raised the minimum price to $2 per acre, and another in 1800 (the Harrison Land Act) reduced the minimum tract size to a half section (320 acres). This 1800 ordinance also allowed for four payments over a five-year period. The purpose of the ordinance was to make land more available to more people. Unfortunately, however, the changes only encouraged speculation, and the desired purpose was not achieved.

A new ordinance in 1820 (passed because of the collapse of the western land boom the year before) was more successful. It did away with credit sales, reduced the size of sale tracts to one-eighth section (80 acres), and lowered the minimum price to $1.25 per acre. Land was sold under this act until 1908.

D. Preemption sales

In 1830, the first preemption act was passed by Congress, in an alliance between the South and the West. Preemption allowed any settler (i.e., squat-

---

[4] Roy M. Robbins, *Our Landed Heritage: The Public Domain 1776–1936* (Lincoln, NE: University of Nebraska Press, 1962), 156–157.

ter) on the public land who had cultivated a tract in 1829 to buy it (up to 160 acres) for $1.25 per acre.

The preemption act was merely a pardon to those who had settled illegally, and once the step was taken to grant amnesty to squatters, it was difficult to reject demands for similar action later on. Thus, for a time, preemption was renewed nearly every time Congress convened.

Following the financial panic of 1837, after much debate by government officials, a new temporary preemption act was passed by Congress in 1838. This act allowed any settler on the public domain who

- was either over 21 or the head of a family;
- was living on the land when the act was passed; and
- had been there for four months preceding the act

to have all the benefits granted in the Act of 1830. Preemption was a major issue in the Presidential campaign of 1840 (Harrison over Van Buren), and the act was again renewed by Congress.

In 1841, a permanent preemption act was passed by Congress, allowing anyone who was the head of a family, a widow, a single man, over 21 years old, and a U.S. citizen or someone who had declared his intention to become a citizen[5] to stake a claim on a tract up to 160 acres and then buy it from the government for not less than $1.25 per acre.

Some lands, however, were not open to preemption. These included (a) reservations, (b) school lands, (c) specific Indian lands, (d) land already sectioned for town sites, (e) mineral and saline lands, (f) land within incorporated towns, and (g) lands already granted for various reasons.

The land involved had to be previously surveyed. There was a requirement that the claimant had to have come to inhabit the land after June 1, 1840. He also had to have improved the land and built a dwelling on it. He had thirty days after settling to file a declaration of his intention to make the claim. Or, if he was already on the land when the act was passed, he had three months to file his declaration. Congress repealed this act in 1891.[6]

E. Donation land grants and price reductions

In 1854, another federal act made public land that had been on the market for thirty years available for 12 cents per acre. There were also other measures taken to lure settlers to some remote areas. It is of note that in the Florida, New Mexico, Oregon, and Washington territories, the federal government offered donation land grants (free land) to almost anyone who would settle there. East

---

[5] Note that aliens were permitted to make claims under all earlier preemption acts.

[6] "27th Congress, Ch. XVI, 5 Stat. 453, 'An Act to appropriate the proceeds of the sales of the public lands, and to grant pre-emption rights.'" *The Preemption Act of 1841*, November 2009, http://www.minnesotalegalhistoryproject.org/ (accessed July 31, 2017).

Florida was extended this privilege in 1842 to attract men who could protect the territory. Any man over 18 or the head of a family who took up permanent residence was entitled to receive 160 acres.

The Donation Land Act for the Oregon Territory passed Congress in 1850. It granted a "donation" of free land—320 acres for each single man and 640 acres for each married man—to those who settled on the land before December 1 of that year. The act required four years of continuous residence on and cultivation of the land in order to gain title. In 1853, that residence requirement was cut in half. Another act in 1854 extended the same donation land benefits to the Washington Territory, which had been divided from the Oregon Territory the previous year. Both acts expired at the end of 1855.

On July 22, 1854, just three days after passage of the Washington Donation Land Act, donation privileges were extended to the New Mexico Territory. The New Mexico donation act provided that donation claims could be switched to cash purchases for $1.25 per acre. That act expired in 1883.

In essence, the donation land experiments were a limited trial of the principle of homesteading before the latter became a national policy.[7]

F. Homestead grants

After the secession of the Southern states, which had opposed the homestead principle, cash sales and preemptions were largely replaced by homestead grants. Under the Homestead Act of 1862, a settler could gain title to public lands without monetary consideration (except a small filing fee) by meeting a five-year residency requirement, if he cultivated and improved the land. Any person who met the age and citizenship requirements of the Preemption Act of 1841 could homestead up to 160 acres (quarter section) of public land. The claimant had to be the head of a household or at least 21 years old. The Homestead Act, however, did not completely eliminate either direct cash sales or preemptions.

One provision of the Homestead Act allowed the homesteader, if he desired, to commute his homestead entry to a cash entry for $1.25 per acre after six months' residence and improvement of the land. Union Army and Navy veterans (those who had served fourteen or more days during wartime) were considered to meet the age requirement automatically. Those who had borne arms against the government or had given aid to its enemies were excluded, but only until January 1, 1867.

Many changes were made to homestead laws by various congressional bills, and an act passed in 1872 made it possible for all Civil War veterans with at least ninety days' service to apply their service time—up to four years—toward the five-year homestead residency requirement.

---

[7] Robbins, 153–154.

Acts passed in 1879 and 1880 made it possible to commute a preemption claim to a homestead claim and vice versa, if the claimant desired. The privileges and guarantees were the same. Preemption was finally repealed by Congress in 1891, with a provision allowing completion of claims initiated before the repeal.

Later bills provided for larger homesteads (320 acres) in the West on certain non-irrigable lands (Act of 1909) and for three-year homesteads (Act of 1912). Stock raising—primarily grazing—homesteads of 640 acres were specified in the Act of 1916.

G. Private land claims

Another type of grant was the *Private Land Claim*. These were claims

usually made by persons who claimed to have grants from foreign sovereigns, by descendants of such persons, by citizens of the United States who settled these lands with the permission of the foreign government, and by U.S. citizens who bought up rights to lands acquired under foreign sovereignty and presented them to the Federal Government for the purpose of acquiring title.[8]

A Private Land Claim was merely an acknowledgment of title by the federal government to those who owned or had been granted land by a foreign government before the U.S. became sovereign in the area concerned. These claims covered a broad period of time and extensive portions of the public domain; portions of fifteen states were involved.

H. Closing of the public domain

The Taylor Grazing Act of 1934, as amended, closed most of the public domain to entry, and grazing lands were left in public ownership, under jurisdiction of the Interior Department.

In 1935, by Presidential order, all public lands were essentially closed to individual entry.

V. RECORDS CREATED BY LAND ENTRIES IN THE PUBLIC DOMAIN

Most records relating to those land entries described above have been preserved. They were originally housed in the General Land Office and, when that office was discontinued, were sent to the National Archives. Though most land entry records for the public domain are in this collection, a few are still in land offices and/or historical societies in the individual states.

---

[8] Anne Bruner Eales and Robert M. Kvasnicka, eds., *Guide to Genealogical Research in the National Archives of the United States*, 3rd ed. (Washington, DC: National Archives and Records Administration, 2000), 298.

The records in the National Archives include the following:

A. Credit entry files

As indicated earlier, most land sold by the federal government between passage of the Harrison Land Act of 1800 and the Act of 1820 (see IV, C, above) was on five years' credit for a minimum of $2 per acre. The Credit Entry Final Certificates, which were issued on completed purchases, are the most important records in this file, but you will also find an occasional assignment filed with these certificates, as well as some other records.

All final certificates filed before the Act of 1820 are called "Credit Prior Certificates," and those filed afterward (under relief legislation) by those who had begun payment before the act was passed, but had not finished, are called "Credit Under Certificates."

Both types of final certificates normally show the following:

> Name and place of residence of the entryman as given at the time of purchase, date of purchase, number of acres purchased, land description, summary of credit payments, and volume and page number of the copy of patent in the ESO [Eastern States Office of the Bureau of Land Management].[9]

Many of the records of the General Land Office (GLO) and the Bureau of Land Management (BLM) are now held by the various Regional National Archives. A listing of the states and their records in possession of these facilities is found on pages 300 through 303 of *Guide to Genealogical Research in the National Archives of the United States* (3rd ed.), edited by Eales and Kvasnicka. For example, the Regional National Archives in Chicago has the records of the Canto, Chillicothe, Cincinnati, Steubenville, Wooster, and Zanesville land offices, 1801–1828. These records include local office registers, tract books, and correspondence.[10]

Also, note the following:

> The Ohio History Connection [formerly the Ohio Historical Society] serves as the custodian of records from Ohio's federal and state land offices, United States Military District and Virginia Military District. The records consist of survey plats and notes, and entry, sale, and payment records. . . . These historical records, which date to the late 18th Century, document the western expansion of a young nation and illustrate some of the earliest exploration of the Ohio wilderness through plats, field notes, and tract and entry books from most of Ohio's land districts, entry books and payment entry and receipt books, journals, and ledgers from six of Ohio's oldest land offices, [as well as] entry and survey books from the Virginia Military District.[11]

---

[9] Ibid., 292.

[10] Ibid., 302.

[11] "Land Records," Ohio History Connection. Ohio History Center, https://www.ohiohistory.org/learn/archives-library/land-records (accessed October 31, 2016).

The Ohio History Connection is at 800 E. 17th Avenue, Columbus OH, 43211.

B. Cash entry files

Beginning with the Act of 1820, most land sold by the government was for cash at a minimum of $1.25 per acre. The Cash Entry Files are arranged at the National Archives under the names of the individual land offices, but there is a master card index to the cash entries for seven states: Alabama, Alaska, Arizona, Florida, Louisiana, Nevada, and Utah.

An individual file contains an application for a tract, a receipt for money, and a Final Certificate authorizing the claimant to secure a patent. In cases where the land was claimed by preemption, the preemption proof may also be in the file. If the tract was entered as a homestead and later commuted to a cash entry, the Homestead Entry File is included.

Ordinarily the most valuable document in a Cash Entry File is the Final Certificate, which shows the following:

> Name of entryman, place of residence at time of purchase, land description, number of acres, date of patent, and volume and page number of the copy of patent in NARA or ESO [Eastern States Office of the Bureau of Land Management]. Testimony of the purchaser in a preemption proof may, in addition, include age, citizenship, date of entry on the land, number and relationship of members of the household, and nature of improvements to the land.[12]

All preemption entries were cash sales and are therefore included in these files. Cash Entry Files cover the period from 1820 to 1908, but the records of all land offices do not cover the entire period as many were opened later.

The Illinois State Archives in Springfield has compiled a computerized database of the Illinois Public Land sales of more than 500,000 public land sales in that state. This indexed database makes it possible to locate the subject land on a map. The information below is included in the index:

> Name of purchaser and record ID number, type of sale, description of land purchased, number of acres, price per acre, total price, male or female purchaser, date of purchase, county or state of residence of purchaser, and volume and page of original land record.[13]

The Illinois State Archives is at the Margaret Cross Norton Building, Springfield, IL 62756. These records can be accessed online through a computerized index at *http://ilsos.gov/isa/landSalesSearch.do*. Note also that some of these records are digitized and indexed on the Ancestry website at *http://search.ancestry.com/search/db.aspx?dbid=3780*. Land ownership maps for multiple states, including Illinois, have also been digitized and indexed by Ancestry and are online at *http://search.ancestry.com/search/db.aspx?dbid=1127*.

---

[12] Eales and Kvasnicka, 292.

[13] *Newsletter*, Chicago Genealogical Society, July/August 1982.

C. Donation entry files

The Florida Donation Entry files are mainly for 1842 through 1850 and are in varying degrees of completeness, depending on the extent to which the title to the land was perfected. If the claimant completed the five-year residency requirement, his complete file contains the following:

> [A] permit to settle, application for patent, report by the land agent, and final certificate authorizing a patent. . . . A permit to settle shows name of applicant, marital status, month and year the applicant became a resident of Florida, and land description. An application for patent shows name of applicant, land description, name of settler (the person actually living on the land), and period of settlement. A final certificate shows the name of applicant, land description, date of patent, and volume and page number of copy of patent in the ESO [Eastern States Office of the Bureau of Land Management].[14]

All files containing Final Certificates are indexed in a master card file at the National Archives.

The Donation Entry Files for Oregon and Washington are filed separately in the National Archives, and those for each state are divided into two series— one for completed entries and one for those that were not completed. Files of both states are indexed. An alphabetical list of the Oregon claims has also been published serially in the *Genealogical Forum of Portland, Oregon* under the title of "Index to Oregon Donation Land Claims." This publication is on microfiche at the Family History Library in Salt Lake City.

Concerning the Oregon and Washington donation files, Eales and Kvasnicka wrote:

> The **Oregon and Washington donation files** for each appropriate land office are arranged numerically in two series. One series relates to patented entries, the other to incomplete or canceled entries. Both series have been reproduced on M815, *Oregon and Washington Donation Land Files, 1851–1903,* 108 rolls [of microfilm].
>
> Abstracts with indexes for both the Oregon and the Washington donation entries are also available on M145, *Abstracts of Oregon Donation Land Claims, 1852–1903,* 6 rolls [of microfilm], and M203, *Abstracts of Washington Donation Land Claims, 1855–1902,* 1 roll [of microfilm]. The abstracts fully identify each claim by name, land office, and patent number, and can be used to locate files on M815. . . .
>
> Documents in a donation file include notification of settlement, which described the land either by legal description or by natural features (metes and bounds), sometimes accompanied by a plat; affidavit of settlement, which shows the settler's date and place of birth and, if applicable, of marriage; proofs of cultivation; oath that the land has been used for cultivation only; for naturalized citizens, proof of citizenship (not filmed on M815), and donation

---

[14] Eales and Kvasnicka, 292, 293. Note that the BLM/ESO office is at 20 M Street SE, Suite 950, Washington, DC 20003.

certificate, which shows name of entryman, place of residence, land description, date of patent, and volume and page number of copy of patent in the National Archives.[15] [Emphasis in original.]

Registers of donation notifications and entries for New Mexico between 1855 and 1871 are reported to be at the Regional National Archives in Denver, gathered from the land offices in Clayton, Folsom, Fort Sumner, LaMesilla, Las Cruces, Roswell, Santa Fe, and Tucumcari.[16] A book with further details on these records is Victor Westphall's *The Public Domain in New Mexico, 1854–1891.* Albuquerque, New Mexico: University of New Mexico, 1965. There is a copy of this book in the Family History Library in Salt Lake City (978.9 R2w).

D. Military bounty land entries

Also located in the National Archives are records of the U.S. bounty land warrants surrendered at the various land offices for land in the public domain or for scrip certificates that could be used to purchase land. All except the War of 1812 warrants (which limited the location to military reservations in Illinois, Arkansas, and Missouri) were assignable, and most were assigned (i.e., sold) by the veterans who received them. These warrants could be exchanged for land almost anywhere in the public domain.

The Virginia bounty land warrants are indexed in two manuscript volumes at the National Archives, entitled *Indexes to Names of Warrantees for Virginia Military Bounty Land Warrants Issued for Continental Line Service, ca. 1789–1839.* Separately, these two volumes are also known as *Virginia Military Warrants, Continental Line, Alphabetical Index to Warrantees* [vol. 30] and *Virginia Military Land Warrants to Whom Issued, Alphabetically Arranged* [vol. 31]. The first volume (volume 30) indexes the Continental Line warrants and is arranged alphabetically by first letter of the surname of warrantee, and thereunder chronologically by warrant number. The second volume (volume 31) relates to Virginia warrants, and surnames are indexed alphabetically by first letter.

The names of Virginia warrantees have also been copied onto cards that are filed in a consolidated bounty land warrant index. The names of these Virginia warrantees are also included in Gaius M. Brumbaugh's *Revolutionary War Records*, Vol. I [the only volume published], 1936. Reprint, Baltimore: Genealogical Publishing Co., 2008, 323–525.

The following are included in Virginia bounty land warrant records:

> The surrendered Virginia bounty land warrant files, 1782–1892, and related documents. A file generally consists of a surrendered warrant, a survey, assignments, and, where appropriate, related documents concerning heirs of

---

[15] Ibid., 293

[16] *Guide to Genealogical Research in the National Archives,* rev. ed. (Washington, DC: National Archives Trust Fund Board, 1983), 225.

the veteran. The file may also show date and place of death of the warrantee, names of assignees and heirs, and places of residence. Often an assignee who had several warrants assigned to them requested that one large tract be surveyed to satisfy the warrants; in such cases, a file will contain more than one warrant. . . .

The volume and page number of the record copy of patent, which is maintained by the Eastern States Office [ESO] of the Bureau of Land Management, is usually found in the file. This is important because the surrendered Virginia bounty land warrant files are arranged by these volume and page numbers.

Finding aids are available to assist in locating surrendered Virginia bounty land warrant case files. Entries in the index to names of warrantees are arranged alphabetically by initial letter of surname. Those in a register entitled "Virginia Military Warrants—Numerical—Continental and State Lines," are arranged by warrant number with the survey number; entries in a register entitled "Surveys for Land in Virginia Military District, Ohio," are arranged by survey number and give the volume and page number that identifies the case file. If only the name of the warrantee is known, it is necessary to use all three finding aids in succession to identify the surrendered bounty land warrant case file.[17]

Because of sales and assignments of warrants, the warrantee and the patentee were often different people. There is also an index to patentees in a manuscript volume at the National Archives entitled *Virginia Military Land Patent Index (vol. 34)*. In addition to the name of the patentee, this index tells the name of the warrantee and the location of the entry file.

Much of Kentucky was settled as a direct result of Revolutionary War bounty land warrants from the Virginia Line. The records of these surveys and grants are at the Kentucky Land Office, Secretary of State's Office, Capitol Building, 700 Capital Avenue, Frankfort, KY 40601. A helpful aid is Willard R. Jillson's *Old Kentucky Entries and Deeds: A Complete Index to All of the Earliest Land Entries, Military Warrants, Deeds and Wills of the Commonwealth of Kentucky*. 1926. Reprint, Baltimore: Genealogical Publishing Co., 2008, 313–392.

Jillson's volume is an index to these warrants. It is arranged alphabetically and includes the name of the warrantee, the number of acres, the warrant number, a description of the warrantee's service, and the date of the warrant. You can access a digitized copy of Jillson's book online at *https://familysearch.org/ search/catalog/74688?availability=Family%20History%20Library*.

The Virginia Military District was originally a significant part of what later became the state of Ohio. After the Revolutionary War, however, Virginia gave up most of these western lands, ceding them to the federal government and retaining only that area bounded on the south by the Ohio River, on the west by the Little Miami River, and on the north and east by the Scioto River. Virginia used this retained land to give bounty land grants to her Revolutionary War veterans. Eventually, however, she gave those lands not claimed by

---

[17] Eales and Kvasnicka, 184–185.

veterans to the United States government, and the government gave them to the State of Ohio.

Records relating to the surveys and grants in the Virginia Military District are at the Ohio History Connection at 800 E. 17th Avenue, Columbus OH, 43211. With regard to these grants, you should be aware of two important works:

> Smith, Clifford Neal. *The Federal Land Series: A Calendar of Archival Materials on the Land Patents Issued by the United States Government with Subject, Tract, and Name Indexes. Parts 1 & 2: Grants in the Virginia Military District of Ohio.* Vol. 4. Chicago: American Library Association, 1972–1973. Entries in these two C.N. Smith books (comprising volume 4) are arranged according to survey number, and each entry lists acreage, adjacent watercourses, county and township, warrant number, and the names of warrantee, patentee, and any others who settled on any part of the land. Every entry is indexed three ways—by name, by county and/or township, and by watercourse. More than 22,000 persons are identified. (This work is on microfilm at the Family History Library in Salt Lake City and was also reprinted by Clearfield Company in 2007 [available at *genealogical.com*].)[18]

> Smith, Alma Aicholtz. *The Virginia Military Surveys of Clermont and Hamilton Counties, Ohio, 1787–1849.* Cincinnati: The author, 1985. This book is available in several places, including the Family History Library. It contains numerous excellent maps and much useful data.

Federal bounty land entries are filed and indexed in various series at the National Archives. Details concerning them are included in the discussion of military records in Chapters 26 and 27. It is unfortunate that fires destroyed the application files relating to more than 14,700 warrants issued between 1798 and 1800, but the basic information from these files had been copied onto cards. The information on each card includes the veteran's name, rank, military unit, warrant number, acreage granted, issue date, and where applicable, the name of the heir or assignee. The cards are interfiled alphabetically with the Revolutionary War pension applications.

Warrants were issued for unspecified public land under the various congressional acts between 1847 and 1855. These acts, as mentioned earlier, differed from prior legislation because they were passed to reward those who had already served rather than to encourage enlistment. Nearly all of these warrants were sold by their recipients.

---

[18] In addition to these two parts of volume 4, this *Federal Land Series* by Clifford Neil Smith includes three other important volumes. Volumes 1 and 3 contain information on land patents in several parts of the public domain between 1788 and 1814. The subtitle of both volumes is *A Calendar of Archival Materials on the Land Patents Issued by the United States Government, with Subject, Tract, and Name Indexes.* Volume 2 includes federal Revolutionary bounty land warrants, 1799 to 1835. Its subtitle is *Federal Bounty-Land Warrants of the American Revolution.*

The files contain no family history information about the warrantee except in the unlikely case that he died while still in possession of the warrant. In that case, the file would contain the names and places of residence of his heirs. All patentees are identified and the location of the land is shown. The files are arranged by year of the basic congressional act, then by the number of acres awarded, and finally by warrant number. The *applications* for these bounty land warrants are arranged alphabetically in two series at the National Archives—one series for those with Revolutionary War service (combined with the pension application files) and one for those with later service. Locating a person's application enables you to locate his file.

No bounty land warrants were issued after passage of the Homestead Act in 1862. Veterans were instead given special privileges under the various homestead acts. Additional detail about bounty land warrant records is found in Chapter 8 of the *Guide to Genealogical Research in the National Archives of the United States* (3rd ed.), edited by Anne Bruner Eales and Robert M. Kvasnicka and published in 2000. The chapter is entitled "Bounty Land Warrant Records."

E. Homestead entry files

Homestead Entry papers contain more family history information than the earlier land entry files. These papers are in the National Archives in Washington and in the Regional National Archives under the names of the individual land offices, usually in two separate series—one series for those who completed their entries and the other for those who did not. The files cover January 1863 through June 1908. In the *Guide to Genealogical Research in the National Archives of the United States*, mentioned above, in Section D ("Other Useful Records"), Chapter 15 ("Land Records"), beginning on page 293, there is information concerning homestead records—as well as other land records—in the National Archives system. The following description is given there of homestead entry files:

> There are generally two types of homestead files for each land office, one for patented homestead entries, the other for unpatented or canceled homestead entries. A patented homestead file usually contains a homestead application; certificate of publication of intention to enter land; testimony of the applicant and two witnesses; final certificate authorizing patent; and, where appropriate, copy of naturalization proceedings or copy of a Union veteran's discharge certificate.
>
> A **homestead application** shows name of entryman, place of residence at time of application, land description, and number of acres. Testimony of the applicant on a **homestead proof** includes land description; name, age, and address of applicant; description of the house and date when residence was established; number and relationship of members of the family; nature of crops; and number of acres under cultivation. A **final certificate** shows name and address of applicant, land description, date of patent, and volume and page number of copy of patent in NARA [National Archives and Records

Administration] and the ESO [Eastern States Office of the Bureau of Land Management].[19] [Emphasis in original.]

All homestead entries commuted to cash entries are in the Cash Entry Files.

F. Private land claim entries

As explained earlier, private land claims were made by persons who were granted or were otherwise in possession of the land they held when the location was controlled by a foreign government before the U.S. became sovereign in the area. The National Archives has records of private land claims records for parts the following fifteen states:

- Illinois, Indiana, Michigan, and Wisconsin (originally in the Northwest Territory)
- Alabama and Mississippi (originally in the Mississippi Territory)
- Louisiana and the Missouri Territory states of Arkansas, Iowa, and Missouri (originally part of the Louisiana Purchase)
- Florida (originally the Florida Cession from Spain)
- Arizona, California, Colorado, and New Mexico (in and adjacent to the southwestern territory ceded to the U.S. by Mexico)[20]

The records arising from these claims vary with both time and territory. Some of the available records include certificates of survey, surveyors' reports, congressional reports, board of commissioners' reports, journals, claims papers, certificates of confirmation, and maps. Many of them are indexed.

> Records relating to Individual claims presented before boards of commissioners or other Federal agencies, 1790–1837, were sent to Congress and transcribed and indexed in *American State Papers: Public Lands,* 8 vols. (Washington: Gales and Seaton, 1832–61). Claims from 1790–1809 are in volume 1; 1809–15 in vol. 2; 1815–24 in vol. 3; 1824–28 in in vol. 4; 1827–29 in vol. 5; 1829–34 in vol. 6; 1834–35 in vol. 7; and 1865–37 in vol. 8. Each volume is indexed [but the indexes are not trustworthy]. A consolidated index has been published under the title *Grassroots of America,* edited by Phillip W. McMullin (Salt Lake City: Gendex, 1972). Most of the reports published in the Gales and Seaton edition were also published in the less complete edition of *American State* Papers issued by Duff Green in 1834.[21]

Regarding the nature of these records, as they are found in the National Archives, Eales and Kvasnicka explain:

> Those **private land claim case files** in R[ecord] G[roup] 49[,] where title to the land has been approved[,] are arranged by state or other geographic

---

[19] Eales and Kvasnicka, 293.

[20] Ibid., 298.

[21] Ibid., 298. Note, also, that *Grassroots of America* was reprinted in 1994 by Southern Historical Press of Greenville, South Carolina. It is also available on microfilm from the Family History Library in Salt Lake City (film number 6051323).

area, thereunder by docket number, with indexes for most states or geographic areas. Case files include correspondence, reports, maps and plats, petitions, affidavits, transcripts of court decisions, and deeds and abstract of title. Because proof of title was required, wills, deeds, marriage certificates, and assignments may be found among these records. For the most part, the case files contain copies of original documents. Many of these records were created during the adjudication of claims by agencies of the United States. These case files do not include the original grant or other documents of the original land transfer, except perhaps some copies in translation. For California, however, there are records, for the most part in Spanish, concerning land claims based on grants made by the Mexican Government, 1822–46.[22] [Emphasis in original.]

G. Land entries 1908–73

Most land entry case files for the period between July 1, 1908, and May 16, 1973, are in the National Archives in one numerical series, filed according to patent number, regardless of the entry type. These include records of cash sales, homestead, timber culture, desert land, Indian allotments, and all other types. There are two card indexes:

- An alphabetical index to applicants. This index identifies the land office and the serial application number. It includes all applications, both those that were rejected, relinquished, or canceled and those where patents were issued.

- An index by state and, thereunder, by land office. This index is based on application numbers and gives the patent numbers assigned to perfected patents.

Each of these files shows the following:

Name of patentee, place of residence, land description [subdivision, section, township, and range], date of patent and patent number. Type of land entry determines the nature of additional information in the file. All copies of patents for the period after June 30, 1908, are in the ESO [Eastern States Office of the Bureau of Land Management]. Most serial patent files are held by NARA; many of the Indian allotment serial patent files, however, are not in the National Archives. Rejected, canceled, or relinquished serial application files for the eastern states, July 1, 1908–1933, arranged by state, thereunder by land office, and thereunder by serial application number, are also in the National Archives. Those for western states are mostly in [the regional National Archives].[23]

H. Land records in the Regional National Archives

The Regional National Archives, described and discussed in Chapter 5, have various land entry records in their collections as noted in the paragraph

---

[22] Ibid., 298.

[23] Ibid., 298.

quoted immediately above. These include the records of the 362 district land offices that operated at various times and locations throughout the U.S. However, these are too extensive to list here. I refer you instead to a National Archives website called "Records of the Bureau of Land Management [BLM]." This site has a state-by-state listing—in some detail—under the number and title "49.9 RECORDS OF DISTRICT LAND OFFICES 1800–1980." The website URL is *https://www.archives.gov/research/guide-fed-records/ groups/049.html#top*. Though this URL is quite long, it is worth the effort involved to take a careful look.

VI. LAND PATENTS FROM THE BLM

In 1989, the Bureau of Land Management, with some project funding from the Department of Energy (DOE), began a project to computerize on compact discs—by means of optical scanning—all of the land patents in the BLM for the states east of the Mississippi River. This project began with the patents for the public lands in Arkansas, and that part of the project was completed in January of 1990.

As DOE workers gained experience with the project, BLM officials expressed a desire to include the land patents for the entire country and to build an index into its system that would facilitate greater use by family history researchers. These records are now all digitized and indexed, making enhanced copies of the patents themselves almost instantly accessible by going to *https://glorecords.blm.gov/search/*. Once on that website, enter the desired details in the spaces provided, then click on "Search Patents" at the bottom of the page. From there, you will be able to see where the land is located on the map and access a copy of the land patent. That copy can also be printed.

In the beginning, the BLM expressed a desire to work with the LDS Family History Library to provide space in each of these records (not the actual document copy) to insert the library's Ancestral File number of each patentee. The idea was to have library volunteers or others insert the Ancestral File numbers as the identities of the patentees were verified. There has been nothing done on this proposal insofar as I can determine.

VII. TEXAS

At the beginning of this chapter, I mentioned that Texas is not in the public domain even though it has no connection with the original states. At the time Texas was annexed by the United States in 1845, Texans considered themselves an independent republic, though Mexico did not agree. (After the battle of San Jacinto in April 1836, Mexico had no actual control over Texas, though such was never admitted.) This presented a unique situation when Texas, then an independent republic, applied for U.S. statehood. Because of that unique situation, special agreements were made concerning the control of the state's public lands and the state's responsibility for its own debts.

44

The United States of America,

To all to whom these Presents shall come, Greeting:

Homestead Certificate No. *426*
Application *745*

Whereas, There has been deposited in the General Land Office of the United States a Certificate of the Register of the Land Office at *Salt Lake City Utah Territory*, whereby it appears that, pursuant to the Act of Congress approved 20th May, 1862, "To secure **Homesteads** to actual **Settlers** on the **Public Domain**," and the acts supplemental thereto, the claim of *William Greenwood* has been established and duly consummated, in conformity to law, for the *West half of the North West quarter of Section twenty seven and the East half of the North East quarter of Section twenty eight, in Township twenty nine South, of Range seven West, in the District of Lands formerly subject to sale at Salt Lake City now Beaver City, Utah Territory, Containing one hundred and sixty Acres.*

according to the Official Plat of the Survey of said Land, returned to the General Land Office by the Surveyor General.

Now know ye that there is, therefore, granted by the United States unto the said *William Greenwood* the tract of Land above described: **To have and to hold** the said tract of Land, with the appurtenances thereof, unto the said *William Greenwood* and to his heirs and assigns forever; subject to any vested and accrued water rights for mining, agricultural, manufacturing, or other purposes, and rights to ditches and reservoirs used in connection with such water rights as may be recognized and acknowledged by the local customs, laws, and decisions of courts, and also subject to the right of the proprietor of a vein or lode to extract and remove his ore therefrom, should the same be found to penetrate or intersect the premises hereby granted, as provided by law.

In testimony whereof, I, *Ulysses S. Grant*, PRESIDENT OF THE UNITED STATES OF AMERICA, have caused these letters to be made Patent, and the Seal of the General Land Office to be hereunto affixed.

Given under my hand, at the City of Washington, the *third* day of *November*, in the year of our Lord one thousand eight hundred and *Seventy Six*, and of the Independence of the United States the *one hundred and first*.

[L.S.]

By the President: *U. S. Grant*

By *D. C. Cone*, Secretary.

W. Clark, Recorder of the General Land Office.

FIGURE 3—BLM LAND PATENT RECORD

Prior to Texas entering the Union, her leaders proposed that the U.S. pay her $10 million public debt in return for title to her public lands. The U.S. Congress rejected this arrangement on two occasions. However, on the third time annexation came before Congress, Texas agreed to assume responsibility for its own public debt if it could retain title to its public lands. This proposal was accepted by Congress as the condition for annexation.[24]

To help you appreciate the unique situation of Texas land, let us look brief-ly at the state's land history. In 1820, Moses Austin left Missouri for Texas, where he made an agreement with the Texas governor to bring 300 families from the U.S. to Texas. Austin returned to his home in Missouri but died shortly after arriving home, leaving his son, Stephen F. Austin, to fulfill the agreement.

Young Austin brought the first settlers into the Brazos Valley in December 1821 only to learn his father's agreement with the governor needed to be rati-fied also by the Mexican congress, a matter that was not finally accomplished until 1823. Under the agreement, Austin allowed each of the 300 families one *labor* (177 acres) of land for farming and seventy-four labors (13,098 acres) for livestock raising. This amounted to one *sitio* or one *square league* (13,275 acres) of land for each settler. He charged the families 12½ cents per acre to cover the expenses of administration and settlement.

By September 1824, 272 families had received grants from Austin, and at about the same time he was given permission to bring another 300 families from the United States.

Shortly thereafter, in March 1825, Mexico passed a Colonization Act under which it contracted with *empresarios* to also bring Mexican families to Texas, where each family would receive a league of land (4,428 acres) by paying $30 in three installments to the *empresario*. If an *empresario* brought in 100 families, he would be entitled to receive five leagues of grazing land and five labors of farming land for himself. However, the Mexican *empresarios* were not serious competition, and Austin's colonies proved to be more popular.

Most early Texas pioneers were Americans, chiefly from Missouri, Ten-nessee, and Kentucky. By 1830, there were some 20,000 Americans in Texas.

Later, after the battle of San Jacinto, when America was recovering from the financial crash of 1837, the Republic of Texas offered every family that would settle within her boundaries 1,280 acres of free land. This gift proved very popular despite unsettled conditions and threats from Mexico. The Texas population grew rapidly as she continued to grant her land under this liberal policy—a policy that continued even after annexation.

PDF files of all Texas land grant records are on file at the State Land Office, 1700 Congress Avenue, Austin, TX 78701, and an index to grant-ees and patentees is online at *http://www.glo.texas.gov/history/archives/land-grants/index.cfm.*

---

[24] Letter from Jerry Sadler, Commissioner of Texas General Land Office, Austin, TX, February 18, 1969.

VIII. OTHER STATE-LAND STATES

As noted at the start of this chapter, the state-land states (in addition to Texas) include those thirteen states that were the original colonies, plus Kentucky, Maine, Tennessee, Vermont, and West Virginia. The fact that the land in those states was not included in the public domain is not an indication that all available land in those states had been granted during the colonial period. Many of these states—especially the newer ones—had considerable ungranted lands. These individual states, however, rather than the federal government, had exclusive control of those lands and were the ones that made the grants.

There were many land grants issued by these states. In fact, the process was not essentially different from what it had been in the colonies. As far as records are concerned, the procedure varied from one state to the next. Some—both before and after the Revolution—recorded and preserved land-grant records with the deeds and other local land records. Others—such as Georgia, Maryland, Massachusetts, Pennsylvania, Tennessee, and Virginia—kept their land-grant records in their state land offices. In my experience, it is often difficult to find the records identifying when an original land title in these states was obtained.

20

Local Land Records

L ocal land records are those records resulting from the fifth phase of American land transfer as defined in Chapter 19. They are the records of land transactions between individual parties under the jurisdiction of a local governmental unit, most often the county. As you use the records of such transactions, the first two basic terms you will need to know are GRANTOR and GRANTEE. In a land conveyance, the seller is the grantor and the buyer is the grantee.

Unlike wills and other probate records, you will not find the original documents in the hands of the recorder. Once a document has been recorded, the original is returned to the person who submitted it for recording. Insofar as I can determine, this has always been true. This practice provides proof to the grantee that the document is in fact recorded and that the world has notice of his title to the property.

I. LAND TITLES

Let us briefly examine the nature of land titles to provide a basis for better understanding land records. Earlier chapters mentioned many of the terms related to land titles, but we need to look at them again solely within the context of land records.

Land, together with whatever is erected on it and/or affixed to it, is called REAL PROPERTY or REAL ESTATE, and the best title a person can hold to that land is a FEE SIMPLE title. In America, fee simple has always meant that the estate would potentially last until the title holder sells it to the party or parties of his choice, devises it to the person or persons of his choice in his will, or lets it descend to his heirs if he dies intestate. The primary obstacles preventing a fee simple title or fee simple estate from being absolute ownership are as follows:

- Those provisions in our land laws that provide for an estate to escheat (see Chapter 16) to the state when there are no heirs. This is a carryover from feudal law.

- Those statutory provisions that allow the property to be taken by the local taxing authority for failure to pay property taxes.

- The power of eminent domain, which gives a government entity and certain others the right to take private lands for public purposes upon payment of just compensation.[1]

There are many kinds of "ownership" (or estates) that are less than fee simple, and most of these—with some limitations—can be sold by the titleholder and can sometimes be left to heirs or devisees. These include LIFE ESTATES, ESTATES IN TAIL (or FEE TAIL), ESTATES UPON CONDITION, ESTATES FOR YEARS, and ESTATES FROM YEAR TO YEAR (or ESTATES AT WILL), plus a few others. Each of these types of estates represents a title to something less than the whole thing. Though some give greater portions of the complete title than do others, none of these constitutes a fee simple title except certain estates upon condition (see below).

A LIFE ESTATE merely entitles the holder to possess title to the property during the period of his own life or the life of some other specified person (life estate *per autre vie*). A dower estate is a life estate, but more is said about that later. We also find some persons selling their lands in their old age, usually to their children or other relatives, while also preserving a life estate for themselves. Thus, they dispose of the fee simple estate before their deaths, without being uprooted from the "old homestead." After the death that terminates a life estate, the future interest that has been created becomes a present possessory interest in fee simple.

In an ESTATE IN TAIL, the ownership is not absolute because of the limitation on the holder that he cannot convey more than a life estate (his own life) in the property and, upon his death, it will descend to some particular class of heir only, usually the heirs of his body (forever). Most estates in tail are created by wills, but not all of them. Should the line and the posterity entitled to the tail estate cease, the estate terminates and the property title reverts (in fee simple) to the estate from which it was created. Tail estates can be general, special, male, or female. Today they are not legal in most states because they make land inalienable (unable to be bought and sold). Should the language of an instrument create an estate in tail, different jurisdictions deal with it in different ways.

An ESTATE UPON CONDITION is based on the happening of some uncertain condition or event. It can be created by such an event (and may be fee

---

[1] This power comes from English common law, but it is primarily controlled and administered by statute.

simple), it can be enlarged (again perhaps fee simple), or it can be terminated by the specified condition. The condition must be valid and must not violate good morals or public policy. Many states have put time limits on conditions that cause forfeiture because the law abhors forfeitures, for they too—like estates in tail—tend to make land inalienable.

Many estates upon condition are created by wills. An example of such an estate is provided by the provision a man makes in his will to provide for his widow by leaving her certain lands "during the space of her widowhood." If she should remarry, her estate in that land would terminate and title would revert to the estate from which it came, that of the deceased husband (unless the provision is ruled to be against public policy).

An ESTATE FOR YEARS usually exists by virtue of a lease. It exists by contract for a definite and specified time, the length of which is not significant. Such an estate usually—but not always—exists and continues by virtue of the payment of rent. Documents creating estates for years are not ordinarily recorded.

Closely related to an estate for years is an ESTATE FROM YEAR TO YEAR. It extends for an unspecified period based on the mutual agreement of the parties. It is sometimes referred to as an ESTATE AT WILL and is very common. The period may be less than a year—even from week to week or from month to month, depending on how rent is reserved.

All of the above types of estates are less than fee simple, except as stated, and can affect the records kept. Let us now examine some of the record types that have arisen out of private land ownership.

II. RECORDS THAT RELATE TO LAND

Some of the records listed here will not be new to you or even new to our discussion; many were introduced in our discussion of probate records. However, as mentioned at that time, land and probate records are typically recorded in different places—in different offices in the county courthouse. I have duplicated some definitions here for the sake of clarify.

Some of the more important records are as follows:

ABSTRACT OF TITLE: An abstract of title is a condensed history of the title to a parcel of real property. It should include a summary of every conveyance of title to the property, all restrictions and express easements, and a statement of all liens or charges against it. It will often include maps, plats, and other aids. In most localities, abstract offices (title companies) have been set up by individuals or corporations and will, for a fee, furnish an abstract of the title to any real estate in the jurisdiction. In some places, the accuracy of the abstracts is guaranteed; in other places it is not. Though the abstract is not a complete record, it can serve as an (expensive) index to the original records that relate to a parcel of real estate. The legal description of the land (by subdivision, section, township, and range) is essential in locating a title at the various title and abstract offices because tract indexing is used. (See the discussion on indexes at the end of this chapter.)

ACKNOWLEDGEMENT: An acknowledgement is a formal statement at the end of an instrument, especially of a deed, after the signature of the person(s) who executed the instrument—the grantor(s)—where an authorized official, such as a notary public, certifies that the person(s) who executed the instrument declared to him that he (or they) signed the instrument and that it was his (or their) own free act and deed. It is sometimes called a *certificate.*

AFFIDAVIT: An affidavit is a written statement of facts made voluntarily and affirmed by the oath of the party making it. The oath is made before some party legally authorized to administer it. An affidavit can be used as evidence. See also DEPOSITION.

AGREEMENT: There are various things upon which two (or more) parties can agree that might be recorded in land records. The term "agreement" simply implies that the parties have given mutual assent to a particular matter that might change some of their rights and/or obligations. A typical example might be the agreement made between George Litzinger and his wife, Elizabeth (of the first part), and John Boardley and Isaac Perryman (of the second part) in Baltimore County, Maryland, on March 31, 1802. They signed an agreement that would

> keep and leave open an alley on the west side of the brick house now occupied by the said Boardley of the width of three feet and running back of the depth of thirty six feet from King Tamany street which alley shall be for the use and benefit of the said parties their heirs or assigns provided always and . . . that the said George Litzinger and Elizabeth his wife their heirs or assigns shall have the privilege and benefit of building over the said alley against the west wall of the said brick house at least thirteen feet from the surface of the earth without the least trouble or interruption of the said Perryman and Boardley their heirs or assigns.

> An agreement is similar to a CONTRACT (*q.v.*), yet the term has broader application.

ANTENUPTIAL CONTRACT: An antenuptial contract is a contract that a man and his bride-to-be execute wherein the property rights of one or the other or both are delineated. Such an agreement is usually made prior to a second marriage and is often for the purpose of securing certain properties for the children of former union(s), though this is not always the case. These settlements are found in the records of most states but are especially prevalent in states with community property laws. They were also common among the Dutch in New Netherland. The following antenuptial contract (which I have redacted significantly) provides for the inheritance rights of the bride-to-be and her daughter by a former marriage:

This indenture made this thirteenth day of June . . . one thousand eight
hundred and one between Patrick Bennet of . . . Baltimore . . . Maryland of the one part Elizabeth McCay of the same place . . . of the
second part and James Bennet of the same place . . . of the third part
WHEREAS a marriage is agreed upon . . . to be shortly . . . solemnised
between . . . Patrick Bennet and Elizabeth McCay Now this indenture
WITNESSETH that . . . Patrick Bennet in consideration of the . . . intended marriage and of the personal estate which . . . Elizabeth McCay
stands possessed of and which . . . Patrick Bennet will be entitled to
and also for... the sum of five shillings . . . to him . . . paid by James
Bennet . . . before the sealing . . . of these presents the receipt whereof
is hereby acknowledged hath . . . transferred and set over . . . unto . . .
James Bennet . . . all that . . . parcel of ground . . . on Fells Point . . .
plat . . . number two . . . TO HAVE AND TO HOLD the said . . . parcel
of ground . . . unto James Bennet . . . until said marriage shall take effect . . . and immediately after the solomnization thereof to the use of
Patrick Bennet . . . during his natural life and from immediately after
the decease of . . . Patrick Bennet in case . . . Elizabeth McCay shall
survive him to the use of . . . Elizabeth . . . in the name of a Jointure[2]
. . . and will . . . pay . . . unto Ann Alley the daughter of . . . Elizabeth
McCay by a former marriage . . . five hundred dollars . . . at . . . the
age of twenty one years or day of marriage . . . and the said Elizabeth
McCay doth . . . agree . . . to accept . . . the provision before made for
her . . . for her Jointure in lieu . . . of all such dower . . . at common
law which she . . . might . . . be entitled to out of . . . any freehold lands
whereof . . . Patrick Benet . . . shall be seized . . . in case . . . Patrick
shall . . . die intestate.

These are also called antenuptial agreements, antenuptial settlements,
and marriage settlements. (Chapter 18 has further discussion.)

ASSIGNMENT: In most cases, the assignments you will find recorded in
land record books have to do with the assignment of property rights,
such as the unexpired term of a lease or of a life estate. However, they
can actually include the assignment of all types of property rights. There
are also occasions where trusts, trust deeds, and mortgages are also the
subject matter of assignments.

BILL OF SALE: A bill of sale is a statement documenting a transfer of
ownership as the result of a sale, and it is not ordinarily a land record.
However, bills of sale, especially those involving the buying and selling
of slaves (because they were considered chattel or personal property),
were frequently recorded in the land-record books.

CERTIFICATE: See ACKNOWLEDGEMENT.

CONTRACT: A contract is a reciprocal agreement made between two or
more persons to do something for their mutual benefit. The law recog-

---

[2] Jointure was an estate provided for the wife on the death of her husband in lieu of dower. In
establishing it, the husband secured for his wife a freehold estate to take effect upon his decease
and to continue at least during her life (again, a life estate but not limited to one-third of the real
property as is dower).

nizes a duty therein and it is enforceable under the law. A contract for the sale of land is made prior to the making of the deed and is completely fulfilled with the delivery of the deed on the one hand and the payment of the agreed-upon consideration (price) on the other. In such a contract, the seller is called the vendor and the buyer is called the vendee. Such documents are seldom recorded, though a person is free to have any document recorded that he chooses, upon payment of the recording fee.

CONVEYANCE: See DEED.

DEED: The deed (or conveyance) is the document of our main consideration in a study of local land records. It is the document by which title in real property is transferred from one party to another. There are different types of deeds but the most common type is the WARRANTY DEED (*q.v.*), which is ordinarily a deed in fee (so called because it conveys a fee simple title). It is usually referred to simply as a deed and that is how I shall refer to it. Various types of deeds are discussed separately on this list under their various titles. (Note especially WARRANTY DEED, QUITCLAIM DEED, and TRUST DEED.)

DEED IN TRUST: See TRUST DEED.

DEED OF DIVISION: See PARTITION.

DEED OF GIFT: See GIFT DEED.

DEED OF PARTITION: See PARTITION.

DEED OF RELEASE: A deed of release is a document executed by a lien holder once the lien, mortgage (trust deed in many states), or other encumbrance has been removed. It returns the complete title to its owner. This document is sometimes referred to as a RELEASE (*q.v.*), but it is quite different from the document ordinarily called a release.

DEED OF TRUST: See TRUST DEED.

DEPOSITION: Depositions were mentioned under probate records, but let me define the term again as it is pertinent to land records. It is the written testimony or declaration of a witness to a certain matter. Such a testimony is not taken in open court but may (under certain conditions) be used there as evidence. It must be made under oath and be properly authenticated by the court official (usually the attorney) in charge of taking it. Depositions were often taken to verify land titles and to help settle land disputes when boundary markers were removed or destroyed and when surveys proved to be inaccurate or based on incorrect reference points. The following document, purporting to be a deposition, but which could more properly be called an AFFIDAVIT (*q.v.*), is one of several documents relating to the same matter. It is typical of those recorded with the local land records:

> A deposition of Nicholas Frost aged about Sixty yeares, or thereabouts, This deponent Sayth that about sixteen or seaventeen yeares since, Thomas Crockett had possession of a necke of Land in Spruse Cricke, lying on the North Side of the cricke, against the field, he now

hath. His possession was had by falling tymber & clearing ground, and made preparation to build an house upon the Sd Land, & further Saith not, Taken upon oath before me Nicholas Shapleigh this 30th of the 4th 1658.

DIVISION: See PARTITION.

DOWER RELEASE: See RELEASE OF DOWER.

GIFT DEED: A gift deed is a deed that transfers real property without normal consideration. Typically, such deeds transfer real estate from a parent to his offspring, but there is no rule about that. The consideration is often stated to be something akin to "for the natural love and affection which I bear towards my son and for other valuable consideration." An example of a gift deed follows:

> Know all men by these presents, that I Richard Kirle of Kittery in the County of Yorke, as well for my natural affection & parentall Love w'h I bear to my well beloved Son in law, Samuell Knight of s[d] Towne & County, as allso for diverse others good Causes & Considerations, me at present especially moving, have freely given & granted, & by these presents do give & grant to s[d] Samuell Knight Six Acres of Land being part of a Town Grant of fiveteen Acres of Land, lying & being in Kittery, s[d] Knight Part shall begin at the Great Cove, & so run sixty eight Pole next to the Land, which is now Remonicks Land, and such breadth, as makes up the forementioned Summ of Acres—To have & to hold all & singular the s[d] six Acres of Land to s[d] Knight, his Heires, Executors, Administrators, & Assignes forever to their own proper Use & Behoof, freely and Quietly without any matter of Challenge or claim, or demand, of me the s[d] Kirle, or of any other person or persons w'soever for me, in my name, by my cause, meanes, or procurement, and without any money or other thing to be yeilded and paid, unto me s[d] Kirle, my Heires, Executors or Assignes, And I the said Kirle all the s[d] Land to the s[d] Knight his Heires, Executors, Administrators, & Assignes, to the use aforesaid against all People doth Warrant & defend by these presents, And farther Know that the s[d] Kirle, hath put s[d] Knight in peaceable and Quiet Possession of the s[d] Land, at the delivering & Sealing of the presents, as wittnesse my hand Seale this twenty seventh day of July one thousand, six hund, & seventy six.

Signed Sealed & delivered in
the presence of us
    his
John *Æ* Green   (signed) Richard Kirle
    marke
Thomas Spinney,

LEASE: A lease is an agreement that creates a landlord-tenant relationship. Because it transfers an estate in real property, it is very much like a deed, and all rights of each party are defined within it. Though the document itself is much like a deed in its format, the title transferred is less than fee simple and its duration is usually specified. The estate that one holds under such an instrument is referred to as a *leasehold estate* or as an *estate for years*. Leases are rarely recorded, as there is no reason for doing so.

LETTER OF ATTORNEY: See POWER OF ATTORNEY.

LIEN: Though liens are not land records, they deserve mention here because they encumber land titles and are thus recorded with the land records. A lien is a claim by one party upon the property of another for security in the payment of a debt. When the debt is satisfied, a LIEN RELEASE is created and recorded. In some (most) states, a MORT-GAGE (*q.v.*) is not considered to create a legal title but merely a lien against the property.

MARRIAGE SETTLEMENT: A marriage settlement can be either an AN-TENUPTIAL CONTRACT (*q.v.*) or a similar postnuptial contract.

MEASUREMENTS OF LAND: As you read old land records, you may come across unfamiliar land measurements. Below are a few of the most common units of measurement you will encounter:

Acre: 43,560 square feet, 160 square rods.

Chain: 66 feet, 22 yards, or 4 rods (100 links).

Furlong: 660 feet or 220 yards (10 chains).

Link: 7.92 inches. There are 25 links in a rod and 100 links (or 4 rods) in a chain.

Mile: 5,280 feet (80 chains, 320 rods, or 8 furlongs).

Perch: 5½ yards or 16½ feet; also called rod or pole.

Pole: 5½ yards or 16½ feet; also called perch or rod.

Rod: 5½ yards or 16½ feet; also called pole or perch.

Rood: As a measurement of length this varies from 5½ yards (rod) to 8 yards, depending on locality. It was also used sometimes to describe area, being equal to one-quarter acre.

MORTGAGE: A mortgage is a conditional transfer of legal title to real property as security for payment of a debt. It is much like a deed in its form, but if the conditions prescribed therein are met (i.e., the debt is paid) the conveyance becomes void. Under common law, actual legal title is transferred by this deed to the mortgagee, and he has the right to possess the land. In many states, especially in more recent times, the common law rule of mortgages has been altered, and no title is transferred to the mortgage holder. A mortgage is regarded instead as a LIEN (*q.v.*) against the property.

PARTITION: When two or more persons hold real estate as cotenants (such as the undivided property left them in a probate settlement) and they wish to divide that property, a partition or *deed of partition* is made and recorded. It identifies the separate parts taken by each party. No additional title is taken or conveyed by any party by such an instrument, but their joint title is divided into separate titles.

PETITION: We discussed petitions in connection with probate records, but they are also common in land records. A petition is a request made to a court for action in a matter that is not the subject of a suit. A good example is provided in the petition recorded in Land Book No. 1 in Kossuth County, Iowa. It was made by the administrators of Thomas Gallion's estate in 1882:

> The petition of E. S. Streeter & J. H. Grover administrators of the Estate of Thomas Gallion of Kossuth County—Iowa respectfully shows to this court That the said Thomas Gallion died on or about the 19th day of August 1881 in said county, leaving an estate to be administered upon. Your petitioners were duly qualified administrators of his estate and letters of administration were issued to them on the 30th day of Sept. 1881 which has never been revoked.
>
> Your petitioners duly made and returned a true inventory of all the personal property, book accounts &c of the said deceased on the 14th day of October 1881.
>
> They also published due notice of their appointment as administrators and notified all parties who were indebted to the estate by such publication to pay the debts due the estate, and all creditors to present their claims duly verified for allowance and payment—all of which will more fully appear by a reference to the papers on file in the clerks office.
>
> The amount of property which has come into the administrators hand is valued at $414.66
>
> The amount which has been paid out for debts and expenses of administration $ 69.00
>
> The amount set aside to the widow as exempt from execution as provided by Law $381.16
>
> The amount debts due from the estate $300.00
>
> The necessary expenses of administration in the future $ 50.00
>
> Total amount due when the estate will be settled $419.00
>
> The above said decedent died possessed in fee of a certain tract of land containing eighty acres situated in Kossuth County Iowa described as follows to wit the South half of South west quarter of sec thirty-six (36) in Township # Ninety seven (97) North of range # twenty Eight (28) west of 5th P. M. Iowa.
>
> The whole of which estate was acquired by him since his marriage. Also the following are the names and ages of the devisees of the deceased to wit:
>
> —Jane Gallion widow of Deceased   age   64
> Thomas S. Gallion son of Deceased   "   40
> John Gallion   "   "   "   "   38
> Maggie Stahl daughter of Deceased   "   35
> James Gallion son   "   "   "   33
> W. J. Gallion "   "   "   "   30
> Robert Gallion "   "   "   "   25
>
> Your petitioners therefore allege that the personal estate in the hands of the petitioners is insufficient to pay the debts and the allowance to

the family and expenses of administration and that it is necessary to sell the whole or some of the real estate for that purpose.

Wherefore your petitioners pray that an order be made by said court directing all persons interested in said real estate to appear before said Court at such time as it may appoint to show cause why an order should not be granted to your petitioners to sell so much real estate as shall be necessary.

And that after a full hearing of this petition and examinations of the proofs and allegations of the parties interested due proof of the publication of a copy of said order to show cause &c an order of sale be made authorizing your petitioners to sell so much, and such parts of the real estate as said Court shall Judge necessary or beneficial or that such or further order May be necessary in the premises.

(signed) E. S. Streater

(signed) J. H. Grover

POWER OF ATTORNEY: When a person is unable to act for himself in a certain matter and appoints another to act for him, the document by which he does so is called a power of attorney or *letter of attorney*. The person thus appointed becomes an *attorney in fact* in the performance of specified acts. If a man who lives in Iowa inherits property from his grandfather who died in North Carolina and wishes to sell that property, he may make a power of attorney authorizing his brother who lives much closer (or anyone else he chooses) to act as his agent or attorney in selling the property. As long as the closer brother acts within the limits specified in the document, he can do all things as if he were actually the Iowa brother. John Cox made such a document in 1810:

Know all men by these presents that I John Cox, of Knox County, and state of Kentucky have made ordained Constituted & appointed, and by these presents do make ordain Constitute & appoint Samuel Cox Junr my true & Lawful attorney, for me & in my name, but For my use to do perform & Transact all my Business In the State of Virginia To make a deed of Conveyance To a Certain tract of Land Lying in Grayson County in the State of Virginia it being the Same Which Robert still Sold as agent for me To a Certain William Byers, To Collect all money or Moneys which may be due me and to Transact any other Business Which may be Necessary for my wellfare and Well Standing in the Said State of Virginia and what ever Lawful act my said attorney may do or Cause to be done for me and in My Name I do by these presents ratify and Confirm, in witness where of I have here unto set my hand and affixed my seal this 28th day of August 1810.

Teste	his
Nathan Cox	John ✕ Cox
Richard Cox	mark

QUITCLAIM DEED: A quitclaim deed is an instrument by which a person releases all title, interest, or claim he may possess or appear to possess in certain real properties without making any warrants thereto. He merely conveys all he has. The title or claim released is *not necessarily* a valid one, but on many occasions, it is the instrument of a valid conveyance of land. One example of a situation that might generate a quitclaim deed would be an error in a land survey. When the error is corrected, the party affected by it often makes a quitclaim deed releasing all claims to the erroneous paper title he held before the correction. A primary use is to remove clouds, or potential clouds, from real estate titles and make the property more saleable.

RELEASE: A release is a document by which a person gives up, to another, his right to something in which he has a just claim. Such a conveyance must, under common law, be to a person who has either possession of or an interest in the property. It is not a unilateral cancellation of rights but must be supported by lawful consideration. A cotenant of undivided lands can transfer his rights to another cotenant by a release. (There is an example of a release in Chapter 18.)

A release is sometimes, erroneously, confused with an ASSIGNMENT (*q.v.*). In most jurisdictions, it is also very different from a DEED OF RELEASE (*q.v.*).

RELEASE OF DOWER: The nature of dower was discussed briefly under probates, but I want to review a couple of essential points here just to show why such documents exist. Dower, of course, is the right to a life estate that a widow has in the real estate of her deceased husband under the common law. One significant thing about dower is that the right attaches to any and all property that her deceased husband procured in fee simple during their marriage. This means that even though a man sells the property, his widow can come back after his death, even if it has been fifty years since the sale, and legally claim her dower rights in that property. Consequently, when a person bought land, he was usually careful to see that the wife of the grantor either signed the deed or executed a release of dower. Through such, she relinquished all right to ever claim dower rights in the property. Though genealogically it may tell no more than her name, the release of dower, by giving that name, provides important evidence that may not be found elsewhere.

Documents releasing a widow's right to dower will most often be found in state-land states. In public domain states, it was more common for wives to sign the deeds.

RELEASE OF MORTGAGE: See DEED OF RELEASE.

SURRENDER: A surrender is much like a deed in its form. However, it involves the giving up of a lease (an estate for years) before its term has expired. It is not a unilateral abandonment of the lease but is made with the mutual consent of both the lessor and the lessee and is legally binding on both.

TAX RECORDS: Through the years, tax records have been widely recognized as important sources of family history evidence. When many of the early census schedules were lost, they were replaced (reasonably well) by contemporaneous tax lists. Others have been published separately, and many others have been microfilmed. In some places, during early periods, you can follow an ancestor through the tax lists as if those lists were a yearly census. We will look later at how tax records can be used to help solve pedigree problems.

TRUST DEED: In most states where trust deeds are recorded in the land records, they are instruments for real property financing and are similar to mortgages. They operate by transferring the title to one or more trustees to secure the payment of the debt. For example, the State of Maryland passed early legislation allowing the legal title to the property of certain insolvent debtors to be transferred to persons who were trustees in behalf of the creditors. The instrument of such a transfer is called a *deed of trust* or trust deed. Though the approach may be slightly different, these records are similar to those found in several other states and in the District of Columbia. The arrangement under which such a trust is established allows the property to be sold in case of default and for the proceeds to pay the debt, then turning all surplus back to the debtor. A trust deed has *nothing* to do with trustees of an organization conveying their title to property.

WARRANTY DEED: A warranty deed is perhaps the most common and most important type of deed of real property. By it, the grantor warrants (by covenant) the title of the property he is selling; and should the title become faulty because of paramount claims against it, or for any other reason, the grantor (or his heirs) may be sued on the warranty. See also DEED.

In many localities, you will also find other kinds of documents, including various court orders (decrees) and miscellaneous probate instruments, recorded in land record books as proof of title. Some states, as discussed in Chapter 15, require the filing of certain final papers of probate with the custodian of local land records to be recorded for that purpose.

The important thing is that you not to be too fussy about what you find recorded in most jurisdictions; just use what documents you find there and the evidence those documents provide as it relates to your ancestral family. In all states, the recording acts provide that almost any document may be recorded upon payment of the recording fee. And most documents affecting land titles are recorded to make those titles secure.

III. USING LAND RECORDS

I have used a great deal of space defining and describing land records, but I have said little about their value in family history research. And knowing all about those records is pointless unless they contain valuable information.

My earlier observation about land records being among the best sources for American family history research is true. Land records and probate records are, in fact, the American researcher's "bread and butter," and what was said about the general value of land records in Chapter 19 is especially true of those records associated with private land ownership. Consider the following:

- A large percentage of your American ancestors were probably land owners.

- Good land records exist right from the beginning of most of the early permanent settlements in America.

- The older records uniquely contain much more family history data than their modern counterparts.

Your understanding of these facts will help you appreciate the significance of this much-overlooked family history source—a source that, I am sorry to say, is not among those records that have any priority for being indexed on the important family history websites.

A. Relationship information

You already know that local land records contain the names of men's wives, a useful tool in a man's identification. But did you know that these records also contain many other statements of relationship? Someone has suggested that statements of relationship (other than husband and wife) are found in about 10 percent of the early American deeds—and the earlier the better. My own experience suggests that this figure is probably about right, but in some localities, the percentage is somewhat higher—much depends on local custom. But, regardless of what the percentage might have been, the important thing is that if any reasonable possibility exists of your finding a relationship in a deed that will help solve a family history problem, you ought to be ready and willing to search for that deed. There are many such possibilities.

This brings us back to an old theme, one you need to indelibly stamp on your memory: You *must* search the records for everyone of your surname (including spelling variations). Remember that in your quest to find relationships stated in records, it is impossible to know in advance what the result is going to be. You cannot afford to pick and choose in this matter if you want to be successful in your research.

To illustrate some of the possibilities let us look at a few representative samples from deeds of Baltimore County, Maryland. One of the most helpful deeds is the one where joint heirs in an estate combine as cotenant grantors to sell their inherited property. Consider the following example:

> This Indenture made this twenty fifth day of April in . . . Eighteen hundred and one between Ignatius Diggs and Charlotte his wife formerly Charlotte Weaver and Lewis Weaver of Baltimore County of the one part and Joshua Jones of the Same County of the other part WHEREAS Daniel Weaver by

his last Will and Testament bearing date the 22d March 1797 did devise and bequeath as follows. . . .

[The deed then goes on to quote part of the will in which Daniel Weaver named his son Daniel Weaver, daughter Elizabeth Hesson and daughter Charlotte Weaver as beneficiaries, and then continues.] . . . WHEREAS the said Daniel Weaver [the son] after having Complied with the Conditions aforesaid departed this life intestate leaving the aforesaid Charlotte and Lewis TOGETHER with Elizabeth Hesson now the Wife of Benjamin Morrison and John Weaver now under age his heirs and legal representatives. Now this Indenture WITNESSETH that the said Ignatius Diggs and Charlotte his wife and Lewis Weaver for . . . three hundred and eighty five Dollars. . . .

This is as far as we need to go. There is a lot of good relationship information in the above-cited deed. Relationship information like this is often found in deeds where there are co-grantors. Now let us look at a quotation from another deed:

This indenture made this twenty second day of September in the year of our Lord one thousand eight hundred and one by and between Andrew Boyd the Elder of the City of Baltimore of the one part and Elizabeth Boyd and Mary Boyd of said City and daughters of the Said Andrew Boyd of the other part. [James P. Boyd signed this deed as a witness.]

The foregoing is a deed of gift, and a quite unusual one at that—it has co-grantees. Here is another interesting deed:

This indenture made the thirtieth day of May in the year of our Lord eighteen hundred and one between John Hollins of the city of Baltimore in Baltimore County and state of Maryland Merchant Samuel Smith of the same County and State Esquire and Margaret his wife William Patterson of the same County and State Esquire and Dorcas his wife William Lee Forman of the same City County and State Merchant and Jane his wife and Joseph Spear of the same City County and State Merchant and Barbara his wife which said Margaret Smith Dorcas Patterson Jane Forman and Barbara Spear are the daughters of William Spear deceased late of Baltimore County and State aforesaid Merchant of the one part and Martin Eichelberger of the same City County and State Merchant of the other part WHEREAS by a decree of . . . chancellor of the said State of Maryland made in a cause depending in the High Court of Chancery of the said State between Ephraim Robinson and other Plaintiffs and Mary deceased and their respective husbands have agreed to join with the Spears heirs of John Spear deceased defendant bearing date the first day of July in the year seventeen hundred and ninety-nine it was by the said Chancellor . . . adjudged ordered and decreed that the before named John Hollins be and he was thereby appointed trustee for making sale of the real estate late of the said deceased or so much thereof as would be necessary for the payment of his just debts. . . . by public auction . . . and whereas the said Children of the said William Spear deceased and Sisters of the said John Spear also deceased and their respective husbands have agreed to join with the said John Hollins as trustee . . . In the conveyance.

Documents with better family history evidence are scarcely found.

Also, well buried in land records are relationships of persons who are neither grantor nor grantee. These, of course, are much harder (in fact often impossible) to find, but their value cannot be denied. Consider the following:

> THIS INDENTURE made this Sixteenth day of June in . . . one thousand eight hundred and one Between John Tolley Worthington of Baltimore County and State of Maryland of the one part and Caleb Merryman of the said County and State of the other part WHEREAS William Ridgley of John by his deed of indenture bearing date the thirteenth day of April in . . . One thousand Seven hundred and Ninety five and recorded among the Land records of Baltimore County Court in Liber WGN° TT folio 73 for the Considerations therein mentioned did Convey unto the said John Tolley Worthington . . . all that part of a tract called Well's mannor . . . in the County aforesaid which was devised to the said William by the last Will and Testament of his father John Ridgley late of Baltimore County deceased.

This deed provides collateral evidence of the relationship between William and John Ridgley but, as good as it is, that evidence would be virtually impossible for the Ridgley researcher to find since it would not be indexed under either of those names. However, the deed is referring to a will where that same relationship is probably stated and which is likely quite findable. If land records ever come to the top of records to be digitized and indexed on the important family history websites, it is my hope that all names in every deed will be included in those indexes.

B. Place information

In addition to stating relationships, deeds and related records are also useful because of the places of residence they state for both grantors and grantees. In all of the instruments just quoted, you will note that this was true, and that information is of great value. However, it is usually of even greater value if the party you seek is stated to be from a place other than where the deed was recorded. If, for example, the grantee buys property before he moves into the county, the deed tells his immediate origin and can facilitate an extension of research. And if the grantor sells his land in a given place after he moves away, the deed will tell where he has gone and facilitate your search for him and his family in later records.

C. Land descriptions as a means of proving connections

Very often, the researcher will trace a pedigree back to a situation where an ancestor has one or more contemporaries with his same name. In such cases, it is impossible, on the face of it, to distinguish one from the other in existing records. In circumstances like this, land descriptions *can* sometimes provide evidence to help us make the right connection. The technique is quite simple if the approach fits your situation. Let us look at the approach.

You tackle the problem in conventional fashion—i.e., you work from the known to the unknown, gathering data from the land records on all persons of your surname. If you do this, the process will not be overly complicated and will involve no special research techniques. And your findings can be easily analyzed as you tabulate and evaluate the evidence you find.

Not every problem can be solved by using land descriptions. In fact, this approach can work only when two specific conditions are present:

1. There is a *positive identification* of our ancestor at the time he disposes of a specific tract or parcel of land.

2. There is a direct statement of relationship—preferably a lineal relationship—between your ancestor and someone else in the instrument by which that ancestor acquired his title to the property.

You must have evidence that your ancestor owned a specific parcel of land and that he disposed of it by a deed (or will) in which you have positively identified him as the grantor. (There must be *no* possibility of this person being his like-named counterpart.) You might identify him by the name of his wife—this is very common—or by his signature or mark, or by some other means. Regardless of your method, that identification is essential.

The more deeds of this nature you find, the better will be your chances for success. You must note carefully the descriptions of the lands being sold. (This is quite easy where the Rectangular Survey system was used but is more difficult if the land was described by metes and bounds—unless the tract was called by a specific name, as is sometimes the case.)

Next, you must identify the instrument (will or deed) by which your ancestor acquired his title to that tract of land. If the land was acquired from a relative and a statement of relationship between your ancestor and that relative is given, you are in luck. Any relationship thus stated increases your chances for solving the problem—but of course lineal connections are preferred. You may find the land in question devised to him in his father's (or other relative's) will, and a will can serve your purpose as well as a deed.

It all comes down to this: If you find your ancestor John X selling 100 acres of land of the same description as William X sold to his son John X sixteen years earlier, you have a pretty good case. This can be tricky, though, because sometimes tracts are divided or combined with other tracts when they are sold.

D. Other tricks for hard cases

When clues to identity are hard to find and family connections are scarce, it is worthwhile to go into the land records in greater depth to mine the hidden value so often overlooked. Consider the following approaches. Though they are often time-consuming, they can be worth all the time they take:

1. Look for companion documents. When you have identified a land record of interest to you, you should look at all of the deeds for a few pages before and a few pages after it. In this search, look for two things.

First, identify any records where the parties are the same (or obviously connected) and where the land is in the same general area. Study these records, abstract them (see next chapter), and identify what useful data pertinent to your problem they might contain.

2. Check for deeds on adjoining properties. Tract books, land surveys, plat maps, and property descriptions in deeds to or from your ancestor often give the names of those persons whose property is adjacent to his. Deeds pertaining to those adjacent tracts may contain valuable data on the subject property. Always consider that the two owners may be related, that they may have come together from the same place of origin, or that the properties may have been two parts of the same original patent or grant. Clues of great worth (and even specific details) relative to these and other matters that are not in your ancestor's deeds might be found in such documents.

3. Locate and plat out the property description of your ancestor's land on a county map. This can be helpful in many ways, but most importantly, it shows you the location of the property in relation to such things as cemeteries and churches—information that may prove invaluable. If the land is in a public land state, you can prepare township-range model sheets using the diagram in Figure 1 of Chapter 19. Using a blank model sheet, locate the subject property. Next, look up the section in the tract book and list all real property within a two-mile radius and check it out. Records relating to these adjacent tracts just might contain pertinent data or useful clues, as already stated.

4. Names of the owners of the adjacent property can also be used in connection with the census records to identify whether your ancestor is the landowner in question when there is more than one person with the same name.

5. Account for both the acquisition and disposition of every tract of our ancestor's land. Elizabeth Shown Mills suggested in her presentation to the National Genealogical Society's 1985 conference in Columbus, Ohio, that you make an "in" and "out" table with five columns. In column 1, write the land's legal description; in columns 2 and 3, tell the date and means of acquisition; and in columns 4 and 5, tell the date and means of its disposal. By failing to account for both the "ins" and the "outs," you risk missing important clues and/or family history evidence.[3]

6. It is also recommended that you check tract books (or land-entry books), where applicable, to determine if your ancestor got his land in the public domain from the federal government, and if so, then seek the details of the grant or purchase in appropriate records.

---

[3] From personal notes taken by the author at the conference.

IV. TAX RECORDS

There are various kinds of tax records—in fact, you seldom find two that are exactly the same—but they can generally be divided into three main types:

1. Real property tax records
2. Personal property tax records (primarily livestock and slaves)
3. A combination of the other two

These are all useful records, but those records that show persons taxed for personal property often have an advantage because they pick up persons who were established in the community but who owned no land.

Depending on locality and time, tax records on real property usually show the amount of land; its location (including on what watercourse); the persons in whose name it was originally entered, surveyed, and patented; and its appraised valuation.

Not all states kept good early tax records, so this is not a source you will use with every problem. However, you need to keep it in mind. Let us look at Kentucky, where some of the best tax lists were kept in early periods. Figure 1 illustrates the worth of these records. This illustration follows the surname Cobb through twenty-three years of tax schedules in Owen County. Note carefully the nature of the information and the knowledge that can be gained when you consider everyone of the surname of interest, every year, over a long period. (In this example I actually stopped before I would have ordinarily done so.) There is no reason to stop if the family is still there.

I know that these records leave many questions unanswered, but when other records—such as deeds, probate records, marriage records, etc.—are used in conjunction with this tax information, you can tell quite a lot about the persons and families involved.

Tax lists are usually kept in columnar form, as you can observe. For this example I cheated a little and put everything on one standardized form, but the forms of the actual schedules vary somewhat from year to year as witnessed by some of the spaces left blank on my form. Also, you should know that some of these lists have other minor columns that I have omitted. As you study the example, you will observe that there is nothing spectacular about tax lists. They just contain good basic data that might somewhere, sometime, provide clues needed to help solve a family history problem.

FIGURE 1—KENTUCKY TAX LISTS

Name	Land (acres)	County	Water course	In whose name entered	In whose name surveyed	In whose name patented	White males over 21	Blacks over 16	Total Blacks	Horses and mares	Value of land per acre	Total valuation	chn. 4-14	chn. 7-17
1819:														
Cobb, William							1			1		$40		
Elisha							1			2		$90		
Asa							1			1		$40		
John	100	Owen	Eagle	Phillips & Young	same	same	1			3		$500		
Daniel							1			1		$40		
1820:														
Cobb, Thomas	100	Owen	Eagle	H. Marshall	same	same	1	1	1	4		$1,000		
William							1			1		$50		
John	100	Owen	Eagle	Phillips & Young	same	same	1			2		$500		
Elisha							1			2		$80		
Asa							1			1		$50		
Daniel										1		$40		
1821:														
Cobb, Asa							1			1		$30		
William							1			1		$30		
Elisha							1			1		$60		
Daniel							1			1		$40		
John	100	Owen	Eagle	Phillips	same	same	1			2	4	$500		
Thomas	100	Owen	Eagle	Marshall	same	same	1	1	1	4	5	$1,050		

FIGURE 1—(continued)

Name	Land (acres)	County	Water course	In whose name entered	In whose name surveyed	In whose name patented	White males over 21	Blacks over 16	Total Blacks	Horses and mares	Value of land per acre	Total valuation	chn. 4-14	chn. 7-17
1822:														
Cobb, William	100	Owen	Eagle	Marshall	same	same	1			2		$70	3	
Asa							1			1		$30		
Elisha							1	1	1	1	2	$65	1	
Thomas							1			4		$1,050	4	
Daniel							1			1		$40	3	
1823:														
Cobb, Asa							1			2		$60		
Elisha							1			1		$50		
Daniel	100	Owen	Eagle	Marshall	do	do	1			1		$50		
William							1			1		$100		
Thomas							1			4		$1,250		
John							1							
1824:														
Cobb, Thomas	100	Owen	Eagle	Marshall	do	do	1			4		$1,200		
William							1			1		$80		
Elisha							1			1		$50		
Asa							1			2	3	$75		
Daniel							1					$80		
1825:														
Cobb, William	100	Owen	Eagle	Weaver	same	same	1			1	3	$540		
Daniel							1			2		$150		
Asa							1			1		$100		
Elisha										3		$150		

FIGURE 1—(continued)

Name	Land (acres)	County	Water course	In whose name entered	In whose name surveyed	In whose name patented	White males over 21	Blacks over 16	Total Blacks	Horses and mares	Value of land per acre	Total valuation	chs. 4-14	chs. 7-17
1825 (cont'd):														
Cobb, Thomas	100	Owen	Eagle	Marshall	same	same	1			5	3	$1,450		
same	300	Owen	Stevens	May & Co.	same	same								
1826:														
Cobb, Thomas	100	Owen	Eagle	Weaver	same	same	1			5		$950		
Elisha							1			2		$100		
William	100	Owen	Eagle	Weaver	same	same	1			2		$325		
Asa							1			1		$65		
Daniel							1			1		$40		
1827:														
Cobb, William	100	Owen	Eagle	Weaver	do	do	1			2		$330		
Thomas	100	"	"	Marshall	do	do	1			4		$750		
Elisha	100	"	"	Weaver	do	do	1			1		$200		
Daniel	100	"	"	"	do	do	1			2		$280		
John	50	"	"	Asburn	do	do				2				
same	27	"	"	May & Co.	do	do	1					$350		
Asa	97½	"	"	Weaver	do	do				2		$200		
1828:														
Cobb, John	102	Owen	Eagle	May & Co.	do	do	1			2	3	$356		
Elisha	100	"	"	Weaver & c	do	do	1			1	2	$250		
Thomas	100	"	"	Marshall	do	do	1			4	6	$750		
Daniel	100	"	"	Weaver	do	do	1			1	2.50	$280		
Asa	107	"	"	"						2	2	$239		

FIGURE 1—(continued)

Name	Land (acres)	County	Water course	In whose name entered	In whose name surveyed	In whose name patented	White males over 21	Blacks over 16	Total Blacks	Horses and mares	Value of land per acre	Total valuation	chn. 4-14	chn. 7-17
1829:														
Cobb, Asa	97½	Owen	Eagle	Weaver	do	do	1			2	2	$750	3	
Elisha	100	"	"	"	do	do	1			2	2	$250	3	
Daniel	60	"	"	Marshall	do	do	1			2	5	$350	4	
Thomas	100	"	"	Weaver	do	do	1			4	5	$660	3	
William	100	"	"	"	do	do	1			4	3	$460	4	
1830:														
Cobb, Elisha	100	Owen	Eagle	Weaver	do	do	1			2	2.50	$300		
Daniel	60	"	"	"	do	do	1			2	5	$350		
Asa	106	"	"	"	do	do	1			1	2.50	$310		
William	100	"	"	"	do	do	1			3	5	$625		
1831:														
Cobb, Elisha	100	Owen	Eagle	T. Weaver	do	do	1			3	2.50	$350		
Daniel	60	"	"	"	do	do	1			2	5	$360		
Asa	106½	"	"	"	do	do	1			1	2.50	$300		
William	100	"	"	"	do	do	1			3	5	$600		
1832: Tax list is missing														
1833: Tax list is missing														
1834:														
Cobb, Asa	106	Owen	Eagle	Weaver	do	do	1			2	2.50	$325		
Elizabeth	40	"	"	"	do	do				1	3	$150		

FIGURE 1—(continued)

Name	Land (acres)	County	Water course	In whose name entered	In whose name surveyed	In whose name patented	White males over 21	Blacks over 16	Total Blacks	Horses and mares	Value of land per acre	Total valuation	chn. 4-14	chn. 7-17
1834 (cont'd):														
Cobb, Elisha Jr							1			1		$10		
Daniel	100	Owen	Eagle	Weaver	do	do	1			2	5	$560		
Elisha	100	"	"	"	do	do	1			3	3	$410		
1835:														
Cobb, Asa	106	Owen	Eagle	Weaver	do	do	1			2	3	$390		
Daniel	100	"	"	"	do	do	1			3	5	$600		
Elisha	100	"	"	"	do	do	1			4	3.50	$500		
Elizabeth	95									1	2	$270		
Elisha Jr										2		$30		
1836:														
Cobb, Elisha	100	Owen	Eagle	Weaver	do	do	1			3	5	$700		
Daniel	100	"	"	"	do	do	1			3	6	$730		
Elizabeth	40	"	"	"	do	do				1	25	$1,050		
Asa	106	"	"	"	do	do	1			2	3	$458		
Elisha Jr	100	"	Richland	Weaver	do		1			1	3	$330		
1837:														
Cobb, William	100	Owen					1 (under age)			1	2	$260		
Elisha Sr	950	"					1			5	5	$1,493		
Daniel	50	"					1			5	19	$1,200		
Elizabeth	100	"								1	8	$850		
Asa	156	"					1			1	6	$1,061		
Elisha Jr	100	"					1			1	2	$260		

FIGURE 1—(continued)

Name	Land (acres)	County	Water course	In whose name entered	In whose name surveyed	In whose name patented	White males over 21	Blacks over 16	Total Blacks	Horses and mares	Value of land per acre	Total valuation	chn. 4-14	chn. 7-17
1838: Tax list is missing														
1839:														
Cobb, Asa	206										5	$1,030		
Danl	157										6	$942		
Elisha Sr	168										6	$1,008		
Danl F.	100										3	$300		
Wm	100										3	$300		
Elisha Jr	140										2.50	$350		
1840:														
Cobb, Elisha Sr	100	Owen	Eagle				1			3		$753		2
Asa	205	"	"				1			2		$940		3
Daniel F.	100	"	Elk				1			2		$275		
Daniel	155	"	Eagle				1			2		$1,670		1
Elisha Jr	140	"	"				1			2		$323		
William	100	"	Elk				1			2		$375		
1841:														
Cobb, Elisha Sr	110	Owen	Eagle				1			4		$744		3
Asa	207	"	"				1			3		$990		5
William	100	"	Elk				1			2		$350		
Daniel	155	"	Eagle				1			2		$1,076		1
Daniel F.	100	"	"				1			2		$275		
Elijah							1			1		$50		
Elisha Jr							1			1		$40		1

V. COUNTY LAND OWNERSHIP MAPS

Also useful for some time periods and some localities are old county land-ownership maps. There are more than 1,400 maps from forty-six states, covering 1,041 counties, located in the Library of Congress Geography & Map Reading Room, Room LM B01, Madison Bldg., 101 Independence Avenue SE, Washington, DC 20540-4650. Most of these are for counties in the northeastern states, north central states, California, Texas, and Virginia. These comprise, in total, nearly one-third of all American counties. The only states without maps in this collection are Alaska, Hawaii, Idaho, and Wyoming. However, each of the states of Arizona (Pima County, 1893), Nevada (Elko County, 1894), and Oklahoma (Cleveland County, 1900) has a map for only one county in one year. About 7 percent of the maps are of pre-1840 vintage, and about 24 percent were published between 1840 and 1860. About 38 percent were published between 1860 and 1880, and 30 percent between 1880 and 1900.[4]

For a list of available maps, by state and county, go to a website called "Kin Quest" (*http://kinquest.com/usgenealogy/lom.php*). If maps are available for the county of your interest, at the time your ancestor owned land there, microfiche copies of these maps are available for purchase online from the Library of Congress Photoduplication Service (*http://loc.gov/duplicationservices/collections-guide/#loctoggler=2*) based on established fees for reproduction and mailing. Copies may also be obtained by hiring a researcher from the National Capital Area Chapter of the Association of Professional Genealogists. You can contact chapter members through the chapter website (*http://ncac-apg.org/*).

These maps predate county plat books and topographical surveys of the U.S. Geological Survey, and scales vary from 1:3,960 to 1:600,000. Seventy-six percent have scales larger than 1:100,000.[5] In most cases, the names of all landholders at the time the map was made are recorded directly on the map. Thus, their value for family history and historical purposes is obvious (see Figure 2).

There is a published guide/checklist to the land ownership map holdings of the Library of Congress that was compiled in 1967 by Richard W. Stephenson of the Geography and Map Division. This small booklet is identified in footnote 4 of this chapter, but it seems to be out of print and it is very difficult to locate copies.

---

[4] Richard W. Stephenson, comp., *Land Ownership Maps: a Checklist of Nineteenth Century Land Ownership Maps in the Library of Congress* (Washington, DC: U.S. Government Printing Office, 1967), vii–viii. (LC catalog no.: Z6027.U5 U54; LCCN: 67060091). This is an important book, but it is now quite difficult to find. However, most of the information you need concerning these maps is on the Kin Quest website referred to in the text.

[5] Ibid., vii–viii.

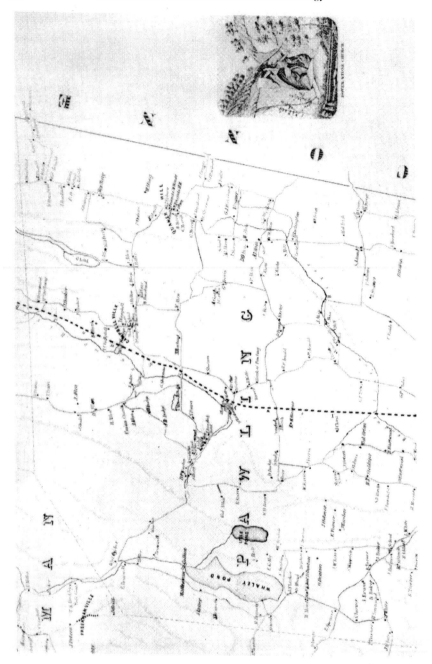

FIGURE 2—LAND OWNERSHIP MAP FOR PART OF DUTCHESS COUNTY, NEW YORK
(1:42, 240—1850—J. C. SIDNEY)

Some plat maps in the National Archives are described in chapter 19 of *Guide to Genealogical Research in the National Archives of the United States,* 3rd ed. (see 19.3, "General Land Office Records," pages 341 and 343). These include approximately 20,000 survey plats used by the General Land Office and more than 22,000 survey plats used by the local land offices. These survey plats are for several states and are available on sixty-seven rolls of microfilm (*Township Plats of Selected States*: microfilm T1234).

VI. AVAILABILITY OF LOCAL LAND RECORDS

Now that you are more familiar with the value and use of local land records, let us look at their availability.

A. Location

In most states, land records are under county jurisdiction, but there are too many exceptions for me to give that as a standing rule. Following is a list of the custodians of these land records in the several states. The record of every recorded land transaction is maintained in the jurisdiction where the land in question happens to lie:

ALABAMA:	County Probate Court.
ALASKA:	Recorder in the judicial district.
ARIZONA:	County Recorder.
ARKANSAS:	Circuit Court in the county.
CALIFORNIA:	County Recorder.
COLORADO:	County Clerk and Recorder.
CONNECTICUT:	City/Town Clerk.
DELAWARE:	County Recorder of Deeds.
DIST. OF COLUMB.:	Recorder of Deeds (1101 4th Street, SW, 5th Floor, Washington, DC 20024).
FLORIDA:	Clerk of Circuit Court in the county.
GEORGIA:	Clerk of County Superior Court.
HAWAII:	Bureau of Conveyances, P.O. Box 2867, Honolulu, HI 96803.
IDAHO:	Clerk's Office in the county.
ILLINOIS:	County Recorder of Deeds. (In counties under 60,000 population, the County Clerk is also the Recorder.)
INDIANA:	County Recorder.
IOWA:	County Recorder.
KANSAS:	County Register of Deeds. (The County Clerk has transfer books recording all transfers before deeds can be recorded by the Register of Deeds.)

KENTUCKY:	County Clerk.
LOUISIANA:	Clerk of Court in the parish.
MAINE:	Register of Deeds in the county. (In Aroostook and Oxford counties, there are two registries in each. Aroostook County has a Northern Registry at Fort Kent and a Southern Registry at Houlton. Oxford County has a Western Registry at Fryeburg and an Eastern Registry at South Paris.)
MARYLAND:	Circuit Court in the county. In Baltimore City, it is the Circuit Court for the city. (All land records for Maryland before the federal Constitution was ratified in 1788 are in the Hall of Records, Annapolis. There are also many pre-twentieth-century records at the Hall of Records, but this is purely at the discretion of county officials and not legally mandated. Some of these records were housed in the State Land Office at Annapolis, but that office was recently abolished and the records transferred to the Hall of Records.)
MASSACHUSETTS:	Registry of Deeds in registry district. (All except five counties have only one registry office per county: Berkshire County has a Northern District at North Adams, a Middle District at Pittsfield, and a Southern District at Great Barrington; Bristol County has a Northern District at Taunton, a Bristol Fall River District at Fall River, and a Southern District at New Bedford; Essex County has a Northern District at Lawrence and a Southern District at Salem; Middlesex County has a Northern District at Lowell and a Southern District at Cambridge; and Worcester County has a Northern District at Fitchburg and a Southern District at Worcester. Be aware of dates of county and district creations.)
MICHIGAN:	Registry of Deeds in the county.
MINNESOTA:	Register of Deeds in the county.
MISSISSIPPI:	Chancery Court in the county.
MISSOURI:	Register of Deeds in the county.
MONTANA:	County Recorder.

NEBRASKA:	Register of Deeds in the county. (In counties of less than 16,000 the County Clerk is ex-officio Register.)
NEVADA:	County Recorder.
NEW HAMPSHIRE:	County Registry of Deeds. (Go to *http://www.nhdeeds.com/* for record access.)
NEW JERSEY:	County Clerk. (All land records prior to 1800 are in the State Library, Bureau of Archives and History, Trenton. A few later ones are also there.)
NEW MEXICO:	County Clerk.
NEW YORK:	County Clerk (except in New York, Kings, Queens, and Bronx counties, where they are in custody of the Register of the City of New York; there is a registry office in each NYC borough).
NORTH CAROLINA:	Register of Deeds in the county.
NORTH DAKOTA:	Registrar of Deeds in the county.
OHIO:	Registry of Deeds in the county.
OKLAHOMA:	County Clerk. (Go to *https://okcountyrecords.com/* for record access.)
OREGON:	Recorder's Office in the county.
PENNSYLVANIA:	Recorder of Deeds in the county.
RHODE ISLAND:	City/Town Recorder of Deeds. (Go to *http://rilandrecords.com/* for record access.)
SOUTH CAROLINA:	Recorder of Deeds Office or Clerk of Courts Office in the county. (Land records prior to 1785 were recorded at Charleston. Records between 1785 and 1868 were kept in the districts with all of their complicated fluctuations. For more information on the history and organization of S.C. districts, see James M. Black, "The Counties and Districts of South Carolina" [*Genealogical Journal*, Vol. 5, No. 3]. There is also a useful research outline on South Carolina research at *http://www.hewat.net/hewat/LDS-history-carolina.html*. This outline was prepared by the LDS Family History Library.)
SOUTH DAKOTA:	Register of Deeds in the county.
TENNESSEE:	Register of Deeds in the county.

TEXAS:	County Clerk. (Go to *https://texaslandrecords. com/* for record access.)
UTAH:	County Recorder.
VERMONT:	Town Clerk in the township.
VIRGINIA:	Circuit Court Clerk in the county or independent city. (See Chapter 27 for further information on courts and jurisdictions in Virginia.)
WASHINGTON:	County Auditor.
WEST VIRGINIA:	County Clerk.
WISCONSIN:	Register of Deeds in the county.
WYOMING:	County Clerk.[6]

When tracing a family in the New England states of Connecticut, Rhode Island, and Vermont, where land records are kept in the town, it is important to search the records of all towns of interest, including "parent" towns, in periods before the newer towns were divided off. This is also true in New Hampshire, where all but the most recent records are in the towns. This is the same principle you follow when you search the records of parent counties in other states.

The LDS Family History Library has extensive collections of local land records on microfilm. These records are an essential source whenever a county's records are filmed or digitized. So, if you have access to that library's collections, either there or at a branch library, you must always check the library catalog for holdings in those localities where your research is centered.

You need to know that there are a few situations where restrictions have been imposed on the use of official records, and the public cannot have direct access to them. In most such cases, however, land records are not included in this kind of restrictive legislation. The Freedom of Information Act pretty much prohibits that result, and the careful researcher can still gain access to these records if proper application is made before visiting the county courthouse. People who examine and research land titles have ready access all the time.

B. Indexes

Most local land records are well indexed, by both the names of grantors and the names of grantees. These are usually separate indexes, but they are combined in a few cases. Thus, you generally have little difficulty putting your hands on most records that relate to your ancestors. There are a few limi-

---

[6] The source of this information in earlier editions was *Martindale-Hubbell Law Dictionary*, 120th ed. (Summit, NJ: Martindale-Hubbell, Inc., 1988), Vol. VIII (used with permission) as well as correspondence with various court officials. In this edition, that information has been updated using websites of the individual states.

tations in these indexes, but you can learn to live with these if you are aware of them. Following are some of the main limitations:

1. **Multiple parties not listed.** If there is more than one grantor or one grantee, the index often lists only the one named first in the instrument. The fact that there are other parties involved is sometimes indicated by merely putting *et al.* (Latin abbreviation for "and others") in the index after the name of the first party.

2. **Legal agents listed instead of landowners.** If a trustee, a guardian, an attorney, an executor, an administrator, a commissioner, a sheriff, a court representative, or any other legal agent (including a court representative who sells land for tax purposes) acting as the grantor in a deed is standing in place of your ancestor, you will not usually find your ancestor's name in the index but will more likely find the name of that legal agent. This makes things difficult because you have no way to know the identity of this person or even that such a sale took place. Suggestions given under "Other tricks for hard cases" earlier in this chapter may prove to be helpful here. This problem is especially difficult because you are not likely to know about these records even though they might be the records most likely to contain helpful family history information.

3. **Indexes not strictly alphabetical.** Most indexes are not strictly alphabetical. They are usually alphabetical only by the first letter or two of the surname, and then—sometimes—alphabetical by the first letter of the given name, then chronological. Before the advent of technology in the recording process, such methods had to be used in order to keep the indexes current with the records. In any case, it is generally necessary in the research process to go through the entire index of the initial letter of our ancestor's surname to find all entries relating to persons of that surname.

4. **Each book indexed individually.** In order to make the indexes as manageable as possible, most recorders indexed each deed book separately. In these cases, the indexes are easier to use, but this practice often necessitates our checking many indexes to cover relevant time periods.

5. **Master indexes often incomplete.** In some localities, records custodians went back and developed master indexes to land records. These master indexes combined the indexes from many separate books and are easy to use because they eliminate the need to check the multiple volumes mentioned above in order to find a few entries.

   These master indexes, however, often lull the researcher into a false sense of security. You need to be aware that these master indexes are often incomplete. Many master indexes were compiled from the indexes to the individual volumes, and it was easy for an indexer to skip entries inadvertently when he was trying to make sure that all entries were in their proper alphabetical sequence. There is also the possibility of names being misread and thus mis-indexed. If you have access to the individual volumes and if the indexes to these individual volumes are available, it is a good idea to check them.

6. **Some indexes are to township and range rather than people.** There are a few states in the public domain (Iowa is a good example) that have no direct indexes to the parties of land transactions. In these states, all land records are indexed according to tract. With that type of index, a line or column in the index is assigned to conveniently sized tracts

GENERAL INDEX TO DEEDS

Ba to Bl   GRANTOR

To find Name by this Table—

GRANTORS		GRANTEES	WHERE RECORDED BOOK VOL. PAGE	DATE OF DEED MONTH DAY YEAR	DATE OF RECORD MONTH DAY YEAR	LOCATION
Black	et ux James	Caroline F May	K 10 440	Dec 17 1873	D 17 1873	Conestoga St City
Bleacher by Shf	John	John Hildebrand	P 10 224	Nov 17 1873	Feb 3 1875	Providence
Black	et ux James	George Varnan	U 10 598	Apr 16 1868	Sep 13 1876	W James St
Blackburn	John A	Joseph C Taylor	D M1s 367	Feb 11 1863	Mar 28 1877	L Britain
Black	John	Henry Stoltzfus Odn	E M1s 127	Apr 1 1879	May 21 1879	Release
Black	James	Abraham A Myers	E M1s 81	Dec 28 1872	Jun 24 1879	S Water St
Blaul	Jacob	Louis Blaul	L 11 299	Mar 29 1880	Mar 29 1880	E Lemon St Lanc
Black	et ux James	James Warren et al	N 11 432	Oct 27 1873	Jul 22 1880	S Water St
Black	John	Elizabeth S Dickey	P 11 289	Feb 18 1881	Feb 21 1881	E Orange St Lanc
Black	et ux James	Anna Martha Miller	P 11 436	Mar 31 1881	Mar 31 1881	133-135 E King StLanc
Black	et ux James	John R Diffenbach	T 11 222	Mar 30 1882	Mar 30 1882	N Duke St Lanc
Blank	Jacob	John B Barbour	W 11 77	Jan 9 1882	Jun 23 1882	E Earl R of W
Blank	John S	John B Barbour	X 11 269	Jan 2 1883	Jan 5 1883	Right of Way
Black	James	Sarah A Musselman	Z 11 394	Apr 2 1883	Apr 2 1883	N Duke St
Black	James R	William Black	Z 11 593	Mar 29 1883	Apr 9 1883	Release
Black	et ux	Eliza E Haldeman	B 12 23	Feb 20 1882	Apr 19 1883	Salisbury
Black	Joseph H	John W Brubaker	D 12 86	Apr 1 1884	Apr 2 1884	Columbia
Black	et ux James	James Moore	E 12 413	May 19 1884	May 24 1884	S Water St
Blair	et ux James	Fanny A Blair	G 12 361	Mar 1 1884	Jan 2 1885	Fulton Twp

FIGURE 3—A PAGE FROM A GRANTOR INDEX

(such as a section, quarter section, platted block, or lot). In these cases, it is necessary to know the subdivision, section, township, and range (or block number) in order to find the records. These indexes are an asset to those who examine land titles and can be valuable to the family history researcher once he has located his ancestor's land, but they are not good finding tools. They usually pose problems for us.

There are some occasions when the survey description of a man's land has been included in his biographical sketch in the local county history. The petition by the administrators of Thomas Gallion's estate in Kossuth County, Iowa, used as an example earlier in this chapter, was located in this way.

In many states, there are several other indexes in addition to those for grantors and grantees. In Idaho, for example, twenty-seven separate indexes are required by statute. Some of these may be useful.

You *must* use the indexes. In spite of some shortcomings, they are good and they provide reasonably easy access to most land records. If you do not have personal access to the records, do not be afraid to write to the record custodian and ask him to check for specific names in his indexes on your be-half. However, be sure your requests are reasonable and that you are willing to compensate him for the copies and for his time spent.

In its microfilming program through the years, the LDS Family History Library always filmed the indexes when it filmed the land records. This practice is still being followed now that the records are being digitized. If you have access to these films or to the digitized records, you will find them easy to use—just as easy as reading the same indexes at the courthouse. And I stress again that when you use indexes, you must consider all possible spellings of the names you seek.

C. Other cautions

You will sometimes encounter situations where an ancestor is not listed in the land record indexes, even though he appears as a landowner on local tax lists. There are four possible reasons why this might be the case:

- He did not record his deed(s).
- You are not looking in the right place in the indexes.
- The name of your ancestor was misspelled in the indexes.
- The indexes are incomplete.

You must not be afraid in such cases to read deed books, deed by deed, for the appropriate time periods. This does not mean reading entire deeds—only enough to identify the names of the parties.

Some deeds are not recorded, and the law does not require that they be recorded. Recording provides protection for the property owner—it is his notice to the world that he has legal title to the property—but it is his responsibility to record the deed in order to take advantage of that protection.

VI. CONCLUSION

I have talked at length about the value of these records to our family history, and I stand by that assessment. I have also talked about using the grantor and grantee indexes. That approach may seem out of step with the research you do on the Internet. Unfortunately, because deeds and land records do not consistently generate the kind of results that some other records—such as census schedules and wills—generate, they are very low on the priority list of records to be indexed on the various family history websites. This means that, for the foreseeable future, most of your research in land records will have to be done the old-fashioned way.

Some of these records are available online, many are available on microfilm—some in the offices of the records custodians, some in state repositories, and some through the Family History Library in Salt Lake City (including FamilySearch libraries and branch libraries). A few of these records, however, are available only in the offices of the records custodians in local county courthouses. That is where they must be searched, along with their indexes. However, whatever is required is worth your effort.

21

Abstracting Probate and Land Records

Considerable time and space have already been spent discussing the importance of taking adequate research notes and picking up all available information relating to every person of our surnames of interest. With the indexed databases of digitized records on the various family history websites, it is easy to save exact copies of documents where these people are listed. However, we are not always fortunate enough to find the documents relevant to our family research included among these indexed databases. This means that there will still be a time—if you are a typical family history researcher—when you will need to actually do "pick and shovel research" and manually extract the information relating to your ancestral families from the records you find.

The purpose of this chapter is to discuss how best to accomplish that task— how to efficiently get the required information out of the records and into your notes in a meaningful and readily usable form without omitting significant evidence. This is especially relevant as it relates to deeds and other land records. However, in many instances, it also relates to wills and the various probate documents.

Though it sounds quite simple, there are some obstacles. In fact, it is often difficult to tell what is important and what is not. Experience teaches best, but perhaps some carefully thought-out suggestions can assist while you are gaining experience.

I. ABSTRACT VS. EXTRACT

There was a brief introduction to abstracts and extracts in Chapter 7, but little was actually said there about their relative value. We need to look at them here in a bit more depth, but first we need to define our terms:

ABSTRACT, used as a verb, means to summarize, abridge, or take essential thoughts only. Chapter 19 mentioned abstracts of title (a noun), and, from the definition of the verb, it should be clear why they were given that name.

EXTRACT, used as a verb, on the other hand, means to take something out of another source in its entirety—to copy it exactly. Whatever is extracted is copied verbatim from its source, as a deed being copied from a book of deeds or a biographical sketch from a book of such sketches.

TRANSCRIBE, also used as a verb, likewise means to copy. However, any copy or reproduction is a transcript (a noun) or a transcription.

Many records need to be extracted. Census schedules, vital certificates, church register entries, tax lists, immigration records, passages from books and newspapers, etc., all fall into this category if you are unable to take photographs, scan the original, or make photocopies. If you can print copies from the Internet database or elsewhere, that is usually what you want to do. This exact reproduction is essential to proper analysis. However, deeds, wills, most other court records, and early military pension and bounty land warrant application papers can be abstracted when exact duplications cannot be made. And there are also occasions when it is more efficient to make abstracts even when photographic copies or scanned images can be made.

It is a good idea to print exact copies of documents whenever possible, and that is an easy process when the documents are online. Exact copies provide a simple way to go back and look again when things do not quite make sense.

Even when the documents are not online, digital photography and portable scanners make it easy to get readable exact copies. However, if the handwriting in the document is legible and if you are careful in the abstracting process, exact document copies are not always required. I should also note, as indicated in Chapter 7 as part of our discussion of research notes, there are now record-keeping programs available that copy documents from the Internet and create links between the persons named in those documents and your research notes. If you use these programs, I offer two suggestions relating to this matter:

- Some record-keeping programs create hyperlinks from your records to the documents in their various database sources. Because such links can get broken and cause the loss of significant documents, do not rely on those links. The link is fine, but you also need to make a copy of each document and download it into the records of your record-keeping program on your computer hard drive.

- Because these record-keeping programs operate on "the cloud," I believe it is a good idea to also preserve a copy on another, more permanent, storage medium, such as a flash drive or an external hard drive.

In this chapter, we deal only with the abstracting of land and probate records. It is especially important that you learn how to abstract these important records because there can sometimes be dozens of documents in one locality relating to your surname(s) of interest. Not only can there be many documents, but there is also much verbiage in those documents not relevant to your research purposes. It is folly to waste time and money copying it, and to do so can add unnecessary bulk to your research notes and increase the amount of time needed for evaluation because of the eventual need to sift through mountains of redundant verbiage to ferret out the essential evidence.

Researchers do not all agree on this issue. Some say it is best to make a verbatim extract of every pertinent record you find or—when possible—photograph, scan, or make photocopies of the records because such copies ensure you have all the information you need and that there are no extraction errors. That argument is valid. However, I believe that if you are careful and precise in your abstracting, you can get everything that is essential and have the same assurance. Your notes will also be much less voluminous and will be easier to evaluate when you get to that stage of the process.

If you choose to go the abstracting route, the only universal rule I can offer is this: GET ALL THE ESSENTIAL INFORMATION. Do not try to be brief just for the sake of brevity. When there is a question about the importance of something, include it. It is better to get too much information than not enough. And as you gain experience, your ability to discern relevance will become more acute.

One thing you can do to help assure that your abstracts will not be misinterpreted is to always use the same pronouns that were used in the document you are abstracting. If a man said in his will: "I leave to my son John such and such property . . .," your abstract should *use the same pronouns he used.* And you must be consistent in this throughout the process.

Some researchers make abbreviated abstracts, copying only dates, names, and relationships from wills; and names, dates, considerations (price), and relationships from deeds. These brief abstracts may be all right on rare occasions, but they do not ordinarily qualify as good research notes. In addition to overlooking significant family history data, it is much easier to make errors when you do not actually read the document but skim through it watching only for those limited morsels of information. A prime example of this is the abstract of George Blackburn's will cited in Chapter 17 where the abstracter, who apparently went through the document picking out the names of George's children, listed two unrelated persons—actually two slaves—as children in the family, and then missed some of his actual children.

As you do your research—if you intend to do good, reliable work, as I hope is the case—you must make fairly detailed abstracts (depending on the specific records, of course). The only requirement is that you get all essential facts!

II. THE NATURE OF THE ABSTRACT

The abstracts you make must fit naturally into your note-keeping system, and your research log must list every record you search. Every abstract must include a complete reference to its source by locality, volume (or book or liber, etc.), and page (or folio)—and to serial numbers of microfilms where appropriate. It must also state clearly the type of record involved and include all dates important to the document—the date made and the date recorded for a deed, and the date made and the date probated (sometimes date recorded) for a will. Sometimes, when people are working with records on the Internet, there is a tendency to forget to record sources accurately—or even to record them at all—as they move quickly from one source to the next.

Some researchers use prepared forms for abstracting different types of records. These are fine, especially for the beginner who may wonder what is significant and what is not. Be careful, however, because there are times when valuable information in a record may not fit the format of the form.

I do not use any forms for abstracting wills and deeds, not because they are bad, but mainly because they require more space and add more bulk to my files. (Usually only one deed or one will is abstracted per page of notes when forms are used, while these limits do not otherwise apply.) If bulky notes do not bother you, you may want to develop and use some types of extraction forms.

A. Abstracting deeds

Whether or not you use a form, there are certain basic kinds of information that *must* be abstracted. In addition to the complete locality, relevant dates, and source information, the following nine items are essential to a deed abstract:

1. Parties to the deed—the grantor(s) and the grantee(s).

2. Places of residence of those parties.

3. Consideration involved—the price paid and any stated terms.

4. Description of the land—including size (acreage) and location. (If metes and bounds were used, this might include a relationship to a watercourse or other body of water, or a road and/or adjacent lands of other persons, and/or a brief history of the title to the land, the beginning of the metes and bounds—such as "Beginning at a sweet gum tree on the shore of William's Bay at the corner of the land belonging to Matthew Quick"— and the name of the tract, if it has one—as in Maryland.) In the public domain states, the land description in terms of subdivision, section, township, range, directions (compass bearings), and distances should all be noted.

5. Relationship information. This includes relationships of all types and between any and all persons—not just the grantor and grantee.

6. Miscellaneous information. (This category is the most difficult to define because you never know exactly what a land record might say. A deed may include special terms, restrictions, or privileges that are significant. A man may have sold land and preserved a right of way through the land he sold. Or he may have reserved a small corner where the family burial plot was located. Anything else of value must be determined from the

record itself. The origin of the grantor's title to the land might also be given and may have particular significance.)

7. Names of witnesses—exactly as they appear. (Today's deeds do not usually have witnesses but rather acknowledgments by notaries.)

8. Signature(s) of the grantor(s). (Though you do not find actual signatures in the land record books in the days before photocopy recording, it is often helpful to know whether a man signed his own name or whether he used a mark, and this is indicated in the deed books.)

9. Any release of dower rights by the wife of the grantor. (Such releases are often—but not always—recorded immediately following the deeds to which they pertain.) In many cases, the wife also signed the deed.

B. Abstracting probate records

As you abstract probate records, there are nine items to consider in addition to the type of document, source, locality references, and essential dates. These are as follows:

1. The name of the testator—the person who made the will.

2. Any additional descriptive information relating to the testator—such as place of residence, occupation, religion, inferences of age or state of health, etc.

3. All persons named in the will should be listed exactly as their names appear in the record, in the order named, and in direct connection with . . .

4. Any relationships stated for those persons to either the testator, to some other person(s), or to each other, and . . .

5. The essentials of the bequests and devises made to these persons. (This should include land descriptions, names of slaves, amounts of money, and all other property mentioned.)

6. Miscellaneous information. (Again, this is a difficult category to define because wills are just as unpredictable as deeds. Usually, however, any special explanations, restrictions, or privileges might fall into this category.)

7. The name(s) of the executor(s) and any relationships or connections that are stated between him (them) and the testator.

8. The names of witnesses—exactly as they appear.

9. The signature of the testator. (As with deeds, it is often useful to know whether a man signed his name or made his mark. This evidence may help provide evidence of a connection sometime. And though the wills in the early registers are not the originals and do not show original signatures, they do indicate if a mark was used, and the scribe often imitated marks from the original documents.)

Now that we have discussed the essentials of abstracting deeds and wills, let us look at some actual documents and abstracts of them. The deeds abstracted here are from the records of Washington County, Virginia, and the wills are from Guilford County, North Carolina.

III. ABSTRACTS OF DEEDS

A. Example No. 1

DEEDS OF WASHINGTON COUNTY, VIRGINIA—BOOK 11 (1831–34), PAGE 6.

This Indenture made this first day of November in the year of our Lord one thousand eight hundred and thirty one Between Jacob Lynch commissioner appointed for the purpose by the County Court of Washington of the one part and Andrew Shannon of the County of Washington and State of Virginia of the other part: Whereas in a suit in chancery depending in the County Court of Washington aforesaid wherein Andrew Shannon is Complt and Hannah Warsham, David S, Joseph, Jonathan M. Warsham and Jesse Lee & Edith his wife, widow and heirs of William Warsham deceased, John & Joseph Warsham, Eliza and Robert Warsham children & sole heirs of Robert Warsham Jr dec^d, Thomas Warsham, Jeremiah Warsham, The children and heirs of Beary Warsham, deed, the children & heirs of Jefferson W. Warsham, dec, John, Maria, Polly, George, and the other five children of Patsey Smith dec^d & Tobias Smith her husband, William Mackey & Ruth his wife, being all heirs of Robert Warsham the elder deceased are defendants, it was on the 18th day of May 1831 adjudged ordered and decreed that Jacob Lynch who is hereby appointed Commissioner for the purpose do convey to the Complt all the lands in the bill mentioned, except the portion of Lee & wife and the interest therein of Polly Rockholds heirs according to the partition between the Complainant and Lee and wife which is hereby affirmed, with covenants of special warranty against himself and his heirs: and the Complt be forever quieted in the possession and enjoyment of the lands hereby decreed to be conveyed: Now therefore This Indenture Witnesseth: That the said Jacob Lynch for and in consideration of the promises Doth hereby grant, bargain & sell unto the said Andrew Shannon and his heirs, the tract of land above mentioned which according to the plot filed among the papers in said suit in Chancery contains one hundred and fifty three acres 135¾ poles, and is bounded as followeth to wit Beginning at two Spanish oaks and poplar N 43º W 78 poles to a black oak, N. 53º W 140 poles to two white oaks & a black oak N. 53º E 160 poles to a double Socerwood & a white oak S. 39º E 88 poles to a Spanish oak and Sugartree 39º 23º E. 144.2 poles to a stake on the patent line S 63º 40º W 54 poles to the Beginning excepting such interest az the heirs of Polly Rockhold dec^d may have therein with all its appurtenances. To Have and To Hold the above described tract of land with all its appurtenances unto the said Andrew Shannon and his heirs forever. And the said Jacob Lynch for himself and his heirs doth covenant with the said Andrew Shannon and his heirs that he the said Jacob Lynch and his heirs, the said tract or parcel of land, except az before excepted, unto the said Andrew Shannon and his heirs against all claim which said Lynch or his heirs, hath acquired thereto under the decree aforesaid will warrant and forever defend

In Witness whereof the said Jacob Lynch hath hereunto subscribed his name and affixed his seal the day & year first written.

(signed) Jacob Lynch

[No witnesses signed.]

This Indenture of bargain and seal was acknowledged in the clerks office of Washington County on the 11th day of November 1831 before David Campbell clerk of the said County by the said Jacob Lynch as his act and deed and admitted to record.

Not only does the above deed challenge the ability of the abstracter, it also suggests that court records in chancery should hold valuable information on the Warsham family. The sad part about a record like this is that the researcher looking for records of the Warsham family may never find it because it is indexed with Jacob Lynch, the court-appointed commissioner, as grantor. (This is one of the problems with indexes to land records we discussed in Chapter 20.)

Now let us see how we can make an abstract:

DEEDS OF WASHINGTON CO, VA—BK 11 (1831–34) P. 6.

Deed from JACOB LYNCH, Commissioner, to ANDREW SHANNON of Wash. Co.—result of suit in Chancery 18 May 1831 in which sd. SHANNON was complt.and the defend's were: "HANNAH WARSHAM, DAVID S., JOSEPH, JONATHAN M. WARSHAM & JESSE LEE & EDITH HIS WIFE, WIDOW & HEIRS OF WILLIAM WARSHAM DECD, JOHN & JOSEPH WARSHAM, ELIZA & ROBERT WARSHAM CHN & SOLE HEIRS OF ROBERT WARSHAM JR DECD, THOMAS WARSHAM, JEREMIAH WARSHAM, THE CHN & HEIRS OF BEARY WARSHAM, DECD, THE CHN & HEIRS OF JEFFERSON W. WARSHAM, DECD, JOHN, MARIA, POLLY, GEORGE, & OTHER 5 CHN OF PATSEY SMITH DECD & TOBIAS SMITH HER HUSBAND, WILLIAM MACKEY & RUTH HIS WIFE, BEING ALL HEIRS OF ROBERT WARSHAM THE ELDER DECD."
By court order LYNCH to transfer all lands mentioned in bill except portion of LEE & wife & interest of POLLY ROCKHOLD'S HEIRS according to partition btw SHANNON & LEE—plot of tract filed with papers in suit— 53 acres, 135¾ poles—Beginning at 2 Spanish oaks and poplar . . . —(no adj. land holders or identifying topographic features named)—no witnesses signed—(signed) Jacob Lynch—1 Nov 1831—Ack. & recd: 11 Nov 1831.

Note that though I used several abbreviations in this abstract, names were never abbreviated unless they were abbreviated in the record. They are always copied *exactly as they appear in the record*. Note also that I have done a lot of capitalizing. This makes the abstract much easier to use and the data therein easier to tabulate and analyze. You can underline with similar effect. Without additional evidence, some of the relationship information in this deed could be very easily misinterpreted. It is impossible to determine whether John, Maria, Polly, and George belong to Jefferson W. Warsham or to Polly and Tobias

Smith. In cases like this, we do as I have done here and copy the information verbatim and put it in quotation marks rather than try to interpret it. By following these procedures, you save yourselves headaches and questions later when you analyze your notes. You can only hope that the records resulting from the suit in Chancery Court will answer most of your questions and tell you the relationships between all of these people. Perhaps the will of Robert Warsham, Sr., will also help you.

B. Example No. 2

DEEDS OF WASHINGTON COUNTY, VIRGINIA—BOOK 11 (1831–1834), PAGE 289.

This Indenture made this 23^d day of July 1833, Between James Mobley of the one part and Peter Mayo of the other part, both of Washington County, Virginia: Witnesseth that the said James Mobley for and in consideration of one dollar to him in hand paid, doth bargain and sell unto the said Peter Mayo and his heirs the following property To wit, two negro boys, one named William about 13 years old, and one named Mark about ten years old, being slaves left him Mobley by his father John Mobley dec^d To Have and To Hold said property unto said Peter Mayo and his heirs against the claims of all persons whomsoever. In Trust: Nevertheless, that if the said James Mobley or his heirs, shall on or before the 23^d day of July 1834 will and truly pay or cause to be paid unto James C. Hayter the just and full sum of three hundred dollars with interest from this day which is justly due him, together with the expense of drawing and recording this Indenture, then this Indenture to be void. And in further Trust that if said James Mobley or his heirs shall fail to pay the said sum of three hundred dollars with interest on or before the 23^d day of July 1833 [*sic*] then it shall be lawful for the said Peter Mayo or his heirs, executors or administrators to proceed to sell the above described property at public sale, to the highest bidder for ready money, having advertised the time and place of sale twenty days by putting up an advertisement for that purpose for that space of time at the front door of the Courthouse in Washington County, and out of the proceeds of said sale to pay said Hayter whatever may be due him of the debt aforesaid the expense of drawing and recording this Indenture, the expense of sale and six per cent to said trustee for his trouble, and the overplus if any to said James Mobley or his heirs, and if the property should not pay the debt, he promises to pay the balance and binds his heirs thereto In Witness whereof said parties have hereunto set their hands and seals this day and year first above written.

(signed) James Mobley
(signed) Peter Mayo

[No witnesses signed.]

At a court continued and held for Washington County the 23^d day of July 1833.

This Indenture in trust between James Mobley of the one part and Peter Mayo of the other part, was acknowledged in court by the said Mobley and Mayo as their act and deed and ordered to be recorded.

As you may have noted from reading it, the above instrument is a trust indenture and was made to ensure the payment of a debt. (It is not a trust deed because it does not deal with real estate, but it is nevertheless recorded in the deed registers.) If, and when, that debt is paid, the indenture becomes void. Let us abstract it:

DEEDS OF WASHINGTON CO. VA.—BK 11 (1831–34) p. 289.

Indenture in trust from JAMES MOBLEY to PETER MAYO, both of Wash. Co. —for $1—2 negro boys, William, age 13, & Mark, age 10—slaves left to MOBLEY by HIS FATHER JOHN MOBLEY, DECD—to secure payment of $300 debt owed by MOBLEY to JAMES C. HAYTER, due 23 July 1834—if debt not pd, property to be sold at public sale by MAYO to pay debt—no witnesses signed— (signed) James Mobley, Peter Mayo—23 July 1833—Ack. & Recd: same day.

C. Example No. 3

DEEDS OF WASHINGTON COUNTY, VIRGINIA—BOOK 12 (1834–1837), PAGE 45.

This Indenture made this 30th day of January in the year of our Lord one thousand eight hundred and thirty between Joseph Warsham and Nancy his wife of the County of Washington and State of Virginia of the one part and John Hacket of the said County and State of the other part Witnesseth that the said Joseph Warsham & Nancy his wife for and in consideration of the sum of _____ current money of the United States to them in hand paid, the receipt whereof is hereby acknowledged do grant bargain and sell unto the said John Hacket a certain piece or parcel of land, lying and being in the County of Washington on the waters of the North fork of Holstein and in the rich Valley being part of two surveys one of 190 acres patented to John McHenry & one of 50 acres patented to Job Crabtree, and bounded as follows, to wit, Beginning at a Sugar tree and Buckeye Sapling on the South line of the said 50 acre survey thence for a division line between said Hackett and Warsham N 9½° W. 61 poles to two Buckeye saplings and a Stake in a rich hollow N 45° W 38 poles to a white oak dogwood and Maple Sapling N 66º 27 poles to a white oak and Dogwood N 3° E 17 poles crossing the creek to a white oak at the mouth of a cave near where a beech stood a corner of the 190 acre survey and with a line thereof S 75º W 90 poles to a white oak and maple N. 84º W 7 poles to a white oak thence leaving said lines S 17º E 39 poles to a Locust bush on the top of a hill S 28½º E 110 poles to a dogwood and small buckeye bush N 55º E 52 poles to the Beginning containing fifty four acres be the same more or less with all its appurtenances. To Have and To Holde, the said piece or parcel of land with all its appurtenances unto the said John Hacket and his heirs to the sole use and behoof of him the said John Hacket and his heirs forever. And the said Joseph Warsham and Nancy his wife for themselves and their heirs do covenant with the said John Hacket and his heirs that they the said Warsham & wife and their heirs, the said piece or parcel of land with all its appurtenances unto the said John Hacket and his heirs against the claims of all persons whomsoever, shall Warrant and will forever defend. In Witness whereof the said Joseph Warsham & Nancy his wife have hereunto subscribed their names and affixed their seals, the day and year first above written.

signed sealed and delivered   (signed) Joseph Warsham

in presence of [No witnesses named.]   (signed) Nancy Warsham

Washington County, to wit,

We Joseph C. Trigg and Tobias Smith justices of the peace of the county aforesaid in the state of Virginia do hereby certify that Nancy Warsham the wife of Joseph Warsham parties to a certain deed bearing date on this 30th January 1830 and hereunto annexed personally appeared before us in our County aforesaid and being examined by us prively and apart from her husband and having the deed aforesaid fully explained to her she the said Nancy Warsham acknowledged the same to be her act and deed and declared that she had willingly signed sealed and delivered the same and she wished not to retract it given under our hands & seals this 30th January 1830.

                                     (signed) Joseph C. Trigg

                                     (signed) Tobias Smith

At a Court held in Washington County the 27th day of October 1834 This Indenture of bargain & sale between Joseph Warsham & Nancy his wife of the one part and John Hacket of the other part was acknowledged in Court by the said Warsham as his act and deed and together with the certificate of the acknowledgment of the said Nancy made thereto ordered to be recorded.

There is nothing unusual about this deed. It is probably very much like most deeds you will find for your ancestors and presents few problems for the abstracter. Your abstract might look something like this:

DEEDS OF WASHINGTON CO, VA—BK 12 (1834–37) p. 45.

Deed from JOSEPH WARSHAM AND WIFE NANCY of Wash. Co. to JOHN HACKET of Wash. Co.—for (price not stated)—tract in Wash. Co. on N. fork of Holstein in the rich Valley, part of 2 surveys (one of 190 acres patented to JOHN McHENRY & one of 50 acres patented to JOB CRABTREE), "Beginning at a Sugartree and Buckeye sapling on S. line of said 50 acre survey . . ." —54 acres—no witnesses signed—(signed) Joseph Warsham, Nancy Warsham—Certif of acknowledgement made by Nancy—30 Jam 1830—Recd: 27 Oct 1834.

D. Example No. 4

DEEDS OF WASHINGTON COUNTY, VIRGINIA—BOOK 12 (1834–1837), PAGE 40.

This Indenture made this tenth day of October in the year of our Lord one thousand eight hundred and thirty one Between Isaiah Austin heir at Law of James Austin deceased of the county of Washington of the one part and John Austin of Atkens Tennessee of the other part Witnesses that the said Isaiah Austin the father and heir at law of James Austin deceased for and in consideration of the sum of two thousand dollars current money of the United States to him in hand paid, the receipt whereof is hereby acknowledged doth grant bargain and sell unto the said John Austin two several tracts of land adjoining each other lying and being in the County of Washington on the waters of the middle fork of holston river, One which was conveyed to the said James by deed bearing date the 4th of October 1823 executed to him by James Edmondson and William Buchanan executors of William E. Buchanan deceased bounded as follows to wit, Beginning on two white oaks and dogwood N. 16½º West 88 poles to a white oak and hickory North 1º East 54 poles to a white oak & Black oak on the side of the knob, South 54½º West 136 poles North 62½º West 36 poles South 29½º West 58 poles South 66° West 146 poles to a black oak on the great road South 57° East 120 poles to a white oak, South 12½ º East 36 poles to a hickory and dogwood North 62° East 114 poles to the Beginning containing two hundred acres be the same more or less. Also one other tract conveyed to the said Isaiah Austin by James Edmondson bounded az follows to wit Beginning at three chestnut oaks on a ridge on said Edmondsons line thence with the same S 27º E 70 poles to two white oaks corner to same S 5º E. 16 poles to a white oak and black oak corner to James Austins land, thence with Austins line S 57° W 136 poles to two hickories and white oaks N 70° W 36 poles to a maple on the side of a Knob S 32º W 58 poles to a white oak S 65° W 76 poles to a stake on said James Austins line thence with Benjamin Sharps line N 37° W 14 poles to a white oak and two hickories Thence N 50° E 122 poles to two white oaks & ash by a swamp thence N 45° E 180 poles to the Beginning. containing ninety five acres with all its appurtenances: To Have and To Hold the said tracts or parcels of land with all their appurtenances unto the said John Auston and his heirs to the sole use and behoof of him the said John Austin and his heirs forever. And the said Isaiah Auston for himself and his heirs doth covenant with the said John Austin and his heirs that he the said Isaiah Auston and his heirs the said tract or parcels of land with all appurtenances unto the said John Auston and his heirs against the claims of all persons whomsoever, shall and will forever defend. In witness whereof the said Isaiah Auston hath hereto subscribed his name and affixed his seal the day and year first above written.

Signed sealed & delivered
in presence of   Isaiah X (his mark) Austin

    John H. Fulton   Bev R. Johnston

    John C. Cummings   Charles S. Bekem

At a Court held for Washington County the 27th day of October 1834 This Indenture of bargain & sale between Isaiah Austin of the one part and John Austin of the other part was proved in court by the oath of John H. Fulton, Beverly R. Johnston and Charles S. Bekem three of the subscribing witnesses thereto to be the act and deed of said Isaiah and ordered to be recorded:

There is the deed; here is an abstract of it:

DEEDS OF WASHINGTON CO, VA—BK 12 (1834–37) p. 40.

    Deed from ISAIAH AUSTIN, FATHER & HEIR AT LAW OF JAMES AUSTIN, DECD of Wash. Co. to JOHN AUSTIN OF ATKENS, TENN. (both names sometimes spelled AUSTON in the deed)—for $2,000—2 tracts adj. each other on middle fork of Holston River—1 conveyed to sd JAMES AUSTIN by JAMES EDMONDSON & WILLIAM BUCHANAN, EXORS

OF WILLIAM E. BUCHANAN, "Beginning on two white oaks and dog-
wood . . ." on the great road (200 acres)—other tract conveyed to ISAIAH
by JAMES EDMONDSON, "Beginning at 3 chestnut oaks on a ridge on sd
EDMONDSON's line . . ." adj. JAMES AUSTIN'S land & sd EDMOND-
SON AND BENJAMIN SHARP (95 acres)—witnesses: JOHN H. FULTON,
JOHN C. CUMMINGS, BEV R. JOHNSTON (In acknowledgement of
court, her name is given as BEVERLY), CHARLES S. BEKEM—(signed)
Isaiah X (his mark) Austin—10 Oct 1831—Recd: 27 Oct 1834.

E. Example No. 5

DEEDS OF WASHINGTON COUNTY, VIRGINIA—BOOK 12 (1834–
1837), PAGE 366.

This Indenture made this first day of December 1835 between Amelia
Conn Senr and Amelia Conn Jr. both of Washington County Virginia. Witnesseth that the said Amelia Conn S^r for & in consideration of the natural
love and affection which she bears unto her daughter the said Amelia Conn
Jr. & for the further consideration of one dollar to her in hand paid hath
granted given bargained & sold to the said Amelia Junnor thirty two acres of
the tract of land on which she the said Amelia Conn Sr at the present resides
to include the dwelling house & spring and to be laid off in convenient form,
To Have and To Hold the same unto the said Amelia Conn Jr. & her heirs
forever. But the said Amelia Sr reserves to herself the right to the possession
and exclusive enjoyment of the said land and premises during her natural
Life at the termination of which the said Amelia Conn Junr or her heirs shall
be entitled to enter upon the same In witness whereof the said Amelia Conn
Senr hath set her hand & seal the day and year first above written.
Attest

David Parks   Amelia IE (her mark) Conn

John Melton

John Parks

This Indenture of bargain & sale between Amelia Conn Sr of the one part
and Amelia Conn Jr of the other part was proved in the Clerk's office of
Washington County on the 2nd day of March 1836 before David Campbell
Clerk of the said County by the oath of David Parks one of the subscribing
witnesses thereto to be the act & deed of said Amelia Senr. At a court held for
Washington County the 22d day of August 1836—

It was proved in Court by the oath of John Parks another witness thereto
to be the act & deed of said Amelia Senr—And at a Court continued and held
for said county the 23^d day of August 1836—It was further proved in Court
by the oath of John Melton another witness thereto to be the act & deed of
said Amelia Senr and ordered to be recorded.

And the abstract:

DEEDS OF WASHINGTON CO, VA—BK 12 (1834–37) P. 366.

Gift deed from AMELIA CONN SR TO HER DAU AMELIA CONN JR,
both of Wash. Co.—for love and affection & $1—32 acres of tract where
AMELIA SR. now resides, including dwelling house & spring, to be laid

off—AMELIA SR reserves right to possession during natural life—witnesses: DAVID PARKS, JOHN MELTON, JOHN PARKS—(signed) Amelia IE (her mark) Conn—1 Dec 1835—Recd: 23 Aug 1836.

Let us look now at the mechanics involved in abstracting wills.

IV. ABSTRACTS OF WILLS

A. Example No. 1

WILLS OF GUILFORD COUNTY, NORTH CAROLINA, BOOK A (1771–1813), PAGE 37.

Whereas Thomas Cox of Richland Creek in Guilford County and North Carolina yeoman being but weak in body but in perfect mind and memory and taking into consideration the certainty of death and ye uncertainty of life hath thought good to make order and appoint this my last will and Testament in manner and form following revoking and disresulting all manner of will or wills before by me made this only to be my last will and Testament.

Imprimis [first]—I commit my soul to Almighty God who gave it me and my body to be decently buried by my brother Solomon Cox and William Wierman who I appoint my Executors to see the accomplishment of this my last Will and Testament and make full satisfaction for all funeral charges and other Worldly debts every where to be paid. —

I leave and give to my beloved wife a fether bed & bed cloaths a side sadle and bridle and the third part of all the remainder part of my personal estate excepting only such particular artickels as are herein hereafter mentioned and given to particular persons.

I leave and give to my son Thomas one hundred acres of land including the improvements whereon I live to him his heirs and assigns forever—I leave and give my son Joshua one hundred acres of land to be laid of for him on the South side of the aforesaid tract and joining Solomon Cox's land to him his heirs and assigns forever. I leave and give my son Daniel one hundred acres of land to be laid of for him on the west side of my son Thomas' land to him his heirs and assigns forever.—I leave and give my son John one hundred acres of land to be laid of for him on the North side of my son Thomas' land to him his heirs and assigns forever.—I leave and give to my son Abner all the remainder part of my lands to be laid of for him where it should be most suitable to be valuable.—I leave and give my daughter Sarah a fether bed.—I leave and give my daughter Martha a fether bed to be made of the benefits of my improvements, and it is my will and desire that my wife shall live with my son Thomas on his place if she so wishes so long as she lives single—and I leave and give to my son Thomas ten pounds prock money—and it is my will and desire that my children have larning at least to read and write.—I leave and give to my son Abner fifteen pounds prock money—and I leave the remainder part of my personal estate to be equally divided among all my children—and it is my will that my sons shall possess everyone his part of my estate at the age of twenty one years and that my daughters shall everyone possess her part at the age of eighteen years—and it is my will that if any of my sons do not live to the age of twenty one years that then his or their lands shall be sold to the highest bider of his brethren and the price thereof be equally divided amongst his brethren—and it is my will that if any of my children do not live to the years above ordered to possess their estates at that then his heirs or their personal estate shall be equally divided amongst the living ones.

Signed and sealed in the
presence of

Wm Garner   (signed) Thomas Cox

Stephen Hussey (jurat)

John Kenworthy   North Carolina, Guilford County,
                                        November Court 1771. Then the
                                        within last will & Testament of
Thomas Cox was proved in open court by the oath of Stephen Hussey one of the subscribing witnesses thereto and motion ordered to be recorded. Then Solomon Cox and William Wierman (who by the Testator were left Executors of the within will) came into court and qualified as such &c.

An abstract of Thomas Cox's will might look like this:

WILLS OF GUILFORD CO, N.C.—BK A (1771–1813) P. 37.

WILL OF THOMAS COX, Richland Creek, Guilf. Co, Yeoman—weak in body, perfect in mind—Exors: MY BROTHER SOLOMON COX & WILLIAM WIERMAN.

To my BELOVED WIFE (NOT NAMED)—certain item of personal property.

To my SON THOMAS—100 acres, including improvements, whereon I now live.

To my SON JOSHUA—100 acres on S. side of aforsd tract—adj. SOLOMON COX.

To my SON DANIEL—100 acres on W. side of SON THOMAS.

To my SON JOHN—100 acres on N. side of SON THOMAS.

To my SON ABNER—all the remainder part of my lands.

To my DAU SARAH—fether bed.

To my DAU MARTHA—fether bed.

MY WIFE to live with my SON THOMAS as long as she is single (if she wishes).

To my SON THOMAS—10 pounds prock[lamation] money.

To my SON ABNER—10 pounds prock money.

ALL MY CHN shall learn to at least read and write.

Remainder of personal estate divided equally among chn.

SONS to possess their part of estate AT AGE 21, and DAUS AT AGE 18.

If son dies before 21, land to sell to highest bidding brother, price thereof equally divided amongst his brethren.

If any child dies before he is of age, personal estate divided equally to living children.

Witness: WM GARNER, STEPHEN HUSSEY, JOHN KENWORTHY.

(signed) THOMAS COX.

Will not dated. Proved: Nov Crt 1771.

The way I have abstracted the above will takes more space than if I had listed one item right after the other with only dashes between, as I did with the deeds. It can be done the other way, but this format makes for easier tabulation and analysis.

B. Example No. 2

> WILLS OF GUILFORD COUNTY, NORTH CAROLINA—BOOK A (1771–1813), PAGE 224.
>
> This first day of February in the year of our Lord one thousand eight hundred and fourteen I Robert Lamb of the State of North Carolina and County of Guilford: being sound in health of bodday minde and memmory do make this my last will and testament at the same time revoking all former wills made by me, declaring this to be my last will & Testament.
>
> Firstly—I give and bequeath unto my three sons namely Samuel, Simeon and John Lam all the lands that I have previously put them in possession of together with there stock and every spicice of property that I have heretofore given them.
>
> I also give and bequeath unto my four daughters and my grand daughter namely Elizabeth White Deborah Hoggatt Ester Hodson Ann Reynolds Margate Balilen each and every of them the whole property which I have heretofour given them.
>
> I allso give and bequeath unto my beloved wife all my household furniture together with all the live stock which I am now in possession of the same to be subject to hir use and benefit during hir natureal life and at hir death the same to be devided eaqually between my three sons my four daughters and my grand daughter as above named—and lastly after my just debts are paid I give and bequeath all the rezidue of all my estate what eaver and whearever to my eight children as above named equally devided between them and at the same time. I appoint my friend Zino Worth and do impower him to act as the Executor of this my last will and Testament to which I have hereunto set my hand and affixed my seal the day and date above mentioned.
>
> Daniel Worth (Jurat)
>
> Benjamin Hall   Robert X (his mark) Lamb
>
> For probate &c. of the foregoing Will—see min. Doc. No. 4 page 409.

There is the will; now let us abstract it:

> WILLS OF GUILFORD CO, N.C.—BK A (1771–1813) p. 224.
> WILL OF ROBERT LAMB of Guilf. Co—in good health.
> To my 3 SONS SAMUEL, SIMEON & JOHN LAM—all lands and property I have previously given them.
> To my 4 DAUS AND MY G DAU ELIZABETH WHITE, DEBORAH HOGGATT, ESTER HODSON, ANN REYNOLDS, MARGATE BALILEN—property I have heretofore given them. To my BELOVED WIFE (NOT NAMED)—all household furniture and livestock now in my possession, during her natural life—at her death to be divided among my 3 SONS, 4 DAUS, AND G DAU.
> All residue to my 8 CHN, above named, equally.

Exor: My FRIEND ZINO WORTH.
Witness: DANIEL WORTH, BENJAMIN HALL. (signed) ROBERT X (his
  mark) LAMB.
Dated: 1 Feb 1814—No date of probate given ("FOR PROBATE, ETC., SEE
  MINUTE DOCKET #4, p. 409.")

Notice that the above will suggests the use of another record. It would be a
serious mistake if we failed to look up the court record (minute docket) where
the information relating to the probate of this will is recorded. I also inserted
commas between some names in this abstract, but only because their placement was obvious.

C. Example No. 3

Some other types of probate records contain very little specific family history information, yet they are significant in other ways. Consider, for example,
the account of the administrator of his activities in probating an estate. Names
and dates are significant, but often little else. Here is an example:

SETTLEMENTS OF ESTATES, GUILFORD COUNTY, NORTH CARO-
LINA, 1844–1853, PAGE 104.

MAY Term 1846
    May 15th 1846—We the undersigned Justices of the Peace in aforesaid
County having met at the house of James S. Watson Admr of Eleanor Watson
Decd in pursuance of an order of Court to us directed proceeding to settle
with said Admr and find as follows:
    Dr. to amount of Sales Vouchers $198.57
    [Immediately following is a long list of accounts, the names of which are
probably, but may not be, without significance. Because of this factor, it is
usually desirable at least to make an abstract of the foregoing and then list the
names. In this account the names were:]
    M.D. Smith, Washington Donnett, Walter McConnel, Sarnl Nelson, Fran-
cis Obriant, Catharine Clark, L. W. Doakes, Rev. John A. Gritter, DR. L. W.
WATSON, James R. McLean, Sarah Mathews, Mrs. Dick.
    [It is not a sure thing, but these names may provide some clues to connec-
tions with other persons when other evidence is considered.]

                                            (signed) F. Shaw J.P.
                                            (signed) E. Denny J.P.

Note that the information in this chapter is given only as a suggestion. I
am not trying to dictate the specific form or content of your abstracts, but to
merely suggest that your abstracts, though brief, must be complete enough to
meet the demands of thorough research. I hope my suggestions and examples
will be helpful and will expedite your research. Remember, above all, that
your notes must be both complete and accurate, because these records (both
land and probate records) are the "bread and butter" sources of American family history research. Relevant evidence found in these records is often limited,

so you are going to need all the information that is there—in exactly the way it appears there. You never know but what you will find the very evidence you need to establish proof of a difficult connection.

22

Court Records and Family History

To some, it may seem strange to include an entire chapter on court records since many of the records already discussed have been court records of one type or another—notably land, probate, and guardianship records. However, other types of court records also have value for the family history researcher and deserve attention.

The story is told of a man who was going down the highway and stopped to help a woman motorist whose car had stalled. When he asked what the trouble was, she replied that she thought something was wrong with the clutch. The man went around and lifted the hood and, after looking inside, went back to report that the motor had fallen from its mounts and was lying on the ground beneath her vehicle. The woman's reply (in all seriousness): "Thank goodness it wasn't the clutch."

Somehow, this woman got the idea that there were only certain things that could go wrong with her car and, if the problem was not one of those, it was of little consequence. The beginning family history researcher often falls into a similar trap as he tells himself that only certain records are of value and that others deserve no serious consideration. Nowadays, the records that are believed to be of value to us are the records that have been digitized and indexed on the Internet. Of course, we all know that some records are better than others by their very nature. However, when you happen to need those other records—when they fit your problem—they are of great importance.

It has been my experience that court records, as a category, though not among the most important records, can be extremely valuable in some cases. When court records exist for your ancestor, or when you find a situation that suggests their probable existence, you need to take heed. Though they are probably not on an indexed database, they are available and should be used.

I. BACKGROUND AND DEFINITION

Roughly, court records are divided into two categories—criminal (public)[1] and civil (private). The records we will discuss in this chapter are the records of actions on civil matters. We will not discuss criminal court records except to define them and to state that there is considerable overlap in records of criminal and civil actions in most courts. Criminal actions deal with the process of bringing public offenders to justice. Crimes are carefully defined and punishments are often established by statute.

Civil actions deal primarily with the protection of individual rights, and most civil actions have two parties (a plaintiff and a defendant) opposed to each other for the recovery of a right or the redress of a wrong that the plaintiff claims to have suffered because of the defendant's acts. It should be noted, however, that non-adversarial proceedings, such as name changes, naturalizations, guardianship proceedings, adoptions, and the like, also have significant family history relevance.

Extensive records are maintained by the courts. Every writ, affidavit, complaint, answer, summons, subpoena, judgment, injunction, petition, motion, deposition, pleading, order, and decree, and all proceedings and testimony of every case, are detailed in court records and filed in systematic order. The extent and volume of these records is almost unbelievable—perhaps even incomprehensible to the nonprofessional.

II. A MISCONCEPTION

The Family History Library in Salt Lake City and other organizations have filmed and digitized some court records besides those already discussed in previous chapters—mainly court minutes, dockets,[2] and court orders—but only on rare occasions has that institution taken steps to preserve copies of the court files themselves (even in some localities where they have filmed, they have certainly not filmed or digitized all of them). Many researchers have received the impression that these microfilmed and digitized records represent all court records available in the localities from which they come—a serious error to make. These copies (both microfilmed and digitized copies) generally represent only a minute portion of the available court records.

With all the records that need to be gathered and preserved to facilitate family history research, most court records have low priority, and that priority is appropriate—but not because they have no value. They can be extremely useful in the right circumstances. Court dockets and minutes are especially

---

[1] Public law is that branch of law that involves the state (the government) in its sovereign capacity. Other forms of public law, of little concern to us here, include Constitutional, administrative, and international law.

[2] A docket is a brief chronological summary of a court's proceedings prepared by the court clerk. In many states, the law requires that the court dockets be indexed.

good[3] because they contain information about judgments, decrees, commissioners' reports and resolutions, and various other court actions. Many research problems can benefit from their use.

Minute and docket entries vary all the way from the simple notation that the action has been continued (carried forward) until a later date to a summary of the activities of an administrator in a probate matter. Some of these minutes and dockets are also indexed, which makes them quite easy to use once you find them.

People who are involved with records preservation have been more inclined to film and/or digitize some types of court records than others. Minutes, dockets, and court orders are bound and easily accessible, while loose files are much more difficult to work with (besides their incredible volume).

In a few cases, as with judgments of the Maryland Court of Appeals, some quite extensive court records have been filmed but, generally speaking, those records designated as "court record books" and "court orders" have only limited value.

If you cannot personally visit the courthouse, you should not hesitate to write to the court where you have an indication that there may be valuable court records pertaining to your ancestors. In a given case, this may be the most intelligent and profitable step you can take.

III. THE AMERICAN COURT SYSTEM

It is impossible, in the limited space here, to explain the intricacies of the American court system, but only to give you an idea of the essential nature of the system. In addition to the distinctions between civil and criminal matters, previously mentioned, there are some other important distinctions in U.S. court records:

1. State courts vs. federal courts
2. Law vs. equity
3. Trial courts vs. appellate courts

Let us now briefly explain these distinctions

1. State courts vs. federal courts

There are two sources of court control—the individual states and the federal government. The federal government, in addition to the U.S. Supreme Court, controls the U.S. Courts of Appeals set up in twelve circuits. Within those twelve circuits are ninety-four U.S. District Courts (plus some other courts that I will not discuss here). Some of these judicial districts include

---

[3] If you have ancestry in North Carolina, never overlook the old minutes of the County Superior Courts, a few of which are on film, and of the old Courts of Pleas and Quarter Sessions, which are almost completely microfilmed. In some states, lists/notices of pending cases involving title to real property—called *lis pendens*—have also been filmed and have some family history value.

entire states. They have jurisdiction over all admiralty and maritime causes, most criminal cases indictable under federal laws, and many civil matters. Each District Court is assigned to and functions within and with one of the twelve judicial circuits.

Courts set up in and by the states are set up under state statute and differ from one state to another. A state's court system is subject to structural change at the will of the state legislature. One thing that may be confusing to those trying to distinguish between state and federal courts is that many of these courts have the same names. Several of the states have District Courts and several others have Circuit Courts. In most states, there are multiple counties in each district or circuit. In New England, however, some states have several districts in each county.

Every state has a Supreme Court, but not every Supreme Court is the same. In most states, the Supreme Court is the court of final appeal, but in New York State, it is a court of general original jurisdiction with only limited appellate authority. Some states have County Courts with ordinary civil jurisdiction, limited criminal jurisdiction, and appellate jurisdiction over cases decided by justices of the peace or magistrates, as well as jurisdiction over probate and guardianship matters. In other states, courts of various other names perform all of these functions. In many states, you will find Courts of Common Pleas, while in still others, there are Superior Courts. Some states have several kinds of—and differently named—courts.

Some states have Justice-of-the-Peace Courts and others have Magistrate Courts; some have both. These courts usually have limited original jurisdiction and may not be courts where records are kept. Some have Family Courts and some have Small Claims Courts, etc., etc., etc. Each state has its own system, and you have to get used to the idea that what is called by one name in one state is probably called by a different name somewhere else.

As you use court records—or seek to use them—you should understand that federal court records usually have limited value to the family history researcher. Most court records that will likely be of interest to you are those generated by the state court system. For many reasons, mostly jurisdictional, only a small percentage of actions are brought in the federal courts.

2. Law vs. equity

At common law, the terms *equity* and *chancery* (which are synonymous) are used to describe one type of court proceeding and the term *law* is used to describe another. Equity means "justice" and relates to impartial justice between two parties whose claims (or rights) are in conflict. Judicial discretion may be exercised by the judge in an equity case, and there is no right to jury trial. Courts of equity are not bound by legal precedent or by specific types of writs or pleadings. They are free to seek impartial justice in the best interest of the parties involved.

In an action at law, the plaintiff seeks to recover monetary damages for injuries to himself, his property, his pocketbook, his reputation, etc. In a suit in equity, however, he seeks to compel another party to do something (specific performance decree) or to stop doing or refrain from doing something (injunction). Equity courts have traditionally handled divorces, foreclosures of liens, receiverships, partitions, trusts, real property controversies, etc.

Two of the most important types of actions at law are actions in *contract* and in *tort*. A tort is a wrong or injury arising out of the law that is not associated with a contract but involving a legal duty, a breach of that duty, and injury as a result of the breach. A tort involves injury to one's person (including his reputation and feelings) or his property. Assault, battery, trespass, misrepresentation, defamation, and negligence are all common torts.

Equity courts and the judicial remedies they provide originated in England as the result of lengthy power struggles between Parliament and the Crown. When Parliament said no legal writs[4] could be created by the King's courts as a source of relief, except those writs that already existed, the Crown named chancellors and created chancery courts, giving them authority to grant equitable relief in those situations where a person had been wronged and the law provided no remedy.

Concerning the early history of American civil actions (equity actions especially), Charles E. Chadman, a legal writer during the first part of the twentieth century, gave the following explanation:

> The American colonies were settled during the most influential period of the chancery court in England, and it, along with other serviceable institutions of the mother country, became engrafted on the judicial system of the various colonies. In most of them [i.e., the colonies], the equity powers were exercised by the royal governor in conjunction with his council, while in Rhode Island, during the colonial period, the [colonial] assembly acted as a court of chancery. In all of the colonies, except Pennsylvania, the chancery existed as a distinct tribunal from the common law courts. In Pennsylvania equity was administered by the law courts and, according to the procedure of the common law, until the middle of . . . [the nineteenth century]. When the colonies became states, they either established separate courts of equity, presided over by chancellors, or conferred the equity powers upon the ordinary law courts with a provision for its exercise according to the forms and procedure of chancery. . . .
>
> The American states and territories may be divided into three groups as regards the method followed of administering equity jurisprudence. These are:—
>
> First. Those states in which separate courts of chancery are maintained, and law and equity are administered by distinct tribunals under different

---

[4] A writ under English law is a predefined cause of action. There were several of these, but they did not cover every possible type of action. If the plaintiff's claim for relief did not fall within the purview of those existing writs, his suit could not be brought and he was barred from seeking legal relief.

modes of procedure. In this group the chancery court is copied after the Court of Chancery in England, and is similar as to powers and jurisdiction. This group . . . [has historically included] Alabama, Delaware, Mississippi, New Jersey and Tennessee.

Second. Those states in which law and equity are still administered in their distinct and appropriate forms, but by the same court. The boundaries between the two as to jurisdiction being jealously guarded, and the chancery jurisdiction not ceasing because the statutes confer the same powers on law courts. The most important member of this group . . . [has been] the federal government of the United States, comprising the various federal courts, which follow[ed] the system uniformly and are not influenced by state legislation. The states . . . [that have historically belonged] to this group are Arkansas, Florida, Georgia, Illinois, Maine, Maryland, Massachusetts, Michigan, New Hampshire, New Mexico, Pennsylvania, Rhode Island, Vermont, Virginia and West Virginia.

Third. This group includes the states and territories which have adopted the Civil Code. In these, the distinction between actions at law and suits in equity is abolished, and all relief is said to be administered through the uniform procedure of civil action. The effect of this is not, however, to abolish entirely the distinction between law and equity, though affording a common method of administration. The fundamental principles of equity are regarded, and it is even quite common to refer to actions involving equity principles as equitable actions, as distinguished from law actions. The abolition of the distinction between suits in equity and law as made by the Codes does not allow of the bringing an action not previously cognizable either in law or equity.[5]

The states of most interest to us here are those that maintained separate courts for dealing with actions in law and equity, Mr. Chadman's first group. As noted, they include Alabama, Delaware, Mississippi, New Jersey, and Tennessee. Of these, Alabama and New Jersey no longer maintain separate courts. New Jersey maintains separation of law and equity, but does so in two separate divisions of the same court. Delaware, Mississippi, and Tennessee still have two separate courts, and they have been joined, in more recent years, by Arkansas.

These states (both the ones with present-day separation and the ones that have changed) are significant because of the need we have as researchers to be aware of two sets of records, both of which might be important. In addition, you should understand that the records of equity courts often have special value because of the nature of their subject matter. For example, the law courts were often incapable of giving adequate relief whenever the subject matter of the dispute was unique, thus sending the matter into equitable jurisdiction. Because of this, lawsuits that related to possession of and title to land were often tried in equity.

---

[5] Charles E. Chadman, ed., *Chadman's Cyclopedia of Law* (Chicago: American Correspondence School of Law, 1912), Vol. 8, 185–187. The reason I have used a source so old is to capture something of the historical background and significance of the American legal system. Obviously much information in such sources is now out of date but the history does not change.

One of the most popular types of equitable actions involving land has been an action for ejectment. An ejectment action provides for the recovery of possession. Its significance to the family history researcher is that the record of the court should contain information on the history of the land and its title, especially significant if the title to the land in question stayed in the same family for several generations—not an uncommon occurrence in earlier times. Under such a circumstance, the court record might provide information on several generations of the family. The dispute may be over the title to an entire tract or it may involve the placement of a boundary that became obscure or was unobserved when relatives owned adjoining tracts.

Today most states maintain no distinction between law and equity causes brought under civil law. The intent is to do justice in each case without concern for cumbersome traditional distinctions. When traditional legal remedies are considered appropriate, they are applied; and when equitable remedies are called for, they are applied. Though there are differences from state to state, most have abolished distinctions between pleadings, parties, sittings, and dockets; however, principles, causes, rights, remedies, and defenses are generally still intact and are available as appropriate. You need to know, however, that many of the states have adopted this approach in relatively recent times.

In the old law courts, a person could not bring a simple action to set aside a contract, to force compliance with it, or to recover damages because of its breach. He would instead bring an action in *covenant* (to recover monetary damages), or *debt* (to recover a specific sum for a contract breach), or *assumpsit* (to recover damages if the agreement was not under seal), or *detinue* (to recover specific chattels [personal property] rightfully taken but wrongfully retained), or *replevin* (to recover specific chattels unlawfully taken).

A damage suit (tort action) would be either in *trespass* (for monetary damages), *trover* (for damages to property or goods by interference or improper detention), or *deceit* (for injury [wrong] committed deceitfully).

3. Trial court vs. appellate court

The trial court is the court of original jurisdiction where a case is tried. The appellate court is the court where a case goes for review when there is an appeal from the decision made by the trial court. To understand the significance of this distinction, you should understand that most cases that are filed never actually come to trial; they are settled or dismissed first. And most cases that are tried are never appealed.

The record of every case that is filed—whether or not it comes to trial—is in the trial court. This fact is a significant indicator of which records—those of the trial court or those of the appellate court—are most valuable to the researcher. Another important factor is the reality that no new evidence may be introduced in a case when that case is appealed. Thus, even if we find a record in the appellate court, there will be no information found there that is not in the trial court record.

Trial court records certainly have the greatest potential value for the researcher, but if a case is discovered in an appellate court, that fact can help you locate the trial court record. The reported opinion of the case in the appellate court will identify the court of original jurisdiction—the information you need to identify the trial court record and find the record.

IV. RECORDS AND OUR ACCESS TO THEM

There are a number of different records kept by the courts that are of interest to us:

- Minute books
- Docket books (or registers of actions)
- Court order books (or judgment books)
- Case files

Minute books are a daily record made by the court. They comprise a chronological record of court actions and proceedings and often include lists of jury members and names of attorneys, as well as information about financial accounts and fee collections. Sometimes the text of a court order is also included.

Docket books contain summaries of all case proceedings. They include a summary of every motion and court order as well as the eventual disposition of each case. Many states require that docket books be indexed.

Court order books contain the text of each court order and judgment.

Case files constitute the bulk of the court's records. They are filed numerically by case number—the number assigned to the case at the time the petition or complaint was filed. These files generally contain all the original papers filed by the attorneys as well as those issued by the court. They include such documents as petitions, motions, indictments, complaints, subpoenas, depositions, affidavits, writs, and judgments or decrees.

Minutes, dockets, and court order books all facilitate access to case files, but dockets deserve special mention here because of their value in helping the researcher find the actual case files. A civil docket entry is an abbreviated account of important court actions in the handling of a case. Every important act of both the court and the parties is docketed, and every docket entry relating to a given case is entered on the same page. State law often requires these docket books to be indexed. And though the dockets themselves often contain valuable bits of information, their chief function, insofar as you as a researcher are concerned, is to provide access to the case files.

In addition to civil dockets, there are various other types of dockets, including trial dockets, execution dockets, and judgment dockets. These differ from civil dockets, but they may also help you locate various court records. The **trial docket** (or trial list) is a list or calendar of cases set for trial during a specified term of the court. An **execution docket** is a list of executions or expropriations made by the sheriff to satisfy rulings of the court against defendants' properties. A **judgment docket** is a listing of the court's judgments (decisions) kept in connection with the judgment book (or order book) in which all judgments of the court are recorded.

The judgment docket and judgment book provide official notice to the world of judgments and court-ordered liens. They are always readily available and are easy to use. The entries in the judgment docket are usually made in alphabetical sequence by the first letter or two of the names of those defendants against whom judgments were entered.

Court order books also differ from civil dockets. They contain only the mandates and directives of the court while the docket books list every paper filed with the court. Court orders are made and entered in response to motions made by the parties to the various court actions. The entries in the court order books are in chronological sequence as those orders are issued by the court. Over a period of time, there may be several entries associated with a specific case.

The case file, which contains the entire record of the specific case, can be found once you learn the case file number from the docket, court order book, or elsewhere.

A. Divorce records

Divorce records were discussed briefly in Chapter 13 but, because they are essentially court records, deserve further discussion here. Some people wonder about the family history value of divorce records because they do not understand them. However, if the divorced couple had minor children, the names and ages of those children—because of child custody and visitation issues—are usually given in the court records (though not on the divorce certificate). Dates of birth (or ages) of both parties, the state or country of birth of both parties, the date and place of their marriage, and the date of and grounds for divorce are all part of the record. The following quotation relates to the divorce registration system in the United States as explained by the U.S. Department of Health and Human Services:

> The registration of divorces in the United States is a State and local function. The civil laws of all States provide for a continuous and permanent divorce registration system in the courts. The registration of divorces in a centralized file in the State office of vital statistics is established in almost all States. Each system depends upon the conscientious efforts of the local attorneys, clerks of court, judges, and other officials in preparing the information needed to complete the original records and in certifying to the information on these records. . . .
>
> Each State has local court districts that contain courts empowered to grant decrees of divorce, dissolution of marriage, and annulment. In States with centralized files, the clerk of court in each district collects the certificates of all divorces occurring in his or her court and transmits the completed forms to the State office of vital statistics.

The clerk of court is required to provide the petitioner or petitioner's attorney the appropriate divorce reporting form with instructions for completing the personal data. The petitioner or attorney completes the personal data on the reporting form and returns it to the clerk of court at the time the petition for divorce is filed. The clerk of court reviews the returned form for completeness and retains it in the court file pending judicial action. The judge verifies that the information necessary to complete the form has been provided to the clerk of court, either before the case is heard or before the final decree is granted. After the final decree is granted, the clerk of court completes the items related to the decree and custody of minor children and transmits the reporting form to the State office of vital statistics.

The State office of vital statistics inspects each record for promptness of filing, completeness, and accuracy of information; queries for missing or inconsistent information; numbers the records; prepares indexes; processes the records; and stores the records for permanent reference and safekeeping.[6]

In most states, the court with authority to grant divorces is the court with jurisdiction over equity matters. There are only a few exceptions to this. Following is a list of the courts in the several states that have jurisdiction in divorce cases. The records are ordinarily kept in these courts and, in many cases, are open to public access:

ALABAMA:	Circuit Court in the county of respondent's (non-filing party's) residence.
ALASKA:	Superior Court in specified areas in the four judicial districts. (The judicial districts are unrelated to the state's boroughs, which are equivalent to counties.)
ARIZONA:	Superior Court in the county of petitioner's (filing party's) residence.
ARKANSAS:	Chancery Court in the county of petitioner's residence, unless petitioner is not a state resident, then county of respondent's residence.
CALIFORNIA:	Superior Court in the county.
COLORADO:	District Court in the county.
CONNECTICUT:	Family Division of Superior Court in the county.
DELAWARE:	Family Court (after 1975) and Prothonotary (up to 1975) in the county.
DIST. OF COLUM.:	Family Court in the district (prior to 1956, in District Court for District of Columbia).
FLORIDA:	Circuit Court in the county.

---

[6] "Appendix B. The Divorce Registration System in the United States," *Handbook on Divorce Registration*. U.S. Department of Health and Human Services, April 1988, https://www.cdc.gov/nchs/data/misc/hb_div.pdf, 17–18 (accessed November 8, 2016).

GEORGIA:	Superior Court in the county.
HAWAII:	Family Division of County Circuit Court.
IDAHO:	Magistrate's Division of District Court in the county.
ILLINOIS:	Family Division of Circuit Court in the county.
INDIANA:	Superior Court, Circuit Court, or Domestic Relations Court in the county.
IOWA:	District Court in the county where either party resides.
KANSAS:	District Court in the county.
KENTUCKY:	Family Court Division of the Circuit Court in the county.
LOUISIANA:	Judicial District Court in the parish.
MAINE:	District Court in the county.
MARYLAND:	Circuit Court in the county.
MASSACHUSETTS:	Probate and Family Court in the county.
MICHIGAN:	Circuit Court in the county.
MINNESOTA:	District Court in the county.
MISSISSIPPI:	Chancery Court in the county.
MISSOURI:	Family Court in the county.
MONTANA:	District Court in the county.
NEBRASKA:	District Court in the county.
NEVADA:	District Court in the county.
NEW HAMPSHIRE:	Family Division of Circuit Court in the county.
NEW JERSEY:	Family Division of County Trial Court.
NEW MEXICO:	District Court in the county.
NEW YORK:	Supreme Court in the county.
NORTH CAROLINA:	Civil District Court Division of the General Court of Justice in the county.
NORTH DAKOTA:	District Court in the county.
OHIO:	Domestic Relations Division, Court of Common Pleas in the county.
OKLAHOMA:	District Court in the county.
OREGON:	Circuit Court in the county.
PENNSYLVANIA:	Court of Common Pleas in the county.
RHODE ISLAND:	Family Court in the county.
SOUTH CAROLINA:	Court of Common Pleas (equity jurisdiction) in the county. (Divorce was not legal in South Carolina until April 1949.)

SOUTH DAKOTA:	Circuit Court in the county.
TENNESSEE:	Circuit Court and Chancery Court in the county (concurrent jurisdiction).
TEXAS:	District Court in the county.
UTAH:	Family Court Division of the District Court in the county.
VERMONT:	Family Court in the county.
VIRGINIA:	Circuit Court in the county or independent city. (See section on Virginia later in this chapter.)
WASHINGTON:	Family Court Department of the Superior Court in the county.
WEST VIRGINIA:	Circuit Court or Family Court in the county (concurrent jurisdiction).
WISCONSIN:	Family Court Division of the Circuit Court in the county.
WYOMING:	District Court in the county.[7]

In addition to the records of divorce kept in the courts listed above, many states have legislation that also requires copies of divorce certificates to be filed with the state department of vital statistics. Generally, these records are quite recent, but there are a few exceptions. Note again, however, that these are certificates of divorce and not the court records. Those states where the certificates are available from the state office of vital statistics are identified in *Where to Write for Vital Records*, the booklet published by the U.S. Department of Health and Human Services.[8] However, if you know the place of the divorce, the best source of these certificates is the county where the divorce was granted. As the *Where to Write for Vital Records* booklet indicates, many state offices have only indexes. Those indexes, however, can help you identify the appropriate county. Also, note that many states have restrictions on who can obtain copies.

Procedures and requirements change, and information on how to find records can be amended at any time. Thus, the researcher should always refer to the most current issue of *Where to Write for Vital Records* for the most current information.

---

[7] The source of this information in earlier editions was *Where to Write for Vital Records* (Hyattsville, MD: United States Department of Health and Human Services, 1998) and *Martindale-Hubbell Law Directory*, 120th ed. (Summit, NJ: Martindale-Hubbell, Inc., 1988), Vol. VIII (used with permission) as well as correspondence with various court officials. In this edition, that information has been updated from court websites of the individual states and by other correspondence.

[8] *Where to Write for Vital Records*, U.S. Department of Health and Human Services, Centers for Disease Control and Prevention, September 16, 2015, https://www.cdc.gov/nchs/w2w/ (accessed November 8, 2016).

TYPE/PRINT IN PERMANENT BLACK INK FOR INSTRUCTIONS SEE HANDBOOK

U.S. STANDARD
CERTIFICATE OF DIVORCE, DISSOLUTION OF MARRIAGE, OR ANNULMENT

COURT FILE NUMBER — STATE FILE NUMBER

DEPARTMENT OF HEALTH AND HUMAN SERVICES - PUBLIC HEALTH SERVICE - NATIONAL CENTER FOR HEALTH STATISTICS - 1989 REVISION

HUSBAND

1. HUSBAND'S NAME (First, Middle, Last): John Alex Stevens
2a. RESIDENCE—CITY, TOWN, OR LOCATION: Raleigh
2b. COUNTY: Wake
2c. STATE: North Carolina
3. BIRTHPLACE (State or Foreign Country): North Carolina
4. DATE OF BIRTH (Month, Day, Year): June 28, 1948

WIFE

5a. WIFE'S NAME (First, Middle, Last): Susan Marie Stevens
5b. MAIDEN SURNAME: Petto
6a. RESIDENCE—CITY, TOWN, OR LOCATION: Oxon Hill
6b. COUNTY: Prince Georges
6c. STATE: Maryland
7. BIRTHPLACE (State or Foreign Country): Maryland
8. DATE OF BIRTH (Month, Day, Year): May 3, 1951

MARRIAGE

9a. PLACE OF THIS MARRIAGE—CITY, TOWN, OR LOCATION: Miami
9b. COUNTY: Dade
9c. STATE OR FOREIGN COUNTRY: Florida
10. DATE OF THIS MARRIAGE (Month, Day, Year): April 8, 1976
11. DATE COUPLE LAST RESIDED IN SAME HOUSEHOLD (Month, Day, Year): February 19, 1988
12. NUMBER OF CHILDREN UNDER 18 IN THIS HOUSEHOLD AS OF THE DATE IN ITEM 11: Number 2 ☐ None
13. PETITIONER: ☐ Husband ☒ Wife ☐ Both ☐ Other (Specify)

ATTORNEY

14a. NAME OF PETITIONER'S ATTORNEY (Type/Print): Jean K. Lovette
14b. ADDRESS (Street and Number or Rural Route Number, City or Town, State, Zip Code): 666 K St., NW Washington, D.C. 20022

DECREE

15. I CERTIFY THAT THE MARRIAGE OF THE ABOVE NAMED PERSONS WAS DISSOLVED ON: (Month, Day, Year): November 12, 1989
16. TYPE OF DECREE—Divorce, Dissolution, or Annulment (Specify): Absolute Divorce
17. DATE RECORDED (Month, Day, Year): November 14, 1989
18. NUMBER OF CHILDREN UNDER 18 WHOSE PHYSICAL CUSTODY WAS AWARDED TO: Husband ____ Wife ____ Joint (Husband/Wife) 2 Other ____ ☐ No children
19. COUNTY OF DECREE: Prince Georges
20. TITLE OF COURT: Circuit Court
21. SIGNATURE OF CERTIFYING OFFICIAL: ▶ Julia L. Thorpe
22. TITLE OF CERTIFYING OFFICIAL: Clerk of Court
23. DATE SIGNED (Month, Day, Year): November 14, 1989

CONFIDENTIAL INFORMATION. THE INFORMATION BELOW WILL NOT APPEAR ON CERTIFIED COPIES OF THE RECORD.

	24. NUMBER OF THIS MARRIAGE—First, Second, etc (Specify below)	25. IF PREVIOUSLY MARRIED, LAST MARRIAGE ENDED: By Death, Divorce, Dissolution, or Annulment (Specify below)	25. Date (Month, Day, Year)	26. RACE—American Indian, Black, White, etc (Specify below)	27. EDUCATION (Specify only highest grade completed): Elementary/Secondary (0-12)	27. College (1-4 or 5+)
HUSBAND	24a Second	25a Divorce	25b August 3, 1973	26a White	27a	4
WIFE	24b First	25c Never Married	25d	26b American Indian	27b	2

PHS T 005
REV 1/89

FIGURE 1—STANDARD CERTIFICATE OF DIVORCE OR ANNULMENT
(Certificates with this format are in current use in many states).

Because of privacy concerns, many states will provide copies of divorce certificates to parties of the action only. However, where the records are available, all that is usually necessary to secure copies of the court proceedings is to write to the proper court, providing the names of the parties and the approximate year of the divorce. If a certificate is desired, write to the custodian identified in the *Where to Write* booklet. State your relationship and the purpose for which the copy of the record will be used. There will be a fee for this service and for the copy.

Because some divorce records are included on the indexed, digitized databases of various family history websites—Ancestry, FamilySearch, FindMyPast, and MyHeritage, etc.—it is always prudent to check there first. Some divorce records are also accessible on state websites. Try entering the name of the state and "divorce records" in your Internet search engine space.

B. Citizenship and naturalization records

1. Background

Naturalization is the granting of citizenship rights to aliens as if they were native-born. Article I, Section 8, Clause 4, of our U.S. Constitution authorized Congress to formulate a "uniform Rule of Naturalization," and, beginning in 1790, Congress began enacting laws to control the naturalization process.

Some naturalization took place in the British colonies during the colonial period, but very few citizens were naturalized. Only Europeans (those from the continent) were not already considered as British citizens. Since that time, however, naturalization of aliens in America has generally been handled in both federal and state courts, and much of our present naturalization policy is based on some of the earliest congressional acts. Though there have been many modifications, the policy has generally been consistent.

The earliest involvement of a government agency in the naturalization process was in 1891 with the creation of the Office of Superintendent of Immigration in the Treasury Department. In 1895, the Office of Superintendent of Immigration was renamed the Bureau of Immigration, and in 1903, it was transferred to the newly created Department of Commerce and Labor.

In 1906, the Bureau of Immigration became the Bureau of Immigration and Naturalization in the newly created Naturalization Service. The next change was in 1913 when the Bureau of Immigration and Naturalization was divided in half to create the Bureau of Immigration and the Bureau of Naturalization, both of which were placed in the new Department of Labor.

In 1933, the two bureaus were once again merged into a single agency, the Immigration and Naturalization Service (INS) within the Department of Labor. In 1940, the INS was moved to the Department of Justice.

In 2003, the INS was abolished and its functions divided between three agencies, and all three were moved to the new Department of Homeland Security. These agencies are the United States Citizenship and Immigration Service (USCIS), Immigration and Customs Enforcement (ICE), and U.S. Customs and Boarder Protection (CBP). Citizenship and naturalization of immigrants is the responsibility of USCIS.[9]

Prior to ratification of the Fourteenth Amendment in 1868, all citizenship was considered to be in the state rather than the nation. In many places, the process of becoming a citizen during the early periods was simple. The immi-

---

[9] "Our History," U.S. Citizenship and Immigration Service, Department of Homeland Security, May 25, 2011, https://www.uscis.gov/about-us/our-history (accessed November 8, 2016).

grant merely signed a statement of allegiance as he came off the boat. Because of this, some of those early books of so-called citizenship lists in Chapter 25 are nothing more than immigration lists. The following are some good examples of this:

> Giuseppi, Montague S. *Naturalizations of Foreign Protestants in the American and West Indian Colonies . . .* 1921. Reprint, Baltimore: Genealogical Publishing Co., 1995.

> Egle, William H. *Names of Foreigners Who Took the Oath of Allegiance to the Province and State of Pennsylvania, 1727–1775, with the Foreign Arrivals, 1786–1808.* 1890. Reprint, Baltimore: Genealogical Publishing Co., 2002.

The Fourteenth Amendment guaranteed *national* citizenship status and extended its full benefits to everyone who was either born or naturalized in the U.S. and subject to its jurisdiction. (This, however, excluded tribal Indians, natives of unincorporated territories, and children of foreign ambassadors.)

There was no comprehensive regulation of naturalization until 1906 when Congress established the Bureau of Immigration and Naturalization and prescribed a specific procedure to be followed concurrently by this new bureau and by those courts with naturalization jurisdiction. Prior to 1906, all naturalization matters resided entirely within the jurisdiction of the courts.

For many years, naturalization was a two-step process that required at least five years. After two years in the United States, an alien could file a "Declaration of Intent" (called "first papers"). Then, after three more years, he could file a "Petition for Naturalization." Once the petition was granted, a "Certificate of Citizenship" was issued. These events were cumbersome, and the records have suffered somewhat because of overlapping jurisdictions.

Historically, there have been three major exceptions to the five-year requirement:

- The **first exception** has been called **"derivative" citizenship** and was applied to wives and minor children of men who became naturalized citizens. Between 1790 and 1922, the wife of a naturalized man automatically became a citizen, as did an alien woman who married a U.S. citizen. And the opposite was true of an American woman who married an alien; she lost her U.S. citizenship.

  Between 1790 and 1940, children under 21 became naturalized citizens when their fathers were naturalized. However, prior to September 1, 1906, information about these wives and children was rarely included in the papers.

- The **second exception**, this one applying between 1824 and 1906, was that **minor aliens who had resided in the United States for at least five years before turning 23** could file both their declarations and petitions at the same time.

- The **third exception** was applicable to aliens who were **U.S. military veterans**. An 1862 law allowed an Army veteran of any war who was honorably discharged and who had at least one year of residency to file his Petition for Naturalization without having previously filed a Declaration of Intent. An 1894 law extended the same privilege to honorably discharged five-year Navy and Marine Corps veterans. Then, near the end of and following World War I, laws were passed that also provided preferential treatment to alien veterans.

In recent years, the naturalization process has begun with the filing of the required paperwork with USCIS. Then, following an investigation by the appropriate government agency (which can be waived), the applicant files a Petition for Naturalization with the clerk of the court where he resides. Next, he is examined by someone from the USCIS office, following which he must appear before the judge of the court for a final hearing. At the hearing, he must be recommended for naturalization by a USCIS representative. An oath of allegiance is then administered and a certificate of naturalization issued.

It is important to remember that prior to 1906 the courts were responsible for the entire process. Naturalization proceedings could take place in any U.S. District Court, in any court of record of the several states, and in the District or Supreme Courts of the territories. The clerk of the court was required to record all proceedings.

In instances where territories are annexed by the United States, all residents of those territories can become citizens by collective naturalization through legislative enactment (as with Hawaii, Texas, Puerto Rico) or by treaty (as with Louisiana, Florida, Alaska, the U.S. Virgin Islands). Immigrants can also be made citizens by legislative action granting amnesty to illegal immigrants, both those who came illegally and those who came legally and overstayed their visas.

There are two books by John J. Newman on naturalization processes and records that are of interest to those who need to use these records in their research:

- Newman, John J. *American Naturalization Processes and Procedures.* Indianapolis: Indiana Historical Society, 1985.
- _____. *American Naturalization Records, 1790–1990: What They Are and How to Use Them.* 2nd ed. North Salt Lake, UT: Heritage Quest, 1998.

2. The location and nature of the records

Many documents relating to naturalizations in federal and state courts, especially the records created after September 26, 1906, are in the Regional National Archives. A detailed list of the holdings in the various archives, by state, is found in the *Guide to Genealogical Research in the National Archives of the United States.*[10] Naturalization records created after September 26, 1906, can best be found at the U.S. Citizenship and Immigration Service (USCIS). Because records prior to 1906 involved only the courts, records of naturalizations in both state and federal courts can still be found in those courts.[11]

USCIS also has important records relating to both immigration and naturalization from 1906 until the end of the current period of restriction (75 years). This agency is authorized—in connection with its Genealogy Program—to make the following five series of the agency's historical records available to researchers:[12]

- Naturalization Certificate Files, September 27, 1906 to March 31, 1956:
These are "copies of records relating to all U.S. naturalizations in Federal, State, county, or municipal courts, overseas military naturalizations, replacement of old law naturalization certificates, and the issuance of Certificates of Citizenship in derivative, repatriation, and resumption cases. Standard C-Files generally contain at least one application form (Declaration of Intention and/or Petition for Naturalization, or other application) and a duplicate certificate of naturalization or certificate of citizenship. Many files contain additional documents, including correspondence, affidavits, or other records. Only C-Files dating from 1929 onward include photographs." [Most of the C-Files are on microfilm only.]

- Alien Registration Forms (Form AR-2), August 1940 to March 1944:
These forms "are copies of approximately 5.5 million Alien Registration Forms completed by all aliens age 14 and older, residing in or entering the United States between August 1, 1940 and March 31, 1944. The two-page form called for the following information: name; name at arrival; other names used; street address; post-office address; date of birth; place of birth; citizenship; sex; marital status; race; height; weight; hair and eye color; date, place, vessel, and class of admission of last arrival in United States; date of first arrival in United States; number of years in United States; usual occupation; present occupation; name, address, and business of present employer; membership in clubs, organizations, or societies; dates and nature of military or naval service; whether citizenship papers filed, and if so date, place, and court for declaration or petition; number of relatives living in the United States; arrest record,

---

[10] Anne Bruner Eales and Robert M. Kvasnicka, eds., *Guide to Genealogical Research in the United States of America,* 3rd ed. (Washington, DC: National Archives and Records Administration, 2000), 87–104.

[11] About two-thirds of all naturalizations take place in 200 federal courts with the other one-third taking place in about 1,800 state courts.

[12] All five quotations in this bulleted list are from "Historical Records Series Available from the Genealogy Program," *U.S. Citizenship and Immigration Services,* February 9, 2016, https://www.uscis.gov/history-and-genealogy/genealogy/historical-records-series-available-genealogy-program (accessed November 9, 2016).

including date, place, and disposition of each arrest; whether or not affiliated with a foreign government; signature, and fingerprint." [These files are on microfilm and are available only for A-numbers 1,000,000 to 5,980,116; A-numbers 6,100,000 to 6,132,126; A-numbers 7,000,000 to 7,043,999; and for A-numbers 7,500,000 to 7,759,142.]

- Visa Files, July 1, 1924 to March 31, 1944:

    "Visa Files are original arrival records of immigrants admitted for permanent residence under provisions of the Immigration Act of 1924. Visa forms contain all information normally found on a ship passenger list of the period, as well as the immigrant's places of residence for 5 years prior to emigration, names of both the immigrant's parents, and other data. Attached to the visa in most cases are birth records or affidavits. Also there may be attached other records such as: marriage, military, or police records." [These files are hard copies only {textual format}.]

- Registry Files, March 1929 to March 31, 1944:

    "Registry Files are records, which document the creation of immigrant arrival records for persons who entered the United States prior to July 1, 1924, and for whom no arrival record could later be found. Most files also include documents supporting the immigrant's claims regarding arrival and residence (i.e., proofs of residence, receipts, and employment records)." [These records are in hard copy only {textual format}.]

- A-Files, April 1, 1944 to May 1, 1951

    "Immigrant Files, (A-Files) are the individual alien case files, which became the official file for all immigration records created or consolidated since April 1, 1944. A-numbers ranging up to approximately 6 million were issued to aliens and immigrants within or entering the United States between 1940 and 1945. The 6 million and 7 million series of A-numbers were issued between circa 1944 and May 1, 1951. Only A-File documents dated to May 1, 1951, are releasable under the Genealogy Program." [These files are in hard copy only {textual format}.]

Past prohibitions against the copying of naturalization records in the courts are now gone. Both uncertified and certified (for an additional fee) copies are now permitted. Many of these records are now available from NARA and can be ordered on the Internet. Go to *https://www.archives.gov/research/naturalization/*.

Those seeking information from the files of the USCIS should use form G-1041, "Genealogy Index Search Request," because no records can be found without using the index. The cost for this search in 2017 is $65. The form and related instructions can be accessed at *https://www.uscis.gov/g-1041* and completed on your computer. Once completed, the form can be printed, signed, and mailed to USCIS Genealogy Program, P.O. Box 805925, Chicago, IL 60680-4120. Searches of USCIS historical indexes are used to determine if the USCIS has records on the subject and, if so, to identify file numbers and other identifiers.

The Works Projects Administration (WPA) undertook a project in the 1930s to make photocopies of pre-1906 naturalization records and index those records. However, the project managed to cover only the courts in New York and four New England states—Maine, Massachusetts, New Hampshire, and Rhode Island—plus a partial index to Connecticut, before the project was terminated. These 5" x 8" photocopies, covering the period 1787 to 1906, are in the Regional National Archives in Boston, together with a card index (Soundex system, as described in Chapter 14). The records in these files consist of

> photographic copies of naturalization documents, usually two pages for each naturalization, containing some or all of the following information: petition for citizenship, oath of allegiance and previous citizenship, place and date of birth, occupation, place and date of arrival in the United States, place of residence at the time of application, and name and address of a witness to these statements. Earlier records contain less information than later ones.[13]

If your immigrant ancestor settled in New Jersey, you will find naturalization records from 1749 through 1810 in the State Library, Archives and History Division, at Trenton. Also in New Jersey, the WPA made a "Guide to Naturalization Records" in the courts of that state (December 1941) as part of their program to inventory vital statistics records (see Chapter 13). In Massachusetts, naturalizations from 1885 to 1931 are on file in the Archives Division at the State House in Boston.

Records of naturalization usually included the following:

- Declarations of Intention
- Petitions for Naturalization
- Depositions
- Certificates of Naturalization

Declarations of Intention are used by applicants to renounce allegiance to foreign governments and to declare their intention to become U.S. citizens. They normally preceded other documents by at least two years and, as already indicated, were sometimes not required if the applicant was a military veteran or entered the country as a minor. Declarations of Intention, prior to 1906 usually showed the following for each applicant:

> [N]ame, country of birth or allegiance, date of the application, and signature. Some show date and port of arrival in the United States.[14]

After 1906, these declarations contained more detail because a more detailed form was used. They included

> such information as applicant's name, age, occupation, and personal description; date and place of birth; citizenship; present address and last foreign address; vessel and port of embarkation for the United States; port and date of arrival in the United States; and date of application and signature.[15]

---

[13] Eales and Kvasnicka, 105.

[14] Ibid., 87.

[15] Ibid., 87.

Petitions for Naturalization were used to make formal application for citizenship by those who had met the residency requirements and who had declared their intention to become citizens. Through September 26, 1906, information on these petitions was limited to the

> name of the petitioner and sovereign to whom he is foreswearing allegiance, and occasionally the petitioner's residence, occupation, date and place of birth, and port and date of arrival in this country. The amount of information given in these early petitions varies but is typically quite limited.[16]

Beginning on September 27, 1906, however, the information contained in these petitions was significantly enhanced to include

> name, residence, occupation, date and place of birth, citizenship, and personal description of applicant; date of emigration; ports of embarkation and arrival; marital status; names, dates, places of birth, and residence of applicant's spouse and children; date at which U.S. residence commenced; time of residence in state; name changes; and signature.[17]

Note, also, that copies of declarations of intention, certificates of arrival, and certificates of completion of citizenship classes were often interfiled with these petitions and that, after 1930, petitions often included photographs of the applicants.

An applicant has the right to choose people to make **depositions** in support of his declaration. These depositions are formal statements supporting the applicant's petition. These, typically indicate the period of applicant's residence in a certain locale, and other information, including the witnesses' appraisals of the applicant's character.[18]

Other papers often added to document a grant of citizenship include records of naturalization and oaths of allegiance. In recent times, these records have been in the form of **certificates**. They are typically found in the court where naturalization took place in a chronological arrangement. They are often in bound volumes with surname indexes. Many of the earlier records are hard to locate because of lack of uniform policy requirements. Thus, court minutes and their related court orders are the only sources for many earlier naturalization records. Also, with regard to these early periods, there are some cases where

> all records for one person have been gathered together in [what has been referred to as] a petition and record, which usually included the petition for naturalization, affidavits of the petitioner and witnesses, the oath of allegiance, and the order of the court admitting the petitioner to citizenship.[19]

---

[16] Ibid., 87.

[17] Ibid., 87.

[18] Ibid., 87.

[19] Ibid., 87.

3. Special helps and other sources of naturalization information

In a case where a naturalized citizen (or an alien seeking naturalization) filed a homestead claim or applied for a passport, that application (homestead and passport) is normally in the National Archives. Passport records are among the General Records of the Department of State, Record Group 59; and homestead records, already discussed in Chapter 19, are in the Records of the Bureau of Land Management, Record Group 49.

These records give the name of the court where the naturalization took place. This information will be valuable if you do not know the location of that event. Also, copies of naturalization records are often included in those other files.

You might also receive help from the 1870 federal census. That census indicated whether males over 21 years of age were U.S. citizens. If an immigrant is reported as a citizen, you know there must be naturalization papers somewhere.

If you know your ancestor was a naturalized citizen, it is worthwhile to spend whatever time is required to locate his naturalization records. Those records can bridge the gap to the ancestral home in the Old World. Remember, however, that persons born in the U.S. are citizens even though their immigrant parents may never have become citizens. If your immigrant ancestor failed to seek American citizenship, there will be no record.

Some naturalization and citizenship records have been digitized and indexed on the various family history websites—including Ancestry, FamilySearch, FindMyPast, and MyHeritage, etc.—and are readily accessible for searching on those sites. You may have success with this, but these records are incomplete, and the records you need may not yet be part of these projects. Because of this, you should not be hesitant about seeking the actual records when evidence suggests that your immigrant ancestor was a naturalized citizen but fails to appear in your search of the indexed databases.

V. LEGISLATIVE RECORDS

In some jurisdictions during some time periods, a few legal issues were handled and resolved by legislative action rather than by the courts. This was true to some extent in virtually every state. Types of actions that might be included vary from state to state, but typical of such matters are legal name changes and divorces.

Records of these legislative actions can be found in the sessions laws of the states involved. These sessions laws are in legislative libraries within the states and in many of the larger law libraries.

VI. ADOPTION RECORDS

Adoption records have, in the past, been almost exclusively closed to public access—sealed by the courts to protect the privacy of those involved, including natural parents, adopting parents, and children—to be opened only by court order for "good cause shown." This is still mostly true, but there are resources now available to assist those who were legally adopted and are seeking to identify their bloodlines. Neither family history nor genealogical curiosity has normally satisfied the "good cause shown" requirement. Even the LDS Church, with its great emphasis on family history, supports this approach. And it is interesting to note that LDS Social Services, which has been involved with thousands of adoptions in the past, no longer handles adoption cases.

In recent years, many adopting families have what are called "open adoptions," with significant interchange between the birth mother (and others in her family) and the adopting family. These arrangements generally seem to work well for all concerned. There are also some jurisdictions that are becoming more sympathetic to the "right" of the adopted child to know his blood parents. The records in these states can be accessed quite easily by those who are deemed to have that right. There are also other things that can be done to trace natural parentage.

For the benefit of those adopted individuals and descendants of adoptees who desire to pursue identification of their bloodlines, I suggest the following books:

Brown, Teresa A. *Adoption Records Handbook*. North Las Vegas, NV: Crary Publications, 2008.

Carangelo, Lori. *The Ultimate Search Book: U.S. Adoption, Genealogy & Other Search Secrets*. Baltimore: Genealogical Publishing Co., 2015.

Rillera, Mary Jo. *Adoption Searchbook*, 3rd ed. Westminster, CA: Tri-adoption Publications, 1993.

Strauss, Jean A. S. *Birthright: The Guide to Search and Reunion for Adoptees, Birthparents, and Adoptive Parents*. New York: Penguin Books, 1994.

Perhaps even more important resources than books, however, are some Internet websites that provide significant help and are able to stay updated with the latest information. I suggest two:

- "United States Adoption Research," is a wiki page on FamilySearch with some helpful resources. It is at *https://familysearch.org/wiki/en/United_States_Adoption_Research*.
- The "Adoption" page on *Cyndi's List* is at *https://cyndislist.com/adoption/*.

The final resource I will mention here, for the benefit of both the adopted person and the birth parent trying to make a connection, is DNA testing, which we discussed in Chapter 9. As more people add their DNA profiles to the bank, there is significant likelihood of finding a close blood relative through which a connection can be made.

VII. NOTE ON VIRGINIA'S INDEPENDENT CITIES

Many family history researchers have difficulty in Virginia research because they fail to allow for the idiosyncrasies of the state's court system. They try to treat Virginia like any other southern state, never looking for records anywhere except in the county. This will probably work well most of the time, but if you will carefully note some of the lists of various courts given in this chapter and in the chapters on wills, land records, and court records, you will see that there are some significant exceptions in Virginia, and some of these date back a long way. This means that some very important records are not found in county courthouses but rather in the cities. Many cities in Virginia are completely independent of the counties in which they are located, and that independence involves their total operation.

As a general rule, once incorporated as a city, a Virginia municipality established its own courts and government separate and distinct from the county in which it was geographically situated. However, there are a few exceptions. The following table shows Virginia's independent cities (as they are called), the county where each is physically located, the year each was incorporated as a town (in parentheses), and the year each was incorporated as an independent city. Other relevant explanations are also included. The asterisks (*) in the list are explained in footnote 20. In spite of having status independent from the counties, several also are county seats of their local counties. These include Charlottesville (Albemarle County), Covington (Alleghany County), Emporia (Greensville County), Fairfax (Fairfax County), Manassas (Prince William County), Martinsville (Henry County), Richmond (Henrico County), Salem (Roanoke County), Staunton (Augusta County), Williamsburg (James City County), and Winchester (Frederick County).

City	County where geographically located	Incorporation date
Alexandria	Fairfax and Arlington counties	(1779) 1852
Bedford	Bedford County*	(1839, as Liberty) 1890 (reverted back to town status in 1912)
Big Lick	(See Roanoke)	
Bristol	Washington County	(1801) 1890 (from town of Goodson) (added additional territory from Washington County in 1970)
Buena Vista	Rockbridge County	(1890) 1892
Charlottesville	Albemarle County	(1801) 1888
Chesapeake	formerly Norfolk County (now defunct)	1963 (by merger of Norfolk County and the City of South Norfolk)

Colonial Heights	Chesterfield County	(1926) 1948
Covington	Alleghany County	(1833) 1954
Danville	Pittsylvania County	(1830) 1890 (North Danville added in 1869)
Emporia	Greensville County*	1967
Fairfax	Fairfax County*	(1874) 1961 (formerly called Providence)
Falls Church*	Fairfax County	(1875) 1948
Franklin	Southampton County*	(1876) 1961
Fredericksburg	Spotsylvania County	(1782) 1879
Fredericktown	(See Winchester)	
Galax	Carroll* and Grayson counties	(1906) 1954 (formerly called Bonaparte)
Hampton	formerly Elizabeth City County (now defunct)	(1849) 1908 (Elizabeth City Co.; town of Phoebus added in 1952)
Harrisonburg	Rockingham County*	(1849) 1916
Hopewell	Prince George County	1916 (City Point added in 1923)
Lexington	Rockbridge County*	1966
Lynchburg	Campbell County	(1805) 1852 (additional territory from Campbell County added in 1970)
Manassas	Prince William County*	1975
Manassas Park	Prince William County*	1975
Martinville	Henry County	(1873) 1928
Nansemond (merged into Suffolk in 1974)	formerly Nansemond County (now defunct)	
Newport News	formerly Warwick County (now defunct)	1896 (city of Warwick added in 1958)
Norfolk	formerly Norfolk County (now defunct)	(1737) 1845 (Berkeley added in 1906)
Norton	Wise County*	(1894) 1954 (formerly called Prince's Flat)
Petersburg	Dinwiddie and Prince George counties	(1784) 1850 (Blandford, Pocahontas and Ravensworth added in 1784) (added additional territory from Dinwiddie and Prince George counties in 1970)
Poquoson	York County*	1975

Portsmouth (now in Chesapeake)	formerly Norfolk County (now defunct)	(1836) 1858
Radford	Montgomery County	(1887) 1892 (formerly called Central City)
Richmond	Henrico and Chesterfield counties	(1782) 1842 (added Manchester —or South Richmond—in 1910 and Barton Heights, Fairmount, Highland Park in 1914)
Roanoke	Roanoke County	(1874) 1902 (formerly called Big Lick) (added additional territory from Roanoke County in 1970)
Salem	Roanoke County	1968
South Boston	Halifax County*	(1884) 1960
South Norfolk	(See Chesapeake)	
Staunton	Augusta County	(1801) 1871
Suffolk	Nansemond County	(1808) 1910 (absorbed Nansemond in 1974)
Virginia Beach	formerly Princess Anne County (now defunct)	(1906) 1952 (Princess Anne County added in 1963)
Warwick	(See Newport News)	
Waynesboro	Augusta County	(1834) 1948 (Basic City added in 1923)
Williamsburg	James City County* and York County	(1732) 1884
Winchester	Frederick County	(1779) 1784 (formerly called Fredericktown) (added additional territory from Frederick County in 1970)[20]

In several of these independent cities, the records date back to their time of incorporation as cities and, in some instances, to their incorporation as towns. If your ancestors lived within the area of any of these cities after they became independent cities, that fact is probably important to your research.[21]

---

[20] Note that those independent cities where I have marked the counties of their location with asterisks *do not* maintain their own records. Their records, in each case, are maintained by the county whose name is marked with the asterisk. Also, there is one more complicated case—the city of Falls Church, where the asterisk has been placed by the name of the city. In Falls Church, current records are in Arlington County, but records prior to 1988 are in Fairfax County.

[21] For your information, there are three other cities in the United States with this same type of independent status: Baltimore, Maryland; St. Louis, Missouri; and Carson City, Nevada.

Though these cities are legally separated from county jurisdiction, I have listed the counties in which they are situated to facilitate your locating them. Many of them, interestingly, are the seats of county government in those counties. As the above list attests, many of these independent cities have only recently achieved such status and, at present, have negligible family history significance. Perhaps there will be others created in the future.

Some of the old Virginia counties no longer exist because they have been absorbed by the independent cities. In such cases, the records of those counties are in the custody of the city courts. The extinct Virginia counties include:

Alexandria County	Became Arlington County in 1920. Much of the area is now in the city of Alexandria.
Elizabeth City County	Now in the city of Hampshire (since 1952).
Nansemond County	Now in the city of Suffolk. (Part was originally in the city of Nansemond, which was absorbed by the city of Suffolk in 1974.)
Norfolk County	Now in the city of Chesapeake (since 1963). (Chesapeake also has records of the former independent cities of Portsmouth and South Norfolk.)
Princess Anne County	Now in the city of Virginia Beach (since 1963).
Warwick County	Now in the city of Newport News (since 1958).

All court records, including land and probate records, are in the jurisdiction of the courts of these cities and not in the county courts, except as noted in footnote 20. Formerly, the courts in these cities were called Corporation Courts but are now called Circuit Courts.

A useful book for understanding Virginia and her history is *A Hornbook of Virginia History*, 4th rev. ed. (Richmond: The Virginia State Library, 1994).[22] I recommend it to anyone with Virginia ancestry.

Another book, important because of the vast amount of information it contains about Virginia records, is Carol McGinnis's *Virginia Genealogy: Sources & Resources*.1993. (Reprint, Baltimore: Genealogical Publishing Co, 2008).

VIII. CASE REPORTS, REPORTERS, AND DIGESTS

Reports of the various state courts of appeal also provide a way to locate some trial court records in the states. These reports are composed of the published opinions of the judges in the appellate courts to which those cases were

---

[22] This book was first published in 1949 with James R. V. Daniel, division director, and others as compilers and editors. The 1994 edition was edited by Emily J. Salmon and Edward D. C. Campbell.

brought. They are accessible using court digests, which provide a table of cases (by both plaintiffs and defendants—by surname only) as well as a subject (or point-of-law) index to the reports. These reports are no substitute for the case files of the trial courts, but they provide a way to locate case files. They give the name of the court of original jurisdiction and the date of the court's decision. This can help you locate briefs and case files.

In addition to the state reports, since the 1880s the comprehensive reporters and digests of the seven regions of the National Reporter Series, the four federal court series, and the supplemental reports for New York State and California are also important.

The regional reporters include some cases from the state appellate courts that are not in the state reports because they contain reports of cases from all courts of appellate jurisdiction. State reports (with few exceptions) are limited to cases in the state Supreme Court.

What may be a useful tool is the table of cases in the *American Digest* (St. Paul, MN: West Publishing Co.). Of special note are volumes twenty-one through twenty-five of the 1911 edition of this publication, wherein is printed "A Complete Table of American Cases from 1658 to 1906." Subsequent editions (published every ten years) update this table of cases. However, note that the *American Digest* is virtually unusable if the surname you seek is common.

All of the various court reports and digests can usually be found in law libraries (at the local courthouse), and occasionally in other libraries.

An aid to finding the proper digests is Frederick C. Hicks's *Materials and Methods of Legal Research*. 3rd rev. ed. (Rochester, NY: Lawyers Cooperative Pub. Co., 1972). An appendix in this book contains a list of the various volumes of court reports, arranged by state.

IX. CONCLUSION

In most states, court records of one type or another go back to the very beginning, thus providing a useful source of family history evidence. However, many of the most valuable court records—the older records and case files—are often stored in out-of-the-way places because they are not in current use and space is scarce. The present records custodian is often unaware of the location (or even the existence) of such records. In some cases, the WPA inventories of the various county courthouses are useful, but often the information therein, which was current in the early 1940s, is somewhat antiquated. In searching for these records, the researcher will do well to employ both diligence and imagination.

The records and files of some court actions are voluminous. You may find hundreds of pages of various kinds of papers in the file of just one case. In such situations, it is certainly impractical for you to copy all of this material into your notes or even to scan or take digital photos; however, you may find it worthwhile to go through the papers and abstract everything of significance and perhaps to even photograph the more relevant pages. It has been my experience that the *complaint* of the plaintiff (the portion at the beginning of the case where the cause is explained, also sometimes called the petition, declaration, or statement of claim), the *answer* of the defendant to the complaint, and the judge's *decree* (the *final judgment*) usually contain the most significance family history information. (This, however, is not to discount the value of other information that may be in the file.) The complaint and the answer, which are the formal allegations and the defenses of the parties, are also called *pleadings*.

Court records, with some justifiable exceptions, are open to the public use. If they are not on film for the locality you need (and they usually are not), you should contact the court or pay a personal visit to the courthouse. And, as has been noted by some examples in earlier chapters, other records will often provide clues to the existence of important court records.

A simple and helpful guide to the use of court records in your research is Genealogical Publishing Company's four-page publication *Genealogy at a Glance: Court Records Research.*[23] You will find it to be clear and concise.

---

[23] Wendy Bebout Elliott, *Genealogy at a Glance: Court Records Research* (Baltimore: Genealogical Publishing Co., 2014).

23

Property Rights of Women as a Consideration

One of the more difficult challenges faced by family history research-ers is that of identifying the women on our ancestral lines. That chal-lenge is the basis of this chapter. It is unfortunate that records relat-ing to women in earlier periods—especially married women—are not only inadequate but are scarce in most of the traditional research sources. There are helps available, and we should be aware of them, but they do not change the reality.[1]

The subject of finding records relating to women is not the focus of this chapter. Unfortunately, even after our best research efforts, the best we can often do is to identify a female ancestor as "Mrs. William Johnson" or what-ever her husband's name happened to be. Our focus in this chapter is, instead, on those legal considerations that will help you better understand and apply whatever evidence you find in your research.

Once a woman was married, there was little trace of her in the records. There were very few occasions where it was perceived as either appropriate or necessary for her to be mentioned in the records. It seems strange to us now, but even in many early church records when children were christened, it was not unusual for the father to be the only parent identified. Historically women had no significant status, either in society or under the law, apart from their

---

[1] I refer you to three books (listed alphabetically by author) that provide useful clues and insights to assist in your search for the identities of your female ancestors:

(1) Sharon DeBartolo Carmack, *A Genealogist's Guide to Discovering Your Female Ancestors: Special Strategies for Uncovering Hard-to-Find Information About Your Female Lineage* (Cincinnati, OH: Betterway Books, 1998).

(2) Marsha Hoffman Rising, *The Family Tree Problem Solver: Tried and True Tactics for Tracing Elusive Ancestors* (Blue Ash, OH: F+W Media, 2011).

(3) Christina K. Schaefer, *The Hidden Half of the Family*, 1999 (Reprint, Baltimore: Genealogical Publishing Co., 2008).

husbands. A husband and wife were essentially considered to be one person, and that one person was the husband. William Blackstone, in his four-volume work, *Commentaries on the Laws of England,* explained it this way:

> By marriage, the husband and wife are one person in law: that is, the very being or legal existence of the woman is suspended during the marriage, or at least is incorporated and consolidated into that of the husband: under whose wing, protection, and *cover*, she performs everything. . . . Upon this principle, of an union of person in husband and wife, depend almost all the legal rights, duties and disabilities, that either of them acquire by the marriage.[2]

An understanding of this phenomenon and of some of its consequences can be very helpful to the us. It will enable us to make a better interpretation of the records. It will give us a greater insight into the content and context of the records. And, in some cases, it will open research possibilities that we might otherwise overlook.

I. BACKGROUND

Under the English common law, upon which American law was based, a single woman (femme [or feme] sole, as she was known in legal terms) had essentially the same property rights as a man, except that she had no political rights (such as a right to vote) attached to her property ownership. A married woman (femme [or feme] covert[3]), however, had no authority to enter into a binding contract of any kind (except as she might be considered to act as an agent for her husband). She had virtually no property rights apart from her husband. Of this situation, as it relates to early North America, Marylynn Salmon writes:

> No [American] colony or state allowed married women, or femes coverts, . . . the legal ability to act independently with regard to property. Only under certain circumstances, at particular times, in precise ways, could a wife exercise even limited control over the family estate, including what she contributed to it. Under property law, the male head of household held the power to manage his own property as well as his wife's.
>
> The one outstanding exception to this generalization concerned wives with separate estates. Under the equitable rules enforced in some of the colonies and states, married women could own and control property separately from their husbands. If their marriage settlements gave them the power to do

---

[2] William Blackstone, *Commentaries on the Laws of England,* Vol. 1 , 430, Oxford, 1765–69, as cited by Marylynn Salmon in *Women and the Law of Property in Early America* (Chapel Hill: University of North Carolina Press, 1986), 200. All quotations from Salmon's work are used with the permission of the publisher. Her work is excellent and goes into detail on this subject. The book's emphasis is on the colonial and early statehood periods and deals exclusively with the colonies and states of Connecticut, Massachusetts, New York, Maryland, Virginia, and South Carolina.

[3] The legal term *femme covert* relates to *coverture* (a married woman's legal status). It means "a married woman." It is used to describe her legal condition—because of her marriage—as being under the cover, protection, and authority of her husband.

so, femes coverts could act as though they were femes soles, or unmarried women, in managing settlement property. Yet even this exception did not spell meaningful independence for American women, for they could make marriage settlements only if their husbands consented. . . .[4]

All of the colonies and states had strict limitations on the right of a married woman to own and dispose of property, though no two jurisdictions took exactly the same approach or achieved the same results. The common-law principle of unity of person was very strong. Even after the laws were changed, those who interpreted the law (usually the judges) often clung tenaciously to the old common-law principles. Salmon offers this explanation of the old common-law doctrine of unity of person:

> Under the common law, women and men gained certain rights and responsibilities after marriage. No longer acting simply as individuals, together they constituted a special kind of legal partnership, one in which the woman's role was secondary to the man's. Restrictions limited a married woman's ability to act at law. At marriage, her husband gained the right and responsibility for prosecuting suits in her name as well as his own. She could not institute a suit without him. In suits involving only the rights of the husband, the wife did not join. Such was the uneven nature of unity of person, which limited the activities of the wife while broadening those of the husband.
>
> After marriage, women acting alone could not execute valid contracts. Nor could they convey the property they brought to their marriages or earned with their husbands. They also lost the power to act as executors or administrators of estates and as legal guardians. With their husbands, however, femes coverts could do all of these things. Coverture notwithstanding, women who contracted, conveyed, and administered jointly rather than alone did so with the sanction of law. Men, in contrast, did not need the consent of their wives in executing most contracts and conveyances, and never needed to join in actions as executors, administrators, and guardians. Men also possessed the legal right to devise their estates, whereas women could do so only with the express consent of their husbands. Even then, their rights extended only to personal property.
>
> Restrictions on feme covert activities were a necessity, given the nature of property law. The inability of wives to act as individuals at law arose as a corollary to their inability to own property. After marriage, all of the personal property owned by a wife came under the exclusive control of her husband. He could spend her money, including wages, sell her slaves or stocks, and appropriate her clothing and jewelry. With regard to real property, his rights were almost as extensive. He made all managerial decisions concerning her lands and tenements and controlled the rents and profits. A conveyance of a woman's real estate was another matter, however. No husband could sell or mortgage real property without the consent of his wife. The common law sanctioned conveyances only when wives freely agreed to them, although "free" consent sometimes was difficult to determine in court.
>
> Unity of person meant that once they married, a man and woman had to cohabit for the rest of their lives. Legal separations or divorces remained rare

---

[4] Salmon, xv.

and were frowned upon among all social classes. The law required men to support their wives and children. If they refused, they could be prosecuted. At death, men had to devise at least two-thirds of their estates to their immediate families. If men died intestate, their families received all of their property.[5]

A basic understanding of some general principles and their effect can be helpful. It is not only valuable during the research process, but it has particular significance as we attempt to interpret the results of our research. Some of the concepts discussed in previous chapters, such as dower and curtesy, take on special significance. More is said about that later in this chapter.

It may prove helpful to explore briefly the requirements and the effects of two specific areas of the law as they relate to unity of person:

- Real estate conveyances
- Laws and customs relating to inheritance

This discussion will also consider the customs tied to the application of the various laws. This is not to suggest that other areas of the law, such as divorces and separate estates, are of no significance—only that they had less significance for most of our ancestors.

II. REAL ESTATE CONVEYANCES

Though the laws relating to the unity of person of a husband and wife robbed the wife of her separate identity, they prevented the husband from selling real property without his wife's consent. This requirement was satisfied in different ways in different places. In Britain, under the common law, an examination procedure was established whereby a court official took the seller's wife into a separate room where she was read the contents of the deed. She was then asked if she agreed. If she did, that fact was noted either by an attached certificate or on the face of the deed itself. Her acknowledgment would forever bar her from claiming any further rights associated with the property involved. This procedure, which became the typical practice in the American South, was supposed to protect the woman from the coercion of her husband. However, one does not need a wild imagination to believe that many women expressed their agreement because they were afraid of what would happen afterwards if they did not (or what might have already happened).

Other southern jurisdictions adopted procedures that required the deed to be executed (signed) by both the husband and the wife in order to be valid and effective. However, this practice of making the husband and wife joint grantors did not usually preclude the private examination. Other jurisdictions had the wife execute a separate document, a document known as a *dower release* (or release of dower), in connection with her private examination and her husband's signing of a deed.

---

[5] Salmon, 14–15.

The approach used in the North was quite different, perhaps because there were no separate equity courts. In early Connecticut, for example, there was no private examination of wives because a wife had no property rights until 1723—not even in connection with her husband. Under Connecticut law, all property belonged to the husband, regardless of how it came into the family. The 1723 law, however, instituted an examination procedure similar to that followed in the South.

Wives in colonial Massachusetts, New York, and Pennsylvania signed deeds as joint grantors with their husbands, but they were not examined privately. The husband was required to acknowledge such a deed as his own, but all that was required of the wife was her signature on the deed itself. The Pennsylvania courts apparently believed that giving women greater rights in conveying real property would be a threat to the security of land titles. Even after laws were passed to resolve this issue, the judiciary often ignored those laws, and the standards for determining compliance were loose and informal.

One of the most significant effects of these early conveyancing laws is that the name of a man's wife usually appeared, along with that of her husband, in the land records. Knowing a woman's given name at least gives us a starting place in our research as we seek to identify her. Also, if a man had a common name—as so many of our ancestors did—the name of his wife on a land record helps us to know if the person selling the property is our ancestor, or if he is another man with the same name. If he is our ancestor, we can initiate further research to identify when and how the property came into his possession—whether it was devised to him by will, inherited by intestate succession, conveyed by deed, or became his because his wife owned it when they married. Family details contained in the earlier document might provide just the evidence required.

III. LAWS AND CUSTOMS RELATING TO INHERITANCE

As we look at the laws associated with unity of person and their effect on inheritance, we shall consider just three questions:

- What happened when a woman's husband died before she did (i.e., the case of the widow)?
- What happened when a man's wife died before he did (i.e., the case of the widower)?
- What happened when a married woman received property, by either inheritance or devise, from her father—or from anyone else who was not her husband?

A. The widow

What happened when a woman's husband died before she did? The circumstances of a woman after the death of her husband were largely dependent on what was provided for by her late husband. Some husbands left wills that adequately provided for the needs of their widows; such women were fortunate. The provisions of such wills varied but, typically, her husband left her a life estate in some or all of his real property, or rights to the property that terminated if she should remarry. There were good and logical reasons for such limitations.

As we have already learned, if the woman were to remarry in the absence of such limitations on her ownership, her new husband essentially became the owner of any real property left to her. And, even if she had only a life estate in the property, the new husband might have full management rights and the right to rents and profits. This result was especially true under the legal practices of New England, where separate estates were seldom recognized. And the result might be more far-reaching than this: even supposing that a woman had a bona fide separate estate and her new husband did not become the owner at the time of their marriage, he would gain full control of the property after her death as a tenancy by the curtesy (which we will discuss later).

Even if a man wanted to give his widow a better title to his property than an estate for life (or estate during her widowhood), it was generally not wise for him to do so. An outright fee simple conveyance or devise might actually defeat his intentions to look after the needs of his surviving widow and to then ultimately leave the property to his children.

The same problem was also inherent in joint tenancy estates and in property held in tenancy by the entirety. If a widow with more than a life estate should remarry, her new husband essentially became the owner of the property—unless a valid separate estate had been created by acceptable legal procedures (in those jurisdictions where separate estates were recognized). Also, if a valid separate estate was created, the new husband—if they had children together and he outlived her—received a life estate in the property in tenancy by the curtesy.

George Washington's will, executed in 1790, provides a good example of a case where the widow was given a limited title to the land (i.e., for her life only):

> To my dearly beloved wife Martha Washington I give and bequeath the use, profit and benefit of my whole Estate, real and personal, for the term of her natural life. . . .

If a man left no will, as was often the case, the law determined what the widow would receive. Under the common law, she received an *estate in dower* in her late husband's real property. Though this was discussed earlier, let us look again at what the common-law tenancy in dower involved.

Common-law dower included a life estate in one-third of the real property that the widow's husband had owned at any time during their marriage. If the marriage produced no children (which is not the likely case with your ancestors), the widow could claim her dower in one-half of her husband's real property.

Note, also, that if a husband made a will leaving his widow less than she could claim by her right of dower, she could renounce the will and take the dower property instead. There were also other reasons why a widow might elect to choose dower over the estate left to her by her husband's will. For example, if the husband was an insolvent debtor, she might be wise to choose dower because a widow always received her dower before the debts of the estate were paid.

Because the widow had only a life estate in the property, it descended after her death to the beneficiaries of her husband's estate. She had no right to sell the property but had the right to all rents and profits. And if she remarried, her new husband would have no rights in the property after her death.

As a life tenant, the widow could do nothing to the property that would diminish its value without risking a lawsuit by the heirs because of her "waste." For example, if the property was timbered, she might not be allowed to cut timber even if that was the only way she could use the property to support herself.

Because the widow's dower rights were attached to all real property owned during the marriage, her right to dower could obviously be a great encumbrance to land titles; it often kept the title tied up for years, even decades— and not just the title, but also the use. The buyer of property subject to dower would not be able to use the property until the passing of the widow. Thus, most buyers took considerable care to ensure that the seller's wife released her dower rights at the time of the sale.

Many sales fell through because the seller's wife declined to consent to the conveyance and sign the deed (or otherwise release her dower rights). Unless the wife publicly acknowledged her willingness to renounce her future right to dower, the conveyance would not bar her later claim to the property. After her husband's demise, she would be free to sue the present owner and be awarded a life estate, and that owner could not get the property back until after the widow's death.

The early common law also gave the widow dower rights in her husband's personal property as well as his real property. By his will, a man was able to give one-third of his personal property to whomever he chose (including persons outside of his immediate family), one-third went automatically to his widow as dower, and one-third went to his children. However, during the seventeenth century this practice changed.

In 1656, Connecticut adopted a statute that provided the widow a share of both the real and personal property of her deceased husband, but the law was in effect only until 1673. By 1700, a man in Connecticut was typically free to dispose of his personal estate as he chose, and no dower rights were attached to it.

Virginia and Maryland both continued to recognize dower rights in personal property into the eighteenth century. An interesting twist developed in Virginia in 1705 when legislation was adopted defining slaves as real property. This law gave the widow dower rights in her husband's slaves, allowing her their use and benefit during her life, and then giving ultimate title to her children, her husband's heirs. This law provided a way for the slaves to be kept in the widow's family even if she decided to remarry. In 1748, legislation defined Virginia slaves once again as personal property.[6]

It should also be noted that most American jurisdictions did not adhere strictly to the common-law rules of dower. They instead created other rights for surviving widows, both to the advantage of the widows themselves and to land titles.

B. The widower

What happened when a man's wife died before he did? Because the husband was the marriage partner who had primary control of all property in the marriage, he tended to fare far better, both legally and economically, when his wife died than a woman did when her husband died. A widow's rights of survivorship, though significant, were inferior in many ways to a surviving husband's rights. Where the widow received a life estate in one-third, or at most one-half, of her husband's property as dower, the widower—if there were children born to the marriage (and this is an important point) —received a life estate in all of his deceased wife's separate real property. This was called *curtesy* or *tenancy by the curtesy.*

Though the husband was unable to sell the property or otherwise dispose of it, he made all managerial decisions and had the right to all rents and profits. Curtesy was conditioned upon the husband's role as guardian of his children, and if there were no children, the wife's separate property went to her heirs. It is interesting, however, that curtesy attached to the property even if the children of the marriage were deceased. It was necessary only that a child had been born alive. The widower's tenancy by the curtesy in his late wife's estate ended upon his death, and the heirs of the wife (usually her children) took title.

C. The married woman who receives property from someone other than her husband

What happened if a married woman received property, by either inheritance or devise from her father—or from anyone else who was not her husband? There will be many times in your research when you will find a married woman receiving property from her father, and less frequently from her brother or some other person who was not her husband. This passing of property may have been by will, by intestate successor, or perhaps by gift deed. Such cases are significant enough to deserve discussion—not because the situation was unusual, but because the results were unusual as compared with the results of similar cases today. It is important to understand these results as you

---

[6] Salmon, 152–154.

seek to understand the circumstances in which your ancestors lived. It is very easy to draw erroneous conclusions if you misunderstand the laws of inheritance and property ownership and how those laws were applied in the times of your ancestors.

Several years ago, when I was teaching an Independent Study class for Brigham Young University, there was one assignment where the students were asked to analyze a will and tell what they thought was the most interesting thing about that will. One provision in that will that got nearly everyone's attention was the testator's devise of a parcel of real estate to his daughter Nancy. The testator, one Lewis Terry, was careful to make clear his intention that this particular devise was meant only for her and not for her husband. The provision reads:

> I will and desire my daughter Nancy Carder, wife of Thomas Carder, free from control or management of her said husband and not subject to the payment of his debts, lot of land number ninety-one (91), district of the third section of said county to her during her natural life . . . .[7]

Most students thought this provision was interesting because it appeared to them that Mr. Terry either did not trust his son-in-law, did not like him, or both. Of course, any of those assumptions might be true, but it is more likely that Lewis Terry was merely interested in creating a separate estate for his daughter—an estate that she could control and not an estate of property that would essentially become the property of her husband through the principle of unity of person.

It was actually quite difficult, often impossible, to create legal separate estates in some jurisdictions. For example, in some colonies, the courts ruled that if a single or widowed woman who owned slaves was to marry, those slaves became the property of her husband. And some jurisdictions said that slaves conveyed or bequeathed to a married woman became the property of her husband.

IV. CONCLUSION

As you can see, legal requirements and common-law principles had a significant influence on the very nature of the records that are now available for family history research. And your understanding of the requirements and the principles involved in a specific situation can greatly affect—either to hinder or help—your research. It is easy to generalize, and I have generalized for purposes of illustration in this chapter, but you must realize that each jurisdiction is somewhat unique. Each had its own system of complex rules—ever-changing rules—relating to the legal status of women and their property rights. Even the existence or nonexistence of a chancery court, with its rules

---

[7] It is interesting that this will of Lewis Terry was dated in May 1851 in Murray County, Georgia, long after you would expect this sort of thing was necessary to preserve his daughter's rights to the property.

of equity (see Chapter 22), had a significant impact on women and their property rights.

These rights are significant, but that is another whole study. If you have further interest in that study, I again commend to you Marylynn Salmon's *Women and the Law of Property in Early America* (see footnote 2 in this chapter for bibliographic information).

The understanding that I hope you will get from this discussion relates to the effect of these legal matters on the nature of the records they generated. This is important to your family history research. It can give you a significant advantage and make you a better researcher. As part of this, I hope the explanations and examples offered here will give you some useful insights and help you understand some very important principles.

24

Church Records and Family History

The story is told of an old cowboy who visited the Grand Canyon for the first time. It is reported that he tied his horse to a tree, then sauntered out to the ledge to look down into the canyon. He later described the experience: "Ah took one look," he said, "and then ah wished ah'd tied m'self to the tree and let the horse look down into the canyon."

This is about the way American church records affect many researchers. These records constitute a vast, relatively unexplored, and little-known source of family history evidence, and they can be awesome to the average family history researcher. However, they are different from the Grand Canyon in that they are not usually as easy to locate—and finding those church records that pertain to our ancestors is usually our biggest problem.

I am not saying that no one has ever made good use of American church records (that would certainly be an error), but I am saying, rather, that church records present some unique challenges, which significantly limit both their usefulness and their use. In New England and the northern colonial states, however, church records present fewer problems and have much wider use than is typical elsewhere in the country.

I should also note that with the digitizing and indexing of many records, some church records have had a high priority. However, this is a rather hit-and-miss proposition in many parts of the United States. You will understand why as we proceed.

I. TYPES OF RECORDS

In a number of respects, the records of many churches are not unlike vital records. They deal with the same essential data—births, marriages, deaths—only in a slightly different way. Rather than recording the actual birth, the church record ordinarily reports the child's baptism or christening—usually a few days later. Instead of keeping a record of a marriage license or bond, the church keeps a record of the actual marriage of the couple and of the banns.[1] And, instead of recording a death, church records are more likely to report a person's burial. However, because of the near proximity of the dates of these events timewise, the church records of these events serve the same purpose; they are useful identifiers, and they were generally kept much earlier than were civil vital records. It is easy to understand why records of these three events—christenings, marriages, and burials—are usually the most important, and certainly the most widely used, church records in family history research. They have ordinarily been kept in books called *registers*.

Another kind of church record with particular value for us is the record that indicates the removal of members from one church congregation or their arrival at another church congregation. Most churches kept records of this type so that faithful members would be welcomed into the fellowship of the church when they moved to a new location, but each church had its own name for these records. The Society of Friends (Quakers) called them *certificates of removal*, the Protestant Episcopal Church (Church of England) called them *letters of transfer*, the Baptists called them *letters of admission*, the Congregationalists called them *dismissions*, and the early Latter-day Saints (Mormons) called them *certificates of membership*.

These records are useful because they facilitate the tracing of a family from one location to another, which is often a difficult task without such assistance. The main problem with these records is that they are usually incomplete.

Other types of church records include confirmations, lists of communicants, membership lists, and excommunications—all of which are frequently recorded in the registers—plus vestry minutes and proceedings (Protestant Episcopal Church), sessions minutes (Presbyterian Church), and other minutes that include financial reports, disciplinary actions and fines imposed on backsliders, and (for the Friends) disownments and manumissions.[2] These records often contain information of significant value to the family history researcher.

It might be well to mention now, though it will be discussed more thoroughly later, that the nature of church records is greatly affected by the position (and by this I do not mean geographical location) of the church in the community. In places where there is a *state church*—one that is recognized by law as the official church and is supported by the government—church records are usually much better and more complete. This underscores one of our main challenges with American church records as a source of family history evidence: the U.S. has a complete separation of church and state. Politi-

---

[1] Banns are a public proclamation, very often read in the local Christian church, of the impending marriage of two people, usually read on three successive Sundays—the point being that these readings of the banns would provide opportunity for timely objections.

[2] Manumission was the formal process of freeing a slave.

cally this is ideal, but it has disadvantages for those who seek family history information.

During America's colonial period, there were state churches in some of the colonies. Many of the New England colonies adhered officially to the Congregational Church; in Virginia, the English or Protestant Episcopal (P.E.) Church had official status. Other colonies—notably Georgia, Maryland, and South Carolina—also held the P.E. Church as a state church at various times. In New Netherlands, the Dutch Reformed Church had state church status.

America was truly unique in her religious development. During settlement, she combined persons from many European nations who brought with them the religions of their homelands, each group trying to make its religion dominant. The English tried hard and, because the colonies were mostly English, they had an advantage.

Though state churches existed in the American colonies, they did not stand unchallenged. Thus, the only remedy left to the framers of the Constitution, in light of the multiplicity of both churches and national origins, was to give the federal government no power over the nation's churches and to provide for free exercise of religion. This is evidenced by the First Amendment's wording that "Congress shall make no law respecting an establishment of religion. . . ."[3]

Though there was never a national church in the United States, some state establishments persisted long after the Revolution—especially in New England. It was not until after the Fourteenth Amendment that the proscriptions of the Constitution were interpreted to apply to the individual states as well as to the federal government.

II. THE NATURE OF THE RECORDS

Perhaps the best way to explain the true nature of church records is to show examples of them; I have chosen here to present examples from the following:

A. The Congregational Church in New England (Maine)

B. The Protestant Episcopal (P.E.) Church in the South (Virginia)

C. The Lutheran Church in the central-Atlantic states (Pennsylvania)

D. The Baptist Church

E. The Society of Friends (Quakers)

We will also discuss the records of the Roman Catholic Church (F) without giving specific examples and then comment briefly on other denominations (G).

Remember that these are only examples and that church records often vary considerably even within the same denomination. There are frequently extensive variances in records of the same congregation when a new minister or a new clerk assumed the record-keeping duties.

---

[3] U.S. Const., Amendment 1.

A. Congregational Church

We begin with a Congregational church—the Second Church of Kittery (Maine). This church, like most Congregational churches, kept a record of baptisms, but you will note that these were not always baptisms of infants, and some important (in our opinion) information was not included in the records. (I have not corrected spelling or grammar in the below examples.)

1. Baptisms

1725—Ap[ril]—David Libby Jun[r]
    Ester his wife
    Mary Smal Jos: wife
    Eban[r] Libby

Sept[r]—Joseph son of Joseph Harn[d] Jun[r]—
    Decem[r]—Catharine my Daughter [the minister]
    Feb. —Sam[l] & Hep[h] child[n] of Sam[l] Hanscom in Privte
    1726—July—Two Children of Nathan Spinney—
    Edward Chapman son Simon
    31— Jno Libby & Ephra[m] Libby, adult—
    Elisha son of John Libby
    Mary Daughter of Rich[d] King

1727—May—Eleanor Daughter of Deacon Tetherly
    June 25—Nath[l] son of Peter Staple—
    July 3d Sab—Tho: Knight—
    Sept 3—David Libby & Son David
    Sam[l] Son of Samuel Winget on her acc[t]—

A few years later the information was a little more detailed, but not much:

1764

Aug 29	Gabriel son of William Tetherly
	Eunice dau of John Spinney J[r]
Sep 24	Jotham, son of Samuel Emery
Oct 1	Nathan Bartlett, Jr, son of Nathan

1765

Apr 21	J. Gowen, wife of William Gowen
May 12	John Kennard owned the covenant & had his child baptized named John
June 9	Mary child of Mr. Tho Hammend & wife who renewed their baptismal covenant
July 14	Joshua son of Jonathan More. 3d Sabbath in Oct Joseph son of William Stacy
Oct 10	Joel & David sons of Ephraim Libby, Jr.
Nov 23	Samuel son of Tobias Shapleigh

2. Communicants

The following is from an undated list (sometime between 1727 and 1746) of "Males Belonging to the Communion." Such lists were also made of female communicants, but they did not often state the given names of married women—only "Mrs.":

Joseph Hamond	Edward Chapman mov'd
Nicᵒ Shapleigh	Christopher Sargent mov'd
Samˡ Hill	Robert Staple
Daniel Fogg	James Staple junʳ
John Staple	Phylip Cooms mov'd
Stephen Tobley	Josiah Paul
William Tetherly	Jeremiah Paul mov'd

3. Dismissions

Also recorded among sundry notes that the minister kept of the church's—and of his own—activities are records of persons moving in and out. These are called *dismissions*:

> June 1749—Had Deacon Simon Emerys Dissmission from the Church of Berwick Read to the Brethren, and then voted for receiving him into communion with us—
>
> July 30, 1778—Jerusha Hanscom was dismissed from this chh & recommended to the 2nd chh of Berwick.
>
> July 7, 1817—Sarah Thimison was dismissed from this chh and recommended to the chh of Xᵗ in Temple.

4. Notes

As mentioned earlier, the ministers in some churches—including this one—kept notes in journal form of some of the church's activities. There is not a lot of information in these notes that is of value to the family history researcher as far as lineal connections are concerned, but they should be considered for their historical value. The following notes are typical:

> Novembʳ 6—1721—
>
> The chh met at the House of Brother James Staple, in order to make choice of Two Suitable Persons for Deacons: And after Prayer to the Great Head of the chh, for Direction in this Important affair—the Members by written votes, chose William Tetherly, & James Staples for this offices.

> Octobʳ 6, 1727
>
> Being yᵉ Lords Day: After the Public Exercises were over I Stay'd yᵉ Brethren of yᵉ chh, & Laid before them yᵉ Error which I apprehended those of oʳ Brethren, viz. Hamᵈ, Tobey, Rogers, Hanscom, Tob: Leighton, in withdrawing communion from this chh & in Continuing in their Separation from it: observed to them yᵗ they had broken their Covenant with us which was to Submit to yᵉ watch & Discipline of this chh, & walk orderly & in Comunion with us: and Laid before them our Duty; which was to call them to an accᵗ & proceed with them in a way of admonition in the first place, Publickly before the chh to bring them to a sense of yʳ disorderly doings.

In addition to these notes and to the lists of communicants given earlier, this church also kept a list of persons admitted to full communion with the church, as follows:

1746, May 18, Admitted Abigail Wittum wife of Eben^r—

1747, Augt 30. Admitted Cumbo, a Negro woman of Capt Bartletts—

1748, Ap^l 10. Admitted Wid^o Judith Gowen—

1751, Augt 4. Jane Remick, wife of Nath Remick—

1754. July. Samuel Fernald—

1754. Decem^r 1: John Heard Bartlett: who had a Liberal Education at Harvard Colledge—

1756 June, Joanna Preble the wife of Edward Preble

5. Burials and marriages

In this particular church, there are no records of burials or marriages preserved, though such is not the case in all Congregational churches.

B. The Protestant Episcopal Church (Church of England)

The Protestant Episcopal Church has generally kept quite good records in America, but many of those records have not survived. The examples used here are from two separate churches—the Augusta Parish in Augusta County, Virginia, where we will take a comprehensive look at vestry minutes,[4] and the Immanuel Church in Hanover County, Virginia, where we will also peek at the vestry minutes but shall be chiefly concerned with church registers.

1. Vestry minutes

The P.E. Church in colonial times had a very close connection with the civil government of Virginia, as already discussed, and many things you will find in the records of the vestry you might more typically find in civil court records if you were in some other part of the country or in a later time period. One example—which will not be illustrated but only mentioned—is those records involved with what was called the processioning of land. This involves the formality of determining the limits and boundaries (metes and bounds) of the several private estates within the parish. The processions tell the amount of land (number of acres) that each person owns. Another example is the record kept of orphans and illegitimate children.

a. *The poor, orphans, and illegitimate children.* The church, through the vestry, was responsible for the material sustenance and physical well-being of parish members and kept careful records of the manner in which this obligation was discharged. In addition to widows, others—including the physically incapable, the habitually poor, and children who were unable to provide for themselves—were objects of special concern. A large portion of the vestry

---

[4] The vestry is composed of a group of church members who oversee and manage the temporal affairs of the church.

minutes was often devoted to them. Bastardy bonds, such as the following, were quite common and have significant family history value:

> 1748/9 KNOW all men by These Presence that we Christopher Finney and
> Feby 14th William Armstrong are held and firmly bound unto James Lockhart
> and John Madison Churchwardens for the Parish of Augusta in the
> just and full sum of Fifty Pounds Curr^t money of Virginia to which
> Payment will and truly to be made and done we bind us and Each
> of our Heirs and Assigns firmly by these Presents as witness our
> Hands and Seals this 14th day of February 1748/9.
>
> THE CONDITION of this obligation is such that whereas
> Sarah Simmons Single Woman hath this day before me Charged
> Christopher Finney Taylor for getting Her with Child which Child
> when Born will be a Bastard and may be Burdensome To our s^d
> Parish of Augusta if the said Finney shall be and appear at our
> next Court to be held for s^d County then & there to do what may
> be by the s^d Child then this obligation to be void or Else to Re-
> main in force and Virtue in Law & c.
>
> Taken before me ⎱ (signed) Christopher Finney
> Robt Cunningham ⎰ (signed) Wm Armstrong

Also, as the result of efforts to remove the care of children from the church, it was also common to find apprenticeship records wherein an orphan or illegitimate child (the record usually indicating which) was bound as an apprentice to some responsible church member. Some illegitimate children were apprenticed to their reputed fathers.

Following is an apprenticeship document for Peter Smith, a child who was deserted:

> THIS INDENTURE Witnesseth that we James Lockhart and John Archer
> Churchwardens of Augusta County at the November Court In the Year of
> our Lord MDCCL it was agreed that the Churchwardens bind out an orphan
> Child belonging to Nicholas Smith named Peter Smith and as he is now Run
> away it appearing to the Court that all his Children is like to become Bur-
> donsome to the Parish of Augusta there being no Persons to care of ye sd
> Children it is ordered y^t ye Churchwardens bind out the sd Peter Smith to
> Elijah McClenachan who appeared in Court & agreed to take the sd Peter
> Smith According to Law Pursuent To which they bind him unto ye s^d Elijah
> McClenachan to serve him his Heirs or assigns untill he shall be full Twenty
> one years of Age he being now Four years of Age during all which Term y^e
> sd Peter Smith his sd master and mistress shall Faithfully serve their Secrets
> keep their Lawful commands everywhere gladly obey he shall do no Dam-
> age to his master or Mistress he shall not Waste his s^d master or mistresses
> Goods nor lend them unlawfully to any He shall not commit Fornication nor
> Contract matrimony during ye sd Term he shall not Play at Cards Dice or any
> unlawful Game he shall not absent himself Day nor night from his said Mas-
> ter or mistresses service unlawfully nor haunt Ale Houses Taverns or Play
> Houses but in all things behave himself as a Faithful servant out to do & ye sd
> Elijah McClenachan shall Teach or cause him to be Taught to Read write and
> Cast up Acct^s & shall Provide for & Procure to him meat Drink Washing &

apparel & all other necessaries fitting for such an apprentice the sd Term and for the true Performance of every the said Covenants & agreements either of the Parties bind themselves to the others firmly by these Presents In witness whereof this XXIJ Day of November 1752 & the sd Elijah McClenachan shall give sd Peter Smith when free such freedom dues as the Law directs likewise to Learn him or cause him to be instructed in the Cooper Trade or some other & c.

Signed Sealed and delivered	(signed) James Lockhart
In Presence of—	(signed) John Archer
Wm Preston	(signed) Elijah McClenachan

b. *Money.* The vestry minutes kept track of money coming into the church from various sources:

1753 Dr To the Parish of Augusta

To Cash paid . . . by Mr John Madison	£30 – 0 – 0
To Ditto by William Henderson a fine	2 – 10 – 0
To Ditto by Widow Smily a fine	2 – 10 – 0
To Ditto by James Greenlee his servants fine	2 – 10 – 0
To Ditto by Andrew Beard for swearing	0 – 10 – 0
To Ditto by Robert Gwin his Daughters fine	0 – 10 – 0
To Ditto collected by James Greenlee Constable for swearing	1 – 0 – 0
To Ditto by John Mason Constable for swearing	0 – 10 – 0
To Ditto by Henry Gay his Daughters fine	2 – 10 – 0
To Jean Campbells Fine	2 – 10 – 0
To a Deposit in his Hands the 6th Augt 1750	52 – 14 – 5
To Interest on the same 2 years	5 – 4 – 0
To Viter Mauck's part of the Quitrent money	4 – 18 – 3
To Cash of John Graham for swearing	1 – 0 – 0
To Cash pd. By David Stuart late Sheriff	1 – 12 – 3

They were also concerned with the exiting of that same money:

2 Nov 1752

David Stuart Sheriff Produced an Acc^t against this Parish out of which he is allowed the sum of £1"15"2 and ordered that he be Paid the same.

Ordered that Margaret Frame be allowed the sum of £6"0"0 for the maintainance of one of Her Children this insuing year it appearing To this Vestry that it is an Object of Charity.

It appears to this Vestry that Hewan Mathers is an object of Charity it is therefore ordered that he be allowed £4 for this Present Year to be laid out at the Discretion of the Churchwardens for Cloaths only.

Ordered that the Revd John Jones be allowed at the rate of £50 p^r annum to commince from the first Day of Sepr 1752 It appearing to this Vestry that the Glebe Buildings are not yet Finished and the said Jones having acquainted this Vestry that John Lewis Gen^t (the undertaker of the same) Agrees to allow him at the Rate of £20" p^r annum until the same be Finished, for which he declares himself Satisfied and acquits this Vestry and Parish of any further charge for the same.

Ordered that a Reader of this Parish be allowed the sum of £6"5 yearly and that the Revd Mr Jones have a Liberty to Choose the same to officiate at ye Court House.

Ordered that Wm Preston be allowed the Sum of £5" p^r Annum to serve as a Clerk for this Vestry and that, to Commence from the first Sepr 1752.

Ordered that a Register Book be Procured for the use of this Parish and Delivered to the Rev^d Mr Jones.

And . . .

1753 To Cash pd the Revd John Jones as Hd Rect	£ 50" 0" 0
To Cash to CoLo James Patton (Asst) Rect	9" 19" 0
To Hewan Mathers one of the Poor of this Parish	4" 0" 0
To 2¾ Gallons of Wine for the Sacrament	1" 7" 6
To Diging a Cellar in the Glebe House	2" 13" 4
To Robert McClenachan H^d order of Vestry	2" 13" 4
To David Stuart & Wm Hinds for carriage of the vestry books	1" 10" 0
To Julian Mauck for keep a Blind Woman	1" 4" 3
To Patrick Porterfield for Nursing an Orphan Child	9" 4" 0
To Widow Thing for Burying John Lowdon	4" 10" 0
To the Quitrents of the Glebe Land for the Years 1747:48:49:50:51 & 52	1" 9" 11½
To Cash to Thomas Moffit at Sundrys one of the Poor	4" 13" 4
To Peter Mauck on Account of a Blind Woman	9" 6" 9
To Lambert Booper an Object of Charity	2" 12" 10

c. *Other matters.* Various other types of notes are also found in vestry minutes. The following is particularly reminiscent of documents arising out of the "poor laws" of England requiring that the parish of origin (called "parish of settlement") be responsible for their poor regardless of where those poor may have removed themselves:

August 6th 1750

On the information of CoL^o John Buckanan that one——— [*sic*] Morrice is lately come into this Parish with a numerous Family who is likely to become chargeable to this Parish Its ordered that the Churchwardens move the said Morrice to the place from whence he came———According to Law and bring in their Charge for the same at the laying of the next Parish Levy unless he give Security for indemnifying the said Parish.

Even biographical material can be found in vestry minutes upon occasion. In the minutes of the Immanuel Church, Hanover County, Virginia, on October 21, 1878, there was recorded the lengthy obituary for one of the churchwardens or vestrymen. It had been copied into the minutes from *The Southern Churchman*:

BASSETT—Departed this life on the 25th of August, 1878, at his residence, Clover Lia in the county of Hanover, George Washington Bassett, Esqr, in the seventy ninth year of his age. By the death of Mr. Bassett, a prominent and valient member of the old fashioned Virginia gentry has been taken away from the few who still survive and the church has been deprived of a wise and devoted member.

Mr Bassett was descended from the ancient and honorable family of the Bassetts of Eltham in the county of New Kent, which for two centuries exercised so prominent an influence in their native county and was so active in the civil and, ecclesiastical affairs of Virginia. The sister of Mrs. Washington, Miss Anna Maria Dandridge, married Mr. Bassett's grandfather and between the families of Mount Vernon and Eltham there was always maintained the most intimate and cordial relations. Early in life Mr. Bassett became a communicant of the Episcopal Church and at once manifested the most active zeal for its prosperity in the neighborhood in which he resided. He sat in many of the conventions of the diocese and was always found in hearty cooperation with those ───── and, devoted, men to whom so much of the prosperity and advancement of the church in Virginia is firstly due.

In the year of 1843, soon after his removal, to his estate in Hanover, Mr. Bassett became much concerned at the prostrate condition of the Church in his neighborhood, and the adjoining counties of King William and New Kent. The parishes had died out and been without rectors or church services for more than half a century. With extraordinary patience and self denial Mr. Bassett awakened the interest and aid of the few Churchmen scattered over the large extent of the country and, the church was reorganized and a clergyman appointed, to labor in the lower part of Hanover County, two parishes in King William and one in New Kent.

Mr. Bassett's money, his time and, personal influence were issued unsparingly bestowed, and, his faithful services were much abundantly rewarded.

He saw the Church of his fathers happily restablished and with slight interruptions it has continued to prosper to this day. So far as ───── judgment may venture it seems certain that but for Mr. Bassett's exertions the Church would, have died out utterly or remained ───── and, useless as he found it in this part of Virginia.

Like so large and sorrowful a number of the prominent families in old, Virginia, Mr. Bassett sustained severe damage to his temporal prosperity from the effects of the late war and, other causes beyond his control. Estates held from a long line of honored ancestry were almost wholly ───── but his patient submission to his Master's dispensations and his unmurmuring acquiescence in what had befallen him without any hope of amelioration were most touching and edifying to witness.

No complaints ever fell from his lips and he seemed heartily thankful for the comforts yet left to him in his declining years.

For heaven his last days were his best days, and it is a most precious memory to his many friends, that the religion of his early manhood was so full of steadfastness and afforded, so many precious consolations when he was wasted and feeble and slowly passing away to his rest in heaven.

The community of which Mr. Bassett was so conspicuous a member for so many years will long remember him as a ───── friend, a hospitable, sympathising neighbor, and though not a perfect, yet an humbel minded, earnest and devoted, Christian.

2. Registers of the P.E. Church

The registers of the Immanuel Protestant Episcopal Church are quite typical of those kept in other churches of the same denomination, though, as mentioned earlier, there are no set patterns—they vary even with each minister. Let us look at some register entries:

a. *Baptisms*

Name of infant	Name of parents	Name of sponsors	Date and age
William Braxton	Carter & Ellen Roy	Parents	1857 April 1 yr
Carter			1857 April 3 yrs
William Roy	Thomas H. & Susan Carter	W^m H Roy & Sally V B Tabb	1857 June 5 yrs
James Bernard	Thos & Sally Q. Gardiner	E. P. Meredith	1857 July 10 2 yrs
Blanch Bell	Mrs. McGehee	Mother & uncles	1857 Sep 8 yrs

Note this Baptism was at Wht Sulphur Springs. The parties of Bolvin County, Miss. (Post Office Victoria)

Charles Pinkney	Thos & Sally Q. Gardiner	E. P. Meredith	1858 May 29 3 mo
Edmon Fitzhugh	Rob^o W. & H. V. B. Tomlin	Parents	1858 July 9 yrs
Thomas Nelson Carter	Thomas H. & Susan Carter	Mrs. Ann Wickham Mrs. Ann Carter	1858 Nov

These baptisms contain quite complete information, but records of baptisms just a few years later were somewhat more informative:

At Hempstead July 5th 1873—
> Ellen Douglas, daughter of W.W. & Fanny Gordon Born Aug 11th 1873 [*sic*]

1874: Nov 16. At the house of James S. & Delia Kelley their child
> Mary Egbert born May 6th last
> Sponsors, Mrs B. B. Bassett & Mrs Annette L. Ingle
> Rev J. E. Ingle of the Diocese of Maryland officiating

1876: Apr 28—At Mrs Blake's, King William Co.
> Rush Aldridge Hunt
> Son of Jones Rush Lincoln (and Elizabeth Aldridge Blake his wife deceased) born Ap 8 1866
> Sponsors Rev E. A. Dalrymple STD, Miss Sophia L. Lincoln—by proxy.

Oct 14th at Hampstead, New Kent.
> Laura Robinson daughter of W. W. & Fanny Gordon born July 10th 1876.

1877:
Oct 5th at the Rectory.
> Lydia Bock, daughter of Francis E. & Emma Keene Habersham born Sept 20th
> Sponsors: Mrs Emma Keene, Miss Ella Habersham, Newton Keene, by proxy.

b. *Confirmations*

Confirmations tell us very little—mostly just names and dates:

Name of candidates	By whom administered	Date
Ella Moore Bassett	Rt Rev Wm Meade D.D.	1857 Nov.
Augusta Lewis	”	”
Sarah Ann Baker	”	”
Thos. H. Carter	”	1860 Nov. 4th
Mary M. L. Newton	”	” ”
Henry Franklin Baker	”	” ”
Mary Louisa ”	”	” ”
Maria Carter Wormly	”	” ”
Bettie A. Polaka	Confirmed in Lexington, Ky	
May Dabney	” Charlottesville, Va	
O. T. Baker	Rt Rev J. Johns D.D.	1866 Nov.
Robt H. ”	”	”
Margt E. ”	”	”
Susan C. L. ”	”	”
Anna J. ”	”	”
Maria Dabney	”	”
Sallie C. Darricotte	”	”

c. *Communicants*

The records are brief, but there is information about some people that could be very helpful.

1. Geo W. Bassett sen
2. Betty Barnett Bassett
3. Geo W. Bassett Jr.
— Judith F. F. Bassett   Removed
4. Carter Warner Wormley
5. Ellen Bankhead Wormley
6. Sallie Lightfoot Wormley
—   Turner   Removed to Frederick, M^d
7. Mary Sheet
8. Susan E. Carter   Withdrawn
— Robert W. Tomlin   Died July 22^d 1862
9. Wm A. R. Brockenborough
— William Sayre   Removed
— Elizabeth Sayre   Died Dec 8th 1860
— Mildred Ruffin   Removed to Frankfort, Ky
— Margaret Tyler   Transferred to St Peters Parish
— Betty Tyler   Transferred to St Peters Parish
10. Wm A Baker   Died June 24, 1873
11. Sarah A. Baker
12. Judith O. Johnson
— Sally A. Gardiner   Removed to Kanawha 1860
— Virginia T. Carroway   Removed and dead
— Ella M. Bassett   Removed to Jefferson C. Nov 1860
13. Annette L. Bassett
14. Sarah A. E. Baker   Removed to California
15. Sarah Eliza Blake   Withdrawn

d. *Marriages*

Name of parties	Where married	Date
Wᵐ A. Tignor & Ann E. Clifton	Immanuel Church	1857 Oct 13ᵗʰ
John Peris Points & Elizᵗʰ Garlick Tyler	Turwood Hannvill	1858 April 18ᵗʰ 11: AM
Henry J. C. Vass & Lavinia Via	Black Creek Church	1858 April 18ᵗʰ 3 PM
Wᵐ Robᵗ Boyd & Margt Farley Smith	Immanuel Church	1859 Sept 28 10: AM
Barnett Bassett Sayre & Mildred Campbell Ruffin	Marlbourne	1859 Oct 4 12 AM

e. *Deaths and funerals*

Wᵐ Roy infant son of Dʳ Thos & Susan Carter died Sunday May 2ᵈ and buried at Pampatake on Monday May 3ᵈ [1857]

James Tyler died July — 1857 and buried by Mr Points

Mrs ———— White aged about 100 buried Oct 2/58

Mrs Bently Waker   Apr 12/59

Miss Polly White   June "

Elisha White   69   Nov 23ᵈ "

C. W . Robt Wate   abt 60   Aug 11 1860

Mrs Eliz Sayre died on 8th Decr Buried Decr 10ᵗʰ at Marlbourne

This infant son of Mrs Sayre 19 "

Susan Cathᵃ daughter of Mrs Blake died 25ᵗʰ & buried 27th Aug 61

Later funeral and death records are typically more informative than the earlier ones:

1876 March 25ᵗʰ

Mrs Harriet Clopton, aged 78, was buried at the cemetery near the dwelling house of her son

March 31—In New Kent County from his residence at The White House. William A. Cooke—aged about 30.

April 25ᵗʰ—At Hampstead, New Kent, Virginia—Jane Farland eldest daughter of Wᵐ W. Gorton Esq. —aged seventeen years. One who belonged to be with Christ!

1877—March 1ˢᵗ. Mrs Maria D. Woodee a recent Communicant of this Church, aged 27 or 28 years was buried at Shinmer [?] Hill this day.

1878—Feb 13: Mʳ James Tucker a citizen of Hanover Co., aged 62, died, It is said of the disease of the heart suddenly.

Apr. 24. Mrs. Judith Johnson—aged 71

August 27ᵗʰ—George W. Bassett Sr.

Born Aug 23, 1800—Died Aug 25, 1878. A Communicant from early life and Warden of Immanuel Church from its organization. When he moved to the County, he found the Colonial Church extinct, and by his efforts, and liberal aid, was Immanuel Church built subsequently— He lies in its cemetery, — May his rest be peace.

Nov 7—Ramaliel Philips, son of William and Caroline Philips, died Nov 6ᵗʰ 1878, aged 19 years, buried in the cemetery of Immanuel.

C. The Lutheran Church

The Lutheran Church was the dominant religion in many areas during the early history of this country, and also had a significant following in other areas. Lutheran records are generally quite complete but, as with the records of other churches, much depends on the minister or clerk. Lutheran Church records are much like the records of some other churches, notably some branches of the Reformed Church. The following examples are from the records of the Goshenhoppen Lutheran Church, Montgomery County, Pennsylvania.

1. Register of families

The register of families contains detailed information on all members of the congregation and their families. The register is arranged by family and looks like this:

> The names of the Members of the Congregation their wives and Children, began in the year 1751.

> 1. John Michael Reiher, age 62 years, born 1689 father John Michael Reiher, Mother Annie Catherine, from Rohrbach near Zinze in Courtebarg. Anno 1732 he came to America. He married

> (1) In the year 1708, Anna Maria, daughter of Dietrich Seeland and Amelia, of Nurnberg, died 1742.

> (2) In the year 1743, Maria Catherine, Reformed, born 1713, died 1750, daughter of Henrich Schneider of Asohpissen in the Palatinate and of Catharine daughter of Abraham Schneider.

> (3) In 1751, Sept 12, Maria Christine, born 1718, Nov 18 at Borna in Electoral Saxony, daughter of George Gerlach and Susanna, who is now with her daughter. Married (1) John Christopher Hoepler, died Aug 18, 1750 at sea, where he was buried.

> The children of this marriage are as follows:

> 1. John Christian, born 1739, Jan 18, bapt 29 ditto
> 2. John George, born 1743, Nov 17. Bapt Nov 18
> 3. John Gottleib, born 1748, Jan 23, bapt Jan 25
> 4. John Henry, born 1750, Dec 11, bapt Dec 20

> In the year 1750, she with her mother and parents in law came to America and married (2) Michael Reiher. Michael Reiher has the following children of the first and second marriage.

> 1. Anna Maria, died
> 2. John Carl, born 1711, Dec 15, bapt. Dec 17
> 3. Anna Maria, born 1712, Dec 5, bapt Dec 8
> 4. John Martin, born 1716, Jan 9, bapt Jan 11
> 5. Anna Sarah, born 1718, March 24
> 6. Anna Catharine, born 1729, Dec 6
> 7. Anna Barbara, born 1745
> 8. George Philip, born 1750

2. Lists of communicants

This is a periodic list of persons who received communion, made approximately every two or three months. In this case the names were arranged more or less alphabetically:

Nov 4 1751

1. Bausberger, Laurence
2. Bauersax, John Nicholas
3. Bausmann, Conrad
4. —— Anna Eva, his wife
5. Berckheimer, Leonhard
6. —— Catharine, his wife
7. Berckheimer, Valentine
8. Bering, Adam
9. Bittner, Henry
10. —— Christinea, his wife

3. Confirmations

The following list was dated June 24, 1752:

1. Elias Schneider, age 18 years, son of Conrad Schneider, see p. ——
2. John Martin Schmidt, age 17 years, son of Henry Schmidt
3. Peter Gabel, 14 years, son of Philip Gabel, see p. ——
4. Christian Hoepler, 13 years, son of John Christopher Hoepler, see p. ——
5. George Philip Gabel, 12 years, son of Philip Gabel, see p. ——
6. Michael Schneider, 16 years, son of Conrad Schneider, see p. ——
7. Anna Margaret Klein, 23 years, wife of John Klein
8. Elizabeth Schmid, 17 years, da. of Martin Schmid
9. Maria Agatha Klingele, 17 years, da. of Georg Frederick Klingel and wife Maria Agnes, of Conestoga, living at Samuel Schuler's
10. Evan Margaret, 15 years, da. of Philip Kresler; her mother Barbara is dead

4. Marriages

(1751)

1. John George Goerkes, single, Lutheran, admitted to the Lord's Supper with his father William Goerkes living in New York, married Anna Zipperle, single, Lutheran, da. of the late Frederick Zipperle and Catharine of Rhinesbeck, who lived at George Weigele, bro. of her mother, Banns published (1) in Old Goshenhoppen, June 30, (2) at same place July 14, (3) at Falkner Swamp July 21. Married at Old Goshenhoppen, July 23, in the church with a wedding sermon. The text was taken from Tobit 4: 1–7, 13–16.

Later marriage records (contrary to normal patterns) have much *less* detail:

(1780)

Jan 11. George Schwenck	and	Susanna Weis
Febr 8. George Lemle	and	Barbara Haas
May 11. Henry Graf	and	Charlotte Schwarz
July 18. Jacob Gros	and	Susanna Klein

5. Baptisms

There was not much change in the information or format in the baptism records over the years. They are all about like these:

(1751)

Children	Parents	Sponsors
Elisabeth	Jacob Grotz	Henry Bittner
b. July 7, 1751	and Elizabeth	and Christina
bapt Aug 4	at Shippack	fr Shippack
Anna Margaret	Henry Bittner	Jacob Grotz
b. July 24, 1751	and Christine	and wf Elizabeth
bapt Aug 4		

There was also a separate baptism record for children born out of wedlock:

> Names of the baptized children, who were born out of wedlock.
>> George Philip, born Febr 16, 1753, bapt Febr 25 1753 in the school-house. His father is said to be Henry Lips, a servant accross the river. The mother is single, named Elizabeth, living at John Fischer's, Godparents: Philip Wenzel and wife Christine, both newcomers.
>> Anna Elizabeth, born Dec 27, 1754, bapt. March 9, 1755.
>> Parents: His father is said to be John Peter Kabel
>> His Mother Anna Barbara Kircher, da of the late John George Kircher, single.
>> Godparents: John Frederick Kircher, single and Elizabeth Schwenck, single, da of the late Peter Schwenck.
>> Barbara, born July 21, 1763.
>> Parents: John Daub, died and Catharina
>> Sponsors: John Kantz and wife Barbara
>> Manli, born 1767, parents: Michael Gaugler and Catharine Gaugler.
>> Sponsors: Kilian Fischer and Elizabeth Nuagesser.

6. Dead who were buried publicly

> 1. Eva Margaret, born 1751, March—died Jan 31, 1752, buried Febr 2nd, in cemetery in front of the Old Goshenhoppen Church, on Sunday before the morning service. Parents: John Jacob Kayser and Anna Maria, Ref.
> 2, Jacob Eckmann, age 65 years, born 1687, from Switzerland, the Canton of H. Gall, born in Runnelshorse, Reformed. Father Librich Eckman, who left only one son, Jacob, and his widow Anna Maria. Anno 1752, July 3 he died and was buried in our Church yard at Old Goshenhoppen on July 4, 1752.

The same is true of the burials as was true of the marriages—there are fewer details on the later ones:

> 1776
>> On April 5, was buried Catharina, da of Henry Hemsinger schoolmaster here, her age 2 years, 8 months.
>> On May 31, was buried Catharine, da of the late Herman Waische, her age 5 years, 10 months.
>> On June 6, was buried Catharine, da of George Boyer, her age 3 years less 5 weeks.

D. The Baptist Church

The Baptist Church records I have chosen to examine (briefly) are those of the Woodbury Baptist Church in Cannon County, Tennessee. The records are called "minutes," and the entries are diverse. They include financial accounts, lists of converts (name only), notations of letters of admission, annual membership lists (also name only), and accounts of church business meetings. Baptisms, marriages, and burials were not recorded. Following are the minutes of a business meeting:

> Saturday Jan. 26, 1889
> Baptist Church of Christ met in Conference at Woodbury. Minutes of last meeting called for and Read and approved. No unfinished business refured to. Bro. J. R. Rushing anonce the minutes of last association. Are on the table, and all can get them that want to. Bro. D. B. Vance give notice of the death of Sister Juda A. Ferrell. A notice from the Clerk of North Fork, Missionary Baptist Church notify the church of this place that Bro. Wm. St. John and wife was Received into that church Oct. 1888 by letter granted them by this church. By motion and 2nd Bro. J. G. Moore, Bro. J. C. New, Bro. D. B. Vance appointed as a commity to examine the windows of the church, come upon some plan of Repairing the same. Investigate the cost of Repairs and Report to the church next meeting. A motion was made to appoint a commitee to see Sister Sue Talley about Dancing. Bro. Moderator appoint the Deacons of the church as the commity. By motion church vote to cloth the committy with the authority to interview all other disorderly members. Bro. J. D. New made a financial report to the church moved and 2nd.

E. The Society of Friends (Quakers)

The last denomination from whose records we will draw specific examples is the Quakers. Regardless of where you go, you will find consistency in the nature of Friends' records. They do not vary extensively either with the passage of time or from one locality to another. The records are based on what they termed a "Meeting" system. The local congregation that meets weekly is called a *Weekly Meeting*. Each Weekly Meeting group also has a *Preparative Meeting* to conduct the business of the congregation. A *Monthly Meeting* comprises several congregations' Weekly Meetings and is the meeting where most church business is transacted and recorded. There are both men's and women's Monthly Meetings. The Monthly Meeting records are generally considered to have the most family history value.

Several Monthly Meetings make up a *Quarterly Meeting* and several Quarterly Meetings unite to make up a *Yearly Meeting*; some branches of the organization also have *Three-Year Meetings*. These latter three meeting levels are mainly administrative, and their records are less useful to the family researcher.

Thomas W. Marshall, writing in the introduction to Hinshaw's *Encyclopedia of American Quaker Genealogy* (Vol. I), made the following observations about Quaker records. Though it is somewhat lengthy, I include it here and recommend careful study of this material if your ancestors have Quaker connections:

> The records kept by Friends Monthly Meetings during the eighteenth and nineteenth centuries usually consisted of a record of births and deaths, a record of marriage certificates, and minutes covering all proceedings and discussions coming before the monthly sessions of the meeting. As the men and women met separately, two sets of minutes were kept. In some meetings the marriage records were kept in the same book with the birth and death records; in others they were kept in a separate book. The birth and death records are never complete. In some cases whole families are omitted; sometimes the older children of a family are recorded and the younger ones omitted. The percentage of births recorded appears to be considerably higher than that of deaths. In only a few meetings was it the practice to record the birth dates and parentage of the father and mother of a family. Place of birth was not usually recorded, for either parents or children.
>
> None of the earlier meeting records contains a list of the membership. When a monthly meeting was divided to establish a new one, all members of the old meeting who lived within the verge of the new automatically became members of the new meeting without any list of their names being entered in the records of either meeting. A person who became a member in this way, unless he took some active part in the affairs of the meeting, was married, or was complained of for some breach of discipline, might continue in membership until the end of his life without his name ever appearing in the records.
>
> The records of marriage certificates are much more complete than birth and death records. In a few meetings every marriage accomplished in the meeting is fully recorded. Others are nearly complete—with only a few marriages missing. Since the regular procedure in the marriage involved two appearances of the couple before both men's and women's meetings prior to marriage and subsequent reports of the committees appointed to attend the marriage ceremony, there is ample record of each marriage in the minutes even though recording of the marriage certificate may have been overlooked. The record in the minutes, however, does not give the names of the parents of the persons married nor the exact date of the marriage. The report of the committee that the marriage had been accomplished was made in the next succeeding meeting, thus fixing the date within a month.
>
> The minutes of sessions of the monthly meetings cover many subjects. . . . During the periods of migration the minutes relating to certificates of membership received and issued are the most numerous and have the greatest interest. Records of disciplinary action against members for violation of the rules of the Society occupy much space. Members were "dealt with" on a great variety of complaints, including fiddling and dancing, drinking intoxicating liquor to excess, serving in the militia or other armed forces, using profane language, fighting, failure to meet financial obligations, marrying contrary to the order used by Friends, deviation from plainness in apparel or speech, joining another religious society, etc. Unless the offending member expressed sorrow for his misconduct and brought a signed paper condemning the same, he was usually disowned. The number so disowned runs into thou-

sands. Many of them, after a shorter or longer time, produced the necessary paper of condemnation and were reinstated in membership. A minute showing that a person presented a satisfactory paper condemning his misconduct, implies that he was retained or reinstated in membership, as the case might be, whether the fact is specifically stated or not. Often, following the disownment of a member (perhaps many years later) the minutes may record a request for membership coming from a person of the same name, but with no reference to previous membership or disownment. In such cases it is usually impossible to tell whether the two minutes refer to the same person or to two individuals with the same name. A great many of those who were disowned never asked to be reinstated but remained outside the Society for the rest of their lives. The names of these persons never appear in the records again.

When individual members of families removed from one monthly meeting to another they were furnished removal certificates setting forth the fact of their membership in good standing and recommending them to the fellowship of the monthly meeting to which they were removing. In the earlier days these certificates were usually prepared and signed in advance and carried by the members to their new place of abode. Later, it appears to have become more the custom to wait until the new home had been established and then send back a request that the certificate be forwarded. A condition to the granting of a certificate was that the member's "outward affairs" be satisfactorily settled. The certificate usually stated that this had been done. When a certificate was issued to a family the fact was generally recorded in the men's minutes so far as it applied to the husband and sons, and in the women's minutes as it applied to the mother and daughters. The names of children were frequently omitted in the minutes of the issuing meeting but were usually recorded by the receiving meeting. The fact that John Jones and family (men's minutes) and Mary Jones and daughters (women's minutes) were granted certificates to the same meeting on the same day does not guarantee that John and Mary were husband and wife. Such an assumption would be correct in the majority of cases but would sometimes be erroneous. Confirmatory evidence should always be sought.

If a man and woman contemplating marriage were members of different monthly meetings they made their declarations of intention in the meeting of which the woman was a member. The man was required to bring a certificate from his meeting stating that he was a member in good standing and free from marriage engagements with others. This certificate did not transfer his membership to the woman's meeting, but only made it possible for him to marry there. After marriage, the wife usually obtained a certificate, issued in her married name, transferring her membership to her husband's meeting.

Marriage contrary to the Friends' order, variously referred to in the minutes as "marriage by a priest," "outgoing in marriage," "marriage contrary to good order," "marriage out of unity," "marriage contrary to discipline," etc., and spoken of in every day speech as "marriage out of the meeting," was the cause of more complaints and disownments than any other single offense. . . . Unfortunately the minutes rarely give the name of the person to whom the offending member was married. The record relating to a woman usually refers to her as Mary Jones, formerly Brown, thus giving a clue which is not available in the case of a man. In a large percentage of cases of marriage contrary to Friends' order, only one of the parties was a member. When both parties to a marriage engagement were members in good standing, there was usually no reason why they might not apply to the meeting, and receive permission to marry under its authority, but there were some exceptions. Marriage between first cousins or others of close relationship was forbidden by the rules of the Society. Parental objection may have been a bar to a marriage in meeting in some cases. In other cases the couple married out of meeting for no other reason than to accomplish their purpose more quickly and without the formality which was necessary to a marriage in meeting.[5]

The examples of Friends' records that follow are from the Monthly Men's Meeting of Smithfield, Rhode Island, and from the Monthly Men's Meeting of Hampton, New Hampshire. These are typical entries taken at random from the minutes:

(SMITHFIELD)

—28th of 1st Mo 1802

This meeting Recd a Certificate of Removal from Swanzy Monthly Meeting in favor of Job Chace his wife Sibel and their Children whose names are Earl, Cromwell, Pillena Joanna and Lamira Chase which being read Excepted and ordered Recorded.

—29th of the 4th Month, 1802

This Meeting Recieved a Certificate of Removal from Southkingstown Monthly Meeting in favor of Alice Rathbom which being Read is Excepted

—Monthly Meeting 30th of the 9th Mo 1802

The women inform that they have come to a conclusion to Disown Rhoda Smith with which this Meeting unites.

Smithfield preparitive Meeting informed this that Reuben Shearman Desires a Marriage Certificate to Uxbridge Monthly Meeting. Chad Smith and William Buffam are appointed to take the necessary care theirin and if nothing appears to hender prepare a Certificate and bring to next Monthly Meeting

—Monthly Meeting 25th of the 11th Mo, 1802

Smithfield Preparatives Meeting inform this that Daniel Inman Proposed Laying his Intention of Marriage with Abigail Mowry before this Meeting he producing a Certificate from Uxbridge Monthly Meeting. And they appeared in this Meeting and Declaired their Intentions accordingly and were Directed to next Monthly Meeting for an answer.

—Monthly Meeting 30th of the 12th Mo, 1802

Smithfield preparitive Meetg informed this Meetg that Elisha Shearman was in the practice of Keeping Company with one not a Member of our Society in order for Marriage Whereupon Rowland Rathborn Joseph Bart-

---

[5] William Wade Hinshaw, ed., "Introduction" to *Encyclopedia of American Quaker Genealogy*, Vol. I, 1936 (Reprint, Baltimore: Genealogical Publishing Co., 1994), ix–xi. (There are seven volumes of Hinshaw's work, in addition to an index volume. The first six volumes were reprinted in the 1990s by Genealogical Publishing Co. and these six volumes are also available from the publisher as e-books. According to *The Source* [edited by Loretto Dennis Szucs and Sandra Hargreaves Luebking], Volume 7 is an abstract of the other volumes as they relate to Indiana meetings. It was prepared by Willard Heiss and published by the Indiana Historical Society in 1972.)

let Seth Kelly and Stephen Aldrich Are appointed with such others as the womens Meetg may appoint to make a visit to the family endeavoring to feel after the mind of Truth theirin and Report their Sence thereon to next Monthly Meetg

Daniel Inman and Abigail Mowry appeared in this Meetg and Continued their intentions of Marriage and Recvd and Answer accordingly and Zaccheus Southwick and Daniel Smith are Appointed to have the Necessary Care theirof according to Discipline and Report to next Monthly Meeting.

This Meetg is informed that James Clemence a member theirof is gone to live a few monthes in the verge of Bolton Monthly Meetg and Desires a few lines to Certify his right of Membership, the Clerk is Directed to furnish him with a Coppy of this Minute

—M M at 27th on 1st Mo 1803

The Committee on the Case of Elisha Shearman inform that they have had an opportunity with him and that he is married out of the good order of friends and Does not appear to them to be in Sutable Disposition of mind to Make friends Satisfaction. This Meetg after Solidly Considering the same Do with the unity of the womens Meetg Disown unity with him as a Member and Elisha Kelly and Rowland Rathborn Are appointed to inform him their of his right to appeal Draft a Testimony of his Denial and report to next Monthly Meetg.

The Committee on the Case of Philip Walden request for his Children report that some care has been taken in sd Matter but not being ready to make full report at this time Sd Case is referd under the same friends Care and Directed to Report to next Monthly Meetg.

The Committee to have Care of Daniel Inman and Abigail Mowry Marriage report that according to their observation it was Conducted in an orderly Manner and that the Certificate is Delivered to the Regester.

—M M on 28th of 4th Mo, 1803

The Committy appointed to Prepare a Certificate for Joseph Bartette to uxbridge Mo Meeting in order for marriage presented one wich Being Read with Some alteration is agreed to and Sined by the Clark.

—6th Mo, 30th, 1803

This Meeting appoints Caleb Pain to read the Testamony of Denial aginst Elisha Shearman at a publick Meeting in this Place and lodge the same with the Regester to be recorded and report to our next Monthly Meeting.

—11 Mo, 24th, 1803

The Women presented a Testimony of Denial against Waty Bartlett formerly Buffum which was read and agreed to in this Meeting.

—4th Mo, 26th, 1804

The Committee appointed to prepare a Removal Certificate for Elisha Thornton Jur to Newbedford Monthly Meeting presented one which being read with some Alterations is approved and signed by the Clerk.

—6th Mo, 28th, 1804

Our Beloved Friend Jonathan Wright attended this Meeting with a Certificate from hopewell Monthly Meeting in Virginia dated 6d of 2th Mo, 1804—Expressive of their Unity with him as a Minister, whose Company and Gospel Labors have been exceptable to us.

(HAMPTON)

Joseph Dow deceaced this Life ye 4th of ye 2th Month 1703

Eastor Green Desesed Y^e 24th of Y^e 7th Month 1703

Abraham Green Juner dyed ye 11th of Y^e 3th month 1703

Thomas Lankster & Y^e widow Musey Kiled ye 19th of Y^e 6th mon 1703

Jeams Pearintun Lost at sea Y^e 12 day of the same. 1718: in his 55 year

Hannah Pearintun: daughter of James Pearingtun and Lydia his wife Born the 14th day of Y^e 2 mo: 1708

Lydia Mussey Pearintun Born ye 10th day of ye 9th mo 1671

1737: The: 3 day of the 10th mo Lydia Pearintun dyed in her: 66 year.

A Record of the Births of the Children of Jonathan Hoag and Comfort his Wife as Followeth (viz)—

Peter Hoag: Son of the afore Said Jonathan Hoag and Comfort his wife Born the: 21 Day of ye: 12th month Called February............ 1738/9

Hephsabe born the: 25th of ye 9th mo Called November 1741

Hussa born the 10th day of the seccond month April...................1744

Anna born the 1st day of the Sixth month Called August 1745

Mary born the 10th day of the Sixth month Called August............1747

Abraham born the 25th day of ye 7th mo Called September 1748

Isaac Born y^e: 7th day of the 7th mo; Old Stile Called September 752

1742

Whereas Jonathan Hardy son of John Hardy of Hampton in the Province of New Hampshier in New-England and Lydia his wife And Bathshabe Stanyan daughter of James Stanyan of Hampton in the province afore said And Ann his wife haveing publickly decleared their Intentions of takeing Each other in Marrage before severall monthly meeting of the people Calld Quakers in hampton and Almsburg according to the good order useed amongst them: Whose proseedings there in after deliborate Considiration Thereof: they apearing Clear of all others Relateing to marrage And haveing consent of parents and Relations Conserned were approved by the said Meeting—

Now these are to Certify all Whom it may Consern that for the full Accomplishing of their sd Intentions this fourteenth day of the seventh month called September Anno Domini one Thousand Seven hundred and forty two: They the Said Jonathan Hardy and Bathshaby Stanyan appeared in a Publick assembley of the aforesd People (and others) Meet to gather for that purpose at our meeting house at hampton afor'sd And sd Hardy takeing sd Stanyan by the hand openly Decleared that he took Bathshabe Stanyan to be his Wife Promiseing through the Lords assistance to be unto her a Kind and Loveing husband untill it Shall please God by Death to seperate us: (or to that Effect) and then and their in sd assembly sd Stanyan publickly decleared that she took Jonathan Hardey to be her Husband promiseing through the Lords assistance to be unto him a true and faithfull Wife untill it shall please God by Death to seperate us or words to ye same Import. And the Said Jonathan Hardy and Bathsaby Stanyan as a farther Confirmation thereof did hereunto

Set their hands (she according to the Custom of Marrage assumeing the name of her husband) And wee whose names are hereunto Subscribed being present at their Solomnizeing of Said Marrage and Subscription as afore sd have here unto set our hands as witnesses the day and year above written—

Jonathan Hardy
Bathshaby Hardy

Phebe dow	Philip Rowell	James Stanyan
Elizabeth dow	Jonathan Hoag	Joseph Stanyan
	Winthrop Dow	Merry Newbegin
	Abraham Dow	Rebeckah Hunt
	Nathan Hoag	Jonathan hoag jr
		Comfort Hoag
		Elizabeth Hunt

F. The Roman Catholic Church

The Roman Catholic Church, as a whole, probably has better records than any other Christian church in the United States. Though not perfect, the sacramental records (parish registers) of the church are exceptional in the completeness of the information they contain. By church edict, the records were carefully kept and well preserved—and the requirements were strict.

There have, however, been some challenges associated with research in records of the Roman Catholic Church for the following reasons:

- Until after the second Vatican Council, 1962 to 1965, the records were kept in ecclesiastical Latin. There has been measured change since that time, though not mandated by the council.

- There are few indexes (as is also true of the records of most other churches).

- Most records are still in the parishes and little effort has been made to centralize them.

- Rules relating to access of these records are somewhat restrictive.

Though some dioceses are bringing in records from their parishes for microfilming and/or digitizing, this has not essentially changed the policy of restricted usage. The efforts being made to preserve the records are for purposes of preservation and not for research. It is a hopeful sign, however, that this is the beginning of more centralization activity.

In recent years, as the favorability of family history has increased, many restrictions have been eased, and most of these records have been made reasonably available for research. Many of these records are now being digitized and indexes are being made available on the popular family history websites, especially on FindMyPast. In April 2017, FindMyPast announced that their website had 30 million U.S. Catholic records. That is a significant milestone, and I trust that number will continue to increase.

To provide a better understanding of Catholic Church records and their availability for research—without giving examples of the records—I quote from an article by Lisa Alzo on the Internet site entitled Archives:

Roman Catholic records offer a wealth of information for genealogists. . . . Follow these three "R's" for research success. . . .

1. Registers

Sacramental records are the first types of documents you should look for when researching your Catholic ancestors. Find these records first in local churches, where they are usually kept chronologically in parish registries. The two most valuable are records of the sacraments of baptism and marriage.

Baptismal records include the date of baptism, child's full name, parents' names (and mother's maiden name), names of godparents (sponsors), and signature of the priest. Other notations or information may be included depending on where the church is located.

Marriage or matrimony records list date of marriage, names of the bride (including maiden name) and groom, and names of two witnesses and the priest. Other details on the registry may include: place and date of birth, occupations, parent's names (including mother's maiden name), parents' residences, and fathers' occupations. If you know the name of the church the bride's family attended, try looking there first for a marriage record, since marriages are traditionally held at the parish of the bride.

While each parish typically kept its own records (and most still do), keep in mind that many early churches didn't have a priest-in-residence, and sometimes their record books traveled with them, or were held locally. So you may need to check other parishes.

If the church closed and the area was no longer served, the records probably went to the diocesan [regional] archives. In a bigger city, when a parish closed, the people might go to a neighboring church, and the record books may have been transferred. It's also not out of the realm of possibility for Catholic Church records to be found in the collections of civil archives, universities or historical societies. Furthermore, if your ancestor lived in a town without a Roman Catholic Church, it's possible their records may be housed at a local church of another denomination.

2. Rites and rights

When researching any record group, it helps to learn any laws that govern access and availability. Studying the history of the Roman Catholic Church will give you benchmark dates to understand how the records are kept and why certain procedures are followed.

Besides baptism and marriage, there are five other sacraments in the Catholic Church: First Communion (typically received around the age of seven in the Latin Rite), Confirmation (usually received several years after First Communion), Reconciliation (not always recorded), Holy Orders (received only by priests and deacons), and Anointing of the Sick (formerly known as Extreme Unction or Last Rites). While these records offer less genealogical value than baptismal or marriage registers, it's always worth viewing them to place your ancestor at a particular location or residence on a particular date, or gain clues such as the name of a sponsor for Confirmation (usually a family member or close friend). . . .

Finally, remember Church records are private records—they don't have to let you look at them.

3. Requests

If you know the name and location of your ancestor's parish and it still exists, send a friendly and precise written request for baptism, marriage, or funeral records to the church office. Include details about your ancestor, such as: name, birthdate, marriage date, etc. (If dates are unknown, do your best to give a close estimate.) Be sure to ask for a copy of the actual page of interest within the official parish register and not just a typed or handwritten abstract of the information. A transcribed record may contain errors, and abstracts or church-issued certificates may not include the margin notes. . . .

In most instances parish priests and their staff are helpful, but they are also very busy. Their first priority is serving their current congregation, <u>not</u> researching your genealogy. Understand that your request may be delayed, denied, or even go unanswered. It's also possible that a secretary or other staff member may not be familiar with the early records or have to go searching for them, especially if the records are not indexed by surname or are misfiled. Therefore, try not to request more than one to two records at a time and be very specific. Although most parishes will not typically charge for records, you should be prepared to pay a fee, if necessary. At the very least, it's always helpful to send a donation to cover any research time and copy costs. (In addition, . . . send a self-addressed stamped envelope). . . .

4. Other records

Deaths, burials, and cemetery records. Parishes may have detailed records of deaths and/or burials (in particular if the church has its own cemetery). Such records can include the name of the deceased (including maiden names), age at death, date and place of death or burial, the name of the informant, and whether the sacrament of Extreme Unction was received. The birthplace of the deceased may also be listed (if the deceased was an immigrant, perhaps even his or her town or village of origin).

Marriage banns, dispensations, and validations. Marriage banns were . . . to help aid in uncovering any information that might indicate the couple was not eligible for marriage. Such announcements were made in the parishes of the bride and groom for three consecutive Sundays before the marriage was to take place. Bans only stated an intention to marry, but the marriage itself may never have actually taken place, so always check for the sacramental registry. . . . Marriage validations (also called blessings or rehabilitations) may exist in the event of the discovery of a close-blood relationship between the two spouses where there was no previous ecclesiastical dispensation, or for other various reasons. Find them at the church or diocesan level.

Status of the souls (*Status animarum*). Beginning in the middle 18th century, many Catholic Churches created parish family books (similar to a census). These registers listed dates of marriage, birth of each child, and death or migration of family members. Such lists are usually available only at churches or archives and not typically microfilmed.[6] [Emphasis added.]

---

[6] Lisa Alzo,"The Three R's of Researching Roman Catholic Church Records," Archives, May 14, 2013, http://www.archives.com/experts/alzo-lisa/researching-roman-catholic-church-records. html (accessed November 15, 2016). [Quotation used with author's permission.]

G. Other denominations

I have not pretended to cover the entire spectrum of church records in this discussion. That would be an impossible task within the limits of this work. You are, no doubt, acutely aware of many of my omissions and probably feel that many other religions and sects might be profitably discussed. I have passed over the records of the Eastern Orthodox Church, the Presbyterian Church, the Methodists (including the Methodist Episcopal Church, which became so strong after the Revolutionary War), and the Anabaptists and their offspring (including the Mennonites, the Amish Mennonites, and the Hutterites).

I have also neglected the Reformed Church groups (Calvinist), which came out of the *Netherlands* (the Reformed Church in America and the Christian

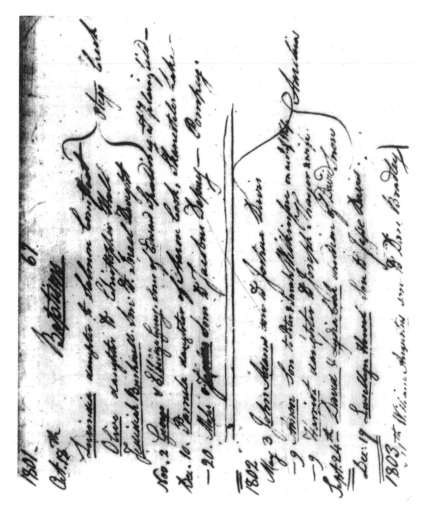

FIGURE 1—PRESBYTERIAN BAPTISM RECORDS

Reformed Church); the *German Palatinate* (the Reformed Church in the United States, which later became the Evangelical and Reformed Church); *Hungary* (the Free Magyar Reformed Church in America); and *France* (the Huguenots). Neither has attention been given to the various splinters from the Lutheran Church that came to America from central Europe. These include the Brethren Churches (also known as Dunkers, Tunkers, and Dunkards) and the Pietist groups (especially the Unity of the Brethren, better known as Moravians). I have also ignored Jewish records and Latter-day Saints (Mormon) records. And on and on . . .

While I regret that further coverage cannot be given, my examples represent an appropriate cross-section of typical American church records and should give you a "feel" for almost any church records you might encounter. It is probably more important to talk about how these records can be located than what they look like. When you find them, you will discover the nature of their contents quickly enough.

III. LOCATING CHURCH RECORDS

A. Problems and solutions

Church records are of no value if you cannot find the ones that fit your specific problems. In America, where church and state are separate and where people with ancestry from all over Europe lived side by side and intermarried, there are two main problems:

- Determining the church with which your ancestor was affiliated
- Locating records of that church in the locality where your ancestor lived

Clues to solve the first problem might come from many sources. Perhaps the family's present affiliation can help you, or the national origin of the family, or even family tradition. You might also find your answer in a will or a deed or on a tombstone. It may be in an obituary. Or there may be a clue in the locality where your ancestor resided—it may have been the settlement of a particular religious denomination—but you must know the locality's history to determine this.

Some people belonged to several churches during their lives. This was quite common on the frontier, because if a town had only one church, that church was usually where the town's residents (especially the Protestants) attended worship services, regardless of former affiliation. In later years obituaries, death certificates, hospital records, etc., contain statements of religious preference.

The second problem may be the more difficult of the two. There are some helps and reference tools to assist in locating church records, but most of these are quite incomplete and may be misleading if you are not aware of their limitations.

Some comprehensive studies of U.S. church records were made in the 1930s and early 1940s as part of the Historical Records Survey under the auspices of the Works Projects Administration (WPA) of the "New Deal." The "Inventories of Church Archives" that resulted from these studies were excellent for the geographic areas and the churches they covered at the time, but much of the information is now outdated. Many of the records have since been moved, and many that were in private hands are now completely untraceable.[7]

We never assume that records of a specific church do not exist just because we have been unable to find them. On the other hand, it would be foolish to say that no church records have ever been lost or destroyed, because, unfortunately, they have. The vestry minutes of the Immanuel Church in Hanover County, Virginia, of which I gave an example earlier in this chapter, show this quite clearly. The biographical sketch (obituary) of George Washington Bassett tells some of the history of the Immanuel Church:

> In the year 1843, soon after his removal, to his estate in Hanover, Mr. Bassett became much concerned at the prostrate condition of the Church in his neighborhood, and the adjoining counties of King William and New Kent. *The parishes had died out and been without rectors or church services for more than half a century.* [Emphasis added.]

Was this a common situation? What about records during that "more than half a century"? What happened to records of the earlier period before the church "died out"? All of these questions should be considered in a study of American church records. The same thing may have happened in hundreds of other churches.

Some people have suggested that many records of the English Church met their doom during the Revolutionary War as part of an act of reprisal against the British, but I am unaware of any specific cases.

B. Finding the records

If you can find early American church records that relate to your ancestors, they are an excellent source of family history evidence. So, let us consider some steps you might take as you begin your search:

- First, consider the possibility that the records are still in the custody of the church where they were kept, if that church still exists.
- Do not be afraid to ask questions—of ministers, chambers of commerce, old-timers, anyone who might know.
- The records of many churches have been published, especially in genealogical and historical periodicals, and are thus available. These are generally not too accessible either from the standpoint of finding the proper periodical or of knowing that an article of value to you even exists. Your best approach is to use the various periodical indexes listed in Chapter 6.

---

[7] See Chapter 13 for a list of the guides to the WPA inventories of church records in the several states.

A few church records are also published in book form (both alone and in conjunction with other records) and you should be aware of this possibility. Go online and look under the locality of interest in your library catalog. A prime example of published church records is Hinshaw's work on the Quakers cited earlier in this chapter.[8] These seven volumes (in eight) contain abstracts of Monthly Meeting records. They are indexed and are quite useful as far as they go. They certainly do not cover all Quaker records, but they are a representative example of published American church records.

In using published church records, as with all published sources, remember that they present secondary evidence and frequently contain copying errors.

- Many church records have been microfilmed or digitized by the churches themselves or by other agencies such as the Family History Library in Salt Lake City. Today many more have been and are now being digitized, and indexes to them are available on the major family history websites. Historical societies often preserve microfilm copies as well as originals; copies are frequently available for sale or you can search the records on-site.

  The Family History Library has microfilmed and/or digitized the records of many churches throughout the U.S., and you may find it worthwhile to check that library's online catalog before making other searches.

- Libraries and historical societies have collected many church records (especially in their local areas and/or for specific denominations) and made them available for searching. One of the big problems is to determine just who has the records. The National Union Catalog of Manuscript Collections and the works produced by the publisher Chadwyck-Healey can help. It is also suggested that the researcher become familiar with resources provided by Chadwyck-Healey to make NUCMC cataloging more available.[9]

C. Some record locations

With no indication of specific congregations or of the actual extent of the records, I offer the following as a partial list of church record depositories in states east of the Mississippi. Further information on the exact nature of the various collections and the addresses of these repositories must be determined from other sources. However, if you are interested in the records of a particular place and/or a specific library or historical society on the following list, it

---

[8] William Wade Hinshaw, ed., *Encyclopedia of American Quaker Genealogy,* 7 vols. (in 8), 1936—. (Vols. 1–6 have been reprinted by Genealogical Publishing Co., Baltimore.) See footnote 3.

[9] For more information, please review the extensive discussion under "Special manuscript collections" in Chapter 12.

is suggested that you enter the name of that place and library/society in your Internet search engine to learn more specifics. In this same way, you can learn about other records in other repositories.

ALABAMA:
1. Samford University, Birmingham—Baptist (Georgia and Alabama)
2. Department of Archives and History, Montgomery— Baptist, Catholic, Church of Christ, Episcopal, Jewish, Methodist, and Presbyterian

ARKANSAS:
1. Hendrix College, Conway—Methodist

CONNECTICUT:
1. Bristol Public Library, Bristol—Congregational (local)
2. Archives of the Episcopal Diocese of Connecticut, Hartford—P.E.
3. Farmington Museum, Farmington—Congregational (local)
4. Connecticut State Library, Hartford—various (more than 700 churches)
5. The Missionary Society of Connecticut, Hartford—Congregational
6. Peck Memorial Library, Kensington—Congregational (local)
7. Wesleyan University Library, Middletown—Methodist

DELAWARE:
1. Delaware Public Archives Commission, Dover—various
2. University of Delaware Library, Newark—Presbyterian, Baptist
3. Historical Society of Delaware, Wilmington—various

DIST. OF COLUM.:
1. American Catholic Historical Association, Catholic University of America—Roman Catholic

GEORGIA:
1. Emory University Library, Atlanta—Methodist

ILLINOIS:
1. Chicago Theological Seminary, Chicago—Congregational
2. Lutheran Church in America, Chicago—Lutheran
3. McCormick Theological Seminary Library, Chicago—Presbyterian (including records formerly at Lane Theological Seminary in Cincinnati, Ohio)
4. Church of the Brethren Historical Library, Elgin—Brethren (Dunkers)
5. Garrett Biblical Institute Library, Evanston—Methodist
6. Knox College Library, Galesburg—Presbyterian, Congregational
7. Bethany Theological Seminary, Oak Brook—Brethren (Dunkers)

INDIANA:
1. Franklin College Library, Franklin—Baptist
2. Archives of the Mennonite Church, Goshen—Mennonite and Amish Mennonite
3. Archives of DePauw University and Indiana Methodism, Greencastle—Methodist
4. Henry County Historical Society Museum, New Castle—Quaker (local)
5. New Harmony Workingmen's Institute Library, New Harmony—Methodist (local)
6. Earlham College Library, Richmond—Quaker
7. Old Catholic Library, Vincennes—Roman Catholic

KENTUCKY:
1. College of the Bible Library, Lexington—Disciples of Christ
2. Margaret I. King Library, U. of Kentucky, Lexington—mainly Baptist and Presbyterian, but also Disciples of Christ and Shaker
3. Filson Club, Louisville—Shaker (Mercer County)
4. Louisville Presbyterian Theological Seminary Library, Louisville—Presbyterian

MAINE:
1. Parson Memorial Library, Alfred—Baptist, Congregational, Methodist (local)
2. Androscoggin Historical Society, Auburn—Baptist (Lewiston)
3. Bangor Public Library, Bangor—various (limited)
4. Hubbard Free Library, Hallowell—Congregational, Unitarian
5. Louis T. Graves Memorial Library, Kennebunkport— ? (local)
6. University of Maine Library, Orono—Baptist (Polermo)
7. Maine Historical Society, Portland—various (scattered locations)
8. Colby College Library, Waterville—local country churches

MARYLAND:
1. Hall of Records, Annapolis—various (more than 400 volumes)
2. Archives of the Archdiocese of Baltimore, Baltimore—Roman Catholic
3. Baltimore Yearly Meeting of Friends (Hicksite), Baltimore—Quaker
4. Baltimore Yearly Meeting of Friends (Orthodox), Baltimore—Quaker (extensive)
5. Maryland Diocesan Library, Baltimore—P.E. (extensive)
6. Maryland Historical Society, Baltimore—P.E. (local)
7. Methodist Historical Society, Baltimore—Methodist

MASSACHUSETTS:
1. Amesbury Public Library, Amesbury—Congregational (local)
2. Amherst College Library, Amherst—Congregational (local)
3. Barre Town Library, Barre— ? (local)

4. Beverly Historical Society, Beverly—Congregational (local)
5. Congregational Library, Boston—Congregational (extensive)
6. Massachusetts Diocesan Library, Boston—P.E.
7. New England Methodist Historical Library, Boston—Methodist (very few registers)
8. Dedham Historical Society, Dedham—Congregational, P.E. (local)
9. Haverhill Public Library, Haverhill—various (nearly 200 volumes)
10. Ipswich Town Hall, Ipswich— ? (local)
11. Marlborough Public Library, Marlborough— ? (local)
12. Universalist Historical Library, Crane Theological School, Tufts University, Medford—Universalist
13. Nantucket Historical Association, Nantucket—Quaker (local)
14. Friends Meeting House, New Bedford—Quaker
15. Andover Newton Theological School Library, Newton Center—Baptist (includes collections formerly in New England Baptist Library)
16. Forbes Library, Northampton—Congregational
17. Northborough Historical Society, Northborough— ? (local)
18. Peabody Historical Society, Peabody—Congregational, Unitarian, Baptist (all local)
19. Petersham Historical Society, Petersham—Church of Christ (local)
20. Berkshire Athenaeum, Pittsfield—Shaker and (mainly) Quaker
21. Essex Institute, Salem—various
22. Shrewsbury Historical Society, Shrewsbury— ? (local)
23. Historical Room, Stockbridge Library, Stockbridge—Congregational (local)
24. Goodnow Public Library, Sudbury— ? (local)
25. Old Colony Historical Society, Taunton—Congregational, Baptist
26. Narragansett Historical Society of Templeton, Templeton— ? (local)
27. Westborough Historical Society, Westborough— ? (local)
28. J. V. Fletcher Library, Westford— ? (local)
29. Winthrop Public Library, Winthrop—Methodist (local)
30. Woburn Public Library, Woburn—Congregational (Woburn and Burlington)
31. Worcester Historical Society, Worcester—Congregational, Baptist, Universalist (local)

MICHIGAN:

1. Michigan Historical Collections, U. of Michigan, Ann Arbor—Presbyterian, Baptist, Congregational, Methodist, et al.
2. Archdiocese of Detroit Chancery, Detroit—Roman Catholic

3. Burton Historical Collection, Detroit Public Library, Detroit—Roman Catholic and various Protestant (extensive)
4. Flushing Township Public Library, Flushing— ? (local)
5. Hope College, Van Zoeren Library, Holland—Dutch Reformed
6. Thompson Home Library, Ithaca—Congregational (local)
7. Jackson City Library, Jackson— ? (Jackson County)
8. Kalamazoo College Library, Kalamazoo—Baptist et al.
9. Port Huron Public Library, Port Huron— ? (local)

MINNESOTA:

1. Pope County Historical Society, Glenwood— ? (local)
2. Blue Earth County Historical Society, Mankato— ? (local)
3. Hennepin County Historical Society, Minneapolis—various
4. Historical Society of the Minnesota Conference of the Methodist Church, Minnesota Methodist Headquarters, Minneapolis—Methodist (extensive)
5. Evangelical Lutheran Church Archives, Luther Theological Seminary, St. Paul—Evangelical Lutheran
6. Historical Committee of the Baptist General Conference, Bethel Theological Seminary, St. Paul—Baptist (extensive)
7. Minnesota Historical Society, St. Paul—P.E. (extensive for state)
8. Weyerhauser Library, Macalester College, St. Paul—Presbyterian
9. Gustavus Adolphus College Library, St. Peter—Evangelical Lutheran

MISSISSIPPI:

1. Mississippi Conference Methodist Historical Society, Millsaps College Library, Jackson—Methodist
2. Mississippi Department of Archives and History, Jackson—Southern Presbyterian

NEW HAMPSHIRE:

1. New Hampshire State Library, Concord—various
2. Dover Public Library, Dover—Baptist (local)
3. University of New Hampshire Library, Durham— ? (local)
4. Dartmouth College Library, Hanover—Congregational
5. New Hampshire Antiquarian Society, Hopkinton—various

NEW JERSEY:

1. Blair Academy Museum, Blairstown—Presbyterian, Methodist
2. Cape May County Historical Association, Cape May—Quaker
3. Monmouth County Historical Association, Freehold—various
4. Drew University Library, Madison—Methodist (including papers formerly held by the Methodist Historical Society of New Jersey)
5. Morris County Historical Society, Morristown—various (local)
6. New Brunswick Theological Seminary Library, New Brunswick—Reformed Church (extensive)
7. Rutgers University Library, New Brunswick—various (on film)

8. Sussex County Historical Society, Newton—various
9. Passaic County Historical Society, Paterson—various
10. Seventh Day Baptist Historical Society, Plainfield—Seventh Day Baptist
11. Princeton Theological Seminary, Princeton—Presbyterian (N.J. Synod)
12. Salem County Historical Society, Salem—Quaker
13. Atlantic County Historical Society, Somers Point—Quaker et al.
14. Somerset County Historical Society, Somerville—various (local)
15. State Library, Archives and History Bureau, Trenton—various

NEW YORK:

1. New York State Library, Albany—various (extensive)
2. Cayuga County Historical Society, Auburn—Congregational
3. Buffalo Historical Society, Buffalo—Baptist, Presbyterian
4. Ontario County Historical Society, Canandaigua—various (local)
5. Cobleskill Public Library, Cobleskill—various (local)
6. New York State Historical Association and Farmers' Museum, Cooperstown—various (Otsego County)
7. Cortland County Historical Society, Cortland—various (local)
8. Green County Historical Society, Coxsackie—various (transcripts)
9. Department of History and Archives, Fonda—Dutch Reformed et al.
10. Pember Library and Museum, Granville—Presbyterian (local)
11. Colgate University Archives, Hamilton—Baptist
12. Hempstead Public Library, Hempstead—various (local)
13. Huntington Historical Society, Huntington—Presbyterian, P.E., et al.
14. Dewitt Historical Society of Tomkins County, Ithaca—Methodist, Presbyterian, et al.
15. Columbia County Historical Society, Kinderhook—various
16. Senate House Museum, Kingston—Dutch Reformed et al.
17. Daughters of the American Revolution Library, LeRoy—various
18. Wayne County Division of Archives and History, Lyons—various (local)
19. Huguenot Historical Society, New Paltz—Huguenot
20. Jean Hasbrouck Memorial House, New Paltz—Dutch Reformed, Methodist
21. Holland Society of New York Library, New York City—Dutch Reformed, Lutheran, French Reformed, German Reformed
22. New York Genealogical and Biographical Society, New York City—various (extensive)
23. New York Historical Society, New York City—P.E. and various
24. New York Yearly Meeting Archives, New York City—Quaker
25. Queens Borough Public Library, New York City—various

26. Society of Friends Records Committee, New York City—Quaker
27. Union Theological Seminary Library, New York City—Presbyterian (defunct parishes in Manhattan)
28. Yivo Institute of Jewish Research, New York City—Jewish
29. Historical Society of Newburgh Bay and the Highland, Newburgh—various (local)
30. Shaker Museum Foundation, Inc., Old Chatham—Shaker
31. Oswego County Historical Society, Oswego—Presbyterian (local)
32. Portville Free Public Library, Portville—Presbyterian (local)
33. Suffolk County Historical Society, Riverhead—various (local)
34. American Baptist Historical Society, Rochester—Baptist (extensive, including Samuel Colgate Baptist Historical Collection formerly at Colgate University)
35. Colgate Rochester Divinity School Library, Rochester—Baptist plus some Dutch Reformed and German Evangelical
36. Saratoga County Historian's Office, Saratoga Springs—various (local)
37. Schenectady County Historical Society, Schenectady—Presbyterian, Dutch Reformed
38. Schoharie County Historical Society, Schoharie—Dutch Reformed, Lutheran, Methodist, Presbyterian
39. Staten Island Historical Society, Staten Island—Dutch Reformed, Methodist
40. Onondaga Historical Association, Syracuse—various (local)
41. Syracuse Public Library, Syracuse—various (transcripts)
42. Syracuse University Library, Syracuse—Methodist (central and western New York)
43. Hancock House, Ticonderoga—Quaker, Presbyterian, Methodist Episcopal, et al.
44. Troy Conference Historical Society, Ticonderoga—Methodist
45. Utica Public Library, Utica—United Presbyterian, Congregational, et al. (of Paris, NY)
46. Waterloo Library and Historical Society, Waterloo—various (local)
47. Westchester County Historical Society, White Plains—Baptist, Congregational, Methodist, Presbyterian

NORTH CAROLINA:
1. Duke University, Durham—Methodist Episcopal (extensive)
2. Guilford College Library, Greensboro—Quaker (extensive)
3. High Point College Library, High Point—Methodist
4. Historical Foundation of the Presbyterian and Reformed Churches, Montreat—Presbyterian, Reformed (extensive)
5. Catawba College Library, Salisbury—German Reformed
6. Moravian Archives, Winston-Salem—Moravian
7. Smith Reynolds Library, Winston-Salem—Baptist

OHIO:

1. Ashland Theological Seminary, Ashland—Brethren (Dunkers)
2. Great Cleveland Methodist Historical Society, Berea—Methodist (especially German Methodist)
3. Mennonite Historical Library, Bluffton College, Bluffton—Mennonite, Anabaptist
4. American Jewish Archives, Cincinnati—Jewish
5. Historical and Philosophical Society of Ohio, Cincinnati—various
6. Western Reserve Historical Society, Cleveland—Shakers et al.
7. Ohio Historical Society, Columbus—Quaker, Freewill Baptist, Methodist, Presbyterian, Shaker
8. Historical Society of the Evangelical United Brethren Church, Memorial Library, United Theological Seminary, Dayton—Evangelical United Brethren and predecessors, Methodist
9. Ohio Wesleyan University Library, Delaware—Methodist, Methodist Episcopal
10. Rutherford B. Hayes Library, Fremont—P.E. (local)
11. Oberlin College Library, Oberlin—Congregational (formerly belonged to Ohio Church History Society)
12. Toledo Public Library, Toledo—Presbyterian (local)
13. Otterbein College Library, Westerville—Evangelical United Brethren
14. Public Library of Youngstown and Mahoning County, Youngstown—various (typescript)

PENNSYLVANIA:

1. Lehigh County Historical Society, Allentown— many local churches (extensive)
2. Old Economy, Pennsylvania Historical and Museum Commission, Ambridge—Harmony Society
3. Tioga Point Museum and Historical Society, Athens— Moravian (local)
4. Archives of the Moravian Church, Bethlehem—Moravian
5. Bethlehem Public Library, Bethlehem—various (typescript)
6. Moravian Historical Society, Bethlehem—Moravian
7. Delaware County Historical Society, Chester—various
8. Presbyterian Historical Society of Coatesville, Coatesville— Presbyterian (local)
9. Bucks County Historical Society, Doylestown—various (extensive)
10. Easton Public Library, Easton—various
11. Ephrata Cloister, Ephrata—Seventh-day Baptists
12. Lutheran Historical Society, Gettysburg—Lutheran
13. Lutheran Theological Seminary Library, Gettysburg—Lutheran

14. Friends Historical Association, Haverford College Library, Haverford—Quaker
15. Historical Society of the Evangelical and Reformed Church, Lancaster—Reformed
16. Lancaster County Historical Society, Lancaster—various
17. Landis Library, Lancaster Mennonite Conference Historical Society, Lancaster—Mennonite
18. Philip Schaff Library, Lancaster Reformed Seminary, Lancaster—Reformed
19. Vail Memorial Library, Lincoln University—various
20. Fulton County Historical Society, McConnellsburg—Presbyterian, Reformed (local)
21. Susquehanna County Historical Society, Montrose—various
22. Historical Society of Montgomery County, Norristown—various
23. Schwenkfelder Library, Pennsburg—Schwenkfelder
24. American Catholic Historical Society of Philadelphia, Philadelphia—Roman Catholic
25. American Swedish Historical Museum, Philadelphia—various (mostly Lutheran)
26. Christ Church Library, Philadelphia—P.E.
27. Department of Records, Society of Friends of Philadelphia, Philadelphia—Quaker
28. Genealogical Society of Philadelphia—various
29. Historical Society of Pennsylvania, Philadelphia—Universalist et al.
30. Historical Society of Philadelphia Annual Conference of Methodist Episcopal Church, Philadelphia—Methodist, Methodist Episcopal (extensive)
31. Lutheran Theological Seminary Library, Philadelphia—Lutheran (extensive)
32. Presbyterian Historical Society, Philadelphia—Presbyterian (extensive, including church records from Lyman C. Draper Collection in State Historical Society of Wisconsin)
33. Historical Society of Western Pennsylvania, Pittsburgh—Presbyterian, Reformed
34. Pittsburgh Theological Seminary Library, Pittsburgh—Presbyterian, Reformed
35. Historical Society of Berks County, Reading—various (local)
36. Lackawanna Historical Society, Scranton—various
37. Scranton Public Library, Scranton—Baptist
38. Monroe County Historical Society, Stroudsburg—various (local)
39. Northumberland County Historical Society, Sunbury—various (local)
40. Friends Historical Library, Swarthmore College, Swarthmore—Quaker

41. Uniontown Public Library, Uniontown—various (local)
42. Washington and Jefferson College Historical Collections, Washington—various
43. Greene County Historical Society, Waynesburg—various
44. Luzerne County Historical Society, Wilkes Barre—Presbyterian (local)

RHODE ISLAND:

1. Newport Historical Society, Newport—Quaker, Congregational, Baptist
2. Moses Brown School, Providence—Quaker
3. Rhode Island Historical Society, Providence—Baptist, Unitarian, Congregational, Quaker

SOUTH CAROLINA:

1. South Carolina Historical Society, Charleston—Congregational, P.E.
2. South Carolina Department of Archives and History, Columbia—P.E.
3. South Caroliniana Library, U. of South Carolina, Columbia—various
4. Wofford College Library, Spartanburg—Methodist

TENNESSEE:

1. McClung Historical Collection, Lawson McGhee Library, Knoxville—Baptist, Methodist, Presbyterian
2. Burrow Library, Memphis—Presbyterian
3. Disciples of Christ Historical Society, Nashville—Disciples of Christ
4. Joint University Libraries, Nashville—various
5. Methodist Publishing House Library, Nashville—Methodist
6. Tennessee Historical Society, Nashville—various
7. Tennessee State Library and Archives, Nashville—various

VERMONT:

1. Vermont Historical Society, Montpelier—Congregational et al.

VIRGINIA:

1. Randolph-Macon College Library, Ashland—Methodist
2. University of Virginia Library, Charlottesville—Baptist, Lutheran, Methodist, Presbyterian
3. Hampden-Sydney College Library, Hampden-Sydney—various (local)
4. Union Theological Seminary Library, Richmond—Presbyterian (extensive)
5. Valentine Museum, Richmond—Quaker (typescript)
6. Virginia Baptist Historical Society, University of Richmond, Richmond—Baptist
7. Virginia Diocesan Library, Richmond—P.E.

8. Virginia Historical Society, Richmond—various
9. Virginia State Library, Richmond—various, including Baptist, Methodist, Quaker, Lutheran, German Reformed, Presbyterian (extensive)[10]

WEST VIRGINIA:

1. West Virginia Department of Archives and History, Charleston— Baptist, Methodist
2. West Virginia Collection, West Virginia University Library, Morgantown—various

WISCONSIN:

1. State Historical Society of Wisconsin, Madison—various
2. Joyce Kilmer Memorial Library, Campion Jesuit High School, Prairie Du Chien—Roman Catholic (local)
3. Racine County Historical Room, Racine—various (local)
4. Waukesha County Historical Society, Waukesha—various (local)

These depositories are few but significant, and it is important that we do all we can to locate those church records we need. After all, if church records can be found, they provide some of the best family history information available for the periods before the start of civil vital records. The examples in this chapter provide ample evidence of that fact. Any effort you expend in pursuit of church records is well used.

A significant source of information relating to American church records is a FamilySearch wiki page entitled "United States, Church Records, 1600s– the Present." It is available on the Internet at *https://familysearch.org/wiki/ en/United_States,_Church_Records,_1600s-the_Present*. Another useful resource, though now somewhat dated and difficult to find, is E. Kay Kirkham's *A Survey of American Church Records*, 4th ed. (Logan, UT: Everton Publishers, 1978).

You should also be aware that some U.S. church records have been digitized and indexed. At the time of this writing, this is a hit-and-miss situation. All I can suggest is that you go to the Internet and see what you can find that might relate to the locality of your research and the denomination(s) to which your ancestors belonged. Use your Internet search engines and make locality searches on the major family history websites for the people and surnames you need to find. If relevant records are there, you should be able to find them. Also, remember to use wildcards and spelling variations when searching these databases.

---

[10] A useful aid for the researcher who will use these records is Jewell T. Clark and Elizabeth Terry Long, comps., *A Guide to Church Records in the Archives Branch, Virginia State Library* (Richmond: Virginia State Library, 1981).

25

Immigrant Ancestor Origins: American Finding Aids

Normally, one of the most difficult problems faced by American family history researchers is the challenge of tracing their ancestors across the ocean to a specific place in the Old World. It does no good, generally, to know they came from England or Germany or Denmark unless you know more precisely where they lived in England or Germany or Denmark. Specific places are essential for continued research.

The purpose of this chapter is two-fold. First, it is to help solve the origin problem. Second, it is to provide assistance in solving related identification problems by using American-generated records. I do not have all the answers for either issue, but I think I can help.

We are primarily concerned with immigration records or ships' passenger lists—the lists that were made when our ancestors (none of whom was native to this country unless they were American Indians) came to this country. The main problems are that there is no complete collection of passenger lists and that some of those available are either difficult to use or have significant information gaps. Though these things are true, much is happening to add to our understanding. The National Archives has an ambitious microfilming program aimed at making the records more accessible.

Because of the rapid pace at which important materials are appearing, it is impossible for any book (including this one) to be completely up to date on the subject. Even the *Guide to Genealogical Research in the National Archives of the United States* (the 3rd edition published in 2000), which I have relied upon heavily, is woefully outdated.

The most comprehensive and up-to-date book on the subject is probably Michael Tepper's *American Passenger Arrival Records: A Guide to the Records of Immigrants Arriving at American Ports by Sail and Steam* (Baltimore: Genealogical Publishing Co., 2009).[1] Tepper's work examines the records in their historical and legal framework and explains what they contain, where they can be found, and how they can be used. It also features expanded coverage of colonial emigration records, finding aids and reference materials, National Archives microfilm programs and publications, current projects, and new developments in immigration research. Though time may quickly date some of the details, Tepper's books will no doubt continue to be the definitive published works on American ships' passenger lists.

We are fortunate that passenger lists are not the only possible source of information about ancestral homes. Court records of various kinds, especially those relating to naturalization and citizenship, are especially significant. Land entry records in the public domain, certificates of vital events, obituaries, probate records, military records, church records, and others (including old letters and family records) may contain the needed information. If so, your problem is less difficult. Consequently, you need to keep your eyes open for this information on foreign origin from the very inception of your research. Because some of these other possibilities were discussed in earlier chapters, we need to look now at immigration records and see just what they are and how they might help.

I. IMMIGRATION RECORDS: THEIR NATURE AND VALUE

There are three types of ships' passenger arrival lists of general interest to us:

A. Customs Passenger Lists
B. Immigration Passenger Lists
C. Customs Lists of Aliens

The National Archives in Washington, DC, has most of the American passenger lists that are in existence. They primarily cover the years between 1820 and 1945. The National Archives also has joined forces with major family history websites (Ancestry, Fold3, and FamilySearch) to make selected microfilm publications and original records available on those websites.

For a listing of these records, with clickable hyperlinks to the websites where the digitized records are located, I refer you to the following National

---

[1] In addition to the work mentioned here, Michael Tepper has compiled several more books relating to passenger lists, all published by Genealogical Publishing Company. See the bibliography later in this chapter.

Archives website: *https://www.archives.gov/digitization/digitized-by-partners*.[2] However, I suggest that you read the following information describing these records before you go to the website.

A. Customs Passenger Lists

An act of Congress in 1819 required the master of every ship coming from a foreign port to file a list of passengers with the district customs collector. These lists are part of Record Group 36 at the National Archives, Records of the U.S. Customs Service. The records included in this category are subdivided into the following:

1. Original lists
2. Copies and abstracts
3. Transcripts from the U.S. State Department
4. Microfilmed card indexes for a few ports prepared in the 1930s by the Works Projects Administration (WPA) and National Youth Administration (NYA), as well as an incomplete supplementary index to seventy-five additional ports and some Mexican and Canadian land border crossing locations

Let us look at each of these:

1. Original Customs Passenger Lists

There are original lists available for the years between 1820 and 1905 (+ or –), but only for the following sixteen ports:

Baltimore, Maryland—1820–91 (with gaps)
Bath, Maine—April 1806[3]
Boston, Massachusetts—1 January 1883–29 July 1891, 1891–99, 1912
Fall River, Massachusetts—June, August, September 1865
Gloucester, Massachusetts—December 1905

---

[2] The page on the National Archives website referred to here is entitled "Microfilm Publications and Original Records Digitized by Our [NARA'S] Digitization Partners." The website contains references and clickable hyperlinks to all the records in the National Archives—and not just immigration records—that have been digitized and indexed by the websites that have partnered with the National Archives—Ancestry.com, Fold3.com, and Familysearch.org. Persons using the research rooms at the National Archives, including the facilities in the Regional National Archives and Presidential libraries, have access to these websites free of charge. You will want to become a frequent visitor to this page as your research moves to different localities and you seek to use many different records. As the site is updated, you will be able to keep abreast of current projects that are relevant to your ancestors and your research objectives. Near the top of the page are instructions on how to utilize this resource most efficiently.

[3] Note that some Cargo Manifests for 1800–1819—and also a few for later periods—have names of passengers who are not on the Customs Passenger Lists. These Cargo Manifests comprise all records in the pre-1820 periods on this list.

Middletown, Connecticut—1822–33

Mobile, Alabama—1820–79 (with gaps)

New Bedford, Massachusetts—1823–99

New Orleans, Louisiana—1820–1902[4]

New York City, New York—1820–17 June 1897, 1840–74, 1875–97 (with gaps)

Newport, Rhode Island—1820–75 (with gaps)

Perth Amboy, New Jersey—1801–37 (with gaps)

Philadelphia, Pennsylvania—1 January 1800–December 1882, 1820–54, 1883–91

Providence, Rhode Island—1820, 1822–31

Provincetown, Massachusetts—1887–89, 1893, 1895–96

Savannah, Georgia—1820–26

These records are in the handwriting of many individuals, and they were not always well cared for, thus are not always easy to read. Because of the neglect they experienced before being transferred to the National Archives, they had to be microfilmed in order to make them available for use. Also, some were not filmed, and others have been transferred by NARA to the Balch Institute for Ethnic Studies, which merged with the Historical Society of Pennsylvania in 2002 (1300 Locust Street, Philadelphia, PA 19107). Also, the Immigration and Naturalization Service (INS) apparently destroyed many of the original immigration records before they were filmed, which is unfortunate.

The Customs Passenger Lists that were filmed by NARA are now available on microfilm in documents relating to the U.S. Customs Service, Records Group (RG) 36. They include the indexes and lists for the following ports:

Atlantic, Gulf, and Great Lakes ports:
   Supplemental index (that excludes New York), 1820–1874, 188 rolls (M334)
   Passenger lists for miscellaneous ports, 1820–1873, 16 rolls (M575)
Baltimore, MD:
   Index (Soundex) to federal passengers, 1820–1891, 171 rolls (M327)
   Index (Soundex) to city passengers, 1833–1866, 22 rolls (M326)
   Passenger lists, 1820–1891, 50 rolls (M255)
   Quarterly abstracts of lists, 1820–1869, 6 rolls (M596)
Boston, MA:
   Index, pre-1848–1891, 282 rolls (M265)
   Passenger lists, 1820–1891, 115 rolls (M277)

---

[4] New Orleans is the only port on this list for which there are original records covering the entire period from 1820 to 1902.

New Orleans, LA:
  Index, 1853–1899, 32 rolls (T527, now with records of the Immigration
    and Naturalization Service, RG85)
  Passenger lists, 1820–1902, 93 rolls (M259)
  Quarterly abstracts of lists, 1820–1875, 17 rolls (M272)

New York, NY:
  Index, 1820–1846, 103 rolls (M261)
  Passenger lists, 1820–1897, 675 rolls (M237)
  Registers of vessels, 1789–1919, 27 rolls (M1066). For an explanation
    of these registers, go to the NARA website, *https://www.archives.*
    gov/research/immigration/customs-records-1820-1891.html.

Philadelphia, PA:
  Index, 1800–1906, 151 rolls (M360)
  Passenger lists, 1800–1882, 108 rolls (M425)[5]

These records were prepared by the ships' masters and generally reveal the
following:

> Name of vessel, name of [vessel] master, port of embarkation, date of arrival,
> port of arrival, and for each passenger, name, age, sex, occupation, country of
> origin, country of intended settlement, and date and circumstances of death
> en route, if applicable.[6]

2. Copies and abstracts of Customs Passenger Lists

The copies and abstracts also cover the period between 1820 and 1905.
Some of these are just the same as the original lists, and in many cases they
can be used to fill gaps in the originals. They were prepared by the customs
collectors and were forwarded (usually quarterly) to the State Department in
compliance with statute.

Many customs officials, in meeting the requirement for generating copies, made abbreviated abstracts of the original lists to forward to Washington.
The National Archives has some of these copies and abstracts of the Customs
Passenger Lists for seventy-one Atlantic Coast and Gulf of Mexico ports, but
there are not records for any port that cover the entire eighty-five-year period.

---

[5] "U.S. Customs Service Records, 1820–ca. 1891, Passenger Lists: Microfilmed Records of
the U.S. Customs Service, 1820–ca. 1891," *National Archives,* August 15, 1916, https://www.
archives.gov/research/immigration/customs-records-1820–1891.html (accessed August 9, 2017).

[6] Anne Bruner Eales and Robert M. Kvasnicka, eds., *Guide to Genealogical Research in the
National Archives of the United States,* 3rd edition (Washington, DC: National Archives and
Records Administration, 2000), 54.

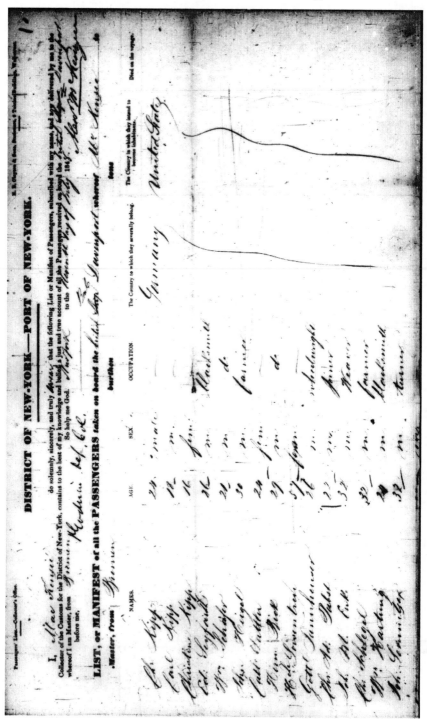

FIGURE 1—CUSTOMS PASSENGER LISTS MANIFEST FOR THE PORT OF NEW YORK

3. Transcripts of Customs Passenger Lists from the U.S. State Department

The transcripts of those lists in the State Department usually included the following:

> [T]he name of the district or port, quarter-year of arrival, and sometimes the port of embarkation. Copies and abstracts contain for each passenger the same information that is found in the original lists, but some information may be abbreviated. For example, some copies and abstracts show only the initials of the given names of passengers.[7]

The National Archives has eight manuscript volumes of these transcripts, which cover only December 31, 1819, to December 31, 1832 (thirteen years). These are volumes 1 through 9, with Volume 2 (September 30, 1820, through September 1821) missing.

The transcripts, which were apparently prepared by the State Department, are arranged by quarter-year of arrival, next by district or port, then by name of vessel, and finally by name of passenger. Below is the information included for each passenger:

> [N]ame, age, sex, occupation, "country to which they belong," "country of which they intend becoming inhabitants," and whether the person died on the voyage. The bulk of these records are for 1820–27. Fewer records were transcribed in 1828–32; and no transcript was made for the period October 1831–September 1832. Less than 30 passengers were recorded for 1819.[8]

The National Archives also has a manuscript volume that relates to a portion of the aforementioned transcripts. It is entitled *Letter from the Secretary of State, with a Transcript of the List of Passengers Who Arrived in the United States from the 1st October, 1819, to the 30th September, 1820* (16th Cong., 2d Sess., S. Doc. 118, Serial 45, Vol. 4).[9] This volume has a typescript index that includes all entries from volume 1 and some entries from the missing volume 2. This volume begins with records that are three months earlier than the other volumes.

State Department transcripts for forty-seven ports are also in the National Archives. These were apparently prepared by the State Department from the abstracts the State Department received from the customs officials at the ports.

You should also be aware of a book entitled *Passengers Who Arrived in the United States, September, 1821–December, 1823.* 1969 (Reprint, Baltimore: Genealogical Publishing Co., 2005).[10] This book, which is indexed, was compiled from the State Department transcripts. It contains more than 15,000 names of passengers—on about 2,000 ships—who disembarked at some forty

---

[7] Ibid., 55.

[8] Ibid., 55.

[9] Ibid., 55.

[10] The U.S. Department of State is listed as the author of this book.

ports. The book is available at the LDS Family History Library, but there is also an indexed database on the Ancestry website (*http://search.ancestry.com/search/db.aspx?dbid=48459*).

4. Microfilmed index cards

The card indexes to the Customs Passenger Lists prepared by the WPA are for the ports of Baltimore (1820–1897), Boston (1848–1891), New York (1820–1846), and Philadelphia (1800–1906). There is also an incomplete index on 188 rolls of microfilm (M334) entitled *Supplemental Index to Passenger Lists of Vessels Arriving at Atlantic and Gulf Coast Ports (Excluding New York) 1820–1874*. This microfilmed index relates to seventy–five ports. There are also indexes to Canadian and Mexican border control sites.

> In general, microfilmed indexes consist of cards that show the following information for each person: name, age, sex, marital status, occupation, nationality, last permanent residence, destination, port of entry, name of vessel, and date of arrival. The indexes may contain all the information sought about the arrival of a passenger, but they are not necessarily complete or infallible. An indexer may have made errors in transcribing information from the lists . . . [and] should be verified by examination of the microfilmed immigration record.
>
> A growing number of published indexes, created by private individuals and organizations, supplement the microfilmed indexes. . . . These can be found in libraries with genealogical collections. They are especially helpful for the period before January 1, 1820, which has few Federal passenger lists, and for the period 1847–June 1896, which has no comprehensive index for arrivals at the port of New York.[11]

5. Observation about these Customs Passenger Lists, copies, transcripts, abstracts, and indexes

You may be disappointed in the Customs Passenger Lists. Their contents, as you will have noted, do not include information on specific places of origin—only country. Though they may be useful for other purposes, they do not solve the problem we set out initially to solve. And even though some of these lists are indexed—and they are the earliest official passenger lists available and the easiest of all available passenger lists to use—they are not as helpful as we wish they were.

B. Immigration Passenger Lists

The earliest Immigration Passenger Lists begin in 1883 and are for the port of Philadelphia. Most other ports have records beginning somewhat later than this, and the records of several ports start in the 1890s. There are also, as you can probably guess, some restrictions on the use of these records. Both the records and their indexes have a "confidential" restriction for fifty years. The in-

---

[11] Eales and Kvasnicka, 53.

dexes—where they exist—are even more restricted because several years are indexed together and cannot be used until all entries on the roll of microfilm are more than fifty years old. An additional problem is that certain indexes are arranged chronologically and thus are alphabetized (by the first letters of the surnames) for each day, after first being arranged by shipping line. You must know quite a bit about the person's arrival to even use the indexes.

Indexes are available for the ports of Boston; New York; Philadelphia; Portland, Maine; and Providence, Rhode Island (among others). All available indexes are listed in Table 3 in *Guide to Genealogical Research in the National Archives of the United States*, by Eales and Kvasnicka.

My research has identified thirty-seven ports for which there are Immigration Passenger Lists in the National Archives—some for only one day. These ports are listed below in alphabetical order by state:

Eagle, Alaska	Dec. 1910–Oct. 1938
San Francisco, California	May 1893–May 31, 1953
Apalachicola, Florida	Sept. 4, 1918
Boca Grande, Florida	Oct. 28, 1912–Oct. 19, 1939
Boynton, Florida	May 9, 1942
Carrabelle, Florida	Nov. 7, 1915
Fernandina, Florida	Aug. 29, 1904–Mar. 12, 1935
Fort Pierce, Florida	May 27, 1939–May 6, 1942
Hobe Sound, Florida	May 4, 1942
Key West, Florida	Nov. 2, 1898–Dec. 14, 1945
Lake Worth, Florida	May 8, 1942
Mayport, Florida	Nov. 16, 1902, Feb.–Apr. 1916
Millville, Florida	Jul. 4, 1916
Panama City, Florida	Nov. 10, 1927–Dec. 12, 1939
Port Inglis, Florida	Mar. 29, 1912–Jan. 2, 1913
Port St. Joe, Florida	Jan. 18, 1923–Mar. 21, 1923
St. Andrews, Florida	Jan. 2, 1916–May 13, 1926
St. Petersburg, Florida	Dec. 15, 1926, Mar. 28, 1936–Mar. 1, 1941
Stuart, Florida	May 6, 1842
Tampa, Florida	Nov. 2, 1898–Dec. 31, 1945
Savannah, Georgia	Jun. 5, 1906–Dec. 6, 1945
New Orleans, Louisiana	Jan. 8, 1903–Dec. 31, 1945
Portland, Maine	Nov. 29, 1893–Mar. 1943
Baltimore, Maryland	Jun. 2, 1892–Jun. 30, 1948, Dec. 1, 1954–May 7, 1957
Boston, Massachusetts	Aug. 1, 1891–Dec. 31, 1943
Gloucester, Massachusetts	Oct. 14, 1906–Mar. 11, 1942
New Bedford, Massachusetts	Jul. 1, 1902–Jul. 1942
Gulfport, Mississippi	Aug. 27, 1904–Aug. 28, 1954
Pascagoula, Mississippi	Jul. 15, 1903–May 21, 1935
New York City, New York	Jun. 16, 1897–Jul. 3, 1957
Philadelphia, Pennsylvania	Jan. 1, 1883–Dec. 31, 1945
Providence, Rhode Island	Jun. 17, 1911–Jan. 1943
Georgetown, South Carolina	Jun. 17, 1923 –Oct. 24, 1939
Galveston, Texas	1893, Jan. 14, 1896–Oct. 35, 1948

St. Albans District, Vermont............................ Jan 11, 1895–Nov. 30, 1954
St. Albans, Vermont..Jul. 9 1929–Jun. 24, 1949
Seattle, Washington ....Jan. 4, 1949–Nov. 29, 1954[12]

It is unfortunate that the Immigration and Naturalization Service destroyed some Immigration Passenger Lists before they were microfilmed, including records for the ports at Port Everglades, Florida; Tampa, Florida; Key West, Florida; Savannah, Georgia; New Orleans, Louisiana; Baltimore, Maryland; Philadelphia, Pennsylvania; San Juan, Puerto Rico; and St. Thomas, Virgin Islands.[13]

The information in Immigration Passenger Lists (or Manifests, as they are frequently called) varies somewhat with time period and with state statute. For Philadelphia, the port with the earliest lists, they contain the following information:

> [N]ame of master, name of vessel, ports of arrival and embarkation, date of arrival, and, for each passenger, name, place of birth, last legal residence, age, occupation, sex, and remarks.[14]

Beginning in 1893, Federal law standardized the form used by all ports to include the following information:

> [N]ame of master, name of vessel, ports of arrival and embarkation, date of arrival, and the following information for each passenger: full name; age; sex; marital status; occupation; nationality; last residence; final destination; whether in the United States before, and, if so, when, and where; and whether going to join a relative, and if so, the relative's name, address, and relationship to the passenger. The format of the immigration passenger lists was revised in 1903 to include race, in 1906 to include a personal description and birthplace, and in 1907 to include the name and address of the nearest relative in the immigrant's home country.[15]

As you can see, these can be very useful records under the right circumstances.

Some of these Immigration Passenger Lists are indexed. One important index, arranged alphabetically by the passengers' names, is called *Index to Passenger Lists of Vessels Arriving at Miscellaneous Ports in Alabama, Florida, Georgia, and South Carolina, 1890–1924*. That index comprises twenty-six rolls of microfilm (T517).

All other indexes are for individual ports. Microfilmed indexes are available for Boston (T790, T521, T617); New York (T519, T612, T621); Philadelphia (T526, T791); Portland and Falmouth, Maine (T524, T793); and Providence, Rhode Island (T518, T792). You need to use the indexes only when the

---

[12] Ibid., Table 3, 66–78.

[13] Ibid., Table 4, 79.

[14] Ibid., 55.

[15] Ibid., 55.

port and the approximate date of arrival are known. If you know the exact date and the port, go directly to the passenger lists.

There is a microfilmed card index for New Orleans from 1900–52 (T618), and Baltimore has indexes from 1897 to July 1952 (T520). There are also indexes for New Bedford, Massachusetts, covering July 1, 1902, to November 18, 1954 (T522).

An 1835 Maryland law required ships' masters to submit lists of passengers arriving in the port of Baltimore to the mayor of the city. This continued until 1866. These "city lists" were microfilmed by NARA along with the Customs Passenger Lists to fill gaps (M255-fifty rolls). Though microfilmed together, the two records are indexed separately. The Soundex index to these "city lists" is on twenty-two rolls of film (M326).

C. Customs Lists of Aliens

Customs Lists of Aliens are perhaps the least significant shipping or passenger lists in the National Archives—not because their information is lacking, but because they relate to only Beverly and Salem, Massachusetts, 1798 and 1800. These records (which cover only about ten ships) were made in compliance with an act of Congress, but the existence of any such records from other ports is currently unknown. There are no indexes because the records are so brief. The records include some or all of the following information:

> [N]ame of vessel, name of master, date of arrival, names of ports of embarkation and arrival, and, for each alien, name, age, birthplace, name of country of emigration, name of country of allegiance, occupation, and personal description.[16]

These brief lists were published in their entirety in *The New England Historical and Genealogical Register* in July 1952.[17]

D. Other immigration records

In addition to the records described above, there are other records relating to immigration located in various depositories around the U.S., including the following:

Massachusetts Archives Division at the State House, 220 Morrissey Boulevard, Boston, MA 02125: Some immigration records, 1848–1891. Holds records that are indexed on 282 rolls of microfilm (M265) at the National Archives.

College of the Holy Cross Library at 1 College Street, Worcester, MA 01610. A collection on Irish immigrants and their descendants in Worcester, 1840–1900.

---

[16] Ibid., 65.

[17] Vol. 106, pp. 203–209.

Burton Historical Collection, Detroit Public Library, 5201 Woodward Avenue, Detroit, MI 48202. Records of the Michigan immigration agency from 1848 to 1880 and papers relating to the Detroit and Mackinac customs offices, 1789–1876.

Holland Museum (formerly the Museum of the Netherlands Pioneer and Historical Foundation), 31 West 10th Street, Holland, MI 49423. Extensive manuscripts relating to the settlement of western Michigan by Dutch immigrants.

Hendrick Hudson Chapter Library, NSDAR, 113 Warren Street, Hudson, NY 12534. Cargo Manifests, 1739–44.

YIVO Institute for Jewish Research, 15 West 16th Street, New York, NY 10011. About 300 autobiographies of Jewish immigrants from Eastern Europe in the 1880s and 1890s, plus some 10,000 letters from European relatives to Jewish immigrants. In 2006, the Yivo Institute published nine of these autobiographies under the title *My Future Is in America: Autobiographies of Eastern European Jewish Immigrants* (edited by Jocelyn Cohen and Daniel Soyer).

Historical Society of Pennsylvania, 1300 Locust Street, Philadelphia, PA 19107. The Gilbert Cope Collection, which includes some ships' registers and other historical and genealogical materials, 1682–1924. This collection has been indexed, and the index is available on microfilm at the Family History Library in Salt Lake City. It was digitized in 2016.

University of Texas Library, 101 E. 21st Street, Austin, TX 78705. Papers relating to German, French, and English immigration to Texas.

The Church of Jesus Christ of Latter-day Saints, Historical Department, 15 East North Temple Street, Salt Lake City, UT 84150. Records of LDS Church members immigrating to the United States from Europe between 1849 and 1932. There are shipping lists from the British Mission (1849–55, 1899–1925), the Scandinavian Mission (1854–96, 1901–20), the Netherlands Mission (1904–14), and the Swedish Mission (1905–32). There is also a card index to these records. Both the records and the index are on microfilm at the LDS Family History Library, 35 North West Temple Street, Salt Lake City, UT 84150.[18]

Some of the records in the above-listed depositories are very good sources while others have little family history value. There are also other useful original immigration records in other places. Use of your Internet search engine can often produce good results.

During the summer of 1984, archivists at the National Records Center in Suitland, Maryland, fortuitously opened some storage crates and discovered extensive passenger lists (at least 10,000 volumes from various ports, mostly

---

[18] For further details, see "LDS Records and Research Aids," Research Papers of The Genealogical Society of The Church of Jesus Christ of Latter-day Saints (Series F, no. 1).

on the West Coast). There were records for the ports of Honolulu, Hawaii; Portland, Oregon; San Diego, California; San Francisco, California; San Pedro, California; Seattle, Washington; El Paso, Texas; Galveston, Texas; Miami, Florida; Newport News, Virginia; Port Huron, Michigan; and Oswego, New York. These records have all been microfilmed and are available at the National Archives. Most have also been digitized and indexed on Ancestry.

Also of interest are the Hamburg Passenger Lists, which cover emigration from Hamburg, Germany, to America between 1850 and 1934 (except during World War I). The 274 rolls of film in this collection are housed currently in the Hamburg State Archive [Staatsarchiv], Bestand Auswandereramt. This record has been digitized and indexed by Ancestry and can be searched on the Ancestry website at *http://search.ancestry.com/search/db.aspx?dbid=1068*. The Family History Library in Salt Lake City also has a copy of the Hamburg Passenger Lists on forty-six rolls of microfilm.

> Usually the list contains the name of each person aboard a ship. It gives the husband's name, plus that of the wife, children and other family members traveling with them. Also given are the ages, occupations or professions and the last place of residence before emigration.[19]

Another German city from which many American immigrants came was Bremen. Bremen also kept passenger lists beginning in 1832. These lists provided the same type of information about emigrants as the Hamburg lists, including their places of origin. Unfortunately, German archivists systematically destroyed all the Bremen records from 1875 to 1908 older than three years because of lack of storage space and, with the exception of 3,017 passenger lists for the years 1920–1939, all other lists were lost in World War II. The surviving records have been indexed and are now available, along with assorted other lists, on a website of the Bremen State Archives (*http://www.passengerlists.de/*). This site shows all of the information found in the records, but there are no digitized images.

There is also a three-volume work for the port of New York covering the years from 1847 to 1867, inclusive. These volumes are called *German Immigrants: Lists of Passengers Bound from Bremen to New York*. They were compiled by Gary J. Zimmerman and Marion Wolfert (Baltimore: Genealogical Publishing Co.) between 1985 and 1988. All three volumes were reprinted in 2006. Zimmerman and Wolfert extracted these records from the Customs Passenger Lists for the port of New York in the National Archives (film M237) where the port of embarkation was identified as Bremen. It has been estimated that these volumes contain about 21 percent of the passengers who sailed from Bremen and arrived in New York during this period.

Another significant project, involving putting ships' passenger lists onto a computer database and publishing them, is going forward at the Temple

---

[19] From the *North Central N.D. Genealogical Record*, as quoted in *Federation of Genealogical Societies Newsletter*, Vol. 9, January/February 1985, 6.

University-Balch Institute Center for Immigration Research in Philadelphia. This project is explained on a Library of Congress website:

> After the National Archives microfilmed many of its passenger manifests in 1978, the originals were loaned to Temple University in Philadelphia for the purpose of compiling statistics on the social, economic, and genetic aspects of immigration, a project directed by Dr. Ira A. Glazier. Subsequently, this effort became a joint project of the newly established Temple-Balch Institute for Ethnic Studies (now the Balch Institute for Ethnic Studies) where storage facilities were available for the thousands of large bound volumes weighing approximately eleven tons. . . .
>
> In transcribing data from the above-mentioned passenger lists into a computer data base, Dr. Glazier acceded to a request that his team include information to benefit those involved in research concerning immigration and immigrant ancestors. The initial effort was a computerized list of Irish passengers published as *The Famine Immigrants: Lists of Irish Immigrants Arriving at the Port of New York, 1846–1851* (Baltimore: Genealogical Pub. Co., 1983–86), currently being expanded to cover English, Welsh, and Scottish immigrants from 1880–1914. The subsequent major undertakings in this project are: *Germans to America: Lists of Passengers Arriving at U.S. Ports, 1850–1893* (Wilmington, Del.: Scholarly Resources, 1988–); *Italians to America, 1880–1899* (Wilmington, Del.: Scholarly Resources, 1992–); and *Migration from the Russian Empire. Lists of Passengers Arriving at the Port of New York, 1875–1914* (Baltimore: Genealogical Pub. Co., 1995–).[20]

The Irish and German records include information on "place of origin," which many of the other records do not. Unfortunately, most of the places given are only countries. By the end of 2013, this project had generated seventy-four published volumes of indexes:

Glazier, Ira A., and Michael Tepper, eds. *The Famine Immigrants: Lists of Irish Immigrants Arriving at the Port of New York, 1846–1851*. 7 vols. Baltimore: Genealogical Publishing Co., 1983–86.

_____, and P. William Filby, eds. *Germans to America: Lists of Passengers Arriving at U.S. Ports, 1850–1897*. Wilmington, DE: Scholarly Resources, Inc., 1988—. There are now sixty-seven volumes in this series.

The Glazier-Filby volumes are available on the MyHeritage website and can be accessed by going to *http://germanroots.com/gtoa.html*. Later projects—that will include Italian, Eastern European, and English emigrants—are promised.

In previous editions of this book, I noted the possible existence of additional passenger lists for the port of New York beyond those kept under federal

---

[20] "Immigrant Arrivals: A Guide to Published Sources," Local History & Genealogy Reference Services. Library of Congress, January 8, 2014, https://loc.gov/rr/genealogy//bib_guid/immigrant/intro.html (accessed November 17, 2016).

statutes and housed in the National Archives. These were records arising from a law passed in 1824 by the New York Legislature entitled "An Act Concerning Passenger Vessels Arriving in the Port of New York." The master of every vessel arriving in the port of New York was required to make a writing within twenty-four hours containing the name, place of birth, last legal settlement, age, and occupation of every passenger.[21] Correspondence dated January 10, 1973, from the Municipal Archives and Records Center of New York reported that they had no knowledge about the existence of these records.[22]

In a renewal of my search for any remnants of these records in late 2016 and early 2017, I had e-mail correspondence with Municipal Archives personnel once again to determine if these records—or any part of them—had perchance been found. As a result of that correspondence, I learned that the Municipal Archives now has "the register of ships arriving in NY dating 1829, 1833, 1838–1849," but that this register "is in pretty bad shape and needs to be examined by conservation before we can provide access to it. It may or may not need . . . reparation." Further correspondence revealed that "the records are open to the public," but, "due to the delicate condition of the volumes, access is provided at the discretion of the archives and conservation departments" and that "the Municipal Archives hopes to eventually digitize these volumes."[23]

Though records for the entire period, beginning in 1824, do not currently exist, there is significant potential value in those that remain. Any request for access to these registers should be made to the New York City Municipal Archives, Department of Records and Information Services, 31 Chambers Street, New York, NY 10007.

E. Published lists

Through the years, there have been numerous books published containing lists of immigrants to America. Many of these lists are very early and, though they certainly do not cover all early immigrations, they can be quite useful. Following is an extensive, but incomplete, list of such books:

Banks, Charles Edward. *The English Ancestry and Homes of the Pilgrim Fathers.* 1929. Reprint, Baltimore: Genealogical Publishing Co., 2006.

————. *The Planters of the Commonwealth.* 1930. Reprint, Baltimore: Genealogical Publishing Co., 2006.

————. *Topographical Dictionary of 2,885 English Emigrants to New England, 1620–1650.* 1937. Reprint, Baltimore: Genealogical Publishing Co., 2002.

---

[21] *City of New York* v. *Miln* [36 U.S. (Pet.) 102].

[22] Letter from Elizabeth M. Eilerman, Assistant Director, dated January 10, 1973.

[23] E-mail correspondence to the author from Rossy Mendez of the NY Municipal Archives dated November 28, 2016, and January 5, 2017.

————. *The Winthrop Fleet of 1630.* 1930. Reprint, Baltimore: Genealogical Publishing Co., 2009.

Bentley, Elizabeth Petty. *Passenger Arrivals at the Port of New York, 1820–1829: From Customs Passenger Lists.* 1 vol. in 2 parts. Baltimore: Genealogical Publishing Co., 1999.

————. *Passenger Arrivals at the Port of New York, 1830–1832.* Baltimore: Genealogical Publishing Co., 2000. This book, together with the one listed immediately above, provide complete coverage of passengers' arrivals at the port of New York from 1820 to 1832. These two works are a direct transcription of the original microfilmed lists in the National Archives (M237).

Bolton, Ethel Stanwood. *Immigrants to New England, 1700–1775.* 1931. Reprint, Baltimore: Genealogical Publishing Co., 2004.

Boyer, Carl, III, comp. and ed. *Ship Passenger Lists: National and New England (1600–1825).* Berwyn Heights, MD: Heritage Books, Inc., 2005.

————. *Ship Passenger Lists: New York and New Jersey (1600–1825).* Berwyn Heights, MD: Heritage Books, Inc., 2007.

————. *Ship Passenger Lists: Pennsylvania and Delaware (1641–1825).* Berwyn Heights, MD: Heritage Books, Inc., 2009.

————. *Ship Passenger Lists: The South (1538–1900).* Newhall, CA: the compiler, 1979.

Brandow, James C. *Omitted Chapters from Hotten's Original Lists of Persons of Quality.* 1983. Baltimore: Genealogical Publishing Co., 2008.

Brock, Robert A. *Huguenot Emigration to Virginia . . .* 1886. Reprint, Baltimore: Genealogical Publishing Co., 2007.

Browning, Charles H. *Welsh Settlement of Pennsylvania.* 1912. Reprint, Baltimore: Genealogical Publishing Co., 2007.

Cameron, Viola Root. *Emigrants from Scotland to America, 1774–1775.* 1930. Reprint, Baltimore: Genealogical Publishing Co., 1999.

Coldham, Peter Wilson. *The Complete Book of Emigrants, 1607–1660.* 1988. Reprint, Baltimore: Genealogical Publishing Co., 2008.

————. *The Complete Book of Emigrants, 1661–1699.* 1990. Reprint, Baltimore: Genealogical Publishing Co., 2002.

————. *The Complete Book of Emigrants in Bondage, 1614–1775.* Baltimore: Genealogical Publishing Co., 1988.

————. *Supplement to The Complete Book of Emigrants in Bondage, 1614–1775.* Baltimore: Genealogical Publishing Co., 1992.

————. *The Bristol Registers of Servants Sent to Foreign Plantations, 1654–1686.* Baltimore: Genealogical Publishing Co., 1988.

Colket, Meredith B., Jr. *Founders of Early American Families: Emigrants from Europe 1607–1657.* Washington, DC: General Court of the Order of Founders and Patriots of America, 1975.

Deiler, J. Hanno. *The Settlement of the German Coast of Louisiana and Creoles of German Descent* (With a New Preface, Chronology, and Index by Jack Belsom). Baltimore: Genealogical Publishing Co., 2009.

DeVille, Winston. *Gulf Coast Colonials: A Compendium of French Families in Early Eighteenth Century Louisiana.* Indexed ed. Baltimore: Clearfield Co., 2007.

_____, trans. *Louisiana Colonials: Soldiers and Vagabonds.* Baltimore: Clearfield Co., 2001.

Dickson, Robert J. *Ulster Emigration to Colonial America, 1718–1785.* Belfast, Ireland: Ulster Historical Foundation, 2010.

Dobson, David. *Directory of Scots Banished to the American Plantations, 1650–1775.* 2nd ed. Baltimore: Genealogical Publishing Co., 2010.

_____. *The Directory of Scottish Settlers in North America, 1625–1825.* 7 vols. 1988–1993. Reprint (Vols. I and II), Baltimore: Genealogical Publishing Co., 1988, 1993; no reprints of Vols. III–VII.

_____. *Dutch Colonists in the Americas, 1615–1815.* 2008. Reprint, Baltimore: Genealogical Publishing Co., 2009.

_____. *The Original Scots Colonists of Early America, 1612–1783.* 1989. Reprint, Baltimore: Genealogical Publishing Co., 2008.

_____. *Ships from Ireland to Early America, 1623–1850.* 3 vols. 1999–2010. Reprint (Vols. 1 and 2), Baltimore: Genealogical Publishing Co., 2008.[24]

Drake, Samuel Gardiner. *Result of Some Researches Among the British Archives for Information Relative to the Founders of New England.* Baltimore: Genealogical Publishing Co., 1969.

Egle, William Henry. *Names of Foreigners Who Took the Oath of Allegiance to the Province and State of Pennsylvania, 1727–1775, with the Foreign Arrivals, 1786–1808.* 1890. Reprint, Baltimore: Genealogical Publishing Co., 2002.

Faust, Albert Bernhardt, and Gaius M. Brumbaugh. *Lists of Swiss Emigrants in the Eighteenth Century to the American Colonies.* 2 vols. 1920, 1925. Reprint, Baltimore: Genealogical Publishing Co., 2007.

Filby, P. William, ed. *Philadelphia Naturalization Records: An Index to Records of Aliens' Declarations of Intention and/or Oaths of Allegiance, 1789–1880, in United States Circuit Court, United States District Court, Supreme Court of Pennsylvania, Quarter Sessions Court, Court of Common Pleas, Philadelphia.* Farmington Hills, MI: Gale Group, 1982.

_____. *Philadelphia Naturalization Records Found in Various Order Books of 92 Local Courts Prior to 1907: An Index to Records of Aliens' Declarations of Intention and/or Oaths of Allegiance, 1789–1880.* Detroit: Gale Research Co., 1982.

---

[24] Note that David Dobson has several other books. Go to the Genealogical Publishing Company Internet page (http://www.genealogical.com) for a complete listing.

Fothergill, Gerald. *Emigrants from England 1773–1776*. 1923. Reprint, Baltimore: Genealogical Publishing Co., 2014.

_____. *A List of Emigrant Ministers to America, 1690–1811*. 1904. Reprint, Charleston, SC: Nabu Press, 2013.

French, Elizabeth. *List of Emigrants to America from Liverpool, 1697–1707*. 1913. Reprint, Baltimore: Genealogical Publishing Co., 1983.

Giuseppi, Montague Spencer. *Naturalizations of Foreign Protestants in the American and West Indian Colonies Pursuant to Statute 13, George II, C. 7*. 1921. Reprint, Baltimore: Genealogical Publishing Co., 1995.

Greer, George Cabell. *Early Virginia Immigrants, 1623–1666*. 1912. Reprint, Baltimore: Genealogical Publishing Co., 2008.

Hackett, J. Dominick, and Charles M. Early. *Passenger Lists from Ireland* (reprinted from the *Journal of the American Irish Historical Society*, vols. 28–29). 1929–31. Reprint, Baltimore: Genealogical Publishing Co., 1998.

Hargreaves-Mawdsley, R. *A Record of the First Settlers in the Colonies of North America, 1654–1685* . . . 1929 and 1931. Reprint, Baltimore: Genealogical Publishing Co., 1967.

Hartmann, Edward George. *Americans from Wales*. Boston: The Christopher Publishing House, 1967.

Hinman, Royal R. *A Catalogue of the Names of the First Puritan Settlers of the Colony of Connecticut; with the Time of Their Arrival in the Colony, and Their Standing in Society, Together with Their Place of Residence, as Far as Can be Discovered by the Records*. 1846. Reprint, Baltimore: Genealogical Publishing Co., 2011.

Hotten, John Camden. *The Original Lists of Persons of Quality: Emigrants, etc., Who Went from Great Britain to the American Plantations, 1600–1700*. 1874. Reprint, Baltimore: Genealogical Publishing Co., 2007.

Jewson, Charles Boardman. *Transcript of Three Registers of Passengers from Great Yarmouth to Holland and New England, 1637–1639*. 1964. Reprint, Baltimore: Genealogical Publishing Co., 2005.

Joseph, Samuel. *Jewish Immigration to the United States from 1881 to 1910*. Charleston, SC: Nabu Press, 2012.

Kaminkow, Marion J., and Jack Kaminkow. *A List of Emigrants from England to America, 1718–1759. Transcribed from . . . Original Records at the Guildhall, London*. Baltimore: Magna Carta Book Co., 1964.

_____. *Original Lists of Emigrants in Bondage from London to the American Colonies, 1719–1744*. 1981. Reprint, Baltimore: Genealogical Publishing Co., 1989.

Knittle, Walter Allen. *Early Eighteenth Century Palatine Emigration*. 1937. Reprint, Baltimore: Genealogical Publishing Co., 2004.

Krebbs, Friedrich. *Emigrants from the Palatinate to the American Colonies in the Eighteenth Century.* Norristown, PA: Pennsylvania German Society, 1953.

Linn, John B., and William H. Egle. *Persons Naturalized in the Province of Pennsylvania (1740–1773)* (Reprinted from *Pennsylvania Archives*, Ser. 2, Vol. II). 1890. Reprint, Baltimore: Genealogical Publishing Co., 2009.

Munroe, J. B. *A List of Alien Passengers Bonded from January 1, 1847, to January 1851.* 1851. Reprint, Baltimore: Genealogical Publishing Co., 2005.

Myers, Albert Cook. *Immigration of the Irish Quakers into Pennsylvania, 1682–1750.* 1902. Reprint, Baltimore: Genealogical Publishing Co., 2009.

Newsome, Albert Ray. *Records of Emigrants from England and Scotland to North Carolina, 1774–1775.* 1934. Raleigh: North Carolina Department of Archives and History, 2007 revision.

Olsson, Nils William. *Swedish Passenger Arrivals in New York, 1820–1850.* Chicago: Swedish Pioneer Historical Society, 1967.

_____. *Swedish Passenger Arrivals in U.S. Ports 1820–1850 (Except New York): With additions and corrections to Swedish passenger arrivals in New York 1820–1850 (Acta Bibliothecae Regiae Stockholmiensis).* Stockholm: Kungliga Biblioteket [National Library of Sweden], 1979.

Putnam, Eben. *Two Early Passenger Lists, 1635–1637.* Baltimore: Genealogical Publishing Co., 1964.

Rasmussen, Louis J. *San Francisco Ship Passenger Lists.* 4 vols. Colma, CA: San Francisco Historic Records, 1965–70. (Part of the *Ship 'n Rail* series, San Francisco Historic Records).

Vol. 1—1850

Vol. 2 —April 1850—November 1851

Vol. 3—November 1851—June 1852

Vol. 4—June 1852—January 1853

Revill, Janie. *A Compilation of the Original Lists of Protestant Immigrants to South Carolina, 1763–1773.* 1939. Reprint, Baltimore: Genealogical Publishing Co., 2008.

Rupp, Israel Daniel. *A Collection of Upwards of Thirty Thousand Names of German, Swiss, Dutch, French and Other Immigrants in Pennsylvania from 1727 to 1776.* 2nd rev. and enl. ed. [with an Index by Ernst Wecken from the Third ed. (1931), and Added Index to Ships]. 1876, 1931. Reprint, Baltimore: Genealogical Publishing Co., 2006.

Schenk, Trudy, Ruth Froelke, and Inga Bork. *Württemberg Emigration Index.* 8 vols. Salt Lake City: Ancestry, Inc., 1986. Note: this work is digitized and indexed on the Ancestry website.

Schlegel, Donald M. *Passengers from Ireland: Lists of Passengers Arriving at American Ports Between 1811 and 1817, Transcribed from* The Shamrock *or* Hibernian Chronicle. 1980. Reprint, Baltimore: Genealogical Publishing Co., 2007.

Scott, Kenneth R., comp. *British Aliens in the United States During the War of 1812.* 1979. Reprint, Baltimore: Genealogical Publishing Co., 1999.

_____. *Early New York Naturalizations: Abstracts of Naturalization Records from Federal, State, and Local Courts, 1792–1840.* 1981. Reprint, Baltimore: Genealogical Publishing Co., 1999.

_____, and Kenn Stryker-Rodda, comps. *Denizations, Naturalizations, and Oaths of Allegiance in Colonial New York.* 1975. Reprint, Baltimore: Genealogical Publishing Co., 2005.

Sheppard, Walter Lee, Jr., ed. *Passengers and Ships Prior to 1684: Reprints of Articles with Corrections, Additions and New Materials by Marion R. Balderston, Hannah Benner Roach, Walter Lee Sheppard, Jr.; Reprints of Related Material by Francis James Dallett, Morgan Bunting, L. Taylor Dickson.* Vol. 1. Philadelphia: Welcome Society of Pennsylvania, 1970. Note: this work is digitized and indexed on the Ancestry website (http://search.ancestry.com/search/db.aspx?dbid=49286).

Sherwood, George. *American Colonists in English Records.* 2 vols. in 1. 1921, 1933. Reprint, Baltimore: Genealogical Publishing Co., 1982.

Simmendinger, Ulrich. *True and Authentic Register of Persons Who in the Year 1709 Journeyed from Germany to America.* Translated by Herman F. Vesper. 1934. Reprint, Baltimore: Genealogical Publishing Co., 1992. This book is widely known as *The Simmendinger Register.*

Skordas, Gust. *The Early Settlers of Maryland: An Index of Names of Immigrants Compiled from Records of Land Patents, 1633–1680, in the Hall of Records, Annapolis, Maryland.* 1968. Reprint, Baltimore: Genealogical Publishing Co., 2009.

Stanard, William G. *Some Emigrants to Virginia: Memoranda in Regard to Several Hundred Emigrants to Virginia During the Colonial Period Whose Parentage is Shown or Former Residence Indicated by Authentic Records.* 2nd ed. 1915. Reprint, Baltimore: Genealogical Publishing Co., 2003.

Stapleton, Ammon. *Memorials of the Huguenots in America, with Special Reference to Their Emigration to Pennsylvania.* 1901. Reprint, Baltimore: Genealogical Publishing Co., 2005.

Strassburger, Ralph Beaver, and William J. Hinke. *Pennsylvania German Pioneers: A Publication of the Original Lists of Arrivals in the Port of Philadelphia from 1727 to 1808.* 2 vols. 1934. Reprint, Baltimore: Genealogical Publishing Co., 2002.

Swierenga, Robert P. *Dutch Immigrants in U.S. Ship Passenger Manifests, 1820–1880: An Alphabetical Listing by Household Heads and Independent Persons.* 2 vols. Lanham, MD: Rowman & Littlefield Publishers, 1983.

Tepper, Michael, ed. *Emigrants to Pennsylvania, 1641–1819: A Consolidation of Ship Passenger Lists from the* Pennsylvania Magazine of History and Biography. 1877–1934. Reprint, Baltimore: Genealogical Publishing Co., 2009.

_____. *Immigrants to the Middle Colonies: A Consolidation of Ship Passenger Lists and Associated Data from the New York Genealogical and Biographical Record, 1879–1970.* Reprint, Baltimore: Genealogical Publishing Co., 1992.

_____. *New World Immigrants: A Consolidation of Ship Passenger Lists and Associated Data from Periodical Literature.* 2 vols. 1988. Reprint, Baltimore: Genealogical Publishing Co., 2008.

_____, ed. *Passenger Arrivals at the Port of Baltimore, 1820–1834, from Customs Passenger Lists.* Transcribed by Elizabeth P. Bentley. 1982. Reprint, Baltimore: Genealogical Publishing Co., 2000.

_____, ed. *Passenger Arrivals at the Port of Philadelphia 1800–1819: The Philadelphia "Baggage Lists."* Transcribed by Elizabeth P. Bentley. 1986. Reprint, Baltimore: Genealogical Publishing Co., 2003.

_____. *Passengers to America: A Consolidation of Ship Passenger Lists from the New England Historical and Genealogical Register, 1847–1961.* Reprint, Baltimore: Genealogical Publishing Co., 2008.

Virkus, Frederick A., ed. *Immigrant Ancestors. A List of 2,500 Immigrants to America Before 1750.* (Excerpted from *The Compendium of American Genealogy*, Vol. VII). 1942. Reprint, Baltimore: Genealogical Publishing Co., 1998.

Yoder, Don, ed. and trans. *Emigrants from Württemberg; the Adolf Gerber Lists.* (Reprinted in the *Pennsylvania German Folklore Society Yearbook*, Vol. X). Allentown, PA: Pennsylvania German Folklore Society, 1945.

_____. *Pennsylvania German Immigrants, 1709–1786: Lists Consolidated from Yearbooks of The Pennsylvania German Folklore Society.* 1984. Reprint, Baltimore: Genealogical Publishing Co., 2006. (Contains two indexes—one to personal names and one to ships).

_____, ed. *Rhineland Emigrants: Lists of German Settlers in Colonial America.* Baltimore: Genealogical Publishing Co., 1998.

The above list of books, though long, is far from complete, and it should not be considered as such; there are many more published immigration sources. Note, also, that information found in many such books is of questionable accuracy (because of its origin) and should be verified before acceptance.

It is exciting to note that these immigration sources have a high priority for digitizing and indexing on the various family history websites.

Of special note to the family history researcher is *A Bibliography of Ship Passenger Lists, 1538–1825*, originally prepared by Harold Lancour and revised by R. J. Wolfe, 3rd ed. (New York: New York Public Library, 1963).

An update of Lancour and Wolfe's work is the 1981 book by P. William Filby entitled *Passenger and Immigration Lists Bibliography 1538–1900*.[25] Filby's work is also a companion to the fifteen-volume work entitled *Passenger and Immigration Lists Index* and its annual supplementary volumes published by Gale Research Company.[26]

F. INS A-Files and C-Files

Since April 1, 1944, the Immigration and Naturalization Service has maintained an individual case file on each immigrant alien, called an A-File. Since April 1, 1956, every A-File has also included records relating to naturalization. Every legal immigrant who arrived since the 1944 date should have records in that file. Today these records are centralized at a National INS Records Center in Washington, DC, where they are filed by Alien Registration Number and indexed by name, date of birth, and place of birth. These records are subject to INS Freedom of Information/Privacy Act Restrictions.[27]

Even earlier than the A-Files, beginning September 27, 1906, until April 30, 1956, the INS maintained what it called C-Files on the immigrants who became naturalized citizens. A C-File on an immigrant contains

> a duplicate copy of naturalization papers and records relating to all U.S. naturalizations dated [during that period], as well as records of renunciations and resumption of citizenship and applications for certificates of derivative citizenship since 1929. These files are maintained on microfilm by the INS in Washington, DC, and are indexed by name, date of birth, and place of birth. C-Files remain subject to INS Freedom of Information/Privacy Act restrictions.[28]

By way of explanation, "derivative citizenship" is citizenship derived from the citizenship of another person. It relates to the citizenship of a child derived from a parent who is a citizen or who is naturalized. The child must be under the age prescribed by the law (usually 18) and must live in the U.S. It includes children adopted from foreign countries. Also, remember that start-

---

[25] P. William Filby, *Passenger and Immigration Lists Bibliography 1538–1900* (Detroit: Gale Research Co., 1981 with 1984 supplement and a 2nd [cumulative] edition in 1988).

[26] P. William Filby and Mary K. Meyer, eds., *Passenger and Immigration Lists Index.* 15 vols. (Detroit: Gale Research Co., 1981 with annual supplements). Note that these index volumes (but not the lists) have been digitized and are on the Ancestry website (http://search.ancestry.com/search/db.aspx?dbid=7486).

[27] Eales and Kvasnicka, 81.

[28] Ibid., 81.

ing on April 2, 1956, all naturalization and citizenship records were filed in the INS A-Files.

G. Ellis Island records

During the sixty-two years between 1892 and 1954, more than 12 million people came through the U.S. immigration facility at the mouth of the Hudson River in New York City. It has been estimated that more than one-third (some say 40 percent) of all Americans can trace their lineage to someone who entered the country through Ellis Island. Because of the shallow water near the island, the ships docked in Manhattan, where the American citizens and first- and second-class passengers were allowed to enter the country after a brief inspection; the steerage passengers were ferried to Ellis Island for further processing.[29] All passengers, however, appear in the records. If your ancestor entered the United States during that period through the port of New York, you would do well to locate him in the Ellis Island records. The process followed at Ellis Island is described as follows:

> Each arriving person faced a "primary inspection" to determine their status, a process which consisted of questioning by an immigration official. . . . The inspector followed defined lines of questioning concerning age, birthplace, amount of money, occupation, and U.S. citizenship or prior U.S. residence, if applicable, to determine whether the person was admissible. If doubt existed about the person's admissibility, the person was referred to a board of special inquiry (BSI). Each board consisted of three members who were appointed by the commissioner of immigration in charge of the local immigration station. . . .
>
> The . . . hearing before a BSI began with the presentation of evidence. The detainee was called before a table or bench to face the seated members of the board, placed under oath, and subjected to questioning by the chairman of the board. The first phase of the interrogation was routine. Basic facts were put into the record: age, birthplace, port of departure for the United States, destination in this country, amount of money in the individual's possession, trade or calling, purpose of migration, and applicable evidence of U.S. citizenship or prior U.S. residency. Witnesses who came to testify . . . were secluded in a separate room . . . [and] were not called to testify until after the detainee had completed their testimony. Usually the board rendered its decision immediately at the end of the hearing. Two out of three board members prevailed. If the decision was to admit, the person was immediately released from detention. If the decision was to deport, the person was kept in detention until deported or until an appeal was completed.[30]

The Ellis Island records are readily accessible. All have been digitized and indexed, and they are online at the Statue of Liberty–Ellis Island website

---

[29] Evan Andrews, "9 Things You May Not Know About Ellis Island," History Stories, November 12, 2014, http://www.history.com/news/9-things-you-may-not-know-about-ellis-island (accessed August 8, 2017).

[30] Eales and Kvasnicka, 82.

(*https://www.libertyellisfoundation.org/passenger*). FamilySearch also has a name index to the lists of 25 million people (not just the immigrants) who went through the port of New York between 1892 and 1924. This index includes clickable hyperlinks to images on the arrival lists on the website.

Everything that has already been said about searching indexes applies here. Some of these records are difficult to read and interpret and were thus subject to indexing errors. You need to be versatile with your spellings—even imaginative—as you seek the records of your ancestors.

I need also to mention Genealogical Publishing Company's *Genealogy at a Glance* publication relating to Ellis Island research.[31] This laminated four-page guide to the Ellis Island records is a significant research aid. There are also other publications relating to Ellis Island research listed in the "Conclusion" section at the end of this chapter.

I also note that there was a fire on June 15, 1897, that destroyed many of the records prior to that date as well as other New York immigration records going back to 1855.

II. LOCATING AND USING IMMIGRATION RECORDS

A. Much useful information

With some family history problems, there is untold value in immigration records. With this in mind, let us review some of the information already given and consider how you can actually locate and use these records.

If your ancestor was an early immigrant, you would certainly not want to overlook the possibility of finding information about him and his origin in one of the available books. If he was a more recent immigrant, the ships' passenger lists may be a worthwhile source to consider—especially the Immigration Passenger Lists where they apply—because of the information they contain about Old World origins. Though the Customs Passenger Lists have informational limitations, they too can be helpful.

Considering that the Customs Passenger Lists give the name, age, sex, and occupation of each immigrant and tell his date of arrival in America—plus the port from which he sailed—they can be useful tools for identifying your ancestor and separating him from all other persons of the same name.

I have already mentioned that the main difficulty in locating people in the Immigration Passenger Lists is the chronological arrangement of the indexes. Generally speaking, these indexes are arranged first by year, then arranged under each year by ship. Under each ship or shipping line, they are arranged, in part, by class of passenger, and then alphabetically by the first letter of the passenger's surname. There are slight variations from one port to another, but all are somewhat difficult to use.

---

[31] Sharon DeBartolo Carmack, *Genealogy at a Glance: Ellis Island Research* (Baltimore: Genealogical Publishing Co., 2011).

There are alphabetical indexes to the Boston port from 1902 to June 30, 1906, and the New York port from June 16, 1897, to June 30, 1902; and the alphabetical card index to the Customs Passenger Lists in the Philadelphia port serves as a partial index to its Immigration Passenger Lists up to 1906. These indexes, located in the National Archives, make the lists easier to use.

Use of the Immigration Passenger Lists poses a challenge. The essence of that challenge is this: It is almost essential to have specific information about a person's immigration before you can find the record of that immigration. You must know the port of entry, and the more specific the date you have, the better off you are. The name of the ship is also very helpful. When you consider that thousands of persons entered the U.S. through some of the larger ports every year, you can appreciate the value of specific information. It is possible to make a general search of passenger lists for a given port, but that approach is not recommended if there is some other way.

There are also records in the National Archives of the names and dates of arrival of the vessels in several ports. These tell the ports from which each ship sailed and, if you know the approximate time, may help you find the name of the ship on which your ancestor arrived. This information on ports of embarkation can save a lot of searching if it is properly used.

B. Our research tactics

As with all records we use in our research, records relating to immigration are not perfect. Because of that lack of perfection, there are certain issues to consider as you plan your research strategy. Errors were made at the time the records were created, and errors were also made when those records were being indexed and/or compiled for publication or for ease of use.

One of the first problems to consider is the proper understanding of names. There may be spelling problems—in both original documents, in compilations, and in indexes. In your search of these records for information relating to your ancestors, you must not only be flexible, but you must also use your imagination to cover relevant possibilities. The spelling issue is compounded when you consider that many immigrants did not speak English, and many of those clerks who recorded names in those records did not speak or understand the languages of the immigrants.

Other issues also require sensitivity as you search these records. It is helpful to know when your ancestor was born (at least an approximate time) to help you distinguish him from other immigrants with the same name. You should know something of his ethnic background and the political history of his country of origin that might be significant in helping you locate the correct record. Also, the more specific you can be about the date of his immigration, the more likely you are to find the correct record. Even when the records are indexed, it is helpful to know the approximate year of immigration. In this regard, remember that the 1900 and 1920 censuses, as noted in Chapter 14, tell the year of immigration for all immigrants.

It is also helpful to know your ancestor's port of arrival. If the port is unknown, it is good to start your research in the records of the ports that have indexes—Baltimore, Boston, New Orleans, Philadelphia, and the miscellaneous Atlantic and Gulf Coast ports—before trying to find him in the records of the port of New York, which has no indexes between 1847 and June of 1896. Also, you should remember that books published for some immigrant groups—such as those who came from specific countries—have indexes that may fit your need.

C. Other helpful resources

Other aids in finding passenger lists are naturalization records, land entry records (especially homestead entries), and passport applications. Naturalization records tell port and date of arrival of the alien in the United States.[32] Homestead entry papers include copies of naturalization proceedings and, of course, show the dates and ports of arrival. They also tell the entryman's place of birth. If a naturalized citizen applied for a passport to travel abroad—perhaps to return to his homeland for a visit—the application papers show his original date and port of arrival in this country.

One of the more useful books published on the subject of locating immigrant ancestors is Neagles' *Locating Your Immigrant Ancestor*.[33] This book discusses the subject and makes helpful suggestions about locating and using records pertaining to those who immigrated to America from other lands. The authors make useful suggestions for those who use these important records.

You should also be aware of three websites with information compiled by Joe Beime on immigration records. One is entitled Finding Passenger Lists & Immigration Records 1820–1940s (*http://germanroots.com/passengers. html*). The second is called Finding Passenger Lists Before 1820: Arrivals at US Ports from Europe (*http://germanroots.com/1820.html*). The third is Emigration and Immigration Records and Resources: Including Ship Passenger Lists and Naturalization Records (*http://germanroots.com/ei.html*).

It is worth your time to visit these websites. All three have links to passenger lists available on the Internet, including those that are digitized and indexed. There is also other significant information to assist in your quest to find your immigrant ancestors, including information about important books, microfilms, and collections.

III. PASSPORT APPLICATIONS

All passport applications filed with the U.S. State Department between 1791 and 1905 are in the National Archives. However, at no time during that period did the law require passports, except during part of the Civil War.

---

[32] See Chapter 22, "Court Records," for more detailed information on naturalization records.

[33] James C. Neagles and Lila Lee Neagles, *Locating Your Immigrant Ancestor: A Guide to Naturalization Records* (Logan, UT: Everton Publishers, 1975).

Many persons secured passports for the protection they afforded while traveling abroad, and this was especially important for immigrants returning to their homelands. The applications from 1810 through 1905 are bound, and there are various card and book indexes covering the period from 1834 to 1905.

The earliest applications were merely letters of request, but other papers often accompanied those letters and were filed with them. The other papers included such documents as expired passports, birth certificates, certificates of citizenship, etc. Regarding record content, the *Guide to Genealogical Research in the National Archives of the United States*, edited by Eales and Kvasnicka, says:

> Passport applications vary in content, information being ordinarily less detailed before the Civil War than afterward. For the period 1791–1905, they usually contain name of applicant, signature, place of residence, age, and personal description; names or number of persons in the family intending to travel; and date of travel. Applications sometimes contain date and place of birth of the applicant, spouse and minor children, if any, accompanying the applicant; and if the applicant was a naturalized citizen, the date and port of arrival in the United States, name of vessel on which the applicant arrived, and where appropriate, the date and court of naturalization.
>
> For the period 1906–1925, the records usually contain name of applicant, signature, and date and place of birth; name, date, and place of birth of spouse or minor children, if any; residence and occupation at time of application; immediate travel plans; physical description; and photograph. The applications are sometimes accompanied by transmittal letters and letters from employers, relatives, and others attesting to the applicant's purpose for travel abroad.[34]

U.S. Passport applications for the years 1795 through 1925 have been digitized and indexed and are on the Ancestry website at *http://search.ancestry. com/search/db.aspx?dbid=1174*.

Passports are a source with value only for those whose ancestor traveled abroad and happened to secure one. However, it was common for immigrants to secure passports when they traveled to their homelands (even when not required by law) because they offered a certain amount of security for the traveler. Many men were in danger of being drafted into military service in their homelands if they went back without a U.S. passport. If your ancestor traveled abroad and secured a passport for his travel, his passport application will be an important document in your research.

IV. CONCLUSION

Properly used, immigration records and passport records can lead to invaluable information about an ancestor's specific places of foreign origin that you may not find in other records. They may also lead to information about

---

[34] Eales and Kvasnicka, 330.

your ancestor after his American arrival. In case his name is common, specific dates and places from these records can help to distinguish him from his contemporaries of the same name.

You need to be aware of the value of these records and, when the occasion is right, to use them wisely. However, you cannot expect them to solve all of your problems.

In addition to all that has been said here, there are some additional publications you may find valuable as you seek to better understand and use those records that relate to immigration:

Bolino, August C. *The Ellis Island Sourcebook.* 2nd ed. Washington, DC: Kensington Historical Press, 1991.

Carmack, Sharon DeBartolo. *Family Tree Guide to Finding Your Ellis Island Ancestors: A Genealogist's Essential Guide to Navigating the Ellis Island Database and Passenger Arrival List.* Cincinnati, OH: Family Tree Books, 2005.

_____. *Genealogy at a Glance: Immigration Research.* Baltimore: Genealogical Publishing Co., 2011.

Colletta, John P. *They Came in Ships: A Guide to Finding Your Immigrant Ancestor's Arrival Record.* 3rd ed. Salt Lake City: Ancestry, 2002.

Wood, Virginia Steele. *Immigrant Arrivals; A Guide to Published Sources.* Rev. ed. 1997. Washington, DC: Library of Congress, 2001 revision. Barbara B. Walsh made those revisions in the 2001 edition under the auspices of the Bibliographic Enrichment Advisory Team (BEAT) of the Library of Congress.

26

Military Records: Colonial Wars and the American Revolution

Much of modern history can be told in wars. Nearly every generation of Americans has known war. From the family history perspective, war is a two-sided coin—it is destructive on the one hand (to human lives, to property, and to records) and it is creative on the other hand (fostering great medical and technical advances, etc., to help people live longer and, from a family history perspective, being the source of many useful records). Thus, in retrospect, we look on past wars with mixed emotions; but as family history researchers, we must be familiar with the diverse effects of war. And, especially, we must be familiar with military records; complete research depends upon it.

I. BACKGROUND AND HISTORY

Even the early colonists in America knew war's sting. From King Philip's War[1] in 1675–76, down to the time of the Revolutionary War with Great Britain, there were few periods of peace. In these earlier periods, the Indians and the French were the main adversaries of the British colonists.

The Revolutionary War, 1775–83, pitted neighbor against neighbor, brother against brother, and father against son as leaders of thirteen of the twenty-two British-American colonies chose to declare their collective independence from the British Crown.

---

[1] This was the first armed conflict between some Native American inhabitants of what is now New England and the English colonists who invaded their land. This rebellion, which resulted in destruction of twelve colonial settlements, was led by the Pokunoket chief, Metacom (the son of Massasoit), who was called "King Philip" by the colonists. Several Native American tribes sided with the colonists.

Following the Revolution, several factors led the United States to declare war against Britain again and ignited another war that lasted for thirty-two months and came to be called the War of 1812. This proved to be a very sad conflict for the Americans because their national capital, Washington, DC, was seized by British troops and burned. This was primarily as payback for U.S. troops burning the city and parliament building in York (now Toronto), the capital of Upper Canada, a year earlier.

Although the War of 1812 was the last war with Britain, the Native Americans—seeing their lands taken over by American settlers as their British ally abandoned them—remained a threat on much of the frontier. Throughout the nineteenth century, various and sundry Indian wars were waged.

In 1846, again mostly as a result of selfish tendencies and the desire for expansion, the U.S. was drawn into war with Mexico. Texas had already been annexed, and American pioneers and settlers had their collective eyes on a great deal more Mexican territory. The Mexican War ended in 1848.

In 1861, as a culmination of many pressures brought to bear by the slavery issue and the secession from the Union of certain Southern states, war was declared—and thus began the most costly war, in terms of human lives and suffering, that America has ever known. The war did not end until 1865, after 364,511 had died and 281,881 more had been wounded. Like the Revolution, this too was a "family affair," as family members fought under opposing flags.

The year 1898 brought war with Spain because of the Cuban insurrection of 1895, and then came the twentieth century with two great world wars and other major military involvements in Korea, Vietnam, the Persian Gulf, and various Middle Eastern countries. These are the highlights in the story of American military activity; for the family history researcher, each war has produced its own records, though many military records created in the twentieth and twenty-first centuries are not yet available for public searching.

II. THE RECORDS

As the term "military records" is used in the next two chapters, it refers to any and all records of all branches of the armed forces—army, navy, air force, marines, coast guard, etc. In this chapter's discussion of the records of the Revolutionary War, there are basically only two types of original source documents that we will consider:

- Service records
- Records of veterans' benefits

These records are important to us because of their significant family history value. And, as we get to Chapter 27, we will add records of draft registration to our discussion. Though they have significance, they are not an item for consideration during any discussion of colonial conflicts or the Revolutionary War.

As you already know, there is little consistency in American family history sources. Many sources are undefinable in terms of specific content, and though we have general ideas about what they contain (or at least what we think they ought to contain), we are never sure what any specific document says until we read it. This phenomenon is just as true of military records as it is of other records—especially those records relating to the early wars.

My only advice here is that you seek out pertinent records and read them—I think you will be pleasantly surprised. Insofar as service records go, you are in a better position to locate information if your military ancestor had an officer's commission, but the enlisted man was, in his later years, more often in a position to receive assistance through veterans' benefits. An excellent guide to those military records located in the National Archives is the book entitled *Guide to Genealogical Research in the National Archives of the United States* (2000), edited by Eales and Kvasnicka, to which frequent references have been made in earlier chapters and which I will lean upon heavily in the next two chapters (even beyond what footnotes might indicate).

As you become familiar with military records, you should be aware that many of the records discussed in this chapter and in Chapter 27 are now on digitized databases and that many of these digitized records have been indexed. The primary Internet location of these military records is the Ancestry-owned website named Fold3 (*https://www.fold3.com/*). The records can be accessed on that site (and in many cases, I will provide URLs that are more specific). There is, however, a subscription fee for use of Fold3, following a seven-day free trial period.

III. COLONIAL WARS

There are no official national records of wars before the Revolution because the United States of America did not exist. The only records that have survived are a few colonial and local militia records—mainly rolls and rosters. These lists are not extensive (nor is the information they contain), but many of the records that exist have been published.

Most of these lists contain only the names of the soldiers and the military organizations in which they served. Their main value is that they give names, dates, and places, allowing you to put people in specific places at specific times—often an important genealogical necessity. In most cases, there were no particular benefits provided for veterans of colonial service, though there were exceptions to this. For example, Governor Dinwiddie and the Council of Virginia offered 200,000 acres of bounty land in the Ohio River Valley to Virginia troops who served in the French and Indian War. Some other colonies did the same, but there are no general records. Any extant records are in the individual states.

A short bibliography of a few published works arising out of the colonial wars follows:

Andrews, Frank DeWitte. *Connecticut Soldiers in the French and Indian War*. Vineland, NJ: The compiler, 1923.

Bockstruck, Lloyd D. *Bounty and Donation Land Grants in British Colonial America*. Baltimore: Genealogical Publishing Co., 2007.

————. *Virginia's Colonial Soldiers*. 1988. Reprint, Baltimore: Genealogical Publishing Co., 2008.

Bodge, George M. *Soldiers in King Philip's War, Being a Critical Account of that War, with a Concise History of the Indian Wars of New England from 1620–1677, Official Lists of the Soldiers of Massachusetts Colony Serving in Philip's War. . .* 3rd ed. 1906. Reprint, Baltimore: Genealogical Publishing Co., 2005.

Buckingham, Thomas. *Roll and Journal of Connecticut Service in Queen Anne's War, 1710–1711*. 1916. Reprint, Charleston, SC: Nabu Press, 2010.

Chapin, Howard Millar. *Rhode Island in the Colonial Wars. A List of Rhode Island Soldiers and Sailors in King George's War, 1740–1748, and A List of Rhode Island Soldiers and Sailors in the Old French & Indian War, 1755–1762*. 2 bks. in 1. 1918 and 1920. Reprint, Baltimore: Genealogical Publishing Co., 1994.

————. *Rhode Island Privateers in King George's War, 1739–1748*. Providence: Rhode Island Historical Society, 1926.

Clark, Murtie J. *Colonial Soldiers of the South, 1732–1774*. 1 vol. in 2. 1983. Reprint, Baltimore: Genealogical Publishing Co., 1999.

Connecticut Historical Society. *Rolls of Connecticut Men in the French and Indian Wars, 1755–1762*. 2 vols. Hartford, CT: The Society, 1903–05. A digitized version of these volumes is available on the FamilySearch website: *https://familysearch.org/search/catalog/684260?availability=Family%20History%20Library*. All information from this source—with a clickable index but no digitized images—is on the Ancestry website: *http://search.ancestry.com/search/db.aspx?dbid=3983*.

DeForest, Louis Effingham (ed.). *Journals and Papers of Seth Pomeroy, Sometime General in the Colonial Service*. Society of Colonial Wars, New York: Society of Colonial Wars in the State of New York at the request of its Committee on Historical Documents (Publ. No. 38), 1926.

Lewis, Virgil A. *Soldiery of West Virginia in the French and Indian Wars; Lord Dunmore's War; the Revolution; the Later Indian Wars . . .* (3rd Biennial Report of Department of Archives and History, 1911.) Reprint, Baltimore: Genealogical Publishing Co., 2006.

New York Historical Society. *Muster Rolls of New York Provincial Troops, 1755–1764*. New York: The Society, 1892. A digitized copy is online at *https://archive.org/details/musterrollsnewy00socigoog*.

Pennsylvania Archives. "Officers and Soldiers in the Service of the Province of Pennsylvania, 1744–1764." *Pennsylvania Archives*, Series 5,

Vol. 3, pp. 419–528. Harrisburg: 1906. It appears that Craig R. Scott, through Heritage Press of Berwyn Heights, MD, republished this work in 2015. It is unknown what enhancements, if any, may have been made.

Rhode Island Society of Colonial Wars. *Nine Muster Rolls of Rhode Island Troops Enlisted During the Old French War, to Which Is Added the Journal of Captain William Rice in the Expedition of 1746* . . . Providence: The Society, 1915. A digitized copy is online at *https://babel. hathitrust.org/cgi/pt?id=loc.ark:/13960/t67375b6r;view=1up;seq=7.*

Robinson, George Frederick and Albert Harrison Hall. *Watertown Soldiers in the Colonial Wars and the American Revolution.* Watertown, MA: Historical Society of Watertown, 1939. A digitized copy is online at *https://catalog.hathitrust.org/Record/010029659.*

Taylor, Philip F. *A Calendar of the Warrants for Land in Kentucky Granted for Service in the French and Indian Wars.* (Excerpted from the *Year Book of the Society of Colonial Wars in Kentucky*, 1917.) Reprint, Baltimore: Genealogical Publishing Co., 2004.

IV. THE REVOLUTIONARY WAR

A. Service records

When the war for American independence began, there was no official United States government and hence very few records were made of the troops who fought—rosters and rolls mainly, as in the colonial confrontations. However, this war was the beginning of U.S. military records, and machinery was set up to make a record of those who served. Though some of these already scant early records have been destroyed by fire, those that remain are still very important.

At the National Archives, there are records that have been abstracted onto 3½" x 8" cards by the Adjutant General's Office. These contain all information from muster rolls (lists of men in a particular military unit), pay rolls, etc., for each individual soldier. Each soldier's cards have been placed in a separate jacket-envelope, which is filed according to whether he served in the Continental Army, in a state organization, or in another branch of the service. These compiled military service records include (1) a name index for the "Continental troops," (2) name indexes for each of the states (with North Carolina, Connecticut, and Georgia being on microfilm), and (3) name indexes for other branches of service.

> Military organizations designated "Continental Troops" were generally state units adopted by the Continental Congress in the first years of the Revolutionary War or [they were] units raised in more than one state. Regular units of the Continental Army raised in only one state are generally listed with that state's military organizations.
>
> The most comprehensive name index is the *General Index to Compiled Military Service Records of Revolutionary War Soldiers* [Sailors, and Members of Army Staff Departments] [*sic*], M860, 58 rolls. This index may refer

the user to more than one jacket-envelope if a soldier served in more than one unit. In addition to the general index, the following state indexes are available: *Index to Compiled Service Records of Volunteer Soldiers Who Served During the Revolutionary War in Organizations from the State of North Carolina*, M257, 2 rolls; *Index to Compiled Service Records of Revolutionary War Soldiers Who Served with the American Army in Connecticut Military Organizations*. M920, 25 rolls; and *Index to Compiled Service Records of Revolutionary War Soldiers Who Served with the American Army in Georgia Military Organizations*, M1051, 1 roll. Additional indexes, which are not microfilmed, are available for soldiers serving in organizations from the states of Delaware, Maryland, Massachusetts, New Hampshire, New Jersey, New York, Pennsylvania, Rhode Island, South Carolina, Vermont, and Virginia.

The original records and copies of records from which the Revolutionary War compiled service records were made are available on microfilm: M246, *Revolutionary War Rolls, 1775–1783*, 138 rolls, and M853, *Numbered Record Books, Concerning Military Operations and Service, Pay and Settlement of Accounts, and Supplies in the War Department Collection of Revolutionary War Records*, 41 rolls. Notations in the lower left corner of the card abstracts frequently indicate the volume number of the original record copied.[2]

There are also some miscellaneous records that, in addition to the various kinds of military service information, have information relating to civilians who performed services, provided supplies, or were mentioned in the records for other reasons. These records are called *Miscellaneous Numbered Records (The Manuscript File) in the War Department Collection of Revolutionary War Records, 1775–1790s*. There are 125 rolls in microfilm publication M859.

> In this varied collection, there are lists of persons on various pension rolls; records removed from pension files and transferred to the War Department; copies of commissions, resignations, enlistment papers, orders, and accounts; and correspondence that includes various lists of individuals. The records relating primarily to military service have been examined, copied, and included in the compiled military service records. [There is also] a name index to persons mentioned [in this record that] has been microfilmed as M847, *Special Index of Numbered Records in the War Department Collection of Revolutionary War Records, 1775–1783*, 39 rolls.[3]

If you have reason to believe that one of your ancestors or a member of his family served in the Revolutionary War, you should carefully read section 5.2.1, "Revolutionary War," of the third edition of the *Guide to Genealogical Research in the National Archives* (2000), edited by Eales and Kvasnicka, beginning on page 128. There are many different kinds of records—orderly books, rosters, oaths of allegiance, receipts, enlistment papers, correspondence, etc.

---

[2] Anne Bruner Eales and Robert M. Kvasnicka, eds., *Guide to Genealogical Research in the National Archives of the United States*, 3rd ed. (Washington, DC: National Archives and Records Administration, 2000), 128, 134.

[3] Ibid., 134.

All of these records are in Record Group 93, War Department Collection of Revolutionary War Records, at the National Archives in Washington as well as in the Regional National Archives.

B. Veterans' benefits

Revolutionary service records are important, but records relating to veterans' benefits for Revolutionary service have more to offer the family history researcher, primarily because most legislation bestowing or making possible such benefits was not passed until many years after the war. Two kinds of benefits were available:

1. Pensions
2. Bounty land

1. Pensions

Pension benefits and the nature of pension records were ably described by Colket and Bridgers in their 1964 guide to genealogical records in the National Archives:

> Pensions were granted by Congress to invalid or disabled veterans; to widows and orphans of men who were killed or died in service; to veterans who served a minimum period of time if they were living at an advanced age; to widows of veterans who served a minimum period of time if the widows were living at an advanced age; and, in some instances, to other heirs. Pensions granted on the basis of death or disability incurred in service are known as death or disability pensions. Pensions granted on the basis of service for a minimum period of time are called service pensions.[4]

There were also some very early pensions granted by the individual states to those who were disabled in the war, many of which were taken over by the federal government beginning in September 1789. In 1792, it became possible for a disabled veteran to apply directly to the federal government for a pension through the U.S. Circuit and District courts.

> All of the contents of all of the files are reproduced on [microfilm publication] M804, *Revolutionary War Pension and Bounty-Land-Warrant Applications Files*, 2,670 rolls . . . An introduction to this microfilm publication is reproduced on each roll . . . [which includes] an excellent explanation of the eligibility requirements of the various resolutions and acts of Congress, 1776–1878, establishing pensions for Revolutionary War service. . . .
>
> A fire in the War Department in 1800 destroyed Revolutionary War pension applications and related papers submitted before that date. Consequently, if a veteran applied for a disability or invalid pension before 1800, the envelope of his file will show his name, the state or organization in which he served, and a file symbol. In place of missing papers, most of the files contain

---

[4] Meredith B. Colket, Jr., and Frank E. Bridgers. *Guide to Genealogical Records in the National Archives* (Washington, DC: The National Archives, 1964), 77.

one or more small cards giving such information as rank, unit, date of enlistment, nature of disability, residence, and amount of pension. The information was transcribed by the Bureau of Pensions from [Class 9 of] *American State Papers, Claims* [pages 58–67, 85–122, 125–128, 135–145, 150–172] (Washington, DC: Gales and Seaton, 1834). This volume contains transcriptions of the eight War Department pension reports based on original applications and submitted to Congress during the period 1792–95. The volume is indexed. The reports themselves are in Records of the U.S. House of Representatives, RG 233, and Records of U.S. Senate RG 46. The 1792 report is in the second volume of a House publication entitled "Reports War Department 1st Cong. 3rd Sess., to 2nd Cong. 2nd Sess." The seven reports of 1794 and 1795 are in a Senate volume entitled *War Office Returns of Claims to Invalid Pensions.* Entries are arranged by date of report, thereunder by state, and thereunder by name of applicant.

Similar reports, 1794–96, were retained by the War Department and are now among the Records of the Office of the Secretary of War, RG 107. They constitute pages 526–612 of a War Department record book, identified on the backstrip as "War Office Letter Book 1791–97." The entries duplicate many entries in the reports submitted to Congress, but some entries are unique. The reports are reproduced as part of M1062, *Correspondence of the War Department Relating to Indian Affairs, Military Pensions, and Fortifications, 1791–1797,* 1 roll.

The 1796 reports were transcribed and printed in "Recently Discovered Records Relating to Revolutionary War Veterans Who Applied for Pensions Under the Act of 1792," *National Genealogical Society Quarterly 46* (March 1958): [pages] 8–13 and (June 1958): [pages] 73–78.[5]

There is also a second microfilm publication that includes up to ten pages (picking the most significant documents) from each file (M805—898 rolls). Many genealogical libraries have these films available. The LDS Family History Library and all of the Regional National Archives have the larger publication.

A book entitled *Pensioners of the United States, 1818,* based on a report dated March 28, 1818, by the War Department and listing all U.S. pensioners (including invalid veterans, widows, and orphans), is also an important source.[6] Some 5,900 pensioners are included.

Notwithstanding the loss of the early pension files, much of the information therein being forever lost, there are extensive records of pensions that were applied for after 1800 under the various acts of Congress. The first service pensions (remember Colket and Bridgers' distinction between disability pensions and service pensions) were granted under an act of March 18, 1818. And the latest service pensions were granted based on an act of February 3, 1853. The qualifications of pensioners became much more liberal during those thirty-five years.

---

[5] Eales and Kvasnicka, 170, 172.

[6] U.S. War Department, *Pensioners of the United States, 1818,* 1818 (Reprint, Baltimore: Genealogical Publishing Co., 2008).

GENERAL SERVICES ADMINISTRATION NATIONAL ARCHIVES AND RECORDS SERVICE	DO NOT WRITE IN THIS SPACE	
ORDER FOR PHOTOCOPIES CONCERNING VETERAN (See reverse for explanation)	RECEIPT NO. 62612	DATE 6-15-68
	SEARCHER	
	FILE DESIGNATION David Hurlbut S 45401 Rev. Sol.	

State of New York / Broome County

On this 9th day of September 1820 personally appeared before Jona Lewis, one of the Judges of Broome Common Pleas David Hurlbut aged 63 years resident in the Town of Lisle in said County who being first duly sworn according to law doth on his oath declare that he served in the revolutionary War as follows — that he enlisted in the Company Commanded by Captain Albert Chapman in Col. Herman Swifts Regiment in the month of August in the year 1777 — and served three years, — Discharged at Peeks Kill, that he made declaration to obtain a pension on the 25th day of April in the year 1818 Number of pension Certificate ___ On I do solemnly swear that I was a resident Citizen of the United States on the 18th day of March 1818 and that I have not since that time by gift sale or in any manner disposed of my property or any part thereof with intent thereby so to diminish it as to bring myself within the provisions of an act of Congress Entitled an act to provide for certain persons engaged in the land and naval service in the Revolutionary War passed on the 18th day of March 1818 And I have not nor has any person in trust for me any property or securities contracts or debts due to me nor have I any income other than what is contained in the Schedule hereunto annexed and by me subscribed

Schedule

One Cow. Two Hogs — one pot, 2 old Kettles — Tea Kettle — old pair of Tongs and Shovel — one Chain and Hooks — two spinning wheels — one Reel five old Chairs — old Chest with drawers — one Table — one old Chest — two wash tubs, 2 pails — three Tubs, 1 Keg — one Skillet — four old meal bags — one old churn — three wooden bowls — one brown Earthen pan. 6 earthen plates, four bowls — one Sugar bowl — four Tea Cups and saucers — Tea Pot cream pot two bottles, pair old Sad Irons — one Pitcher one pair old Steelyards — one old meat barrel eight Gray teeth — one pair of a Plow Irons — one Chain two old axes two old Hoes, two Shares, 1 Crotch — a clo — 1 saw — One old Candlestick one Scythe

Jona Lewis   David Hurlbut

This Deponent further declares, that he is by occupation a farmer but is wholly unable to pursue it or any other business, being only able to mull the house and considered by Physicians to be in a consumption has a wife and 5 Children — the name of his wife Lois, her health not very good yet able the greatest part of the time to do her work in the house aged 44 years. Henry oldest Child living at home aged 14 years Albert aged 13 years Marion aged 8 years Gideon aged 6 years Lovisa aged 3 years — The Children as may be presumed are not able to do but very little towards their support

Jona Lewis,   David Hurlbut

FIGURE 1—VETERAN'S DECLARATION AS PART OF A REVOLUTIONARY WAR PENSION APPLICATION

Perhaps the pension act that took the most significant liberalization steps was the one passed on June 7, 1832. That act made pensions available to all who had served for at least six months, regardless of need. All post-1832 acts also applied to widows of servicemen and veterans as well as to veterans themselves.

At the National Archives, the original pension application papers are in linen-lined envelopes arranged alphabetically by the names of the servicemen/veterans and are completely indexed. The index was first published by the National Genealogical Society in its quarterly magazine between the years 1946 and 1963 (volumes 20, 40, 44, 50). That index has been available in book form[7] for several years and copies are in many libraries. It has also been microfilmed.

2. Bounty land warrants[8]

As the British had done during the French and Indian Wars, the Continental Congress promised free land as an enticement for men to serve in the American Revolution because there was not sufficient money to pay the troops. Some soldiers or—if the soldiers were killed—their heirs took up the land soon after the war (based on an act of 1788) on special reservations set aside for that purpose. Special warrants (bounty land warrants) were issued by the Secretary of War to accomplish this.

Many others took up land under later acts. The last major bounty land act was passed in 1855. It provided 160 acres to anyone who fought in a battle or served for at least fourteen days. The 1855 act applied to all men who had served in any war up to that time and not just to Revolutionary veterans.

Prior to 1830, military land warrants were of three types:

a. Federal warrants for the U.S. Military District of Ohio

b. Virginia warrants (for service in the Virginia State Line) for land in Kentucky

c. Virginia warrants (for service in the Virginia Continental Line) for land in either Kentucky or the Virginia Military District of Ohio

Records of federal bounty land warrants are indexed and are in the National Archives,[9] but that is not the case with the Virginia warrants. An act of the Virginia General Assembly in 1779 established the Virginia Land Office and set up a system for granting bounty land to those who served in the Vir-

---

[7] Frank Johnson Metcalf, Max Ellsworth Hoyt, et al., comps., *Index of Revolutionary War Pension Applications in the National Archives*, rev. ed., NGS Special Publ. No. 40 (Washington, DC: National Genealogical Society, 1966).

[8] In connection with this discussion, you may find it helpful to review the material relating to bounty land warrants in Chapter 19.

[9] More is said later in this chapter about the availability and use of the federal bounty land warrant records.

ginia State Line, the Virginia Continental Line, and the Virginia State Navy. Because the primary purpose of that act was to encourage longer military service, the requirement for such grants was a minimum of three continuous years of military service. Widows and other surviving heirs of deceased servicemen also qualified.

The original papers associated with these Virginia Revolutionary War bounty land warrants are in the Library of Virginia and are included in the Records of the Executive Branch, Office of the Governor (Record Group 3). They are also available on microfilm (twenty-nine rolls) under the record title of "Revolutionary War Bounty Warrants." These files contain all those documents submitted by claimants seeking to prove their qualifications. More information is available on the Library of Virginia website at *http:// www.lva.virginia.gov/public/guides/opac/bountyabout.htm*.

Because all Virginia bounty lands were located in the Virginia Military Districts in what are now the states of Kentucky and Ohio, the records of the surveys and grants are maintained in those states. The Kentucky surveys and grants are in the State Land Office, which is associated with the Secretary of State's office in the state capitol building (700 Capital Avenue, Frankfort, KY 40601). The Ohio surveys and grants are in the Western Reserve Historical Society (10825 East Boulevard, Cleveland, OH 44106).

If the warrantee (the qualifying veteran) died before the process was completed, the record of the surrendered warrant generally provides the names of any heirs who filed their claims, as well as their relationship to the warrantee in each case, their places of residence, and the date the warrant was surrendered.

Significant changes were made in 1830. It became possible, beginning in that year, for federal warrant holders to take up land anywhere in the public domain. Those who had not used their warrants to patent land in the designated reservations could now surrender them or exchange them for scrip certificates (sometimes merely called "scrip"), that allowed them to claim any public land.

The most valuable records relating to bounty land warrants are the papers associated with the applications. However, many bounty land warrant applications filed prior to 1800 are believed to have been destroyed by that same War Department fire that took the early pension applications, but there are records at the National Archives identifying—by name—the 14,757 federal applicants whose papers were destroyed.

All existing federal bounty land warrant applications for those who claimed land based on Revolutionary War service have been interfiled with the Revolutionary War pension application papers at the National Archives and indexed with them in the National Genealogical Society's index mentioned earlier.

> Each file pertains to one or more claims by one or more persons [the veteran, his widow, his children, or other heirs] for pensions or bounty land warrants,

based on the participation of one individual [the veteran] in the Revolution, along with an occasional file relating to claims based on later service.[10]

C. Information in the application files

It is difficult to tell exactly what kind of information you might find in a particular pension or bounty land application file. A file might contain only a single summary card (because of the loss of early records) or the envelope might contain many pages. The information in the complete files varies, but in a typical veteran's bounty land file, you will usually find the following:

1. Name
2. Rank
3. Military unit
4. Period of service
5. Residence
6. Birthplace
7. Date of birth or age at the time of application
8. Property owned (when claims were made on basis of need)[11]

A widow's application usually contains most of the information found in a veteran's file application, plus her name, age, residence, maiden name, marriage date and place, and her husband's death date and place. An application by a child or other heir usually includes most of the information found in a veteran's application, plus the heirs' names, dates and places of their births, their residence, and the date of their mother's death.[12]

In addition, application files often include

> supporting documents such as discharge papers, affidavits and depositions of witnesses, narratives of events during service (to prove that the veteran had served at a particular time even though he might not have documentary evidence), marriage certificates, birth records, . . . pages from family Bibles, and other papers.[13]

Though not all of this information is in every file, there might be other documents, such as affidavits of relatives, in-laws, and neighbors. Some veterans included information that traced all their movements and told of all the places they lived between the time of their service and the time when they filed their applications. And so on. There are many possibilities.

The following is a declaration and power of attorney filed by the heirs of a veteran named Daniel Hurlburt:

---

[10] Eales and Kvasnicka, 170.

[11] Ibid., 169.

[12] Confer Ibid., 170.

[13] Ibid., 170.

State of New Hampshire
County of Coos
 On this Second Day of August AD 1851 Be it known that before me James Washburne Justice of the Peace in and for the County of Coos aforesaid Personally appeared Miles Hurlburt aged 51 years and Betsey Young aged 57 years and Maid oath in due form of Law that they are the Children of Daniel Hurlburt and that there is No widow Living of Daniel Hurlburt who was a Soldier in the revolutionary war and that the Said Daniel Hurlburt Died at Clarksville in the State of New Hampshire on or about the 14 Day of January AD 1829 and that their said Mother Died at Stewartstown New Hampshire on or about the 12 Day of october AD 1849 and that they make this Declaration for the Purpose of receive from the united States any and all money or moneys Back Pay or survey bounties or land or pension that May be Lawfully due them as Children afforesaid and onely Surviving heirs and That Furthermore they hereby Constitute and appoint F E Hassler Washington City D C their tru and Lawful attorney for and in their name to transact and receipt for any Money or Moneys they may be entitled to hereby rectifying and conforming whatsoever their Said attorney legally do in the Premises.

(signed)

Acknowledged Sworn to & Subscribed ⎤   Miles Hubbert
before me the Day and Year afore Said. ⎦   Betsey Yonge
(signed) James Washburn Justice of the Peace

As already noted, a bounty land application file is much like a pension application file in its contents because the same things had to be proven—that service was rendered and that the applicant was entitled to benefits under the law.

D. Using the index

The Index of Revolutionary War Pension Applications in the National Archives prepared by the National Genealogical Society is simple to use. It is arranged alphabetically (with cross-references for variant spellings of surnames). It gives the name of each serviceman; generally the state from which he served; the name of any other claimant (such as a widow), where appropriate; and the number of the pension or bounty land file. The file number may be prefixed with an "S" (indicating that the applicant was a *Survivor* and a pension was granted), an "R" (which means the application was *Rejected*), a "W" (indicating a *Widow's* pension), a "BLWt" (meaning it was a *Bounty Land Warrant* application), or a "BL Rej" (showing that the *Bounty Land* claim was *Rejected*).

There are asterisks (*) by some names in the index to indicate, in each case, that the papers relating to that soldier's application were published in the *National Genealogical Society Quarterly*. The date and page of publication are always given.

The fact that an application was rejected does not mean the applicant was fraudulently seeking a pension for service he never gave. Many applications

O'DONAGHY (or O DONAGHEY), Patrick, N. Y., Agness, W20997

O'DONOHY, Patrick, N. Y., BLWt. 7574. Issued 9/28/1790 to Alexander Robertson, assignee. No papers

O'DORNER (or O DORNEN), Murty, Pa., S40215

ODUM, Seybert, Ga. Agcy., Dis. No papers

O'FERRELL (or O'FARRELL), Dennis, Va., S25072:

OFFICER, James, Pa., S31280

OFFUTT
Jessee, S. C., Obedience, R7769
Nathaniel, S. C., S31887

O'FLAHERTY, John, N. J., BLWt. 8618. Issued 4/20/1792. No papers

O'FLYING (or O FLING, FLING), Patrick, Cont., N. H., War of 1812, S35542, Rejected Bounty Land Claim of 1812. For family history, etc., consult Wid. Ctf. 16785 of Edmund O'Flying, Pvt. U. S. Inf. War of 1812. Also see Claim for bounty land allowed on account of services of Lt. Patrick O'Flying, War of 1812, 23 W. S. Inf. who died Nov. 1, 1815. Wt. 3 for 480 A., Act of 4/14/1816. (No original papers in this claim)

OGDEN
Aaron, N. J., S19013; BLWt. 1610-300-Capt. Issued 6/11/1789. No papers
Barne (or Barney), N. J., S38279, BLWt. 773-200
Benjamin, N. J., S31281
Daniel, N. Y., BLWt. 7563. Issued 7/30/1792. No papers
David, Conn., Sally, W17414
David, N. Y., BLWt. 7581. Issued 7/13/1792. No papers
David, N. Y., Susannah, W24364
Edmond, Conn:, Navy, Sebal, R7777
Eliakim, N. J., BLWt. 8607. Issued 6/20/1789. No papers
Gilbert, N. Y., R7770
James, N. J., Ruth, R7772
Jedediah, N. J., S32419
John, Mass:, Naomi Burnap, former wid., W15618
John, N. Y., BLWt. 7559. Issued 8/26/1790 to Elijah Rose, assignee. No papers
Jonathan, N. Y., S11154
Joseph, Conn., S38277
Joseph, N. J., S11155

OGDEN (continued)
Ludlow, N. J., Comfort, W187
Matthias, N. J., BLWt. 1609-500-Col. Issued 6/11/1789. No papers
Nathaniel, Cont., N. J., BLWt. 1281-100
Nathaniel, N. J., S34454
Noah, N. J., BLWt. 8610. Issued 6/11/1789 to Matthias Denman, assignee. No papers
Obadiah, N. Y., Martha, R7771, BLWt. 45715-160-55
Samuel, N. J., S38273
Stephen, N. Y., Va., S7775
Stephen D., N. J., R7776
Sturges (or Sturgess), Conn., S14049

OGEN, Thomas, Va., BLWt. 12444. Issued 3/1/1794. No papers

OGG, James, R. I., BLWt. 3369. Issued 5/16/1791 to Deborah May, Admx. No papers

OGILBY, George, Pa., BLWt. 10185. Issued 6/25/1794 to Gideon Merkle, assignee. No papers

OGILVIE, Kimbrough, N. C., S14050

OGLE, Benjamin, Va., R7778

OGLESBY
Elisha, Va., S1866
Jesse, Va., Celia, W1987; BLWt. 28525-160-55
Richard, Va. res. of wid. in 1812, Susan, R7779

O'GULLION (see GULLION), John B.

OHARA
(or O HARRO), Francis, Pa., Nancy, BLWt. 233-100
George, N. J., Elizabeth, W5442
John, Va., S25340
John, Md., Susan, W9215
(or OHARRA), Joseph, Pa., Mary, BLWt. 224-100
Patrick, Pa., BLWt. 10184. Issued 4/3/1794 to John Phillips, assignee. No papers

OHL
Henry, Pa., S2030
(or OHE), John, Pa., S22428

OHLEN
Henry G., N. Y., Cathrina, S43100, W19935
Henry G., N. Y., BLWt. 7570. Issued 8/26/1790 to William Carr, assignee. No papers

OHMET, John, Pa., S40218

O'KAIN (or CANE), James, Pa., BLWt. 319-100

FIGURE 2—A PAGE FROM *INDEX OF REVOLUTIONARY WAR PENSION APPLICATIONS,* PREPARED BY THE NATIONAL GENEALOGICAL SOCIETY

were rejected because the veteran was unable to establish sufficient proof of his service. Usually, either discharge papers or the affidavit of a fellow soldier was required. If you have served in the armed services yourself, think how difficult it might be to prove you served if no records of your service were kept. Some other claims were rejected because of insufficient service, remarriage (in the case of a widow), service of a non-military nature, etc.

In several instances, the words "no papers" appear after an applicant's name in the index. This means that the pension application papers have been destroyed, probably by fire, as mentioned earlier.

E. Obtaining copies of the records

The records relating to Revolutionary War service are at the National Archives and Records Administration (NARA), Old Military and Civil Records Branch, Washington, DC. However, it is not necessary to go personally to the National Archives or to a Regional National Archives to check these pension and bounty land files. One alternative is to request copies of papers from these files (on paper, on microfilm, or a digitized copy on a CD) either with an online request or through the mail.

For a prescribed fee (stated on the request form), you can secure a copy of records in the file of any veteran you choose. The required form—NATF Form 85 (see Figure 3)—along with instructions for completing the form, are online at *https://www.archives.gov/veterans/military-service-records/pre-ww-1-records*. If copies of the complete file are not sent to you because of the size of the file, you can order copies of remaining documents by making a specific request. You will be notified of the cost of purchasing these additional copies.

You will be notified when your order is received and will be given a tracking number. Because of the number of requests, it can take up to 90 days to receive your order, so it will pay you to develop a little patience and perhaps work on another project while you wait.

Another alternative, available to many, is to visit a library with the pension and bounty land warrant microfilms. The alphabetical breakdown, film by film, of microfilm publication M804 is described in a 1974 pamphlet entitled "Revolutionary Pension and Bounty-Land-Warrant Application Files: National Archives Microfilm Publications Pamphlet Describing M804." This pamphlet, a copy of which is in pdf format, is on the Internet on the FamilySearch wiki, with the alphabetical listing beginning on page 27. Access is available at *https://familysearch.org/wiki/en/Revolutionary_War_Pension_Records_and_Bounty_Land_Warrants*.

Your best alternative may be to go to the Fold3 website (*https://www.fold3.com/*), a site specializing in military records. On that site, all of these Revolutionary War pension and bounty land warrant application files have been digitized and indexed. Once on the site, click on "Revolutionary." The index is available on both the Ancestry and FamilySearch websites, but you will have to go to Fold3—using the clickable hyperlink—to see the digitized records. Fold3 is a subscription website, but a seven-day free trial is available. The Ancestry site connection is at *http://search.ancestry.com/search/db.aspx?dbid=1995*, and the FamilySearch connection is at *https://familysearch.org/search/collection/1417475*.

Also of some interest may be a three-volume work giving the Family History Library call numbers for all U.S. military records (as of 1985). Note that Volume 1 is the work that will interest you here:

> Deputy, Marilyn, and Pat Barben, comps. *Register of Federal United States Military Records: A Guide to Manuscript Sources Available at the Genealogical Library in Salt Lake City and the National Archives in Washington, D.C.* 3 vols. Bowie, MD.: Heritage Books, 1986.
>
> > Vol. 1—1775–1860
> >
> > Vol. 2 —The Civil War
> >
> > Vol. 3—1866–World War II, and records of various branches of the military

F. Pension payment records

Other possible sources of information about a person who secured a pension for his service during the Revolution are in the records of the Pension Office and those of the Treasury Department, which are now housed in the National Archives. There are a few possibilities.

1. Record of payments to invalid pensioners:

> In addition to pension application files, certain other related records contain material for genealogical research. Documentation of pension payments appears in two record groups. In Records of the Veterans Administration [which is one of the referenced groups], RG15, are Pension Office record books of **payments to invalid pensioners,** 1801–15. . . .
>
> Pension Office records include one volume for payments to invalid pensioners labeled "Revolutionary War and Act of Military Establishment, Invalid Pensioners Payments, March 1801 through September 1815." Microfilmed as M1786, Record *of Invalid Pension Records to Veterans of the Revolutionary War and the Regular Army and Navy, March 1801–September 1815,* 1 roll.
>
> Many of the pensioners were Revolutionary War veterans whose papers were presumably destroyed in the War Department fires of 1800 and 1814. The entries, which record semiannual payments, are arranged by state, thereunder alphabetically by initial letter of surname. An entry shows name and rank of pensioner, state in which payment was made and amount paid in March and September of each year. If the pensioner died or moved to another state during the period of the records, the fact is indicated, and in some cases the date of death is shown.[14] [Emphasis in original.]

2. Final payment vouchers for pensioners paid by agencies in the states of Alabama, Arkansas, California, and some of those paid by agencies in Connecticut were combined with related Revolutionary War pension application files.[15]

---

[14] Ibid., 176.

[15] Ibid., 173.

NATIONAL ARCHIVES TRUST FUND BOARD NATF Form 85 (rev. 07-2017) OMB Control No 3095-0027 Expires 07-31-2020

NATIONAL ARCHIVES ORDER FOR COPIES OF FEDERAL PENSION OR BOUNTY LAND WARRANT APPLICATIONS *(See Instructions page before completing this form)*

SECTION A. 1. INDICATE BELOW THE TYPE OF FILE TO BE SEARCHED *(Check ONE box only)*
If we locate the file you identify below, we will make copies as indicated. There is no charge for an unsuccessful search.

☐ **Full Pension Application File-Civil War, 1860 and Later:** The cost for copies is $80 for the first 100 pages and $.70 per additional page *(see Instructions).*

☐ **Pension Documents Packet:** *(See Instructions.)* The cost for copies is $30.

☐ **Full Pension Application File Pre-Civil War:** The cost for copies is $55.

☐ **Bounty-Land Warrant Application:** The cost for copies is $30.

1. Reference Number:	Reference Number: Enter the date you fill out the form (example – MMDDYY = 012315). Enter the number of the request being submitted in the last two boxes. If you are submitting four forms and this is your second, you would enter 02. A completed reference number example is: 01231502.

F [ ] [ ] [ ] [ ] [ ] [ ] [ ] [ ]
  M   M   D   D   Y   Y   #   #

REQUIRED MINIMUM IDENTIFICATION OF VETERAN - MUST BE COMPLETED OR YOUR ORDER CANNOT BE SERVICED

2. VETERAN *(Give last, first, and middle names)*	3 BRANCH OF SERVICE IN WHICH HE SERVED ☐ ARMY ☐ NAVY ☐ MARINE CORPS

4. STATE FROM WHICH HE SERVED	5. WAR IN WHICH, OR DATES BETWEEN WHICH, HE SERVED	☐ If service was Civil War, UNION SERVICE ONLY. See Instructions.	6. KIND OF SERVICE ☐ VOLUNTEER ☐ REGULAR

PLEASE PROVIDE THE FOLLOWING ADDITIONAL INFORMATION, IF KNOWN

7. UNIT IN WHICH HE SERVED *(Name of regiment or number, company, etc., name of ship*	8. IF SERVICE WAS ARMY, ARM IN WHICH HE SERVED *If other, specify* ☐ INFANTRY ☐ CAVALRY ☐ ARTILLERY	9 RANK ☐ OFFICER ☐ ENLISTED
10. PENSION/BOUNTY LAND FILE NO.	11. IF VETERAN LIVED IN A HOME FOR SOLDIERS, GIVE LOCATION *(City and State)*	12. PLACE(S) VETERAN LIVED AFTER SERVICE
13. DATE OF BIRTH	14. PLACE OF BIRTH *(City, County, State, etc.)*	17. NAME OF WIDOW OR OTHER CLAIMANT
15. DATE OF DEATH	16. PLACE OF DEATH *(City, County, State, etc.)*	

18 Your completed order is available either as a paper reproduction or as a .pdf. Delivery of .pdf files can be done via USPS on CD/DVD or through NARA's electronic transfer system. Check one box below for selection*.

☐ **Paper Copies** ☐ **CD/DVD** ☐ **Electronic Transfer** email address: _____

* If no selection is made, paper copies will be generated; a certified copy cannot be generated of a .pdf
** Download speeds will vary based upon file size and your internet connection. A valid email address is necessary for electronic transfer.

SECTION B. THIS SPACE IS FOR OUR REPLY TO YOU

We were unable to search for the file you requested above. No payment is required. Your request is returned because:

☐ SECTION A.1 IS NOT CHECKED and we are unable to determine which type of file you are requesting.

☐ MORE THAN ONE FILE IS CHECKED IN SECTION A 1. Except for Revolutionary War service, these are two different files and must be searched separately.

☐ REQUIRED MINIMUM IDENTIFICATION OF VETERAN WAS NOT PROVIDED. Please complete blocks 2 (give full name), 3, 4, 5, and 6 and resubmit your order.

☐ MORE THAN ONE VETERAN'S NAME appears in Block 2.

☐ THE FILES YOU REQUESTED ABOVE ARE NOT IN THE CUSTODY OF THE NATIONAL ARCHIVES. There are no bounty land warrant applications for service after 1855. We do not have pensions based on Confederate service. Please see the instruction sheet for this form or the attached leaflets or information sheets.

SECTION C. CREDIT CARD INFORMATION AND YOUR SHIPPING ADDRESS (REQUIRED)

CREDIT CARD TYPE: _____
(see Instructions for credit cards we can accept)

Signature:	Exp. Date:	Card Validation Code (See Instructions):

Day Time Phone (Required):	e-mail Address (Preferred):

	Last Name	First Name, MI			Last Name	First Name, MI
Shipping Address	Street		(check here if shipping address is same as billing address)	**Billing Address**	Street	
	Street				Street	
	City	State	ZIP or Postal Code	Country (if not USA)		City	State	ZIP or Postal Code

FIGURE 3—NATF FORM 85

3. There are twenty-three volumes of pension payments from the records of the Treasury Department that cover 1819 through 1871. These records have been microfilmed as *Ledgers of Payments, 1818–1872, to U.S. Pensioners Under Acts of 1818 Through 1858, from Records of the Office of the Third Auditor of the Treasury* (T718—twenty-three rolls of film). Entries in these volumes are arranged according to the act of Congress under which they were obtained and the pension agency involved. The information necessary to locate an entry in these volumes can be found in the pension application file (i.e., the name of the veteran, the name of the pensioner, act of Congress under which latest payment was made, and the amount of payment if there was more than one pensioner with the same name). There is a typewritten "Key to the Pension Payment Volumes Relating to Revolutionary War Pensioners" at the National Archives that will help guide you to the entry you seek.

With regard to cards prepared from these pension-payment volumes, as well as the payment vouchers, Eales and Kvasnicka explain:

> The name of every Revolutionary War veteran listed in the registers of payments to U.S. pensioners, available on microfilm T718 [see above] . . . was placed on a card along with location of the pension agent's office, act authorizing payment, date of pensioner's death, and date of either the last or final payment. Cards for veterans whose vouchers were located were annotated with an asterisk. The same procedure was followed for widows and invalid pensioners if the ledgers indicated that a final payment had been made after their deaths.
>
> These cards and vouchers are not available to researchers. The National Archives staff will search the index cards and the segregated vouchers. If the voucher requested by a researcher (in person or by letter) is not among these files, no further search will be made unless the researcher has examined microfilm publication T718 and found evidence that final payment was made. In this case, the researcher must furnish the name of the pensioner, the act under which the pension was paid, date of death, and date of final payment. Final payment vouchers of pensioners paid by agencies in Alabama, Arkansas, California, and some of those paid by Connecticut agencies were consolidated with the related Revolutionary War pension application files[16]

Items 1 and 2 above are in the National Archives in Record Group 15, Records of the Veterans' Administration (as are the pension and bounty land applications), and item 3 is in Record Group 217, Records of the U.S. General Accounting Office.

G. Books on Revolutionary War soldiers

Other important sources of information on those persons who served in the Revolutionary War are the many books that have been published on the subject. Hundreds of books have been written (especially relating to the several states and even counties and towns), all of them providing information

---

[16] Ibid., 173.

about those who served. There are rosters, lists of soldiers buried in this or that place, histories, lineages, etc., any of which may be helpful in determining if your ancestor served in the Revolutionary War.

Do not overlook these possibilities. Most libraries, especially genealogical libraries and libraries in the localities concerned, have many such books. These books are essential when you consider that so many of the original records have been either lost or destroyed.

A number of books with lists of participants in the Revolutionary War are in the following list. Some also have information relating to later wars. The more general books are listed first, followed by those that relate to specific states:

Bockstruck, Lloyd DeWitt. *Bounty Land Grants Awarded by State Governments.* 1996. Reprint, Baltimore: Genealogical Publishing Co., 2006.

_____. *Revolutionary War Pensions: Awarded by State Governments 1775–1874, the General and Federal Governments Prior to 1814, and by Private Acts of Congress to 1905.* Baltimore: Genealogical Publishing Co., 2011.

Brown, Margie G., comp. *Genealogical Abstracts, Revolutionary War Veterans, Scrip Act 1852.* Lovettsville, VA: Willow Bend Books, 1997.

Callahan, Edward W. *List of Officers of the Navy of the United States and of the Marine Corps, from 1775 to 1900 . . .* New York: L.R. Hamersly, 1901. Most of the men listed in this volume served after the Revolutionary War. A digitized copy is online at *https://archive.org/details/listofofficersof00unit.*

Dandridge, Danske. *American Prisoners of the Revolution.* 1911. Reprint, Baltimore: Genealogical Publishing Co., 2007.

Dickore, Marie, trans. *Hessian Soldiers in the American Revolution: Records of Their Marriages and Baptisms of Their Children in America 1776–1783.* Cincinnati: D. J. Krehbiel Co., 1959.

Eelking, Max von. *The German Allied Troops in the North American War of Independence, 1776–1783.* Translated and abridged from German by J. G. Rosengarten, 1893. Reprint, Baltimore: Genealogical Publishing Co., 2002.

Ellet, Elizabeth Fries. *The Women of the American Revolution.* 3rd ed. 3 vols. New York: Baker and Scribner, 1849. Amazon.com has had this work available on CD. A digitized copy is also online at *http://archive. org/stream/womanamrevol02ellerich#page/n9/mode/2up.*

Hamersly, Thomas H. S., comp. *Complete Regular Army Register of the United States for 100 Years (1779 to 1879).* Washington, DC: T.H.S. Hamersly, 1881, A digitized copy is online at *http://archive.org/stream/completeregulara1881hame#page/n7/mode/2up.*

_____. *General Register of the Navy and Marine Corps, Arranged in Alphabetical Order for 100 Years, (1782–1882).* Washington, DC: T.H.S. Hamersly, 1882. Digitized copies can be accessed online at *https://catalog. hathitrust.org/Record/000114723*.

Hayward, Elizabeth M. *Soldiers and Patriots of the American Revolution.* Ridgewood, NJ: The author, 1947.

Heitman, Francis Bernard. *Historical Register of Officers of the Continental Army During the War of the Revolution, April 1775 to December 1783.* 1914, 1932. Reprint, Baltimore: Genealogical Publishing Co., 2008.

Kaminkow, Marion J. and Jack. *Mariners of the American Revolution.* 1967. Reprint, Baltimore: Genealogical Publishing Co., 1993.

Neagles, James C. *Summer Soldiers: A Survey & Index for Revolutionary War Courts-Martial.* Salt Lake City: Ancestry Publishing Co., 1986.

Peterson, Clarence Stewart. *Known Military Dead During the American Revolutionary War, 1775–1783.* 1959. Reprint, Baltimore: Genealogical Publishing Co., 2009.

Pierce, John. *Pierce's Register: Register of the Certificates Issued by John Pierce, Esquire, Paymaster General and Commissioner of Army Accounts for the United States. To Officers and Soldiers of the Continental Army Under Act of July 4, 1783. First Published 1786 in Numerical Order.* 1915. Reprint, Baltimore: Genealogical Publishing Co., 2012.

Saffell, William T. R. *Records of the Revolutionary War:* [Bound with: *Index to Saffell's List of Virginia Soldiers in the Revolution* by J. T. McAllister]. 3rd ed. 1894 and 1913. Reprint, Baltimore: Genealogical Publishing Co., 2002.

U.S. Bureau of the Census. *A Census of Pensioners for Revolutionary or Military Services, 1840* [Published with *A General Index to a Census of Pensioners. 2 vols. in 1*], 1841, 1965. Reprint, Baltimore: Genealogical Publishing Co., 2005.

U.S. Department of the Interior. *Rejected or Suspended Applications for Revolutionary War Pensions.* 1852. Reprint, Baltimore: Genealogical Publishing Co., 2003.

U.S. House of Representatives. *Digested Summary and Alphabetical List of Private Claims Which Have Been Presented to the House of Representatives [from the First to the 31st Congress, Exhibiting the Action of Congress on Each Claim].* 3 vols. 1853. Reprint, Baltimore: Genealogical Publishing Co., 1997.

U.S. Secretary of War. *Pension Roll of 1835: The Indexed Edition in Four Volumes.* 4 vols. 1835 and 1968. Reprint, Baltimore: Genealogical Publishing Co., 2002.

_____. *Revolutionary Pensioners. A Transcript of the Pension List of the United States for 1813* ... 1813. Reprint, Baltimore: Genealogical Publishing Co., 2002. This book was out of print in 2016.

U.S. Senate. *Pension List of 1820: Letter from the Secretary of War Transmitting a Report of the Names, Rank and File of Every Person Placed on the Pension List in Pursuance of the Act of the 18th March, 1818, Etc. Washington.* 1820. Reprint, Baltimore: Genealogical Publishing Co., 2000.

U.S. War Department. *Pensioners of the United States, 1818.* 1818. Reprint, Baltimore: Genealogical Publishing Co., 2008.

Alabama

Mell, Annie R. W. *Revolutionary Soldiers Buried in Alabama.* [This is Vol. X of *Publications of the Alabama Historical Society.*] Montgomery: Alabama Historical Society, 1904. A digitized copy of this volume is online at *https://archive.org/details/revolutionarysol00mell.*

Owen, Thomas M. *Revolutionary Soldiers in Alabama.* 1911. Montgomery: Alabama Department of Archives and History, 2009 update. A digitized copy is online at *http://archives.alabama.gov/al_sldrs/~start. html.*

Connecticut

Connecticut Historical Society. *Lists and Returns of Connecticut Men in the Revolution, 1775–1783* [Vol. 12 of Connecticut Historical Society Collections]. Hartford: The Society, 1909. A digitized copy is online at *http://archive.org/stream/listofofficersof00unit#page/134/mode/2up.*

Johnston, Henry P., ed. *Record of Service of Connecticut Men in the I, War of the Revolution; II, War of 1812; III, Mexican War* [Connecticut Historical Society Collections]. Hartford: Case, Lockwood, and Brainard Co., 1889. A digitized copy is online at *http://archive.org/stream/waroftherevolution00recorich#page/n29/mode/2up.*

Middlebrook, Louis F. *History of Maritime Connecticut During the American Revolution, 1775–1783.* 2 vols. Salem, MA: Salem Institute, 1925. Hyperlinks to digitized copies of both volumes are online at *https://catalog.hathitrust.org/Record/001262389.*

Richards, Josephine Ellis, ed. *Honor Roll of Litchfield County Revolutionary Soldiers.* Litchfield, CT: D.A.R., 1912. A digitized copy is online at *https://archive.org/details/honorrolloflitch00daug.*

Rolls and Lists of Connecticut Men in the Revolution, 1775–1783 [Connecticut Historical Society Collections, Vol. 8]. Hartford: Case, Lockwood, and Brainard Co., 1889. A digitized copy is online at *https://archive.org/details/rollslistsofconn08conn.*

District of Columbia

Ely, Selden Marvin. *The District of Columbia in the American Revolution, and Patriots of the Revolutionary Period Who Are Interred in the District or in Arlington* [Records of the Columbia Historical Society, Vol.

21]. Washington, DC: The Society, 1918. This book is online at *https://books.google.com/books?id=ZUHrL7tQVS8C&printsec=frontcover&source=gbs_ge_summary_r&cad=0#v=onepage&q&f=false*, beginning on p. 129.

France

Ministère des affaires étrangères. *Les Combattants Francais de la Guerre Americaine, 1778–1783* (Senate doc. 77, 58th Congress, 2d sess.). 1905. Washington, DC: Imprimerie Nationale, 1905. This book is written in French. A digitized copy is online at *http://archive.org/stream/combattantsfranc00fran#page/94/mode/2up*.

Georgia

Blair, Ruth, and Georgia Department of Archives and History. *Revolutionary Soldiers' Receipts for Georgia Bounty Grants*. Atlanta: Foote and Davies, 1928.

Hitz, Alex Mayer, comp. *Authentic List of All Land Lottery Grants Made to Veterans of the Revolutionary War by the State of Georgia*. 2nd ed. Atlanta: Georgia Secretary of State, 1966.

Knight, Lucian L. *Georgia's Roster of the Revolution . . .* 1920. Reprint, Baltimore: Genealogical Publishing Co., 2012.

McCall, Mrs. Howard H. *Roster of Revolutionary Soldiers in Georgia*. 3 vols. [Vol. 1, 1941; Vol. 2, 1968; Vol. 3, 1969]. Reprint, Baltimore: Genealogical Publishing Co., 2004.

Illinois

Cliff, G. Glenn. *List of Officers of the Illinois Regiment, and of Crockett's Regiment Who Have Received Land for Their Services*. Frankfort, IL: S.A.R., 1962.

Meyer, Virginia M. *Roster of Revolutionary War Soldiers and Widows Who Lived in Illinois Counties*. Chicago: Illinois D.A.R., 1962.

Walker, Harriet J. *Revolutionary Soldiers Buried in Illinois*. 1917. Reprint, Baltimore: Genealogical Publishing Co., 2007.

Walker, Homer A. *Illinois Pensioners Lists of the Revolution, 1812, and Indian Wars*. Washington, DC: 1955.

Indiana

O'Byrne, Mrs. Estella. *Roster of Soldiers and Patriots of the American Revolution Buried in Indiana*. 2 vols. Brockville, IN: Indiana D.A.R., 1938 and 1966. (Volume I was reprinted by Genealogical Publishing Co., Baltimore, in 1999.)

Waters, Margaret R. *Revolutionary Soldiers Buried in Indiana. Three Hundred Names Not in the Roster by Mrs. O'Byrne*. 2 vols. 1949 and 1954. Reprint in 1 vol., Baltimore: Genealogical Publishing Co., 2007.

Kentucky

Quisenberry, Anderson C. *Revolutionary Soldiers in Kentucky* [Excerpted from *Year Book, Kentucky Society, S.A.R.*]. 1896. Reprint, Baltimore: Genealogical Publishing Co., 2006.

Wilson, Samuel M. *Catalogue of Revolutionary Soldiers and Sailors of the Commonwealth of Virginia to Whom Land Bounty Warrants Were Granted by Virginia for Military Services in the War of Independence* [Excerpted from *Year Book, Kentucky Society, S.A.R.*]. 1913. Reprint, Baltimore: Genealogical Publishing Co., 2003.

Maine

Flagg, Charles Alcott. *An Alphabetical Index of Revolutionary Pensioners Living in Maine.* 1920. Reprint, Baltimore: Genealogical Publishing Co., 2005.

House, Charles J. *Names of Soldiers of the American Revolution [from Maine], Who Applied for State Bounty Under Resolves of March 17, 1835, March 24, 1836, and March 20, 1836, as Appears of Record in Land Office.* 1893. Reprint, Baltimore: Genealogical Publishing Co., 1996.

Houston, Ethel Rollins. *Maine Revolutionary Soldiers' Graves.* Portland, ME: Maine D.A.R., 1940.

Miller, Frank Burton. *Soldiers and Sailors of the Plantation of Lower St. Georges Who Served in the War for American Independence.* 1931. Reprint, Baltimore: Genealogical Publishing Co., 1999.

Maryland

Brumbaugh, Gaius Marcus, and Margaret R. Hodges. *Revolutionary Records of Maryland, Part I.* 1924. Reprint, Baltimore: Genealogical Publishing Co., 2003.

McGhee, Lucy K. *Pension Abstracts of Maryland Soldiers of the Revolution, War of 1812, and Indian Wars Who Settled in Kentucky.* Washington, DC: The author, 1952.

Archives of Maryland. *Muster Rolls and Other Records of Service of Maryland Troops in the American Revolution, 1775–1783* [Archives of Maryland, Vol. 18, 1900]. Reprint, Baltimore: Genealogical Publishing Co., 2000.

Newman, Harry Wright. *Maryland Revolutionary Records.* 1938. Reprint, Baltimore: Genealogical Publishing Co., 2002.

Secretary of the Commonwealth. *Massachusetts Soldiers and Sailors of the Revolutionary War.* 17 vols. Boston: Wright and Potter Printing Co., 1896–1908.

Michigan

Silliman, Sue I. *Michigan Military Records* [Michigan Historical Commission Bulletin 12]. 1920. Reprint, Baltimore: Genealogical Publishing Co., 2008.

Mississippi

Welch, Alice T. *Family Records, Mississippi Revolutionary Soldiers*. Jackson, MS: Mississippi D.A.R., 1956.

Missouri

Houts, Alice K. *Revolutionary Soldiers Buried in Missouri*. Kansas City: The author, 1966.

McGhee, Lucy K. *Missouri Revolutionary Soldiers, War of 1812 and Indian Wars Pension List*. Washington, DC: 1955.

New Hampshire

Batchellor, Albert Stillman, ed. *Miscellaneous Revolutionary Documents of New Hampshire, Including the Association Test, the Pension Rolls, and Other Important Papers* [New Hampshire State Papers Series, Vol. 30]. Manchester, NH: John B. Clark Co., 1910. A digitized copy is online at *http://archive.org/stream/miscellaneousrev00batcrich#page/n7/mode/2up.*

Hammond, Isaac W., comp. and ed. *Rolls of the Soldiers of the Revolutionary War, 1775–1782*. 4 vols. [New Hampshire State Papers Series, Vol. 1 of War Rolls and no. 14 of the Series]. Concord, NH: Parsons B. Cogswell, 1885. A digitized copy is online at *http://archive.org/stream/rollsofsoldiersi14hammrich#page/n1/mode/2up.*

New Jersey

Stryker, William S. *Official Register of the Officers and Men of New Jersey in the Revolutionary War.* 1872 and 1911. Reprint, Baltimore: Genealogical Publishing Co., 1997, with added *Digest and Revision* by James W. S. Campbell.[17]

New York

Fernow, Berthold. *New York in the Revolution* [Vol. 1 of *New York State Archives* and Vol. 15 of *Documents Relating to the Colonial History of the State of New York*]. Albany: Weed, Parsons & Co., 1887. A digitized reproduction of a microfiche copy is online at *http://archive.org/stream/cihm_53998#page/n407/mode/2up.*

Mather, Frederic Gregory. *The Refugees of 1776 from Long Island to Connecticut*. 1913. Reprint, Baltimore: Genealogical Publishing Co., 2005.

---

[17] The index to this volume, called *Index to Stryker's Register of New Jersey in the Revolution,* as prepared by the Historical Records Survey of the WPA in 1941, was reprinted by Clearfield Company in 2005 and is available for purchase on the Genealogical Publishing Co. website, http://www.genealogical.com.

Muster and Pay Rolls of the War of the Revolution, 1775–1783. 2 vols. New York: New-York Historical Society, 1916. This work is digitized and indexed on the Ancestry website at *http://search.ancestry.com/search/db.aspx?dbid=6154.*

Roberts, James A., comp. *New York in the Revolution as Colony and State.* Vol. I. 2nd ed. Albany: Brandow Printing Co., 1898. A digitized copy is online at *http://archive.org/stream/newyorkinrevolut00newy#page/n9/mode/2up.*

State Comptroller's Office. *New York in the Revolution as Colony and State.* Vol. II. Albany: J.B. Lyon Co., 1904. A digitized copy is online at *http://archive.org/stream/newyorkinrevolut02newyuoft#page/n3/mode/2up.*

Tallmadge, Samuel, et al. *Orderly Books of the Fourth New York Regiment, 1778–1783* and *The Second New York Regiment, 1780–1793.* 2 vols. Edited and transcribed by Almon W. Lauber. Albany: University of the State of New York, 1932. This work is digitized and indexed on the Ancestry website at *http://search.ancestry.com/search/db.aspx?dbid=11659.*

North Carolina

Daughters of the American Revolution, North Carolina. *Roster of Soldiers from North Carolina in the American Revolution.* 1932. Reprint, Baltimore: Genealogical Publishing Co., 2008. This book is digitized and indexed on the Ancestry website at *http://search.ancestry.com/search/db.aspx?dbid=10162.*

Ohio

Daughters of the American Revolution, Ohio. *Official Roster of the Soldiers of the American Revolution Buried in the State of Ohio.* 3 vols. Columbus: Ohio DAR, 1929, 1938, 1959. This work is digitized and indexed on the Ancestry website at *http://search.ancestry.com/search/db.aspx?dbid=20105.*

Pennsylvania

Gearhart, Heber G. *Revolutionary War Soldiers Buried in Pennsylvania: Listed According to Counties.* New York: F.H. Hitchcock, 1926.

Linn, John B., and William H. Egle. *Pennsylvania in the War of the Revolution: Associated Battalions and Militia, 1775–1783* [Pennsylvania Archives, Ser. 2, Vols. 13–14]. Harrisburg: F.K. Meyers, 1890–92. A digitized copy is online at *http://archive.org/stream/pennsylvaniainwa01linniala#page/n25/mode/2up.*

"List of Officers and Men of the Pennsylvania Navy, 1775–1781" [Pennsylvania Archives, Ser. 2, Vol. 1, pp. 243–434]. Harrisburg: Pennsylvania Archives, 1896. A digitized copy is available online at *http://www.worldvitalrecords.com/indexinfo.aspx?ix=wvr_listofofficersandmenzpennsylvanianavy1775z.*

Rhode Island

Cowell, Benjamin. *Spirit of '76 in Rhode Island* [with an Analytical and Explanatory Index by James N. Arnold]. 1850. Reprint, Baltimore: Genealogical Publishing Co., 2012.

South Carolina

Boddie, William Willis. *Marion's Men; a List of Twenty-five Hundred.* Charleston: The author, 1938. The copies now available seem to be retypings of the original book "with corrections."

Burns, Annie W. *South Carolina Pension Abstracts of the Revolutionary War, War of 1812, and Indian Wars.* 12 vols. Washington, DC: 1930.

Ervin, Sara Sullivan. *South Carolinians in the Revolution.*1949. Reprint, Baltimore: Genealogical Publishing Co., 2008.

Moss, Bobby Gilmer. *Roster of South Carolina Patriots in the American Revolution.* 1985. Reprint, Baltimore: Genealogical Publishing Co., 2009.

Pruitt, Jayne C. C. *Revolutionary War Pension Applicants Who Served from South Carolina.* Fairfax, VA: Charlton Hall, 1946.

Revill, Janie. *Copy of the Original Index Book Showing the Revolutionary Claims Filed in South Carolina Between August 20, 1783 and August 31, 1786.* 1941. Reprint, Baltimore: Genealogical Publishing Co., 2003.

Salley, Alexander S., Jr., ed. *Accounts Audited of Revolutionary Claims Against South Carolina.* 3 vols. Columbia: Historical Commission of South Carolina, 1935–43. Digitized copies of all three volumes can be accessed at *https://catalog.hathitrust.org/Record/008557568.*

_____, ed. *Stub Entries of Indents Issued in Payment of Claims Against South Carolina Growing Out of the Revolution.* 12 vols. Columbia: South Carolina Department of Archives and History, 1910–57.

Tennessee

Allen, Penelope Johnson. *Tennessee Soldiers in the Revolution: A Roster of Soldiers Living During the Revolutionary War in the Counties of Washington and Sullivan.* 1935. Reprint, Baltimore: Genealogical Publishing Co., 2008.

Armstrong, Zella. *Some Tennessee Heroes of the Revolution.* 1933. Reprint, Baltimore: Genealogical Publishing Co., 2002.

———. *Twenty-four Hundred Tennessee Pensioners: Revolution, War of 1812.* 1937. Reprint, Baltimore: Genealogical Publishing Co., 1996.

Vermont

Crockett, Walter H. *Soldiers of the Revolutionary War Buried in Vermont: And Anecdotes and Incidents Relating to Some of Them.* 1903–04. Reprint, Baltimore: Genealogical Publishing Co., 2007.

Goodrich, John E., comp. and ed. *Rolls of Soldiers in the Revolutionary War, 1775–1783*. Rutland, VT: The Tuttle Co., 1904.

Virginia

Brumbaugh, Gaius Marcus. *Revolutionary War Records: Virginia*, 1936. Reprint, Baltimore: Genealogical Publishing Co., 2008.

Burgess, Louis Alexander. *Virginia Soldiers of 1776: Compiled from Documents . . . in the Virginia Land Office*, 3 vols. 1927–29. Reprint, Baltimore: Genealogical Publishing Co., 2008.

Dorman, John Frederick, abstr. and comp. *Virginia Revolutionary Pension Applications*. 45 vols. Washington, DC: The author, 1958 – c. 1995. Links to digitized copies of Volumes 1 through 10, and to searches in Volumes 11 through 45 are at *https://catalog.hathitrust.org/Record/000306233*.

Eckenrode, H. J. *List of Revolutionary Soldiers of Virginia* [Special Reports of Dept. of Archives and History, 1911 and 1912]. 2 vols. Richmond: Virginia State Library, 1912 and 1913. Digitized copies of these volumes are online at *http://archive.org/stream/listofrevolution09virg#page/n5/mode/2up* and at *http://archive.org/stream/listofrevolution00virg#page/n3/mode/2up*.

Gwathmey, John H. *Historical Register of Virginians in the Revolution: Soldiers, Sailors, Marines, 1775–1783*. 1938. Reprint, Baltimore: Genealogical Publishing Co., 1996.

McAllister, Joseph T. *Virginia Militia in the Revolutionary War*. Hot Springs, VA: McAllister Publishing Co., 1913. A digitized copy is online at *http://archive.org/stream/virginiamilitiai00mcal#page/n5/mode/2up*.

Saffell, William T.R. *Records of the Revolutionary War: Containing the Military and Financial Correspondence of Distinguished Officers, Names of the Officers and Privates of Regiments, Companies, and Corps, with Dates of Their Commissions and Enlistments . . .* 3rd ed. [This book is bound together with the] *Index to Saffell's List of Virginia Soldiers in the Revolution* by J. T. McAllister. 3rd ed. 1894 and 1913. Reprint, Baltimore: Genealogical Publishing Co., 2002.

Stewart, Robert Armistead. *The History of Virginia's Navy of the Revolution*. 1934. Reprint, Baltimore: Genealogical Publishing Co., 1993.

Wilson, Samuel M. *Catalogue of Revolutionary Soldiers and Sailors of the Commonwealth of Virginia to Whom Bounty Land Warrants Were Granted by Virginia for Military Service in the War for Independence*. 1913. Reprint, Baltimore: Genealogical Publishing Co., 2002.

West Virginia

Johnston, Ross B. *West Virginians in the American Revolution*. c. 1959. Reprint, Baltimore: Genealogical Publishing Co., 2005.

Lewis, Virgil A. *Soldiery of West Virginia in the French and Indian War; Lord Dunmore's War; the Revolution; the Later Indian Wars . . .* 1911. Reprint, Baltimore: Genealogical Publishing Co., 2006.

Reddy, Anne Waller. *West Virginia Revolutionary Ancestors Whose Services Were Non-military and Whose Names, Therefore, Do Not Appear in Revolutionary Indexes of Soldiers and Sailors.* 1930. Reprint, Baltimore: Genealogical Publishing Co., 2009.

In connection with, and in addition to, this list, you should also be aware of a list of "Selected Genealogical Research Aids: Revolutionary War" published as "Table 6" in *Guide to Genealogical Research in the National Archives of the United States*, 3rd ed., edited by Eales and Kvasnicka (pages 129 through 131). Many of the works included in Table 6 are not on the list of books in this chapter.

V. USING REVOLUTIONARY WAR RECORDS

Many beginning family history researchers overlook Revolutionary War records as a research source mainly because they do not recognize valid clues. Many do not even think about the possibility that their ancestor may have served unless they read somewhere that he actually did. However, there are several clues that might suggest the need for considering these records:

- Any time the line on which you are working was in America prior to the time of the war, you must consider these records. Even if a lineal ancestor did not serve, perhaps a relative (maybe a brother) of the same surname did, and records of his service or his pension application would provide useful information about your ancestors and his family—names, dates, and places especially.

- If a known male ancestor was in America at the time of the Revolution and was of age to serve, the possibility of service must certainly be considered.

- If a known ancestor was born in America within the period beginning just before the war and ending two decades after it, you must consider the possibility that his (or her) father served, even though you may not know the father's name. The index to pensioners provides a ready list of servicemen (at least those who applied for pensions) of the surname you seek who served from the state or the general region from which your ancestors came. Books about Revolutionary War veterans in the state(s) where your ancestors lived might also help suggest some possibilities to you.

The digitized and indexed database on the Ancestry website (*http://search.ancestry.com/search/db.aspx?dbid=1995*) gives you an opportunity to examine the records relating to soldiers of the same surname for any possible connection that you can explore elsewhere. However, if your ancestral line is not traced back to this time period, there is seldom good reason to spend your time searching records of soldiers of this war. You have too little to go on. There will be ample time to use these records when your line is extended to that period of time and when research and analysis indicate the need for their use.

VI. LOYALISTS AND THE REVOLUTIONARY WAR

Perhaps your people were in America before the Revolution but you can find no evidence of their service. There may be a number of reasons for this, including the possibility that they belonged to a pacifist church such as the Society of Friends (Quakers). But, on the other hand, there is also the possibility that they were sympathetic to the cause of the Crown rather than to that of the revolutionaries.

If you do not know where your ancestors were during the Revolution because you have not traced them that far, but you find them coming out of Canada (or even Florida or the West Indies) in later years, the same possibility exists. It is estimated that as many as one-third (some say one-half) of the colonists were loyal to the Crown. Among the Loyalists were British government officials and their friends, English Church ministers, and others whose positions and/or wealth depended on British sovereignty.

Technically speaking, all of those persons were not Loyalists, though often called such—proBritish or Tories, yes, but not true Loyalists. A true Loyalist was one who actively participated in the war to aid the cause of the Crown, usually in British uniform. The Tories did suffer, especially if they refused to take an oath of allegiance, but their property was not usually confiscated and they were not generally charged with treason as were their Loyalist cousins.

Many of these Tories have been called Loyalists—in fact, all of those who went to Canada were so called—but many Tories went other directions too (and they were free to do so). However, there is generally no record of loyalism or of confiscation of property in the former American homes of those Tories who immigrated to Canada. Also, those Tories were not eligible for Canadian land grants.

In addition to Canada and Florida, many Loyalists and Tories went to the West Indies (especially Jamaica) and some returned to Britain. Canada, however, seemed to be a favored place; in Upper Canada (now Ontario), it is said that 80 percent of the settlers came from the American colonies.

A. Printed Loyalist sources

Some of the printed sources on Loyalists (and Tories) from the American Revolutionary period are as follows:

Allen, Thomas B. *Tories: Fighting for the King in America's First Civil War*. New York: Harper Paperbacks, 2011.

_____, and Todd W. Braisted. *The Loyalist Corps: Americans in Service to the King*. Trenton, NJ: FoxAcre Press, 2011.

Bell, David Graham. *American Loyalists to New Brunswick: The Ship Passenger Lists*. Halifax, Nova Scotia: Formac Publishing Co., 2015.

Bradley, Arthur Granville. *Colonial Americans in Exile; Founders of British Canada.* New York: E. B. Dutton and Co., 1932.

Brown, Wallace. *The King's Friends. The Composition and Motives of the American Loyalist Claimants.* Providence: Brown University Press, 1965.

————. *The Good Americans: The Loyalists in the American Revolution.* New York: William Morrow and Co., 1969.

Bruce, R. M. *Loyalist Trail.* Kingston, Ontario: Jackson Press, 1965.

Campbell, Wilfrid. *Report on Manuscript Lists in the Archives Relating to the United Empire Loyalists, with Reference to Other Sources.* Ottawa: 1909. A digitized copy of this 30-page booklet is online at *http://archive. org/stream/reportonmanuscri00publuoft#page/n1/mode/2up.*

Canniff, William. *History of the Settlement of Upper Canada (Ontario): With Special Reference to the Bay of Quinte.* Toronto: Dudley and Burns, Printers, 1869. A digitized copy is online at *http://archive.org/ stream/cihm_00468#page/n1/mode/2up.*

Chadwick, Edward Marion. *Ontarian Families: Genealogies of United Empire Loyalists and Other Pioneer Families of Upper Canada.* 2 vols. Toronto: Rolph, Smith & Co., 1895. A digitized copy is at *http://archive.org/ stream/ontarianfamilie01chadgoog#page/n4/mode/2up.* There is also an indexed digitized copy on Ancestry at *http://search.ancestry.com/search/ db.aspx?dbid=27968.*

Chartrand, René. *American Loyalist Troops 1775–84 (Men-at-Arms).* Oxford, UK: Osprey Publishing, 2008.

Clark, Murtie June. *Loyalists in the Southern Campaign of the Revolutionary War, Volume 1: Official Rolls of Loyalists Recruited from North and South Carolina, Georgia, Florida, Mississippi, and Louisiana.* 1981. Reprint, Baltimore: Genealogical Publishing Co., 2003.

————. *Loyalists in the Southern Campaign of the Revolutionary War. Volume II: Official Rolls of Loyalists Recruited from Maryland, Pennsylvania, Virginia, and Those Recruited from Other Colonies for the British Legion, Guides and Pioneers, Loyal Foresters, and Queen's Rangers.* 1981. Reprint, Baltimore: Genealogical Publishing Co., 1999.

————. *Loyalists in the Southern Campaign of the Revolutionary War, Volume III: Official Rolls of Loyalists Recruited from the Middle Atlantic Colonies, with Lists of Refugees from Other Colonies.* 1981. Reprint, Baltimore: Genealogical Publishing Co., 1999.

Coldham, Peter Wilson,[18] comp. *American Loyalist Claims, Volume 1* [Abstracted from the Public Record Office Audit Office Series 13, Bundles

---

[18] There is an informative article about the historian Peter Wilson Coldham on the FamilySearch wiki (https://familysearch.org/wiki/en/Peter_Wilson_Coldham). It includes a listing of his many articles and books relating to family history. Also, many of the books listed in the article are digitized and have hyperlinks on the FamilySearch wiki site.

1–35 & 37]. Washington, DC: National Genealogical Society, 1980. There is a hyperlink to a digitized version of this volume at *https:// familysearch.org/search/catalog/89435?availability=Family%20His tory%20Library*. The volume includes Loyalist claims from New York, New Jersey, New Brunswick, part of New Hampshire, Nova Scotia, Virginia, and part of Georgia; it is indexed. See footnote 19, near the end of this chapter, for more information.

_____. *American Migrations, 1765–1799: The Lives, Times, and Families of Colonial Americans Who Remained Loyal to the British Crown Before, During and After the Revolutionary War, as Related in Their Own Words and Through Their Correspondence.* Baltimore: Genealogical Publishing Co., 2000. A digitized copy is on the Ancestry website and can be accessed by entering the book title in your search engine.

Craig, Gerald M. *Upper Canada: The Formative Years, 1784–1841.* New York: Oxford University Press, 2013.

Cruikshank, Ernest A. *The Settlement of the United Empire Loyalists on the Upper St. Lawrence and Bay of Quinte in 1784.* Toronto: Ontario Historical Society, 1934.

DeMond, Robert O. *Loyalists in North Carolina During the Revolution.* 1940. Reprint, Baltimore: Genealogical Publishing Co., 2004.

Evans, G. N. D. *Allegiance in America: The Case of the Loyalists.* Reading, MA: Addison-Wesley Publishing Co., 1969.

Flick, Alexander Clarence. *Loyalism in New York During the American Revolution* [Studies in History, Economics and Public Law, Volume XIV]. New York: Columbia University Press, 1901. A digitized copy is online at *http://archive.org/stream/loyalisminnewyor00flic#page/n9/mode/2up*.

Fraser, Alexander. *United Empire Loyalists, Evidence in the Canadian Claims: The Second Report of the Bureau of Archives for the Province of Ontario.* 1905. Reprint, Baltimore: Genealogical Publishing Co., 1994. A digitized copy of the 1905 edition is online at *http:// archive.org/stream/report03archgoog#page/n6/mode/2up*.

Gilroy, Marion, comp. *Loyalists and Land Settlement in Nova Scotia.* 1937. Reprint, Baltimore: Genealogical Publishing Co., 2002.

Hancock, Harold Bell. *The Loyalists of Revolutionary Delaware.* 1940. Plainsboro Twp., NJ: Associate University Press, 1977.

Harrell, Isaac Samuel. *Loyalism in Virginia: A Thesis in History.* Durham, NC: Duke University Press, 1926.

Jasanoff, Maya. *Liberty's Exiles: American Loyalists in the Revolutionary World,* Reprint ed. Pontiac, MI: Vintage, 2012.

Jones, E. Alfred. *Loyalists in Massachusetts, Their Memorials, Petitions and Claims.* 1930. Reprint, Baltimore: Genealogical Publishing Co., 1995.

———. *Loyalists of New Jersey: Their Memorials, Petitions, Claims, etc., from English Records.* 1927. Bowie, MD: Heritage Books, 1988.

Jones, Caleb. *The Orderly Book of the Maryland Loyalist Regiment, June 28, 1778, to October 12, 1778.* 1891. Reprint, Baltimore: Genealogical Publishing Co., 1996.

Newman, Peter C. *Hostages to Fortune: The United Empire Loyalists and the Making of Canada,* Canadian Origin ed. Toronto: Touchstone Books (Simon & Schuster), 2016.

The Old United Empire Loyalist List (reprint of *The Centennial of the Settlement of Upper Canada by the United Empire Loyalists, 1784–1884*). 1885. Carlton Place, Ont.: Global Heritage Press, 2005, CD 2010.

Orderly Book of the Three Battalions of Loyalists Commanded by Brigadier-General Oliver de Lancey, 1776–1778 [To Which is Appended "A List of New York Loyalists in the City of New York During the War of the Revolution"]. 1917. Reprint, Baltimore: Genealogical Publishing Co., 2005.

Paltsits, Hugo Victor, ed. *Minutes of the Commissioners for Detecting and Defeating Conspiracies in the State of New York. Albany County Sessions, 1778–1781.* 2 vols. Albany: The State of New York, 1909. Digitized copies of these volumes are online at *http://archive.org/stream/minutesalbanycou01newyrich#page/n8/mode/1up* and *http://archive.org/stream/detectingdefecting02paltrich#page/n7/mode/2up.*

Peck, Epaphroditus. *Loyalists of Connecticut.* New Haven: Yale University Press, 1934. There is a hyperlink to a digitized copy of this booklet at *https://catalog.hathitrust.org/Record/006583205.*

Pringle, J. F. *Lunenburgh or the Old Eastern District: Its Settlement and Early Progress.* Cornwall, Ont.: Standard Printing House, 1890. A digitized copy of this book is online at *http://archive.org/stream/lunenburgh00prinuoft#page/n3/mode/2up.*

Raymond, William O. *Loyalist Transport Ships, 1783.* Saint John: New Brunswick Historical Society, 1904.

Reid, William O. *The Loyalists of Ontario: The Sons and Daughters of the American Loyalists at Upper Canada.* 1973. Reprint, Baltimore: Genealogical Publishing Co., 1994.

Ryerson, Adolphus E. *The Loyalists of America and Their Times: 1620 to 1816.* 2 vols. 1880. London: British Library [Historical Print Editions], 2011. A digitized copy of volume II of the original is at *http://archive.org/stream/loyalistamerica02ryeruoft#page/n5/mode/2up.*

Sabine, Lorenzo. *Biographical Sketches of Loyalists of the American Revolution.* 2 vols. 1864. Reprint, Baltimore: Genealogical Publishing Co., 2005.

Siebert, Wilbur Henry. *The American Loyalists in the Eastern Seigniories and Townships of the Province of Quebec* [Transactions of the Royal

Society of Canada]. 1913. Rochester, NY: Scholar's Choice, 2015. A digitized copy of the original booklet is at *http://archive.org/stream/ americanloyalist00siebuoft#page/n1/mode/2up*.

————. *The Colony of Massachusetts Loyalists at Bristol, England*. Primary Source ed. 1912. Charleston, SC: Nabu Press, 2014. A digitized copy of the original of this small booklet is at *http://archive.org/stream/ colonyofmassachu00sieb#page/n7/mode/2up*.

————. *The Flight of American Loyalists to the British Isles*. Columbus, OH: F. J. Heer Co., 1911. A digitized copy of this booklet is at *http://archive.org/ stream/flightamericanl00siebgoog#page/n6/mode/2up*.

————. *The Legacy of the American Revolution to the British West Indies and Bahamas: A Chapter Out of the History of the American Loyalists*. 1914. Reprint, Provo, UT: Repressed Publishing, 2014. A digitized copy of the original is at *http://archive.org/stream/legacyamrev00siebrich#page/ n3/mode/2up*.

————. *The Loyalists and Six Nation Indians in the Niagara Peninsula* [Transactions of the Royal Society of Canada]. 1916. Charleston, SC: Nabu Press, 2011. A digitized copy of the original book is at *http:// archive.org/stream/loyalistssixnati00siebuoft#page/n1/mode/2up*.

————. *Loyalists of East Florida, 1774 to 1785*. 2 vols. DeLand, FL: Florida State Historical Society, 1929.

_____. *The Loyalist Settlements on the Gaspé Peninsula* [Transactions of the Royal Society of Canada]. Ottawa: The Royal Society of Canada, 1914.

————. *The Refugee Loyalists of Connecticut* [Transactions of the Royal Society of Canada]. Ottawa: The Society, 1916. A digitized copy is at *http://archive.org/stream/refugeeloyalists00sieb#page/n1/mode/2up*.

————. *The Temporary Settlement of Loyalists at Machiche, P.Q.* [Transactions of the Royal Society of Canada]. Ottawa: The Royal Society of Canada, 1916.

Singer, Charles G. *South Carolina in the Confederation*. 1941. Chatham, MI: Porcupine Press, 1977 facsimile of 1941 edition.

Smith, Paul H. *Loyalists and Redcoats: A Study in British Revolutionary Policy*. Chapel Hill: University of North Carolina Press, 1964.

Starke, James H. *The Loyalists of Massachusetts, and the Other Side of the American Revolution*. Boston: W.B. Clarke Co., 1910. A digitized copy is at *http://archive.org/stream/loyalistsofmassa00staruoft#page/ n7/mode/2up*.

————. *The United Empire Loyalists* [United Empire Loyalist Transactions]. Toronto: The United Empire Loyalists of Canada, 1917.

United Empire Loyalists' Association of Canada, Toronto Branch. *Loyalist Lineages of Canada, 1783–1983*. 2 vols. Toronto: Generation Press, 1983 and 1991.

Upton, L. F. S. *The United Empire Loyalists: Men and Myths.* Toronto: Copp Clark Publishing Co., 1969.

Van Tyne, Claude Halstead. *The Loyalists in the American Revolution.* New York: The MacMillan Co., 1902. A digitized copy is at *http://archive. org/stream/loyalistsinamer00vantrich#page/n5/mode/2up.*

Wallace, W. Stewart. *The United Empire Loyalists. A Chronicle of the Great Migration* [Vol. 13 of "Chronicles of Canada"]. 1914. Reprint, Toronto: Glasgow, Brook and Co., 1972. A digitized copy is at *http:// archive.org/stream/unitedempireloya00walluoft#page/n13/mode/2up.*

Walton, Jesse M. *Quaker Loyalist Settlement, Pennfield, New Brunswick, 1783.* Aurora, Ont.: The author, 1940.

Wright, Esther Clark. *Loyalists of New Brunswick.* Fredericton, N.B.: The author, 1981.

Yoshpe, Harry Beller. *Disposition of Loyalist Estates in the Southern District of the State of New York.* New York: Columbia University Press, 1939.

The New York Public Library has a collection of American Loyalist claims papers, and the New Jersey State Library, Archives and History Department (185 W State Street, Trenton, NJ 08608), has records of New Jersey Loyalists whose estates were confiscated. There is also information about Loyalists from Sussex County, New Jersey, in an article by Thomas B. Wilson in *The Ontario Register* entitled "Notes on Some Loyalists of Sussex County, New Jersey" (Vol. 2, No. 1, 1969, pages 31–47).

A current periodical of importance to those interested in Loyalists and their records is the *Loyalist Gazette.* It is published twice yearly by the United Empire Loyalists Association of Canada. More information is available on the organization's website: *http://uelac.org/.*

B. Canadian Loyalist sources

Concerning official Loyalist sources in Canada, I quote from a genealogical booklet prepared by the Public Archives of Canada and published by the Queen's Printer and Controller of Stationery in Ottawa (1967 edition):

> A list of Loyalists in Upper Canada, compiled in the Office of the Commissioner of Crown Lands, and presently kept in the Crown Lands Department in Toronto, records names, contemporary residence and descendants; we [the Public Archives of Canada in Ottawa] have a transcript of this list. A similar list also in our holdings was retained in the Executive Council Office. Comparable lists were not compiled in other colonies.
>
> The Audit Office Series (A.O. 12 and A.O. 13) is perhaps the most rewarding source for the genealogist. The first of these contains evidence in support of Loyalist claims for losses sustained during the American Revolution together with the proceedings of the investigating commission, and the second records the evidence of claimants only. It should be emphasized

that by no means all of the Loyalists who suffered losses as a result of adherence to the Crown submitted claims, often because of the considerable expense entailed. These records give location of former residence in the various American colonies, size of families, often the dependents' names, details of military service and residence at the time of the claim. . . . These records are on microfilm [at the Public Archives]. The originals are in the Public Record Office [now the National Archives], London, England. The Series is completely indexed.

A further source, though one generally listing heads of families with the number of dependents, is the nominal lists and returns of Loyalists in the Haldimand Papers [which list the settlers by township], the originals of which are in the British Museum [now the British Library], in London. We [the Public Archives] have transcript copies of these lists, completely indexed.[19]

The Family History Library in Salt Lake City also has a microfilm copy of these two Audit Office Series (A.O. 12 and A.O. 13), plus their indexes. In addition, Ancestry has digitized and indexed these records. They are online at *http://search.ancestry.com/search/db.aspx?dbid=3712*.

I should also state here that there is a more current edition available of the "Tracing Your Ancestors in Canada" pamphlet than the one I have quoted here. Though the more recent edition does not include the above information, it is a useful resource. If you enter that title in your Internet search engine, you will be given many options—from a pdf file to a copy you can download and print.

---

[19] Public Archives of Canada, "Tracing Your Ancestors in Canada" (Ottawa: The Queen's Printer and Controller of Stationery, 1967), 17–18. Note that claim records in the Audit Office Series (A.O. 13) are being abstracted in a series being published by the National Genealogical Society, called *American Loyalist Claims*. The first volume (NGS publication no. 45) was compiled by Peter Wilson Coldham and published in 1980. The work is on the list of Loyalist works earlier in this chapter. It also has an index, which greatly facilitates its use.

27

Military Records: After the Revolution

I. BETWEEN THE REVOLUTION AND FORT SUMTER

The records arising out of the American Revolution, though they contain less information than some that followed, set a pattern for the records of later wars. And, as we look at these other wars, we observe that the same kinds of records (speaking generally) were also kept in relation to those who served in later wars:

- Service records
- Records of veterans' benefits

However, with the passage of time, another type of record also came into existence. We know these as draft registration records. They first appeared during the Civil War and became a fact of life in nearly every war that followed.

As we consider the records of wars between the Revolution and the American Civil War, we will again divide the records by categories rather than by war, but there are only these two categories because there was, as yet, no draft.

As indicated at the beginning of Chapter 26, many of these military records are now becoming available on indexed digitized databases on the Internet. There is a listing of the digitized military records on the Fold3 website at *https://go.fold3.com/records/military/*. And, as we look to the future, perhaps the day will come when all of these records will, at least, be on digitized databases (because no one is microfilming any more), and perhaps even indexed. However, with the volume of records involved, that day is still likely far off.

A. Service records

1. Compiled military service records—Army (similar to those made on 3½" x 8" cards for Revolutionary soldiers) exist for those who served during the post-Revolutionary period, including the following:

a. *Records for the period between the Revolution and the War of 1812 (called the post-Revolutionary War period).* These records are part of Record Group (RG) 94 at the National Archives, microfilm publication M905, on thirty-two rolls of microfilm. The films contain the records of volunteer soldiers serving between 1784 and 1811, but not including those who served in the Revolutionary War.

> The military service records of volunteer soldiers were abstracted onto cards from muster and pay rolls, descriptive rolls, returns, hospital records, prison records, accounts for subsistence, and other material. The card abstracts for each individual soldier were placed in a jacket-envelope bearing the soldier's name, rank, and military unit. This jacket-envelope, containing one or more abstracts and, in some instances, including one or more original documents relating specifically to that soldier, is called a **compiled military service record.**
>
> A compiled military service record is only as complete as the material about an individual soldier or [his] unit. A typical record shows the soldier's rank, military unit, dates of entry into service, and discharge or separation by desertion, death, or dismissal. It may also show age, place of birth, and residence at time of enlistment.[1] [Emphasis in original.]

These records have been digitized and, along with a description of the records, are on the Fold3 website (*https://www.fold3.com/browse/246/hH9i9bnSa*).

b. *Records for the War of 1812.* These are compiled military service records dated 1812–1815. Most are arranged by military unit within each state or territory. The information is the same as in the compiled service records of the post-Revolutionary War period. The Fold3 website has a digitized index to these records plus digitized copies of four series of the records themselves—records of more than 34,000 soldiers:

1) War of 1812 Service Records—Mississippi   29,632 records
2) War of 1812 Service Records—Lake Erie   4,113 records
3) War of 1812 Service Records—Chickasaw Indians   281 records
4) War of 1812 Service Records—Creek Indians   128 records

c. *Records of Indian and related wars.* These wars took place between 1817 and 1857. The information in the records is about the same as in those service records already mentioned except that the state from which the soldier served is not always identified. A table showing the microfilmed indexes to the combined service records of volunteers during the various Indian Wars is on page 138 of the *Guide to Genealogical Research in the National Archives of the United States,* 3rd. ed., edited by Eales and Kvasnicka (Washington, DC: National Archives and Records Administration, 2000). Digitized copies of the enlistment records—all of them arranged alpha-

---

[1] Anne Bruner Eales and Robert M. Kvasnicka, eds., *Guide to Genealogical Research in the National Archives of the United States,* 3rd ed. (Washington, DC: National Archives and Records Administration, 2000), 127.

betically—are on the Fold3 website at *https://www.fold3.com/browse/248/hXexiVV7MOIgn5tVl.*

d. *Records of the Mexican War, 1846–48.* These records contain all the information included in those of the previously mentioned wars, plus the soldier's age is sometimes given. A name index to these service records is called *Index to Compiled Service Records of Volunteer Soldiers Who Served During the Mexican War* (M616—forty-one rolls). The enlistment records can also be accessed on the Fold3 website at the same URL as listed above for the Indian and related wars.

Each series of these compiled service records is indexed, and each set of records—except those of the Mexican War—has indexes to the various states and the non-state organizations from which the men served. This means that it is usually easier to locate a soldier's service record if you know the state from which he served or the organization with which he served. That information can be found in the serviceman's pension-application records if a pension was claimed.

These compiled service records are all located in Record Group 94, Records of the Adjutant General's Office, at the National Archives. And, as already indicated, all digitized copies of these records are on the Fold3 website.

2. Miscellaneous military records, 1784–1815, are also in Record Group 94. These records consist of the following:

a. *Post-Revolutionary War manuscripts*

b. *Miscellaneous records of the War of 1812*

c. *Prisoner-of-war records of the War of 1812*

The first two of these record groups have master card indexes that include all names, but the prisoner-of-war records are only partially indexed. There is not a significant amount of family history information in any of these records, and most of the information of value is also in other service records.

3. Naval service records are varied but are not unlike the Army service records. However, they are slightly more complete during this early period. Naval service records in the National Archives include the following:

a. *Records relating to commissioned naval officers.* There are several series of these, mostly in Record Group 45. Among them are the following series:

1) *Register of officers, May 1815–June 1821.* This listing, which is alphabetical by first letter of surname, gives each officer's name, rank, date appointed to that rank, age, and remarks of his superior officer concerning his promotion potential.

2) *Statements of the place of birth of officers, 1816.* This one manuscript volume includes the name, age or date of birth, and place of birth for each officer included. Unfortunately, it is composed almost exclusively of officers whose surnames began with the letters *C* and *D.*

3) *Statements of the place of birth and residence of officers, 1826.* The entries are alphabetical in two manuscript volumes (but exclude chaplains and pursers). The record shows the name, state or territory of birth, state or territory from which appointed, and state or territory of which each officer was a citizen.

4) *Records of officers serving in 1829.* This is one indexed manuscript volume that claims to outline the service record of every officer then serving in the Navy.

5) *Statements of service written by officers, 1842–43.* There are two bound manuscript volumes that were essentially filled out by the officers themselves, from memory, in response to a questionnaire. The statements outline the service record of each officer then serving, up to the end of 1842. There are also two manuscript volumes with letters of transmittal and supplemental biographical statements by some naval officers.

6) *Abstracts of service of officers (in lettered volumes).* These include all naval officers who served between 1798 and 1893 (including noncommissioned officers). There are fifteen separate bound manuscript volumes, A–O. Volumes J and O are each bound in two parts. Each volume covers a specific time period. Some are indexed; others are alphabetical. For each officer, the record shows name, date of appointment, dates of changes in rank, and the nature of each officer's termination of service. (Note that these are in RG 24, M330—nineteen microfilm rolls.)

7) *Records of officers in numbered volumes.* There are thirty-eight manuscript volumes relating mainly to naval officers commissioned between 1846 and 1902, with some later entries. There is a master index, and an individual officer's entry usually gives his name, birth date, birthplace, date of entering duty, ranks held, duty stations, place of residence, and date and place of death.

8) *Register of engineer officers.* This manuscript volume relates to officers of the Navy Engineer Corps between 1843 and 1899. Each entry shows name, date of birth, place of birth, date of appointment, date of death or retirement, place of death, and a detailed service record.

b. *Registers of admissions of midshipmen or cadets.* These registers relate primarily to those admitted to the U.S. Naval Academy at Annapolis between 1849 and 1930; they are arranged chronologically by date of appointment. An appointee's entry gives name, birth date (early registers give age instead), signature, name of parent or guardian, and place of residence. Information relating to midshipmen is meager.

c. *Records of enlisted men.* These records relate to men who enlisted in the Navy between 1798 and 1956. The following are included in these extensive records:

1) Muster rolls and payrolls of vessels between 1798 and 1844. They are in bound manuscript volumes and are not indexed. However, each volume ordinarily relates to only one vessel for a specific time period, with some vessels having several volumes. They are maintained alphabetically by the names of vessels, and each volume is arranged chronologically. The volumes relating to the Frigate *Constitution*, 1798–1815, are all indexed.

These records often enable a researcher to follow a man throughout his naval career because many entries show the name of the vessel from which a man came or to which he went upon reassignment. If you find your ancestor on the Frigate *Constitution*, or you learn from other sources—such as pension records—that he served on a certain vessel, you can often trace him through his entire naval service in these rolls.

Muster and pay rolls through 1859 are in Record Group 45. Those for 1860–1900 are in Record Group 24; some are microfilmed.

2) *Muster rolls and pay rolls of shore establishments.* These mainly cover 1805–49 and 1859–69. They are in bound manuscript volumes, arranged the same as those rolls for vessels in number 1), above. The information and the usage are essentially the same.

3) *Registers of enlistments.* This is the best source of information on Navy enlisted personnel. There are three manuscript volumes covering 1845–54, and they are arranged alphabetically by the first letter of the surname. Volumes One and Two are continuous from 1845 to 1853; Volume Three is for 1854 only. These registers are indexed and the index, on microfilm, is incorporated into the Index to *Rendezvous Reports, Before and After the Civil War, 1846–61 and 1865–84* [see item 4), below]. Each register entry shows name, date and place of enlistment, birthplace, and age. There is also a "remarks" column, often containing information on names of ships and duty stations to which assigned as well as discharge date.

4) *Weekly returns of enlistments at naval rendezvous.* These records cover 1855–91 and are bound in chronological volumes. The entry for each enlistee shows his name, date of enlistment, term of enlistment, rating, birthplace, age, occupation, personal description, and sometimes residence. Reference to any previous naval service is also included. The non-Civil War returns are indexed with the registers of enlistment in item 3) above (RG 24, T1098—thirty-two rolls).

5) *Jackets for enlisted men.* These jackets are arranged alphabetically for 1842–55 and normally show name, full service record, and place of residence after service.

6) *Certificates of consent.* This one manuscript volume covers 1838 to 1840 and contains certificates signed by parents or guardians allowing youths between ages thirteen and eighteen to become naval appren-

tices and serve until age twenty-one. A certificate gives the boy's name, his birth date, and the name of his parent or guardian. The certificates are arranged chronologically, and there is no index. They are also in RG 24.

4. Marine Corps service records also have significance for some. They include the following:

  a. *Records of commissioned officers*

    1) *Letters of acceptance.* There are three manuscript volumes dated 1808–62. Volume 1 is alphabetical by surname and covers 1808–16. The other two volumes are arranged chronologically and cover years 1812 to 1862. Each letter shows name, date commission was accepted, and (after 1830) state or territory of birth, and state or territory from which appointed. Some also give the place of residence.

    2) *Card list of officers.* These alphabetically arranged cards, covering 1798 to 1941, show only name, year of appointment, and rank.

  b. *Records of enlisted men*

    1) *Service records.* These records are in individual jackets (one for each man) and cover 1798–1895. Within each year, they are arranged by the first letter of the enlistee's surname and then by date of enlistment. There is a group of cards [see item 2), below] showing the enlistees' names and their dates and places of enlistment. These cards are an index to these records. The jackets themselves usually contain information relating to name, date of enlistment, place, term of enlistment, age, personal description, occupation, and sometimes the date and circumstances of separation from the Marine Corps.

    2) *Card list of enlisted men.* These are the cards mentioned in number 1), above, and cover 1798 to 1941.[2]

5. There are also books available that contain rolls, rosters, and biographical information of servicemen during the period between the Revolution and the Civil War. Many libraries have good collections. You will want to look at the bibliography at the end of this chapter as well as the bibliography in Chapter 26. Some of the books listed there relate to this period of military history as well as to the Revolution.

B. Veterans' benefits

1. There are four series of pension records that relate to men who served between the Revolution and the Civil War and, depending on the time or the war of your ancestor's service, you may find value in one or more of them.

---

[2] All the preceding information on service records between the Revolution and the Civil War was taken from (1) Colket and Bridgers, *Guide to Genealogical Records in the National Archives,* 65–76; (2) Guide to Genealogical Research in the National Archives, rev. ed., 89–95 and 111–119; and (3) Eales and Kvasnicka (eds.), *Guide to Genealogical Research in the National Archives of the United States,* 3rd ed., 156–164.

a. *The "Old Wars" (or "Old War") series* relates to death and disability claims for service during this entire period under various congressional acts (the first in 1790). The claims concern service in the regular Army, Navy, or Marine Corps during the War of 1812, Mexican War, Indian wars, and, in some cases, the Civil War. The files are alphabetical, and there is a microfilm index to the entire series, 1815–1926 (RG 15, T316—seven rolls). This index is called *Old War Index of Pension Files, 1815–1926.* An entry in the index shows the

> name of the veteran; name and class of dependent, if any; service unit; application, file and certificate number; and state from which the claim was made. Cross-references to files in other series are included when appropriate.[3]

According to Colket and Bridgers, the pension files themselves contain the

> name, rank, military or naval unit, and period of service of the veteran. If he applied for a pension, it shows his age or date of birth, place of residence, and sometimes place of birth. If the widow applied, it shows her age and the place of her marriage to the veteran, and her maiden name. If the veteran left orphans, it shows their names, ages, and the places of their residence.[4]

b. *The War of 1812 series* contains papers relating to claims based on service between 1812 and 1815. These pensions were granted primarily under acts passed in 1871 and 1878.[5] The files are arranged alphabetically.

Interfiled with these pension papers at the National Archives is a subseries relating to death and disability claims that was previously a part of the "Old Wars" series. There are also some War of 1812 bounty land warrant applications from the post-Revolutionary War series. These additions greatly enhance the value of the files because the records of many more soldiers are included, and these added records had their origin soon after the war.

Regarding these War of 1812 pension files, Eales and Kvasnicka explain that they are

> arranged alphabetically by name of veteran. The alphabetical name index is available as M313 [in RG 15], *Index to War of 1812 Pension Applications Files,* 102 rolls. Each frame shows the face side of a jacket-envelope containing relevant documents. Given are the name of a veteran; name of the widow, if any; service data; pension application and certificate numbers; and/or a bounty land warrant application number, if any. Certain pension application files in the War of 1812

---

[3] Eales and Kvasnicka, 173.

[4] Meredith B. Colket, Jr., and Frank E. Bridgers, *Guide to Genealogical Records in the National Archives* (Washington, DC: The National Archives, 1964), 82.

[5] The fact that service pension legislation was not passed until so long after the war is a major limitation on the value of these records. Relatively few servicemen, and even few widows, lived that long.

series can be located through the use of the Remarried Widows Index, which is available on microfilm as M1784 [in RG 15], *Index to Pension Application Files of Remarried Widows Based on Service in the War of 1812, Indian Wars, Mexican War, and Regular Army Before 1861*, 1 roll.[6]

c. *The Mexican War series* of pension records is based on an act passed by Congress in 1887; it provided benefits for service performed between 1846 and 1848. Pensions were available to veterans who served at least sixty days and to the unremarried widows of veterans. A few of the death and disability files formerly included in the "Old Wars" series are now also part of this series. Several different documents are in the files, though every pensioner's file will not contain all of them. The files are arranged alphabetically, and there is an alphabetical name index on microfilm—*Index to Mexican War Pension Files, 1887–1926* (T317 in RG 15, fourteen rolls). The pension application files from the "Old Wars" series that are now included here relate to men who were disabled or killed in the Mexican War.

> Entries in the index show name of the veteran; name and class of dependent, if any; service data; and application number and state from which the claim was made. Certain pension application files in the Mexican War series can be located through the Remarried Widows Index on M1784 [in RG 15, one roll] . . .[7]

Colket and Bridgers explained these pension files:

> A veteran's declaration shows the name of the veteran; the dates and places of his birth, his enlistment, and his discharge; and the places of his residence since service. The declaration of a widow seeking a pension shows the same information about the service of the veteran; her name, age, and place of residence; the date and place of her marriage to the veteran, with the name of the person performing the ceremony; and the date and place of the death of the veteran. A filled-out questionnaire shows the maiden name of the wife; the date and place of the marriage of the couple and name of the person performing the ceremony; the name of a former wife, if any, and the date and place of her death or divorce; and the names and dates of birth of living children.[8]

Pension records for the Mormon Battalion, which participated in the Mexican War, are on twenty-one rolls of microfilm (RG 15, T1196). The title of these files is *Selected Pension Application Files Relating to the Mormon Battalion, Mexican War; 1846–1848*.

d. *The Indian Wars series* resulted from an act of Congress in 1892 and other later acts. The 1892 act provided service pensions for veterans of wars between 1832 and 1834 and their unremarried widows. Later acts

---

[6] Eales and Kvasnicka, 173.

[7] Ibid., 174.

[8] Colket and Bridgers, 83.

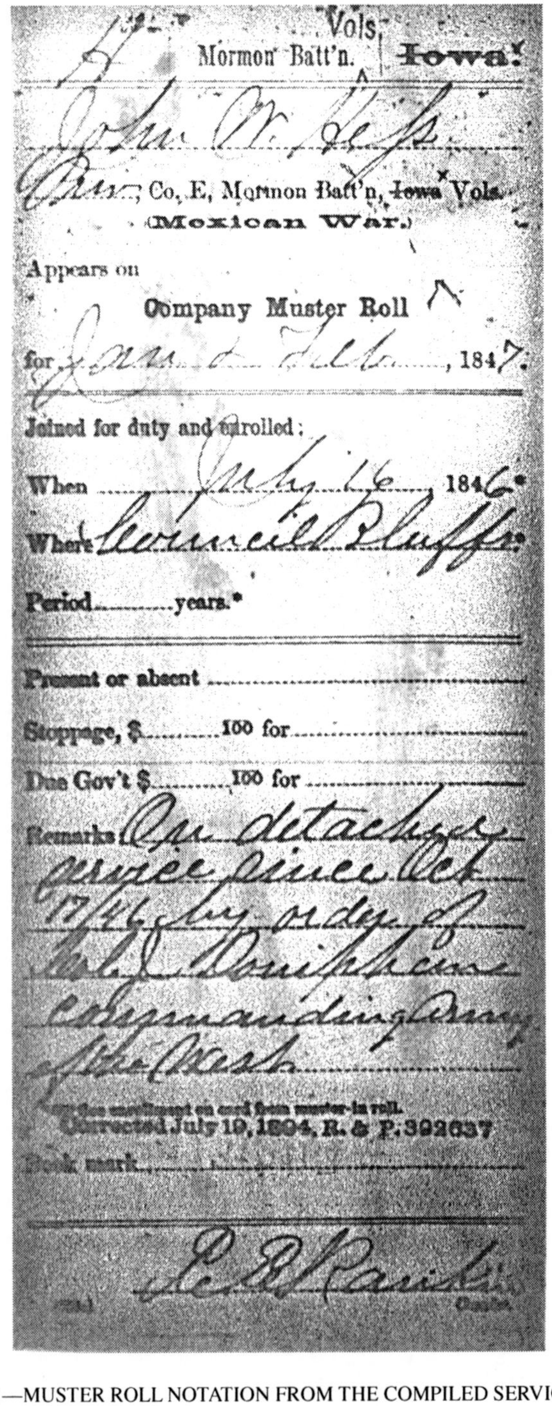

Vols.
Mormon Batt'n. | ~~Iowa~~.

John W. Hess

Priv.; Co. E, Mormon Batt'n, ~~Iowa~~ Vols.
(Mexican War.)

Appears on
Company Muster Roll
for Jan & Feb, 1847.

Joined for duty and enrolled:
When July 16, 1846.*
Where Council Bluffs.*
Period .... years.*

Present or absent ....
Stoppage, $........100 for ....
Due Gov't $........100 for ....
Remarks: On detached service since Oct 17/46 by order of Col J Doniphan commanding Army of the West

*[illegible] enrollment on card from muster-in roll.
Corrected July 10, 1894, R. & P. 392637

Book mark: ....

[illegible]

FIGURE 1—MUSTER ROLL NOTATION FROM THE COMPILED SERVICE RECORDS OF THE MEXICAN WAR extended the benefits to all who served in Indian wars between 1817 and 1898. There are also some files in this series that were previously part of the "Old Wars" series.

The files are arranged alphabetically, but there is also a microfilm index to this series at the National Archives called "Index to Indian Wars Pension Files, 1892–1926" (RG 15, T318—twelve rolls). Entries in that index show

> name of the veteran; name and class of dependent, if any; service data; and application number and, for an approved claim, pension certificate number and state from which the claim was made.
>
> For pension application files concerning men who were disabled or killed in Indian wars and in whose behalf no service claims were made, *see* the records in the Old Wars series. For pension applications relating to persons who served in an Indian campaign during the War of 1812, Mexican War, or Civil War, *see* the pension indexes relating to claims based on service in that war.[9]

Concerning the contents of actual service files, Colket and Bridgers explained that the information in the files

> varies depending upon the act under which the pension was applied for, the number of years of the veteran's survival after the war, and whether or not he was survived by a widow. A file contains some or all of the following information: the name, Army unit, and place of residence of the veteran; a summary of his Army record; his age or the date of his birth; the place of his birth; date and place of his marriage; the date and place of his death; and the names of their surviving children, with the date and place of birth of each.[10]

Access to *some* files in all four of the above-described pension series can be obtained by using the first part of the *Remarried Widows Index*. This index is in two parts—one relating to non-Revolutionary War claims prior to the Civil War and the other relating to the Civil War and all post-Civil War military service before World War I. The index is alphabetical by the names of the remarried widows. The name of the woman's former husband, his service unit, and the file or certificate number are included.

As with Revolutionary War pension application files, copies of these pension application files can also be ordered by mail using NATF Form 85. (See the illustration of this form [Figure 3] in Chapter 26.)

2. Bounty-land warrant applications for all service after the Revolutionary War—except those relating to the War of 1812—are filed in one series. Applications for bounty land based on service in the War of 1812 are interfiled with the Revolutionary War pension claims, as noted earlier.

---

[9] Eales and Kvasnicka, 174.

[10] Colket and Bridgers, 85.

These bounty-land application files are much like those for the Revolutionary War—many, in fact, were granted under the same legislation. They are merely filed separately. There is no index to the files in this later wars series, but they are filed alphabetically by the names of the veterans.

The final bounty land act, passed by Congress in 1855, authorized issuance of warrants for 160 acres to anyone who served for at least fourteen days or in a battle. The files relating to approved applications are identified by a number that begins with the abbreviation "B.L.Wt," followed by the warrant number, the number of acres in the grant, and the year of the act under which the claim was submitted (often just the last two digits of that year).

Files of disapproved applications are in the same file and are identified with the abbreviation "B.L.Rej [or Reg]," followed by the assigned register number and the year of the act involved. There is little difference in the contents of these two types of files.

The information in a bounty land application file usually includes

> the name, age, residence, military unit, and period of service of the veteran. If the applicant was an heir, the file should also show the name, age, and place of residence of the widow or other claimant, and the date of the veteran's death. If the application was approved, the file shows the warrant number, number of acres granted, year of the act, and where appropriate, name of the assignee. Two or more claims under different acts may have been filed together if they related to the service of the same veteran.[11]

Both the pension application files and the bounty land application files are in RG 15, Records of the Veterans Administration, at the National Archives. As of 2017, it does not appear that these records have been either microfilmed or digitized. However, copies can be obtained by using NATF Form 85.

You should also note that much of the information found in pension and bounty land application files is the very information you need to locate a soldier's service record.

II. THE CIVIL WAR, 1861–65

You have probably noticed that military records are quite typical of most family history sources in that the later records have more information than the earlier ones. This fact holding true, records of the Civil War are better than the records of any of the wars we have already discussed. And now, for the first time, we can appropriately divide the records into three types:

- Draft registration records
- Service records
- Records of veterans' benefits

---

[11] Eales and Kvasnicka, 181.

A. Draft registration records

There were three classes of "consolidated lists" that were created because of draft legislation passed by Congress in March 1863:

- Lists of all men subject to military duty between the ages of 20 and 35 years and unmarried men above age 35 years and under age 45
- Lists of married men aged above 35 and under 45
- Lists of veterans and of those currently serving (i.e., volunteers)

The principal draft records of the Washington office of the Provost Marshal General's Bureau that relate to individual men are the Union Army consolidated lists.

> Most [of these lists] are in bound volumes, arranged by state, thereunder by enrollment or congressional district, and thereunder by class [the three classes listed above]. . . . Entries in each class are arranged in rough alphabetical order by initial letter of surname. Each entry shows name; place of residence; age on July 1, 1863; occupation; marital status; state, territory, or country of birth; and, if Class III, the military organization.[12]

There are also descriptive rolls that are the principal records of the enrollment districts. These are

> arranged by state, thereunder by number of enrollment or congressional district. The rolls are chiefly in bound volumes. Arrangement of the entries varies considerably from district to district. Some are not indexed; some are indexed by initial letter of surname; and some are indexed by place of residence.
>
> An entry often shows, in addition to information in the corresponding consolidated list, the physical description, place of birth, and whether accepted or rejected for military service. Entries in many volumes, however, are not complete.[13]

Both the consolidated lists and the descriptive rolls are valuable, but in both cases, it is necessary to know the congressional district in which a man lived in order to find him. If you know the county where he lived, you can determine the congressional district by checking the *Congressional Directory for the Second Session of the Thirty-Eighth Congress of the United States of America* (Washington, DC, 1865), a photocopy of which is in the National Archives central search room.

The National Archives also has a list of Civil War districts that gives, for each state, the names of the counties in each congressional district. National Archives personnel in the Military Archives Division will determine the congressional district and search the draft records for you if you know the county where the person was living—or, if he was living in a large city, the ward of the city.

---

[12] Ibid., 144.

[13] Ibid., 144.

If this sounds complicated, you will be pleased to learn that the Union Army draft records have been digitized and are indexed on the Ancestry website (at *http://search.ancestry.com/search/db.aspx?dbid=1666*). Earlier cautions given concerning the use of indexes also apply here.

B. Service records

The Union Army service records

> exist for nearly all soldiers who were accepted for service in the Union Army as militiamen or volunteers, 1861–65, whether or not they actually served. Records relating to soldiers who participated in actions that occurred between 1861 and 1865 are included in the records of the Civil War, even if the actions were unrelated to the war, such as Indian warfare.
>
> Records of enlisted men sometimes include information about age, residence, occupation at the time of enlistment, and physical description. Personal papers occasionally give additional information about residence, family, or business of officers and enlisted men. Information about heirs is sometimes found in records concerning hospitalization or death in service.[14]

There are also some important guides to Civil War service records, as noted in the third edition (2000) of *Guide to Genealogical Research in the National Archives of the United States*, edited by Eales and Kvasnicka:

> A comprehensive description of the various records available is given in *Guide to Federal Records Relating to the Civil* War,[15] compiled by Kenneth W. Munden and Henry P. Beers (Washington: National Archives and Records Service, 1962; reprinted 1998). Some information also appears in *War of the Rebellion: A Compilation of the Official Records of the Union and Confederate Armies,* 128 vols. (Washington: War Department, 1880–1901). This publication is available on microfilm as M262, *Official Records of the Union and Confederate Armies, 1861*–1865, 128 rolls, and was reprinted by the National Historical Society, Gettysburg, PA, 1971–72 and again in 1985. . . . The name index may enable researchers to discover actions in which their ancestors participated.[16] The National Archives produced two research aids to this compilation. The researcher may wish to consult M1036, *Military Operations of the Civil War: A Guide Index to the Official Records of the Union and Confederate Armies, 1861–1865, Volume 1, Conspectus,* 1 roll, and M1815, *Military Operations of the Civil War: A Guide-Index to the Official Records of the Union and Confederate Armies, Volumes I–V,* 18 fiche.[17]

---

[14] Ibid., 139.

[15] The correct title of this book is *Guide to Federal Archives Relating to the Civil War.* A digital copy is online at http://archive.org/stream/guidetofederalar00mund#page/n3/mode/2up.

[16] In this important work, there are 70 volumes arranged in four series. They are available in many libraries and online at http://ebooks.library.cornell.edu/m/moawar/waro.html.

[17] Eales and Kvasnicka, 141.

Concerning the nature and arrangement of Civil War service records, Colket and Bridgers explained that they consist of

> card abstracts and documents relating to individual soldiers, such as voluntary enlistment papers, prisoner-of-war papers, hospital bed cards, and death reports. The cards and sometimes the documents relating to one soldier are filed in a jacket envelope. The jacket-envelopes for men in State organizations are arranged by name of State; thereunder by arm of service such as cavalry, artillery, infantry; thereunder numerically by regiment; thereunder alphabetically by name of soldier. The jacket-envelopes for men in other organizations such as the U.S. Sharp Shooters are arranged similarly. Many of the documents relating to individual soldiers in State organizations are not filed in the jacket-envelopes with the related card abstracts but are filed separately in alphabetical order at the end of the file for the State. Some jacket-envelopes include cross-references to the names on the regimental papers that are filed with the muster rolls.
>
> In addition to these basic files, there is a separate file of card abstracts pertaining to both volunteer and Regular Army staff officers, which is arranged alphabetically by name of officer.[18]

There is no master index to these Civil War service records, but rather a separate name index for each state and for each organization that was not connected with a specific state. This means that, in order to locate the service record of your Union Army ancestor, you must know the state from which he served or the organization with which he served. Table 9 on page 140 of the third edition of *Guide to Genealogical Research in the National Archives of the United States,* edited by Eales and Kvasnicka, gives the microfilm publication numbers for both the indexes and the compiled service records, state-by-state. The records of many states have not been filmed or digitized.

These service records, according to Eales and Kvasnicka, contain the same information on each soldier as do the compiled service records of the earlier wars, plus

> the date of a change in his rank, and the date, place, and nature of his discharge. For some soldiers there is a voluntary enlistment paper or an abstract that shows his age, the town or county of his birth, his occupation, and a personal description. If the soldier was hospitalized, a bed card shows his age, nativity, evidence of whether or not he was married, his place of residence, and the date and occasion of his being wounded. If he died in service, a casualty sheet shows the date and place of his death.[19]

Many of the Civil War service records have been digitized and are indexed on the Fold3 website at *https://go.fold3.com/records/civil-war/.*

Some other records that relate to Union Army service include the following:

1. Service histories of volunteer units. At the same time that service records for the individual Union Army soldiers were compiled, the War Depart-

---

[18] Colket and Bridgers, 55.

[19] Eales and Kvasnicka, 56.

ment also compiled histories of volunteer units. These have been microfilmed as *Compiled Records Showing Service of Military Units in Volunteer Union Organizations* (RG 94, M594—225 rolls).

2. Burial records of soldiers. These records are very incomplete. Nearly all of them relate to soldiers buried at U.S. military installations. There are four volumes relating to burials in the U.S. Soldiers' Home in Washington, DC, 1861–68. These are the most complete of the Civil War soldiers' burial registers.

> Entries in these volumes also show rank; place of residence before enlistment; name and residence of widow or other relative; age; cause, place, and date of death; and date of burial.[20]

Other registers have even less information, but, at a minimum, they have the soldier's name, his military organization, and the date and place of his burial. Some compiled lists of Union soldiers buried at the U.S. Soldiers' Home, 1861–1918, give the name, military organization, date of death, and place of burial for each soldier. These lists are alphabetical, but there is a separate set of lists for each state from which these soldiers served.

There are also some lists of soldiers buried in national cemeteries, mainly between 1861 and 1865 (some as late as 1886). These lists give the same information as the lists of soldiers buried at the U.S. Soldiers' Home mentioned above. These lists are arranged alphabetically by state of burial.

> For each state, there are three kinds of lists: on one, the names are arranged by cemetery, on another by military organization, and on another alphabetically by initial letter of surname of the soldier. Lists arranged by surname, however, exist only for Connecticut, Delaware, District of Columbia, Iowa, Maine, Maryland, Massachusetts, Michigan, New Hampshire, New Jersey, Pennsylvania, Rhode Island, Vermont, and Wisconsin. An entry usually shows the name of the soldier, military organization, date of death, and place of burial.[21]

Information on the burials of Union soldiers in private and public cemeteries during the Civil War is in a twenty-seven-volume publication called *Roll of Honor.* These books were published by the U.S. Quartermaster Department between 1865 and 1971.

> Entries are arranged by name of cemetery, thereunder alphabetically by name of soldier; they show the date of death. An accompanying *Alphabetical Index to Places of Interment of Deceased Union Soldiers* (Washington: U.S. Quartermaster Department, 1868) pertains to volumes 1–13. The National Archives has an unpublished place index to all 27 volumes. . . .
>
> The Cemetery Service, National Cemetery System, Veterans Administration, 810 Vermont Ave. NW, Washington, DC 20420, has alphabetically arranged carded records identifying practically all **soldiers who were buried**

---

[20] Ibid., 193.

[21] Ibid., 192.

in national cemeteries and other cemeteries under Federal jurisdiction from 1861 to the present.[22] [Emphasis in original.]

A group known as the Sons of Union Veterans of the Civil War (SU-VCW) has undertaken, in recent years, what it calls a Grave Registration Project. The project's purpose is to document the graves of Civil War veterans, both Union and Confederate, wherever they may be. This indexed database is online, and there are no usage fees involved. It can be searched by going to *http://suvcwdb.org/index.php?r=site/search.*

This project—which began in 1996—is ongoing, and the SUVCW is looking for people to participate. The project involves making visits to graveyards. For more information, go online to *http://suvcwdb.org/.*

3. Headstone applications. Between 1879 and 1925, the Federal Government, by an act of Congress, erected headstones on the graves of Union servicemen, wherever they were buried. (Other acts have provided headstones for those who served in the Revolutionary War and in other wars.)

> Applications for headstones were made by relatives of the deceased veteran, veterans associations, local or state governments, or civic groups. Each application shows the name and address of the applicant for the headstone, name of veteran, military organization, rank, years of service, place and date of burial, and sometimes date and cause of death.
>
> Applications are in several series, with most arranged by state of burial, thereunder by county, and thereunder by cemetery. . . . A few of the applications that relate to servicemen who were buried at branches of the National Home for Disabled Volunteer Soldiers are arranged by name of the home, thereunder by date of application.
>
> Alphabetically arranged cards document the applications dated 1879–1903. Each card shows the soldier's name, military organization, name and location of cemetery where buried, date and place of death, and date of applications. These cards have been microfilmed as M1845 [in RG 92], *Card Records of Headstones Provided for Deceased Union Civil War Veterans, ca. 1879–ca. 1903,* 22 rolls.[23]

These headstone application cards have been digitized and indexed; they are on the Ancestry website at *http://search.ancestry.com/search/db.aspx?dbid=1195.*

4. Naval service records

There are also significant records relating to those who served in the Union Navy.

a. *Age certificates of officers.* These records were created by an act of Congress passed in December 1861 relating to the retirement of officers.

> The certificates are in four volumes, two for 1862 and two for 1863.
> The entries in each series are arranged alphabetically by surname of

---

[22] Ibid., 193.

[23] Ibid., 193.

officer and are indexed. Each certificate is signed by the officer and shows name, rank, and date of birth. These volumes are in RG 24.[24]

b. *Biographies of officers.* There are three indexed manuscript volumes of these biographies. They were prepared about 1865 and contain detailed information (though both the content and the amount of detail vary significantly). Their chief shortcoming is that coverage was very incomplete.

c. *Registers of candidates for admission to the U.S. Naval Academy.* These records cover 1849 to 1930, but with some gaps. They are in RG 45 and are filed chronologically by date of appointment. Most entries show candidate's name, residence, date and place of birth, and signature. They also give the name, residence, and occupation or profession of the candidate's parent or guardian.[25]

d. *Records of Navy enlisted men.* There are several series of bound volumes of muster rolls and pay rolls. For the period between 1860 and 1900, there are 366 volumes. These volumes are in three separate series and are arranged alphabetically within each series by the names of the ships.

> The volumes contain, for each person aboard, information concerning enlistment, whether entitled to an honorable discharge, personal description, date received on board, and applicable data concerning transfer, discharge, desertion, or death.[26]

Muster rolls and payrolls for shore establishments are also arranged alphabetically by the names of the stations and then chronologically. To use these records, it is necessary to know when and where the person served.

In addition to those records listed here, there are also many records relating to service during the pre-Civil War period that overlap into the Civil War era and often extend beyond. These records were discussed earlier in this chapter.

A great number of naval records are located at the National Archives at College Park, MD. Many of these records have been digitized and indexed and are online and accessible for research on the FindMyPast website: *http:// search.findmypast.com/search-world-Records/civil-war-sailors-1861-1865.*

B. Veterans' benefits

Veterans' benefits for those who served in the Civil War were almost exclusively pensions. As mentioned in Chapter 19 in our discussion of land entry records in the public domain, no bounty land warrants were issued for Civil War service. Insofar as land was concerned, Civil War veterans (both Union

---

[24] Ibid., 156.

[25] Ibid., 157.

[26] Ibid., 158.

and Confederate) were given special consideration in Homestead legislation.

All pension applications relating to military service between 1861 and 1934 are filed in one series, but this excluded certain Indian wars already discussed and World War I.[27]

The pension applications of interest to us here are called the "Civil War and Later" series and, in addition to Union Army Civil War pensioners, also include pension applications relating to service in the Spanish-American War, the Philippine Insurrection, the Boxer Rebellion, and the Regular Army. Both death/disability pensions and the service pensions are included in this series. As mentioned earlier, a few naval death and disability pensions from the early part of the Civil War are also in the "Old Wars" series.

Both the information and the documents in the files of the Civil War and Later series vary significantly, depending upon the act of Congress under which the applicant sought relief—as well as other factors. Civil War veterans with Union Army, Navy, or Marine service were all included, but Confederate veterans were not.

> The information in the files varies depending on the act under which the pension was applied for, the number of years the veteran survived after the war, and whether or not . . . survived by a widow or other dependent.
>
> The number and type of documents in the Civil War and later series vary greatly from file to file. Documents of the greatest genealogical interest include the declaration of the veteran, declaration of the widow, statement of service from the War or Navy Department, personal history questionnaire, and documents relating to the termination of pensions.
>
> The records are arranged numerically by application, certificate, or file number. Index cards, arranged alphabetically by surname of veteran, have been microfilmed as T288, *General Index to Pension Files, 1861–1934*, 544 rolls. A card shows the name of the veteran, name and class of dependent, if any; service data; application number or file number and state from which the claim was filed. Also available on microfilm is M1785, *Index to Pension Application Files of Remarried Widows Based on Service in the Civil War and Later Wars and in the Regular Army After the Civil War*, 7 rolls.
>
> Because the alphabetical index often shows several veterans with the same name, it may be difficult to identify the file desired without time-consuming research. This difficulty can be resolved if the researcher knows the military or naval unit the veteran served in or the given name of the veteran's widow. It is also helpful to know, in addition, the residence or date of birth of the veteran. Such information appears on the award cards. . . .
>
> Pension Office **award cards** record payments to pensioners on the rolls, 1907–33, except for World War I pensioners. Arranged alphabetically by surname of pensioner, the cards were microfilmed as M850, *Veterans Administration Pension Payment Cards, 1907–1933*, 2,539 rolls. Each card shows name of pensioner, military unit, date of the act and certificate or file number

---

[27] Should the "Indian Wars" series of pension applications fail to disclose a pension application for a veteran of one of the later Indian wars, a search of the "Civil War and Later" series is recommended.

under which payment was made, and date the pension began. Some cards show place of residence and date of death of a pensioner, names of the pension agencies from which or to which jurisdiction was transferred, and name of widow or other recipient of death benefits. The cards are sometimes useful in identifying Civil War or other pension application files that cannot be identified from the microfilmed indexes.[28] [Emphasis in original.]

There are two indexes to these files—an alphabetical name index (name of veteran), and an organization index for use if you know the state and the organization in which he served.[29] The latter has advantages if you have the necessary information to use it. The "Veterans' Schedules" of the 1890 census can be of assistance here (see Chapter 14). Also, some of these files can be accessed through use of the second part of the *Remarried Widows Index* mentioned in the previous quotation.

Copies of Union Army service and pension files can be obtained from the National Archives through use of NATF Form 85, discussed in Chapter 26. The index to these files—but *not* the files themselves—is on Ancestry at *http://search.ancestry.com/search/db.aspx?dbid=4654*.

With regard to the widows of Navy veterans, also be aware of the following:

> About 7,000 rejected applications make up a separate publication, M1274, *Case Files of Disapproved Pension Applications of Widows and Other Dependents of Civil War and Later Navy Veterans ("Navy Widows' Originals") 1861–1910*, ca. 8,500 microfiche. Also available is M1391, *Lists of Navy Veterans for Whom There are Navy Widows' and Other Dependents' Disapproved Pension Files ("Navy Widows' Originals") 1861–1910*, 15 microfiche.[30]

C. The other side of the war: the Confederacy

As the Confederate troops evacuated Richmond in 1865, the Confederate military records were taken to Charlotte, North Carolina, by the adjutant and inspector general, who transferred them to a Union officer. From there, they were taken to Washington, DC, along with various records captured during the war. In 1903, the Secretary of War, who had custody of those records, persuaded the governors of most of the Southern states to lend their military personnel records to the War Department for copying. These records now comprise a substantial portion of the War Department Collection of Confederate Records and are in Record Group 109.

---

[28] Eales and Kvasnicka, 174, 176, and 177.

[29] The alphabetical index is called *General Index to Pension Files, 1861–1934* (T288—544 rolls). The organization index is called *Organization Index to Pension Files of Veterans Who Served Between 1861 and 1900* (T259—165 rolls).

[30] Eales and Kvasnicka, 176.

The Confederate Army relied even more heavily on the draft than did the Union. They started drafting men earlier in the conflict (Act of April 16, 1862), and the reach of their draft laws was much broader. They began by drafting men between 18 and 35, and finally settled on all men between 17 and 55—for three years of service. Unfortunately, there are no known Confederate draft records in existence.

It is also unfortunate that records relating to the Confederate forces are not as complete as are those of Union Army troops. However, there are records and you need to be aware of them. The National Archives has three series of **Compiled Military Service Records** of Confederate troops. These have all been microfilmed and have also been digitized and indexed. You can access these records, as well as a complete description and instructions on their use, on the Fold3 website at *https://www.fold3.com/ page/367_confederate_compiled_military_service_records#description.*

These compiled Confederate service records were brought together on cards by the War Department from various sources, including prisoner of war records, prisoner parole records, muster rolls, returns, rosters, pay rolls, appointment books, hospital registers, etc. All cards relating to the same individual soldier are generally in the same jacket-envelope. There are three series of these records:

- Those filed by state (by far the largest series)
- Those for troops in non-state organizations
- Those for officers and enlisted personnel doing their jobs

There is a consolidated alphabetical name index (RG 109, M253—535 rolls) as well as an index for each Confederate state. If you know the state from which the soldier served, that is usually the best place for your research to start.

For the benefit of those who wish to use these microfilm records, Table 11 on page 145 of the third edition of *Guide to Genealogical Research in the National Archives of the United States*, edited by Eales and Kvasnicka, gives the microfilm publication numbers for both the indexes and the compiled service records for each of the fifteen Confederated states. The compiled records

> consist of cards on which the War Department . . . recorded information abstracted from Union prison and parole records and from captured and other surviving Confederate records. They are similar to those for Union Volunteers. In addition to the usual information found on compiled military service records, some of these show facts about a soldier's imprisonment. If he was captured, they may show the date of his release and parole, or if he died in prison, the date of his death. References to the original records are included on the cards. Researchers should note, however, that original records rarely contain any additional information.[31]

---

[31] Ibid., 144.

There are also various minor records in the National Archives, including some "Citizens Files" and some "Amnesty and Pardon Records," which primarily provide information on places of residence for those involved.

As with other military records, the originals of the Confederate records in the National Archives are available by using NATF Form 85.

Also, note that the individual Southern states offered pensions for their disabled and indigent veterans and to widows of veterans. Pensions were applied for and issued by the state of residence and not the state of service. Records relating to the pension applications are available for research as explained in the following list:

ALABAMA: Alabama began granting pensions in 1867. The records are digitized and indexed and are available on the Ancestry website at *http://search. ancestry.com/search/db.aspx?dbid=1593.* The original applications are in the Alabama Department of Archives and History, 624 Washington Avenue, Montgomery, AL 36130. Also, Ancestry has a digitized and indexed record of Confederate pensions in Alabama, Texas, and Virginia at *http://search.ancestry. com/search/db.aspx?dbid=1677.*

ARKANSAS: Arkansas began granting pensions in 1891. Information from the pension applications (but not digitized copies) is on the Ancestry website at *http://search.ancestry.com/search/ db.aspx?dbid=2281.* On the FamilySearch website, the records are digitized and indexed. Be aware that there are two sets of records. One is of the applications for "Ex-Confederate" pensions, 1891 to 1931; it is on the FamilySearch website at *https://familysearch.org/ search/collection/1921864.* The second is a record of applications for "Confederate" pensions, 1901–1929, on FamilySearch at *https:// familysearch.org/search/collection/1837922.* The originals of both are at the Arkansas History Commission, 1 Capitol Mall #215, Little Rock, AR 72201. Neither the difference between, nor the reason for, these two types of pension is clear.

FLORIDA: Florida began granting pensions in 1885. The pension applications are digitized and indexed on the FamilySearch website at *https://family search.org/search/collection/1913411* and on the Florida Memory website at *https://www. floridamemory.com/collections/pensionfiles/*.

GEORGIA:

Georgia began granting pensions in 1879. The pension applications are digitized and indexed on the Georgia Archives website at *http:// vault.georgiaarchives.org/cdm/landingpage/ collection/TestApps*.

KENTUCKY:

Kentucky began granting pensions in 1912. The pension applications are digitized on the FamilySearch website at *https://familysearch. org/search/collection/1916017*. They were not indexed at the time of this writing.

LOUISIANA:

Louisiana began granting pensions in 1898. The pension applications are digitized, but the records require some browsing because the state's index is in alphabetical ranges of names. The records are on FamilySearch at *https://familysearch.org/search/ collection/1838535*.

MARYLAND:

Maryland granted no pensions for service in the Confederacy.

MISSISSIPPI:

Mississippi began granting pensions in 1900. The pension applications are digitized, but the records require some browsing because the state's index is in alphabetical ranges of names. The records are on FamilySearch at *https:// familysearch.org/search/collection/1936413*. The original records are at the Mississippi Department of Archives and History, 200 North Street, Jackson, MS 39201.

MISSOURI:

Missouri began granting pensions in 1911. The pension applications are digitized and are in four separate categories: (1) approved pension applications, (2) disapproved pension applications, (3) approved soldiers' home applications, and (4) disapproved soldiers' home applications. Some browsing is required because the state's indexes are in alphabetical ranges of names. The records are on FamilySearch at *https://familysearch. org/search/collection/1865475*.

NORTH CAROLINA:

North Carolina began granting pensions in 1885. The pension applications are digitized, but some browsing is required because the state's indexes are in alphabetical ranges of names. These records are on FamilySearch at *https://familysearch.org/search/collection/ 1911763*. The original applications are at the North Carolina Department of Archives and History, 109 E. Jones Street, Raleigh, NC 27601.

OKLAHOMA:

Oklahoma began granting pensions in 1915. Index cards have been prepared as a finding aid. The cards are organized alphabetically by name, and they often contain other significant information about the applicant. The index cards have been digitized and indexed and are online at Ancestry: *http://search.ancestry. com/search/db.aspx?dbid=9236*. The application files are available at the Oklahoma Department of Libraries, 200 NE 18th Street, Oklahoma City, OK 73105.

SOUTH CAROLINA:

South Carolina began granting pensions in 1916. There appear to be no digitized records or indexes available. The records are in the Department of Archives and History, World War Memorial Building, 8301 Parklane Road, Columbia, SC 29223. The Family History Library in Salt Lake City has some information available concerning pensioners from Abbeville, Anderson, Charleston, Chester, Fairfield, Laurens, Lexington, Pickens, Union, Williamsburg, and York counties; check the library catalog.

TENNESSEE:

Tennessee began granting pensions in 1891. The Tennessee State Library and Archives in Nashville has an index to these pension records online at *http://share.tn.gov/tsla/history/military/ pension007.htm*. The pension application files are digitized on the FamilySearch website at *https://familysearch.org/search/collection/ 1874474*. They can be searched using the aforementioned index. The files themselves are in the Tennessee State Library and Archives, 403 7th Avenue North, Nashville, TN 37243.

TEXAS:

Texas began granting pensions in 1899. The Texas State Library and Archives has the pension application records. That library also has an online index to those records at *https://www.tsl.texas.gov/apps/arc/pensions/*, but not all counties are represented in the index. There is also a published index to Texas Confederate pension papers by John M. Kinney, *Index to Applications for Texas Confederate Pensions*, Rev. ed. (Austin: Archives Division, Texas State Library, 1977). The Texas State Library and Archives is at Texas Capitol, 1201 Brazos Street, Austin, TX 78701. Also, Ancestry has a digitized and indexed record of Confederate pensions in Alabama, Texas, and Virginia at *http://search.ancestry.com/search/db.aspx?dbid=1677*.

VIRGINIA: Virginia began granting pensions in 1888. The Library of Virginia (800 E. Broad Street, Richmond, VA 23219) has an indexed digitized database of those pension records. It can be accessed directly at a website with a very long URL: *http://lva1.hosted.exlibris group.com/F/?func=file&file_name%20=find-b-clas10&local_base=CLAS10&_ga=1.1713 72128.1784624344.%201471040647*. Also, Ancestry has a digitized and indexed record of Confederate pensions in Alabama, Texas, and Virginia at *http://search.ancestry.com/search/db.aspx?dbid=1677*.

III. MILITARY ACTIONS FOLLOWING THE CIVIL WAR

The American Civil War cost more American lives than any other war in American history. Recent recalculations say that the number of war dead (including both Union and Confederate) was approximately 750,000—twenty percent higher than previous estimates. That bloody war was formally ended with General Robert E. Lee's formal surrender at the McLean house in the village of Appomattox Court House, Virginia, on April 9, 1865, but this did not end American involvement in war. The most recent wars, however, have been so recent that most records relating to them have some restrictions. However, let us look at some of the available records that you ought to know about.

Not including the skirmishes with the Indians discussed previously, perhaps the major military and naval confrontations during the period prior to World War I had to do with America's encounters with Spain and the Philippines—the Spanish-American War in 1898 and the Philippine Insurrection from 1898 to 1901.

A. Spanish-American War

Because of this war with Spain—fought mostly in Cuba and the Philippines—the United States acquired Puerto Rico, Guam, and the Philippines; Cuba became independent.

There is a card index to the service records of the more than 250,000 American troops who served in the Spanish-American War (RG 94, M871, 126 rolls). It is entitled *General Index to Compiled Service Records of Volunteer Soldiers Who Served During the War with Spain.*

> Each index card gives name, rank, and unit in which the soldier served. Cross-references are included to names that appeared in the records under more than one spelling.
>
> Some index cards refer to "miscellaneous personal paper," but there are no compiled service records for individuals whose index cards contain this entry. The papers themselves follow the jacket-envelopes for most units. The War Department apparently accumulated these papers to be interfiled with the regular series of compiled service records but never did so.[32]

There is a general comprehensive index plus a separate index for each state and unit of U.S. Volunteers (including the Puerto Rican Regiment), but in 2016, the only microfilm publication of service records is for the volunteers from Florida.

The comprehensive index identifies

> the compiled service records of volunteers regardless of their military units. It has been reproduced as M871, *General Index to Compiled Service Records of Volunteer Soldiers Who Served During the War with Spain,* 126 rolls. Each index card gives name, rank, and unit in which the soldier served. Cross-references are included to names that appeared in the records under more than one spelling.[33]

There are also separate indexes for each of the states, as well as for each unit of U.S. volunteers. Only those indexes for the states of Louisiana (M240, 1 roll) and North Carolina (M413, 2 rolls) were available on microfilm in 2016.

The microfilmed Florida service records are entitled *Compiled Service Records of Volunteer Soldiers Who Served in the Florida Infantry During the War with Spain* (RG 94, M1087, 13 rolls). That microfilm is also available at the Family History Library in Salt Lake City (FHL films 1002433–558).

With regard to the service records themselves, it should be noted that

> volunteers served in [1] existing state militia units accepted into Federal service, [2] additional units raised in states and territories, and [3] units raised

---

[32] Eales and Kvasnicka, 148.

[33] Ibid., 148.

directly by the Federal Government. Because methods of enlistment varied, compiled military service records for these soldiers are arranged in four sub-series: [1] records of state units arranged alphabetically by state; [2] records of volunteers from the continental territories; [3] records of volunteers raised directly by the Federal Government; and [4] records of volunteers from Puerto Rico. The compiled service records are further arranged by organizational breakdown ending with the regiment or independent battalion or company. Under each unit, service records are arranged alphabetically by surname of the soldier.[34]

According to Colket and Bridgers, these service records contain

> the name, rank, and military organization of each soldier; the dates and places that he was mustered in and out; his place of residence; his occupation; and, if single, the name and address of a parent or guardian.[35]

As mentioned earlier in this chapter, all pension records for the war with Spain are in the "Civil War and Later" series. These pension records are in the National Archives, Record Group 94, Records of the Adjutant General's Office.

B. Philippine Insurrection

The Philippine Insurrection (1899–1901) arose almost immediately following the war with Spain when the Philippine people—who had declared their independence from Spain during that war—rebelled when two things happened. First, the 1898 Treaty of Paris gave ownership of the Philippines to the United States. Second, President William McKinley declined to grant independence. Before these matters were settled, the lives of more than 4,200 American servicemen were lost (plus 2,900 wounded). There were also 20,000 Filipino soldiers and 500,000 Filipino civilians killed during the conflict. Though the Filipinos failed to win the conflict, they continued to seek independence, which was finally granted to them on July 4, 1946.

Many servicemen who fought in the Philippines during the Spanish-American War also served during the Philippine Insurrection because they were still there when the rebellion began. However, Congress also authorized the raising of more troops for the conflict. Recruits were sought from all states and territories, as well as from the Philippines.

One challenge for those who search the records of the Philippines Insurrection is that the names of volunteer units did not include the names of the states or territories as part of their official titles, as had been the custom in earlier conflicts. This was true even when all of the recruits came from the same place.

> The compiled military service records are arranged by regiment number and name, thereunder jacket-envelopes are arranged alphabetically by surname

---

[34] Ibid., 148.

[35] Colket and Bridgers, 58.

of soldier. Only Americans who served in regiments formed in the United States and in the Philippines are represented. No records relating to Filipinos are represented. No records relating to the Puerto Rican Regiment, U.S. Volunteers, which was organized for service in Philippines but remained in Puerto Rico, are filed and indexed with the compiled service records of the Spanish-American War.

A general comprehensive index was published on microfilm as M872, *Index to Compiled Service Records of Volunteer Soldiers Who Served During the Philippine Insurrection*, 24 rolls. There is no compiled service record for a soldier whose index card contains a cross-reference to the miscellaneous papers. This is a separate series of personal papers following the compiled service records. . . . [T]hese were apparently accumulated by the War Department for interfiling that never took place.[36]

C. Boxer Rebellion and other later records

The Boxer Rebellion in China in 1900 was a peasant uprising—essentially ignored by the Chinese government—which attempted to drive all foreigners and Christians from the country. Some 5,000 American troops (Marines, sailors, and infantry) were involved in this action, but no special or separate service records were compiled. Records relating to this service are included among the records of the regular Army, which are discussed later in this chapter.

D. Other military records of the post-Civil War period

Many of the records relating to service in earlier periods overlap into this post-Civil War period, as you may have already noted; but there are a few other records in the National Archives coming exclusively out of this period that deserve our mention:

1. *Quarterly Returns of Naval Enlistment on Vessels, 1866–91*, are arranged by year in forty-three volumes at the National Archives. Those between 1866 and 1884 are indexed with the Weekly Returns of Enlistments at Naval Rendezvous mentioned earlier [under A, 3, c, 4]. The returns within each volume

   are arranged by number, thereunder by quarter, thereunder by name of vessel, and thereunder by date of enlistment. Most entries show, under the name of the vessel, the name of the enlisted individual, date and term of enlistment, rating, a reference to any previous naval service, place of birth, age, occupation, and personal description. Some entries show place of residence. Returns for the years 1866–84 were indexed, and the index entries were incorporated into T1098 [*Index to Rendezvous Reports, Civil War, 1861–65, 31 rolls*].[37]

---

[36] Eales and Kvasnicka, 150.

[37] Ibid., 158.

2. *Naval Apprenticeship Papers, 1864–1889*, are alphabetically arranged (first two letters of surname) at the National Archives as part of Record Group 24, Records of the Bureau of Naval Personnel.

> They consist of forms filled out by parents or guardians and, for the years 1864–69, testimonials of character. Each apprenticeship paper shows the name of the apprentice, place of service, date of entrance into service, place and date of birth, and name, residence, and relationship of parent or guardian.[38]

3. *A Register of Naval Apprentices, 1864–1875*, is indexed and has to do with apprentices who served on the training ships *Sabine, Portsmouth,* and *Saratoga*.

> An entry shows the name of the apprentice, date and place of birth, date and place of enlistment, name of parent or guardian, and date of detachment from the service. The single register is indexed by initial letter of surname. [This register is part of Record Group 24, Records of the Bureau of Naval Personnel.][39]

4. *A Register of Living and Retired Marine Corps Officers, 1899–1904*, relates primarily to officers who served in the Spanish-American War.

> An entry shows the name of the officer, date and place of birth, state from which appointed, and service record, 1899–1905 [RG 127].[40]

5. *Records of Soldiers' Homes, 1866–1938*. If a soldier happened to spend time in a home for soldiers, the records of that home provide another possibility of finding information about him. There are branches of the National Home for Disabled Volunteer Soldiers as indicated by the following list. There are records available for these homes:

> Tuskegee, AL (formerly a hospital, founded 1933, no records)
> Sawtelle, CA (Pacific Branch, founded 1888)
> St. Petersburg, FL (St. Petersburg Home, founded 1930, no records)
> Danville, IL (Danville Branch, founded 1898)
> Marion, IN (Marion Branch, founded 1888)
> Leavenworth, KS (Western Branch, founded 1885)
> Togus, ME (Eastern Branch, founded 1866)
> Biloxi, MS (Biloxi Home, founded 1930, no records)
> Bath, NY (Bath Branch, founded 1929)
> Dayton, OH (Central Branch, founded 1867)
> Roseburg, OR (Roseburg Branch, founded 1894)
> Hot Springs, SD (Battle Mountain Sanitarium, founded 1907)
> Near Johnson City, TN (Mountain Branch, founded 1903)
> Kecoughtan, VA (Southern Branch, founded 1870)
> Wood, WI (Northwestern Branch, founded 1867).[41]

---

[38] Ibid., 159.

[39] Ibid., 159.

[40] Ibid., 161.

[41] Ibid., Chart 15, 192.

Each branch of the National Home for Disabled Volunteer Soldiers kept an indexed historical register, and each veteran who was admitted was assigned a number. The veteran kept that number even if discharged from the home and later readmitted. Existing register books are part of the Records of the Veterans Administration, Record Group 15. Each patient had one page in the register book. The third (2000) edition of *The Guide to Genealogical Research in the National Archives in the United States* edited by Eales and Kvasnicka described that page and its contents:

> Each page of the register is divided into four sections: *military history, domestic history, [soldiers'] home history, and general remarks.* The veteran's *military history* gives the time and place of each enlistment, rank, company and regiment, time and place of discharge, reason for discharge, and nature of disabilities when admitted to the home. The *domestic history* gives birthplace, age, height, various physical features, religion, occupation, residence, marital status, and name and address of nearest relative. The *[soldiers'] home history* gives the rate of the pension, date of admission, conditions of readmission, date of discharge, cause of discharge, date and cause of death, and place of burial. Under *general remarks* is information about papers relating to the veteran, such as admission paperwork, Army discharge certificate, and pension certificate. Information also was entered about money and personal effects if the member died while in residence at the branch. [Emphasis added.][42]

6. *The United States Soldiers' and Airmen's Home.* This institution in Washington, DC, was created by Congress in 1851. It was originally named the United States Military Asylum, then later the U.S. Soldiers' Home. There were also some short-lived branches of this institution in East Pascagoula, MS (also called Greenwood's Island); New Orleans, LA; and Harrodsburg, KY. The Airmen component of the home's title was added in 1942 with the creation of the Air Force from the Army Air Corps.

> Records of greatest genealogical value . . . consist of general and monthly registers of members, hospital records, and death records. To use the records, the researcher must know which home the subject of research lived in and the approximate date of admission, hospital treatment, or death. . . . Entries are arranged chronologically, thereunder alphabetically by member's surname. An entry usually shows the name of the resident, name of the home, date of admission, military history, physical description, date and place of birth, occupation at the time of admission, marital status, size of family, and remarks. [There are also] [a]dditional members' registers, dated 1852–1941, which show the same information. . . .

---

[42] Ibid., 191.

[T]here are also muster rolls and returns that in part duplicate the information in the members' registers.[43]

Records for the U.S. Soldiers' Home include hospital records, 1872–1943; death records, including registers (1852–1942) and certificates (1876–89 and 1913–29); and case files for deceased members, 1880–1942.

IV. THE REGULAR ARMY OR REGULAR ESTABLISHMENT

The military records discussed thus far have dealt mainly with servicemen who enlisted or who were drafted for service in connection with the various wars. However, throughout U.S. history there have been men who enlisted in the service without regard to whether there was a war. Many of these men, of course, were professional soldiers. Early records of the regular Army are fragmentary, but they do exist. There are muster rolls covering the period between 1791 and 1912 and registers of enlistments, 1784–1914, in addition to special records for those who had officers' commissions. Of all these papers, the enlistment papers and registers of enlistments contain the most family history information.

The enlistment papers are in jacket-envelopes and filed alphabetically, for the most part, in three separate series (1784–1815 | 1798–July 14, 1894 | July 15, 1894–October 31, 1912). The files for all three of these series are at the National Archives in Record Group 94, Records of the Adjutant General's Office. These papers are similar to what the military now calls the soldier's "personnel file":

> Enlistment papers generally show the soldier's name, place of enlistment, date, by whom enlisted, age, occupation, personal description, regimental assignment, and certification of the examining surgeon and recruiting officer. Papers relating to enlistments after July 15, 1894, include descriptive and assignment cards, prior service cards, certificates of disability, final statements, inventories of effects, and records of death and interment, if applicable. The highest of the handwritten numbers on the front side of each enlistment paper, at the top center, identifies the enlistment register entry for that soldier.[44]

Enlistment registers are also at the National Archives for the period between 1798 and 1913. They are arranged more or less alphabetically. Each entry relates to a single enlistment, but the entries vary in their detail. Some entries prior to 1815 were quite brief.

> The register entries for the period 1798–June 30, 1821 contain soldier's name, military organization, physical description, date and place of birth, enlistment information, and remarks. Complete service information is not given for every soldier; in particular, the date or reason for termination of service may not be supplied. Entries in the remarks column contain cryptic

---

[43] Ibid., 191–192.

[44] Ibid., 120.

references to the source record from which the information was obtained. A partial key to the references, generally a two-initial abbreviation of the title of the original record, appears in volume 1 of the enlistment registers. Source documents cannot always be identified.

Registers for the period 1 July 1821–1914 are uniform in content. A two-page entry contains the same information that appears on the enlistment paper, as well as information relating to the termination of service. The termination information came from muster rolls and other records. The left-hand page gives the enlisted man's name, date and place of enlistment, by whom enlisted, period of enlistment, place of birth, age, civilian occupation at the time of enlistment, and personal description.

The right-hand page gives the unit number and arm of service, company, and information relating to separation from service. If the individual was discharged, the date, place, and reason for discharge are given, as well as rank at time of discharge. Additional information, such as notations concerning courts-martial or desertions, appears in the remarks column. For the period 1821–1914, the remarks column does not show the source of the information.[45]

Pension files for soldiers in the Regular Establishment are filed in the National Archives with the pensions of the other series.

V. WORLD WAR I AND BEYOND

A. World War I draft registration

During 1917 and 1918, there were three registrations for the draft based on a law passed on 18 May 1917. The first registration was on 5 June 1917 and included all men ages 21–31. The second registration was on 5 June 1918 and included all those men who had turned 21 since the first registration. The third registration also included men 18 to 21 and 31 to 45. It began on 12 September 1918. All local draft boards ceased operation and closed on 31 March 1919.

Both citizens and immigrants were required to register. Note, however, that many men who registered did not serve, and many of those who enlisted in the military did so without registering. Both of my grandfathers registered as the law required, but neither was drafted; they were exempted because they had families relying on their support.

There are draft registration cards for more than 24 million men, which was about 98 percent of men in the U.S. who were born between 1872 and 1900 and about 25 percent of the total U.S. population in 1917–1918.

Under each state, the draft registration cards are arranged by city or county and then by local draft board. Under each draft board, the cards are alphabetical by surname. They comprise National Archives microfilm publication M1509 (4,582 rolls) in Record Group 163, Records of the Selective Service System (WWI), 1917–1939. The Family History Library has these records on microfilm and also has indexed digitized images of the records at *https://*

---

[45] Ibid., 121.

familysearch.org/search/collection/1968530. Ancestry also has digitized and indexed copies of these records at *http://search.ancestry.com/search/db.aspx?dbid=6482.*

The cards and the questions were slightly different for each of the three registrations. The first registration used a card with twelve questions to be answered by the registrant, the second had ten such questions, and the third had twenty questions. Most of the differences were in the wording of the questions. There were also questions on the card that were answered by the draft board official.

If you are unable to find the person you are looking for in these records, you will want to consider spelling variations. You might also consider browsing the records on the microfilm. This is a very doable task, except in heavily populated areas—as long as you know where your ancestor lived. If your ancestor lived in a more populated area, the Family History Library has a microfilm that will help—film #1,498,803, National Archives Microfilm Publication M1860: "Boundary Maps of Selected Cities and Counties of World War I Selective Service Draft Registration Boards, 1917–18". This film has maps that show draft board jurisdictions of the more populated cities, thus facilitating direct access to the records.

The information included on the draft registration cards was as follows:

- Full name (all 3 registrations)
- Home address (all 3 registrations)
- Date of birth (all 3 registrations)
- Place of birth (registrations 1 and 2)
- Age in years (registration 3)
- Occupation (registrations 1 and 3)
- Name of employer (all 3 registrations)
- Place of employment (all 3 registrations)
- Name and address of nearest relative (registrations 2 and 3)
- Citizenship status (all 3 registrations)
- Marital status (registration 1)
- Race (registrations 1 and 3)
- Prior military service—rank and service branch (registration 1)
- Dependents (registration 1)
- Claimed exemption (registration 1)
- Signature of registrant (all 3 registrations)
- Previous military service (registration 1)
- Grounds of exception (registration 1)
- Name and address of nearest relative (registrations 2 and 3)
- Father's birthplace (registration 2)

The local draft board answered these questions:

- Physical description—height and build, eye and hair color (all 3 registrations)
- City, county, and state of local draft board (all 3 registrations)
- Date of registration (all 3 registrations)

B. World War II draft records

You will also want to take note of the World War II draft registration cards for what is called the "Fourth Registration" or the registration of old men. This was a registration in 1942 of men born between April 28, 1877, and February 16, 1897, inclusive. These draft registration cards, for men who were ages 45 to 65, contain

> information supplied by each registrant, including name, address, date and place of birth, age, name and address of employer, and physical description. The cards are arranged alphabetically by state, thereunder alphabetically by name of registrant.[46]

These records have all been digitized and indexed. They are on the Ancestry website at *http://search.ancestry.com/search/db.aspx?dbid=1002.*

C. Service records

Access to these more recent military service records (the Official Military Personnel Files [OMPF]) is essentially limited to the records of those who separated from the military more than sixty-two years ago. This includes the records of all military personnel—not just World War I veterans. The National Archives website explains:

> In an effort to expand access to and ensure the preservation of the records, the National Archives and Records Administration (NARA) together with the Department of Defense (DOD) developed a schedule, signed July 8, 2004, making the Official Military Personnel Files (OMPF) permanent records of the United States. This schedule mandates the legal transfer of these files from DOD ownership to NARA ownership 62 years after the service member's separation from the military [by death, discharge, or retirement].
>
> As part of the initial transfer, the records of 1.2 million veterans who served with the United States Navy and Marine Corps were opened to the public in July 2005. In addition, 200 OMPFs of "Persons of Exceptional Prominence" (PEP files)—such as Presidents, members of Congress and the Supreme Court; famous military leaders; decorated heroes; celebrities; and other cultural figures who served in the military—were also made available to the public for the first time. [PEP records are released ten years after the person's death]. . . .
>
> In November 2007, NARA opened to the public 6.3 million OMPFs of former military personnel who served in the United States Army (includ-

---

[46] Ibid., 150.

ing Army Air Corps and Army Air Forces), Navy, Marine Corps and Coast Guard. In September 2009, marking the 62nd anniversary of the creation of the United States Air Force, NARA accepted the first block of Air Force records into its custody. . . .

Based on a rolling date of 62 years, all military personnel records will eventually become *archival records*, open to the general public.[47]

The archival records (i.e., the "official" designation of those records in the National Personnel Records Center at St. Louis) include the following:

Army[48]	Enlisted personnel:	discharged between 1912 and 62 years ago
	Officers:	discharged between 1917 and 62 years ago
Navy	Enlisted personnel:	discharged between 1885 and 62 years ago
	Officers:	discharged between 1902 and 62 years ago
Air Force	All personnel:	discharged between 1947 and 62 years ago
Marine Corps	All personnel:	discharged between 1905 and 62 years ago
Coast Guard	All personnel:	discharged between 1898 and 62 years ago

Unfortunately, there is a significant gap in the available records on the above list. That gap relates to a fire at the National Personnel Records Center in July 1973 that destroyed approximately 16 to 18 million military personnel files.

The destroyed records included approximately 80 percent of the records of Army personnel discharged between November 1, 1912, and January 1, 1960, and 75 percent of the records of Air Force personnel discharged between September 25, 1947, and January 1, 1964. (This included all Air Force personnel with names, alphabetically, after Hubbard, James E.).

Although there are no other copies of the destroyed records and no indexes, the NPRC uses "alternate sources" as they seek to reconstruct basic service data in response to research requests. There have also been significant efforts made to restore many of the fire-damaged records.

As of this writing, these military service records are neither microfilmed nor digitized. However, requests for copies of these records can be made, and the requested records can be obtained. It is necessary, however, for the requester to provide some basic information, including the complete name as used in the service, the service number, service branch, birth date and place, and dates of service. If the desired records would have been affected by the 1973 fire, give as much additional information as possible. It is helpful if the place of discharge, last assigned unit, and place of entry into the service can be provided.

---

[47] "The National Archives at St. Louis: Military Personnel Records," *National Archives*, August 15, 2016, http://www.archives.gov/st-louis/archival-programs/division.html (accessed January 11, 2017).

[48] This includes Army Air Corps and Army Air Force personnel.

Copies can be requested in person at the National Personnel Records Center Archival Research Room in St. Louis (1 Archives Drive, St. Louis, MO 63138) or by mail. If you are making a request by mail, you can send a letter or (preferably) a Standard Form (SF 180), "Request Pertaining to Military Records," to the NPRC. A link to download a pdf copy of this form (along with related instructions) is online at *https://www.archives.gov/veterans/military-service-records/standard-form-180.html*. Be sure to read the instructions. At the time of this writing, the fee for a copy of a routine file of five pages or less was $25. For six or more pages, the fee was $70.

I also note here that veterans can obtain copies of their own service records even though sixty-two years have not passed since discharge. Their next-of-kin (unremarried widow or widower, son, daughter, father, mother, brother or sister—or the official representative of any of these) can also obtain copies of these records. Requests can be made online at *http://vetrecs.archives.gov/VeteranRequest/home.html*, or by using form SF180, as above.

VI. STATE MILITARY RECORDS AND RECORDS RELATING TO CIVILIANS

In addition to those military records already discussed, many states have collections of records relating to soldiers from their state who gave military service. Also, state militia and other state-troop records are often useful family history tools, and the state's Adjutant General or other record custodian can be a great benefactor to your research.

If you have forebears who served in state military organizations, you should plan to use these records as well as any books that might be published about the military men and military history of the individual states.

Many of these records have been published in genealogical periodicals, and many others have been microfilmed. If you have access to the LDS Family History Library's collections, check the library catalog for the states of your interest. Also, you should not hesitate to use your Internet search engine in your search for these records.

You should also be aware of records relating to civilians during wartime. A summary of such records found in the National Archives is in Chapter 10 of *Guide to Genealogical Research in the National Archives of the United States* (3rd ed.), edited by Eales and Kvasnicka, pages 201–208.

VII. PRINTED MILITARY SOURCES

There are several books relating to those who have served in the armed forces of this country since the Revolution. It would be impossible to name all such books here, especially since most of them relate to servicemen from specific states and other geographic areas. However, a brief bibliography follows:

Blakeney, Jane. *Heroes: U.S. Marine Corps 1861–1955: Armed Forces Awards, Flags.* Washington, DC: Blakeney Publishers, 1957.

Boatner, Mark Mayo III, et. al. *The Civil War Dictionary.* Rev. ed. New York: David McKay Co., 1988.

Cullum, George Washington. *Biographical Register of the Officers and Graduates of the U.S. Military Academy at West Point, N.Y, from Its Establishment, in 1802 . . .* 3 vols. 3rd ed. Boston: Houghton, Mifflin Co., 1891. There was also a fourth volume supplement published in 1901. This fourth volume is online at Google Books. The URL is too long to include here, but the digitized book can be readily accessed by entering the basic information into your Internet search engine.

Hamersly, Lewis Randolph. *The Records of Living Officers of the U.S. Navy and Marine Corps.* 7th ed. rev. New York: L. R. Hamersly & Co., 1902. Note that there are various editions from 1870 to 1902. Digitized copies of all are online and can be easily accessed using your Internet search engine.

————. *Officers of the Army and Navy (Regular and Volunteer) Who Served in the Civil War.* Philadelphia: L. R. Hamersly & Co., 1894. A digitized copy can be accessed online at *https://catalog.hathitrust.org/ Record/000318878.*

Moore, Frank, ed. *The Portrait Gallery of the War, Civil, Military, and Naval: A Biographical Record.* New York: G. P. Putnam, 1864. A digitized copy of this book is online at *http://archive.org/stream/ portraitgalleryo01moor#page/n7/mode/2up.*

Peterson, Clarence Stewart. *Known Military Dead During the Spanish-American War and the Philippine Insurrection, 1898–1901.* Baltimore: The author, 1958. A digitized copy of this book is online at *https://babel. hathitrust.org/cgi/pt?id=wu.89058339128;view=1up;seq=9.*

Powell, William H. *List of Officers of the Army of the United States from 1779–1900, Embracing a Register of All Appointments in the Volunteer Service During the Civil War and of Volunteer Officers in the Service of the United States.* 1900. Reprint, Detroit: Gale Research Co., 1967. A digitized copy of the original volume is at *http://archive.org/stream/ listofficers00powerich#page/n7/mode/2up.*

————. *Records of Living Officers of the United States Army.* Philadelphia: L. R. Hamersly, 1890. A digitized copy is at *archive.org/stream/ powellsrecordsl00powegoog#page/n5/mode/2up.*

————. *Officers of the Army and Navy (Volunteer) Who Served in the Civil War.* Philadelphia: L. R. Hamersly, 1893. A digitized copy of this book is available at *archive.org/stream/officersofarmyna01powe#page/n5/ mode/2up.*

————, and Edward Shippin, eds. *Officers of the Army and Navy (Regular) Who Served in the Civil War.* Philadelphia: L. R. Hamersly & Co., 1892. A digitized copy of this book is available at *http://archive.org/stream/ officersofarmyna00powe#page/n3/mode/2up.*

Schuon, Karl. *U.S. Marine Corps Biographical Dictionary; the Corps' Fighting Men, What They Did, Where They Served*. New York: Franklin Watts, Inc., 1963. A digitized copy of this book can be accessed from *https://catalog.hathitrust.org/Record/000333712*.

———. *U. S. Navy Biographical Dictionary: The Corps' Fighting Men; What They Did; Where They Served*. New York: Franklin Watts, Inc., 1963. A digitized copy of this work is online at *http://archive.org/ stream/usmarinecorpsbio017890mbp#page/n5/mode/2up*.

Simmons, Henry Eugene, comp. *A Concise Encyclopedia of the Civil War*. New York: A. S. Barnes and Co., 1965.

U.S. Adjutant General's Office. *Official Army Register*. Washington, DC: Military Secretary's Office, 1802—. The title has varied somewhat over the years: *Register of the Army of the United States; The Army Register of the United States; Army Register; Official Army and Air Force Register*. Several of these registers are digitized and online. The 1907 edition is at *http://archive.org/stream/officialarmyreg04offigoog#page/ n3/mode/2up*. Those editions for the Civil War years, 1861–1865, are digitized and on the Ancestry website at *http://search.ancestry.com/ search/db.aspx?dbid=31389*. The book itself has an index.

U.S. Bureau of Naval Personnel. *Register of Commissioned and Warrant Officers of the Navy of the United States and of the Marine Corps*. Washington, DC: U.S. Government Printing Office, 1825—. Digitized registers are available for several years. Internet links to digitized registers from 1825 to 1970 are at *https://catalog.hathitrust.org/Record/000523460*.

Refer also to the bibliographies in Chapter 26. Many of the works listed there also relate to post-Revolutionary servicemen and military history as well as to the Revolutionary War.

VIII. WHEN TO USE MILITARY RECORDS

Chapter 26 discussed various circumstances that require sensitivity in relation to the use of Revolutionary War records. The same principles apply to the use of all American military records. If your ancestor lived at a time when he could have served in a war (or if any close relatives of his [or hers] could have served in a war), you must consider a search of military records as a research necessity. Do not wait until you find a clue that your ancestor had military experience. Just make your search in the records of the appropriate war and see what you discover.

However, any clues about military service you have can be helpful. They can help you focus on your target with greater accuracy. I have mentioned many times the increased usability of military records when you have specific data on the organization to which the serviceman belonged, or at least the state from which he served. Such clues can be found in various places; family records, old letters, Bibles, tombstones, obituaries, local histories, church records, vital records (especially death certificates), etc., are all likely sources. In addition, where Civil War service records are concerned, you must know the state in order to use the records.

There is no specific time sequence during a search when military records should be used—this varies from problem to problem—but usually they are one of the first sources to consider once you begin research on an individual who may have had military service or may have had a close relative who did. This is because the information found in these records is often of such a nature that it facilitates the use of other sources and suggests other possibilities.

IX. CONCLUSION

In concluding this discussion, let me restate the basic fact that makes the use of these records so important: Wars have been an integral part of American history and, as such, have produced indispensable records of significance to the family histories of literally millions of people. These are records that not only hold the key to successfully extending many pedigrees but also contain information that can help you see your ancestors as the real people they were and not just as names on your pedigree chart.

In addition to the material in these last two chapters, study carefully the material relating to military records in the latest edition of *Guide to Genealogical Research in the National Archives of the United States,* edited by Eales and Kvasnicka. Section B (chapters 4–14) of that book holds a vast store of information about military records as a family history resource. Also, in this age when books relating to family history research are becoming quickly outdated, it may be even more important for you to study the information on military records on the National Archives website than it is to study that book. Access to that information begins at *https://www.archives.gov/research/military.*

28

Cemetery and Burial Records

I. BACKGROUND

Many inexperienced family history researchers get the idea that if they have found a death certificate or an obituary or a church register entry of a burial, they have found all the important information arising out of a death. They are sometimes right, but there are occasions when it is a serious mistake to overlook gravestones and other cemetery records. This situation reminds me of a cartoon I saw showing a junior executive standing before his boss's desk receiving the following bit of wisdom: "We've never doubted your ambition and drive and self-discipline, Higgins. It's your lack of ability that concerns us."[1] Perhaps it would be appropriate to say that cemetery and burial records are to death certificates, obituaries, and church burial registers what ability is to ambition, drive, and self-discipline. Without them, something significant is missing and you just might not get the job done. Also, you will frequently find that these other sources (i.e., death certificates, obituaries, and burial registers)—or any one or more of them—do not exist and hence cannot be used.

There are two kinds of cemetery records in which family history researchers have interest:

- Gravestone and monument inscriptions
- Records kept by cemetery management and caretakers (sextons' records)

There is a great deal of variation in both the completeness and the accuracy of both kinds of these records, as you will see from the following examples, but because of the very nature of the information they deal with, they must be considered important and should be investigated early in your research.

---

[1] Used with permission of *The New Yorker*. All rights reserved.

727

There are five different kinds of cemeteries in America:

1. *The churchyard*, where members of the congregation are buried right on the church grounds. This custom was brought to America from the Old World and was especially prevalent in the colonial states.

2. *The church-owned cemetery*, neither connected with nor adjacent to the church building, but owned and operated by the church.

3. *The government-owned cemetery*—either town, city, county, state, or national—owned collectively by the people and supported and maintained by tax monies.

4. *The privately owned, non-church cemetery*—usually owned by a corporation and operated as a business enterprise. The U.S. has many of these, and they are especially common in more recent years.

5. *The family cemetery*. This is often just a small corner of the family farm or estate, perhaps in a grove of trees in an out-of-the-way location, set aside for the burial of family members and relatives. Many of these still exist, but they are seldom created today because of zoning and permit requirements as well as concerns about maintenance, power lines, proximity to water supplies, neighbors, property resale values, and access by future generations of family members.

All five of these cemetery types are common in America, and each presents its own problems for the family history researcher—whether it be difficulty in locating, no sexton's records, lack of proper maintenance, or some entirely different issue.

One of the more difficult challenges is to determine where a burial took place. If your ancestor lived in a large—or even a medium-sized community—there are usually several possible places. Two of the best sources to help solve this problem are obituaries and death certificates, but both of these have limitations if the death was early.

Once you find the name of the cemetery, it is not usually difficult to determine its location. Local government officials, church officials, funeral directors, and old-timers can frequently provide the answer to that question. However, there are situations where this can also be a problem.

We will talk later about how to find the cemetery and its records, but let us look first at some typical gravestone inscriptions to see how they might help us.

II. GRAVESTONE AND MONUMENT INSCRIPTIONS

A. From the Rexburg Cemetery, Madison County, Idaho:

Charlotte Helena
Dau. of
Peter & Charlotte Flamm

Died Apr. 5, 1891
aged 3 Ys, 8 Ms, 7 Ds.

Melissa Henry Smith
Born July 11, 1827
Wood Co., Virginia
Died June 15, 1896

In memory of Mary A. Roberts
& infant son
Wife of Alfred Ricks
Born Oct. 7, 1870
Died Jun. 30, 1892
We trust our loss will be their gain,
And that with Christ, they've gone to reign.

James Eckersell
Aug. 5, 1839–Mar. 6, 1917

FARNSWORTH
Albert S.
1891–1895
Blanche
1906–1909
Ralph
1913–1914

Jacob Spori
Born Mar. 26, 1847
Died Sept. 27, 1903

Magdalena R. Spori
Born Feb. 6, 1851
Died Sept. 14, 1900

John Plain Smith
May 14, 1843

His Wife
Elizabeth Andrews
Feb. 6, 1846
Dec. 6, 1915

Sons
Mickle A.
  Aug. 8, 1883
  Jan. 19, 1905
Joseph A.
  Dec. 1, 1881
  July 19, 1908

B. From the Long Cemetery, between Spencer and McMinnville, Tennessee:

Harriet Grissom
April 5, 1852–October 27, 1883
Daughter of Elisha and Elizabeth Boulding
Wife of S. B. Grissom

S. B. Grissom
November 14, 1847–November 1, 1908

William Grissom
March 7, 1797–December 23, 1869

Evey Grissom
May 1, 1797–Jan 25, 1816
Wife of William Grissom

C. From Spencer Cemetery No. 1, Spencer, Tennessee:

BURDIN WHEELER
TENNESSEE—1 LT. ELLIOTT'S CO.
LAUDERDALE'S TENN. MTD. INF.
CHEROKEE WAR 1887

D. From Sycamore Cemetery at Gassaway (near Woodbury), Cannon County, Tennessee:

Mollie E., Dau of
G. G. & Martha Melton
Wife of Geo. Hancock
Born May 22, 1862
Died February 11, 1894
"Blessed are they which do
hunger and thirst after
righteousness for they
shall be filled."

Selmar, Son of
G. E. and M. E. Hancock
Born May 10, 1883
Died February 6, 1900
Aged 16 y's, 8 m's, & 25 d's

Polly, Wife of Bartlet Marcum
Mother of Arch Marcum
Born January 24, 1807
Died May 7, 1855

Jacob K. King
Born March 5, 1844
Died August 2, 1897
Aged 53 Y's, 4 M's, 27 D's
'Think of me as you pass by.
As you are now, so once was I.
As I am now so you must be.
Prepare for death and follow me."

Mathie D. Keaton
June 15, 1897–Dec. 11, 1918
Enlisted Oct. 29, 1918 at
Woodbury, Tennessee
Died at Camp Wadsworth, S.C.
Buried at Sycamore Church
December 15, 1918.
"Dearest brother thou hast left us.
Here thy loss we deeply feel
But tis God that has bereft us.
He can all our sorrows heal."

A. H. Markum
Born September 29, 1846
Died March 23, 1903
Aged 56 yrs. 5 m. 24 days
A. Markum & A. H. Owen
Married May 6, 1864
Joined the M. E. Church S. 1892

Pvt. John E. Hancock
Co. F. 57, Pis. Inf.
June 7, 1896
Died Oct. 10, 1918 in France.

E. From Highland Cemetery, Carter County, Tennessee:

Laura Etta Singleton
Feb. 4, 1853
Age 77 yrs. 1 mo. 2 days
Died March 6, 1930
"Member United Daughters of Confederacy"
She done all she could.

James Calvin Singleton
Nov. 12, 1843
Sept. 25, 1928
Served his country
In Co. A, 5th
Bat., N. C. Calvery [*sic*]
Southern Confederacy
Blessed are the dead which die in the Lord.

F. From the Dorsey graveyard, on a farm at Monongalia, West Virginia:

[All on one stone]
Mary E. Dorsey, born June 28, 1828, died Feb. 14, 1863
Emma L. Dorsey, born Sept. 10, 1860, died Apr. 10, 1863
Delia T. Dorsey, born Mar 10, 1831, died Aug 7, 1910
Warren C. Dorsey, born Oct 2, 1911, died Dec 16, 1911
Marion Hough Dorsey, born May 17, 1875, died Dec 16, 1900

It is plain, even from these few examples, that the information recorded on gravestones is unpredictable and often very enlightening. You never know what might be on a gravestone until you see it. Usually you can count on finding at least a name and a death date (which do not help particularly unless you cannot obtain that information from other sources), but often, especially on those gravestones that are not too recent, you can find a wealth of important family history data. Dates of birth, places of birth, places of marriage, names of parents, names of spouses, names of children, religious affiliation, and military service (even the specific organization and the war) can all be found on gravestones. The foregoing examples have illustrated this.

III. ACCESS TO CEMETERY RECORDS

A. Online records

Various local chapters of the Daughters of the American Revolution (DAR) have undertaken extensive projects of copying gravestone inscriptions. DAR projects have gathered inscriptions from thousands of cemeteries. The Works Projects Administration (WPA) undertook similar projects during the Great Depression of the 1930s, but not so extensively. The Daughters of the Utah Pioneers (DUP) and the Idaho Genealogical Society have likewise engaged in these projects, as have many others. Also, gravestone inscriptions frequently have been published in genealogical and historical periodicals.

In more recent years, there have been extensive projects to gather gravestone information and publish it on the Internet. In August 2017, a website called Find a Grave (*https://www.findagrave.com/*) claimed to have 162 million grave records. That certainly does not cover everyone who has died, but it is a significant number—keeping in mind that there are many other similar websites.

Another significant website, BillionGraves (*https://billiongraves.com/*), claims to be the world's largest resource for searchable Global Positioning System (GPS) cemetery data, and to be "growing bigger and better every day." Members of the public are invited and encouraged to add the Billion-Graves app to their cell phones and contribute gravestone images to the database when they visit cemeteries. This app can be downloaded on the Bil-lionGraves website.

Other gravestone sites include Interment.net (*http://www.interment.net/US/index.htm*), Ancestors at Rest (*http://ancestorsatrest.com/cemetery_records/*), and Nationwide Gravesite Locator (*http://gravelocator.cem.va.gov/*). There is also a clickable list of cemetery websites on a site called Online Cemetery Records and Burial Index (*http://deathindexes.com/cemeteries.html*).

B. The personal cemetery visit

Even though you may have found the record you want online, there is still an advantage to actually going to the cemetery to view, as a whole, all of the graves in the family burial plot. People are usually related in some way or they would not have been buried in the same plot. That very circumstance may provide another clue that will facilitate your research.

It is best to go to the cemetery yourself, if you can, because you will be aware of all aspects of the family history problem and will be in an excellent position to capitalize on clues that others might overlook. However, it is certainly permissible to send your agent to read gravestones for you. There is value in gravestone inscriptions that have been transcribed and published, or even photographs of the gravestones, but a publication is a poor substitute for a personal visit.

There are two reasons why transcribed and printed gravestone inscriptions are inferior to the personal visit:

- There is always the possibility of transcription errors. (Note that digital photography and the Internet have helped with this problem.)
- The arrangement of these sources often causes confusion about which person is buried in which plot, hence confusion about who is related to whom and just how they might be related.

These shortcomings, however, may not be too serious and, in some cases, may be outweighed by virtues. For example, the ravages of time and nature may have since rendered some ancestral gravestones unreadable. Or "progress" may have destroyed or moved the cemetery. Or vandals may have damaged or destroyed valuable monuments. Where these things have happened, the transcripts are a welcome alternative.

When you venture to the cemetery on your own, be prepared and equipped to handle any contingency. I do not want to discourage you, but you will find that many cemeteries have suffered from neglect. Some have been abandoned and are thus overgrown with weeds, bushes, and briars. Some headstones may be overgrown with grass and weeds and/or covered with dirt. You need to be prepared to deal with these problems.

You may find that some gravestones have even sunk into the ground or have tipped over. You will also find that many inscriptions have become eroded beyond legibility. It is ironic (but interesting to note) that gravestones that have sunken or are overgrown with brush have often withstood the erosive forces of time better than others because they had nature's protection.

When you visit old cemeteries, do not wear your best clothes. You might also find it helpful to take along tools—consider hand-held pruning shears and trowels—to cut through the thickets and dig out buried gravestones. A good stiff-bristled (*not wire*) brush will also be useful for cleaning off the dirt. And an eroded inscription can often be made readable by rubbing soapstone or the side of a stick of chalk over it. There are a number of techniques that different people use, but you must not do anything that would mar or deface a gravestone or monument in any way. Some people clean the inscription sufficiently and then take a photograph. Digital cameras and smartphones are ideal for this purpose. This way your copy is always accurate. Digital photography is a wonderful thing because you can see immediately if the photographic image is clear and legible.

C. Accuracy

Be careful of the information on gravestones. Most of it is probably accurate, but remember that an engraver can make errors as easily as can a printer. Also, many gravestones were not installed on the graves until several years after the deaths of those who are buried, and the dates have often been supplied from a family member's memory. Be especially watchful for errors in dates of one day, one month, or one year—these are the most easily made errors and are thus the most common.

IV. SEXTONS' RECORDS

Historically, a sexton was a church employee who was caretaker of the church buildings and graveyard. In more recent times, the title has been applied to the person who keeps the records of a cemetery and oversees the care of grounds and facilities. The records kept by various sextons vary in their content and nature even more than do gravestone inscriptions. For a small family cemetery, there will be no sexton's records at all. In fact, you are fortunate if most graves have gravestones on them. Church cemeteries seldom have any record of burials aside from what is kept in the church's registers (and, with some churches, a book telling which church member owns which plot). Most other cemeteries—those owned by government entities and those that are privately owned—must maintain some type of record. Sometimes these are merely books or plats showing lot ownership, which can save you a great deal of wandering and wondering when you are looking for family graves in a large cemetery.

Some cemeteries have extensive records on everyone who is buried there—sometimes significantly more complete than the information on the gravestones, but you never know this until the gravestones have also been checked. In more recent years, the nature of these records has been the subject of legislation in many states.

Let us look at two typical examples of sextons' records (of the not-too-recent variety).

A. From the town of Skowhegan, Somerset County, Maine:

Lot No. _____24_____   _____Timothy Snow_____

Date of decease	*Name of person interred*	*Age*
1867—Aug 7	Ravmond Snow Child removed from Snow's tomb	Aged 22 years
1880—Sept 23	Timothy Snow	Aged 77 years 6 mos
Sept 18, 1881	Lilliam M. Brageton	ˮ 3 month 10 days
Aug 19, 1897	Lirluri [?] G. Tracy, Dau of T. Snow	ˮ 36 years

These records are indexed and then arranged numerically by plot number, based on the physical location of those plots within the cemetery. Relationships are often stated in these records, though they are not always asked for.

If the ownership of a burial plot changed hands (after the death of the purchaser), it was typical for the old owner's name to be crossed out and the new owner's name entered on the record. Both names are usually readable and indexed. If a deceased person's remains were relocated to another plot or to another cemetery, the record usually gives the details of the move. Also, purchase dates for some of the plots are given.

B. From Spanish Fork City Cemetery, Utah County, Utah:

Name in full	Johnson, William
Father	John Peterson
Mother	Vilborg Thordurson
Husb. or wife	single
When born	27 April 1868
Where born	Westmania Island, Iceland
When died	7 March 1882
Cemetery where buried	Spanish Fork, Utah

In this cemetery, the cards are filed alphabetically by the name of the persons buried. It is also interesting to note that married women were listed under their maiden surnames, which is quite unusual. This would make a record difficult to find if you were not aware of that fact. Also, though the name of the person's spouse was called for, it was seldom given. Most cards said only "married" in the "Husb. or wife" field. Many spaces were often left blank on these cards. Very few cards gave a specific birthplace, as does our sample card, but usually only the state or the foreign country.

These examples are typical of sextons' records; they are not unlike those you might find for your ancestors in numerous localities. The records are generally in the custody of the present sexton or in the office of the county or town clerk. If not, the personnel in these offices will be able to tell you where they are kept.

The information found in these records is basic family history data and, unless you already have it, it is information you need for your records. Remember, however, that the evidence is mostly secondary (especially for older persons), and is no more reliable than the informant who provided it—and we seldom have knowledge of that person's identity. Also, as with most other records, the more recent records are better in many respects than are those of older vintage.

V. HELP IN FINDING THE RECORDS

We have already discussed how difficult it might be to determine a place of burial, and I might add that even knowing the name of the cemetery does not solve all of your problems. Large cemeteries are usually easy to find (they are probably listed in the phone directory), but smaller ones, especially family cemeteries, can be more difficult.

It is not impossible to solve location problems, however. One writer suggests three possible sources of help:

1. Ask—chambers of commerce, city hall, anyone who might know or who would know whom to ask.
2. U.S. Government Geological Survey maps of the locality have sufficient detail that even tiny graveyards are pinpointed.
3. Know the laws of the state that govern cemetery and burial policy.[2]

VI. RECORDS OF FUNERAL DIRECTORS

Another record, closely related to those already discussed in this chapter, deserves mention. This is the record kept by the funeral director (formerly called a mortician or an undertaker) who performed the pre-burial duties for the deceased. Today, though a physician is responsible for specifying the underlying cause of death, the funeral director is usually responsible for initiating and filing the death certificate. Also, he will frequently work with family members in preparing and submitting the obituary. He also assists with programs for the funeral service. Most funeral directors also maintain private records equally as good as any official records that are kept.

Some funeral director records contain useful information not included on the death certificate. For example, they often give the name of any insurance companies with whom the deceased person's life was covered, and insurance companies also have extensive personal data in their files. However, you must remember that both mortuaries and insurance companies are private entities, and their records are available only at the discretion of company officials.

It has been my experience that most funeral directors are very cooperative and more than willing to help you find information in their records. However, because their records are private, any information they make available to you from those records is provided as a favor and not as a legal obligation.

Since the beginning of vital records in America, death certificates have asked for the name and address (usually only the city) of the funeral director. Your local funeral director has a directory, the *American Blue Book of Funeral Directors* (New York: National Funeral Directors' Association) that is published biennially. It can help you locate names and addresses, or you can find those names and addresses in local telephone directories. There are also other directories available, including one called *The Funeral Home & Cemetery Directory* (formerly the *National Yellow Book of Funeral Directors*).

You might try logging into a website formerly called Switchboard and now called WhitePages.com (*http://www.whitepages.com/*), clicking on the "Busi-

---

[2] Richard H. Hale, "Cemetery Records as Aids to Genealogical Research" (Area I, no. 15), World Conference on Records and Genealogical Seminar (Salt Lake City: Genealogical Society of The Church of Jesus Christ of Latter-day Saints, 1969).

ness" tab, and entering the term "funeral home." Next, enter the name of the city and state in the spaces provided. You will get a list of funeral homes in that city, followed by other nearby funeral homes—closest ones first. This will give you information about the businesses—including phone numbers and addresses—that is reasonably current.

If a person died in a location away from where he resided, a funeral director at the place of death often handled the body. He usually embalmed it there and prepared it for the return home. This is good to remember when you are looking for the funeral director's records and cannot locate them in the home town. When the problem is recent, the obituary may provide a clue to this kind of situation, and the death certificate (always filed in the state of death) will provide specific information. It is good to remember that many people did not die in the places where they were buried.

Some funeral directors' records go back more than 100 years,[3] but they do not have to be that old to be valuable. As with death certificates, if they deal with persons who died in old age, these records can bridge two or three generations of time. They can provide names, dates, places, etc., that are invaluable to continued research—but only secondary evidence of the "facts" that they state.

VII. CONCLUSION

In American family history research, there are many sources to consider, and we often have no inkling of what the specific content of a particular source might be until we see the actual record. This uncertainty and the necessity of possessing a knowledge of myriad sources make American research the most difficult genealogical research in the Western world (and also the most interesting and challenging). Though this uncertainty is characteristic of records relating to burials, you may take comfort in the knowledge that these records are a fundamental kind of source. You always know that the information you discover in them will provide evidence of names, dates, places, and relationships—though secondary and not always completely correct.

As a final note to this chapter, I need to mention Sharon DeBartolo Carmack's four-page research guide to cemetery research in Genealogical Publishing Company's *Genealogy at a Glance* series.[4] This handy guide gives practical and insightful advice relating to cemetery research—especially as it relates to your personal visits to ancestral cemeteries and finding and using these records.

---

[3] Norman E. Wright and David H. Pratt, *Genealogical Research Essentials* (Salt Lake City: Bookcraft, 1967), 282, report finding records as early as 1841.

[4] Sharon DeBartolo Carmack, *Genealogy at a Glance: American Cemetery Research* (Baltimore: Genealogical Publishing Co., 2012).

Index

A.P.G. Quarterly (Association of
  Professional Genealogists), 265
Abate, Frank R., 119
Abbreviations in records, 31–36
Abstract, extract, transcribe—
  definitions of, 529–530
Abstract, nature of, 531–532
Abstract of [land] title, 497–498
Abstracting documents,
  Deeds,
    Essential information,
      532–533
    Examples, 534–541
    Guidelines, 529–531
  Probate records,
    Essential information, 533–534
    Examples, 541–545
  Reasons for, 161–162
Abstracting deeds, essential
  information, 532–533
Abstracting probate records,
  essential information, 533–534
Abuttals, 403
Access Genealogy (website), 205
Accouchement, 403
Account (probate), 452–453
Accredited genealogists, 21–22
Acknowledgement (of a deed, etc.),
  498
Adams,
  Arthur, 270
  James Truslow, 117
Administration, 403

Administration bond, 453
Administrator, 403
Administratrix, 404
Adoption records, 567–568
Affidavit, 498
Affinity, 404
African American family history,
  248
African American research, "At a
  Glance" guide, 140
Afro-American Historical and
  Genealogical Society, 266
Agnation, 404
Agreement, 498
Agricultural schedules, *see* Census
  records
Alabama,
  Agricultural schedules, 375
  Cash entry files (public domain
    land), 483
  Census population schedules,
    320, 351, 360 (fn)
  Church records, 614
  Confederate pension records, 709
  Court records, 552
  Customs Passenger Lists, 628
  Divorce records, 556
  Guardianship records, 464
  Land records, 521
  Military records, 668
    Books, 673
  Mortality schedules, 369
  Private land claims, 489

Slave schedules, 374
Social statistics schedules, 376
Vital records, 292
Wills, 435
Alaska,
Cash entry files (public domain land), 483
Census population schedules, 320
Divorce records, 556
Guardianship records, 464
Immigration Passenger Lists, 633
Land records, 521
Wills, 435–436
Albany, NY, 297
Allen,
James B., 251–252
Penelope Johnson, 678
Thomas B., 681
William, 262
Allen County Public Library, 18, 102, 128–129
Alzo, Lisa, 608
Amazon Cloud Drive, 193
AmericanAncestors.org (website), 203, 205
American and British Genealogy & Heraldry (Filby), 142
American Battle Monuments Commission (website), 205
American Biography, a New Cyclopaedia, 262
American Civil War Research Database, from Alexander Street (website), 100
American Digest (West Publishing Co.), 573
American Genealogist, The (periodical), 10 (fn), 125, 265
American Library Directory, 125
American Medical Association, 283
American Places Dictionary, 119
American Society of Genealogists, 265

American Statistical Association, 282
American University, 18
Ancestral File, 60
Ancestral Quest (software), 208
Ancestry.com (website), 73, 100, 112, 198, 199, 202, 208, 210–216, 297, 298, 299, 301, 302, 303, 369, 483, 637, 680, 687
"At a Glance" guide, 140
Community page, 215
Comparison to other large commercial sites, 230
Extras, 215
Hire an Expert page, 215
Historical Newspaper Collection, 275
Outside resources relating to, 216
Research on, 212–214
Other research tactics, 229–230
Support Center page, 215
Ancestry DNA, 197
Ancestry's family history wiki (website/wiki), 191, 215
Ancestry's Red Book, 121, 215
Ancient Faces (website/wiki), 190
Ancillary administration, 404
Andrews,
Evan, 647
Frank DeWitte, 656
Andriot, John I., 117
Antenuptial contract, 453–454, 498–499
Appleton's Cyclopaedia of American Biography, 262
Apps, *see* Computer applications
Appurtenance, 404
Archives.com (website), 203
Archives of Maryland, 675
ArchivesUSA (website of Chadwyck-Healey), 271–273
Arizona,
Cash entry files (public domain), 483

Census population schedules, 320, 366–367
Community property laws, 419
Divorce records, 556
Guardianship records, 464
Land records, 521
Mortality schedules, 369
Non-government local research aids, 133
Private Land Claims, 489
Vital records, 292
Wills, 436
Arkansas,
Census population schedules, 320, 360 (fn)
Church records, 614
Confederate pension records, 709
Court records, 552
Divorce records, 556
Guardianship records, 464
Land records, 521
Military records, 668
Private land claims, 489
"Research in the States" guide (NGS), 141
Slave schedules, 374
Vital records, 292
Wills, 436
Armstrong, Zella, 678
Arnold Collection of Rhode Island Vital Records, 301
Ashby, Charlotte M., 283, 317, 349, 368, 377
Assignment, 404, 499
Assignment of dower, 454
Association of Professional Genealogists (APG), 27, 265, 519
"At a Glance" research guides, 140–141
Atlas for Georgia History, 118
Atlas of American History, 117
Attest, 404
Attorney, 404

Augustan Omnibus, The (periodical) (Augustan Society), 265
Avotaynu, The International Review of Jewish Genealogy (periodical), 265
Ayer Directory of Newspapers and Periodicals, 124
Ayer Directory of Publications, 268, 275–276

Babcock, Charles, 195
Backblaze (computer file backup), 193, 194
Balch Institute for Ethnic Studies, 638
Baltimore, 281, 296
Bancroft, Hubert Howe, 260
Banks, Charles Edward, 639–640
Baptist Church, 600
Barbour Collection (Connecticut), 297
Barbour, Lucius Barnes, 297
Barkley, Carolyn L., 140
Batchellor, Albert Stillman, 676
Beckstead, Gayle, 133
Beime, Joe, 650
Bell,
Carol Willsey, 135
David Graham, 681
Beneficiary, 404
Bennett, Archibald F., 93 (fn)
Bentley, Elizabeth Petty, 640
Bequeath/bequest, 404
Bibliographies,
"At a Glance" guides, 140–141
Bibliographies, 125–128, 258
Biographical works, 261–263
Compendium genealogies, 270
Compiled lists (dictionaries, directories, lists, registers, etc.), 259–261
Evidence, 96–97
Family history websites, 202–204, 230

Genealogical and historical periodicals, 265–267
Indexes, 139
Guides to original sources,
Government publications, 132–133
Non-government local research aids, 133–136
Special publications, 138–139
Texts and specialized sources, 136–138
Immigration records, 638, 639–645, 652
Indexes,
To multiple source types, 130–131
To periodicals, 128–129
To published genealogies and pedigrees, 129–130
Locality data sources,
Atlases and maps, 116–119
Gazetteers, 119–122
Other Internet resources, 122–23
Specialized locality sources, 121–122
Military records,
Colonial wars, 655–657
Loyalist sources, 681–686
Post-Revolutionary, 723–725
See also Revolutionary War List below
Revolutionary War, 671–680
Non-government local research aids, 133–136
Passenger and immigration lists, 639–646
Published records, 269
Special manuscript collections, 270–273
Women, helps for research on, 575 (fn)
Bill of sale, 499
Biographical Dictionary of the American Congress, 1774–1961, 263

Biographical works, 142, 261–263
Biography Index, 130
Blackstone, William, 576
Blair, Ruth, 674
Blakeney, Jane, 723
Blessings, Patrick J., 135
Blogs, *see* Family history blogs
Blois, John T., 123
Bluegrass (periodical) (Kentucky Genealogical Society), 265
Board for Certification of Genealogists (BCG), 4, 22–24, 25, 27, 83, 96, 136
Boatner, Mark Mayo, III, 724
Bockstruck, Lloyd D., 656, 671
Bodge, George M., 656
Bodie, William Willis, 678
Bolino, August C., 652
Bolton, Ethel Stanwood, 640
Bond, 404, 455
Bonner, James C., 118
Bork, Inga, 643
Boston, 281, 282, 296
Boston Public Library, 102
Boston University, 18
Boundary changes, effect on record locations and research, 73–77
Bounty land,
Post-Revolutionary, 477–478
Revolutionary, 477
Bowen, Murray, 239
Bowman, Alan P., 139
Boyer, Carl, III, 640
Bradley, Arthur Granville, 682
Braisted, Todd W., 681
Branches and Twigs (periodical) (Genealogical Society of Vermont), 265
Brandow, James C., 640
Bridgers, Frank E., 110, 132, 659, 660, 694 (fn), 695, 696, 698, 702, 714
Brigham, Clarence Saunders, 126, 274
Brigham Young University, 17, 18

Brigham Young University-Hawaii, 18

Brigham Young University-Idaho, 18

Family History website, 205

Britain,
Vital records, 281

Brock, Robert A., 640

Brooklyn Historical Society, 103

Brother's Keeper (software), 181

Brown,
Ann N., 134
John H., 262
Margie G., 671
Stuart E., Jr., 126
Teresa A., 568
Wallace, 682
William Bradford, 277

Browning, Charles H., 640

Bruce, R. M., 682

Brumbaugh, Gaius M., 485, 641, 675, 679

Bryant, Pat, 119

Buckingham, Thomas, 656

Buffalo and Erie County Public Library, 103

Buffalo, NY, 297

Build a Better GEDCOM (website/wiki), 191

Bulletin, The (periodical) (Genealogical Forum of Oregon), 265

Bureau of Land Management, 482, 491

Burgess, Louis Alexander, 679

Burial records, *see* Cemetery and burial records

Burns, Annie W., 678

Burroughs, Tony, 136

Bush, Angie, 140

BYU Idaho Family History (website), 205

Calendar change, effect of, 53–56

California,
Agricultural schedules, 375
Census population schedules, 320
Community property laws, 419
Divorce records, 556
Guardianship records, 464
Immigration Passenger Lists, 633
Land records, 521
Military records, 668
Mortality schedules, 369
Non-government local research aids, 133
Private land claims, 489
"Research in the States" guide (NGS), 141
Vital records, 292
Wills, 436

California State Library—SUTRO Library, 101

Callahan, Edward W., 671

Cameron, Viola Root, 640

Campbell,
Edward D.C., 572 (fn)
Wilfrid, 682

Canniff, William, 682

Capitalization in records, 36–37

Cappon, Lester Jesse, 126

Carangelo, Lori, 568

Card catalogs, 206

Card files and computer indexes, not recommended, 162

Carmack, Sharon DeBartolo, 140, 575, 648, 652, 738

Carson, Dina C., 124

Carty, Mickey Dimon, 134

Caution, need for, in analysis of research findings, 158

Cavaliers and Pioneers: Abstracts of Virginia Land Patents, 473

Caveat, 455

Cemetery and burial records,
Access to records,
Online, 732–733

Personal cemetery visit,
733–734
Accuracy of records, 734
"At a Glance" guide to American
cemetery research, 738
Background, 727–728
Challenges in use of, 728
Funeral director records,
737–738
Gravestone inscriptions,
728–732
Kinds of cemeteries, 728
Sextons' records, 734–736
*Census of Pensioners for
Revolutionary or Military
Services, 1840, A*, 672
Census records,
"At a Glance" guide, 140
Availability and use, 348–349
Census of Pensioners, 1840, 365
Colonial censuses, 366
Definition and historical
background, 315–317
Examples of use, 390–396
Census records—Federal schedules,
Benefits and uses, 379–386
1790, 379–380
1800–1840, 380
1850–1870, 380–381
1880, 382
1880–1940, 382–386
Contents, 1790–1870 (chart),
318–319
Glossary of terms, 377–378
Important census data (chart),
320–331
Indexes, use of, 348
Indians, 367
Information found in, 244
Information relating to veterans,
366
Limitations, 386–389
Location and availability,
348–349

Military service information in,
365–366
Missing schedules, 349–350
Population schedule forms,
1790–1940, 332–347
Recent schedules, restricted, 354,
359
Research techniques, 348
Rules for successful searching,
396–398
Schedule forms (illustrations),
332–347
Similarities and differences,
1880–1940, 382–386
Census records—non-population
schedules, 317
Agricultural schedules, 374–375
Defective, dependent, and
delinquent classes, 377
Manufacturing schedules,
375–376
Mortality schedules, 282, 283,
368–374
Slave schedules, 374
Social statistics schedules, 376
Census records—special helps,
Soundex indexes, 359–361
Special enumerations, 365,
366–368
State censuses, 366
Street index, 1910, 361–364
Vital registration and, 282–283
When to search, 389–390
*Central Illinois Genealogical
Quarterly* (Decatur Genealogical
Society), 265
Central New York Genealogical
Society, 267
Certified Genealogical Lecturers, 22
Certified Genealogists, 22
Chadbourne, Ava Harriet, 122
Chadman, Charles E., 420, 421,
551–552
Chadwick, Edward Marion, 682

Chadwyck-Healey, publishers,
271–273, 613
Chapin, Howard Millar, 656
Chartrand, René, 682
Chattel, 404–405
Chaucer, Geoffrey, 12
Chemist, as research example, 6–7
Cherokee research, "At a Glance"
guide, 140
Chicago Genealogical Society, 483
Chronicling America (website), 124
Church of England, *see* Protestant
Episcopal Church
Church of Jesus Christ of Latter-day
Saints, The, 248
Historical Department, 636
Interest in and commitment to
family history, 216, 237–238
Church records,
As source of information on
ancestral origins, 626
Challenges in using them,
586–587
Denominations whose records
are not covered, 610–611
Problems and solutions in
locating, 611
Published, 612–613
Record locations, 613–623
Records of movement between
congregations, 586
Registers, 586
Steps to assist in finding,
612–613
Citizenship and naturalization
records, *see* Naturalization
records
City directories, 73, 125
*City Directories of the United
States, 1860–1901*, 121
Civil War Soldiers & Sailors
System (website), 205
Clark,
Jewell T., 623 (fn)
Murtie J., 656, 682

Cliff, G. Glenn, 674
Clifford, Karen, 136
Cline, Inez H., 139
Cloud, the,
And computer backup programs,
194
Concerns about, 194–195
Definition and explanation,
192–193
Popular programs, 193–194
Cloud Security Alliance, 194
Clues, helpful, 77
Coddington, John, 278
"Code of Ethics and Conduct"
(BCG), 22–24
Cohen, Saul B., 119
Coldham, Peter Wilson, 640, 682,
683, 687 (fn)
Colket, Meredith B., 110, 132, 640,
659, 660, 694 (fn), 695, 696,
698, 702, 714
College of the Holy Cross Library,
635
Colletta, John P., 652
Colorado,
Census population schedules,
320, 367, 368
Common-law marriage, 305
Divorce records, 556
Guardianship records, 464
Land records, 521
Mortality schedules, 369
Private land claims, 489
"Research in the States" guide
(NGS), 141
Vital records, 292
Wills, 436
*Columbia Gazetteer of the World,
The*, 119
Common law, 405
Common-law marriage, 305–306
Common sense in research, 77
Community property laws, 405, 419
Community Trees (FamilySearch
program), 61

Compendium genealogies, 269–270
Compiled and published sources,
    61–62, 255–273
    Limitations of, 276–278
Compiled lists (dictionaries,
    directories, registers, etc.),
    259–261
Computer applications (apps), 176
Computer database, definition,
    201–202
Computer hardware, 177
Computer programs, 176
Computer-related terms/definitions,
    177–180
Computer software, 176, 177
Computer systems, 176
Computer technology, guidelines
    for use in genealogical research
    (by NGS), 234–235
Congregational Church,
    Baptisms, 588
    Burials, 590
    Communicants, 588–589
    Dismissions, 589
    Marriages, 590
    Notes, 589–590
Connecticut,
    Agricultural schedules, 375
    Census population schedules,
        321
    Church records, 614
    Customs Passenger Lists, 628
    Divorce records, 556
    Families, 298
    Gazetteers, 119–120
    Gravestone inscriptions, 298
    Guardianship records, 464
    Land records, 521, 524
    Loyalists during Revolution, 684
    Military records, 668
    Mortality schedules, 369
    Naturalization records, 565
    Non-government local research
        aids, 133
    Vital records, 280, 297, 298
    Widows' inheritance rights, 581
    Wills, 436
Connecticut Genealogical Society,
    265
Connecticut Historical Society, 101,
    656, 673
Connecticut Nutmegger, The
    (periodical) (Connecticut
    Genealogical Society), 265
Connecticut State Library, 101, 298
Conrad, J.A., 124
Consanguinity, 405
Consideration, 405
Contract, 500
Conveyance, 405, 500
Copies of original records, potential
    problems with, 92
Corbitt, David Leroy, 122
Corporeal property, 405
Correct research procedures,
    importance of, 143–144
Correspondence in research,
    Analyzing and tabulating results
        of, 166
    Appearance of letters, 172
    Checklist, 173–174
    Documenting sources, 166
    Formulas for success, 167–171
    Identifying potential
        correspondents, 172
    Necessity of, 165
    Objectivity in, 171–172
    Organizing and filing, 165, 166
    Records relating to, 162–163
    Tracking on research log, 163,
        165
Correspondence log, no longer
    recommended, 163
Côté, Richard N., 135
Cotenancy, 405
Coulter,
    Ellis M. 260
    Willa M., 260
County divisions, effect on
    research, 73–77

Court records,
  "At a Glance" guide, 140, 574
  Case files, 554
  Case reports, reporters, and
    digests, 572–573
  Court order books, 554, 555
  Definition and background, 548
  Differences in court names, 550
  Docket books, 549, 554
  Execution dockets, 554
  Extent of, 548
  Judgment dockets, 555
  Law vs. equity, 550–553
  Minute books, 549, 554
  State vs. federal, 549–550
  Trial dockets, 554
  Trial vs. appellate, 553–554
  Value and use, 547
  See also Adoption records;
    Divorce records; Legislative
    records; and Naturalization
    records
Court systems in U.S., 549–554
  Law vs. equity, 550–553
  State vs. federal, 549–550
  Trial vs. appellate, 553–554
Coverture, 576 (fn)
Cowell, Benjamin, 678
Craig, Gerald M., 683
Crandall, Ralph, 134
Crandell, Jill, 147
Crockett, Walter H., 678
Croom, Emily Anne, 136
Crossroads (periodical) (Utah
  Genealogical Association), 265
Crowther, George Rodney, III, 129
Cruikshank, Ernest A., 683
Crume, Rick, 60
CSI: Dixie (website), 205
Cullum, George Washington, 724
Curtesy, 406, 582
Curtilage, 406–407
Customs Lists of Aliens, 635
Customs Passenger Lists, 627–632
  Arrangement of indexes,
    648–649

  Copies and abstracts, 629
  Microfilmed index cards, 632
  Original lists, 627–629
  Record content, 629
  Transcripts from U.S. State
    Department, 631–632
Cutter library classification, 109
  Modified use by Family History
    Library, 109 (fn)
Cyndi's List (website), 60, 136,
  146, 199, 203, 568

Dallas Public Library, 104
Dandridge, Danske, 671
d'Angevillle, Count Howard H.,
  270
Daniel, James R. V., 572 (fn)
Danis, Jan Shelton, 111 (fn)
Database, definition, 201–202
Daughters of the American
  Revolution (DAR),
  Library, 101
  Library catalog, 126
  North Carolina, 677
  Ohio, 677
  Website, 205
Davidson, Katherine H., 283, 317,
  349, 368, 377
Davis,
  Robert Scott, Jr., 133
  Walter G., 260
Death notices in early newspapers,
  273–274
Decatur Genealogical Society, 265
Decedent, 407
de Colange, Leo, 119
Decree of distribution, 455–456
Deeben, John P., 136
Deed, definition, 500
Deed of release, 500
Deeds, examples of abstracts,
  534–541
DeForest, Louis Effingham, 656
Degree of relationship, 407–408
Deiler, J. Hanno, 641

Delaware,
Census population schedules, 321
Church records, 614
Court records, 552
Divorce records, 556
Guardianship records, 464
Land records, 521
Mortality schedules, 369
Probate jurisdictions, 70
Probate records, 441
Slave schedules, 374
Vital records, 298–299
Wills, 436
Delaware Genealogical Society Journal, 265
DeMond, Robert O., 683
Denver Public Library, 101
Deoxyribonucleic acid, *see* DNA
Deposition, 457, 500–501
Descendancy research, 234
Descent and distribution, 408
Detroit Public Library, 102, 636
Detroit Society for Genealogical Research Magazine, 265
Deville, Winston, 641
Devine, Donn, 82, 91, 96
Devisee, 408
Dewey Decimal Classification System, 107, 108
DeWitt, Donald L., 138
Dickore, Marie, 671
Dickson, Robert J., 641
Digital Public Library of America (DPLA), 61
Digitize, definition of, 201
Digitizing of records, 201
Directories
Of libraries and societies, 125
Of newspapers and periodicals, 124
Directory of Family "One-name" Periodicals, 124
Directory of Genealogical and Historical Periodicals in the US and Canada, 124

Directory of Genealogical Periodicals, 124
Directory of Genealogical Societies in the U.S.A. and Canada, 125
Discrepancies, solving, 67 (fn)
Distribution, 457
District of Columbia,
Census population schedules, 321, 351
Church records, 614
Common-law marriage, 305
Divorce records, 556
Guardianship records, 464
Land records, 521
Military records,
Books, 673–674
Mortality schedules, 369
Slave schedules, 374
Wills, 436–437
Divorce and common-law marriage, 306
Divorce records, 306, 555–560
DNA testing as family history tool,
Autosomal testing, 197
Discussion and explanation, 196–198
In adoption research, 568
Y chromosome and mtDNA testing, 198
Dobson, David, 641
Documentation, importance of, 5, 144, 209–210
Dollarhide, William, 76, 118
Donation land grants, 479–480
Donee/donor, 408
Dorman, John Frederick, 679
Dower, 408, 580–582
Dower release, *see* Release of dower
Drake,
Samuel F., 262
Samuel Gardner, 641
Draughon, Wallace R., 134
Dropbox (cloud site), 193, 194
Duplication of effort, 145
Dwelling house, 409

Eales, Anne Bruner, 110, 111, 365,
376, 377, 481, 482, 483, 484,
485, 486, 488, 489, 490, 563,
565, 566, 625, 629, 631, 632,
634, 635, 646, 647, 651, 655,
658, 660, 664, 668, 670, 680,
690, 694 (fn), 695, 696, 698,
699, 700, 701, 702, 703, 704,
705, 707, 708, 713, 714, 715,
716, 717, 718, 719, 721
Easement, 409
Eastman, Dick, 265
*Eastman's Online Genealogical
Newsletter*, 265
Eckenrode, H. J., 679
Eelking, Max von, 671
Effects, 409
Egle, William H., 561, 641, 643,
677
Eichholz, Alice, 121, 215
Eilerman, Elizabeth M., 639
Ellet, Elizabeth Fries, 671
Elliott, Wendy Bebout, 140, 574
Ellis Island,
"At a Glance" research guide,
140, 648
Fire in 1897, 648
Records, 647–648
Ely, Selden Marvin, 673
Enation, 409
Encryption, 179 (fn)
Encyclopedia of Genealogy, The
(website/wiki), 191
Endowment, 409
Enfeoff, 409
England, *see* Britain
English language, Early Modern,
30–31
Entail, 409
Ervin, Sara Sullivan, 678
Escheat, 409, 496
Espenshade, A. Howry, 122
Essex Institute, 301
Estate, 409
Evans, G. N. D., 683

Evernote,
"At a Glance" guide, 140, 147
Cloud usage, 193
For record keeping, 146–147
Everton, George B., 76
Evidence,
Circumstantial or indirect, 85–86
Collateral, 89–90
Conflicting, 93–96
Considering origin/source of,
206, 209
Definitions relating to, 80–82
Direct, 85
Evaluating, 157–159
Hearsay, 90–91
Indirect or circumstantial, 85–86
Original and derivative, 91
Other writings about, 96–97
Primary, 87
Relevance and weight, 91
Secondary, 87–89
Types of, 85–92
Other writings about, 96–97
vs. Sources, 91
When it does not make sense, 92
Ewell, Barry J., 187
Execution, 409
Executor, 409
Executrix, 409
Extract—definition, *see* Abstract,
extract, transcribe

Facebook (website), 188
Facts,
Definition, 81
Importance of, in research,
13–14, 235
Families, compiling complete,
10–12, 68–69, 143
Family Chronicle (periodical), 267
Family group form, 63
Family Historian (software), 181,
208
Family histories and genealogies,
256–258

Family history
  Definitions, 3–5
  Professions, 21–22, 24–26
  Relationship to other subjects,
    142
  Use of this title, 3
  What and why of, 237–239
  Writing, 249–251
Family history blogs, 191–192
Family History Centers (LDS), 61,
  100, 210
FamilyHistory.com (website), 203
Family History Department (LDS),
  139
Family History Guide, The
  (website), 19, 230–233
Family History Library of The
  Church of Jesus Christ of
  Latter-day Saints, 19, 22, 104,
  107, 259, 264, 302, 303, 441,
  468, 524, 549, 613, 632, 636,
  660, 687
  "At a Glance" guide, 140
  Classification system, 108
  Library catalog, 61
Family history professions,
  Computer technology, 25
  Editorial work and writing, 25
  Education for, 15–19
  Freelance record searchers, 24–25
  Library and archives work,
    24–25
  Professional researchers, 21–24
  Teaching, 25–26
Family history research,
  Comparison to research in other
    fields, 5–7
  Courses and classes, 18–19
  Issues relating to, 206
  Key to success in, 26
  Objectivity in, 251–252
  Steps needed to keep on track,
    206–210
Family history software programs,
  180–181, 206, 207–208

Family history websites, 199–200,
  Google-sponsored website list,
    205–206
FamilyLink.com (website), 203
Family.me (website), 188
Familypedia (website/wiki), 190
Family records, as source of
  information on ancestral origins,
  626
FamilySearch.org (website), 60,
  100 (fn), 112, 202, 216–223,
  299–300, 301, 302
  Accounts, 218
  Adoption research, 568
  App gallery, 222
  "At a Glance" guide, 140
  Family Search Catalog, 61
  Family Tree program on, 190,
    218–219
  Help Center, 219
  Homepage, 218
  Indexing, 217–218
  Libraries, 105–106
  Partnerships, 217
  Research tactics, 230
  Search options, 219–222
  Training materials, 222–223
  Wiki, 71, 118, 123, 136, 141,
    190, 222, 623
Family Tree Builder (software), 208
Family Tree DNA, 197
Family Tree Heritage (software),
  181
Family Tree Magazine, 19, 60, 181,
  204, 230, 265
Family Tree Maker (software), 181,
  207–208
Family Tree program on Family
  Search.org, 190, 218–219
Family Tree University, 19
Family tree, your personal,
  Official offline, 206, 207–208
  Official online, 206, 160, 207
Farmer, John, 260
Faust, Albert Bernhardt, 641

Federation of Genealogical Societies (FGS), 16, 17, 129, 265, 363, 637

Fee simple, 410

Female ancestors, "At a Glance" guide, 140

Fernow, Berthold, 676

Feudal system, 410

FGS Voice (periodical) (Federation of Genealogical Societies), 265

Fiduciary, 410

Fief, 410

Field, Thomas P., 122

Filby, P. William, 121, 126, 130, 142, 259, 638, 641, 646

Filson Club Historical Quarterly, 265

Filson Historical Society, The, 102, 265

FindMyPast (website), 100, 129, 202–203, 223–225
 Comparison to other large commercial sites, 230
 Partnerships, 223
 Research on site, 224–225
 Other research tactics, 230
 Settings, 224
 Site use without membership, 224

Fisher, Carleton E., 128

Fixture, 410

Flagg, Charles Alcott, 675

Flick, Alexander Clarence, 683

Flickr (website), 189

Florida,
 Cash entry files (public domain land), 483
 Census population schedules, 321, 360 (fn), 367, 368
 Common-law marriages, 306
 Confederate pension records, 709–710
 Court records, 552
 Divorce records, 556
 Donation land grants, 479–480
 Guardianship records, 464
 Immigration Passenger Lists, 633
 Land records, 521
 Loyalists during Revolution, 682, 685
 Mortality schedules, 369
 Non-government local research aids, 133
 Private land claims, 489
 "Research in the States" guide (NGS), 141
 Slave schedules, 374
 Vital records, 292
 Wills, 437

Focus, determining your research, 206, 208

Fold3.com (website), 100, 112, 203, 205, 655, 690, 691, 708

Folio, 410–411

Forms,
 Blank, for recording family history data, 62–63
 For extracting record information, 162

Forms, *see* Message boards, forums, and special projects

Fothergill, Gerald, 642

Four-S formula for correspondence, 169–171

France, Military records, Books, 674

Franklin, Nancy Gubb, 361

Fraser, Alexander, 683

Freedmen's Bureau Records, 248

Freehold estate, 411

French,
 Elizabeth, 642
 John Homer, 120

Froelke, Ruth, 643

Fryxell, David A., 118, 204, 216

Fulcher, Robert Carlton, 135

Gale Directory of Publications and Broadcast Media, 268, 275

Gannett, Henry, 121

Gazetteer of the State of Michigan,
      123
*Gazetteer of the United States of
      America, A*, 119
Gazetteers, 71, 120, 133
   As research tool, 119–121
   United States general, 119
Gearhart, Heber G., 677
GEDCOM files, importing, 211,
      226
Genealogical and historical
      periodicals, 19
   Accessing old editions, 267–268
   Discussion and list of, 264–269
   Project of Genealogical
      Publishing Company, 264
   Use in research, 267–269
Genealogical conferences, seminars,
      and workshops, 16–18
Genealogical courses and classes,
      18–19, 26
Genealogical Forum of Oregon, 265
Genealogical Institute on Federal
      Records (Gen-Fed), 16
Genealogical Journal (Utah
      Genealogical Association), *see
      Crossroads*
*Genealogical Magazine of New
      Jersey, The*, 266
*Genealogical Periodical Annual
      Index (GPAI)*, 129, 268
Genealogical Proof Standard (GPS),
      79, 83–85, 214
Genealogical Publishing Co., 297,
      604 (fn)
Genealogical seminars, *see*
      Genealogical conferences,
      seminars, and workshops
Genealogical societies, 15–16
Genealogical Society of New
      Jersey, 103, 266
Genealogical Society of
      Pennsylvania, 267
Genealogical Society of Vermont,
      265, 267

Genealogical Standards, 83, 96
Genealogical workshops, *see*
      Genealogical conferences,
      seminars, and workshops
*Genealogies of Connecticut
      Families*, 298
Genealogist, The (periodical)
      (American Society of
      Genealogists), 265
Genealogists,
   Comparison to researchers in
      other fields, 5–7
   Professional, *see* Family history
      professions, Professional
      researchers
Genealogy (*see also* Family history)
   And historical background, 12–13
   And law, 79
   And science, 9–10
   Definitions and explanation, 3–5
   Educational opportunities, 15–19
   Family history connection, 3–5
   Of places, 73
   Places, importance of, 13, 73–77
   Professions, *see* Family history
Genealogybank.com (website), 203
Genealogy.com (website), 199, 203
Genealogy Today (website/wiki),
      190
General Land Office, 482
General Society of Mayflower
      Descendants, 266
Genetic Genealogy Basics, "At a
      Glance" guide, 140
Geographical dictionaries, *see*
      Gazetteers
Georgia,
   Agricultural schedules, 375
   "At a Glance" guide, 140
   Census population schedules,
      321, 351, 360 (fn)
   Church records, 587, 614
   Common-law marriages, 306
   Confederate pension records,
      710

Counties, 119
Court records, 552
Customs Passenger Lists, 628
Divorce records, 557
Guardianship records, 464
Immigration Passenger Lists, 633
Land grant records, 494, 521
Loyalists during Revolution,
    682, 683
Military records,
    Books, 674
Mortality schedules, 369
"Research in the States" guide
    (NGS), 141
Slave schedules, 374
Vital records, 292
Wills, 437
Georgia Department of Archives
    and History, 674
*Georgia Genealogical Society
    Quarterly*, 266
Gift deed, 501
Gilbert Cope Collection, 636
Gilroy, Marion, 683
Giuseppi, Montague S., 561, 642
Glazier, Ira A., 638
Goodrich, John E., 679
Goods, 411
Goods and chattels, 411
Google "Advanced Search" page
    184–186
Google Drive (cloud), 193
Gordon, Thomas F., 121
Government published research
    aids,
    National, 132
    State, 132–133
    See also Non-government local
        research aids
Grasssroots of America, 489
Great Migration project, 304
Green, Fallon N., 137
Greenlaw, William P., 130
Greer, George Cabell, 642
Gregory Gerould, Winifred, 126, 274
Guardian, 411

Guadian *ad litem*, 411
Guardianships,
    Court jurisdiction, 462–466
    Value of records, 466–468
*Guide to Genealogical Research in
    the National Archives* (Rev. ed.,
    1983), 110, 111 (fn), 367, 485,
    694 (fn)
*Guide to Genealogical Research in
    the National Archives* (3rd ed.,
    2000, Eales and Kvasnicka), 110,
    111, 112, 365, 376, 377, 481,
    482, 483, 484–485, 486, 488,
    489, 490, 563, 565, 566, 521,
    625, 629, 631, 632, 634, 635,
    646, 647, 651, 655, 658, 660,
    664, 668, 670, 680, 690, 694
    (fn), 695, 696, 698, 699, 700,
    701, 702, 703, 704, 705, 707,
    708, 713, 714, 715, 716, 717,
    718, 719, 721
"Guidelines for Family History
    Researchers" (NGS), 26–27
"Guidelines for Sound Genealogical
    Research" (NGS), 27–28
"Guidelines for Use of Computer
    Technology . . ." (NGS), 20,
    234–235
"Guidelines for Using Records
    Repositories and Libraries . . ."
    (NGS), 45–46
Guild of One-Name Studies, 60
*Guinness Book of World Records,
    The*, 424
Gwathmey, John H., 679

Hackett, J. Dominick, 642
Hait, Michael, 140
Hale,
    Charles R., 298
    Richard H., 737
Hale Collection (Connecticut), 298
Haley, Alex, 238
Hall,
    Albert Harrison, 657
    Henry, 262

Hamburg Passenger Lists, 637
Hamer, Philip May, 126
Hamersly,
    Lewis Randolph, 726
    Thomas H. S., 671–672
Hammond, Isaac W., 676
Hancock, Harold Bell, 683
Handwriting, reading difficult,
    41–42
Handybook for Genealogists, The
    (Everton), 76
Hansen, Holly, 121
Hardy, Stella Pickett, 270
Hargreaves-Mawdsley, R., 642
Harold B. Lee Library, 104
Harrell, Isaac Samuel, 683
Harrison Land Act, 476, 478
Hartman, Edward George, 642
*Harvard Encyclopedia of Ethnic
    Groups*, 131
Hathaway, Beverly West, 134
Hawaii,
    Census population schedules,
        321
    Divorce records, 557
    Guardianship records, 464
    Land records, 521
    Wills, 437
Hawkeye Heritage (periodical)
    (Iowa Genealogical Society), 266
Hayward,
    Elizabeth M., 672
    John, 119
Headright grants, 473–474
Heir, 411
Heirs and assigns, 411
Heirs of the body, 411
Heitman, Francis B., 260, 672
Hendrick Hudson Chapter Library,
    NSDAR, 636
Hendrickson, Nancy, 137, 216
Heredis (software), 181
Hereditament, 411
HeritageQuest Online (website),
    100, 205

Herringshaw, Thomas W., 262
Hicks, Frederick C., 573
Hill, May Davis, 242, 243
Hinke, William J., 644
Hinman, Royal R., 260, 642
Hinshaw, William Wade, 604, 613
Historic Map Works (website), 76,
    100, 116
Historical considerations in family
    history, 244–248
Historical Newspapers Collection
    (Ancestry website), 275
Historical Society of Pennsylvania,
    104, 636
History of the Great Lakes States
    (website), 122
Hitz, Alex Mayer, 674
Hodges, Margaret R., 675
Hoffman, Marian, 126
Holcomb, Brent Howard, 135
Holland Museum (Michigan), 636
Holland Society of New York, 103
Holmes, Frank R., 260
Home and family sources, 58,
    239–241
Home study classes, 18–19
Homestead land grants, 480–481
Hoosier Genealogist: Connections
    (periodical) (Indiana Historical
    Society), 266
Hornbook of Virginia History, A, 572
Hotten, John Camden, 642
House, Charles J., 675
Houston,
    Ethel Rollins, 675
    Martha Lou, 139
Houston Public Library, 104
Houts, Alice K., 676
Hoyt, Max Ellsworth, 139
Huber, Leslie Albrecht, 188
Hummel, Ray O., Jr., 122
Humphrey, John T., 140

ICAPGen, 22
iCloud (cloud), 193

Idaho,
  Census population schedules,
    321
  Common-law marriages, 306
  Community property laws, 419
  Divorce records, 557
  Guardianship records, 464
  Land records, 521, 527
  Mortality schedules, 369
  Vital records, 292
  Wills, 437
Idaho Falls FamilySearch Library,
  106
*Idaho Genealogical Society
Quarterly*, 266
Illinois,
  Agricultural schedules, 375
  Cash entry files (public domain
    land), 483
  Census, 1910 Soundex problem,
    361
  Census population schedules,
    322, 351
  Church records, 614
  Court records, 552
  Divorce records, 557
  Guardianship records, 464
  Land records, 521
  Military records,
    Books, 674
  Mortality schedules, 369
  Non-government local
    research aids, 133
  Private land claims, 489
  "Research in the States" guide
    (NGS), 141
  Vital records, 292
  Wills, 437
Illinois State Archives, 483
*Illinois State Genealogical Society
Quarterly*, 266
Immigration and Naturalization
  Service (INS),
  A-Files and C-Files, 646–647

Immigration Passenger Lists,
  Challenges in using, 649–650
  Destroyed lists, 634
  Record content, 634
Immigration records, other,
  Bremen, Germany, passenger
    lists, 637
  Cargo manifests, 636
  Gilbert Cope Collection, 636
  Hamburg Passenger Lists, 637
  Irish to Massachusetts, 635
  Jewish immigrants, 636
  LDS Church members, 636
  Massachusetts Archives
    Division, 635
  Michigan immigration, 636
  National Records Center,
    636–637
  New York passenger lists,
    638–639
  Texas immigration (German,
    French, English), 636
  See also Passenger lists, published
Incorporeal property, 411–412
Indenture, 412
Independent cities,
  In Virginia, 569–572
  Other states, 571 (fn)
*Index to American Genealogies
and to Genealogical Material . . .*
  (Munsell), 130, 268
Index to Genealogical Periodicals
  (Jacobus), 268
Indexed records on Internet
  websites,
  Explanation, 201
  Extent of, 202
  Getting involved in indexing,
    217–218
Indexes,
  Concerns about, 41
  To multiple source types,
    130–131
  To original sources, 139

To periodicals, 128–129
To published genealogies and
pedigrees, 129–130
Indiana,
Census population schedules,
322
Church records, 615
Common-law marriages, 306
Divorce records, 557
Gazetteers, 120
Guardianship records, 464
Land records, 521
Military records,
Books, 674
Mortality schedules, 369
Non-government local research
aids, 134
Private land claims, 489
"Research in the States" guide
(NGS), 141
Vital records, 292
Wills, 437
Indiana Historical Society, 266
Indiana State Library, 102
Infant, 412
Information, definition, 80
Institute of Genealogy and
Historical Research (IGHR), 16
Intermarriage, 412
International Association of Jewish
Genealogical Societies (IAJGS),
17
International Commission for the
Accreditation of Professional
Genealogists, *see* ICAPGen
Internet family history websites,
important, 202–206
International Genealogical Index
(IGI), 61
International Society of Genetic
Genealogy, 197
Internet Genealogy (periodical),
266
Internet resources, 122–123

Internet search engines, use of,
181–187
Boolean logic, 182–183
Clues for efficient use, 186–187
Google "Advanced Search"
page, 184–186
Keyword helps, 186–187
Punctuation and symbols
used, 183–187
Minus sign, 183
Number ranges, 184
Quotation marks, 183
Search operators, 184
Wildcards (placeholders),
183–184
Words ignored by, 187
Internet social media use, 187–189
Internet video chat connections, 59
Intestate, 412
Inventory, 457–458
Iowa,
Agricultural schedules, 375
Census population schedules,
322
Common-law marriage, 305
Divorce records, 557
Guardianship records, 464
Land records, 521, 526
Mortality schedules, 369
Private land claims, 489
Vital records, 292
Wills, 437
Iowa Genealogical Society, 266
Iscrupe, William L. and
Shirley G. M., 135
Issue, 412
Item, 412

Jacobson, Judy, 137
Jacobus, Donald Lines, 4, 5, 10, 11,
48, 51, 79, 128, 256–257, 268,
277 (fn), 278
Jarboe, Betty M., 127
Jasanoff, Maya, 683

Jenkins, Warren, 120
Jewish Genealogical Society of
   Illinois, 266
Jewson, Charles Boardman, 642
Jillson, Willard R., 486
Johnson,
   Arta F., 127, 137
   William Perry, 134, 139
Johnston,
   Henry P., 673
   Ross B., 679
Joint tenancy, 406
Jones,
   Caleb, 684
   E. Alfred, 683, 684
   Thomas W., 96
Joseph, Samuel, 642
*Journal of the Afro-American
   Historical and Genealogical
   Society*, 266
Jurisdictions, background and
   definition, 69–70

Kaminkow,
   Jack, 121, 123, 260, 642, 672
   Marion J., 127, 258, 259, 260,
      642, 672,
Kane, Joseph Nathan, 121
Kansas,
   Agricultural schedules, 375
   Census population schedules,
      322
   Common-law marriage, 305
   Divorce records, 557
   Guardianship records, 464
   Land records, 522
   Mortality schedules, 369
   Vital records, 293
   Wills, 437
Kansas City Public Library, 102
Kansas Genealogical Society, 267
Kemp, Thomas Jay, 133, 287, 296
Kennedy, Imogene Kinard, and
   Leon, 135

Kentucky,
   Bounty land warrants, 486
   Census population schedules,
      322, 360 (fn)
   Church records, 615
   Confederate pension records, 710
   Divorce records, 557
   Guardianship records, 464
   Land records, 522
   Military records,
      Books, 675
   Mortality schedules, 370
   Non-government local research
      aids, 134
   Owsley County, 74–76
   "Research in the States" guide
      (NGS), 141
   Slave schedules, 374
   Specialized locality sources, 122
   Vital records, 293
   Wills, 437
Kentucky Ancestors (periodical)
   (Kentucky Historical Society),
   266
Kentucky Genealogical Society,
   265, 267
Kethley, T. William, 303
Kilbourn, John, 120
King Philip's War, 653
Kirkham, E. Kay, 121, 623
Knight, Lucian L., 674
Knittle, Walter Allen, 642
Konrad, J.A., 124
Kozub, Mary Lou, 133
Krebbs, Friedrich, 643
Kurzweil, Arthur, 137
Kvasnicka, Robert M., 110, 365,
   376, 377, 481, 482, 483, 484,
   485, 486, 488, 489, 490, 563,
   565, 566, 625, 629, 631, 632,
   634, 635, 646, 647, 651, 655,
   658, 660, 664, 668, 670, 680,
   690, 694 (fn), 695, 696, 698,
   699, 700, 701, 702, 703, 704,

705, 707, 708, 713, 714, 715, 716, 717, 718, 719, 721

Lancour, Harold, 127, 646
Land entry records (public domain),
    As source of information on
        ancestral origins, 626
    History, 477–481
    Indexes, 483, 484, 485, 486, 487, 489, 490, 491
    Location, 481–491
    Record types, 481–491
    Research aids, 481–491
    Value and use, 481–491
Land estates, kinds of, 496–497
Land grant records,
    Colonial,
        Cash sales, 471, 474
        Definition and background, 469–471
        Grants to the colonies, 470
        Headright grants, 473–474
        Non-grant transfers, 474
        Process explained, 471–473
        Published, 473–474
        Record types, 471–474
        Value, 474
    Public (federal) land,
        Bounty land, 477–478, 662–664
        Cash entry files, 483
        Credit entry files, 482–483
        Donation land grants, 479–480
        Early land sales, 478
        Homestead grants, 480–481
        Land entries, 1908–1973, 490
        Preemption sales, 478–479
        Private land claims, 481
    State-land states, 470, 494
Land measurements, 502
    Metes and bounds, 413
    Rectangular Survey System, 415, 475–476, 477
Land Ordinance of 1785, 475

Land Ordinance of 1787, 476
Land ownership maps, 519–521
Land ownership maps of Arphax
    Publishing, 117
Land patents,
    In the colonies, 472
    In the public domain (BLM), 491
Land records, importance to family
    history research, 400–401, 469
Land records, local,
    Abstracting, *see* Abstracts, Deeds
    Availability, 521–524, 528
    Definition and background, 495
    Devise by will, 429
    Importance of, 400–401, 469–470
    Indexes, benefits and limitations, 524–527
    Jurisdictions, 521–524
    Limitations, 524–527
    Plat maps, 521
    Record types, 497–506
    Situations that generated, 470–471
    Use in hard cases, 510–511
    Value and use, 506–511
    See also Deeds
Land sales by federal government, 478–479
Land titles,
    Limitations on fee simple, 496
    Nature of, 495
Land transfers, historical phases of, 470–471
Land, using descriptions of to prove
    pedigree connections, 509–510
Lands, tenements, and
    hereditaments, 412
Language changes, 29–32, 46–50
Larson, Denise R., 137, 140
Las Vegas FamilySearch Library, 106
Latin terms, 39–40
LDS Family History Library, *see*

Family History Library of The Church of Jesus Christ of Latter-day Saints

Leary, Helen F. M., 78, 80–81, 84, 85, 135

Lease, 501–502

Leasehold, 412

Legacy (definition), 412

Legacy (software), 208

Legacy Family Tree (software), 181

Legal instrument, 413

Legal research, 572–573

Legal terminology/definitions, 402–418

Legatee/legator, 413

Legislative records, 567

Leonard, John W., 262

Letter formula for correspondence, 167–169

Letter of attorney, *see* Power of attorney

Letters of administration, 458–459

Letters testamentary, 459

Lewis, Virgil A., 656, 679

Libby, Charles T., 260

Libraries,
    Catalogs on Internet, 101, 107
    Classification systems, 107–109
    Importance of, 99
    Important, 101–105
    Internet resources at, 100
    Role of, in research, 100–101

Library classification systems, 107–109

Library of Congress, 101, 118, 122, 123, 124, 128, 131, 138, 258, 271, 275, 652

Library of Congress Classification System (LC), 107–108

Library of Virginia, 104, 302

Lichtman, Allan J., 137, 238, 239, 241, 243, 250

Lien, 502

Life estate, 413

Life events as helps to understanding family history, 244–248

Linn, John B., 643, 677

Litigation, 413

Living DNA, 197

Local histories as family history sources, 123, 244, 258–259

Locality analysis,
    Place (county) divisions, 73–77
    Tools for, 70–73

Logan FamilySearch Library, 106

Long,
    Elizabeth Terry, 623
    Helen, 258

Look-alike letters, 38–39

Los Angeles FamilySearch Library, 105

Los Angeles Public Library, 101

Louisiana,
    Cash entry files (public domain land), 483
    Census population schedules, 323, 360 (fn)
    Community property laws, 419
    Confederate pension records, 710
    Customs Passenger Lists, 628, 629
    Divorce records, 557
    Guardianship records, 464
    Immigration Passenger Lists, 633
    Land records, 522
    Loyalists during Revolution, 682
    Mortality schedules, 370
    Private land claims, 489
    Slave schedules, 374
    Vital records, 293, 296
    Wills, 437

Loyalist Gazette, 686

Loyalists, *see* Military records— Revolutionary War

Luebking, Sandra Hargreaves, 138, 215, 269 (fn), 604 (fn)

Lutheran Church,
    Baptisms, 600

Confirmations, 599
Dead buried publicly, 600
Lists of communicants, 599
Marriages, 599
Register of families, 598

MacEntee, Thomas, 195
Mackenzie, George Norbury, 270
Magruder, James Mosby, 139
Maine,
    Agricultural schedules, 375
    Census population schedules,
        323
    Church records, 615
    Customs Passenger Lists, 627
    Divorce records, 557
    Guardianship records, 464
    Immigration Passenger Lists, 633
    Land records, 522
    Military records,
        Books, 675
    Mortality schedules, 370
    Naturalization records, 565
    Specialized locality sources, 122
    Vital records, 299–300
    Wills, 437
Manufacturing schedules, *see*
    Census records
Manuscript collections, special,
    270–273
*Map Guide to the U.S. Federal
    Censuses, 1790–1920*, 76, 118
Maps,
    As research tools, 116–119
    Use of, in research, 72–73
    Websites as sources, 74–76
Marks and signatures, *see*
    Signatures
Marriage notices in early
    newspapers, 273
Marriage records, *see* Vital records
Martin, Kim I., 139
Maryland,
    "At a Glance" guide, 140

Census population schedules, 323
Church records, 587, 615
Confederate pension records, 710
Court records, 549, 552
Customs Passenger Lists, 627,
    628
Divorce records, 557
Guardianship records, 464
Immigration Passenger Lists, 633
Land grant records, 494
Land records, 522
Loyalists during Revolution,
    682, 684
Military records,
    Books, 675
Mortality schedules, 370
"Research in the States" guide
    (NGS), 141
Slave schedules, 374
Vital records, 300
Widows' inheritance rights, 581
Wills, 437–438
*Maryland Genealogical Society
    Journal*, 266
Maryland Historical Society, 102
Massachusetts
    Agricultural schedules, 375
    "At a Glance" guide, 140
    Census population schedules,
        323
    Church records, 615–616
    Court records, 552
    Customs Lists of Aliens, 635
    Customs Passenger Lists, 627,
        628
    Divorce records, 557
    Gazetteers, 120
    Guardianship records, 465
    Immigration Passenger Lists, 633
    Land grant records, 494
    Land records, 522
    Loyalists during Revolution,
        683, 685
    Mortality schedules, 370

Naturalization records, 565
Vital records, 280, 282, 293, 300–301
Wills, 438
Massachusetts Archives, 301, 635
Matchette, Robert B., 111
Mather, Frederic Gregory, 676
Maussan, William A., 130
Mayflower Descendant: A Quarterly Magazine of Pilgrim Genealogy and History (New England Historic Genealogical Society), 266
Mayflower Families Through Five Generations project, 304
Mayflower Quarterly (General Society of Mayflower Descendants), 266
McAllister, Joseph T., 679
McAuslan, William Alexander, 130
McCall, Mrs. Howard H., 674
McCarthy, Joe, 423, 425, 447
McGhee, Lucy K., 675, 676
McGinnis, Carol, 134, 136, 140, 572
McLane, Mrs. Bobby Jones, 139
McMullin, Phillip W., 489
Measurements of land, 502
Meli, Annie R. W., 673
Mendez, Rossy, 639
Mesa FamilySearch Library, 105
Message boards, forums, and special projects, 198–199
Metcalf, Frank Johnson, 139
Metes and bounds, 413
Meyer,
    Mary Keysor, 125, 130, 646 (fn)
    Virginia M., 674
Meyer's Directory of Genealogical Societies in the U.S.A. and Canada, 268
Meyerink, Kory L., 140, 269
Meynen, Emil, 127
Michigan,
    Agricultural schedules, 375

"At a Glance" guide, 140
Census population schedules, 323–324
Church records, 616–617
Common-law marriages, 306
Court records, 552
Divorce records, 557
Guardianship records, 465
Land records, 522
Military records,
    Books, 676
Mortality schedules, 370
Private land claims, 489
"Research in the States" guide (NGS), 141
Vital records, 293
Wills, 438
Mid-Continent Public Library, 102
Middlebrook, Louis F., 673
Midwest African American Genealogy Institute (MAAGI), 17
Milden, James Wallace, 127
Military records,
    As family history source, 244, 653
    As source of information on ancestral origins, 626
Military records—Between Revolution and Civil War, 689–699
    Background, 689
    Indian and related wars, 690–691
    Marine Corps service records, 694
    Mexican War, 691
    Miscellaneous military records, 1784–1815, 691
    Naval service records, 691–694
    Pensions, 694–698
    Pre-War of 1812, 690
    Rolls, rosters, etc., 694
    Service records, 689–694
    Veterans' benefits records,
        Bounty land warrants, 698–699

War of 1812, 690–691
  "At a Glance" guide, 140
Military records—Civil War,
  699–712
  Burial records of soldiers,
    703–704
  Confederate records, 707–712
  Compiled Military Service
    Records, 708
  Draft registration records,
    700–701
  Headstone applications, 704
  Histories of volunteer units,
    702–703
  Naval service records, 704–705
  Service records, 701–702
  Veterans' benefits, 705–707
Military records—Colonial wars,
  Books, 655–656
  Definition, 654
  History and background,
    653–654
Military records—Kept by states,
  723
Military records—Post-Civil War,
  Boxer Rebellion, 715
  Other records, 715–718
  Philippine Insurrection, 714–715
  Spanish-American War, 713–714
Military records—Printed sources,
  723–725
Military records—Regular army/
  regular establishment, 718–719
Military Records—Relating to
  civilians, 723
Military records—Revolutionary War,
  "At a Glance" guide, 140
  Audit Office Series (Canadian),
    687
  Books, 671–680
  Canadian Loyalist sources,
    686–687
  *Index to Revolutionary War
    Pension Applications*, 665

  Information in case files,
    664–665
  Loyalists in the war, 681–687
  Books, 681–686
  Obtaining copies of records,
    667–668
  Pension payment records,
    668–670
  Service records, 657–659
  Using the records, 680–681
  Veterans' benefits records
    (pensions and bounty land),
    659–664
  See also Land records
Military Records—World War I and
  later,
  Draft records, WWI, 719–721
  Draft records, WWII, 721
  Service records, 721–723
Miller, Frank Burton, 675
  Julie, 92
  Larry L., 122
Mills, Elizabeth Shown, 78, 82 (fn),
  96, 97, 137, 152, 511
Milner, Anita Cheek, 274
Ministére affaires étrangère, 674
Minnesota,
  Agricultural schedules, 375
  Census population schedules,
    324, 351, 366
  Church records, 617
  Common-law marriages, 306
  Divorce records, 557
  Guardianship records, 465
  Land records, 522
  Mortality schedules, 370
  Vital records, 293
  Wills, 438
Mississippi,
  Census population schedules,
    324, 360 (fn)
  Church records, 617
  Common-law marriages, 306
  Confederate pension records, 710

Court records, 552
Divorce records, 557
Guardianship records, 465
Immigration Passenger Lists, 633
Land records, 522
Loyalists during Revolution, 682
Military records,
    Books, 675
Mortality schedules, 370
Private land claims, 489
Slave schedules, 374
Vital records, 293
Wills, 438
Missouri,
Census population schedules,
    324
Confederate pension records, 710
Divorce records, 557
Guardianship records, 465
Land records, 522
Military records,
    Books, 676
Mortality schedules, 370
Non-government local research
    aids, 134
Private Land Claims, 489
"Research in the States" guide
    (NGS), 141
Slave schedules, 374
Vital records, 293
Wills, 438
Moiety, 413
Money, 413
Montana,
Census population schedules,
    324–325
Common-law marriage, 305
Divorce records, 557
Guardianship records, 465
Land records, 522
Mortality schedules, 370
Vital records, 293
Wills, 438
Moore, Frank, 724
MooseRoots.com (website), 204

Morasha (periodical) (Jewish
    Genealogical Society of Illinois),
    266
Morgan,
    Dale, 118
    George G., 137, 140, 216
Mormon Church, *See* Church of
    Jesus Christ of Latter-day Saints
Mortality schedules, *see* Census
    records
Mortgage, 502
Morton, Sunny Jane, 230
Moss, Bobby Gilmer, 678
Movable estate, 413
Movables, 413–414
Mozy Home (cloud), 193, 194
Munroe, J.B., 643
Munsell, Joel, 130, 268, 270
*Muster and Pay Rolls of the War of
    the Revolution, 1775–1783* (New
    York), 677
Myers,
    Albert Cook, 643
    Lorraine F., 126
MyHeritage (software), 181
MyHeritage.com (website), 100,
    189, 203, 208, 225–229, 638
    Accounts on, 225–226
    Availability, 225
    Comparison to other large
        commercial sites, 230
    Dealing with matches, 226–227
    Getting started on, 225–226
    Involving other people, 227
    Library edition, 225
    Menu options, 227–229
    Other research tactics, 230
    Partnerships, 225
MyHeritage DNA, 197

Naming practices,
    Given names, 50–52
    Nicknames and pet names,
        52–53
Nason, Elias, 120

National Archives (NARA), 18,
109–114, 374, 490
Address, 113
Immigration records, 638
Partner websites, 112
Regional archives, 113–114, 482,
660
Research assistance, 113
Website, 114, 205
National Archives Trust Fund
Board, 139
National Board of Health, 283
*National Cyclopaedia of American
Biography, The*, 262
*National Directory of Weekly
Newspapers*, 124
National Endowment for the
Humanities, 124
National Gazetteer, The, 119
National Genealogical Society, 15,
16, 18–19, 20, 26, 27, 45, 46 (fn),
104, 234–235, 266, 348, 511,
687 (fn)
*National Genealogical Society
Quarterly*, 266, 665
National Historical Records
Commission, 139
National Office of Vital Statistics,
317
*National Union Catalog of
Manuscript Collections
(NUCMC)*, 270–273, 613
Nationwide Gravesite Locator
(website), 205
Natural affection, 414
Natural heirs, 414
Naturalization records,
A-Files, 564, 646
Alien Registration Forms,
563–564
As source of information on
ancestral origins, 626
Availability, 564–565
Background and history,
560–562

C-Files, 646
Certificates, 566
Declarations of Intention, 565
Location and nature, 562–566
Naturalization Certificate Files,
563
Petitions for Naturalization, 566
Registry files, 564
Special helps and other records,
567
Visa Files, 564
Neagles,
James C., 138, 650, 672
Lila Lee, 138, 650
Nebraska,
Agricultural schedules, 375
Census population schedules,
325, 367, 368
Divorce records, 557
Guardianship records, 465
Land records, 523
Mortality schedules, 370
"Research in the States" guide
(NGS), 141
Vital records, 293
Wills, 438
Nebraska State Historical Society,
103
Neff, Lewis Edwin, 130
Nevada,
Cash entry files (public domain
land), 483
Census population schedules,
325
Common-law marriages, 306
Community property laws, 419
Divorce records, 557
Guardianship records, 465
Land records, 523
Mortality schedules, 370
Non-government local research
aids, 133
Vital records, 293
Wills, 438

New England,
  Church records, 585, 587
  Marriage records, 303, 304
  Non-government local research
    aids, 134
  Vital records leader, 303
  Widows' property rights, 580
New England Historic Genealogical
  Society, 16, 102, 266, 267, 268,
  301, 303
*New England Historical and
  Genealogical Register* (New
  England Historic Genealogical
  Society), 128, 266, 298, 635
New Hampshire,
  Census population schedules,
    325
  Common-law marriage, 305
  Church records, 617
  Court records, 552
  Divorce records, 557
  Guardianship records, 465
  Land records, 523, 524
  Land records jurisdictions, 70
  Loyalists during Revolution, 683
  Military records,
    Books, 676
  Mortality schedules, 370
  Naturalization records, 565
  Non-government local research
    aids, 134
  Probate records jurisdictions, 70
  Vital records, 294, 301
  Wills, 438–439
New Hampshire State Library, 103
*New Haven Genealogical
  Magazine*, 10 (fn)
New Jersey,
  Census population schedules,
    325, 351
  Church records, 617–618
  Court records, 552
  Customs Passenger Lists, 628
  Divorce records, 557
  Guardianship records, 465

Index of Wills, Inventories, Etc.,
    139
  Land records, 523
  Loyalists during Revolution,
    683, 684, 686
  Military records,
    Books, 676
  Mortality schedules, 370
  Naturalization records, 565
  "Research in the States" guide
    (NGS), 141
  Slave schedules, 374
  Vital records, 282, 294
  Wills, 439
New Jersey Historical Society, 103
New Mexico,
  Census population schedules,
    326, 367, 368
  Community property laws, 419
  Court records, 552
  Divorce records, 557
  Donation land grants, 479–480
  Guardianship records, 465
  Land records, 523
  Mortality schedules, 370
  Non-government local research
    aids, 134
  Private land claims, 489
  Probate records, 441
  Vital records, 294
  Wills, 439
New Netherlands, 53, 587
New Orleans, 281, 296
New Orleans Public Library, 102
New York City,
  Loyalists during Revolution, 684
  "Research in the States" guide
    (NGS), 141
  Vital records, 281, 296
New York State,
  Agricultural schedules, 375
  Census population schedules,
    326, 351
  Church records, 618–619
  Court records, 550

Customs Passenger Lists, 628, 629
Divorce records, 557
Gazetteers, 120
Guardianship records, 465
Immigration Passenger Lists, 633
Land records, 523
Loyalists during Revolution, 683, 684, 686
Marriage records, 303
Military records,
    Books, 676–677
Mortality schedules, 370
Probate records, 401
Vital records, 294
Wills, 439
New York Genealogical and Biographical Record (New York Genealogical and Biographical Society), 103, 266
New-York Historical Society, 656
New York Public Library, 103, 264
New York State Library, 103
Newberry Library, 102
Newberry Library Genealogical Index, 130
Newhard, Malinda E. E., 134
Newman,
    Harry Wright, 675
    John J., 562
    Peter C., 684
Newsholme, Sir Arthur, 281
Newsome, Albert Ray, 643
Newspaper and periodical directories, 124
NewspaperArchives.com (website), 100, 275
Newspapers,
    As family history source, 273–276
    Issues relating to their use, 274–275
    Reference works relating to, 274
Newspapers.com (website), 124, 204, 275

Newspapers in Microform: United States, 1948–1972, 124
Next-of-kin, 414
Niles, John M., 119
Non-government local research aids, 133–136
Non-original sources, *see* Secondary sources
North Carolina,
    Agricultural schedules, 375
    "At a Glance" guide, 140
    Census population schedules, 326, 351, 360 (fn)
    Church records, 619
    Confederate pension records, 710–711
    Court records, 549 (fn)
    Divorce records, 557
    Gazetteers, 120
    Guardianship records, 465
    Land records, 523
    Loyalists during Revolution, 682
    Military records,
        Books, 677
    Mortality schedules, 371
    Non-government local research aids, 134–135
    Probate records, 441
    "Research in the States" guide (NGS), 141
    Slave schedules, 374
    Specialized locality sources, 122
    Vital records, 294
    Wills, 439
North Carolina Genealogical Society Journal, 266
North Dakota,
    Census population schedules, 326–327, 367–368
    Divorce records, 557
    Guardianship records, 465
    Land records, 523
    Mortality schedules, 371
    Vital records, 294
    Wills, 439

Noyes, Sybil, 260
NUCMC, see National Union
Catalog of Manuscript
Collections
Nugent, Nell M., 473
Numbers, problems with, 39

Oakland FamilySearch Library, 105
O'Byrne, Mrs. Estella, 674
Obituaries,
As source of information on
ancestral origins, 626
In early newspapers, 273–274
OCLC, *see* Online Computer
Library Center
Officers of the Army and Navy
(Regular and Volunteer) Who
Served in the Civil War, 262
Ogden FamilySearch Library, 106
Ohio,
Agricultural schedules, 375
"At a Glance" guide, 140
Census population schedules,
327, 351
Church records, 620
Common-law marriages, 306
Divorce records, 557
Gazetteers, 120
Guardianship records, 465
Land records, 523
Military records,
Books, 677
Mortality schedules, 371
Non-government local research
aids, 135
"Research in the States" guide
(NGS), 141
Specialized locality sources, 122
Wills, 439
Ohio Genealogical Society, 266
Ohio History Connection, 482, 487
Ohio Records and Pioneer Families
(periodical) (Ohio Genealogical
Society), 266

Oklahoma,
Census population schedules,
327
Common-law marriage, 305
Confederate pension records, 711
Divorce records, 557
Guardianship records, 465
Land records, 523
Mortality schedules, 371
Non-government local research
aids, 135
"Research in the States" guide
(NGS), 141
Vital records, 294
Wills, 439
Old Southwest, "At a Glance"
guide, 140
Olsson, Nils William, 643
Omni Gazetteer of the United States
of America, 119
Omohundro Institute of Early
American History and Culture,
267
On Board (periodical), 81 (fn), 84
Online Computer Library Center
(OCLC), 272
Oral Genealogies, 60
Orange County FamilySearch
Library, 106
Ordinary, 414
Oregon,
Census population schedules,
327
Divorce records, 557
Donation land grants, 479–480
Guardianship records, 465
Land records, 523
Mortality schedules, 371
"Research in the States" guide
(NGS), 141
Vital records, 294
Wills, 439
Oregon Genealogical Society
Quarterly, 267

Oregon Historical Society, 104
Original sources, guides to,
　131–139
Orphan, 414
Orthography, 30–32
Ostroff, Harriet, 271
Our Archives (website/wiki), 191
Outbuildings, 414
Overbury, Sir Thomas, 13
Owen, Thomas M., 673
Oxford English Dictionary, 32

Paltsits, Hugo Victor, 684
Partition, 414, 502
Parturition, 414
Passano, Eleanor Phillips, 130
Passenger lists,
　As family history source, 244
　Finding aids, 650
　Published, 635–639
*Passengers Who Arrived in the
　United States, September, 1821–
　December, 1823*, 631
Passport applications, 650–651
pCloud (cloud), 193
Pease, John C., 119
Peck, Epaphroditus, 684
Pedigree Resource File, 60
Pedigree(s),
　Analyzing with "T" chart, 65–68
　Connected to royalty, 11
　Lengthy, 11
Pennsylvania,
　"At a Glance" guide, 140
　Census population schedules,
　　328
　Church records, 620–622
　Common-law marriages, 306
　Court records, 552
　Customs Passenger Lists, 628,
　　629
　Divorce records, 557
　Gazetteers, 121
　Guardianship records, 465

Immigration Passenger Lists, 633
　Land grant records, 494
　Land records, 523
　Loyalists during Revolution, 682
　Military records,
　　Books, 677
　Mortality schedules, 371
　Non-government local research
　　aids, 135
　"Research in the States" guide
　　(NGS), 141
　Specialized locality sources, 122
　Vital records, 297
　Wills, 439
Pennsylvania Archives, 656–657
*Pennsylvania Genealogical
　Magazine* (periodical)
　(Genealogical Society of
　Pennsylvania), 267
*Pennsylvania Magazine of History
　and Biography*, 268
*Pensioners of the United States,
　1818*, 660
Per stirpes, 414
Periodical directories, *see*
　Newspaper and periodical
　directories
Periodical Source Index (PERSI),
　128–129
Periodicals, *see* Genealogical and
　historical periodicals
Personal property, 414
Personal representative, 414
Peterson, Clarence Stewart, 672,
　724
Petition, 459, 503–504
Pfeiffer, Laura Szucs, 137
Philadelphia, 281, 297
Pictures/photographs, 160, 242–243
Pierce, John, 672
Pilgrim News Letter, 277
Pinterest (website), 189
Pittsburgh, PA,
　Vital records, 297

Pittman, Hannah D., 270
Places, importance in research, 13
  See also Locality analysis
Pleadings, 415
Pocatello Regional FamilySearch
  Library, 106
Political correctness, 4 (fn)
Poorly preserved records, 45
Pope, Charles Henry, 260
Ports, Michael A., 140
Postnuptial contract, 459
Potter, Dorothy Williams, 140
Powell,
  Kimberly, 137
  William H., 724
  William S., 120
Power of attorney, 504
Preemption land sales, 478–479
Preliminary survey, 6, 57–63, 206,
  208
  Compiled and published sources,
    61–62
  Home and family sources, 58–59
  Keeping records of, 62, 156–157
  Secondary sources on Internet,
    59–61
Preston, Jeannine Tussey and
  Joseph A., 134
Pringle, J. F., 684
Printed secondary sources, 255
  See also Compiled and published
  sources
*Printed Sources: a Guide to
  Published Genealogical Records*
  (Meyerink), 269
Private land claims, 481
Probate,
  Definition, 415
  Legal requirements, 419–421
  Philosophy, 418–419
  Process, 450–452
Probate law in the U.S., 199–200
Probate records,
  Abstracting, *see* Abstracts,
    Probate records

As source of information on
  ancestral origins, 626
Content and value, 400–401
Definition and background,
  399–400, 447
Limitations, 401–402
Record types, 452–462
Proclamation money, 415
*Professional Genealogy: A Manual
  for Researchers, Writers, Editors,
  Lecturers, and Librarians*, 78
Professions, *see* Family history
  professions
Progeny, 415
Pronouns, usage in this book, 4 (fn)
Proof,
  Definition, 81–82
  Difficulty, 79
  Standard of (GPS), 79, 83–85,
    214
Protestant Episcopal Church,
  Money, 592–593
  Other matters, 593–594
  Poor, orphans, and illegitimate
    children, 590–592
  Registers, 595–597
  Vestry minutes, 590–592
Prothonotary, 415
Pruitt, Jayne C. C., 678
Public Library of Cincinnati and
  Hamilton County, 103
Published sources, *see* Compiled
  and published sources
Punctuation, 38
Purdue University's Online Writing
  Lab, 152
Putnam, Eben, 643
Puzzilla (website), 233–234

Quakers, *see* Society of Friends
Quisenberry, Anderson C., 675
Quit rent, 415
Quitclaim deed, 504–505

Rand-McNally's Pioneer Atlas of the American West, 118

Random Acts of Genealogical Kindness (website), 74, 117

Randymajors.com (website), 76

Rasmussen, Louis J., 643

Raymond, William O., 684

Real property, 415

Receipt, 459–460

Record content, uncertainty of, 69

Record keeping processes, 143

Recorded documents, 506

Records of research, *see* Research notes

Rectangular survey, 415, 475–477

Reddy, Anne Waller, 680

Reference works/sources,
  Definition, 115
  Guides to locality data, 116–123
  Guides to non-original sources, 123–131
  Guides to original sources, 131–139
  Other useful research guides, 140–142

Register of wills, 416

Reid, William O., 684

Relationships, changes in terms, 47–49

Release of dower, 505

Relict, 416

Reminder notes, 161

Rennick, Robert M., 122

Renunciation, 461

Repositories of unpublished/ archival records, helps in locating, 271–272

Research,
  Area searches, 156
  Complete, 10–12, 68–69
  Cycle/process, 5–9, 159
  Definition, 4
  Family traditions and other clues, place of, 77–78
  Guides, 116–142
  How different from our experience, 4–5
  Knowledge vs. tools, 14–15
  Nature of, 5–9, 19–20
  Technological perspective, 19, 20

"Research in the States" guides (NGS), 141

Research Libraries Information Network (RLIN), 272

Research logs,
  Adaptability to preliminary surveys and area searches, 156–157
  As tables of contents to research notes, 153, 164
  Purpose and use, 149–153, 210

Research notes,
  Area searches, 156
  Computerized, 146–149
  Copies of records/documents, and correspondence, 145
  Evaluating/analyzing information in, 157–159
  Footnotes on family group worksheets, 158
  Identifying purpose of every search in, 145
  Importance of keeping proper, 144, 209–210
  List of essentials in, 163–164
  Methods of keeping, 145–149
  On paper, 149
  Organizing, 153–156
  Preliminary surveys, 156–157
  Preservation of, 163, 164
  Relating to correspondence, 162–163
  Reminder notes, 161
  Requirements of good, 144–145, 166–167
  Research logs, *see* Research Logs (main entry)

Research reports, *see* Research Reports (main entry)

RSS (blog syndication), 191

Research objectives, identifying, 206, 208–209

Research reports, importance in record-keeping process, 159–160, 164

Research results, sharing, 160

ResearchTies (computerized record-keeping program), 147–149, 193

Researchers, expectations for, 14–15

Revill, Janie, 643, 678

Rhode Island,
Census population schedules, 328
Church records, 622
Common-law marriage, 305
Court records, 552
Customs Passenger Lists, 628
Divorce records, 557
Gazetteers, 119–120
Guardianship records, 465
Immigration Passenger Lists, 633
Land records, 523, 524
Military records,
Books, 678
Mortality schedules, 371
Naturalization records, 565
Probate jurisdictions, 70
Vital records, 294–295, 301–302
Wills, 440

Rhode Island Society of Colonial Wars, 657

Rice, Franklin P., 301

Richards,
Josephine Ellis, 673
Kenneth W., 133

Ricks College, *see* Brigham Young University-Idaho

Rider, Fremont, 130, 131

Right of way, 416

Rillera, Mary Jo, 568

Rising, Marsha Hoffman, 137, 575

Riverton FamilySearch Library, 106

RLIN, *see* Research Libraries Information Network

Robbins, Roy M., 478, 480

Roberts,
Gary Boyd, 264, 298
James A., 677

Robie, Diane C., 133

Robinson, George Frederick, 657

Rogers,
Augustus C., 262
Ellen Stanley, 129

Rolls and Lists of Connecticut Men in the Revolution, 1775–1783, 673

Roman Catholic Church,
Challenges associated with research, 607
Deaths, burials, and cemetery records, 609
Marriage banns, dispensations, and validations, 609
Parish family books, 609
Registers, 608
Requests, 609
Rites and rights, 608

RootsMagic (software), 181, 207, 208

Roots Tech conference, 17

RootsWebb (website), 199, 204

Rose, Christine, 97, 137

Rosenbloom, Joseph R., 262

Rottenberg, Dan, 138

Rubincam, Milton, 48 (fn), 137, 278

Rupp, Israel Daniel, 643

Russell, George Ely, 129

Ryerson, Adolphus E., 684

Sabine, Lorenzo, 684

Sacramento FamilySearch Library, 106

Sadler, Jerry, 493

Saffell, William T. R., 672, 679

St. George FamilySearch Center, 106

St. Louis County Library, 103

St. Louis Genealogical Society Quarterly, 267
Sale bill, 461–462
Salley, Alexander S., Jr., 678
Salmon,
  Emily J., 572 (fn)
  Marylynn, 576, 577, 578, 584
Salt Lake Institute of Genealogy (SLIG), 17
San Diego FamilySearch Library, 106
Sanborn, Melinde Lutz, 304
Sanders,
  Edith Green, 127
  Patricia, 133
Savage, James, 261
Saye, A. B., 260
Schaefer, Christina K., 138, 575
Scharf, John Thomas, 258
Schenk, Trudy, 643
Schlam, Rebecca, 132
Schlegel, Donald M., 644
Schleifer, Jay, 138
Schneider, David, 238
Schreiner-Yantis, Netti, 126
Schuon, Karl, 725
Schweitzer, George K., 127, 133, 135
Scott,
  Craig R., 140
  John and James, 120
  Kenneth R., 644
Seal, 416
Search engines, *see* Internet search engines
Seattle Public Library, 105
Secondary research, *see* Preliminary Survey
Secondary sources, 40–41, 59–61, 123–131
Seizin, 416
Separate examination, 416
Settlement (final account), 462
Sharing research results, 160
Shattuck, Lemuel, 282, 317

Shelley, Michael H., 122
Sheppard, Walter Lee, 644
Sherwood,
  Adiel, 120
  George, 644
Shipley, Renee, 181 (fn)
Sidings, 416
Siebert, Wilbur Henry, 684, 685
Signatures, 44–45
Silliman, Sue I., 676
Simmendinger, Ulrich, 644
Simmons, Henry Eugene, 725
Simplicity, need for in record keeping, 144
Singer, Charles G., 685
Skordas, Gust, 261, 644
Slave schedules, *see* Census records
Slocum Robert B., 127, 262
Slosson, Edwin E., 26
Smith,
  Alma Aicholtz, 487
  Alvin, death of, 93–94
  Clifford Neal, 487
  Drew, 140, 147
  Jessie Carney, 138
  Joseph, Jr., ancestry, 94–95
  Paul H., 685
Smithsonian,
  National Museum of African American History and Culture, 248
  Transcription Center, 248
Smolenyak, Megan, 138
Social media use, *see* Internet social media use, 187–189
Social statistics schedules, *see* Census records
Society of Friends,
  Examples of Monthly Meeting minutes, 604–607
  Explanation of meetings and records, 602–604
Source, The (Szucs and Luebking), 138, 215, 269, 375, 604 (fn)

Sources,
  Original and derivative, 91
  vs. Evidence, 91
South Carolina,
  Agricultural schedules, 375
  Census population schedules,
    328, 360 (fn)
  Church records, 587, 622
  Common-law marriage, 305
  Confederate pension records, 711
  Divorce records, 557
  Guardianship records, 465
  Immigration Passenger Lists, 633
  Land records, 523
  Loyalists during Revolution,
    682, 685
  Military records,
    Books, 678
  Mortality schedules, 371
  Non-government local research
    aids, 135
  Probate records, 441
  "Research in the States" guide
    (NGS), 141
  Slave schedules, 374
  Wills, 440
South Carolina Historical Society, 104
South Dakota,
  Census population schedules,
    328–329, 351, 367, 368
  Common-law marriages, 306
  Divorce records, 558
  Guardianship records, 465
  Mortality schedules, 371
  Vital records, 295
  Wills, 440
*Southern Genealogist's Exchange
  Quarterly*, 267
Special projects, *see* Message
  boards, forums, and special
  projects
Special publications, 138–139
Spelling issues, 30–32, 42–44
Sperry, Kip, 42, 60, 127, 129, 133,
  134, 135, 205, 268

Spiros, Joyce V. Hawley, 133, 134,
  136
Stanard, William G., 644
Standard of Proof, *see* Genealogical
  Proof Standard (GPS)
Standard Periodical Directory, 268
Stapleton, Ammon, 644
Starke, James H., 685
State Historical Society of Missouri,
  103
Stemmons,
  Diane, 138
  John D., 138
Stephenson,
  Noel C., 79
  Richard W., 118, 519
Stern, Malcolm H., 138
Stewart, Robert Armistead, 131,
  679
Stinson, Helen S., 136
Stirpes (periodical) (Texas State
  Genealogical Society), 267
Strassburger, Ralph Beaver, 644
Strauss, Jean A. S., 568
Stryker, William S., 676
Stryker-Rodda, Kenn, 138
*Subject Directory of Special
  Libraries and Information
  Centers*, 125
SugarSync (cloud), 194
Surety, 417
Surrender, 505
Surrogate, 417
*Survey of American Genealogical
  Periodicals and Periodical
  Indexes, A*, 268
Swem, Earl G., 129, 268
Swenson, Milton D., 350
Swierenga, Robert P., 645
Szucs, Loretto Dennis, 138, 215,
  269 (fn), 375, 604 (fn)

"T" chart use, 65–68, 208
Tail, estate in, 417
Tallmadge, Samuel, 677

Tax records, 505–506, 512–518
Taylor, Philip F., 657
Taylor Grazing Act, 481
Technological resources, 180–199
Technology,
  Future of, 175
  In perspective, 20
  Innovation and proliferation,
    175–176
Telephone and city directories, 73,
  125
Temple University-Balch Institute
  Center for Immigration
  Research, 637–638
Tenancy by the entirety, 405
Tenancy in common, 406
Tenant, 417
Tenements, 417
Tennessee,
  Agricultural schedules, 375
  Census population schedules,
    329, 348, 360 (fn)
  Church records, 622
  Confederate pension records, 711
  Court records, 552
  Divorce records, 558
  Guardianship records, 465
  Land grant records, 494
  Land records, 523
  Military records,
    Books, 678
  Mortality schedules, 371
  Non-government local research
    aids, 135
  "Research in the States" guide
    (NGS), 141
  Slave schedules, 374
  Social statistics schedules, 376
  Vital records, 295
  Wills, 440
Tenure, 417
Tepper, Michael, 625–626, 638,
  645
Testamentary bond, 462

Texas,
  Agricultural schedules, 375
  Census population schedules,
    330, 351
  Common-law marriage, 305
  Community property laws, 419
  Confederate pension records,
    711–712
  Divorce records, 558
  Guardianship records, 466
  Immigration Passenger Lists, 633
  Land history, 491–493
  Land records, 524
  Mortality schedules, 371
  Non-government local research
    aids, 135
  "Research in the States" guide
    (NGS), 141
  Slave schedules, 374
  Vital records, 295
  Wills, 440
Texas State Genealogical Society,
  267
Textbooks and specialized reference
  sources, 131, 136–138
Thernstrom, Stephan, 131
This Week Magazine, 423, 425
Thorndale, William, 118
Titles (with names), 49–50
TNG (website/wiki), 191
Toedteberg, Emma, 127
Tories, *see* Military Records—
  Revolutionary War
Torrey, Clarence Almon, 303
Towle,
  Laird C., 134
  Leslie K., 129
Township Atlas of the United States,
  117
Traditions, 77
Transcribe—definition, *see*
  Abstract, extract, transcribe
Trapp, Glenda K., 129
Tree Searcher, The (periodical)
  (Kansas Genealogical Society), 267

Tree Shaker (periodical) (Kentucky Genealogical Society), 267
Tree Talks (periodical) (Central New York Genealogical Society), 267
True, Ransom B., 263
Trust deed, 506
Trust/trustee, 417
23andMe.com (website) 197
Tyler's Quarterly Historical and Genealogical Magazine, 264

Ulrich's International Periodicals Directory, 268
United Empire Loyalists Association of Canada, 686
"United States Adoption Research" (FamilySearch wiki page), 568
United States Congress (as author), 263
United States Constitution, 315, 587
United States, general,
    Gazetteers, 119
    Specialized locality sources, 121–122
University of Texas Library, 636
University of Washington, 18
Upton, L. F. S., 686
U.S. Adjutant General's Office, 725
U.S. Bureau of the Census, 672
U.S. Bureau of Naval Personnel, 725
U.S. Department of the Interior, 672
US GenWeb Project, 117, 141–142, 199, 205
U.S. Geological Survey, 519
U.S. House of Representatives, 672
U.S. Library of Congress, *see* Library of Congress
U.S. Newspaper Directory, 1690–Present, 124
U.S. Secretary of War, 672
U.S. Senate, 673
U.S. Territorial maps, 117
U.S. War Department, 660, 673

Utah,
    Cash entry files (public domain land), 483
    Census population schedules, 330
    Common-law marriage, 305
    Divorce records, 558
    Guardianship records, 466
    Land records, 524
    Marriage law, 408
    Mortality schedules, 371
    Slave schedules, 374
    Vital records, 295
    Wills, 440
Utah Genealogical Association, 265
Uxor, 417

Van Tyne, Claude Halstead, 686
Vermont,
    Census population schedules, 330
    Church records, 622
    Court records, 552
    Divorce records, 558
    Guardianship records, 466
    Immigration Passenger Lists, 634
    Land records, 524
    Military records,
        Books, 678–679
    Mortality schedules, 371
    Probate jurisdictions, 69
    Vital records, 302
    Wills, 440
Vermont Genealogist (periodical), 267
Vermont State Archives and Records Administration, 302
Virginia,
    Agricultural schedules, 375
    "At a Glance" guide, 140
    Bounty land warrants (Revolutionary War), 485, 486
    Census population schedules, 330, 360 (fn)
    Church records, 587, 622–623

Confederate pension records, 712
Court records, 552
Divorce records, 558
Guardianship records, 466
Independent cities, 569–572
Land grant records, 494
Land records, 524
Loyalists during Revolution,
   682, 683
Military district, 486–487
Military records,
   Books, 679
Mortality schedules, 371
Non-government local research
   aids, 135
Records of defunct counties, 572
"Research in the States" guide
   (NGS), 141
Slave schedules, 374
Specialized locality sources, 122
Vital records, 279–280, 295,
   302–303
Widows' inheritance rights,
   581–582
Wills, 440
Virginia Genealogical Society, 473
Virginia Genealogies, 126
Virginia Genealogist, The
   (periodical), 267
Virginia Historical Index (Swem),
   268
Virginia Historical Society, 267
*Virginia Magazine of History and
   Biography* (Virginia Historical
   Society), 264, 267
Virginia State Library, information
   pamphlet, 136
Virkus, Frederick A., 128, 270, 645
Vital records (birth, marriage, death)
A source of information on
   ancestral origins, 626
Availability, 306–309
Beginning and background,
   279–284
Certificates, 288–291

Definition, 279
Divorce records, *see* Divorce
   Records (main entry)
Early laws, 279–280
Marriage and divorce records,
   283, 303–307
   See also Divorce records
      (main entry)
Obtaining copies of, 306–309
Record problems, 310–312
Standardization, 283–284
Town meeting records, 309–310
Value and use in research,
   284–286
WPA inventories of, 287–296
Vogt, John, 303

WPA inventories, 573
WPA List of Vital Records, 292–296
   See also Works Projects
      Administration
Wakelyn, Jon L., 263
Wales, *see* Britain
Walker,
   Harriet J., 674
   Homer A., 674
Wallace, W. Stewart, 686
Walsh, Barbara B., 128, 652
Walton, Jesse M., 686
War records, *see* Military records
Ward Maps of United States Cities,
   118
Warrant, 462
Warranty deed, 506
Washington, George, will of, 580
Washington (state),
   Agricultural schedules, 375
   Census population schedules,
      331
   Community property laws, 419
   Divorce records, 558
   Donation land grants, 479–480
   Guardianship records, 466
   Immigration Passenger Lists, 634
   Land records, 524

Mortality schedules, 371
Vital records, 295
Wills, 440
Washington DC, *see* District of
Columbia
Waters, Margaret R., 674
Webb, Walter, 131
Webinars, 19
Websites, accuracy of information
on, not guaranteed, 74
Welch, Alice T., 676
WeRelate (website), 190
West Virginia,
Census population schedules,
331, 360 (fn)
Church records, 623
Court records, 552
Divorce records, 558
Guardianship records, 466
Land records, 524
Military records,
Books, 679–680
Mortality schedules, 371
Non-government local research
aids, 135
"Research in the States" guide
(NGS), 141
Vital records, 295
Wills, 440
Western Illinois University, 18
Western Maryland Genealogy
(periodical), 129
Western Reserve Historical Society,
104
Westphall, Victor, 485
Where to Write for Vital Records
(U.S. gov't pamphlet), 132,
286–287, 296, 308, 358, 359
*Who Was Who in America,
Historical Volume, 1607–1896,*
263
Who's Who in America . . ., 263
Wikipedia (website), 30–32, 181,
424
Wikis, 189–191

Family tree wikis, 190
Reference wikis, 190–191
Special topic wikis, 191
WikiTree (website/wiki), 190
*William and Mary Quarterly,
The* (periodical) (Omohundro
Institute of Early American
History and Culture), 264, 267
Williams, Ethel W., 77
Will contest, 418
Wills,
Abstracting, examples, 541–545
Administration, 243–244
Availability for research, 441
Codicils, 425–426, 427
Contests, 430–432
Definition and background, 423
Finding and using, 435–444
Indexes, 443–444
Kinds of, 424–426
Legal requirements, 419–421
Probate process, 426–430
Published and abstracted,
441–442
Record problems, 433–435
Value and use, 432–433, 445
See also Probate records
Wilson,
Samuel M., 675, 679
Thomas B., 686
WinFamily (software), 181
Wisconsin,
Census population schedules,
331
Church records, 623
Divorce records, 558
Guardianship records, 466
Land records, 524
Mortality schedules, 371
Private land claims, 489
Vital records, 295
Wills, 440
Wisconsin Historical Society, 105
Witcher, Curt, 138
Wolfe, R. J., 646

Wolfert, Marion, 637
Women in family history,
    Difficulty in identifying,
        575–576
    Effect of marriage, 576–579
    In the American Revolution, 671
    Inheritance laws,
        Husband died first (left
            widow), 579–582
        Inheritance by woman from
            non-husband, 582–583
        Wife died first (left widower),
            582
    Property rights, 576–578
    Real estate conveyances,
        578–579
    Separate estates, 580
Wood, Virginia Steele, 128, 652
Word divisions, 39
Works Projects Administration
    (WPA), Inventories, 292–296,
    573
WorldCat website, 116, 273
World Conference on Records
    (1969, 1980), 139
Wright,
    Esther Clark, 686
    Norman E., 738

Writ, 551 (fn)
Wyoming,
    Census population schedules,
        331
    Divorce records, 558
    Guardianship records, 466
    Land records, 524
    Mortality schedules, 371
    Non-government local research
        aids, 135
    Vital records, 296
    Wills, 440

Yannizze Melnyk, Marcia D., 138
YIVO Institute for Jewish Research,
    636
Yoder, Don, 645
Yonkers, NY, 297
Yoshpe, Harry Beller, 686
Younger children, 418
Your Genealogy Today (periodical),
    267

Zabriskie, George Olin, 44
Zimmerman, Gary J., 637

CPSIA information can be obtained
at www.ICGtesting.com
Printed in the USA
LVOW10s1701220318
570811LV00013B/784/P